Early Adventurers On
The Western Waters

Volume III, Part 1
The New River of Virginia
in Pioneer Days
1745-1805

by

Mary B. Kegley

Printed by Walsworth Publishing Company, Marceline, Missouri
for Kegley Books
P.O. Box 134
Wytheville, Virginia, 24382

*This book is dedicated to the memory
of Dr. W. R. Chitwood, an enthusiastic
researcher, author, and collector of history.*

"An adventurer is an optimist who is courageous enough to take the risk to discover, much to his delight, that the grass is greener on the other side of the mountain."

Mary B. Kegley

New River.

Photo by F. B. Kegley

PREFACE

Mary Kegley has done it again!

All historians, genealogists, and serious researchers of economic and cultural history should rejoice upon the publication of her latest book, *Early Adventurers on the Western Waters,* Volume III.

In this new work, Mary Kegley continues her documentation of Wythe County history, focusing on the settlement and development of the eastern segment of the county. Her sources include early surveys, grants, deeds, wills, birth, death, and marriage records, lawsuits and documents filed with them, which she has located not only in Virginia and other states, but also in England and Germany as well. The author has also consulted hundreds of sources not readily accessible to the general researcher: journals, family Bibles, histories, personal letters and private papers, tax lists, military records, DAR papers, U. S. census reports, pension applications, and cemetery censuses. She has corresponded with and interviewed descendants of many of the early adventurers. The scope of her research is truly spectacular.

Following the advice of her mentor, F. B. Kegley, Mary does indeed ''let the records speak for themselves.'' And what a wealth of records, facts, and details she presents! Each statement in this compilation of thousands of facts is painstakingly documented, showing its source, not in footnotes, but in the text itself.

If you wish to answer the question, ''What's in a Wythe County name?,'' study this book. If you want to know the origin of place names, the names of creeks and mountains in the area, consult this book. If you have problems identifying different branches of the same family, or sorting out people who have the same name, read this book.

The consummate researcher, genealogist, and historian, Mary Kegley uses her encyclopedic knowledge of early documents to weave a truly remarkable tapestry of regional history. The lives and fortunes of many of the early adventurers are all intertwined, as this account so clearly shows. For me, the most interesting chapters in the book are the 124 family sketches, which track early settlers and their families from their arrival in this part of Virginia, which became Wythe County in 1790, until they disappear from the scene. Kegley reveals many unknown facts about such early adventurers as the Austins, James McGavock, John Chiswell, the Calhouns, the Grahams, the Jacksons, and the Crocketts, to name only a few. Kegley's study of early settlers reveals that English, German, Welsh, Irish immigrants, and their Negro slaves lived, interacted, and worked here, literally making history.

In these pages, the author not only gives the vital records of the families but she also includes their land transactions, their wills, their children, their personal property, their slaves, all of which is of significant historical, genealogical, sociological, economic and cultural value to students of the past.

In this book, several historical inaccuracies and errors are gently corrected, family traditions are shown to be just that, and a few individuals turn out to be less than heroic. When ''the wish appears to be father of the thought,'' Kegley sets the record straight.

The text of this historical tour de force is enlivened and illuminated by many photographs of people, houses, historical sites, and panoramic landscapes (many of them taken by the author), and includes original maps, documents, and other records of the people who first settled at such evocative places as Poplar Camp, the Lead Mines, Austinville, Fort Chiswell, Foster Falls, Crocketts Cove, or on the waters of New River, Reed Creek, Cripple Creek, and other places along the Great Road and other historic roads that crossed Wythe County. Of especial interest is the development of the lead mining industry at Austinville, and the Fort Chiswell settlement.

Mary Kegley is to be congratulated on her devotion to history and her considerable effort to research, to write, and to publish the documented facts about these early adventurers on the Western Waters.

Mack H. Sturgill

INTRODUCTION

On January 10, 1994, the major part of the writing of this continuation in the series of *Early Adventurers on the Western Waters* was completed. Every day for years, the work of research and writing continued, and on that day the goal was accomplished. Of course maps, photos, index, bibliography, layout, and all those "other" things that go into the making of a book had to be completed, but the major part of the work had been finished.

Trying to describe what these sections of the history of the *Early Adventurers* are about is like describing social groups of interrelated families who settled in close proximity to each other, and were connected many ways and many times through two hundred years of history. As you read these pages, you will see the family relationships, the customs of keeping land in the family, of living close to each other, of intermarriage with neighbors, and many times "cousins." You will also see that houses were simple, small, and generally surrounded by numerous outbuildings...the spring house, loom house, kitchen, barn, and so forth. The contents of the cabins and early homes were generally only revealed at death, therefore each inventory, appraisal, and sale gives some insight into life in the early days.

The "Early" part of the title of this book was intended to refer to records between 1745 and 1800, and this part of the "Adventurers" does that, but more. As the geographic area of study moved west of Montgomery and Pulaski counties, the time frame became later. As a result, there are many instances where the records themselves extend past the Civil War. However, the emphasis is on the beginnings of the eastern part of present Wythe County. The early residents of the lead mines community, Fort Chiswell and Crockett's Cove as well as those settlers who moved up Cripple Creek to the present Smyth County line are featured in the sketches of the families.

Most of the maps were prepared from deeds and surveys found in the records, platted out and then fitted to the USGS maps which, for the most part, show present road systems. Approximate locations of the early settlers were then identified and drawn on the maps presented in the book. Photographs came from several sources: the Dr. W. R. Chitwood Collection, the F. B. Kegley Collection, the Mary B. Kegley Collection, with contributions from various individuals added. Many of the places were visited in 1993 and 1994, and photographs were taken by the author showing present conditions. Other landmark places were gone. Documentation is placed at the end of each paragraph so that future historians may be able to find the full text of the references. Often there are several citations, as each one may provide a different portion of the paragraph.

When the writing was nearing completion, it became evident from typing on the word processor in a single space format that there was much more text than expected, and consequently the volume planned to be number three became Volume 3, Parts 1 and 2, with the index in Part 2. And still the western part of Wythe County waits to be done!

It has been more than ten years since the first two volumes were published. What happened in between would take another book to explain, but the major work was a three-year project which resulted in *Wythe County: A Bicentennial History*. Smaller works included the *County Courthouses of Virginia, Old and New*, four picture albums of places and people, three church-related books, and two books of tax assessment records. And yes, hours and hours spent "digging out" the court records from the clerk's office, and the basement of the courthouse, where most of the lawsuits were filed.

The first two volumes of *Early Adventurers on the Western Waters*, have received high praise from their users, and can be found in libraries and homes all over the United States, in Canada, England, Northern Ireland, and Australia. The aim has been to provide basic information about the families who came into this region, not trying to tell their whole life story, and seldom mentioning their ancestry or place of prior residence. The purpose was to find them here and tell what happened after they arrived, based on the records, using as little as possible of family stories, or history of accomplishments of some illustrious ancestor. Some people have provided detailed records about their families before they came to this area, hoping I would include the information. The best I could do was give the references so that a subsequent researcher would be able to verify the statements. Very little interpretation of the records is given, for my aim was to do as Mr. F. B. Kegley told me many times, "Let the records speak for themselves."

So, I will "let them speak!"

Mary B. Kegley

ACKNOWLEDGMENTS

Many people have assisted me in the preparation of this book, and I acknowledge that it could not have been done without them. Anna Ray Roberts, George Mattis, and Brenda King at the Wytheville Community College Library have cheerfully assisted me in every request I have made, and have been able to provide me with the information needed. Anna Ray also provided me with photographs of the Newland place, and led me to other research on that family. Thanks so much.

The pictures have come from various sources. I acknowledge with gratitude the use of the F. B. Kegley Collection and the Dr. W. R. Chitwood Collection, and I thank Mrs. Chitwood for allowing me to select photos from her deceased husband's collection. Without these two collections many of the pictures appearing in the book would not have been available, as both collections extend over many years, and many of the places photographed are now gone. Michael Keesling generously shared his Keesling research with me. Other individuals have been generous too. These include Agnes Graham Sanders Riley, Davy Davis, Jimmy Spraker, Irene Sayers, Rush Crockett, and Doris Collins. To all of them my special thanks.

Several individuals, well acquainted with their own communities, have assisted me in exactly locating house places, and to them I am especially grateful. These include S. Rush Crockett, Helen Umberger, Thomas M. Jackson, Jimmy Spraker, Hayden Horney, and Doris Collins.

Ralph Bryant provided information about Jesse Evans and his Missouri location. Robert Eddystone Johnson provided enough family information on the Jacob Davis and Johnson families to lead me to more detailed records which I otherwise would not have had. Mr. Johnson also provided a drawing of the Jacob Davis home on Cripple Creek. Thanks for your assistance.

Janet Sayers, Bert Sayers, Irene Sayers, Crockett Harrison, and Alba Scott have all provided me with information on the Sayers families. Many authors have given me permission to use references in their publications, especially Vera Boyatt with her work on the Cassell families. Michael Kessling generously shared his Keesling research with me. Other authors and compilers of information have left their works behind, and have made my writing and research much easier. To all of them I acknowledge a debt of gratitude.

Jo White Linn of North Carolina and I discovered there were several connections between Rowan County and Wythe County. Jo was kind enough to share her research with me, especially in regard to Hugh Montgomery. She helped make the story more complete. Thanks for sharing, Jo.

Bev Repass Hoch traveled with me when I was on picture-taking outings, and I was delighted to have her company and assistance. Ernest Wilson took me flying on several occasions so I could try my luck at aerial photographs, some of which are included in the book. Thanks for the many trips to the river.

Hayden Horney, Clerk of the Wythe County Circuit Court, and his capable staff, Brenda, Ann, Janet, and Teresa, have all given me assistance in locating cases, bonds, and other records on a regular basis. The old records have been published here with permission of the clerk. Thanks to all of you.

My experts added much to this effort. Betsy MacCord has again been my editor, catching errors and omissions I would never have seen. Her expertise has indeed made this a better volume than if I had tried to do it all myself. And Betsy, if there are still errors or omissions, I take the blame, for I know you tried to keep me in line. Thanks for your many hours of excellent editing. Susan Thigpen prepared the ''boards'' for camera-ready shooting and scanned the many photographs and maps with ease and a practiced hand. Thanks for a job well done, Susan.

The introduction written by Mack H. Sturgill, an author of several Southwest Virginia books, was written after reading my entire manuscript. This was a labor of love because of its length and detail, and took much time and effort. His kind words are very much appreciated and his suggestions for additions and corrections were accepted with thanks.

Shirley Johnson-Grose, representative of Walsworth Publishing, and employees of the Missouri location, have given me every assistance in putting the details into place so that the work could be completed on time.

As is often the case when writing a book over such a long time period, there is a tendency to omit some people who have donated time, or photographs, or have written me to clarify family records. I did not intentionally leave you out. To all of you who helped me in any way, my thanks to you as well.

Mary B. Kegley
P.O. Box 134
Wytheville, Virginia 24382

ILLUSTRATIONS

TABLE OF CONTENTS

Virga. ſcⁱ Be it remembred that on the 25ᵗʰ day of may 1790 a commission of the peace & the county court in Chancery & of Oyer & Terminer for the County of Wythe Directed to Walter Crockett Jaˢ McGavock W Davis A Boyd & Jaˢ Newell R Sayers W Ward W Love Jno Adams J.T. Sayers David McGavock Flower Swift & W Thompson bearing date the 12ᵗʰ Feby. 1790 were produced & recui⁰ whereupon the Sᵈ Walter Crockett took the Oath according to law & the Oath of a Justice of the peace of the County Court in Chancery & of Oyer & Terminer all which Oaths were administred to him by Jaˢ McGavock & Andrew Boyd & then the Sᵈ Walter Crockett administred all the afore Sᵈ Oaths to James McGavock Andrew Boyd Wⁿ Davis Jaˢ Newell R Sayers Wⁿ Ward Wᵐ Love Jno Adams J T Sayers David McGavock Flower Swift Jehu Stephens & Wᵐ Thompson.

On May 25, 1790, the Wythe County Court held the first session and Walter Crockett took the oath of a justice of the peace. He, in turn administered oaths to Jas. McGavock, W. Davis, A. Boyd, Jas. Newell, R. Sayers, W. Ward, W. Love, Jno. Adams, J.T. Sayers, David McGavock, Flower Swift & W. Thompson.

Traced by Mary B. Kegley from the original found in the first Wythe County Order Book. *See also*, page 183.

SECTION I
The Land Seekers

Introduction

There is no doubt that available land was one of the major enticements for people to move to the Southwest part of Virginia beginning about 1745. The land companies and their records confirm the extent of the interest. The French and Indian War kept the settlements from developing during the 1750s and 1760s, but when the treaties were signed and the land was once more in the hands of the Virginia government and the land companies, there was a new surge of migration. The Loyal Company continued to deal with its extensive claims and its many land seekers. The Commissioners of Montgomery and Washington Counties came to verify titles in the 1780s (See, *Early Adventurers*, Volumes 1 and 2).

Following the American Revolutionary War, there was another major development on the Western Waters. Soldiers and their families moved to new locations; solid citizens felt the call of the Kentucky bluegrass country, and from New York, Pennsylvania, New Jersey, and other northern locations, they migrated southward. As each new phase of development took place, the one common denominator was the quest for land. Often it was just a few weeks or months after arrival that the adventurer claimed his piece of Southwest Virginia. This quest for land (cheaper, better, or just some) is evident in the entry books, survey records, deed books, and lawsuits.

In the early days of settlement, entries and surveys were made in compliance with the rules of the land companies, such as Patton's Woods River or Great Grant, and Dr. Walker's Loyal Land Company. Many settlers of Montgomery County (now Wythe, Pulaski, Carroll, Grayson, Smyth and Tazewell) counties claimed their land in the 1780s, but not usually under any land company. By the time of the 1780s and certainly by 1790 when Wythe County was formed, most of the best farm land had been claimed and only pieces of vacant land remained. These latter tracts were generally chosen based on treasury warrants from the Land Office in Richmond. There was, however, an exception. The Commissioners of Montgomery and Washington Counties in the 1780s often authorized a survey for land which had been held under the land companies many years before.

Treasury warrants could be for a large number of acres, and several entries could be made on the same warrant until the authorized number of acres had been claimed. The entry book was kept in the clerk's office and notified the surveyor and his assistants that the land could now be surveyed.

The surveyor went to the premises and, generally speaking, ran the lines and wrote the description of the property and drew a map or plat in the surveyor's or plat book, designating the way the land was claimed, who claimed it, the number of acres, and the date of completion. The surveyor noted the location of the property, but because there were no towns or villages, except the county seats, the tracts of land were located by creeks, rivers, and their branches. Blacksburg, Christiansburg, Wytheville, Newbern and others did not exist prior to 1790s. In order to describe the land, line trees, such as red oak, white oak, black oak, sycamore, among others, were marked so each person would know the tract boundaries. Often the surveyor mentioned adjoining owners. Occasionally, a settler would want all of his holdings put in one survey called an inclusive survey, in which case all of his claims were listed. Approval for this type of survey had to come from the court.

It should be emphasized that entries and surveys do not necessarily indicate ownership of land. It was a way to show the intent of the settler to claim a certain place for himself, but until he actually had the patent or grant, he did not have ownership as we know it today, and he had no legal right to make a deed. He may have had a right to the land in question, and his claim was worth something, but the ultimate ownership was a patent or grant from the State Land Office. He would not have been considered a ''squatter'' either, because there was a way to claim land in an orderly manner--stake a claim, enter the land, get a survey, pay fees, and wait for the patent or grant to be issued.

After making an entry, the next step to finalize ownership was to send the description of the survey and the plat to the Land Office with the required fees. If no one else claimed the land through a caveat (usually one to two years depending on the time period), the grant signed by the Governor of Virginia or his agent, was issued to the settler. Prior to the American Revolution, the grants were generally referred to as patents, but often the scribe who wrote the deeds did not know the difference, so in the records of Southwest Virginia the terms are often interchangeable. In both cases, the documents came from the government, and these records can be found at the Virginia State Library, Archives, either in abstract or full form.

After receipt of the grant or patent, a deed could be made in order to sell the property. Prior to receiving the title from the government, the only way to transfer the land was by assignment, when the seller then issued or transferred the title bond for the land. These were not recorded. An entry and a survey, either one or both, could be assigned. Because no deed was made until the purchase money was paid in full, and because people often died or moved away before this took place, many cases were brought before the courts to obtain the deed to the property.

For further information on entries and how the land was taken up, see Kegley and Kegley, *Early Adventurers*, Vol. 1, where abstracts of the entries in Montgomery County Entry Book A, and Kegley, *Early Adventurers*, Vol. 2, where the Commissioner's records are published. Because Montgomery County was the mother county of several counties, the work of abstracting the land entry books continues in this volume. Some entries are for what is now West Virginia, some for the counties of Floyd, present Montgomery, part of Giles, Bland, Wythe, Carroll, Grayson, and part of Smyth. When Wythe County was formed it covered parts of Bland, Tazewell, Smyth, Pulaski, and most of Carroll and Grayson as well as all of present Wythe County. The only way to tell from the entry where the land was located is by knowing the names of the creeks. Most are still on the topographic maps today, but of course a few have changed names.

CHAPTER I
Montgomery County Entry Book B

Montgomery County Entry Book B, located at the Circuit Court Clerk's Office, Christiansburg, Virginia, has records extending from April 8, 1783, to February 20, 1787, for settlers on the waters of the New, Kanawha, Gyandott, Clinch, and Holston rivers. Abstracts follow below, for the 370 pages of Entry Book B. The Montgomery County Entry Book A was published in previous Kegley publications. Wythe County Surveys and Entries appear elsewhere in this book. All information in square brackets was provided by the author.

p. 1

April 8, 1783, ELIZ'TH [ELIZABETH] MADISON, assignee, etc. treasury warrant, 500 acres on north and principal fork of Mud River, a branch of Gyandott, beginning about two miles above the mouth and extending up the said fork on both sides; also 500 acres adjoining and above the above entry and extending up the fork on both sides.

pp. 1-5

WILLIAM WARD, on several treasury warrants, 500 acres adjoining Mr. Madison's entry on the North Fork of Mud River and extending up the fork on both sides (withdrawn); also 500 acres beginning and adjoining and above the last entry and extending up the said fork on both sides (withdrawn); 500 acres beginning adjoining and above the last entry and extending up said fork on both sides (withdrawn); also 500 acres beginning adjoining and above last entry (withdrawn); also 500 acres on Middle Fork of Mud River beginning at the mouth of said fork and extending up it on both sides (withdrawn); 500 acres beginning adjoining and above last entry and extending up said fork on both sides (withdrawn); 500 acres beginning adjoining and above the last entry (withdrawn); 500 acres beginning adjoining and above last entry and up said fork on both sides (withdrawn); also 500 acres the same as above (withdrawn); also 500 acres the same (withdrawn); 500 acres as assignee of George May, beginning adjoining and above the last entry (withdrawn); 500 acres beginning and above the last entry and running up the fork on both sides (withdrawn); and 500 acres the same (withdrawn); assignee of Thomas Rowland, assignee of George Bright, on treasury warrant, 500 acres beginning adjoining and above the last entry and extending up the forks on both sides (withdrawn); as assignee of James Crown, on treasury warrant, 1,744 acres on branch of South Fork of Mud River on bank of which is a large triple poplar marked EW (withdrawn);

p.5

April 12, 1783, JOHN RICHISON, Commissioner's certificate, 400 acres on Little Reed Island, branch of New River.

DAVID MILLER, assignee of Christopher Elm, Commissioner's certificate, 128 acres on branch of Cripple Creek.

p.6

DAVID MILLER, assignee of William Meek, Commissioner's certificate, 82 acres on Sugar Run, a branch of Cripple Creek.

April 14, 1783, FREDERICK MOORE, Commissioner's certificate, 312 acres on both sides of Middle Fork of Reed Creek.

WILLIAM HAMILTON, assignee of Arthur Hamilton, Commissioner's certificate, 300 acres on branch of South Fork of Reed Creek, including a survey made in 1753 or 1754.

April 26, 1783, CHARLES DAVIES, preemption warrant, 1783, for 1,000 acres to include the horseshoe of Cole River, which is on one side of the falls.

THOMAS FARLER, assignee of Walter Crockett, attorney for James Clerk, on treasury warrant, 300 acres part thereof, on Richland Creek, branch of Big Blue Stone, to begin two miles above the mouth and running up the same on both sides, to include improvements claimed by William Perdew.

p. 7

April 30, 1783, JOHN BRECKINRIDGE withdraws his entry of 1,000 acres made 7 September last, at the mouth of Ducking Creek and enters the same on the east side of the Gyandott River opposite the mouth of said Ducking Creek (withdrawn).

JOHN BRECKINRIDGE, assignee of John Love, attorney for Joseph Love, preemption warrant, 1783, no acres stated, adjoining the settlement granted Joseph Love in September last by Commissioners and entered with surveyor 1782, to begin at the mouth of the creek and to extend up both sides of the river (withdrawn).

THOMAS NELSON, ESQR., assignee of John Jenkins, preemption warrant, 1782, for 1,000 acres adjoining the settlement on Mine Mill Creek and the land of John Brawley and Will: Rutherford [New River near the Lead Mines].

THOMAS MADISON and CO., preemption warrant for 1,000 acres adjoining his settlement called the Pasture and lands called Bingaman's Bottom.

p. 8

May 3, 1783, HEZEKIAH CHINA [CHANEY], assignee of Walter Crockett, attorney for James Clerk, on treasury warrant, 1782, 200 acres part thereof, on McCenely [McKinley] Run below and adjoining his settlement [New River].

JOHN STUDIVAN, assignee of Walter Crockett, attorney for James Clerk, treasury warrant, 1782, for 200 acres part of same, land on Eagle Bottom Creek, branch of New River to include his improvements.

WILLIAM BUSTARD, assignee of Walter Crockett, attorney for James Clerk, treasury warrant, 1782, 100 acres part thereof, between the land he lives on and that of Danl. Pearse [Pierce] on Chestnut Ridge [Cripple Creek of New River].

WILLIAM MOORE, state warrant, 1782, 186 acres assigned by James Newell, assignee of Walter Crockett, attorney for James Clerk, on the South Fork of Holston joining Abraham Godding to include his improvements.

ISHAM HARRIS, on state warrant, 1782, 200 acres assigned by James Clerk's attorney, on head of Dry Branch on the south side of Archey Reagh to include his improvements [Cripple Creek of New River].

p. 9

May 3, 1783, RICHARD COX, state warrant, 1782, 300 acres assigned by Walter Crockett, attorney for James Clerk, 100 acres entered on New River adjoining Thomas Kenworthy, to include his improvements; 200 acres on Reed Island Creek, joining Richard Shockley to include Dodson's improvements (withdrawn).

JAMES WALLEN, assignee of Thomas Jones, assignee of Peter Saunders, state warrant, 1781, 300 acres on Dry Fork of Wilsons Creek to include Solomon Cocks' improvement and for the use of said Cox; also 200 acres for the use of Edmund Wood and joining said Wallen land.

JOHN STONE, assignee of Richard Muse, assignee of Walter Crockett, state warrant, 1782, 140 acres on Beaver Dam Fork of Elk Creek, to include the improvements.

p. 10

May 5, 1783, WILLIAM NORTON, assignee of Walter Crockett, attorney for James Clerk, on treasury warrant, 150 acres on Elkhorn Creek, branch of Crooked Creek, to include the improvements; also 100 acres on Crooked Creek at the mouth of the branch called "crooked oak branch" to begin on the north side of the creek; also 100 acres on Crooked Creek below the mouth of Elkhorn.

ALEXANDER EDWARDS, assignee of William Norton, assignee of James Clerk's attorney, on treasury warrant, 200 acres on head branches of fork of Chestnut Creek, to include the improvements.

HENRY PICKRILL, assignee of William Norton, assignee of James Clerk's attorney, 150 acres on head of Cold Creek, to begin at the chestnut near the head of the creek, to include the improvements.

p. 11

CHARLES MORGAN, assignee of William Norton, assignee of James Clerk's attorney, on treasury warrant, 100 acres on North Fork of Crooked Creek, near the lower Pine Swamp.

SAMUEL JACKSON, assignee of William Norton, assignee of James Clerk's attorney, treasury warrant, 100 acres on Crooked Creek below the mouth of Elkhorn, beginning on north side of the creek, also 50 acres on the Pilot Ridge, to include the improvements.

CHARLES HINNEGAM, assignee of William North, assignee of James Clerk's attorney, on treasury warrant, 50 acres on North Fork of Chestnut Creek, to begin on the west side, to include his improvements.

p. 12

May 13, 1783, GEORGE RICHARDSON, on treasury warrant, 1,000 acres on Cole River about five to six miles below the fork of said river, adjoining a survey made in 1783 for Elizabeth Madison; also 1000 acres on two treasury warrants, 1783, adjoining and below the above entry (deleted).

SAMUEL STANDFIELD, assignee of William Norton, assignee of James Clerk's attorney, on treasury warrant, 100 acres on Cold Creek, to begin on the south side.

p. 13

JOHN PICKERRAL, assignee of William Norton, assignee of James Clerk's attorney, on treasury warrant, 200 acres on Cold Creek, branch of Chestnut Creek, to begin at the headwaters of a small branch below his plantation to include his improvements.

FLOWER SWIFT withdraws his entry of 18 November last and enters same adjoining the last mentioned entry of John Pickerrel and for his use.

THOMAS JOHNSTON, assignee of William Norton, assignee of James Clerk's attorney, on treasury warrant, 200 acres on Reddux Mill Creek, branch of Chestnut Creek, to begin at a chestnut on the right hand side of the road that leads to Flower Gap to Captain Swift's, to include his improvements.

p. 14

THOMAS DUNN, on treasury warrant, 1782, 221 acres part thereof, adjoining his settlement of 400 acres on the (blank) side of the same extending on both sides of the Great Road, between Ingram's and Peek (Peak) Creek.

DAVID DOAK, assignee of James Doak, on treasury warrant, 1781, 100

5

acres part thereof, joining his patent line, Adam Walker's and Lewis Able, to include a spring.

LEWIS ABELL [ABLE], on treasury warrant, 100 acres adjoining his entry of 225 acres made 5 March.

THOMAS HUFF, assignee of James Clerk's attorney, on treasury warrant, 1782, no acres given, adjoining his entry made 18 November last on the west side.

p. 15

THOMAS HUFF withdraws his entry of 221 acres made May 9, 1782 and enters same, adjoining the last mentioned entry of 500 acres.

May 10, 1783, RICHARD CHAPMAN withdraws his entry January 7, 1783, the warrant assigned by James Clerk's attorney, dated 1782, and enters 90 acres to begin corner to land he lives on, on a ridge along a line of the land to extend to a hollow known by the name of "dry hollow"; (21 acres withdrawn); also by virtue of the above 50 acres which was assigned to him by Richard Chapman, enters same lying at Moredock McKinsie's line (Walkers Creek). [This entry may be for a different person, the record is not clear].

May 17,1783, WILLIAM BOLES, on treasury warrant, assigned by Walter Crockett, attorney, for James Clark, 1782, 200 acres part thereof, to begin at James Byrn's line and to extend down the creek as far as a small ridge to include small improvement made by John Davidson and Falkner Elliott on Strubbles [Stroubles] Creek.

p.16

May 23,1783, THOMAS WILLIAMS, assignee of John Walter, assignee of James Clerk's attorney, on treasury warrant, 500 acres, issued 1782, enters 170 acres on Little Reed Island Creek, joining William Williams, Ric'd Shockley and John Walter (Watter?), to include his improvements.

JACOB ELLIOTT, assignee of James Clerk's attorney, enters 200 acres on above warrant, on Chestnut Creek, to include the improvements.

JOHN WILLIAMS, assignee of James Clerk's attorney, on treasury warrant, 1782, 150 acres on Chestnut Creek, adjoining Benjamin Hargrove, to include the improvements.

DAVID RICE, on above warrant, enters 150 acres on Little Piney Creek, waters of Chestnut Creek, to include the improvements.

EDWARD HARDEN, by virtue of a warrant and assignee of John Walter, 150 acres on Little Reed Island Creek, adjoining Thomas Morgan.

p. 17

NICHOLAS STILLWELL, assignee of James Clerk's attorney, on treasury warrant, 1782, 150 acres on Wolf Glade Creek, adjoining John Walter (Watter?)

WILLIAM McMULLEN, assignee of James Clerk's attorney on treasury warrant, 1782, 220 acres on Long Branch of Wolf Glade Creek, joining Abraham Vanhouser, William Bobbitt and James Cock.

JOSEPH LAWS, on above warrant, 200 acres on Bailey's Mill Creek, branch of Big Reed Island Creek, joining Daniel Witcher's, to include the improvements.

JEREMIAH WILSON, assignee of James Clerk's attorney, on treasury warrant, 500 acres, 1782, enters 240 acres on Little Reed Island Creek, joining William Williams, and Owen Adkins, on both sides of the creek, to include his improvements.

JOHN WALTERS, treasury warrant, 110 acres on Beaver Dam Creek above Bobitt's Ford.

p. 18

JOHN WALTERS, on several treasury warrants, 300 acres on Beaver Dam Creek, adjoining his former survey.

ABSOLUM BURTON, assignee of John S. (L.?) Jones, assignee of William Woods, on treasury warrant, 1782, 450 acres on top of the mountain where the road leads from Henry County to Montgomery County known by the name of Flower Gap.

JOHN L. (S.?) JONES, on above warrant, 250 acres on the mountain near the above entry on the north side of the waters of Crooked Creek on a line between Henry and Montgomery counties; also 300 acres on Little Reed Island Creek, at a place known by the name of Little Meadows.

May 27,1783, WILLIAM LEGGIT, assignee of John Wiley, on Commissioner's certificate, 400 acres on small branch of Middle Fork of Holston, to include the improvements.

WILLIAM DAVIES withdraws his entry made on McAdams' improvement and enters 100 acres on head of Holston, between his own and Andrew Vaught's line.

p. 19

JOHN ALSUP, assignee of Peter Saunders, on treasury warrant, 1782, 200 acres on west end of Buckeye Mountain, joining White's survey on head of Wattry Branch; also 150 acres on Bear Spring beginning about 15 poles above the head of sd. branch.

May 29,1783, JAMES YOUNG, assignee of Michael Krantz, on Commissioner's certificate, 200 acres on Reed Creek on the Great Road, to include improvements.

JAMES McDONALD, Commissioner's certificate, 400 acres on Lick Run, to include improvements; for same on preemption warrant for 100 acres adjoining his settlement of 400 acres.

May 30, 1783, THOMAS FLOWER, assignee of John Witcher, assignee of Benjamin Bailey, assignee of William Witcher, on treasury warrant, on Greezy Creek, at a place called Round Meadow to include a small improvement (withdrawn August 21, 1783 and warrant given to Wm. Spurlock).

pp. 20-25

June 2, 1783, WILLIAM WARD, assignee of James Trotter, assignee of Neil Alexander, state warrant, 1783, 500 acres on South Fork of Mud River (withdrawn); nine tracts of 500 acres each adjoining and above the first entry (all p. 22, withdrawn); 200 acres including one whole piece of low ground nearly resembling a horseshoe on west side of the Gyandott River, being the next bottom on the west side of the above falls; 300 acres on the east side of the Gyandott opposite the above entry, beginning 40 poles above the mouth of a branch which empties into the river (withdrawn); 500 acres beginning at the mouth of a small branch on the east side, two computed miles below the falls of the Gyandott (withdrawn); 2,000 acres, beginning on the west side of the Gyandott nearly opposite the lower end of the last entry including the land belonging to several branches which empty into the river on each side and belonging to a small creek on the east side about 110 poles below which is an old lick on the bank of the river (the clay resembles chalk); 500 acres beginning adjoining the last entry and down both sides; 250 acres beginning on the east side and adjoining the last entry; 250 acres beginning at a point on a cedar ridge on the east side and about one-half mile below last entry and down, nearly opposite Thos. Huff's cabin built 1772; 1,500 acres on east side of the Gyandott River, opposite to Thomas Huff's cabin and has a remarkable lick in the bank a little above the mouth called the high bank lick; 1,500 acres beginning at the high bank lick; 1000 acres on the west side of the big flat at the foot of a hill which ends the last entry; 1,000 acres on east side of the Gyandott beginning at the high clay bank.

pp. 25-26

June 4, 1783, JOSEPH PAULEY, assignee of Samuel Shannon, on treasury warrant, 1782, 130 acres assigned to him, on Walkers Creek joining his settlement on the southwest side, to include the dwelling house.

PATRICK NAPPER, assignee of Walter Crockett, attorney for James Clark, on treasury warrant, 1782, 100 acres on south side of Walkers Creek, adjoining Thomas Farley, Taylor and Thos. Napper's land (80 acres withdrawn); also 100 acres on the north side of Walkers Creek adjoining Captain George Pearis, Taylor and Thomas Farley's; 200 acres on the north side of Walkers Creek joining his own, Thomas Napper and Taylor's on Little Sugar Run (155 acres withdrawn); also 100 acres at the mouth of Mill Creek extending up and on both sides (withdrawn).

June 7,1783, ANDREW COCK, assignee of Moses Grier, treasury warrant, 1782, 250 acres on branch of Crooked Creek called Wolf Glade, beginning below the wagon road.

June 9,1783, JEREMIAH PATRICK, assignee of Frederick Edwards, withdraws 90 acres entered Oct. 21, 1782, and enters the same adjoining his survey made Nov. 2, 1782 at ye west side (31 acres withdrawn).

June 17, 1783, JOHN BAXTER, Commissioner's certificate, 400 acres on Clover Branch of New River to include the improvements, same on preemption warrant, 200 acres on Clover Branch of the New River.

p. 27

FREDERICK SLIMP [SLEMP], Commissioner's certificate, 250 acres on South Fork of Holston, to include the improvements.

JOHN COX, Commissioner's certificate, 400 acres on Peach Bottom Creek, at the mouth, to include the improvements.

EDWARD WILLIAMS, assignee of James May, Commissioner's certificate, 400 acres on Rocky Branch of New River, to include the improvements.

JAMES NEWELL, assignee of James Clerk's attorney, treasury warrant, 1782, 300 acres on Rock Creek of New River to include Will Sexton's, Benjamin Sexton's, Charles Sexton's and Jno. Sexton's improvements.

WILLIAM SEXTON, assignee of James Clerk's attorney on above treasury warrant, 130 acres on Rock Creek adjoining Edward Williams.

PETER COLEHEP, on above treasury warrant, 80 acres joining survey of William Ewins [Ewing?], on Cripple Creek, to include the improvements.

p. 28

June 17,1783, JAMES NEWELL, assignee of Walter Crockett, attorney for James Clerk, treasury warrant, 1782, 500 acres, enters 265 acres on a branch of Peach Bottom Creek, to begin near the mill belonging to George Reeves on said branch (withdrawn and entered on p. 295 and assigned to Jos. Crockett); also 235 acres on Cripple Creek for the use of Peter Colehep and Fredrick Bransteter.

JOHN FALIAFIRE [should be TALIAFERRO], assignee of Stephen Dance, treasury warrant, 1782, 400 acres joining the Carolina line to include Henry Hardin's improvements on branch of Crab Creek.

JOHN SMITH, assignee of Fredrick Edwards, assignee of Walter Crockett, attorney for James Clerk, 1782, 100 acres part of a treasury warrant, joining Thomas Quirk and David Taylor on east side of Pine Run.

p. 29

JAOB [index has JACOB] NYCEWANDER [NICEWANDER], assignee of Fredrick Edwards, assignee of Walter Crockett, attorney for James Clerk, 1782, 32 acres joining his old survey; also 67 acres adjoining the same (withdrawn).

June 18, 1783, JEREMIAH FARMER, assignee of Walter Crockett, attorney for James Clerk, on treasury warrant, 1782, 220 acres on Dry Branch, branch of Little River to begin on the north side (withdraws 150 acres and assigned to Samuel Landon); also 280 acres on branch called Little Elkhorn Branch of Meadow Creek (withdrawn and assigned to S. Landon).

June 23, 1783, MOSES BAKER, warrant for 500 acres assigned by Peter Saunders, enters 100 acres on Fox Creek, branch of New River, adjoining Thomas Douglas's.

DANIEL PEIRCE, state warrant for 500 acres, 1782, assignee of Walter Crockett, attorney for James Clerk, enters 221 acres on Reed and Cripple Creek adjoining Wm. Busterd and George Vaught.

p. 30

WILLIAM JAMES, assignee of Peter Gulipher, assignee of Thomas Hamilton, assignee of Colin Campbell, assignee of James Piper, on state warrant, enters 59 acres on the head of the South Fork of Holston, adjoining George Martain.

JAMES NEWELL, on state warrant, assigned by Rich'd Muse, assignee of Walter Crockett, attorney for James Clerk, 100 acres joining Johnston's and to extend towards Tuttle's Mill Branch (withdrawn April 30, 1790).

JOSEPH GLOVER, on state warrant, 1782, assigned by Rich'd Muse, assignee of Walter Crockett, attorney for James Clerk, 50 acres on New River to include his improvements.

June 24, 1783, JACOB CAIN, on state warrant, 1782, assigned by Crockett as attorney for James Clerk, 403 acres on New River to include his improvements.

p. 31

THOMAS JONES, on treasury warrant, 200 acres assigned by Manitree Jones, 104 acres entered formerly, now enters remaining 86 acres [should be 96?], on New River at the mouth of Brush Creek to include Sergener's improvements.

August 8, 1783, MICHAEL DRAKE, assignee of John Certain, assignee of Walter Crockett, attorney for James Clerk, 200 acres on Doe Creek, including the mill seat and from it across towards the foot of Doe Mountain, to include small improvement made by Philip Williams.

August 8, 1783 "The following entries made with John Preston since he obtained office of surveyor of Montgomery County."

JACOB ZEGLAR, assignee of Walter Crockett, attorney for James Clerk, treasury warrant for 500 acres issued 1782, enters 100 acres joining George Fielder and to extend towards Michael Price, Senr., on Toms Creek and head of Indian Run.

DANIEL WITCHER, assignee of Ben Lankford, treasury warrant, 1783, 480 acres on Road Creek, waters of Big Reed Island, to include his mill and improvements.

p. 32

August 14,1783, THOMAS HUTCHESON, assignee of Robert Sawyers, on treasury warrant, enters 94 acres head of the Cove near Newberry's Nobb at a place called the "flatt spring," head of Sawyer's Mill Branch.

August 15,1783, MICHAEL DRAKE, assignee of John Certain, assignee of Walter Crockett, attorney for James Clerk, 150 acres between Fredrick Miller and David Price on Spruce Run, waters of Sinking Creek, branch of New River.

August 19,1783, BENJAMIN BAILEY, assignee of Saml. Duval, assignee of John Mays, on treasury warrant, 1781, 17 acres on Big Reed Island of New River for James Gray; also 36 acres on Mine Road beginning at a chestnut marked with a J, waters of Reed Island Creek.

August 22,1783, JACOB BAUGHER, assignee of Jno. Preston, treasury warrant, 1782, 225 acres on East River beginning at six miles fork and at the mouth of same to include spring and extending up Rich Valley along the road leading to Bluestone River.

p. 33

JOHN HENDERSON, preemption warrant, 1783 for 1,000 acres enters same, adjoining his settlement at junction of New River with Ohio to include the vacant land on both sides between two surveys of George Washington and opposite one for Andrew Lewis.

August 27, 1783, ABRAHAM MORGAN, assignee etc. Commissioner's certificate, 50 acres at the mouth of Spruce Run of New River; same on Commissioner's certificate, 50 acres at the mouth of "Bare" Spring, branch of New River.

August 28,1783, MILTON ADKINS, assignee of Richard Chapman, assignee of Walter Crockett, on treasury warrant, 1782, for 500 acres, enters 80 acres on east side of New River at the mouth of Spruce Run, to include the saltpeter cave.

p. 34

ROBERT FRISTO, assignee of Saml. Peircefold, on state warrant, 1782, 113 acres above and adjoining his survey and to include Emos [Enos] Johnston's improvements; above warrant is given up with another plot made on sd. warrant.

September 4,1783, WILLIAM WARD, assignee of James Trotter, assignee of Neil Alexander, state warrant, part entered 500 acres on Mill Creek, branch of Sandy River emptying into it near fork on east side of both forks including falls of said creek (withdrawn); 500 acres adjoining and above last entry (withdrawn); 500 acres adjoining and above Thos. Huff's entry of 50 acres made September 12, 1781 on Salt Spring and to cross the stream issuing from said spring, 12 feet below the head thereof (withdrawn).

p. 35

WILLIAM WARD, 500 acres at "french furnace" ten computed miles above the falls of Buffaloe River (the largest stream between the mouth of the Gyandott and Sandy River) beginning at the lick below the furnace (withdrawn); 500 acres at forks of the "first considerable branch" of said Buffaloe River above the falls (withdrawn); 310 acres at the mouth of Peter Huff's Creek and eastern branch of Gyandott beginning about two miles up said creek from the mouth and down both sides of the creek to the mouth including

10

about 50 acres of low grounds opposite the mouth; also 1000 acres at "fish dam shoal" on Gyandott adjoining Thomas Huff's survey made at the mouth of Crawleys Creek.

p.36

GEORGE TROTTER, state warrant for 3,375 acres, 1783, enters 1,000 acres on Cain Creek about 12 miles above ford (fork?) of Sandy River on east side beginning at the mouth of said creek and extending up on both sides; also 1,000 acres adjoining his first entry at the mouth of Cane Creek; also 1,000 acres adjoining and above first entry at the mouth of Cain (Cane) Creek; also 375 acres residue of state warrant adjoining first entry on the mouth of Cain Creek.
GEORGE BERRY, state warrant, 572 acres, 1782, on Gyandott, beginning near point of a cedar ridge and below a high bank lick on east side of the river (270 acres surveyed, balance withdrawn).

p. 37

EVAN WILLIAMS, military warrant, 50 acres, 1780, assigned by Ephraim Ward, assignee of John Alcorn, joining Joseph Eaton, to include part of the big glade [on New River].
JOSEPH EATON, state warrant, for 272 1/4 acres, 1782, enters land adjoining his own and Evan Williams' settlement [New River].
JOHN BAXTER, state warrant, 169 acres, 1782, assigned by Saml. Ewing, enters same adjoining his own settlement [New River].
PEIRCE NOWLAN, Commissioner's certificate, 300 acres on Chestnut and Meadow creeks
JOSEPH JUSON, state warrant, 1,087 acres, 1782, enters 400 acres on Crooked Creek, branch of New River, to include his improvements.

p.38

EVAN WILLIAMS, military warrant, 50 acres, 1780, assigned by Ephraim Ward, assignee of John Alcorn, adjoining Joseph Eaton, to include the big glade. [Repeat of entry on page 37 ?]
JOSEPH EATON, state warrant, for 272 1/4 acres, 1782, enters land adjoining his own and Evan Williams settlement [New River]. [Probably a repeat of entry on p.37].
JOSEPH JUSON, state warrant, 13,087 acres, 1782, enters 400 acres on Crooked Creek, branch of New River, to include his improvements. [Probably a repeat of entry on p. 37].
JACOB HEADY, state warrant, 1782, assigned by Manitree Jones, assignee of James Powell, 200 acres on Chestnut Creek to include his improvements.
ABRAHAM HEADY, on above warrant, enters 100 acres on Chestnut Creek, to include his improvements.

p. 39

SAMUEL MUNSON, state warrant, 1782, assigned by Manitree Jones, assignee of Jas. Powell, 148 acres on Meadow Creek, to include his improvements.
STEPHEN WHITMIRE, on above warrant, 460 acres on Meadow Creek, to include his improvements.
STEPHEN REEDER, assignee of Thedues [Thaddeus] Cobly [Cooley], assignee of James Clerk's attorney, 250 acres on west side of Queen's Knob joining Red (?) Coleby [Cooley] and Jno. Heldreth.

pp. 39-40,

ARON LEWIS, treasury warrant, 1783, 400 acres beginning at County line

11

and running up Laurel Fork to join Richland tract; 200 acres on both sides Laurel Fork, a little above Richland tract, including a large spring branch; also 200 acres on Laurel Fork, including a large spring with a tree growing in it below where Clinch Road takes up the mountain; also 100 acres below the forks of said creek; also 600 acres beginning at the forks of Laurel Fork and up the South Fork towards the Elk Lick (surveyed 90 and 590 (510?) and sent to Wythe); also 200 acres on forks including the place Thos. Robbins now lives on.

September 7, 1783, ISHAM CHRISTIAN, treasury warrant, 1782, 217 acres beginning at Thomas Christian's, corner on Brush Creek.

September 8, 1783, JOHN WILSON, treasury warrant, 1782, 55 acres in Rich Valley, on north side of Walkers Mountain, joining an open line of his survey made by Hugh Fulton.

p.41

HENRY CEMENTS [CLEMENTS?], assignee of John Wilson on above warrant, 56 acres adjoining Wilson's survey, on Valley path at the upper end.

September 16, 1783, HENRY CEMENTS [CLEMENTS?], on treasury warrant, 1782, 100 acres on south side of John Wilsons, 300 acres surveyed under Walkers Mountain.

September 17, 1783, SOLOMON AKERS, assignee of Israel Lorton, assignee of Walter Crockett, attorney for James Clerk, state warrant of 500 acres, 1782, enters 65 acres on east side of 34 acres surveyed for Harrison, to begin with the line of said survey and run east course for quantity.

THOMAS ALLEY, assignee of James Breckenridge, assignee of George May, on state warrant of 500 acres, 1781, enters 200 acres part on the east side of Little River, adjoining his old survey, to include pair of race paths near the round nob [knob].

p. 42

September 20, 1783, HENRY DAVIS, treasury warrant, 1782, 440 acres on Big Reed Island Creek joining the land he now lives on.

September 29, 1783, REUBEN KEITH, preemption warrant, 1783, enters same, _____ acres adjoining his warrant; also preemption of 300 acres, 1782, adjoining his settlement; also another preemption of 600 acres, 1783, adjoining his settlement.

September 30, 1783, JOSEPH HOWE, assignee of Joseph Cloyd, assignee of Ephraim Dunlop, treasury warrant, 1782, 80 acres on New River, adjoining Mulberry Bottom, on northwest side.

p.43

October 1, 1783, EDM'D CLONCH, assignee of Wm. Foster, treasury warrant, 400 acres on Cramberry [Cranberry] Creek, waters of Crooked Creek, branch of New River.

October 2, 1783, LAZARUS DENNY, assignee of James Newell, preemption warrant, 1,000 acres, 1782, enters 100 acres of it on Meadow Creek.

NICHOLAS AUNSBAUGH, assignee of Adam Dean, state warrant for 1,000 acres, 1782, enters 93 acres on Cripple Creek.

October 3, 1783, THOMAS BURK, assignee of Walter Crockett, attorney for James Clerk, treasury warrant, 500 acres, 1782, enters 59 acres on Doe Run of New River; also 140 acres on west side of New opposite where he now lives; also 44 acres on east side of New River joining his patent land; also 18 acres on the west side of the New River.

JOHN BOYER, assignee of Thomas Burk, assignee of James Clerk's attorney Walter Crockett, on last mentioned warrant, 160 acres on west side of New River opposite the mouth of Sinking Creek.

October 4, 1783, HENRY CRUTCHER, on treasury warrant, 1783, 250 acres beginning at a place called Gap Branch and on the fork of the river [Gyandott] and up the north fork on both sides (withdraws 100); 250 acres at a place known by the name of "old beaver pond," on both sides of the Gyandott about three miles above the last mentioned entry (surveyed 158 acres; surveyed 92 acres); 200 acres to include Leonard Huff's Lick on Gyandott at the mouth of Elk Creek to include the spring (surveyed 210 acres and 40 acres); 300 acres on Gyandott, the main stream below Bear Creek (withdraws 100; also 200 acres); 200 acres about four computed miles above the forks of Gyandott to extend up Clear Fork, on both sides to include the spring.

October 9, 1783, DAVID BUSTARD, assignee [blank] on warrant [blank], 270 acres on head spring of Cripple Creek.

PETER CREAGER, on above warrant, 165 acres on Cripple Creek.

ANDREW BRANSTETER, on above warrant, 165 acres on Cripple Creek.

LAZARUS DENNY, on above warrant, 50 acres on Meadow Creek.

TIMOTHY MURPHEY, on warrant, 140 acres on Meadow Creek, to include his improvements.

JOHN COGGWIL, on above warrant, 50 acres on Meadow Creek

GEORGE KEITH, on above warrant, 436 acres on Elk Creek

GEORGE POWERS, on above warrant, 67 acres on Cripple Creek.

MICHAEL WHITMIRE, on above warrant, 171 acres on Meadow Creek

JOHN COX, on above warrant, 75 acres on Crab Creek; also 225 acres on Peach Bottom Creek.

JAMES NEWELL, on above warrant, 100 acres joining Redm'd [Redmond] McMahan on both sides of branch below Wooton's improvements.

JAMES NEWELL, on above warrant, 150 acres on both sides of Meadow Creek, joining Jacob Grigg's (withdrawn and entered on p. 296).

WILLIAM TOLLIEUR [TOLLIVER] on above warrant, 100 acres on Meadow Creek

JOHN WAGNON [WAGNOR?], on above warrant, 50 acres on Meadow Creek.

October 10, 1783, WILLIAM KIDD, on Commissioner's certificate, 200 acres on a branch of Bluestone, to include improvements.

October 13, 1783, NATHAN BELL, treasury warrant, 1782, 160 acres on Little Snake Creek on Big Reed Island of New River; also 154 acres in forks of Island Creek of Big Reed Island of New River.

October 16, 1783, JOHN GRILLS and JOSEPH CLOYD, treasury warrant, 1783, 200 acres on east end of Burks Garden on branch known by the name of East End Branch, to include headwaters.

October 17, 1783, JACOB ZEGLAR, state warrant, assigned by Walter Crockett, attorney for Jas. Clerk, 100 acres adjoining Fredrick Miller, Jas. Mann, and David Price, on south side of Sinking Creek on road to Greenbrier.

WILLIAM FULTON, assignee of Elijah Gartan on treasury warrant, 1783,

1,115 1/2 acres on Gyandott (withdrawn).

October 25, 1783, BENJAMIN TURMAN, assignee of James Turman, state warrant, 451 1/2 acres beginning at the lower side of Town Creek being the first big creek below the mouth of Richland Fork on east side of Sandy Creek;

p. 48,

BENJAMIN TURMAN, 300 acres on east side of Sandy Creek opposite mouth of Big Paint Lick; also 150 acres up Richland Fork on east side of Sandy; also 100 acres up the Richland Fork on east side of Sandy River; also 150 acres on first big bottom above the mouth of Big Paint Lick Creek on east side of Sandy River (all withdrawn).

HENRY WILLIS, state warrant, not dated, 100 acres on east side of New River including Carter's improvements beginning on an island opposite the mouth of Rich Creek and to extend down to the mouth of Wolf Creek.

November 8, 1783, JOHN BUCKLEY and SETH CALDWELL, treasury warrant, assigned by Nicholas Johnson, 1783, 98 acres on Malata Hill joining James Johnson and Thomas Burk (withdrawn); also 100 acres adjoining James Johnson and James Brumfield; 100 acres on Little Stoney Creek of New River.

November 10, 1783, EDWARD McDONALD, state warrant, not dated, 1,000 acres on main Gyandott River on west side to begin at the big red bank opposite an entry for William Ward, 12 supposed miles below the falls.

pp. 49-50

WILLIAM WARD (of Greenbrier County), assignee of Richard Mathews, two state warrants, one of 2,000 acres, 1782, and the other for 500 acres in 1782, on Peter Huff's Creek, branch of Gyandott, above and adjoining the survey of William Ward's (Botetourt County) and up the creek for quantity; also 1,500 acres on Gyandott to include all low grounds from John Preston's survey at the mouth of Elk Creek to the mouth of Beaver Creek; also 1,000 acres on Gyandott to include low grounds from Thos. Huff's survey at the big spring to William Ward's entry next and above Crowley's; also 1,000 acres on Gyandott to include the low grounds from Thos. Huff's survey at the mouth of Crawleys Creek to W. Ward's entry next above the falls; also 500 acres on lowermost branch that empties into Mud River on lower side, beginning one computed mile from the mouth of said branch.

p. 50

WILLIAM WARD (of Botetourt County), withdraws his entry of 300 acres made opposite his entry above the falls and enters it adjoining and below said entry to extend until it joins his next entry of 500 acres down the river.

December 6, 1783, FRANCIS KEATLY, assignee of Thomas Edgar, 50 acres on state warrant, 1780, west side of New river adjoining his old survey of James Adare for which he obtained a Commissioner's certificate.

December 29, 1783, GEORGE PEARIS, preemption warrant, enters (no acres given), on high land joining the Mulberry Bottom between Ingles' survey and Joseph Howe's entry that joins a survey of John Howe's 400 acres.

p. 51

January 2, 1784, JOHN CROCKETT, assignee of Fredrick Edwards, assignee of Peter Hollis, treasury warrant, 70 acres on Long Hollow, being a branch of Reed Creek known as Cove Creek.

THOMAS MONTGOMERY, assignee of Frederick Edwards, assignee of James Clerk's attorney, and of Peter Hollis, 300 acres in the Cove, head of

Peek [Peak] Creek, east of Sam'l Smith's line, to include vacant lands adjoining his patent lines.

FREDERICK EDWARDS, assignee of James Newell, treasury warrant, 1782, 100 acres adjoining his and Mr. Boyd's patent lines.

JOSEPH BAKER, assignee of Fredrick Edwards, assignee of Peter Hollis, 626 acres joining Edwards, and to extend eastwardly along said Edward's patent line.

p. 52

January 7, 1784, DAVID PRICE, assignee of James Clerk's attorney, on treasury warrant, 50 acres joining survey of 38 acres made for John Lewis, Esq. in '58 (or 68?), below the same on Sinking Creek.

February 3, 1784, CHARLES ZIMMERMAN, assignee of Stophel Zimmerman, treasury warrant, 1782, 55 acres on Reed Creek adjoining John Davies, Senr.'s survey near Lick Mountain.

February 11, 1784, WILLIAM EWING, assignee of Andrew Porter, preemption warrant, 100 acres on the southwest side of Jas. Douglass' patent land, on Cripple Creek of New River.

February 12, 1784, THOS. HUFF, assignee of William Preston, administrator of Will: J. (S.?) Madison deceased, state warrant, 920 acres on Gyandott at a place known as the big Horse Shoe.

p. 53

RICHARD REYNOLD, assignee of Wm. Perkins, treasury warrant, 375 acres at the mouth of Mud River and up said river and down the Gyandott in the fork.

January 13, 1784, FRANCIS PRESTON, on state warrant, 1,000 acres on Cole River about five computed miles below the fork of said river, adjoining the survey for James Breckenridge in 1784 (?), to begin at the lower corner of the survey; also 1,000 acres on treasury warrant adjoining and below the above entry on Cole River.

p. 54

February 24, 1784, JOHN SMITH, 200 acres on Sinking Creek below David Price's mill to extend along lines of said Price and John Price and across the creek to the land of John Miller, to include a good mill seat, iron mine, and two springs on the bank of the creek on opposite side of the iron bank.

JACOB BOUGHER [BAUGHER ?], state warrant, 400 acres joining his former entry made on the East River; 150 acres on Island Creek at a place called Buffeloe Lick, about two computed miles from the mouth joining and near Adam Clendenning's settlement (withdrawn per order of Capperton who purchased of Bougher); 100 acres about two miles above the last entry joining Sam'l Pack's on Island Creek; 50 acres adjoining William Wilson's bottom at the upper end of New River (for the use of Will: Wilson).

JOHN CALLAWAY, state warrant, assigned him, enters 900 acres, joining his entry on the mouth of Sandy Creek and to extend up the Ohio and to include the survey made by Crawford.

p. 55

HENRY WILLIS, assignee of John Smith, state warrant, 100 acres on the southwest side of New River to begin opposite the mouth of Rich Creek and to extend up the river near the mouth of Wolf Creek, and to include an island.

February 26, 1784, JAMES BRECKENRIDGE, assignee of Lettice Breckenridge, assignee of John Breckenridge, treasury warrant of 1000 acres, 1781, on

South Fork of Cole River between four and eight miles below the forks.

pp. 55-56

FRANCIS PRESTON, Assignee, etc., treasury warrant, 1000 acres on Main South Fork of Cole River between four and eight miles below the forks to join James Breckenridge, at the mouth of a creek (N.B., the above mentioned creek is called Prestons Creek); also 2000 acres below and adjoining the entry for James Breckenridge at the mouth of a small creek; also 2,000 acres on south branch of Cole River known as Horse Creek, to begin about four computed miles above the mouth and to include a "cain brake" on said creek; also 400 acres on Crab Creek, branch of New River to join Will: Boles, George Taylor, Senr., and Joseph Popecofer, to include small spring where John Taylor made a small improvement and on the south side of Taylor's land.

JOHN SMITH, assignee, 100 aces on south side of Crab Creek, corner to Mathias and Isaac Peterson, and to run with Isaac's. and to include a spring.

p. 57

FRANCIS FARLEY, assignee of James Breckenridge, assignee of George May, treasury warrant, 500 acres, 1781, enters 10 acres on an island of New River, below Culberson's Bottom, opposite where he now lives.

March 1, 1784, JOHN CALLOWAY, assignee of John Ward, assignee of Charles Lynch, treasury warrant, 5,774 acres, 1783, enters 2,000 acres at the forks of South Fork of Cole River, waters of New River to begin about a mile below the forks; also 3,744 acres on South Fork of Cole River adjoining and above the last entry at the forks

p. 58

JOHN CALLOWAY, assignee of Will: Mead, state warrant for 6,117 acres, 1782, enters 2,000 acres on South Fork of Cole River between two and four miles above the forks to begin at the mouth of a south branch of same, at a large "bent" in the river.

JOHN CALLAWAY, on state warrant, 2,000 acres on main Cole River adjoining and above a survey of James Breckenridge made in 1784, and to begin on corner of said survey and to include a spring and running into the river on the north side; also 2,117 acres, the remainder of the warrant, on the Ohio at the mouth of the Sandy to begin about a mile above the mouth and down the Ohio and up the Sandy on both sides to include the survey made by Crawford (withdrawn).

pp. 59-60

PHILIP SNIDOE [SNIDOW], military warrant, 45 acres on the northeast side of New River adjoining Jacob Certain, to include Brumfield's improvements.

March 2, 1784, THOMAS FARLEY, preemption warrant, 200 acres, 1783, on head of Sugar Run, a branch of Walkers Creek of New River to include the place known as "Martain's Cabbin."

March 3, 1784, EDMOND LYNE, assignee of Joseph Cooper, treasury warrant, 1,546 3/4 acres on Little Cole River at the mouth of Little Horse Creek about ten to twelve miles from the forks.

pp. 59-60

MORDACI HORD, on treasury warrant, 2,382 1/2 acres on west fork of Little Cole River at an old Indian camp; also 188 3/4 acres adjoining and above Edmond Lyne's entry on west side of Cole River at the mouth of Buffaloe Creek.

EDM'D LYNES, assignee of George Hamilton, on treasury warrant, 1781 1/2 acres on the west side of Cole River beginning at the mouth of Buffaloe Creek.

March 25, 1784, JOHN LIGGIT, on treasury warrant for 200 acres, enters 7 acres adjoining Wm. Patterson, William Ligget, William Lockhart and John Campbell on the main road that leads down the Middle Fork of Holston, to begin corner to Patterson; also 195 acres adjoining Will: Lockhart, Will: Liggit, Pat: Campbell on Willes's Run and Sugar Run branches of South Fork of Holston beginning corner to Campbell.

March 21, 1784, ANDREW COCK, treasury warrant, 75 acres to begin at the mouth of Little Snake Creek and down Big Reed Island Creek.

March 26, 1784, COLO. ALEXANDER STEWART, assignee of Robert Simpson, assignee of William Hunter, assignee of Michael Ryan on treasury warrant for 10,000 acres, 1783, enters 19 tracts of land: seven tracts for 400 acres; eight tracts for 200 acres; one tract of 800 acres; one tract for 500 acres, one for 100 acres and one for 1,000 acres. Land located on East River above the rock house on Island Creek, on Round Bottom, branch of the New; below the mouth of Bluestone; below the little falls on New River at the black oak bottom, branch of the New; below the mouth of Bluestone; below the little falls on New River at the black oak bottom; on Camp Creek; on Mountain Creek; on Wolf Creek; on Black Lick Creek which empties into the Bluestone; on Richland Creek; on and near the mouth of Brush Creek; on Millitons Fork, branch of Bluestone; Laurel Creek of Bluestone (parts withdrawn).

WILLIAM MOORE, assignee of Adam Dean, treasury warrant, 150 acres adjoining his own land on east side of George Forbess on the north and John Baxter [New River].

April 3, 1784, JOHN SMITH, on treasury warrant, 400 acres on Morrises Creek to adjoin improvements made by John Grills on northwest side of said improvement and to join patent line of James Thompson and Colo. Ingles's land (withdrawn).

HENRY BANKS, treasury warrant, 800 acres on head of Kimberlin Fork of Walkers Creek to join Robert Garret and to include the Sugar Camp (withdrawn and re-entered); also 1,000 acres, to begin at the Hunting Camp on Garden Fork of Wolf Creek to run down on both sides of the creek and to include three salt peter caves in the side of a mountain (withdrawn); 800 acres on Nobusiness [Creek], to begin at the mill seat about 3/4 mile above James Breckinridge and Elizabeth Madison and to run up both sides for quantity.

RICHARD BAILEY, assignee of John Lumsden, 300 acres on head of East River at the mouth of Owens Valley (surveyed 75, and 225 acres withdrawn); 200 acres on the mouth of Black Lick Creek joining the Bluestone at the lower end of Clover Bottom (175 acres surveyed and 25 acres withdrawn); also 200 acres on branch of Brush Creek to include William Day's improvements (surveyed 183 acres and 17 acres withdrawn); 300 acres joining John Davidson's line along East River Mountain (surveyed 209 acres and 91 acres withdrawn); 300 acres on Brush Creek called Low Gap at the head of South Fork of Black Lick Creek (withdrawn); 200 acres joining Ezekiel Clay's improvements on South Fork of Bluestone to run with Clay and Clover Bottom (surveyed 990 acres, 110 acres withdrawn); 100 acres on North Fork of Bluestone at Militon's Ford.

April 10, 1784, JOHN SMITH, assignee, etc., 120 acres on East River to begin at Davidson's Creek near the head of a sinkhole spring and up the valley to include David Ingles' improvements and to join John Ingless' land on head of Bluestone (surveyed 119 acres); 500 acres on state warrant on Garden Fork of Wolf Creek to begin at Joseph Hix improvements by small creek, to include Hixes improvements and the hunting camp; also 800 acres on Kimberlands Fork of Walkers Creek to join on the northwest side of William Anderson and to include Michael Daughterty's cabin (withdrawn).

pp. 66-67

HENRY BANKS, state warrant, 900 acres on Munsey's Mill Creek, branch of Walkers Creek to begin near the mouth of the north fork to include the hunting camp.

MRS. ELIZA. MADISON, 1,200 acres on treasury warrant on Jacobs Cove at the head of Jacobs Fork, branch of the Sandy River.

ROBERT EVANS, state warrant, 60 acres on Walkers Creek to join his own and the land of Thos. Evans.

JURETY EVANS, assignee of John Smith, state warrant, 150 acres adjoining Thos. Evans and Wm. Munsey on Walkers Creek (withdrawn August 1786).

HENRY BANKS, 900 acres on Wolf Creek to include Shered Adkins improvements and to extend up said creek near the mouth of Clear Fork for quantity; also 1,000 acres in gap of the mountain on Lick Fork of Walkers Creek and to run on both sides of the road that leads from said creek to Bluestone.

April 17, 1784, JOHN NICKLES, assignee of Henry Crutcher, treasury warrant, 10,000 acres, 1783, enters 100 acres on New River to begin at the lower end of Brushy Bottom at his corner tree.

HENRY CRUTCHER, on above warrant, 200 acres at the mouth of 5 mile Fork of East River.

JOSEPH CLOYD, state warrant, 40 acres joining the lower end of his patent land on Back Creek so as to include the mill seat.

p. 68

April 22, 1784, CHRISTIAN BIRKMAN, assignee of John Smith, assignee of John McClenahan, assignee of Richd. Eubank, on treasury warrant, 70 acres between his land and Muddy Fork of Wolf Creek.

April 23, 1784, JOHN CRAIG, Commissioner's certificate, 400 acres at Peirce's Ferry on New River to include improvements.

THOMAS MUSE, on preemption warrant, 1,000 acres, 1783, on east side of New River joining Bingeman's Bottom .

JAMES BABER, on treasury warrant, 1,220 acres, 1782, enters same on Brush Creek to begin where road crosses the creek leading from Gleaves [Cripple Creek of New River], withdrawn.

JOHN BAXTER, preemption warrant, 200 acres, 1783, adjoining his settlement [New River].

p. 69

April 23, 1784, AUGUSTINE WEBBER, on treasury warrant for 500 acres enters 150 acres to begin where the ridge joins Stephens Nobb [Knob], and running between Webber and William Bouren (Bourne), on Elk Creek.

SAMUEL SMITH, on treasury warrant, 796 1/2 acres, 1782, enters 75 acres in the Cove, joining his patent line.

JOHN TANNER, on treasury warrant 796 acres, 1782, enters 261 acres adjoining a survey on Chestnut Creek.

WM. HAMBLETON, treasury warrant, 500 acres, 1781, assigned by Thos. Hambleton, assignee of Collen Campbell, assignee of James Piper, 100 acres on Chestnut Creek, to include Jas. Pendires' improvement.

p. 70

THOS. RODGERS, assignee of James Newell, preemption warrant 1,000 acres, 1784, enters 200 acres joining the lower end of Jas. Wade's land to include improvement.

April 27, 1784, ALEXANDER EWING, preemption warrant, 100 acres, 1782, adjoining his settlement on South Fork of Cripple Creek.

May 1, 1784, JOHN SMITH, 250 acres above Christian Birkman's on Muddy Fork of Wolf Creek to include McDoffet's improvements and to join Alexr. Mcfarland's and Birkman (50 acres withdrawn); also 200 acres on Wolf Creek to begin about 3/4 miles below Christian Birkman's and to join Potter's improvements and Brit's Bottom, for the use of James Britt.

May 5, 1784, HENRY CRUTHCER, 8,500 acres part of 10,000 acres warrant, 1783, to begin at John Calloway's and to run up main stream and the county line 15 miles and then right angles one mile from said creek (withdrawn by John Smith to whom it was assigned.

WM. LS. LOVELY, assignee, etc. on state warrant, 740 acres on Connolly's Branch, known as Lovely Mount.

p. 71

May 8, 1784, HENRY TROLLINGER, SENR., preemption warrant 400 acres enters 200 acres on new River on north side of Peppers Road to join Joseph Cloyd; also 100 acres, 400 poles above the above entry (surveyed 75 acres).

May 26, 1784, JOHN SMITH, treasury warrant, 300 acres dividing waters of Clinch River and Wolf Creek to begin at the white oak on the road and to run to Rich Mountain and down and along the mountain to join Butler's land and to include Gray's improvements on head spring of the Clinch; also 200 acres on both sides of the great road that leads up Walkers Creek and to join William Light and to include improvements made by Diver on branch of Walkers Creek; also shoo [school] house near Britain's line (surveyed 200 acres and assigned to Evans).

[NOTE: The index lists John Smith of Botetourt County and John Smith of Montgomery County. The above entry is for John Smith of Botetourt County]

May 27, 1784, JAMES SIMPSON, on Commissioner's certificate, 400 acres on Cedar Run, to include improvements.

JOHN WHITSELL, on treasury warrant, 1782, assigned by George Bower (Bowen?), 200 acres on Cripple Creek adjoining George Kinzer, Fred. Bransteter, and James Crawford.

HENRY BANKS, on several treasury warrants, enters 18 tracts of land containing from 400 acres to 3,000 acres located in Burks Garden, Wright's Valley on Bluestone River; Abbs Valley, Walkers Creek, Dismal Creek (to include three mill seats), Kimberlains Fork of Walkers Creek, Wolf Creek, Lick Fork, Walkers Creek, Munseys Mill Creek, Hazel Creek, and Lockhart's Lick Branch.

p. 73

June 22, 1784, DAVID SMITH, assignee of Thomas Patton, on treasury warrant for

1,480 acres, 1782, enters 400 acres on North Fork of Holston and on both sides and joining Peter Groseclose's upper survey, and Jones.

FRANCIS PRESTON, 100 acres (void).

JOHN SMITH, on treasury warrant, 400 acres Burks Garden and in east end of same to begin at the head of a spring corner to William Ingles deceased, and by a glade on James Thompson's patent line (courses given).

p. 74

JAMES THOMPSON, 100 acres on west end of Burks Garden on Haw Ridge to include small improvement by Joseph Hicks; also 600 acres nigh east end of Burks Garden between Thompson's patent line and William Ingles, and along lines of tract surveyed under the Commissioner's certificate for Richard Grills, etc. (*et als*)

June 24, 1784, JERH. WILSON, assignee of Thos. Muse, on state warrant, 1,883 3/4 acres, 1783, enters 100 acres on south side of New River at the mouth of Meadow Creek to include improvements.

ELISHA BEDSOLL, part of above warrant, enters 180 acres on both sides of Chest. [Chestnut] Creek joining the lower end of his plantation to include his improvements.

p. 75

SOLOMON COX, state warrant, 1,883 3/4 acres, 1783, assigned by Thos. Muse, 540 acres part of both sides Cole Creek, branch of Chestnut Creek, to include his improvements.

THOMAS DAVIS, JUNR., on above warrant, 100 acres on east side of Chestnut Creek, to include his improvements.

JOHN COCKS, on above warrant, 50 acres on both sides of Chestnut Creek, to include his improvements.

JAMES JONES, on above warrant, 50 acres on east side of New River to include his improvements.

JAMES NEWELL, JUNR., on above warrant, 150 acres on South Fork of Holston, joining A. Gooden, Jervis Smith, and Jno. Wiseman (withdrawn May 27, 1786); also 150 acres to include Peter Razor's improvement where said Razor now lives (withdrawn 31 May 1798 and assigned to Peter Razor).

June 25, 1784, GIDEON MOSS, preemption warrant of 1,000 acres, 1783, enters same joining his settlement on Pine Branch of Peek Creek.

p. 76

JAMES THOMPSON, treasury warrant for 500 (?) acres in western end of Burks Garden on both sides of a path that goes through the gap.

June 28, 1784, HUGH FULTON, treasury warrant, 190 acres on North Fork of Holston, known by the name of Bell's improvements.

June 29, 1784, THOS. SPEAREY, assignee of Henry Banks, treasury warrant, for 75 acres not dated, to begin above the mouth of Byrn's Meadow Run and Strouples [Stroubles] Creek, (surveyed 30, balance withdrawn); also treasury warrant for 75 acres, 1783, enters same along said Speary's unmarked line opposite his barn (withdrawn).

JOHN SMITH, 250 acres at the mouth of Jacobs Fork to include ''the big cain brake'' on east side of Sandy

p. 77

July 4, 1784, ROBERT EVANS, assignee of Henry Banks, treasury warrant, 1783, 75 acres to include the house he now lives in, on Walkers Creek, and to join his own line.

July 12, 1784, THOMAS CONNALLY, assignee of John Preston, assignee of William Moore, assignee, etc., 105 acres adjoining Edward Hail, on Walkers Creek (withdrawn).

PETER HUTCHISON, assignee of James Clerk, treasury warrant for 500 acres, 1782, enters 200 acres on Wolf Creek below round bottom about 2 1/2 miles.

PHILADELPHIA GRILLS, assignee of John Smith, treasury warrant, 75 acres on northwest side of New River below the mouth of Falling Spring to include John Grills, Senr.'s, corn field.

p. 78 omitted in original

p. 79

MOSES LINSEY, assignee of John Smith, 200 acres on Walkers Creek to join Herbertson's unmarked line; 4 acres on west side of Herbertson's to include Birch's improvement on dividing waters of Walkers and Wolf creeks.

JOHN MAYES, assignee of John Smith, treasury warrant, 75 acres on both sides Walkers Creek to join the upper side of Cofman's survey and to include Moses Lindsey's improvements (surveyed for Thomas Dunn).

JAMES RICE, assignee of Thomas Smith, treasury warrant, 100 acres on Walkers Creek, to include his improvements between McGayers and Lambert.

p. 80

July 24, 1784, PATRICK NAPIER, assignee of James Clerk's attorney, treasury warrant, 500 acres, enters 130 acres of same, adjoining his survey on Whitney, on south side thereof.

JAMES JOHNSON, assignee of Richard Chapman, treasury warrant, 50 acres on Walkers Creek, beginning at a big spring about four miles from the mouth and both sides of the creek to join Farler's line (withdrawn March 2, 1787).

July 29, 1784, JOHN HENDERSON, assignee of Hugh Fulton, treasury warrant, 150 acres on both sides of Walkers Creek, joining the west end of his corn right survey.

DAVID KIRKWOOD, assignee enters 100 acres on both sides of South Fork of Reed Creek between John Philipy and Will: Litz (surveyed 100 acres).

EMOS [ENOS] JOHNSON, assignee of Thos. Smith, 164 acres on fork of Crab Orchard Creek, branch of Walkers Creek, between James Rice and Philip Lambert.

p. 81

July 31, 1784, JOHN NEWLAND, treasury warrant, 1782, 150 acres adjoining his patent land on Cripple Creek being surplus of his patent beginning corner to his patent land.

FRANCIS KINCANNON, assignee of Charles Allison, on Commissioner's certificate, 400 acres joining Crockett's patent line to include improvements.

HOWARD HAVEN, assignee of James Clerk's attorney, treasury warrant, 500 acres, enters 250 acres joining and below John Compton's on Bluestone.

WILLIAM HENLY, treasury warrant, part assigned by Thos. Muse and returned to the land office, 50 acres joining the land he lives on [Cripple Creek].

JAMES NEWELL, on above warrant, 200 acres on Cripple Creek joining the upper end of Wm. Gleaves and heirs of Robert Porter, deceased.

JOHN GIBSON, ESQR., of Bedford, treasury warrant, 700 acres on Greasy Creek of Reed Island Creek, known as Turman's Camp (Jno. Preston to find the warrant).

PATRICK NAPPER, assignee of Walter Crockett, attorney for James Clerk, state warrant for 130 acres at the mouth of Little Sugar Run of Walkers Creek and New River, adjoining Taylor's patent land.

August 4, 1784, WILL: BELL, assignee of Henry Davies, 493 acres beginning at the bank of the New River on west side about 200 yards above Mine Mill Creek extending down the river and up Mill Creek to Jinkins improvement including the mill, works and improvements.

JAMES BYRNSIDE withdraws his entry of 200 acres on Lick Creek, branch of New River, known as Farler's cabbin and enters 200 acres on branch of Bluestone called Mountain Creek and to begin two miles above David Frazer's cabin and enters same at Camp Creek, branch of Bluestone about four miles from the mouth of Puncheon Camp and down both sides (withdrawn).

August 17, 1784, ABRAHAM DILLOW, Commissioner's certificate, 400 acres on Peek [Peak] Creek to include improvements.

August 26, 1784, JAMES PARBERRY, assignee of John Breckenridge, state warrant, 2000 acres, 1782, enters same on south side of Gyandotte River of Ohio, adjoining James Madison's survey at "great falls."

September 6, 1784, JOHN GEORGE SREADER [SHCROEDER, SHRADER], warrant now in this office, 150 acres on Pine Run adjoining William Foster, Andrew Boyd, Andrew Crockett, and Adam Renner's [Runner's].

September 15, 1784, JAMES WILSON, LEVI HOLLINGSWORTH, CHARLES WILLING, BERNARD GRATZ and DOWSEY PENTECOST, assignee of James Summers, treasury warrant, 5000 acres, 1783, as follows, surveys for Pentecost & Co., a total of 340 entries appear for this company, each entry containing 1,000 acres. They were located on the waters of Gyandott Creek and Sandy Creek.

MICHAEL GRATZ and COMPANY, on seven warrants granted Colonel Wm. McWilliams, 1783, with a total of 14,000 acres, beginning three miles up from the mouth of the first creek emptying into the Ohio about seven miles below the Big Kanahwa and to extend eastwardly toward the military survey on Kanahwa; also based on nine warrants granted Jno. B. Simpson, 1783, 13,000 acres, beginning at the southeast of the first entry; and 9,000 acres on five warrants granted Charles McRoberts, 1783, above and adjoining the second entry; 2,000 acres on a warrant granted Saml. Peche (?), 1783, adjoining his third entry; 2,000 acres on warrant granted William Trotter, 1783, adjoining first and second entries.

September 18, 1784, WILLIAM SAMPLE, 10,000 acres granted Alexr. Dick (?), 1783, beginning three miles up from the mouth of the second creek emptying into the Ohio about 15 miles below the Big Kanahwa and extending along back of the military surveys; also on four warrants granted Joseph Smith, 1783, 8,000 acres above and adjoining the second entry; also on two warrants, granted Joseph Smith, 1783, 4,000 acres above the third entry in forks of the creek.

PHILLIP and JAMES MOORE, and WM. SAMPLE, on four warrants granted David Anderson, 1783, 28,000 acres beginning three miles above mouth of second creek and on the back of the military warrant; also on four warrants granted David Anderson, 1783, 22,000 acres below and adjoining the first entry on back of the military surveys; same on three warrants granted David Anderson, 1783, 10,000 acres above and adjoining said entry.

WM. THOS. TAYLOR, on three warrants granted Joseph Smith, 1783, for 6,000 acres on second creek emptying in below the Kanahwa adjoining the upper entry made for Wm. Sample.

September 18, 1784, DOCTOR PETER POULUS, 2,000 acres on warrant granted Colonel Wm. McWilliams, 1783, in forks of above creek adjoining Wm. Thos. Taylor.

JNO. IRVIN and ROBERT COCHRAN, on two warrants granted Colonel Wm. M. McWilliams, 1783, for 4000 acres to begin on the bank of the Ohio about six miles below the Big Kanahwa at the mouth of a small creek.

WILLIAM SAMPLE, 1,000 acres on warrant granted David Anderson, 1783, on bank of the Ohio about 14 miles below the Big Kanahwa.

September 22, 1784, ISHAM CHRISTIAN withdraws his entry made 1784 for 150 acres; also 90 acres of 165 acres on the same date and enters 240 acres on Fork of Brush Creek to begin about 60 poles above fork lick.

September 23, 1784, GEORGE ERWIN withdraws 60 acres, part of an entry made in 1782 and an entry of 100 acres made 1782, and enters 160 acres on head branch of Walkers Creek at the Poplar Camp and running along Walkers Mountain.

September 23, 1784, JOHN LIGGIT withdraws 2 acres, part of an entry made 1784 and 5 acres entered at the same time and located 7 acres on a treasury warrant on the top of a hill below Wm. Patterson on both sides of the great road [Middle Fork of Holston?].

September 27, 1784, BASIL PARTHER and JOHN SMITH, 1,000 acres on 12 Pole Creek, branch of the Ohio, to begin 100 poles below the main forks (marginal note states "Prather's and Smith's entry layes nearly an east course from the forks of the main (?) Sandy River").

JOHN SMITH, on sundry warrants, enters 19 tracts of land containing 17,800 acres on the Ohio between the mouth of the Sandy and Gyandotte, on a creek emptying into Cole River (all withdrawn).

SOLOMON HARRISON, treasury warrant, 100 acres adjoining W.(?) Beard's on the head of Plumb Creek, on both sides of the creek, assigned to John Preston, assignee of Henry Banks, 1783.

September 28, 1784, JAMES McDOWELL, assignee of Andrew Waggoner, on a treasury warrant for 2,000 acres, 1783, enters 1,000 acres on Sandy Creek, beginning about one pole southwest of corner of Penticost's and Company entry number 242; also 1,000 acres on Sandy Creek about one pole from southeast corner to Penticost and Co., entry number 240.

September 30, 1784, JOHN SMITH, on treasury warrant in entry #1 on the 27th of the month enters seven tracts of 1,000 acres each on a creek emptying into the Coal River (all withdrawn).

October 1, 1784, JOHN HUTSELL, on treasury warrant assigned by Stephen Chaplan (Chappell?), 10 acres on the north side of Reed Creek, adjoining Henry Helvey and Wiley's patent line; also 20 acres on north side of Reed Creek adjoining Helvey's and John Davies, Senr.; also Wiley's patent land; also 50 acres adjoining Edward Murphy (withdrawn).

October 5, 1784, VAN SWEARING, preemption warrant, 1,000 acres, 1784, on east side of South Fork of Sandy to include a cabin built by Swearhan and others in 1776; also preemption warrants of 1,000 acres, 1784, enters nine tracts of 1000 acres each on Sandy Creek to include cabins built by Swearingham and others and one tract to include the "rich graves"; one on Gyandotte to include five cabins.

THOMAS TEAS, treasury warrant, 4,000 acres, 1783, assigned by Wm. L. Lovely, assignee of William McWilliams, 1,500 acres on the west side of the great Kanahwa (withdrawn); 1,500 acres on west side of Great Kanahwa adjoining the above.

October 6, 1784, JOHN COX, assignee of James Clerk's attorney, 400 acres on George Reeves Mill Creek, branch of Peach Bottom Creek, adjoining Reeves' 100 acres at the fork of Peach Bottom.

JOHN PARTAIN, assignee of Andw. Cocks, 200 acres to begin at Major Ward's line on Burks Fork on both sides, to join Ward and W. Lawson's (surveyed with his entries on pp. 333 and 345).

RIC'D [RICHARD] MUSE withdraws entry on Brush Creek and enters same on Walkers Creek at lower end of Wm. Smith's settlement and joining Thos. Dun on north side.

JOSHUA HANKS, assignee of Thos. Muse, 350 acres on Chestnut Creek joining Will: Readox and Solomon Cox, Sr. (?).

ISHAM CHRISTIAN withdraws his entry 1784 and enters 240 acres on Davies Fork beginning on south side.

GEORGE RICHARDSON, two treasury warrants, 1783, 1,000 acres on Gyandott adjoining a place known as the Big Horseshoe; also 1,000 acres on warrant, 1783, on creek known by the name of Breckinridge Creek running into Cole River below the forks of New River.

JOHN BOYD, Commissioner's certificate, 350 acres at a great spring on Reed Creek, agreeable to a survey made 16 December 1753 by Thomas Walker.

JAMES FINLEY, treasury warrant, 500 acres, 1782, entered 150 acres joining his patent land and the land of William Phips and Jehu Stephens.

THOMAS QUIRK, preemption warrant, 400 acres adjoining his settlement on Reed Creek, and the lands of Robt. Sayers and Hugh Montgomery.

MICHAEL MADDEN, assignee of Christian Snidoe, assignee of Peter Saunders, treasury warrant, 1782, 35 acres under Salt Pond Mountain on Sinking Creek to include the place he lives on.

THOMAS HUFF, treasury warrant, 200 acres on Burks Fork of Reed Island to join Ward's; also 200 acres between his land and Burks Fork of Reed Island. MATHIAS PETERSON, assignee of Jacob Zegler, assignee of James Clerk's attorney, treasury warrant, 150 acres on Crab Creek joining his patent and Mathew Smith and Wm. Mynatt (withdrawn).

p. 164

December 19, 1784, JAMES BYRNSIDES withdraws his entry of 200 acres, 1784, and enters same on a branch of Bluestone known by the name of Little Pipe Stem at Dillion's Camp and southwest over the ridge and down the branch of Big Pipestem (survey for James Hines); also withdraws 100 acres entered in 1784 and enters the same on branch of Lick Creek, branch of New where the branch forks (surveyed 27 acres, withdraws 73 acres).

JOHN HUTSELL, treasury warrant, assigned by Stephen Chaplain [Chaplian?], 160 acres, part thereof, beginning corner to Edward Murfey's [Murphy's] corner to include part of a branch that runs into Cove Creek, branch of Reed Creek to take in a spring by Calhoon line and to join the lines of Calhoun, Walter Beaty, and George Huttsall.

December 20, 1784, JAMES PARBERRY, assignee of Robert B. Chew, 1,000, on forks of Cole, joining Mordaci Hord.

p. 165

WILLIAM WILLSON, assignee of Walter Crockett, attorney for James Clerk, treasury warrant, 1782, 100 acres adjoining his settlement on New River, and on the west side of the same.

December 29, 1784, MICHAEL DRAKE, assignee of John Certain, assignee of James Clerk's attorney, withdraws 100 acres entered 1783 and enters 50 acres of the same between Salt Pond Mountain and Philip Williams, on Sinking Creek (withdrawn).

January 4, 1785, HENRY BANKS, assignee of William Hall, warrant 1782, 506 acres on Sandy River at first big creek that empties into the river which is about six miles below the mouth of Shelby Creek to include large yellow lick.

January 8, 1785, RALPH STAFFORD, assignee of Joseph Cloyd, 100 acres on Peppers Road between Colo. Cloyd's, Morgan, and Craig, to include a spring.

p. 166-170

THOMAS CUNNINGHAM, assignee of James Addair, assignee of Charles Lewis, 200 acres, 1784, adjoining the Sinking Spring and John Craig, to include the Hazel Hollow on Sinking Spring Run.

GEORGE PEERY, 70 acres on balance of warrant, adjoining his entry on Maiden Spring of Clinch which includes Emmons cabins on both sides of the creek.

January 10, 1785, COLO. ALEXR. STEWART, assignee of Robert Simpson, assignee of William Hunter, assignee of Michal Ryan, warrant for 10,000 acres, 1783, enters in part, 21 tracts of land from 100 to 300 acres in size, on East River and its branches, on Bluestone and Pine River; many of them were withdrawn.

p. 171

MICHAEL PRICE, SENR., assignee of Alexr. Stuart, treasury warrant, 100 acres on Strobles [Stroubles] Creek at forks below his mill and below both forks.

pp. 171-175

January 10, 1785, COLO. ALEXANDER STUART withdraws 200 acres of first entry, 50 acres of the second entry, 100 acres of the 4th entry, 50 acres of the 5th entry, 200 acres of the 6th entry, 100 acres of the 7th entry, 50 acres of the 8th entry, 400 acres of the 10th, 200 acres of the 11th, and 600 acres of the 16th, and 200 acres of the 17th entry, and 200 acres of the 20th, and enters 3,050 acres in numbered tracts 41 to 51 inclusive. Land was located on Island Creek, Simmons Fork of Lick Creek, at the mouth of Lick Creek where Adam Clendening entered 50 acres; on Hacketts fork and at the mouth of Lick Creek; on head of Little Pipe Stem to include Rich Ridge on Maple Branch of Island Creek; on Bluestone below Clay's land where Adam Clendening made an entry; on big branch of Bluestone opposite Clover Bottom; on Black Lick Creek, branch of Bluestone; also withdraws 91 acres of the 9th entry, and 10 acres of the 12th, and 100 acres of the 14th, and enters 50 acres on the south side of the Bluestone opposite where Milintons Fork empties (surveyed with the 15th entry).

p.175

January 11, 1785, ISIAH PURDUE, assignee of Alexander Stewart on warrant, 1781, 4 acres on Wolf Creek to include his mill seat.

THOMAS GULLY, assignee as above, enters 45 acres on New River at the lower end of Havens' rough land opposite where he lives.

ADAMS CLENDENNING, assignee of William Duncan on military warrant, 50 acres on Black Lick joining Clay's land on upper side of Rupth (Kupth?) Creek, to include the mill seat; 100 acres adjoining his own on new River and above the same (withdrawn).

pp. 176-177

SAML. [SAMUEL] PECK, assignee of William Fulton, 100 acres on west side of Will Willson's old improvement to begin on Island Creek and along Wilson's line.

January 18, 1785, SHEDERICK HARREMAN, assignee of Jacob Riff, assignee of John Hawkins, 2,000 acres, 1783, 400 acres on Ohio joining Genl. Washington; 200 acres joining the lower end of G. Washington's survey on the Big Kanahwa; 500 acres on Big Hurrican [Hurricane] Creek; 400 acres on Little Hurricane Creek; 300 acres at the head of Davies Bottom beginning at Little Creek and to include vacant land on warrant of 4,000 acres, 1783, and 2,000 acres assigned to him and Jacob Rife, and they enter the same adjoining a survey of George Mercer's on the Ohio on south side (withdrawn 400, surveyed 1,000 acres).

HENRY BANKS, on warrants for 20,000 acres, enters same to join George Mercer on the Ohio containing 13,532 acres and survey of G. Washington of 10,990 acres and survey of John Henderson of 1,400 acres in forks between Ohio and Kanahwa at the mouth of the Kanahwa (notice to survey 14 May, 1785).

p. 178

JACOB RIFE and SHADERACK HARREMAN, assignee of John Hawkins, warrant for 2,000 acres, 1783, enters same adjoining John McMullan's right of settlement in Tees Valley and branch of Big Kanahwa (withdrawn per order of Harreman April 15, 1786).

January 19, 1785, JAMES CLERK, warrant for 500 acres on Bluestone in Wright's Valley, to begin at Brown's upper corner and to extend up the valley to join Jno. Lesley's improvement and to include improvement made by Wright formerly.

JOHN SMITH, on part of a treasury warrant, 130 acres on Clear Fork of Wolf Creek, to begin at the corner of Thomas Smith's land (withdrawn).

JAMES SKAGGS, assignee of James Clerk's attorney, warrant for 285 acres joining Richard Whitt's entry of 100 acres, Simpkins line, Lorton's line as purchased of John Dispain.

SAMUEL ANDREWS, assignee of William Christian, on treasury warrant, 1781, 130 acres between the land of Jeremiah Pate, purchased of the Loyal Company and Israel Lorton's on Meadow Creek.

HENRY BANKS, warrant, 1783 for 380 acres on Burks Fork of New River.

January 21, 1785, ARCHER MATHEWS and THOMAS TEES, assignees of William McWilliams, on three treasury warrants, 4,000 acres each, enters 12, 1,000 acres joining John Jones settlement and including the land between John Madison's entries on Hurrican (Hurricane) Creek and the Great Kanahwa.

HENRY BANKS, assignee of Jno. Hawkins, treasury warrant, 1783, enters same adjoining the last mentioned and extending north for quantity (surveyed with last entry in one survey).

MICHAEL CAIN, land warrant for 3,000 acres, enters same on Sixteen Mile Creek emptying into the Great Kanhawa, to begin at G. Washington's survey (2,253 acres surveyed and 747 acres to be surveyed).

DAVID STEEL, assignee of Andrew Keen(?) assignee of John Barnhas (Barbhas?), assignee of Martin Carney, assignee of Frederick S. Guin, land warrant for 3,000 acres enters 1,000 acres beginning 100 poles below the upper corner of 513 acres surveyed for John Henderson, on the Ohio and to extend to another survey of sd. Henderson containing 900 acres to include a salt spring on second branch below the mouth of Big Kanahwa.

January 22, 1785, GEORGE BOOTHE, land warrant assigned by James Hines, assignee of James Clerk's attorney, 200 acres on Mill Creek, branch of Meadow Creek joining the lands of Samuel Langdon, Thompson, and Shorten Smith.

ABRAHAM CHRISTMAN, assignee of James Charlton, land warrant, 1782, for 60 acres joining his mill place on Crab Creek and George Taylor's line and Hankins, Dowess, and Peterson's lines; 56 acres adjoining Hanks and bounded by Harris, Stony Batter and Dowess.

ROBERT SIMPKINS, assignee as above, warrant for 50 acres adjoining his own on the west side of Little River waters, also joining Saml. Arther.

JAMES SIMPKINS, assignee as above, warrant for 50 acres joining Saml. Langdon and Colo. James Robertson.

SAML. LANDGON, assignee of Jeremiah Farmer, 120 acres on Little Elkhorn, branch of Little River.

MITCHEL OUREY (AUREY) MONTGOMERY, assignee of Js. Clerk's attorney, warrant for 100 acres on Dry Meadow, waters of Meadow Creek (surveyed 96 acres).

JAMES SIMPKINS, assignee of Mathias Peterson, assignee of Jacob Zeglar, assignee of James Clerk's attorney, warrant for 100 acres joining Lorton's, Arthur's and Jervis lines (surveyed 100 acres).

EDMUND LINES, warrant withdrawn his entry of 3 March 1784, at the mouth of Buffalo Creek and enters adjoining Will: French, Joseph Morris, and Samuel Morris on main Gyandott (1,781 1/2 acres entered. Surveyed for Jas. Hines).

THOMAS HUFF, warrant for 250 acres to begin about eight miles from the mouth of Poplar Camp Creek at two large poplars at an old camp, warrant for 14,000 acres assigned by Jacob Rubsaman, assignee of. Dd. [David] Leith [Leitch]; surveyed with another entry, Book C, p. 182.

January 24, 1785, JOHN CUMPTON, assignee of John Smith, 300 acres on south side of his land to include Beaver dams, also to join George Peerey and James Cartmel, and to extend to the mountain on treasury warrant, 1783.

p. 184

January 31, 1785, DAVID STEEL for WILLIAM PICKLES and WILLIAM SAMPLE, three warrants of 2,000 acres each enters 6000 acres adjoining entry of 10,000 acres for Philip and James Moore and William Sample on second creek below the Great Kanahwa about 16 or 18 miles down the Ohio.

WILLIAM SAMPLES, assignee of Joseph Smith on two treasury warrants, 2,000 acres each, enters by Captain David Steel, 4,000 acres above and adjoining 10,000 acres for Philip and James Moore and sd. Samples; also on three land warrants of 1,000 acres each, enters 3,000 acres joining the 9,000 acres entered for Michael Gratz and Company on the first creek below the mouth of the Big Kanahwa.

p. 185

JAMES ERWIN, assignee of William Pickle and Sampels, assignee of Joseph Smith, on two land warrants of 1,000 acres each, enters same by Captain David Steel, below and adjoining 22,000 acres in the name of Philip and James Moore and Wm. Sample on the Ohio below the Great Kanahwa.

WILLIAM GREENOUGH, assignee of James Boverd, assignee of Martin Carney, on treasury warrant, 2,000 acres entered by David Steel, to begin at the entry of 14,000 acres for Gratz and Company on the first creek below the mouth of the Big Kanahwa; also assignee of William Gibson, assignee of Martin Carney on warrant for 2,000 acres entered by Captain David Steel adjoining 13,000 acres of Gratz and Company on first creek below the mouth of Big Kanahwa.

p. 186

GEORGE WELSH, assignee of David Steel, assignee of Peter Roliter, 1,690 acres, part of 3,386 1/4 acres on warrant granted Roliter, 1783, and part of warrant granted Robt. Henderson for 337 acres in all, 2,000 acres adjoining entry by William Greenough below the Big Kanahwa.

GEORGE BOOTHE withdraws 50 acres made 22nd instant, assignee of James Hines and enters same adjoining Shorten Smith and Meredith and running south of Pilot Mountain and to join Smith's place at another part on a branch of Mill Creek of Little River.

p. 187

February 1, 1785, ISRAEL LORTON, warrant for 100 acres between Presgroves', Arthur's, and the sawmill place on Meadow Creek.

February 2, 1785, DAVID STEEL, assignee of Andrew Zeans assignee of John Barniths (?), assignee of Martin Kerney, assignee of Fre. [Frederick] S. Guin, treasury warrant for 3,000 acres not dated, enters 500 acres part thereof, beginning on the bank of the Ohio below Green Bottom or Cain Brake, and about ten miles above the Guyandot at the lower end of a military survey; also on sd. warrant, February 3, 1785, 1,000 acres, beginning on the back line of the survey for John Henderson, on the Ohio below the mouth of the Great Kanahwa and with a line of his 400 acre survey, corner to survey of sd. Henderson of 1,000 acres on preemption warrant.

p. 188

February 4, 1785, HENRY HUNIGAN, warrant for 790 acres joining Kerr's, Alford's and Herald's [waters of New River].

February 10, 1785, WILLIAM DAY, assignee of David Croutch, on two land warrants, 150 acres adjoining Robert Curren's on the north side.
HENRY STOBOUGH, assignee of Preston, 330 acres on south side of Sinking Spring line (surveyed 315 acres, and surveyed 15 acres for Philip Hack).

February 19, 1785, THOMAS TEAS, warrant for 400 acres on 9 Mile Creek, on south side of Kanahwa, beginning one mile 1/4 from mouth to include an old improvement at a large clay lick.

p. 189

February 22, 1785, JOHN SMITH, treasury warrant, 130 acres on south side of Clintch [Clinch] between Major Trigg and Jno. Peerey to include big branch and to extend near Saml. Walkers.

February 28, 1785, MICHAEL DRAKE, warrant for 200 acres on Walkers Creek, branch of New River beginning at a big spring on a new cut road joining Cox, including the meetinghouse and along James Polly's land.
WILLIAM BROWN, assignee of James Clerk's attorney, 200 acres in Wright's Valley, joining his own and up the Valley about 2 1/2 miles to include Jeremiah Pate's improvements.

p. 190-192

March 1, 1785, JACOB RIFE, assignee of Christopher Bryan, assignee of John McMullin, preemption warrant, 1784, 1,000 acres in Teases Valley, adjoining right of settlement obtained from John McMullin.
JOHN ALLSOP withdraws 50 acres on Bear Spring and enters the same on Meadow Branch and on north side of Buckeye survey to begin about 40 poles above the cabin on the same branch.

March 4, 1785, ROBERT EWING, treasury warrant, 703 acres, 1782, and assigned by Alex. Willey, enters same as follows: 100 acres to begin at Godfrey's Antrem's northeast corner near the road that runs from Antrem's to Sproul's; also 100 acres on North Fork of Holston to begin on the river at the north side of the river on Antrem's line; also 100 acres on North Fork of Holston to begin on a path that runs from James Gillaspyes to Jno. Buchanan's about ten poles from the top of the main dividing ridge between Gillaspyes and Buchanan's on north side of sd. Ridge, and to run a northeast course; also 50 acres to begin where Thomas Gillaspyes line crosses the path that runs from Gillaspyes to William Richardson's; also 300 acres to begin at the top of a main dividing ridge in a path that runs from Godfrey Entrem's to John Buchanan's.
JAMES GILLASPY, on part of the above treasury warrant, 50 acres to begin at his southwest corner of an old survey.
JOHN CHAPMAN, assignee of Rich'd Chapman, assignee of James Clerk's attorney, on treasury warrant, 15 acres on east side of New River to join Richard Chapman.

p. 193

March 25, 1785, COLO. ANDREW DONALLY and JOHN ARCHER, treasury warrant, 516 acres, 1782, assigned by John Lockridge, 200 acres at the mouth of Loon Creek, below the Big falls of Chanukah; also 100 acres at the first large island below the mouth of Elk to include the island.

WILLIAM MORRIS, assignee of John Archer, assignee of Mary Bridger, assignee of James Mitchell, assignee of Jas. Clark, on treasury warrant, 1782, 400 acres in Campbell's Bottom between Leonard and William Morris.

p. 194

JOHN JONES withdraws his entry of 1782 of 400 acres below the point, and enters 200 acres in partnership with Wm. Morris on Paint Creek about two miles up; and the remaining 200 acres for Leonard and Wm. Morris joining the right of settlement obtained from Wm. Morris at the mouth of Kitchem's Creek.

March 29, 1785, THADEUS COOLEY, warrant assigned by Stephen Reeder, assignee of J. Clerk, 150 acres joining the southwest side of the land he lives on (83 acres surveyed).

JAMES NEWELL, preemption warrant, 200 acres joining John Francis on Cripple Creek and west side of Henry Francis and Will: Gleaves, beginning on Henry Francis' line on a rocky point; 300 acres joining the widow Porter, Rodger Oats, Stephen Saunders, James and Robert Wiley, on south side of Cripple Creek.

p. 195

PATRICK JOHNSON, warrant for 50 acres enters the same along the lines of an old survey on the main fork of Reed Creek.

April 6, 1785, CALAB KIRK, assignee of Zachirah Standly, assignee of John Boswell, warrant for 1,200 acres, enters same on a creek supposed to be nine miles below the mouth of Cole Run, on head of which hunters have made an encampment.

JOHN MICHIE, assignee of John Jackson, warrant for 500 acres, above and adjoining last mentioned entry.

p. 196

CALEB KIRK, assignee of Zackariah Standly, assignee of John Boswell, on warrant for 976 1/4 acres, adjoining and above the last entry.

JOHN MICHIE, assignee of Nathl. Thomason, assignee of William Roe, warrant for 500 acres, above and adjoining the above entry.

April 11, 1785, GEORGE PEERY withdraws 30 acres entered 19 May, 1782, and assigned same to Wm. Peery who enters same on Hurricane Branch of Clinch adjoining land purchased of John Peery.

THOMAS McGEORGE withdraws his entry at the mouth of Mill Creek and assigns it to Benjamin Turman, 1,400 acres on a warrant granted to Caleb Hall for 5,468 acres, 1782, enters the 1,400 acres joining and below the first bottom below an entry opposite the mouth of Paint Creek and crossing Sandy Creek to extend on both sides of Paint Lick Creek and the painted trees, 699 acres of this entry lying in Fayatte County [Kentucky] and remainder in Montgomery County [Virginia].

April 12, 1785, PATRICK NAPIER, warrant of 30 acres, enters part thereof on a branch that come in from Jeys (?) Mill Creek, beginning where Captain Pearis's road crosses the branch.

ALBERT GALLATIN and SAVARY de VALCONLON, 100 acres on treasury warrant, 1783, granted Michael Ryan, on largest island in Ohio between mouth of Great Kanahwa and the mouth of Sandy so as to include the whole island, the sd. island being opposite a survey for George Mercer and supposed to be about six miles below the mouth of the Great Kanahwa; 1,900 acres on Great Kanahwa beginning at the lower end of Dr. Craig's survey and to include vacant land between Craig's and Genl. Washington's; 5,000 acres on treasury warrant, 1783,

p. 198, granted David Anderson, on Great Kenhawa and Cole River beginning at confluence of both on lower side of Cole River to include all the vacant land between entries of John Madison on Kanhawa and those of Thomas Upton, Genl. Lewis and Charles Davies at or near the falls of Cole River;

p. 199, 4,000 acres on treasury warrant, 1783, granted Richard Noel, Junr., on Great Kanhawa to include vacant land on it between entry of 50 acres for James Byrnsides, adjoining and above G. Washington's survey in forks of Kanhawa at Cole River and several entries made in Price's Bottom and near it a little below and opposite the mouth of Elk River; 8,000 acres on three treasury warrants, one granted Michael Ryan, one granted David Anderson, one granted Philip Slaughter on Great Kanhawa to include vacant land on it between an entry of Andrew Donally at the great falls and entries made in Campbell's Bottom and near it (little above and opposite Elk River); 4,000 acres added to the foregoing entry on three treasury warrants, 1783, granted John Lewis and Richard Claiborne, so the whole is 12,000 acres; 7,000 acres on three treasury warrants

p. 201, granted Frederick S. Guion, 1783, granted to Simon Welch, and two exchanged land treasury warrants in 1784 granted Saml. McCraw in exchange for part of treasury warrant, 1783, on Twelve Pole Creek, branch of the Ohio that empties into the Guyandotte and Sandy River beginning at the upper end of Mr. Duval's upper entry and extending up both sides of said creek and up the main fork of it 15 miles; "the aforesaid entry is to be laid off in as many surveys as will extend so far up leaving room for entry of Prather and Smith at the forks of the creek and also for several entries made by James and Wm. Madison, Thos. Huff and Wm. Ward on Buffaloe Creek, if that creek proves to the same with the main Twelve Pole if those interfere with this."

p. 202

April 18, WILLIAM CHRISTIAN and DANIEL TRIGG, executors of the estate of WILLIAM INGLES, deceased, on treasury warrant, 1782, for 676 1/2 acres, enters 200 acres on Clinch River; 476 1/4 acres on Clinch to include the place marked out by the Loyal Company for Obidiah Garwood.

April 19, 1785, JOHN SMITH, 150 acres on both sides of Clinch to begin at the mouth of Plum Creek (surveyed with his entry of 27th instant, see page 203a).

p. 203

April 26, 1785, ISAAC SPRATT, on warrant of Richard Muse, 400 acres joining William Hayes on east and Godfrey Antrim on west, on a creek emptying into the North Fork of Holston on the north side

GEORGE POWERS, assignee of George Kinser, enters 100 acres with no location given [perhaps Cripple Creek].

PETER RAZOR, preemption warrant, assigned by James Newell, 50 acres on South Fork of Holston joining Ruben Debor [Debord], Michael Plankenpicker and Joshua Jones.

HENRY CLEMENTS, 100 acres joining David Bustard [no location, perhaps on Cripple Creek].

DUNCAN GULLION, 300 acres on head of Sally Run joining Stophel Brown and Harklerader [Harkrader], withdrawn April 26, 1790.

31

p. 203 (a), JOHN BURROW (BARRON?) on warrant granted Peter Brown, 1782, for 490 2/3 acres enters 300 acres on ridge path joining the head of Falling Spring and Dry Hollow (surveyed 185 acres).

ISAAC SKAGGS, 100 acres on head of Strouds Branch joining Conrood Wall and James Skaggs.

JAMES ADAIR, on said warrant, 90 2/3 acres adjoining his old line and Peppers Road (surveyed 90 acres).

SAMUEL BAILEY, assignee of James Clerk's attorney warrant for 500 acres, enters 200 acres joining William Canterbury on east side of headwaters of Mill Creek.

April 27, 1785, JOHN SMITH, state warrant, 150 acres on Clinch joining his entry 19th of month on south side beginning at mouth of Plumb Creek (surveyed 90 acres).

p. 204

May 12, 1785, DANIEL HOWE, assignee of Joseph Howe, assignee of Joseph Cloyd, assignee of Ephraim Dunlop, 35 acres on Back Creek to begin at his patent line.

May 14, 1785, MITCHEAL OURY MONTGOMERY, 50 acres on part of a treasury warrant granted him by Saml. Bailey, on Mill Creek, branch of Meadow Creek to begin at the first branch above Romines Mill and running along Israel Lorton's line, Peter Romines line and joining Lorton's new survey.

May 20, 1785, ROBERT EWING withdraws 33 acres out of 300 acres entered March 4, 1785, and enters same to begin in a lick on a path that runs from John Buchanan's over Brushy Mountain to Poor Valley.

p. 205

May 18, 1785, DANIEL CARLEN, assignee of Patrick Henry, on warrant of 1,000 acres, 1781, enters 50 acres on west side of John Fanning's line; 100 acres on Cramberry Glade beginning at a white oak marked DC and running up and down Cramberry Creek at Captain Swift's muster ground; 50 acres on military warrant, 1780, "the first entry is made by virtue of this military warrant and the second by ye land office treasury warrant. It is a mistake in making the entry, Preston SMC [Surveyor of Montgomery County]."

GEORGE TAYLOR, by virtue of land granted to James Clark, 80 acres lying between George Taylor, Senr. lines, Hankins, and Popecofer's land on Crab Creek; 70 acres joining George Taylor, Senr., Smith and Sperry's lines, and running towards Garlick and Wolrick Taylor's lines (surveyed 60 acres, 10 acres withdrawn).

May 20, 1785, JOHN BELL, assignee of Sam'l Bailey, warrant for 50 acres joining John Bell, Junr., lines on waters of New River.

p. 206, CURTIS ELLIOTT, assignee of Saml. Bailey, 100 acres on Howerton's Spring Branch.

May 26, 1785, SAMUEL ANDREWS, assignee of William Davidson, assignee of Walter Davidson, assignee of James Clerk's attorney, on treasury warrant, 1782, 100 acres adjoining his entry of 30 acres joining Capt. Lorton and Jeremiah Pate (surveyed 64 acres with sd. entry).

PETER ROMINE on above warrant, 50 acres between Richard Whitt's, Nathan Romine and Isreal Lorton's lines on Mill Creek, branch of Meadow Creek [branch of Little River].

MITCHEL OUREY MONTGOMERY, assignee of Samuel Andrews, 50

acres beginning at Shilling's line on Little River and with Jervis' line "to pitch of a hill upon the waggon road."

p. 207, JACOB PATE, assignee of Samuel Andrews, assignee as in the last entry, 200 acres to begin at William Greson's [Grayson's] corner on Little River above Gresons [Grayson's] plantation and up the river to the "chinckquipine" ford and crossing a bent of said river (surveyed 93 acres, withdrawn 107 acres.

May 30, 1785, WILLIAM HALL, on treasury warrant, 500 acres, 1782, assigned to Mathew Dickey by John Walters, assignee of Walter Crockett's attorney for James Clark, enters 100 acres on east side of Chestnut Creek on the north side of Fanning's line and running along Iron ridge towards Crooked Creek.

MATHEW DICKEY, on above warrant, 100 acres beginning at Fanning's east line along east side of Iron Ridge

DAN'L CARLIN, on preemption warrant, assignee of James Newell, assignee of John Fanning, 200 acres to begin at the corner of Fanning's survey on settlement right on west side of Chest. [Chestnut] Creek.

p. 208, DANIEL CARLIN, on treasury warrant, no acres stated, to begin at a white oak some distance from Chestnut Creek, on east at the lower end of John Fanning's to include a ridge of iron ore.

June 18, 1785, ANDREW BROWN, assignee of Nich's [Nicholas] Wyrick, on treasury warrant 372 acres on Read [Reed] Creek, joining George Keagly and Jacob Pruner.

JOHN HARKARADER, on above warrant, 160 acres on Reed Creek adjoining the survey of Stople [Stophel, Christopher] Brown's to include his improvements.

JACOB RIFE and SHADERACK HARRIMAN withdraws 400 acres from their entry of 2,000 acres on January 18, 1785 and enters same on John McMullin to join their former entry on the lower side.

RICHARD MYNATT, assignee of Walter Crockett, attorney for James Clark, 500 acres on treasury warrant, on waste land between Stony Batter, Rich'd Hankins, A. Chrisman, John Harrison, Wm. Hankins, Chtr. [Christina?] Crewey's lines.

p. 209, HENRY BANKS and JOHN HAWKINS, on treasury warrant, 2,200 acres part thereof, on Pain Creek of Great Kanhawa to begin about ten miles above the mouth of said creek near an old camp and about one-half mile below a creek emptying into same on the upper side.

June 22, 1785, JACOB GABERT, assignee of Saml. Gibson, treasury warrant, 973 acres, 1782, from head to mouth of Sandy River including all the vacant lands.

June 23, 1785, RICHARD MASON, assignee of Wm. Hastley (?), assignee of Anthony Crethers, assignee of Colo. Alexr. Dick, on a number of treasury warrants, 30,000 acres on north side of Mud River, a fork of Gyandotte adjoining and above survey for Samuel Jones on sd. river beginning corner to Jones.

p. 210-211

RICHARD MASON, assignee of Wm. Rankin, treasury warrant, not dated, 2,430 acres part on Mud River, fork of Gyandotte adjoining and above survey of 5,000 acres made for Wm. Beard on sd. river, to begin corner to Beard; also 13,026 1/2 acres on Mud River, fork of Gyandotte adjoining and above survey made for Wm. Breckinridge on sd. river.

JAMES CARNOGHAN, assignee of John Campbell on a number of treasury warrants, 30,000 acres on Mud River, a fork of Gyandotte, adjoining survey

33

for Samuel Jones, to begin at a sugar tree corner to Jones.

SAMUEL JONES, treasury warrant, 40,000 acres on Mud River, fork of Gyandott about 30 computed miles above the mouth and to begin about 1/2 mile above the mouth of a small creek; also 25,000 acres on Mud River fork of Gyandotte adjoining and above a survey made for Richard Mason; also 20,000 acres on Mud River adjoining and above a survey for William Breckinridge.

WILLIAM BEARD on a number of treasury warrants, 5,000 acres on Mud River joining a survey for Samuel Jones for 20,000 acres.

JACOB RUBSAMEN, assignee of David Leitch, on treasury warrant, 5,000 acres on Mud River, fork of Gyandott adjoining and above Samuel Jones survey of 25,000 acres (surveyed for Cuthbert, Bullitt and Triple).

p. 212

June 24, 1785, WYATT POWELL, treasury warrant 972 1/2 acres, 1782, on South Fork of Mud River, fork of Gyandott to begin about three miles up south fork and to join James Breckinridge survey at mouth of said fork.

WILLIAM WARD, of Botetourt County, withdraws all entries made 8 April 1783, also 10 acres of the first entry on June 2, 1783, also 5 on September 4, 1783, and one on November 29, 1783.

JOSEPH BAKER, assignee of Frederick Edwards, assignee of Peter Hollis withdraws part of his former entry and enters 150 acres on Ephraim Ward's Branch, also 300 acres to include land between Peirce's, Frank Johnson, and Tuttle.

THOMAS UPTON, assignee of William Hamilton, 400 acres adjoining his and Davies preemption warrant on New River.

p. 213

WILLIAM FARLER, assignee of John Smith, 5 acres beginning on a line of Begley's survey and to include the salt petre cave not far from said land on waters of Walkers Creek.

SAMUEL WALKER, assignee of Henry Banks, on two warrants of 100 acres each, 200 acres on Clinch joining Abram Trigg's upper line where it crosses the Clinch.

June 26, 1785, JOHN TAYLOR and WILLIAM WYNNE, on warrant 1,138 acres on Clear Fork of Sandy Creek above and below Mathias Harman's camp (568 acres withdrawn per John Taylor's verbal order May 29, 1786).

June 28, 1785, DAVID CLAY, assignee of Joseph Baker, assignee of James Clerk, on treasury warrant, 500 acres, enters 400 acres on Rich Creek and down the Bluestone to include Ezekial Clay's improvements (entry withdrawn and assigned to Farley).

MITCHELL CLAY, assignee of said warrant, enters 100 acres on Bluestone joining Clover Bottom and David Cloyd.

pp. 214-217

RALPH STEWART, 100 acres on the north side of New River joining Mitchell Clay's.

July 4, 1785, GEORGE BOOTHE, on treasury warrant, 50 acres assigned by Peter Romine, assignee of William Davidson, assignee of Walter Davidson, assignee of James Clerk's attorney enters same and 80 acres of another warrant, land on Plumb Creek of New River, adjoining the widow Beard, William Taburn [Tabor] and Bingerman's [Bingaman's], and to be on the west side of Taburn's [Tabor's] and running towards Jno. [John] Charlton's and east to

34

Taburn's [Tabor's] and south to Seven Mile Tree on the big road and along the road towards the New River to a fork of the road, on a branch of Meadow Creek (surveyed 109 acres, which was assigned to William Tabor and by him to John Winters).

July 5, 1785, JAMES BRUMFIELD, warrant for 5 acres on west side of New River adjoining the big cave claimed by Philip Snidoe to include the salt petre cave in the clift. "Snidoe cave is in at the lower end of sd. Snidoe line."

July 23, 1785, GEORGE TROTTER withdraws his entries made 4 Sept. 1783.

THOMAS SPEARY withdraws his second entry made June 29, 1784 which was for 75 acres and enters the same joining Mathew Smith, Abram Christman and the land sd. Speary lives on, on Stroubles Creek (surveyed 28 acres and the balance was withdrawn).

August 5, 1785, CUTHBERT, BULLITT and FRANCIS TRIPLETT, on treasury warrant, 1784, 5,000 acres on south side of Mud River beginning at the lower corner of James and Mathew Vaughn's land.

JAMES GLENTWORTH, on treasury warrant, 1783, 1,000 acres on Gyandotte River below the mouth of Mud River, fork of same, to begin at Myn's (?) corner below the mouth of sd. Mud River.

CUTHBERT, BULLIT and FRANCIS TRIPLETT, on two treasury warrants, 5,000 acres on Mud River, fork of Gyandotte adjoining and above the survey of 13,026 1/2 acres for Richard Mason for same, on two treasury warrants, of 5,000 acres each enters same on Mud River, fork of the Gyandotte, begin corner to Richard Mason; also on treasury warrant, 7,000 acres part thereof on Mud River, fork of Gyandotte, corner to survey of Jones.

JOHN SKAGGS, warrant assigned by Thomas Upton, 200 acres to begin at a bent of New River below the War Ford (withdrawn); 100 acres beginning at the steep gut below the War Ford (withdrawn); 400 acres on head of North Fork of Cole River beginning at the lick (withdrawn); 100 acres at the mouth of Piney on upper side and up the New River (withdrawn); 100 acres on Glade Creek beginning at the creek and down the same and then up New River (withdrawn); 200 acres below Brookses Bottom at head of an island including the island (withdrawn); 200 acres at the upper end of Brookses Bottom and beginning at the lower end at the Bottom (withdrawn).

August 10, 1785, WILLIAM FULTON withdraws his entry made 17 October 1783 on treasury warrant for 11,115 1/2 acres (delivered to John Millstead).

August 15, 1785, ANDREW REID, attorney in fact for Samuel Culberson agreeable to Honorable General Court of Virginia held at Richmond Oct. 12, 1784 which ordered a grant for 400 acres in the right of settlement on the land in Montgomery County known as Culberson's Bottom.

p. 218

August 18, 1785, GEORGE BOOTH, assignee of Mitchell Montgomery, 50 acres on treasury warrant, land on branch of Plum Creek on east side of John Charlton's adjoining Henry Bingeman and running to William Tabor's corner and with said Tabor line.

August 21, 1785, JOHN LEGGET enters 50 acres on treasury warrant, on Middle Fork of Holston, joining William Patterson and John Campbell, beginning corner to William Patterson on south side of Middle Fork of Holston.

August 29, 1785, CALAB KIRK, assignee of William Prentis, assignee of David Anderson on 1,000 acres, treasury warrant, 1783, land on east side of Morris Griffith's Nob and running to Inglishes line.

JOHN BOSWELL, 1,200 acres on treasury warrant, 1783, to adjoin above entry and to run on Inglishes line.

September 12, 1785, JACOB GARDNER, assignee of William Prentis, assignee of David Anderson, treasury warrant, 1,000 acres not dated, on headwaters of Clear Fork of Wolf Creek to include Benson's and Isaac Gray's improvements, and to extend to Buckhorn Ridge on north side of Rich Mountain on the south side.

ZACHARIAH STANLEY, assignee of Richard Anderson, treasury warrant, 400 acres on south side of Rich Mountain to begin where a path crosses the mountain between William Wynn and Thompson's on southeast course to Thompson and then a west course down the Valley to include Henry and Brookes' improvements on waters of Clinch.

JOHN BOSWELL, on treasury warrant, 1,200 acres on Clinch to begin at William Wynn's said east corner and towards Rich Mountain to include improvements and an old mill built by said Wynn and to Hensly's line and with it to Harman's.

ZACHARIAH STANDLEY [STANLEY], on treasury warrant, granted Butler Bradburn being a duplicate, enters 581 1/4 acres on Walkers Creek, on Daniel Justice and Richard Muse's lines (withdrawn).

September 13, 1785, JOHN RICHARDSON, assignee of Solomon Stephens, assignee of Thos. McGeorge, on treasury warrant, 200 acres on Clapboard Creek to adjoin William Grayson's survey and below the same to include improvements made by John Gordon (surveyed 190 acres and assigned to Nat. Muncy).

September 19, 1785, WILLIAM LOCKHART, assignee of John Craig (weaver), assignee of Colonel Joseph Cloyd, on treasury warrant, 190 acres on west side of John Craig's.

JOHN GRILLS warrant granted Henry Banks for 75 acres, enters 50 acres adjoining his entry of 50 acres on the northwest side.

JOHN CRAIG (weaver) on warrant assigned in part by Colonel Joseph Cloyd, 100 acres on Hazel Hollow on east side of land.

WILLIAM THOMPSON, assignee of John Taylor, assignee of James Clerk's attorney, on treasury warrant, not dated, 50 acres adjoining land sd. Thompson now lives on and down to another tract of sd. Thompson which he purchased of James King on Maiden Spring Fork of Clinch; 150 acres above Jn. Sharp's survey on Maiden Spring Fork of Clinch known by the name of Puncheon Camp.

SAMUEL CECIL, assignee of James Clerk's attorney, on treasury warrant, 500 acres joining on three sides the land he formerly lived on, also joining Morgan, Cloyd, and Smith, on Neck Creek [of New River].

ZACHARIAH STANLEY, assignee of James Clerk's attorney on treasury warrant, not dated, 500 acres to begin above McEmmon's alias McAddams' improvements on the creek William Thompson lives on, on waters of Clinch, to include McEmmons' improvements.

September 25, 1785, MICHAEL WOODS withdraws his warrant and entries 1780 and warrant is delivered to John Burnisdes per his order.

September 20, 1785, JOHN WALRAVEN, assignee of Andrew Porter, on treasury
warrant, 100 acres on the Cove or joining George Breckenridge on east side
of Captain Adams.

JOHN GODFREY YOUNK [YONTS?], assignee of James Finley, treasury
warrant, not dated, 255 1/2 acres on Pine Run, between and joining Nicholas
Cline, John Etter, and Adam Napp's [Knipp's]. Surveyed 149 acres, withdraws 106 acres.

GEORGE PEARIS, on preemption warrant, 65 acres on Dry Fork of Wolf
Creek between end of Wolf Creek Mountain and Big Spring Mountain; also
40 acres on sd. warrant, adjoining his corn right next to the mountain.

WILLIAM INGLEDOVE, 100 acres on treasury warrant, assigned by Robt.
Sayers on south side of Paxton's Glade and joining sd. survey (withdrawn and
entered for Earhart Zimmerman).

GEORGE PEECK [PECK], on preemption warrant, not dated, 58 acres on
north side of the land he lives on, on waters of Neck Creek [New River]; also
88 acres on north side of same, and also 154 acres on White Glade on path to
Pepper's Ferry adjoining Alexander Page's (all on one warrant, 154 acres
withdrawn).

October 7, 1785

MORDACCI HORD, on treasury warrant, 1783, 1,000 acres on north side of
West Fork of Little Cole River near an Indian Camp; also 1,000 acres on Horse
Creek or Breckenridge Creek emptying into Cole River below the forks.

October 8, 1785, THOMAS SHANNON, assignee of Samuel Shannon, on treasury
warrant, 926 acres, enters 224 acres part thereof, on Big Walkers Creek above
the mouth of Little Walkers Creek (surveyed 208 acres, 16 acres withdrawn).

PATRICK McELYEA on above warrant, 70 acres on north side of Walkers
Mountain nearly opposite to the big crossing of Walkers Creek.

October 10, 1785, THOMAS SMITH, assignee of Henry Banks, on treasury warrant,
not dated, 27 acres on Clear Fork of Wolf Creek to include Lindsday's
improvements; 40 acres adjoining his entry on Wolf Creek on south side of
sd. entry joining Jacob Dooley's (surveyed with sd. entry).

HENRY BAGLEY, assignee of Henry Banks, on three treasury warrants, not
dated, 350 acres on Walkers Creek between Joseph Pauley's and John
Bagley's land and joining Walkers Mountain.

JOSEPH PAULEY, assignee of Henry Banks, on treasury warrant, not dated,
100 acres on south side of former entry.

WILLIAM SPENCER, SENR., on four treasury warrants, 150 acres each,
assigned by Henry Banks, land on Greasy Creek on Reed Island to include
Turman's Camp.

ABNER LESTER, assignee of Samuel Andrews, assignee of William Davidson,
assignee of Walter Davidson, assignee of Walter Crockett, attorney for James
Clerk, on treasury warrant, not dated, 26 acres part thereof, on Peliham (?)
Branch to begin at an old line.

October 13, 1785, MICHAEL MILLER, assignee of Henry Banks, on treasury warrant, not dated, 75 acres to include Beech Springs about one mile and half from where John Young now lives.

p. 228

October 18, 1785, HENRY LAMBERT withdraws his entry 12 Sept. 1782, on Reed Creek joining Wampler, Stailey and the meetinghouse [St. Paul Lutheran] land.

GEORGE WAMPLER, assignee of Henry Lambert, assignee of John Montgomery, treasury warrant, not dated, 150 acres, enters 50 acres of same, joining Ratliff's Marsh, Black, and John Willson, on Reed Creek; 100 acres on Reed Creek adjoining Copeheifer[Copenhaver], Moore, and Ratliff Marsh, that part purchased by Rev'd John Brown.

October 20, 1785, RICHARD CHAPMAN, on treasury warrant assigned by James Clerk's attorney, 130 acres on East River opposite where Edward Hale lives to include the place known as Alsup's Camp; 130 acres one and half miles above last entry on East River to include Nob Lick.

October 31, 1785, SHADERICK HARRIMAN withdraws entry of 400 acres on January 18, and enters same over against the mouth of Elk Creek to begin one-half mile above little creek that comes through a small bottom of William Morrises to join river ridge (withdrawn per order April 15, 1786).

November 1, 1785, MATHEW DICKEY, assignee of John Kerr, preemption warrant for 100 acres on Chestnut Creek, joining Flower Swift, Jerh. [Jeremiah] Clonch, and Dickey.

p. 230

JAMES NEWELL, assignee of Meshack Turner, on treasury warrant, 128 1/2 acres adjoining Mathew Dickey, John Fannen, Jereh. Clonch, on both sides of Chestnut Creek.

November 5, 1785, WILLIAM INGLEDOVE withdraws his entry 30 September 1785 and enters 100 acres joining Paxtons Glade, on east side [Reed Creek].

November 8, 1785, WALTER BEATY, on treasury warrant, 150 acres, adjoining on north side of Patrick Calhoun's patent land [Reed Creek].

PETER PINKLEY, 36 acres between south side of Jno. Vance's patent land and land surveyed for Charles Simmerman [Reed Creek].

p. 231

JAMES NEWELL, on preemption warrant, 234 acres, 1784, enters 100 acres on same on Chest. [Chestnut] Creek, joining Ben Hartgrove, David Read, and John Williams.

ABRAM POWELL on above warrant, 1,346 acres on both sides of Chest. [Chestnut] Creek, joining John Williams

MATHEW DICKEY, on treasury warrant, 500 acres, 1782, assigned to him by John Walters, assignee of Walter Crockett, attorney for James Clerk, 52 acres entered on both sides of Chestnut Creek, joining Flower Swift's and Ben Hartgrove.

November 17, 1785, JAMES BYRNSIDES withdraws his entry December 18, 1781, 470 acres and located on North Fork of Cole River where Toney's stationed camp was this fall, including the camp, likewise a lick with both forks; also withdraws 100 acres entry known by Hick's improvements made 1781, and locates same adjoining above entry some distance below the forks of the creek to an island in the main fork (withdrawn).

pp. 232-233

November 18, 1785, COLO. ALEXR. STEWART, on treasury warrant, 200 acres on branch of Bluestone called Muddy Fork emptying in on west side about one-half mile above McGuyar's Mill (surveyed 113 acres withdrawn 87 acres). WILLIAM BOWLES, assignee on treasury warrant, not dated, 100 acres joining Hornbaragar and own land on north side and on northeast of H. Lower, and between the Great Road that leads from Peppers to Hans Meadows and sd. Hornbarigar's.

JOHN SMITH, on treasury warrant, 150 acres adjoining southwest of above entry to join Hornbaragar on Crab Creek to include Harman Lower's improvements (surveyed for Henry Lower, 80 acres; warrant 1783 for 4,000 acres to Michl. Ryan).

December 2, 1785, COLO. ALEXR. STEWART, on treasury warrant 1,500 beginning at Suiter's improvements at the foot of Lick Mountain opposite George Peck's beginning about one-half mile below said improvements and running up along side of mountain two miles above a spring known as the Big Spring at Workman's improvements; also 1,500 acres to include the whole vacant land on Clear Fork of Wolf Creek; also 200 acres on Cove Fork emptying into Clear Fork (surveyed 175 acres, and 25 acres withdrawn); also 300 acres on Laurel Fork of Wolf Creek beginning where the road from Walkers Creek to Bluestone crosses the creek (surveyed with his third entry January 28, 1786).

CHARLES HAYS, assignee of Colo. Stewart, on treasury warrant, 140 (?) acres at the mouth of Clear Fork of Wolf Creek; 180 acres below Joseph Daughterty's plantation on Wolf creek joining his land; also 100 acres about 2 miles below Joseph Daughterty on Wolf Creek at a place known as the Big Spring (withdrawn).

p. 234

December 3, 1785, ELIZABETH MADISON, on part of a treasury warrant for 200 acres on head branch of Laural and Gourd Creek of Little River to include Bobbit's land.

December 4, 1785, JOHN SMITH, on treasury warrant, not dated, 200 acres on north west side of F. Nestor's survey and to extend to Tobias Phillips.

December 5, 1785, GEORGE BOOTH, on treasury warrant, 93 acres on branch of Mill Creek, south side of Abner Lester's place.

December 8, 1785, MOSES HICKENBOTTOM, on treasury warrant, 1782, 400 acres on north side of Clinch Mountain between Pancake Bottom and Emmons Cabbin on Maiden Spring Fork (withdraws 250 acres, surveyed 150 acres).

HENRY ASBURY, 200 acres on south side of Morrises Nob, joining William Thompson (withdrawn July 8, 1787).

p. 235

December 12, 1785, DANIEL CARLAND [CARLIN], assignee of John Edwards, assignee of Isham Webb, assignee of Peter Saunders, treasury warrant, not dated, 500 acres on Crooked Creek to include iron bank on north side of creek on copprass hill.

December 16, 1785, PETER RIFE, assignee of Michael Price, assignee of Alexander Stuart, on treasury warrant, 100 acres adjoining Taylor and Rowland to include a spring.

CHRISTIAN CROCKLY, assignee of Henry Banks on treasury warrant, not dated, 100 acres on Burks Creek on branch known by the name of Thorney Hollow to join Jacob Pate on north side and running towards Brushy Run.

p. 236

HARMAN LOUR [LOWER], assignee of Howard Havin, on treasury warrant, 1782, 200 acres on Crab Creek to begin at Major Taylor's corner and to run along Keese's and Bowls' lines (surveyed for Henry Lour).

GEORGE FRY, assignee of James McCorkle, on treasury warrant, 67 1/2 acres part thereof, beginning the north side of Nob Mountain and running across the big ridge northwest and thence southwest and thence west joining along George Fry, Senr.'s line (surveyed 56 acres).

DAN'L HARMAN, assignee of John Smith, treasury warrant, 1783, 200 acres on Clintch [Clinch] River, on northeast side of survey for Garwood which he now lives on and to join Wynn.

December 17, 1785, WILLIAM FREYSEY, assignee of Henry Banks, on treasury warrant, 1783, 150 acres beginning on south side of Walkers Creek and to run up the creek and to join Thos. Napper's land that he now lives on and to run with said Napper's line and up the creek to include salt petre cave and improvements and to run down the other side of the creek and to join John Chapman's entry on lower end of Napper's land.

p. 237

December 20, 1785, MURDOCK McKINSIE, assignee of Christian Snidoe, on treasury warrant, 80 acres part thereof, on east side of his survey made 1782 on Walkers Creek, about two miles from the mouth to include his house and clearing and other appurtenances.

December 22, 1785, GEORGE WILLIAMS, assignee of Jacob Scilar, assignee of James Clerk's attorney, on treasury warrant, 20 acres part of which is not yet surveyed in his entry of January 24, 1783, on west side of land he lives on and on both sides of Sinking Creek and to join George Fry and Parker Lucas' lands.

pp. 238-241

January 19, 1786, JOHN SMITH, on treasury warrant, 500 acres of which was assigned by Henry Crutcher, entries as follows: by John Toney's direction according to agreement, 500 acres on North Fork of Cole River to begin at the mouth of Sycamore Creek to include bottom land. " N.B. the north fork mentioned in this entry empties into the Cole River about 16 miles below the mouth of Shockley Fork on the same side of Cole River" (surveyed 230 acres and 270 acres withdrawn); 500 acres at the mouth of North Fork of Big Cole River, to begin near the confluence of said forks and to extend up and down both forks and the main stream to include a large bottom below the forks on south side and a large rock known by the name of Big Stone (surveyed 186 acres, and 207 acres and 107 acres withdrawn); 762 acres on Big Cole River to begin at the mouth of Elk River and to extend down and on both sides Cole River to include bottom known as Canal (Carol?) Bottom, about four computed miles below the mouth of North fork of River mentioned in the first entry of this date (surveyed 186 acres, 143 acres, and 439 acres); 200 acres on Big Cole River to begin in a small cain brake on north side of sd. river opposite the mouth of Bear River and down and on both sides of sd. river to include a beech bottom on south side, about 5 1/2 computed miles below the fork mentioned in the first entry; 500 acres at the big turn hole on Cole River and up and down and on both sides and up a branch that empties into Cole River on north side about 3/4 miles above the turn hole which is about 6 1/2 computed miles below the fork "These two entries surveyed as follows: 125, 195, 96, 60, 129, and 100 withdrawn;" 500 acres on Big Cole River to begin at a small sand lick on north bank of the river about 8 miles below the junction of the forks to include good bottom land (surveyed 456 acres and 44 acres withdrawn); 800 acres on Big Cole River, beginning adjoining and below last entry and to include some beech bottoms (surveyed 125 acres and 655 acres withdrawn); 2,400 acres on Big Cole River to begin at a small island opposite the mouth of Wolf Creek which empties into Cole River on south side and about 10 computed miles below the junction of fork and up and on both sides of Wolf Creek to include sand lick and bottom with some small cane in it above lick and up and down and on both sides of Big Cole River to include an island a small distance below the mouth of said branch (surveyed 167,164, 162, 182, 127, 136, and withdrawn 1,518 acres); 300 acres on North Fork of Cole River, to begin above the mouth of the creek where Toneys made a station camp in September 1785, which is about 13 miles above the junction of said forks being the same creek whereon James Burnsides made an entry 17 November 1785 to include bottom which lies at the mouth of Dry Run (surveyed 212 acres, withdrawn 88 acres); 200 acres on North Fork of Big Cole River to begin at a small sand lick about two miles above the mouth of Dry Run (withdrawn); 600 acres beginning at the white oak lick on head of Little Bluestone branch of Big Bluestone to include Hale's Camp and all good land adjoining.

JOHN TONEY, assignee of John Roe, assignee of John Alsup, assignee of Peter Saunders, on treasury warrant, 100 acres of which is assigned, enters same on head of Kavenaugh's Run which empties into New River at the lower end of Brush Bottom (surveyed 77 acres, and 33 acres withdrawn).

January 23, 1786, JAMES BYRNSIDES withdraws the following entries: 200 acres of third entry December 18, 1781 and 73 acres of second entry made December 19, 1784, and enters 250 acres part thereof adjoining his settlement and preemption in Culbertson's Bottom on New River.

p. 242

January 23, 1786, JAMES BYRNSIDES, JUNR., assignee of James Byrnsides, Senr., on treasury warrant, 223 acres part there of, on Cole River, beginning at first narrows "which are so confined that it is not passible for a man on horseback," about 6 computed miles from Upton's and southwest side of said river running 20 poles down to the river and down the river 60 poles.

HENRY BANKS, assignee of Michael Ryan, on treasury warrant, 2,000 acres, enters 1,215 acres on Bluestone beginning about 15 poles on south of Pipe Stem Nobb.

HENRY BANKS, assignee of Robert B. Chew on two treasury warrants, 3,000 acres each, 1783, enters three tracts of 1,000 acres each, two tracts of 3,000 acres each, and one tract of 2,000 acres on Piney River, adjoining Byrnsides entry on Bacon Town; on Paint Creek including the painted trees (withdrawn); and land about 4 miles where the Laurel begins on branch of Paint Creek emptying in on north side at an old hunting camp; also on a creek that empties into Cole River opposite a large buffaloe lick to begin about one mile above the mouth of said creek; and one 3,000 acres on treasury warrant, assigned by Robert B. Chew on sd. last mentioned creek beginning adjoining and above the last entry including the forks of the creek; and 2,000 acres on treasury warrant, assigned by Robert Chew on branch that empties into the Cole River at the lower end of James Burnsides, Junr.'s entry.

p. 244

ABRAM CHRISTMAN [CHRISMAN], assignee of treasury warrant, 75 acres on Crab Creek, beginning above his mill and joining Peterson's patent

41

land, crossing mill pond, and with several courses of Taylor's lands, also joining Mathew Smith and line of another tract of sd. Christman (withdrawn April 16, 1787).

JOHN SMITH and DANL. HARMAN, assignees of Henry Banks, 150 acres on Linconshire and branch of Clintch [Clinch], including Jacob Harmon's improvements and adjoining the lands of Wm. Ingles.

pp. 245-247

January 27, 1786, JOHN SMITH, treasury warrant, 150 acres adjoining an entry made 18 November 1785, on north side and to run on both sides of the road that leads from Pepper's Ferry to Hands Meadows and to join Shell's entry and to include Keysey's place.

JEREMIAH PATRICK withdraws second entry 21 October 1782, and enters 400 acres on head of Sand Bar Branch, joining Hugh Patrick's land called Bradley, on New River.

BENJAMIN STEWART, on three treasury warrants, 6,343 acres, 1781, enters 2,000 acres on Gyandott that empties in below Huff Creek on same side, beginning about 1/4 mile above the mouth (1,000 acres withdrawn February 22, 1787, also 300 acres); 400 acres on creek that empties in on north side of Gyandott about one mile higher than last mentioned where there is a large lick (200 acres withdrawn); 200 acres on same creek about two miles higher up beginning at a lick on the south side of the creek (withdrawn); 1,000 acres on Gyandott where there is a cain brake, about 4 or 5 miles above the mouth of a creek (withdrawn February 23, 1787); 500 acres on branch of Gyandott called Little Elk to begin at a lick (250 acres withdrawn); 500 acres at the mouth of a creek about 5 miles above a cain brake (250 acres withdrawn); 500 acres on same creek about five miles high where the creek forks (withdrawn 250 acres); 250 acres at the fork of Gyandott River; 500 acres on Gyandott opposite a big bottom (250 acres withdrawn).

FRANCIS KEATLEY withdraws 20 acres of entry made December 6, 1783, 30 acres being surveyed and enters at a line of survey made for James Adair below the mouth of East River, extending from Whitstone's Ridge.

January 28, 1786, GIDEON MOSS, treasury warrant, 792 3/4 acres joining Jacob Groce, Hugh Patrick, and Adam Hance on Peck [Peak] Creek.

pp. 248-249

ALEXANDER STEWART withdraws the following, made on 5th entry January 10, 1785, 100 acres; and withdraws 15 acres from the 8th entry of said date; 14th entry of sd. date, being 150 acres; 15th entry of sd. date, 150 acres; 16th of sd. date, 100 acres; and enters sd. land as follows: 300 acres added to entry on Harman's Branch emptying into Brush Creek and up Brush Creek to Parris line and below mouth of the creek (surveyed with 5th entry January 10, 1785, No. 59); 300 acres on branch of Brush Creek near the head and down to upper end of Pearis's land (surveyed 299 acres, withdraws 10 acres, No. 60); 400 acres added to entry on right hand fork of Laurel Creek above where the road crosses from Laurel Creek to Bluestone (surveyed No. 61); 180 acres to be added to entry at Big Spring on Wolf Creek below Joseph Doughertie's, the place whereon Hayes made an entry (surveyed No. 62); 600 acres on Wolf Creek beginning at Joseph Dougherty's and running up to mouth of Clear Fork and out to the foot of the mountain (withdrawn No. 63); sd. Stewart also withdraws 1st and 2nd entry December 2, 1785, of 1,500 acres each except 205 acres joining George Peck's above him and 200 acres above Stafford's between him and Sallard's and 354 acres along foot of Rich Mountain opposite Sallard's, Wiley's and Dial's; also enters 200 acres in Rich Valley between East River and Stoney Ridge (surveyed with other entry, No. 64).

ABSOLEM STAFFORD withdraws his entry 22 December 1782 per his order by Major Stewart

ANDREW DIAL, assignee of Alexander Stewart, assignee of William White, assignee of French Strother, treasury warrant, enters 123 acres on Clear Fork of Wolf Creek, joining and above the land of John Crompton and joining and below the land of McElyea, the same where Absolem Stafford withdraws above.

p. 250

WILLIAM KIDD, assignee as in last entry, 100 acres on west side of North Fork of Clinch River, bounded by William Cecil's and Henry Mars', on south side of Baptist Valley Ridge on small spring that empties into Maxwell's Mill Creek.

SAMUEL SALARDS, assignee, 150 acres on Clear Fork of Wolf Creek, beginning on spur of mountain on south side of creek and extending up to Rich Mountain (withdraws 60 acres per A. Stewart who made entry).

January 30,1786, JOHN PRICE, assignee of Michael Price, Senr., assignee of Alexr. Stewart, treasury warrant, 85 acres joining Michael Price, Senr., and Henry Price, Junr., and with their lines towards the New River.

January 31, 1786, MICHAEL PRICE, SENR., assignee of Alexander Stewart, on above warrant, 100 acres on both sides of Toms Creek joining his own land and James Bain, Jr. and including the old mill seat.

p. 251

January 31, 1786, JOHN SMITH, treasury warrant, 150 acres on northeast side of Peter Stephens' and Isaac Christman's on Stroubles Creek adjoining Wm. Mynatt's and extending towards the Roanoke [River]; 150 acres joining John Black and Philip Barrier to begin at the head of a spring above John Black's and towards the Roanoke and with Barrier's entry; 450 acres running with lands of Emanuel Harles, James Buchanan, Edward Bilip, and Jacob Shull, and extending towards the Brush Mountain (surveyed Abram Trigg).

February 3,1786, MURDOCK McKINSIE, assignee of George Pearis, 36 acres on west side of Walkers Creek, beginning corner to his own land.

MATHEW FRENCH, assignee, 100 acres, beginning corner to former survey on north side of Wolf Creek (surveyed 69 acres and withdraws the balance).

p. 252

February 5, 1786, JOHN CHARLTON, assignee of Richard Mynatt, 50 acres on treasury warrant on south and southeast side of Beard's line, and joining John Harrison's, Rich'd Hankins' and William Tabert's [Tabor's] land.

February 7, 1786, DAVID PRICE, assignee, 500 acres on creek known as Cane Brake Bottom Creek at back of C. W. Grubb's survey; also 50 acres between Gap Mountain and own on Greenbrier Creek.

February 7, 1786, MATHEW DICKEY, assignee, 300 acres on Chestnut Ridge and New River on south side of Dickey's line on Iron Ridge, and running west across Herbert's old road.

p. 253

JOSEPH ONEY, assignee of James Dever, assignee of William Caldwell, treasury warrant, May 19, 1783, enters 100 aces beginning at lower corner of Harman's land on south side of Walkers Creek (withdrawn per James Devor's

43

order who made entry for Oney, August 1786).

PHILIP LAMBERT, assignee of Joseph Oney, 100 acres joining Harman on upper side extending up Walkers Creek

February 10, 1786, JOSIAH BAKER, assignee of Thomas Patton, treasury warrant, 1782, 720 acres of which are assigned, enters same adjoining Thorn Spring and Thomas Patton on Thorn Spring Branch of Peeck [Peak] Creek.

JOHN SMITH, treasury warrant, 120 acres on north side of his entry on Clinch, 19 April 1785, beginning near Crab Orchard Creek.

p. 254

JOHN LYBROOK, assignee of James Brumfield, assignee of Peter Saunders, treasury warrant, 1782, 500 acres, enters 80 acres as follows: 40 acres between mouth of Sinking Creek and New River on south side of creek between Palsor Lybrook and George Fry, Senr.; 40 acres on Sinking Creek joining Palsor Lybrook and extending down to New River below the mill.

February 15, 1786, PATRICK NAPIER withdraws 80 acres of first entry made 4 June 1783, and 155 acres of 3rd entry of sd. date and 50 acres made on Whitney Branch.

THOMAS PASLEY HAMMON, assignee of Patrick Napper, assignee of James Clerk's attorney, treasury warrant, 500 acres, enters 275 acres as follows (no further details in original).

p. 255

RICHARD CHAPMAN, 100 acres beginning on the upper end of his line on north side of Wolf Creek (surveyed 25 acres and 60 acres, and 4 acres).

February 16, 1786, MATHEW FRENCH, assignee enters 31 acres on both sides of Wolf creek, joining John Pain's survey on north side (withdrawn).

February 17, 1786, MICHAEL DRAKE, assignee of John Certain, assignee of James Clerk's attorney, 50 acres on east point of Nob Mountain to include spring on head of a hollow about 1/2 mile from Parker Adkins (withdrawn).

February 17, 1786, ROBERT HUNTER, assignee of Francis Preston, 150 acres on south side of Nob Mountain on Spruce Run, branch of New River.

PETER CLINE, assignee of John Wiley, assignee of Thos. Wiley, assignee of Thomas Reynolds, on treasury warrant, 200 acres as follows: 90 acres in bent of New River joining Major Taylor's and to James Adair's line (withdrawn); 110 acres at the mouth of Crab Creek and to join Major Taylor's (withdrawn).

p. 256

February 23, 1786, ADAM HANCE, assignee of Gideon Moss, assignee of Hugh Patrick, treasury warrant, 500 acres, enters 250 acres joining Andrew Stobough, Capt. Patton, Edward Corder, and Meredith Reins, to include walnut hollow.

February 27, 1786, DAVID WALLACE and JAMES HAVIN, assignee of William Brown, 150 acres on treasury warrant, to begin at James Cartmil's line and joining James Havens and extending to William Lasley's on north side of Bluestone Mountain and south side of Bluestone Creek.

RICHARD WHITT, assignee of John Taylor, assignee of Malchai (?) Deamwood, treasury warrant, 129 acres joining his own on west and John Spain's on east, on Meadow Creek.

pp. 257-259

March 3, 1786, HENRY BANKS on a number of treasury warrants,, enters part thereof, 78 acres on branch of Glade Creek coming in on the south side about a mile above the ford; 95 acres on headwaters of Glade Creek including large

44

meadow; 500 acres on North Fork of Cole River that heads against the Gyandott; 1,300 acres on South Fork of Cole River that heads against Gyandott; 3,338 acres on South Fork of Cole River joining his own land; 328 aces on Cooper's Run and Bluestone, 1,345 acres one-half mile from White Oak Lick; 380 acres on Cooper's Creek and French Gut; 416 acres on Joe's Ridge and Cooper's Creek; 1,000 acres at Nathan's Ridge about a mile north of ford of Glade Creek; 500 acres on northwest of headwaters of Glade Creek; 500 acres on northwest of headwaters of Glade Creek; 500 acres on Laurel Creek between sd. creek and Droop Mountain; 2,000 acres under Pipe Stem Knob on north side; 2,138 acres on Cole River crossing from Piney to Gyandott including a large marsh; 228 acres on Joe's Ridge waters of Glade Creek; 150 acres on north side of Joe's Ridge and Cooper's Creek; 135 acres on west end of Joe's Ridge on waters of Glade Creek; 214 acres on waters of Glade Creek on south side; 263 acres on Cooper's Run and Glade Creek.

p. 260

March 3, 1786, ROBERT CURREN, assignee of John Craig, assignee of Joseph Cloyd, warrant issued 1782, 75 acres part assigned to him, on head of Dry Hollow joining David Ross's unmarked line [New River].

PATRICK JOHNSON, 30 acres on south side of Pine Ridge on Reed Creek, joining Love's, Fullen's and Henry Bean's.

March 6, 1786, HENRY GRUBB, assignee of Robert Sayers, warrant for 100 acres on south branch of Tates Run called Stophel [Stuffles] Run and both sides of Creek to Michael Crigger's line and then to Barnett Houck's.

p. 261

March 8, 1786, JAMES MATHEWS, treasury warrant, 200 acres of which assigned to him by John Lucas, assignee of John Minster and enters same on Laurel Branch of Greasy Creek to begin at the foot of a steep hill.

JOHN LUCAS, assignee of John Minster on above warrant, 200 acres on Indian Creek to begin at "plant bed hollow" near John Dunkin's; also 200 acres on Reed Island Creek to begin at Holley Spring (Grayson).

March 10, 1798, WILLIAM THOMPSON, assignee of James Thompson, warrant for 60 acres on Back Creek, branch of New River, adjoining land known as patent land, Joseph Cloyd, and Peter Dinges.

p. 262

GIDEON MOSS withdraws 150 acres of entry 28 January last and enters same adjoining Thomas McClanahan's survey on waters of Peeck [Peak] Creek agreeable to lines run by William Breckenridge in 1783 (withdrawn March 5, 1792).

March 17, 1786, WILLIAM MORRIS, assignee of John Skaggs, assignee of George Snuffer, on warrant for 1,500 acres assignee of James Hay, assignee of Henry Banks, assignee of Malcolm Hart, and a warrant for 500 acres assignee of James Hay, assignee of Henry Banks and by warrant for 100 acres, enters same as follows: 200 acres about 1/4 mile above War Ford on New River beginning at mouth of a branch that proceeds from a salt spring; 300 acres on east fork of Cole River and on east side of sd. river at a large rock; 100 acres beginning on east fork Cole River and west side of fork about 1/4 mile below the rock house fork at first opening where the river and hills part. N.B. it being the nearest fork of the river to the Kanhawa against whose waters Paint Creek and Cabin Creek interlock; 500 acres joining and below the above entry; 1,000 acres joining and below above entry.

pp. 263-266

March 17, 1786, WILLIAM MORRIS and ANDREW DONALLY, assignees of Henry Banks, assignee of Malcolm Hart, 15 treasury warrants for 1,000 acres each, and treasury warrant for 1000 acres assigned by Charles Donally, and another 1,000 acres, 500 of which are assigned to Morris by Andw. Donally, being a preemption warrant, enters 17 tracts of 1000 each, on Sandy Creek; part of each entry was located in Fayatte [Fayette] County, Kentucky.

p. 266

JAMES HENDERSON, military warrant, 2,000 acres, enters 1,000 acres joining and below Benjamin Turman's at the mouth of Town Creek; 1,000 acres joining the above entry; 50 acres on a military warrant, assigned by Richard Foster.

p. 267

BENJAMIN TURMAN, assignee of James Turman, withdraws entries made on 25 October 1783 for 1,051 1/2 acres and re-enters 451 1/2 acres beginning lower side of Town Creek being the first big creek below the mouth of Rich Land Fork on east side of Sandy Creek opposite mouth of Big Paint Lick Creek; 300 acres on first big bottom above the mouth of Big Paint Lick Creek on east side of Sandy.

p. 268

March 26, 1786, WILLIAM CALHOON [CALHOUN], assignee of Dan'l Creamer, assignee of John Taylor, assignee of Benjamin Turner (Turman?), assignee of David Anderson, treasury warrant, 150 acres on both sides of Nicks Creek [Holston], joining James Culton's patent line (withdraws 100 acres and assigned warrant to Adam Dutton).
DANIEL CREAMER on above warrant, 150 acres adjoining William Paterson and Robert Shannon's line including part of Crow's spring branch; 200 acres on head of big branch that crosses the road between Atkins and James Culton.
PETER CLINE, assignee of John Wiley, assignee of Thomas Wiley, assignee of Thomas Reynolds withdraws entry of 17 February 1786 and enters sd. 200 acres joining Adair and Helvy between Peppers wagon road and sd. places, New River (this entry transferred to James Adair and survey made in his name).

April 3, 1786

JOHN MILLER, assignee of James Clerk's attorney, treasury warrant, 61 acres beginning at David Price's, below his mill and with Michael Price's line and to his corner.

p. 269

April 4, 1786, ABRAM TRIGG, assignee of John Wylie, assignee of Thomas Wylie, assignee of Thomas Reynolds, treasury warrant, 121 acres adjoining land whereon he lives, adjoining Rife, Barnett, Banks and John Wiley.
MATHEW DICKY, assignee of treasury warrant, 10 acres on west side of Chestnut Creek and on north side of Captain Kilcannon's [Kincannon's] and Captain Carlon's [Carlin or Carland] line, including a bank of iron ore.

p. 270

April 8, 1786, WILLIAM DAY, assignee of Adam Hance, assignee of Gideon Moss, treasury warrant, 100 acres joining Adam Waggoner's patent line, adjoining Piper and another corner of Waggoner land; 60 acres assignee of David Croutch, beginning north corner of new survey; also 80 acres joining Sinking

46

Spring survey on southwest side including Trolinger spring near Sinking Spring.

JOHN LUCAS, assignee of John Minster, treasury warrant, 250 acres on Sproull Run, joining David Price's land near Nob Mountain.

p. 271

April 10, 1786, JAMES NEWELL and JAMES McCORKLE withdraw 500 acres, part of a preemption warrant and enter 100 acres joining Flower Swift and Mathew Dickey (withdrawn); 200 acres on Meadow Creek joining Sam'l Muson and Timothy Murphey (withdrawn 27 May 1786).

JOHN LEEDY, assignee of James Newell and McCorkle, 150 acres joining Nicholas Tarter and Stophel Brown (withdrawn 27 May 1786).

ROBERT CALHOON [CALHOUN], on above warrant, 100 acres between Thomas Crow and William Calhoon on the Holston (withdrawn May 27, 1786).

HENRY GRUBB on above warrant, 100 acres joining Michael Wampler, Jacob Kinser and his own land on branch of Tates Run.

p. 272

JOSHUA JONES, assignee as above, 200 acres on South Fork of Holston to include his iron works; 50 acres adjoining his own survey.

April 15, 1786, JACOB RIFE and SHADERAK HARRIMAN withdraws 2,000 acres joining John McMullan's settlement on Tees Valley, branch of Big Kanhawa.

WILLIAM MORRIS and SHADERACK HARRIMAN, assignees of John Hawkins, treasury warrant, 1783, 2,000 acres to join Jacob Rife's settlement right.

SHADERIK HARRIMAN withdraws his entry of 400 acres made 31 October 1785; also entry of 300 acres made 18 January 1785.

p. 273

THOMAS TEES withdraws his entry made 6 October 1784 and assigns 1,500 acres to William Morris.

WILLIAM MORRIS, SHADERICK HARRIMAN, THOMAS TEAS and WILLIAM NEEL, 3,000 acres from one warrant, 1,000 acres from another and 1,500 acres from another (lodged in surveyor's office in Greenbrier), 700 acres, enters part thereof, 4,000 acres, joining the last entry of William Morris and Harriman.

WILLIAM MORRIS, SHADERICK HARRIMAN, and THOMAS TEES, part of the above warrant, 800 acres on Cole River joining Henry Banks' survey on small creek that empties into Cole River about 1/4 mile from the mouth; also 500 acres to begin one mile above main fork of Cole River.

p. 274

WILLIAM MORRIS and SHADARAK HARRIMAN on part of the above warrant, 200 acres joining General Washington's on Cole River; 100 acres below survey made for Thomas Upton on Cole River; 600 acres on creek below the point about one mile down the Ohio to join survey of said Morris on sd. creek and to join Mercer's survey.

p. 275

TOBIAS PHILIPS, assignee of David Shockley, treasury warrant, 2,318 acres, 1783, enters 370 acres on Greasy Creek of Big Reed Island, branch of New River.

April 27, 1786

PETER HELVEY, assignee of Henry Patton, assignee of William Mares,

47

treasury warrant, 280 acres on head of Falling Spring Branch to begin at Ingles' corner and to run near Cloyd's and along Peck's line.

HENRY BANKS on a number of treasury warrants, enters 2,000 acres on branch of Cole River called Big Mash (?) Fork.

p. 276

JAMES BYRNSIDES, military warrant assigned by Jacob Salmon, 150 acres on southwest side of Great Kanhawa opposite John Prior's improvements and above the mouth of Cole River to join Thomas Upton's.

April 28, 1786, HENRY CLEMENTS, assignee of James Newell, warrant for 150 acres to join William Ewing's patent land and on both sides of Sugar Branch [of Cripple Creek of New River] to begin the upper corner of William Ewing's.

May 1, 1786, JAMES DEVOR, treasury warrant, 50 acres part thereof, on Walkers Creek, 150 poles above his house; 40 acres adjoining Henry Harmon's on north west side to begin between him and Daniel Harman (both withdrawn).

pp. 277-278

May 2, 1786, MARTHA GATLIFF withdraws her entry September 6, 1782 and by treasury warrant, enters 100 acres on west side of New River at a place called the Round Bottom.

May 3, 1786, JOHN SMITH, treasury warrant, enters part thereof, 200 acres joining Henry Willis on New River (surveyed 100; also 45 acres, withdraws 55 acres); 300 acres joining survey of James Addair by John Toney's direction to begin at Whetstone Ridge (surveyed 77 acres withdraws 233 acres); 300 acres about 3/4 mile from point of Whetstone Ridge on Kentucky Road and to include some sinkhole land (surveyed 194 acres and withdrew 106); 296 acres at a place called three nobs (knobs); 300 acres at head of Laurel Creek on dividing waters between sd. creek and head of Christian's fork.

May 4, 1786, SAMUEL THOMPSON, PATRICK HENRY, ESQR., THOMAS MADISON, WALTER CROCKETT, JEHU STEPHENS, THOMAS QUIRK, JAMES McCORKLE, and MANASSAS FRIEL, assignees of John Preston, assignee of Thomas Huff, assignee of Walter Crockett, attorney in fact for James Clerk, treasury warrant, 500 acres, 1782, enters 100 acres joining Samuel Thompson on southwest side to begin about 100 yards from Tates Run on south side and near the lower end of a meadow, including all the vacant land between sd. Thompson and Jehu Stephens and extending up to Reed Creek.

p. 279

May 8, 1786, SAM'L THOMPSON, MICHAEL WALTERS and ELIZA. MADISON, assignees of John Preston, assignee of Thomas Huff, assignee of Walter Crockett, attorney for James Clark, treasury warrant, enters 600 acres on south side of Reed Creek adjoining John McNitt, George McNitt, and William Phips, on south side and Jehu Stephens on east (withdrawn).

pp. 279-280

May 11, 1786, JOHN MONTGOMERY, JUNR., assignee of John Crockett, assignee of Thomas Muse, treasury warrant, 200 acres Reed Creek on south side John Montgomery, Senr.'s patent line.

JOHN MONTGOMERY, SENR., assignee of John T. Sayers, on treasury warrant, 50 acres on south side long glade including both sides of the wagon road leading from Boiling Springs on Reed Creek to the Lead Mines; also 50 acres near the head of a draft that runs through Bentley's plantation, and empties into Reed Creek below the Boiling Spring.

JOHN CROCKETT, assignee of Richard Muse, treasury warrant, 139 acres on east side of branch where Richard Muse lives, on a branch of a creek which leads to the mill at the Lead Mines; also 130 acres on a draft on south side of the long glades including both sides of a path leading to Baker's mill to include a place called Wards Bottom (85 acres withdrawn and another 85 acres withdrawn, March 9, 1788).

ANDREW CROCKETT, assignee of John T. Sayers, treasury warrant, 150 acres on New River adjoining his own patent land on south side (withdrawn April 15, 1790).

p. 281

JAMES CROCKETT, assignee of Andrew Crockett, assignee of James T. Sayers, treasury warrant, 100 acres lying near mouth of Sinclair's Branch beginning at a line of the place the widow Sinclair now lives on (withdrawn April 17, 1790); also 150 acres west side of the place he now lives on (withdrawn Oct. 21, 1792).

May 15, 1786, WILLIAM DAY, assignee of Adam Hance, treasury warrant, 60 acres, adjoining his entry of 60 acres of April 8.

JOHN DAY, assignee of Adam Hance, treasury warrant, 100 acres on Back Creek adjoining his own patent land on the east side.

May 17, 1786, SAMUEL THOMPSON, MICHAEL WALTERS and ELIZ'TH MADISON withdraw entry made 8th instant.

p. 282

SAMUEL THOMPSON, MICHAEL WALTERS, and ELIZ'TH MADISON, as assignees of John Hawkins, on treasury warrant, 3,000 acres, 1783, 600 acres of which were assigned to Thompson, Walters, and Madison jointly and severally, enter 600 acres south side of Reed Creek adjoining John McNitt, George McNitt, and William Phipps on south side and entry of James Finley made 6 Oct. 1784 east side thereof (withdrawn May 26, 1786 and reentered p. 285).

SAMUEL THOMPSON, THOMAS MADISON, WILLIAM BARTLOT, and MICHAEL WALTERS, jointly and severally assignees of John Hawkins, treasury warrant, 500 acres on south side of Reed Creek adjoining David Ross on west and extending to John Davies, Henry Helvy and John McNitt on south side (withdrawn and reentered p. 285).

p. 283

ABRAHAM TRIGG and JOHN INGLES, assignees of John Wiley, assignees of Thomas Wiley, assignees of Thomas Reynolds, treasury warrant, 365 acres east side of New River including a piney mountain joining John Ingles, James Skaggs, Hezekiah Whitt, Peter Sping, William Lewis Lovely, and Conrood Wall's land.

HENRY HARMAN, assignee of Sam'l Parcifield, Francis McGuire, Philip Lambert, Henry Bagley, Andrew Thompson, and Sarah Parcifield, Commissioner's certificate, 800 acres on Walkers Creek, part surveyed for the Loyal Company 1753 or '54, 500 acres to be laid off on lands of Daniel Harman and land Henry Harman, Junr. lives on; 300 acres whereon Holston Muncey now lives (surveyed 116 acres, surveyed 86 acres).

May 21, 1786, JAMES COULTON, assignee of John Hankins, part of a warrant enters 100 acres to begin east corner of patent land on south side of sd. land and to extend with sd. lines to within 30 poles of Nicks Creek (Holston).

May 26, 1786, DANIEL TRIGG, assignee of Adam Dean per order of Capt. James McCorkle, 1786 (withdrawn) entries made by Adam Dean Nov. 4, 1782 on treasury warrant, 1782, for 1,000 acres (sd. entries contain 819 acres) and enter part as follows:

DANIEL TRIGG, JAMES McCORKLE, ABRAM TRIGG, assignees of Adam Dean on treasury warrant, 1782, 200 acres on west side of New River opposite John Grason [Grayson], beginning 100 yards above said bar hollow (withdrawn and assigned to William and Robert Currin).

MATHIAS CRUMB, assignee of Henry Patton, preemption warrant granted William Mares, 1783, 300 acres between Henry Trolinger, Thomas Patton, and Nenian Cloyd, including two springs which rise out of level ground and runs about 200 yards and sinks near Thomas Patton's line on north side of the great road.

SAM'L THOMPSON, THOS. MADISON, ELIZABETH MADISON, MICH'L WALTERS, and WILLIAM BARTLITT, assignees of John Hawkins part of a treasury warrant of 3,000 acres, 1783, enters 2,900 acres beginning adjoining David Ross on southwest side and on south side of Reed Creek and running up the creek to join John Davis, Henry Helvey, Jno. McNitt, Geo. McNitt, and Wm. Phipps on their south sides and entry of Jas. Finley made 1784 on east side.

May 26, 1786, THOMAS MADISON, treasury warrant, 1,895 1/2 acres, 1782, assigned by John and Francis Preston, assignee of Wm. Preston, enters same as follows: beginning at the south corner of Gose's survey assignee of Benj'n Retherford at his upper corner and thence with lines to Chinia's [Chaney's] land and with lines of his three surveys on south side of sd. survey to James Campbell's survey and Jas. Davies survey and with it on east side of his spring branch and down the same including it on both sides and to lands of Henry Francis, deceased, and with lines up the creek to Andrew Porter, heir-at-law of Robert Porter, deceased, and with his lines to Stephen Sanders and with his line to Jno. Kerr's lines and with his lines to Robt. Wylie's and with his to Cyphers and with his line to his upper corner (marked No. 1). [Land is located on Cripple Creek].

May 26, 1786, same on treasury warrant, 1781, assigned by Jno. Preston assignee of Jas. Breckenridge, assignee of John Brackenridge, beginning lower end of last entry and with Francis' lines to Randolph Retherford and with his lines to Wm. Gleaves and with his lines to Thos. Hobbs and with said lines to Jas. Baber's and with his lines to Benj'n Rogers and with his lines to Wm. Henley's and with his lines to Jas. Davis (marked No. 2). [Land is located on Cripple Creek]; also 500 acres on treasury warrant, 1783, assigned by Jno. Preston, assignee of Walter Crockett, attorney for James Clerk, adjoining Samuel Thompson, Thos. Madison, Elizabeth Madison, Mich'l Walters and Wm. Bartlett, and to join Jas. Finley and with his lines to William Phipps and with his line to upper corner (withdrawn, marked No. 3). [Land is located on Reed Creek]; also 1,100 acres on treasury warrant for 500 acres, 1781, and assigned by Jno. and Francis Preston, assignees of Wm. Preston and George May, and four treasury warrants of 150 acres each, 1783, assigned by Jno. Preston, assignee of Henry Banks, beginning on lower end of Creager's survey on

Tates Run and on south side of Grub's late survey and with it to Tates Run and up the same to Jacob Kettering's and with his lines (surveyed 220 acres).

p. 289

May 26, 1786, JOHN CROCKETT, treasury warrant, 150 acres, 1783, assigned by Jno. Preston, assignee of Henry Banks, on Cripple Creek and on north side of same from the land Jas. Newell lives on, to include a high ridge between Sam'l Smith and Jas. Newell (withdrawn).

GILBERT MOORE, 10 treasury warrants of 150 acres each, 1783, beginning on the south side of Michael Kettering's and to join Henry Grub and Stoffle [Christopher] Kettering's and Bar'd Houk's (withdrawn June 26, 1786).

p. 290

May 26, 1786, ANDREW CROCKETT, treasury warrant of 1,209 1/2 acres, 1782, 400 acres assigned by Jacob Fouts, assignee of Jno. Montgomery, enters 150 acres adjoining Isaac Runion to include both sides of Runion's Mill Branch; also 100 acres on north side of Reed Creek, on branch running in below Ben Smith (withdrawn October 21, 1792).

JAMES CROCKETT, part of the above warrant, assigned by Andrew Crockett, assignee of Jacob Fouts, assignee of Jno. Montgomery, 150 acres to join the lower end of Jno. Creager's and upper end of David Sloan's on Purgatory Branch (withdrawn April 17, 179 [blank]).

p. 291

May 26, 1786, ANDREW CROCKETT, six treasury warrants of 150 acres each, 1783, assigned by Jno. Preston, assignee Henry Banks, 500 acres Macks Creek beginning at mouth of said creek and up and down the river and up and down the creek on both sides (withdrawn); 400 acres to begin at the fork of Clapboard Branch and running up both forks (withdrawn).

FRAN. WALKER, treasury warrant, 1,000 acres, 1783, as assigned by Robt. B. Simpson, beginning in Holbert Ellison's [Allison's] line near Pine Run and to join Neil McGlister

p. 292

May 26, 1786, ANDREW CROCKETT, on four treasury warrants, 1783, 150 acres each, assigned by John Preston, assignee of Henry Banks, enters 250 acres on Clapboard Branch joining and above entry of 400 acres; also 250 acres or Raccoon Branch of New River joining and above Mrs. Loveday (withdrawn); also 100 acres joining his entry of 11th instant on southeast side.

p. 293, May 26, 1786

FRANCIS WALKER and JAMES CROCKETT withdraw 500 acres and entry made jointly this date and enter 500 acres to begin on bank of Reed Creek at the Grassy Ford adjoining Sloan's land (withdrawn April 7, 1790).

JEHU STEPHENS, on treasury warrant, 500 acres assigned by Thos. Quirk, assignee of Jas. Clerk's attorney and enters same joining his own land, Wm. Love's, Hezekiah Chinia [Chaney's], Jno. Cypher's and Gose's on Sugar Run and lands of Reagh on Cripple Creek.

pp. 293-294

May 27, 1786, THOS. MADISON on treasury warrant, 150 acres, 1783, assigned by John Preston, assignee of Henry Banks, beginning corner to John Baxter's survey and Andrew Stot's land, Hester McCain and Evan Williams [New River]; also 2,000 acres on treasury warrant, 1783, assigned by Henry Banks, assignee of William McWilliams, beginning on Jas. Baber's line on Mill Creek and to George Ewing's and with his line to Mich'l Least and with his line to Adam Dean's land known as Black's Fort and with Dean's line west to Wm. Henley and to Haunsbaugh (Ansbach?) survey and with the lines down the branch to Benjamin Rogers and with Baber's line to the beginning (500 acres withdrawn July 1, 1786 and entered for J. W. G.).

p. 295

JOHN CROCKETT withdraws his entry of 26th instant and enters same 150 acres adjoining John Montgomery Senr.'s entry of 50 acres on west side near the head of a draft that runs through Bentley's plantation and empties into Reed Creek below the Boiling Spring in said creek.

JAMES CROCKETT, part of a treasury warrant of 500 acres, 1782, assigned by Jas. Newell, assignee of Jas. Clerk's attorney, enters 265 acres of an old survey of Mr. Andrew Boyd, including both sides of a path that goes from said Crockett's to Wm. Pearce's (withdrawn April 17, 1790).

p. 296

May 27, 1786, JAMES McCORKLE, treasury warrant, 500 acres, 1781, assigned by Jno. and Fran. Preston, assignees of Wm. Preston; also 25 acres, 1782, assigned by John Kerr, beginning corner to Rich'd Muse.

FRAN. PRESTON, part of a treasury warrant for 500 acres, 1782, assigned by Jno. Preston, assignee of Thos. Huff, assignee of Jas. Clerk's attorney, enters 400 acres beginning on Mine Mill Creek in the line of Julius Rutherford and to Wm. Moer's [Moores] line, and to John Baxter's near the wagon road leading from Fort Chiswell to lead mines and westwardly to Joseph Evans and back to Muse's.

p. 297

THOMAS QUIRK, preemption warrant, 1,000 acres, 1782, enters 100 acres part of same, adjoining his own, Josiah Ramsey, Jno. Montgomery, and Jas. McDonald.

GEORGE WAMPBLER [WAMPLER], treasury warrant, 1782, assigned by Michl. Staphey [Steffey], 80 acres adjoining his entry of 50 acres made Oct. 18, 1785; also 304 1/2 acres, the balance beginning in a line of Mr. Brown's old survey and to join Wolf's land, Geo. Kinser, and his own patent land.

p. 298

THOMAS MADISON, treasury warrant, 1783, assigned by Jno. Preston, assignee of Henry Banks, beginning on the bank of the creek corner to Colo. Stephens on Reed Creek; this entry to contain 2,000 acres beginning adjoining above entry at the west corner and to the corner of Colonel Stephens' land on Reed Creek and to James Finley's line.

p. 299

JAMES McCORKLE, treasury warrant, 1783, assigned by Henry Banks, on military warrant for 50 acres dated 1780, assigned by Jno. Taylor, beginning corner to Rich'd Muse.

May 29, 1786, ADAM DEAN withdraws eight entries made Nov. 4, 1782.

p. 300

ADAM DEAN on treasury warrant, 300 acres on branch of Cripple Creek adjoining on north side of the land he lives on and on south of his survey known by the name of Black John Rutherford's place.

JOHN TAYLOR, withdraws 569 acres of his entry made between him and William Wynne, 26 June 1785, being part claimed by sd. Taylor.

pp. 300-301

JAMES CAMPBELL, HEZEKIAH CHINA [CHANEY], SAMUEL SMITH,

and JOHN TAYLOR, treasury warrant 1,000 acres, 1782, 500 of which is assigned to Campbell by Adam Dean and 500 acres of which is assigned by Dean to Sam'l Smith and he to Campbell, 250 acres, and by Campbell assigned to China, 313 acres and by Campbell assigned by Stephen Saunders 61 acres, and 63 acres assigned by Campbell to Smith; another warrant of 1,138 acres in the name of John Taylor and Wm. Wynne and by sd. Taylor assigned to Stephen Saunders, 254 acres, the whole amount is 1,569 acres, they enter the same on Cripple Creek, beginning northeast corner to Capt. Love's survey on east side of Kerr's Branch and running along Mr. Madison's entry to Gose's corner and from there to George Powers, and then to Cullop's and then to Peter Kinser's survey and then to Daniel Peerce's and to Vaught's mill place and then to James Douglas and William Ewing and back to Cap. Love's (marginal note states James Campbell withdraws 250 acres, Jno. Taylor withdraws 200 acres, 1798; Stephen Saunders withdraws 250 acres; Hezekiah China withdraws his part 19th April).

p. 301

May 31, 1786, ABRAHAM GOAD, assignee of John Smith of Botetourt County, on treasury warrant, 200 acres made by Commissioner's Certificate, on north branch of Burks Fork of Reed Island Creek.

pp. 301-302

JAMES GOARD [GOAD], assignee of Tobias Phillips, assignee of David Shockley, treasury warrant, 1783 for 2,318 acres, enters 200 acres of same, beginning at the mouth of a spring branch above the mouth of Laurel Branch opposite Lettice Breckenridge's entry of 50 acres, extending across Laurel Branch and includes [survey?] made by him 7 or 8 years ago (withdrawn and enters it May 31 in the name of Jacob Nester).

p. 302

May 31, 1786, ABRAHAM GOARD [GOAD], assignee as above, enters 200 acres on waters of Greasy Creek beginning corner to land purchased by John Witcher, assignee of Benjamin Bailey; 200 acres on Burks Fork to join entry of 200 acres made this day.

JOHN COX, SENR., assignee as above, 100 acres on head of Camp Branch

p. 303

WILLIAM SPENCER, JUNR., assignee as above, 200 acres on waters of Greasy Creek beginning corner to Abram Goard [Goad] bought of John Witcher, assignee of Benjamin Bailey.

FREDERICK NESTOR, assignee as above, 500 acres to begin on Ephraim Witcher's line on Greasy Creek, and down the creek and up Laurel Fork on both sides, for quantity.

June 13, 1786, ANDREW KINCANNON, assignee of Adam Dean, treasury warrant, 2,081 acres, enters same, 50 acres on New River about one mile from Wallens and on south side of the river at a white oak marked AK on side of a ridge about one-half mile from the river, to include the iron ore bank; 50 acres on New River and on north side to begin at the white oak marked AK and to include iron ore bank near Wallins Bottom.

p. 304

June 13, 1786, FLOWER SWIFT, assignee of Andrew Kincannon, assignee as above and on above warrant, 40 acres adjoining his own, and Mathew Dickey to include his mill and mill seat on waters of Chestnut Creek.

ANDREW KINCANNON, assignee as above, and warrant as above, 560 acres adjoining Michael Farmer's and Elisha Walling's entry on Iron Ridge and to join Daniel Carland, Andrew Kincannon, and the Widow Clonch.

June 16, 1786, ZACHARIAH STANLEY, assignee of John Hawkins, on treasury warrant, 300 acres on branch of Crab Creek joining Jacob Hornbarriger, and Joseph Popecofer.

DANIEL TRIGG, ABRAM TRIGG, WILL HALL, JAMES McCORKLE, assignees of Adam Dean, treasury warrant, 1782, beginning on a path leading from Bell's Meadows to Col. Trigg's 350 yards from where the path crosses the run (125 acres withdrawn and assigned to Curtis Eliott, per Col. D. Trigg's order and 300 acres withdrawn by Wm. Hall's order Oct. 13, 1792).

p. 305

June 19, 1786, PATRICK HENRY, treasury warrant, 1,800 acres, not dated, beginning corner to Gideon Moss' survey and with lines to join Wm. Hampton's survey of 285 acres and with his line to Daniel Collon's and to include Peak Creek Mountain (withdrawn June 23, 1786 and re-entered on p. 311 on June 24).

June 20, 1786, JOSEPH DAY, treasury warrant, 300 acres enters 90 acres part of same, on north side of the Fork of Elk Creek, of New River, beginning at his old corner.

RICHARD MUSE withdraws his entry joining Jacob Cain and Charles Deverax and enters 100 acres on branch of Walkers Creek, adjoining William Smith and Moses Justice survey on the east side.

p. 306

THOMAS TEES, certificate of settlement for 400 acres and 1000 acres preemption, enters 1,400 acres as follows: 400 acres on Great Kanhawa adjoining survey of James Craig at the upper end; also 1000 acres on Great Kanhawa and adjoining the above to the mouth of Cole River.

HENRY CARTER, assignee of John Preston on state warrant for 58 (68?) acres on south side of the land he lives on and to join John Harrison [Meadow Creek of Little River, branch of New River].

p. 307

ZACHARIAH STANLEY, JOHN SMITH, and JEREMIAH BELL, assignees of Francis Graves, treasury warrant, 3,000 acres, part of same, on Rich Mountain near the head of the Clinch, beginning where the path crosses from the old waggon's field to Burks Garden and to extend to Morris Griffith's Nob (withdraws 2,000 acres; withdraws 400 acres; withdraws 40 acres by Jereh. Bell in 1794; and 100 acres withdrawn by Jrh. Bell, 1795).

GEORGE TAYLOR, on above warrant, 30 acres on Crab Creek which is to be added to entry of 80 acres, 1783, 10 acres he withdrew from entry of 70 acres made sd. day and adds the same to sd. entry of 80 acres, whole to be 120 acres (309 acres withdrawn May 4, 1796).

June 20, 1786, FRANCIS PRESTON withdraws entry of 400 acres made Feb. 26, 1784.

p. 308

June 21, 1786, GEORGE PECK, assignee of Francis Preston, assignee of John Preston, part of a treasury warrant for 1,511 acres, 160 acres of which was assigned to him, enters the same to adjoin and to be added to his entry on White Glades (withdrawn).

June 23, 1786, GEORGE BOOTH, assignee of William Tabor, assignee of John Minster, treasury warrant, 3,000 acres, 1784, enters 100 acres of same adjoining Abner Lester's land on Meadow Creek (withdrawn per order of

Ezekial Howard to whom it was transferred); 400 acres joining Col. James Robertson, James and Robert Simpkins and William Tabor on Meadow Creek (withdraws 323 acres, Jan. 6, 1787).

JEREMIAH FARMER withdraws his second entry made 18 June 1783.

SAMUEL LANGDON withdraws his entry 22 Jan. 1785.

MOSES WINTERS assignee of Jeremiah Farmer on two treasury warrants, part assigned by Samuel Langdon, assignee of Geo. Booth, assignee of John Minster, 300 acres, 430 acres on former warrant, the whole 730 acres entered as follows: on Pounding Mill Branch of Meadow Creek, to join John Lawrence's land he lives on and the land of Peter Romine and to extend to Rosberry's Meadows.

p. 309

CHRISTOPHER CYMMERMAN [SIMMERMAN], assignee of Frans. Preston, assignee of John Preston, treasury warrant, part of same, 100 acres adjoining David Love, George Kegley, Daniel Wisely, George Erwin and his own, including a good spring and the Pine Ridge.

June 24, 1786, FRANCIS PRESTON, assignee of John Preston, treasury warrant, enters 1,000 acres, part of same, on Tates Run, branch of Reed Creek, beginning at Jacob Kinser's corner next to Lick Mountain and to extend to Rev. John Brown's, and to George Wampler's late survey and corner to Younce's (surveyed 46 acres and 140 acres).

p. 310

June 24, 1786, FRANCIS PRESTON, 251 acres on Tates Run, branch of Reed Creek, beginning on Jacob Kinser's line on south side of Michael Wampler's and to Stophell's Run and up the same to Jacob Kittring's and with his lines to Stophell Kittring's.

JAMES McGAVOCK on military warrant, 3,000 acres, 178- (blank), granted McGavock for services in the last war, enters 1,000 acres at the forks of a road leading from the lead mines to Fort Chiswell and Boiling Spring and to run with the road to Joseph Eaton's line crossing the road and with Eaton's eastward and to join Evan Williams and with his to forked white oak and from there to join a small survey for sd. Williams on north side and back from sd. survey and with several courses to the beginning (withdrawn).

pp. 311-313

PATRICK HENRY, ESQ., THOMAS MADISON and COMPANY, assignees of Patrick Henry, treasury warrant, on Peeck [Peak] Creek, to begin where Gideon Moss's land joins William Hampton and with Hampton to Daniel Collins to include the highest and most eastwardly part of Peeck [Peak] Creek Mountain (#9).

THOMAS MADISON and COMPANY, assignee of James Hawkins, assignee of David Anderson, part of treasury warrant for 4,000 acres, enters 1,000 acres adjoining above entry on west end and extending westwardly and southwestwardly on south side of Peeck [Peak] Creek Mountain (#10); also on the last mentioned warrant, 1,000 acres on lead Mine Mill Creek, branch of New River, to begin at William Rodgers and to John Rodger's land and to Richard Muse's land and to join entry of James McCorkle (#11); for same, on same warrant, 750 acres on Dry Branch to begin at corner of George Ewing's old and new surveys on branch next to Iron Mountain and joining Minetree Jones (#12); also on same warrant, 250 acres on Cripple Creek, joining George Ewing, Samuel Ewing, Charles Nuckolls, Adam Dane [Dean], and

Michael Lease (#13, surveyed 192 acres); for same on same warrant, 250 acres on Tates Run, beginning corner to Henry Grubb's last survey and with said land to where it joins Michael Kettring and with his line to where it joins Grubb's patent land (#14); for same on same warrant, 750 acres on west side of New River to begin at William Herbert's corner next to Andrew Stott's and with Herbert's to the river and down the same to John Craig's and with his lines to Johnson's and then to Baker as purchased of Tuttle, and then to Stott's and to the beginning (#15).

p. 314

THOMAS MADISON COMPANY, treasury warrant, 1,023 3/4 acres assigned by James Nuckolls, enters the land as follows: 500 acres on Reed Creek to join David McGavock and Wm. Campbell on the north side and George Wampler's last survey on west side and Thomas Meese and Thomas Copeheifer's [Copenhaver's] on south side and back from sd. lands southwardly (#16, withdrawn April 27, 1790); for same, 523 3/4 acres joining Joseph Eaton on north and northwest side and Richard Muse on east and back from sd. lands towards the Big Glades [New River} (#17).

DAVID MAY and ALEXANDER SMITH, assignee of John Smith, on treasury warrant, 2,195 acres, 1783, as follows, 1,000 acres on north side of Peeck [Peak] Creek Mountain and joining Thomas Madison on the west and another entry of Madison of 1000 acres.

p. 315

June 24, 1786, MARY EWING, assignee of James Newell, assignee of James Nuckolls, treasury warrant, 1783, 100 acres part of warrant on east side of New River, beginning corner to Paul Razor's survey on the river bank and down the river to where Razor's survey begins on high "clift" of rocks near the bank; 250 acres on west side of New River corner to Sam'l Ewing's (dec'd) patent land on river and with lines to Jones' corner.

p. 316

June 26, 1786, JAMES FINLEY assignee of James Clerk's attorney, treasury warrant, enters 57 acres between Jehu Stephens and his own patent to begin at Stephen's corner on Reed Creek (withdrawn 26 June 1786 and re-entered).
FRANCIS PRESTON, assignee of Henry Banks, treasury warrant, 150 acres joining entry of Sam'l Thompson and others May 4, 1786, on the south and to the beginning corner of Henry Grubb's survey and to Michael Crigger's and to join Jehu Stephens and with entry of Thompson and others to Thompson's patent land, and then to Michael Kittring's.
JAMES FINLEY, assignee of Jas. Clerk's attorney, treasury warrant, 57 acres lying between Jehu Stephens and his own patent and surveyed land on both sides of Reed Creek beginning at Stephens, Love's and his own corner and with Stephen's lines.

p. 317

JACOB KETTERING, treasury warrant, no acres given, enters the balance of a warrant, beginning at his last corner of new survey to join Geo. Wampbler's [Wampler's] and Stoffle Kettering's and running towards Spreaker for quantity.
JEHU STEPHENS, treasury warrant, 500 acres assigned by Thomas Quirk, assignee of James Clerk's attorney, enters same; 100 acres running from the head of Fox Grape Branch to Captain Finley's survey and to join Finley's new entry and to join Stephen's old line; 350 acres to begin at upper end of the old survey and towards mountain branch.

THOMAS MADISON, MICHAEL WALTERS, SAM'L THOMPSON, SAM'L MEREDITH, RAND'H McGAVOCK, JNO. HAWKINS, GEO. MADISON, on treasury warrant, 3,000 acres, 1783, beginning on Stony Fork about three miles above Nicholas Tarter's and then west and south towards the head of Reed Creek and down the creek including both sides of the main fork to join Sam'l Doak's land (withdrawn 26 June 1786 and entered on p. 319).

June 26, 1786, JAMES McGAVOCK, military warrant, 3,000 acres granted to McGavock for service in the last war, enters 400 acres, part of same, to begin at Colonel Stephens' east corner and with his lines to Captain Love's and with his lines and then leaving sd. lines and extending with James Campbell's entry to Gose's corner and Thos. Madison's entry to Cypher's and with his to Love's and then to the beginning (withdrawn).

THOS. MADISON, MICHAEL WALTERS, SAM'L THOMPSON, SAM'L MEREDITH, RANDOLPH McGAVOCK, and GEORGE MADISON, on treasury warrant, 3,000 acres, 1783, assigned by Jno. Hawkins to Sam'l Meredith and he to the company, beginning on Stony Fork of Reed Creek about three miles above Nicholas Tarter's and west and south to the fork of the creek and down the fork including it on both sides to the main fork to join Sam'l Doak (withdrawn per order Sam'l Meredith April 1, 1789).

June 27, 1786, JOHN LEEDY, assignee of James Nuckolls, treasury warrant, 150 acres to join Nich's Tarter and Stoffle [Christopher] Brown.

WILLIAM GLEAVES, treasury warrant assigned by Jas. Nuckolls, 100 acres on Cripple Creek, adjoining Buffalo Ford at the lower end.

June 28, 1786, THOMAS QUIRK, ALEX'R SMITH, HUGH McGAVOCK, and JOHN, JOSEPH, and JACOB KENT, preemption warrant, 1,000 acres, 1782, and also part of treasury warrant of 1,000 acres, assigned by Jas. Nuckolls, 900 acres on north side of New River to join John Plank, William Scrugs, and Randol Fugate.

June 29, 1786, MICHAEL CORMANY, treasury warrant, assigned by Jas. Clerk's attorney, 100 acres to join his own and Peter Etter and Jno. Boyd.

MATHEW DICKEY, treasury warrant, assigned by Francis Preston, 500 acres, enters 100 of same on Peach Bottom Creek, to include the big fall.

July 1, 1786, JAMES McGAVOCK, DAVID McGAVOCK, HUGH McGAVOCK, JAS. McGAVOCK, JUNR., and MICH'L DOUGHERTY, part of a military warrant of 3,000 acres and part of a treasury warrant for 1,500 acres, on the north side of Reed Creek, beginning near John Montgomery and to join Hutchison, Glasgow, Allcorn and Ramsey, and to include Newberry's Knob and a small lick (withdrawn). The same McGavocks as above and Dougherty withdraw the above entry and enter the same on the north side of Reed Creek near Jno. Montgomery's land and east with line and northeast to Thomas Hutcheson, and then to Glasgow's and then west to join his and Jno. Alcorn's across the mountain and to Josiah Ramsey's down the creek to the beginning and to include a small lick in the gap of the mountain (withdrawn).

July 3, 1786, JAMES CROCKETT and WILLIAM LEWIS LOVELY, assignees of Henry Banks, treasury warrant, 1,500 acres between Sinclair's Branch and Pine Run, beginning on Cornelius Linues (?), line adjoining Thompson Sayers.

JACOB SPANGLER, assignee of George Kinser, treasury warrant, 100 acres on Indian Creek, branch of North Fork of Holston, on south side of Brushy Mountain, joining James Willson on north and on Burk's old path.

July 4, 1786, JOHN DAY, assignee of Adam Hance, treasury warrant adjoining his patent on east side of Back Creek.

p. 323

HENRY PIPER, assignee of Adam Hance, treasury warrant, 100 acres joining his old survey on north side.

WILLIAM DAY, assignee of Zachariah Stanly, treasury warrant, all vacant land between his survey and Waggoner's old line.

July 5, 1786, MEREDITH RAINS, assignee of Zachariah Stanley, treasury warrant, 100 acres on northwest side of old survey.

DAVID CROUCH, assignee of Zachariah Stanly, treasury warrant, 150 acres on north side Ingram's and adjoining his own.

GEORGE LEOMAN [LOWMAN?], assignee of Zachariah Stanly, treasury warrant, 200 acres joining the waters of Bullick [Bullock] Pen Branch.

p. 324

July 7, 1786, JOHN COX, assignee of Tobias Phillips, assignee of David Shockly, treasury warrant, 100 acres Laurel Fork of Reed Island, and running over towards the waters of Burks Fork and on the west side of Hays' Nobbs.

WILLIAM JONES, assignee of Tobias Phillips, treasury warrant, 75 acres on south side Greasy Creek beginning at Pranhamas [Branham's?] corner running on east side of sd. William Jones patent land; also 36 acres on Big Reed Island Creek beginning opposite his land on said creek.

DAVID BRANHAM, assignee of Tobias Phillips, treasury warrant, 221 acres east side Greasy Creek beginning at Clements corner.

p. 325

JAMES PRANHAM [BRANHAM?], assignee of Jeremiah Bell, assignee of Zachariah Stanly, treasury warrant, 100 acres on east side of Big Reed Island Creek, beginning at the last corner to Wm. Jones' land.

July 9, 1786, JOHN SMYTH, ZACHARIAH STANLY and JEREMIAH BELL, treasury warrant, 8,000 acres, enters 300 acres on Big Reed Island Creek between John Burk, William Lyns, and James Branham, beginning on John Burk's line.

PETER ROMINES, assignee of Jeremiah Bell, assignee of Zachariah Stanly, treasury warrant, 100 acres on both sides of Poplar Branch (surveyed for Ezekiel Howard to whom land is transferred; withdrawn 28 acres).

p. 326

July 9, 1786, JEREMIAH BELL, out of his Smyth and Stanly warrant for 8,000 acres, enters 200 acres on both sides of Big Reed Island, beginning at Elk Island.

JEREMIAH BELL, JOHN SMYTH, and [Zachariah] STANLY, on treasury warrant for 8,000 acres, enters 300 acres on Big Reed Island Creek and Greasy Creek, beginning at the Panther Branch, including the improvements where Peter Ross lived, known by the name of Rosses cabin.

JEREMIAH BELL, 500 acres on above warrant, enters ____[blank] acres, on head of Mirey Fork of Greasy Creek, part on Burks Fork on Indian Ridge, including improvements made by William Jones and James Branham.

p. 327

ZACHARIAH STANLY, JOHN SMYTH, and JEREMIAH BELL, on above warrant, enters 200 acres on Licking Fork of Indian Creek, adjoining Edmund Vance's survey on the upper side.

July 10, 1786, WILLIAM PEERY, assignee of Zachariah Stanly, 100 acres on Buckhorn Ridge on Clear Fork of Wolf Creek between fork and Laurel Fork.
DAVID HUGHS withdraws 100 acres that lie below Bear Creek on north side of Guyandotte and enters same on south side of Walkers Creek on branch about halfway between How's path and gap of Walker's Mountain to include a large spring.

p. 328

HENRY BANKS, treasury warrant, 12,300 acres on loop waters of New River about eight miles from the mouth of a large creek; also 12,300 acres same location, two miles below the right hand fork of large creek about four miles southeast of Paine Creek on which War Road leads along to go down to the New River.

p. 329

THOS. UPTON, treasury warrants 1782 and 1783, for 2,057 3/4 acres after withdrawing entries before in this book, land on Great Kanhawa to join settlement and preemption about one mile above Davises Creek.

p. 330

August 7, 1786, STEPHEN CHAPLAIN [CHAPELL?] withdraws entries made 1783 and enters 100 acres on Reed Creek.
GEORGE KEAGLEY, assignee of Stephen Chaplain [Chappell?], treasury warrant, 50 acres, to join Wanalator's (?) line on one side and his own old survey and his new survey on the other.

August 14, 1786, JOHN THOMAS, assignee of Benjamin Dawson, treasury warrant, 500 acres on Walkers Creek adjoining Stumps, James Thompson, and John Crow's surveys (withdrawn by Eam (?) Thomas 10 May 1788 (?).

August 16, 1786, JAMES EVANS, assignee of Jurety Evans, assignee of John Smith, treasury warrant, 130 acres on south side of South Fork of Walkers Creek joining Will Davies on east side near improvements made by Cox.
WILLIAM EVANS on above warrant, 20 acres balance of warrant on south side of South Fork of Walkers Creek, including the first branch that runs out of Walkers Mountain, and from Walkers Creek to the mountain.
PHILIP LAMBERT, assignee of Henry Bagley, assignee of Henry Banks, 22 acres adjoining Joseph Oney on southeast side and his own land on south side and towards the mountain.

p. 332

PHILIP LAMBERT, assignee of Joseph Oney, assignee of James Devor, assignee of William Caldwell, 100 acres, added to entry of February 7, 1786 (Walkers Creek).

August 17, 1786, DAVID CULBERTONS, assignee of Samuel Helton, assignee of David Robinson, assignee of George Thompson, treasury warrant, 1,000 acres enters 100 acres on branch of Little River, called Burks Run, joining where Jeremiah Farmer lives at the lower side of said land to include Thomas Evans' improvements.
RANDOLPH SMITH, assignee as above on sd. warrant, 100 acres on Burks Fork of Big Reed Island Creek to begin at Wards line at the creek.

THOMAS HUBBARD, assignee as above, 100 acres on Burks Fork of Big Reed Island Creek, to begin at Wards line and to run south and east.

p. 333

JOHN PARTAIN, assignee as in above entry, 150 acres on Burks Fork of Big Reed Island Creek, joining 200 acres on north side in Sugar Tree Bend.

JOHN TAYLOR, assignee of Jeremiah Bell, treasury warrant, 100 (200?) acres joining Richard Hankins lower place where Edward Hankins lived.

MOORE BELL, 300 acres at the mouth of Cooked [Crooked] Creek, both sides of New

DUNCAN GULLION, 150 acres on Reed Creek joining Nicholas Wyrick and George Houck under Pine Ridge (surveyed 142 acres and 8 acres withdrawn).

p. 334

WILLIAM TABOR, assignee of John Minster, treasury warrant, 200 acres on Plumb Creek, adjoining former entry made 28th Feb. 1783, and added to the same and both laid off in one survey (surveyed 100 in part ''ch'd'' surveyed in full for H. Bingaman).

August 21, 1786, HENRY TROLLINGER, preemption warrant for 400 acres, 1782, enters 86 acres on Clear Fork of Wolf Creek and joining a survey of Jacob Waggoner's on Mile (Mill?) Branch.

JOHN McDONALD, assignee of Henry Banks, enters 50 acres on south side of Brush Mountain and joining the land he lives on, on north side and Bryan McDonald survey made 1783 on east side, and Joseph McDonald's.

September 8, 1786, JAMES DEVOR withdraws two entries made May 1, 1786, and enters them on north side of South Fork of Walkers Creek joining James Polly's line to include a spring, 100 acres.

p. 335

September 12, 1786, THOMAS GODFRY, assignee of Patrick Napier, assignee of Walter Crockett, attorney for James Clark, 100 acres on treasury warrant, beginning at William Kavanough's on north side of Wolf Creek, including survey of Elisha Perdue; also 50 acres at the head of James Johnson's spring branch under Wolf Creek Mountain on north side.

September 13, 1786, MOSES WINTERS, assignee of George Booth, assignee of part of a treasury warrant of 3,000 acres, enters 200 acres on north side of the hill called Pilot Mountain, the timbered land.

MOSES WINTERS withdraws 118 acres of entry made 25 June and added to 150 acres above and enters it at a place called Shilling's Meadow, joining Israel Lorton, joining with How's meadow, and to join the line with his land on Great Elkhorn.

p. 336

September 15, 1786, THOMAS HUFF, assignee of Joseph Morris, assignee of Elijah Creek, assignee of Abram Penn, treasury warrant, 1,000 acres, 1783, enters 500 acres on Little Reed Island Creek at Ronald's Camp.

September 18, 1786, SETH STRATTON, 100 acres on treasury warrant, both sides South Fork of Lick Creek adjoining Daniel Stratton on the east; also 100 acres on part of warrant between James Wilson's survey and Joshua Entrum's plantation on North Fork of Holston, joining Walkers Mountain.

September 19, 1786, JOHN WHITSELL, assignee of Jehu Stephens on treasury warrant, 100 acres on Reed Creek, between Jacob Craford and Sam'l Ewing's.

October 1, 1786, JOHN CHAPMAN, assignee of William Treasy (?), assignee of Henry Banks, treasury warrant, 10 acres joining land Richard Chapman sold and the place Isaac Chapman lives on, including several salt petre caves.

October 10, 1786, HENRY CLEMENTS, assignee of Leonard Straw, treasury warrant, 100 acres head of Holston joining Joseph Davises line on south side between the sd. line and the mountain.

LEONARD STRAW, treasury warrant, 100 acres joining John Leedy and Nicles [Nicholas] Tarter, and 100 acres joining his own and William Lewis, warrant dated 1782; 20 acres joining Michael Venrick, John Ounchill [Hounshell], and his own, warrant of 500 acres, 1782, assigned by James Clerk.

JEREMIAH BELL, JOHN SMITH, and ZACHARIAH STANLEY, treasury warrant, 107 acres on Clapboard Creek to begin at Nathaniel Munsey's lower corner, place he now lives.

CASPER WEBBER, assignee of Henry Patton, treasury warrant, 100 acres on branch called Mill Creek of Walkers Creek to begin at lower side of Henry Harman survey and to join Nathaniel Brittain's lines.

Oct. 10, 1786, GEORGE LOWMAN, assignee of Henry Patton, preemption warrant, enters 200 acres beginning on north side of Crouthcer's old survey and with same and crossing the spring branch (surveyed for Henry Wysor; warrants dated 1783, granted to James Patton).

HENRY PATTON, preemption warrant, beginning on east end of Waggoner's old survey of 70 acres on Sinking Spring and to join with Henry Stobough and Henry Piper, 100 acres dated April 14, 1783, granted to James Patton; 100 acres at the head of a draft corner to Waggoner's 70 acres and north with same to John Piper then south and west.

Oct. 10, 1786, RICHARD ESTIS, treasury warrant, 50 acres beginning on upper end of Edward Hale's survey on south side of Wolf Creek.

ISAIAH PURDUE, warrant assigned by Richard Chapman, 50 acres beginning at lower corner of Will: Cavenner's [Cavenough's] line and east to join James Ross.

THOMAS PICKENS, preemption warrant of 400 acres assigned by Thomas Soward, 320 acres on White Glades, beginning near Cecil's and 80 acres joining the land he lives on, on the east side (surveyed for Thomas Cecil).

October 22, 1786, THOMAS QUIRK, JOHN HARVIE, THOMAS MADISON, PATRICK HENRY, JUNR., JOHN STEWART, ZACH. ROWLAND, JOSPEH KENT, JAMES CROCKETT, ANDREW CROCKETT, JOHN T. SAYERS, JOHN CROCKETT, WILLIAM WADDELL, JOSEPH CROCKETT, JR., ROBERT KENT, JOHN BROWN, HUGH McGAVOCK, preemption warrant, 1785, 1,000 acres joining Andrew Boyd on Little Pine Run and joining James Simpson and John T. Sayers, and Cornelius McGlister's old line, James Lowthers, Randolph Fugate and Andrew Crockett's line.

JOHN VAUGHT, treasury warrant, 409 acres, 1781, assigned by John Creager, assignee of Mary Howard, 150 acres joining his survey and Peter Razor, Zachariah Plankpickle, and Henry Vaceses (Vice's?); 50 acres joining Nilson and Sharod James patent line; 200 acres on north side of Iron Mountain joining Ferral Darter's survey on the south side.

October 22, 1786, THOMAS DUNN, assignee of Samuel Finley, assignee of Henson Gardner, assignee of Robert Sayers, treasury warrant, 1782, 230 acres adjoining the survey for Sam'l Finley and between Philip Lambert's on a branch of Crab Orchard waters of Walkers Creek (surveyed 90 acres and balance withdrawn).

JEREMIAH BELL, assignee of Zachariah Stanly, 80 acres on west side of Henry Piper and joining Henry Trolinger on southwest side (withdrawn Oct. 26, 1787).

THOMAS TEES, preemption warrant, 1786, 1,000 acres on Great Kanhawa adjoining his settlement right to the mouth of the Cole River and up the same.

ANDREW REID, attorney for Samuel (?) Culbertson, preemption warrant, 1786, 600 acres adjoining Culbertson's Bottom on southwest side of New River corner to survey made for Thomas Farler and to include an island.

JOHN AUGUST, assignee of Arthur Campbell, assignee of James Retherford, treasury warrant, 100 acres on Middle Fork of Holston, joining Robert Shannon and John McMillan, and towards the land William Patterson lives on (withdrawn and assigned to W. Ward and Joseph Patterson).

ARTHUR CAMPBELL, assignee of James Retherford, treasury warrant, 100 acres on branch of Middle Fork of Holston called Mill Creek; 200 acres on said warrant on branch of Middle Fork of Holston, called Mill Creek, beginning where the county line crosses the creek, near the head.

October 26, 1786, JOHN WARD, assignee of John Smith, treasury warrant, 862 (?) acres on Burks Fork adjoining settlement as marked by John Taylor.

JOHN CALLOWAY, assignee of Thomas Anderson, assignee of Ed. Winston, assignee of Wm. Christian, treasury warrant 1,000 acres on Greasey Creek branch of Reed Island to include the survey of 554 acres made for Calloway, to run on both sides of Wm. Penurton (?). Withdrawn Nov. 10, 1794).

JAMES CAMERON, assignee of George Kinser, assignee of Michael Venrick, treasury warrant, 220 acres on North Fork of Holston, and north side of Walkers Mountain and both sides of Burks old path.

PETER SPANGLER, assignee of James Thompson, 200 acres on North Fork of Holston lying between his own and James Willson.

JOHN TAYLOR, assignee of John Neal, assignee of William Neal, treasury warrant, 282 acres, 1783, enters part, 167 acres on Middle Fork of Greasy Creek, joining James Calaway's survey at the lower end, beginning corner to Callaway's survey.

JOHN PARTAIN, 50 acres joining an entry of 200 acres on Sugar Tree Bent on Burks Fork (surveys with entries pp. 161 and 333).

RICHARD STEGALL, 50 acres at the end of the Indian Ridge adjoining his right of settlement.

ZACHARIAH STANLEY, JOHN SMITH and JEREMIAH BELL, treasury warrant, 107 acres on Clapboard Creek joining Nathaniel Muncey's survey and to include James Cooly's improvements.

JOHN TAYLOR and JONATHAN ISHAM, 500 acres on west fork of Little

River in the Shanese Hollow to join Thomas Huff, William Spurlock and Andrew Bradley (333 acres withdrawn and entered for Alex Orr; withdrawn in full 4-7-94).

p. 346

October 27, 1786, ABRAHAM STOBOUGH, assignee of John Taylor, treasury warrant, 100 acres joining the land he lives on and lines of Peter Penner's and Conrod Wall's on Plum Creek and Connolley's Branch.

THOMAS DUNN, assignee of John Smith, assignee of John Levell (?), treasury warrant, 1782, for 1,518 acres, enters part thereof, 300 acres on Crab Orchard a branch of Walkers Creek joining Brushy Mountain (surveyed 46 acres with Prunty's certificate and balance withdrawn).

November 1, 1786, ALEXANDER MITCHELL, assignee of John Taylor, treasury warrant, 50 acres below the land John Bell now lives on, opposite side of Little River about one mile below the mouth of Meadow Creek to include the improvements.

p. 347

JOHN BELL, assignee of Henry Banks, treasury warrant, 100 acres to begin at a spring where the old fort stood and down the spring branch and up Little River to the branch, and up the branch to the head of a meadow [this appears to be Bell's Fort mentioned in other records].

JOHN BELL, assignee of John Smith, treasury warrant, 20 acres adjoining the above.

SAMUEL FERGUSON, assignee of John Smith, treasury warrant, 200 acres on head of Bluestone adjoining John Peerey's to include his improvements as marked out by Sam'l Walker.

p. 348

November 22, 1786, DAVID ROSS, treasury warrant for 1,000 acres, 1783, enters same, adjoining New Dublin to surround the old tract and the last survey of 500 acres.

December 1, 1786, JOHN MONTGOMERY withdraws two entries of 50 acres 1786 and enters 100 acres adjoining entry of 200 acres, to be laid off in one survey.

p. 349

GEORGE KINSER withdraws 50 acres of entry adjoining David Doak's and Henry Newman's and 101 acres made on the head of Reed Creek on the north side of Brushy Mountain and assigns the warrant to Peter Stiffy.

PETER STIFFY, assignee of George Kinser, 150 acres on head of South Fork of Reed Creek, adjoining John Staffy's and Michael Knave's [Neff's] (surveyed 140 acres).

December 3, 1786, JOHN BUCKLEY and WILLIAM CALDWELL, treasury warrant, 305 (365?) acres at the foot of Buckeye Mountain and north and south side of same joining Bear Spring survey and Paul Whitley's, Jacob Strayles, John Kirk, and Ralph Bogle; 200 acres on Chinquepine Spring, branch of Walkers Creek, joining Paul Whitley and towards the land of Sam'l Cecil, deceased.

p. 350

December 15, 1786, JOSEPH STEPHENS, assignee of Dan'l How, assignee of Joseph How, assignee of Joseph Cloyd, assignee of Ephraim Dunlop on treasury warrant, assignee of Dan'l Howe, treasury warrant, 90 acres on Stroples [Stroubles] Creek, adjoining Thomas Sperey [Sperry], Abraham Christman and Peter Stephens.

December 19, 1786, MICHAEL MILLER, assignee of John Smith, treasury warrant, 30 acres on Doe Creek in the Cow Camp Hollow on the east side of his house and to join Jeremiah Davis' 70 acres on west side of his land about a mile from his house.

JAMES BOBBIT, assignee of Moore Bell, 397 acres on treasury warrant, to begin on south side of branch of Big Reed Island Creek, the said branch emptying into the river at the old ford of Reed Island Creek.

p. 351

MOORE BELL, treasury warrant, 400 acres on Big Reed Island Creek, and part of Laurel Fork on the dividing ridge.

ROBERT GOAD, assignee of Zachariah Stanley, treasury warrant, 49 acres on Big Reed Island Creek, on both sides of the river above the old patent.

WILLIAM LOCKHART, assignee of Henry Patton, preemption warrant, 34 acres joining John Craig in Hazel Hollow on the northeast side of Craig's land.

p. 352

ZACHARIAH STANLEY, JOHN SMITH, and JEREMIAH BELL, treasury warrant, 300 acres on Clear Fork of Wolf Creek, to begin on south side of the creek and to extend to the foot of Rich Mountain; also 200 acres on Clear Fork of Wolf Creek to begin at George Peck's corner on the north side of the creek.

DANIEL WAGGONER, assignee of Zachariah Stanley, treasury warrant, 100 acres on Clear Fork of Wolf Creek beginning at southeast corner of Adam Waggoner's patent land.

p. 353

HENRY TROLINGER, assignee of Zachariah Stanley, treasury warrant, 117 acres on the North Fork of Kimberlain's Fork of Walkers Creek beginning by Muncey's Creek.

DANIEL CARLIN withdraws 250 acres on Crooked Creek and enters it on Little Reed Island Creek, in some open barrens on south of Poplar Camp Mountain, to include the iron ore bank on the south side of the brushy ridge.

ANDREW HATFIELD, treasury warrant, 106 acres entered after withdrawing his entry made Dec. 2, 1782, on the west side of an old survey and joining it and up and down the Big Stony Creek; warrant to him for 500 acres assigned by James Brumfield, assignee of Peter Saunders.

pp. 354-356

January 4, 1787, GEORGE WILLIAMS, assignee of John Smith, assignee of John Lovell, treasury warrant, 1782, 43 acres adjoining his entry of 20 acres and to be laid off together in one survey; also 50 acres on south side of Nob Mountain, beginning at a Grassy Spring opposite the head of George Fry's spring.

January 6, 1787, EDMUND NAPIER, assignee of John Taylor, treasury warrant, 100 acres on Spruce Run, to begin at the mouth on the south side and to extend up the run to include a mill seat and to join Alexr. (?) Elly (?)

GEORGE BOOTH, assignee of John Minster, treasury warrant, waters of Meadow Creek; also 500 acres assigned by George Turnbull, joining Joseph Fiffer on Mill Creek, George Thompson, and William Canterburry's, extending towards Samuel Canterburry's land.

JOHN LAWRENCE, assignee of John Minster (Minter?), on treasury warrant, 1784, 390 acres adjoining the survey of James Simpkins, William Walton, Rich Hill, Robert Simpkins, and another tract of James Simpkins, James Roberts, and George Boothe.

JAMES HOWARD, assignee of George Turnbull, treasury warrant, 1783, for 1,553 3/4 acres, enters part, 400 acres joining Moses Winters and Joseph Fiffer, and up Mill Creek on the north side with Fiffer's (50 acres withdrawn); 100 acres joining Samuel Lester on Little River and on both sides of the river; 100 acres on a branch of Little River on top of Pilot Mountain at the head thereof; 200 acres joining Henry Carter on east side and upon a branch of Meadow Creek.

January 8, 1787, HENRY ASBERRY withdraws his entry of 8 December 1785, on treasury warrant, 1782, and enters same, 200 acres, to begin on south side of Maiden Spring, branch of Clinch River, opposite the mouth of Thompson Creek, on the north side of Clinch Mountain.

p. 357

January 17, 1787, ALEXANDER ORR, assignee of Robert Calvert, treasury warrant, for 693 3/4 acres, 1783, enters part, 200 acres on Walkers Creek joining Robt. Smith on north side of his land and on southwest side.

January 20, 1787, JOHN WM. HOWE, treasury warrant, 1781, 100 acres joining and at the northeast end of an old entry at the clay lick on Brush Creek, including Meadow ground and part of wood land under the ridge.

p. 358

January 20, 1787, JOHN WM. HOWE, assignee of Edw'd Coughran, assignee of Isaac Taylor, assignee of Uriah Akers, treasury warrant, 50 acres, 1780, located about one mile up the Five Mill Fork of East River, including the Rock House (withdrawn).

DANI'L HOWE, assignee of John Wm. Howe, treasury warrant, 1781, 100 acres on Back Creek at the east side of his patent line to join Brown's, Pekins [Pickins] and Cicil [Cecil].

ALEXR. STEWART, treasury warrant, 200 acres on Harmans Branch which empties into the north side of the East River; also 300 acres on branch emptying into the south side of the East River at the foot of Christian's land to begin below the fork of said branch and up both branches to the head and from the head to the top of Christian Mountain.

p. 359

January 22, 1787, NICHOLAS SNIDOE, treasury warrant, 150 acres on Blue Spring Branch, a branch of Cripple Creek, adjoining John Newland and to extend to the Chestnut Ridge.

February 2, 1787, WILLIAM BOWLEN, assignee of John Taylor, assignee of Robt. Calvert, treasury warrant, 693 3/4 acres, 1782 (?), enters part thereof, 100 acres beginning at John Chapman's corner and to another corner of John Chapman.

pp. 360-361

February 5, 1787, JOHN GARWOOD, assignee of Lovell H. Dogan, treasury warrant, 44 acres on North Fork of Holston, beginning about four poles from Hayses, west line of a survey he lives on.

HENRY BANKS, treasury warrant for 100,000 acres, enters part thereof, 60,000 acres to begin at the head spring of Big Harricane (Hurricane) Creek, corner Banks upper survey on said creek and to join Banks survey of 23,800 acres back of Genl. Washington's land on Kanawha below the mouth of Cole River and to extend back of the surveys on the Harricane (Hurricane) towards Cole River and the Gyandott River, to be laid off in one or more surveys as most convenient; also 20,000 acres to begin adjoining Banks 3,210 acres on

65

a creek emptying into Cole River on the upper side about 160 poles below the second falls of same; also 20,087 acres to begin adjoining the lowermost survey of said Banks in loop of 12,300 acres lying near the great falls of the New.

p. 362

February 7, 1787, HENRY BANKS withdraws 1,000 acres his entry of 23 January 1786, and enters same as follows: 500 acres on Great Kanhawa beginning at the lower corner of Geo. Washington's about two miles above the mouth of same and to run up the river with Washington's land; 500 acres on the Ohio beginning two miles below the mouth of the Great Kanhawa at the upper corner of George Mercer's.

February 9, 1787, HENRY BANKS, assignee of Malcolm Hart, treasury warrant, 500 acres, 1783, on Piney River to include a large rock on the lower side of the river about 100 yards above the War Road that leads down Paint Creek.

February 10, 1787, JAMES WHITE withdraws second entry of 9 May 1782, being 425 acres and assigns the same to William Love.

p. 363

February 10, 1797, WILLIAM LOVE, assignee of James White, treasury warrant, 1782, enters 425 acres part of same, on south side of a survey for David Miller March 17, 1775, and to the south side of Isham Harris to include the Cedar Springs and the iron ore bank.

JAMES JOHNSON, assignee of John Taylor, treasury warrant, 120 acres on Little Stoney Creek, beginning at Thomas Marshall's line and Christian Snidow's line known as "lower lick pond"; also 46 acres joining David Johnson's to begin at a place known as the sink hole; also 134 acres in Turkey Hollow about 50 miles below the spring on the north side of the hollow.

p. 364

February, 10, 1787, JOSHUA JONES, PETER RAZOR, and BENJAMIN JOHNS (JOHNSON ?), assignees of Henry Patton, treasury preemption warrant for 200 acres, on South Fork of Holston, on both sides to include the ironworks (withdraws 30 acres August 8, 1788).

February 10, 1787, JOSHUA JONES on above warrant, 100 acres at the north corner of the land he lives on and to extend to Walker Crockett's patent line on the south side of the South Fork of the Holston.

JOSHUA JONES, PETER RAZOR, BENJAMIN JOHNS (?), assignees of John Alcorn, treasury warrant, 50 acres on south side of Jones' land to begin on north side of Chestnut Ridge, to include a bank of iron ore; also 54 acres to begin on north side of John Vaut's [Vaught's] land and towards Peter Razor's to include the bank of iron ore.

p. 365

February 12, 1787, THOMAS MARSHALL, assignee of John Taylor, treasury warrant, on south side of the land he lives on, on Mallato Hill and towards Christian Snidoe's and Little Stoney Creek (surveyed with entry of 50 acres).

February 16, 1787, JAMES BRUMFIELD, assignee of Peter Saunders, treasury warrant, 100 acres on Little Stoney Creek, joining Caldwell on east side; 115 acres joining Johnson and Hatfield.

CHRISTIAN SNIDOE [SNIDOW], assignee of Jacob Brillmore, assignee of Peter Saunders, 70 acres on north side of Stoney Creek, to include the Pounding Mill.

February 19, 1787, THOMAS EVANS, assignee of Henry Banks, treasury warrant, 125 acres on Claboard Branch of New, including Mary (?) Davis's improvement.

HENRY PIPER, preemption warrant, 1787, for 1,000 acres, enters part thereof, 100 acres adjoining the land he lives on and David Waggoner's and to join William Day.

February 20, 1787, THOMAS BURK, assignee of John Young, treasury warrant and a military warrant, 100 acres to begin near Coopley's in the hollow called Camping Hollow to include the Camping Hollow Spring.

p. 367, JOHN SMITH, treasury warrant, 150 acres to begin at the mouth of Tugs [Tug] River, to include the bottom.

ABRAHAM GLIMPH, assignee of John Taylor, treasury warrant, 100 acres between the lines of Madden and John Goneng (?) on Doe Creek.

JOSEPH ADKINS, treasury warrant, 240 (?) acres to begin on his east corner towards Culton's to include the spring.

JOHN LEGGETT, treasury warrant, 50 acres joining William Calhoon and Joseph Adkins, to include the bank of iron ore (surveyed 30 acres, withdrew 20 acres).

EDWARD CROW, treasury warrant, 100 acres to join his own on southwest side of the South Fork of Holston.

GEORGE MARTIN, assignee, treasury warrant, 150 acres to join Gab'l Scott and William Moore, on South Fork of Holston (48 acres certified to Wythe County).

p. 368,

February 20, 1787, JENKIN WILLIAMS, assignee, treasury warrant, 100 acres to include the falls of Stailey's Creek on the South Fork of Holston River.

CHRISTLEY VAUGHT, 60 acres joining his own, and David Bustard on head of Cripple Creek.

PHILLIP DUTTON, 150 acres on Cripple Creek to join his patent land.

JOHN LESLEY, 50 acres on Dry Branch to join Bransteter, on Cripple Creek.

WILLIAM HARBART, 190 acres in gap of Poplar Camp Mountain, also 100 acres joining his own and William Ross' patent land.

CHARLES HENIGER, 175 acres Crooked Creek, to include Poplar Knob.

p. 369

THOMAS PENSON, 300 acres on New River to include his improvements.

JOHN BRYANT, 120 acres on Meadow Creek.

SAMUEL JACKSON, 370 acres on Chestnut Creek, to include his improvements.

MATHEW DICKEY, 100 acres north and northeast of his survey as purchased of Elisha Walling.

JAMES NEWELL, 150 acres to join James Chester, John Cox and an old survey of Walkers on Little River.

MINITREE JONES, 200 acres to join his own at Wallens Bottom.

JAMES CHESTER, 95 acres at the mouth of Little River and up both sides and on the west side of Little River.

JAMES BLEVINS, 40 acres at the mouth of Little River and up said river and down New River.

p. 370

JOHN FROST, 94 acres joining John McCoy and Flower Swift.

THOMAS SHANNON, assignee of Samuel Shannon, treasury warrant, 50 acres adjoining Henry Long between that and Rockey Bend of Walkers Creek; also 100 acres, assignee of Alexander Stewart on North Fork of Sugar Run, adjoining Thomas Farley and south side of Wolf Creek Mountain.

JEREMIAH WARD withdraws his entry made and joining the lead mines and enters 200 acres on headwaters of Little River, known as Conaways or Bollinds (?) cabin, joining Black Ridge.

JOSEPH and MAYO CARRINGTON, assignee of Frances Graif (?) on two treasury warrants, 10,000 acres on Mud Fork of Gyandott, adjoining a survey of Rich'd Mason.

CHAPTER II
Wythe County Entry Book 1

The entries of Wythe County were most often based on treasury warrants, allowing individuals to claim vacant land. In Entry Book 1, of Wythe County, there are also a few entries based on military warrants for service in the French and Indian War or the Revolution. For further information on how land was taken up, see Kegley and Kegley, *Early Adventurers*, Vol. 1 and Kegley, *Early Adventurers*, Vol. 2, or *see above*.

The geographic area covered by these entries includes present Wythe, Bland, Grayson, Carroll, part of Smyth, part of Pulaski, and part of Tazewell counties. The land was located on the New, Holston and Clinch rivers and their branches.

These records which extend from July 27, 1790 through December 26, 1793, are from the first 126 pages of Entry Book 1. Additional records for later years can be found in the same book. All information in square brackets was provided by the author. The following records are abstracts of the original.

Wythe County Entry Book 1

p. 1, July 27, 1790, JOSEPH ERWIN, enters 100 acres on treasury warrant, 1790, assigned by Robert Adams, assignee of Samuel McCraw, on Reed Creek, to include all the vacant land between Walter Kincer, Henry Newman, John Gullion, Adam Walker, Peter Hedrick, and George Kinder (withdrawn and assigned warrant to Jacob Kinder).

July 28, 1790, JOSEPH ERWIN, 50 acres on same warrant, on Reed Creek adjoining William Thompson and entry of William Ward and to run to Brushy Mountain (withdrawn and assigned to William Thompson).

July 28, 1790, WILLIAM BOUREN [BOURNE], enters [no acres stated] on treasury warrants, assigned by Robert Adams, assignee of Samuel McCraw, 1790, beginning in Matthew Dickey's line and above the falls on Peach Bottom Creek, and both sides, including the head of Rockey Creek, and round or between some of George Reeves' surveys, in one or more surveys as may best suit the situation of the vacant land.

p. 2, July 28, 1790, JESSE EVANS, assignee of Robert Adams, assignee of Samuel McCraw on treasury warrant, 1790, enters [no acres stated] on Cedar Run, branch of Reed Creek, beginning at Stophel [Christopher] Simmerman's, John Davis', and John McNut's corner and going towards George Kegley's, Daniel Etter's and Edward Murphey's to Peter Binkley's and to Charles

Simmerman's and George Armbrister's and to McNutt's for quantity. Marginal note states May 30, 1793, 265 acres of this entry surveyed for Susanna Helvey, Henry Helvey, and Jacob Helvey; May 30, 1793, 88 acres surveyed for John McNutt; March 10, 1796, 50 acres surveyed for Daniel Etter; balance withdrawn at different times.

August 5, 1790, JOHN BUCKLEY and SAML. ROBINETT, 400 acres entered on treasury warrant, 1781, on Brush Creek, branch of New River beginning on Ozborne's old road near the forks, including the "oar" bank at the forks and to Brushy Ridge, and to include other ore banks for quantity. ("Sent to Grayson," written in the margin.) Sam'l Robinett withdraws 50 acres and reenters May 8, 1791.

p. 2, August 6, 1790, STEPHEN REEDER, assignee of Robert Adams, assignee of Sam'l. McCraw, enters 40 acres on part of a treasury warrant, 1,000, 1790, adjoining Joseph Erwin, Nowell, and his own land.

p. 3, August 9, 1790, JAMES MONTGOMERY, SENR. [SR.], assignee of Robert Adams, assignee of Sam'l. McCraw, 150 acres on treasury warrant, 1790, on Peek [Peak] Creek, branch of New River, beginning on the southwest corner of his old survey.

August 9, 1790, JOSEPH CROCKETT, by the above warrant, enters 50 acres beginning on the old patent line on the south side of Reed Creek, towards Aerhart Simmerman's and Ross' line.

August 18, 1790, PHILIP LAMBERT, on above warrant, 100 acres on north side of Walkers Creek, adjoining Francis(?) McGuire and Capt. William Davis, on which he now lives, near the foot of Walkers Big Mountain and running up the valley to McGuire's.

August. 24, 1790, WILLIAM BELCHY, enters 50 acres on treasury warrant, 1782, on north side of Clinch Mountain joining Pat Campball [Campbell], John Young, and Isaac Moore.

p. 4, August 24, 1790, GEORGE KINDER, on a state warrant assigned by Robert Adams, 1790, enters 28 acres to include part of his old improvements.

August. 24, 1790, NATHL. FRISBAY [FRISBY], on treasury warrant, assigned by James Newell, enters 1,000 acres on Crooked Creek, branch of New River, joining Thomas Harbert's known by the name of Paxton's place, the lands of Jacob Colson, the lands where Chas.(?) Cole built a mill on Wolf Glade Creek, and the lands of Jas. Cock known by the name of Hoozer's place, in one or more surveys.

September 1, 1790, JONAS FORTNEY, 25 acres on treasury warrant, 1790, assigned to him by Robert Adams, assignee of Sam'l. McCraw, adjoining Daniel Wysley [Wiseley], James Finley, and William Phipps.

p. 5, September 6, 1790, JAMES FINLEY, enters 7 acres on treasury warrant, 1790, assigned by Robert Adams, assignee of Sam'l. McCraw, adjoining William Phipps and said Finley's old patent line on the south and to include head of "Cole Pitt" Hollow.

September 17, 1790, JAMES WILSON, 100 acres on treasury warrant, 1790, assigned by Robert Adams, assignee of McCraw, adjoining Frederick Slush [Sluss] on the north, and the lands of Jacob Spangler, and to include Wilson's old improvements.

p. 6, September 23, 1790, RITCHARD ELKINS, assignee of John Preston, assignee of James Hines, assignee of Samuel Lewis, on treasury warrant, 1782, 50 acres on Clear Fork of Wolf Creek.

Oct. 2, 1790, ROBERT SAYERS, enters 250 acres on treasury warrant, 1790, assigned by Robert Adams, assignee of Sam'l McCraw, beginning corner to Sayers and George Hancock's line to include the vacant land adjoining Symmerman's [Simmerman's], John Shaver, and others.

September 9, 1790, NICHOLAS WYRICK, assignee of Dunkin Gullion, assignee of William Neel, assignee of Thomas Rutledg [Rutledge] on treasury warrant, 1782, enters 40 acres on north side of his own plantation whereon he now lives.

p. 7, August 30, 1790, PETER KETTERING, enters 100 acres on treasury warrant, 1790, assigned by Ro. [Robert] Adams, assignee of Sam'l McCraw, on Elk Creek, branch of New River, adjoining Robt. Bedwell's and up the north side of the creek to Stophle [Christopher] Gose's line. (Sent to Grayson.)

August 30, 1790, DAVID MILLHANKS, enters 30 acres on treasury warrant beginning at a spring on Steely's path.

August 30, 1790, THOMAS POLLEY, enters 50 acres on treasury warrant, 1790, assigned by Robt. Adams, assignee of Sam'l McCraw on main Walkers Creek beginning on Henry Begley's line and to include vacant land between said line and Joseph Polley.

p. 8, October 4, 1790, HOLTON MUNCEY, enters 50 acres on treasury warrant, 1790, assigned by Robert Adams, assignee of Samuel McCraw, adjoining a high ridge and beginning on Andrew Thomson's line next to Sam'l Munsey.

October 4, 1790, PHILIP YAUGER [YOUNGER, YANGER?], 30 acres on treasury warrant, 1790, assigned by Robert Adams and Sam'l McCraw, adjoining the lands of Jas. (Jos.?) Polley and Nath'l Britton, beginning on Yauger's line to include part of the main road.

October 4, 1790, ADAM WEATHERHOLT, 200 acres on treasury warrant assigned by James Newell, adjoining _____ Summerling, Bengn. [Benjamin] Sexton, William Sexton and James Cole, to include the lands whereon Michael Coker now lives.

October 9, 1790, HENRY UMBARGER, enters 40 acres on treasury warrant, 1782, assigned by Dunkin Gullian, assignee of William Neel, assignee of Thomas Rutledge, on Walkers Creek joining said Umbarger and widow Henderson.

p. 9, October 9, 1790, SAM'L MONCY [MUNCEY], JUNR. [JR.], enters 50 acres on treasury warrant, 1790, assigned by Robert Adams, assignee of Samuel McCraw, on Clear Fork, beginning on line of survey made for Laurence Murry, to include the improvements made by Joseph Baker.

October 19, 1790, WILLIAM BELL, 87 acres on treasury warrant, 1782, on the north side of Crooked Creek, joining Jacob Coleson and Joseph Juson, to include the iron bank.

October 27, 1790, BURKETT CEVIL, enters 50 acres on treasury warrant, 1790, on Holston River joining Christopher Elms.

p. 10, JEREMIAH BELL, assignee of Robert Adams, 100 acres on Clear Fork of Wolf Creek, branch of New River, beginning the upper end and southwest corner of the land George Peck now dwells on, to run to his land and Stewart's and towards Rich Mountain.

LAURENCE KETTERING, 400 acres, Commissioner's certificate, 1782, on South Fork of Reed Creek adjoining John Woods' land recovered from Jacob Kettering to include his improvements.

November 19, 1790, JAMES McGAVOCK, military warrant for 3,000 acres, 1780, enters 2,092 acres, part thereof; also 200 acres on treasury warrant, 1781, on south side of Lick Mountain adjoining William Rogers and between that and John Montgomery.

p. 11, September 28, 1790, PHILIP HARKERADER, 150 acres on treasury warrant, assigned by Robert Adams, assignee of Samuel McCraw, on headwaters of North Fork of Holston, adjoining Barny Gullion, Michael Walters, and John Messersmith.

September 28, 1790, WILLIAM FINLEY, 500 acres on treasury warrant, assigned by Robt. Adams, assignee of Sam'l McCraw, adjoining Gasper Rader and up the north side of Queens Nob, till opposite dividing line between Finley and Frederick Leonard and round Finley's plantation and around Reader's plantation to include the big ridge.

pp. 11-12, September 29, 1790, JACOB KINDER, assignee of Joseph Irwin, assignee of Robert Adams, on treasury warrant of 1,000 acres, 1790, enters 100 acres as follows: 50 acres adjoining Adam Walker, Peter Hederick, George Kinder, Henry Newman; also 50 acres adjoining Henry Newman, John Gullion, George Kinder and Walter Kinsor.

p. 12, JOSEPH POLLEY, 50 acres, treasury warrant, assignee of Robt. Adams, assignee of Sam'l McCraw, beginning at the north of Paulley's Spring Branch, including both sides of the creek.

December 4, 1790, GEORGE CALDWELL, 150 acres, treasury warrant, assigned by Robt. Adams, on Flat Mountain, beginning on north side including lands on both sides of the mountain.

p. 13, December 8, 1790, RITCHARD ELKINS, assignee of John Preston, assignee of James Hines, 50 acres on treasury warrant, 1782, adjoining Stanley's lower line and south side of Clear Fork.

December 15, 1790, CHRISTOPHER ELMS, 50 acres, treasury warrant, adjoining Elms and William Patterson, deceased, and John Snido.

January 4, 1791, JAMES MURPHEY, assignee of Cherles [Charles] Copland [Copeland], treasury warrant, 1782, 50 acres on Cove Creek of New River, beginning at John Adams, near saw pit by the foot of Brushy Mountain on patent line and to include vacant land between lines and Brushy Mountain.

p. 14, January 5, 1791, NATHANIEL LANDERS, assignee of Enoch Osborn, assignee of James Clerk, treasury warrant, 17__ [not legible], 90 acres on Saddle Creek, adjoining Ephrem Osburn on lower side and land of Ezekial Young, beginning where waggon road crosses Saddle Creek; also as assignee of Enoch Osborn and Clerk's attorney, 40 (10?) acres on treasury warrant, 1782, adjoining Stephen Jones, to include improvements made by Robert Pannington.

January 14, 1791, NATHAN WARD, assignee of Enoch Osborn, and Clerk's attorney, treasury warrant, 1782, 100 acres on Saddle Creek, joining Ephraim Osborn above the creek.

pp. 14-15, January 14,1791, WILLIAM BOUREN [BOURNE], treasury warrant, 1790, 1500 acres joining Mathew Dickey's line that includes the ''oar'' bank and running round the survey of Geo. Reeves, joining Capt. Cox and crossing Peach Bottom, joining Reeves on the south side of the creek and Howell's land.

p. 15, January 14, 1791, WILLIAM MULLEN, assignee of Wm. Bouren [Bourne], treasury warrant, 100 acres on open line of survey made by Sam'l Stampfield, and running towards Thomas Car's and Nath'l Ward's.

February 1, 1791, JAMES CAMMARN [CAMERON], assignee of James Murphey,

71

assignee of Charles Copeland, 200 acres, treasury warrant, 1782, adjoining the old survey and Jacob Spangler, Geo. Baugh, and Esau Bradly. Note: James Camron assigns 100 acres of this warrant of this entry to Geo. Kincer.

JOSEPH FLETCHER, treasury warrant, assigned by Robert Adams, 100 acres Walkers Creek beginning at corner of Fletcher's line and to be laid off to include vacant land adjoining said line and John Cox, Senr., on south side of Wolf Creek.

p. 16, February 2, 1791, JOSEPH FLETCHER, treasury warrant assigned as above, 25 acres on Wolf Creek, beginning where Fletcher's old line crosses the creek to run with line so as to include the vacant land towards John Cox, Junr's.

February 12, 1791, GASPER RADER, treasury warrant assigned by Robt. Adams, 100 acres adjoining sd. Rader, Cole, Crockett and William Finley and to extend towards Brushy Mountain for quantity.

February 26, 1791, MOSES (?) LINDSEY, assignee of James Murphy assignee of Charles Copland [Copeland], 50 acres adjoining his own land on Walkers Creek and to run down the spring branch.

February 14, 1791, JOHN COX, SENR., 100 acres (error)

p. 17, JOHN COX, SENR., on treasury warrant, 1790, assigned by Robt. Adams, assignee of Sam'l McCraw, 50 acres on W. [Wolf?] Creek, to include vacant land between sd. Cox and vacant land on south side of sd. line on both sides of the creek.

March 5, 1791, JEREMIAH PATRICK, treasury warrant, 1782, assignee of James Clerk, 100 acres, beginning on bank of New River and to extend to top of high ridge near Captain Carter's corner, then direct line to Racoon Branch and south side of said branch.

March 8, 1791, JOHN CROCKETT, treasury warrant, 1782, assigned by Henry Banks, assignee of Geo. Rice, assignee of Geo. Tucker (?), 100 acres on Cove Creek on north side of John Thompson's and towards the line of Geo. Sheleday.

p. 18, GEORGE DAVIS, treasury warrant, 1782, assigned by John Crockett, assignee of Henry Banks, assignee of George Rice, assignee of Geo. Tucker, 100 acres adjoining Ross and John Davis, Senr.

March 8, 1791, SAMUEL ROBINETT, treasury warrant, 1791, 50 acres on Little Fox Creek to include the limestone quarry.

pp. 18-19, March 8, 1791, JOSEPH DAVIDSON, treasury warrant, 1782, 150 acres assigned by James Murphy, assignee of Chares [Charles] Copland [Copeland], beginning in Charles Hays' line on Buckhorn Ridge, and to include Laurel Fork of Wolf Creek, to include the bottom, known as Red Oak Bottom.

p. 19, March 20, 1791, FREDERICK MOORE, assignee of James Murphey, assignee of Charles Copland, 50 acres, joining John [should be Jehu] Stephens and Jacob Darter on south side of Brushy Mountain (withdrawn).

March 14, 1791, ANTHONY TONKERY [TONCRAY], treasury warrant assigned by Robert Adams, assignee of Sam'l McCraw, 100 acres adjoining David Ross on east and southeast to extend towards Lick Mountain and to include the ridge of pine timber.

p. 20, March 26, 1791, JOHN ALSUP, treasury warrant, assignee of Sam'l Muncey, assignee of Robt. Adams, 50 acres on Clear Fork of Wolf Creek, beginning on the north side, ten rods below the old corner of Adam Waggoner's survey and to run up Rich Hollow towards Buck Horn.

PHILIP YOUNGER, 6 acres on Walkers Creek joining his own, including a field to extend towards Thomas Pauley's.

WILLIAM McGUIR [McGUIRE], treasury warrant, assigned by Murphey, 100 acres on Bluestone, adjoining John Cumpton, on south and up and down East River Mountain for quantity.

p. 21, March 30, 1791, JOHN MERCER [this may be intended for MUSSER], treasury warrant, 1,500 acres, 1790, 100 acres assigned by Walter Crockett, assignee of Robt. Adams, on head branch of Middle Fork of Holston.

March 15, 1791, SHERAD ADKENSON, treasury warrant, 1790, 87 acres beginning on George Peck's line and up Clear Fork of Wolf Creek on the north side.

April 11, 1791, JAMES ANDERSON, treasury warrant, 1790, 100 acres assigned by Robt. Adams, assignee of Sam'l McCraw, beginning at the lower end of an entry made by Stephen Creech, on which Anderson now lives, on Wilson Creek of New River.

p. 22, April 10, 1791, PETER STOUT and JOHN HILL, 100 acres, treasury warrant, 1783, assignee of James Newell on Chestnut Creek of New River, beginning on Flower Swift's southeast corner adjoining lands of Joseph Meas.

April 12, 1791, BENJAMIN HOLSTIEN [HOLSTON], treasury warrant, assigned by Robert Adams, 150 acres on Elk Creek of New River, beginning corner to Robert Bedwell's land he now lives on near the creek.

p. 22, April 25, 1791, HENRY COOK, treasury warrant, assigned by Robt. Adams, assignee of Sam'l McCraw, 120 acres on Cripple Creek adjoining John [should be Jehu] Stephens, Wm. Love, and Peter Spangler.

p. 23, April 28, 1791, JOSEPH ERWIN, treasury warrant, assigned by James Murphy, 10 (?) acres on Reed Creek, joining Erwin's old patent line and up the creek to join his new survey on north side of the creek.

April 28, 1791, JACOB YAUGER, treasury warrant, assigned by James Murphey, 50 acres on Walkers Creek, adjoining George Pearce and James Venater, on south.

May 10, 1791, JACOB FANNING, 700 acres on treasury warrant, assigned by James Murphy, assignee of Chs. [Charles] Copland [Copeland], on the Long Branch of New River, joining Mathew Dickey's, William Alon [Allen?] and Frost.

p. 24, WILLIAM DAVIS, treasury warrant, assigned by James Murphey, 50 acres on Walkers Creek adjoining Capt. Peirce (note, 45 acres of this entry to George Peerie [Peery], who withdraws it and assigns to Jos. Davison, Sept. 10, 1794).

p. 24, WILLIAM ADAMS, treasury warrant, 1790, 55 acres adjoining Robert Breckeridge [Breckenridge] and John Adams, on both sides of the Big Road.

June 2, 1791, NATHAN WARD, treasury warrant, assigned by Wm. Bouren [Bourne], 1783, 100 acres on Cole Creek, beginning on a conditional line between Joseph Hank and Nathan Ward, to include vacant land adjoining sd. line and lands of Enock Cox and John Pickerel (67 acres withdrawn and added to another entry, 1,150 acres made June 15, 1791).

June 9, 1791, JAMES BOGELL [BOGLE], treasury warrant assigned by Robt. Adams, 100 acres on Walkers Creek adjoining Joseph Fletcher's and "ridge where water runs under and raises again."

p. 25, June 11, 1791, CHRISTOPHER GOSE, treasury warrant, 1782, 250 acres on branch of Elk Creek known as Turkey Fork, adjoining survey of sd. Gose on north and running south side of the branch for quantity.

June 15 (25?), 1791, CHRISTOPHER GOSE, on above treasury warrant, enters 52 acres on branch of Elk Creek to include the place known as "flag ponn" [pond].

June 15, (25?), 1791, GEORGE KINCER, treasury warrant, assigned by James Murphy, 90 acres Rich Valley, joining his old entry and lands of John Stroup (Shoup?); also 100 acres in Rich Valley, waters of Holston, warrant assigned by James Camron, assignee of James Murphey, joining John Stroup (entry assigned to Adam Geerhart).

p.26, June 15, 1791, JEFFRY HELDRITH, treasury warrant, assigned by Robert Adams, 70 acres in Rich Valley on Holstain [Holston], beginning on east corner of his own land and to join Sutherland and to include a pond.

p. 26, June 15, 1791, NATHAN WARD, treasury warrant, 1783, 150 acres assigned by William Bouren [Bourne], on Cole Creek and Chestnut Creek of New River, joining his old survey, on southeast and Thomas Carr's and Maurice Davice [Davis'], to include improvements of John Swainy.

June 23, 1791, THADDEUS COOLEY, treasury warrant, assigned to him, 20 acres joining his own line on southeast and to join Edward Murphey, also 100 acres adjoining his own and Joseph Heldreth.

p. 27, July 18, 1791, BENGERMIN [BENJAMIN] HOLSTAIN [HOLSTON], treasury warrant, assigned by Robt. Adams, 50 acres on Elk Creek to include improvements made by John Harper.

July 25, 1791, AQUILA GREER, assignee of Abram Jones, assignee of Peter Saunders, treasury warrant, 200 acres, 1781, 28 acres on branch of Big Fox Creek, beginning at Abram Jones' line and to include Greer's claim.

July 25, 1791, AQUILA GREER, treasury warrant, 1781, 1,000 acres, 100 of which was assigned by Aron Jones, assignee of Thomas Jones, assignee of Peter Saunders, enters 50 acres beginning corner to Solomon Cox and to include part of Low Gap between said Cox and Wm. Greer (28 acres withdrawn Feb. 23, 1792, and adds warrant to this entry).

pp. 28-29, July 25, 1791, WILLIAM NEAL, treasury warrant, 1,478 acres, 1782, enters 515 acres on Reed Creek adjoining an entry of 385 acres and to extend up the creek for quantity; on treasury warrant as above, 100 acres on the North Fork of the Holston River, adjoining the lands of Andrew Lammie and James Buchanan on the south to include the vacant land round and adjoining the same; on treasury warrant as before, 400 acres adjoining his former entry on the South Fork of Reed Creek and entry of Duncan Gullion's of 100 acres, to extend down said creek and to include Downing's improvements. Withdraws 67 acres and assigns to Dan'l Herman, Nov. 20, 1794; also 200 acres on Reed Creek to include Adam's Dutton's improvements and joining an entry of Prestons and William Davis.

p. 29, August 3, 1791, PETER BISHOP and JOHN BISHOP, treasury warrant for 1,000 acres, assigned by Wm. King, assignee of Philip Pennalton, 1781, enters 300 acres adjoining Peter Bishop, Philip Fry, and to extend up to Lick Mountain so as to include part of the road leading to the gap on the north side. WILLIAM NEEL, assignee of Daniel Kidd, treasury warrant, 1,875 acres, 1781, and treasury warrant, 1782, for 1,936 acres, enters 200 acres on Reed Creek to join Christopher Brown's on west side to include Leedy's improvement.

p. 30, August 4, 1791, HENRY VICE, treasury warrant, 1,400 acres, 1782, enters 279 acres in Valley of South Fork of Holston, joining John Vaught and Jervis Smythe.

August 5, 1791, WILLIAM BARTLETT, treasury warrant assigned by Robert Adams, 75 acres adjoining Joseph Heldreth on which he now lives, and survey for

Joseph Heldreth's patent land near where John Belshy lives, and to include Joseph's spring and dwelling house.

p. 31, August 9, 1791, WILLIAM ORR, treasury warrant, 4,000 acres, 1783, enters 100 acres in Rich Valley on North Fork Holston and joining Reece Bowen, dec'd and lands of Foster and Jeffery Heldrith, and to extend towards Walkers Mountain.

August 10, 1791, JOHN SHANNON, assignee of William Neel, treasury warrant, 1,498 acres, 1782, enters 200 acres on Big Spring, Middle Fork of Holston, beginning about 50 poles below the spring and running southeast towards Staleys Creek, including the spring.

August 12, 1791, WILLIAM BARTLETT, treasury warrant, 100 acres adjoining Joseph Heldrith's patent land, Henry Humburger's [Umbarger's] and said Heldrith's old survey (Loyal Co.).

DAVID McGAVOCK, assignee of William Bouren [Bourne], assignee of Alexander Taite (?), treasury warrant, 2,000 acres, 1783, enters 165 acres on South Fork of Reed Creek joining Robert Cowden, to include the survey made 1783 in the name of said McGavock and William Campbell.

p. 32, August 15, 1791, JOHN HERKERADER, treasury warrant, 2,000 acres, 1783, enters 250 acres part thereof which was assigned by William Bouren [Bourne], agreeable to courses formerly run by James Taylor; also 50 acres to join the conditional line between Matthew Lindsy and Christopher Brown and to join the patent on the west and to include the old entry made by John Montgomery on which there is a small improvement made by John Goff.

August 15, 1791, AIRHART ZIMMERMAN [SIMMERMAN], assignee of David Johnson, assignee of James Murphy, assignee of Charles Copeland, treasury warrant, 500 acres, enters 100 acres on Reed Creek, joining his own land and lands of Joseph Crockett, David Ross, and George Davis.

STOPHEL [CHRISTOPHER] ZIMMERMAN [SIMMERMAN], assignee of William Bourn [Bourne], assignee of Alexander Taite, treasury warrant, 2,000 acres, 50 acres entered as follows: 11 acres on Reed Creek between his other surveys and one of 85 acres and another of 235 acres; also 39 acres joining the 235 acres and the lands of George Hutsell and Daniel Etter.

p. 33, August. 16, 1791, JACOB RABASS [REPASS], treasury warrant, 1000 acres, assigned by William King, assignee of William Pendleton, 1781, enters 100 acres joining the lands he now lives on, on the east, to include vacant land between Philip Umbarger, Thaddeus Cooley, and Andrew Brown.

DANIEL RABASS [REPASS], assignee of William Bouren [Bourne], assignee of Alexander Taite, treasury warrant, 1790, 100 acres joining Michal [Michael] Brown on the east and Joseph Heldreth's old and new surveys.

August 16, 1791, MICHAEL BROWN, by last mentioned warrant, enters 200 acres, beginning on John Finley's patent line on the west side of Sally Run and joining Stophel [Christopher] Brown and entry of William Neel and lands of John Herkerader, to include the vacant land whereon Nicholas Castle now lives.

p. 34, August 16, 1791, JACOB RABASS [REPASS], by the last mentioned warrant, enters 100 acres joining Wm. Finley, Conrod Rader, Yost Smythe, and Michael Brown [waters of Reed Creek?].

WILLIAM KING, assignee of William Pendleton, treasury warrant, 1,000 acres, 1780, enters 100 acres joining Jacob Kincer and Stophle [Christopher] Kettering, on branch of Tates Run to include both sides.

75

MICHAEL CASTLE, by last mentioned warrant, enters 200 acres on branch of Reed Creek adjoining whereon sd. Castle now lives on south, and Jacob Toblar, Lawrence Kettering, David Vaught and John Rouse.

FREDERICK CASTLE, on last mentioned warrant, 60 acres joining his own lands on the south and Daniel Pirkey, David Vaught, and John Mangle (withdrawn and assigned to William Ward, Oct. 25, 1794).

August 17, 1791, JAMES FINLEY, assignee of Robert Adams, 7 acres adjoining William Phipps line and own old patent line on the south and to include "Colepitt" Hollow.

p. 35, August 18, 1791, JACOB BLESSY [BLESSING], assignee of Nicholas Wyrick, assignee of Dunken Gullion, assignee of William Neel, assignee of Thos. Rutlidg [Rutledge], treasury warrant, 1782, enters 40 acres on Reed Creek under the north side of Pine Ridge joining his other entry, George Houk's patent and Duncan Gullion.

DUNCAN GULLION, assignee of William Neel, assignee of Thos. Rutlidge, treasury warrant, 48 acres adjoining William Wyrick and George Houck, both sides of Reed Creek; also treasury warrant, assigned by Walter Crockett, attorney for James Clark, 1782, 83 acres adjoining Jacob Pruner and Martain Wyrick, agreeable to courses run before by Robert Adams [surveyor of Wythe County].

p. 36, WILLIAM WYRICK, assignee of Duncan Gullion, assignee as above, 100 acres on north side of Pine Ridge to include land he now lives on.

WILLIAM BARTLET, assignee of John Heldreith, treasury warrant, 625 1/2 acres, 1780, enters 132 acres; also 75 acres, assignee of Robert Adams, joining Joseph Heldrith, to be laid off in one survey and to include the vacant land (Michael Walters assignee of Bartlet, 100 acres, Oct. 10, 1794 (?)).

JOSEPH ERWIN, assignee of Robert Adams, assignee, 100 acres joining George Kinder (Kincer?) on east, Peter Hedrick on south and down the creek to his own patent land.

WILLIAM WARD, assignee of Robert Adams, 60 acres on Reed Creek, adjoining Fredrick Castle, Jacob Baugh, and former entry of sd. Ward.

p. 37, August 19, 1791, WILLIAM BARTLETT, assignee of Robert Adams, assignee, treasury warrant, 4,000 acres, 1783, 250 acres on Reed Creek to include the plantation Martin Wyrick now lives on, adjoining Andrew Brown and Stephen Chappel (withdrawn and warrant re-assigned).

AARON LEWIS, treasury warrant for 2,333 1/2 acres, 1783, 600 acres part at the forks of Lorrel Fork and with South Fork towards the Elk Lick.

August 20, 1791, HUGH McGAVOCK, treasury warrant, 2,000 acres, 1783, assigned by David McGavock, assignee of William Bourn, assignee of Alexander Taite, 165 acres beginning and between the Marks [Max] Meadow [Meadows] tract at the foot of Brushy Mountain and patent land of John Miller.

THOMAS VAUGN [VAUGHAN], assignee of William Bouren [Bourne], assignee of Alexander Taite, treasury warrant, 100 acres beginning on Sturgeon's Branch and up the branch on both sides for quantity.

p. 38, August 20, 1791, THOMAS HASH on the above warrant, 100 acres in forks of Fox Creek adjoining his own survey.

FRANCIS STURGION, on the above warrant, 50 acres on the north side of Fork "Knobb," beginning in the Nettle Cove.

August 20, 1791, JOHN PHILLIPPY, assignee of Robert Adams, 300 acres adjoining Adam Kettering, Leonard Litz, John Stiffy, Leonard Straw (100 acres withdrawn and assigned to Peter Razor and Joshua Jones; 100 acres withdrawn and re-entered; 50 acres withdrawn and assigned to Joseph Philippy).

August 22, 1791, THOMAS FORGUSON, assignee of Robert Adams, 110 acres on Clear Fork of Wolf Creek, including Thomas Wylie's improvements.

WILLIAM INGLEDOVE, 150 acres, treasury warrant, assigned by Robert Adams, beginning at Rosses little field and with Rosses line to the creek and across the creek to include White's Bottom and across Armbruster's [Armbrister's] line to his own entry (100 acres surveyed, balance withdrawn).

p. 39, August 22, 1791, JACOB REBASS [REPASS], assignee of Robert Adams, 100 acres adjoining Finley on Sally Run, adjoining Big Henry Humbarger [Umbarger], Joseph Heldreth, Michael Brown, and John Harkerader's, and with lines formerly run by McNeel.

ROBERT DAVIS, treasury warrant, 1,200 acres, 1781, enters 830 acres on Middle Fork of Holston adjoining William Davis, Adam Dutting [Dutton], and his own land where John Musser now lives and Henry Birkheart now lives (200 acres withdrawn Jan. 1796, balance withdrawn Nov. 1796); also 400 acres in Rich Valley on North Fork of Holston, adjoining Peter Grosecloss [Groseclose], Esau Bradly and heirs of Thos. Dunn, dec'd.

p. 40, STEPHEN REEDER, assignee of Robt. Adams, treasury warrant, 4,000 acres, 1783, enters 182 acres, part thereof to wit: 50 acres on Stony Fork of Reed Creek, adjoining Nicholas Darter, John Nowell, and his own bought of Joseph Irwin; also 87 acres on southwest side of Queens "Knobb," adjoining Joseph Heldrith.

August 23, 1791, JOHN TAUTON [TOTTEN?] assignee of William Bourn, treasury warrant, 4,000 acres, 1783, enters 200 acres in Rich Valley on North Fork of Holston, beginning on west side of Jeffrey Heldreth's line, taking head of a spring that runs into the river above Mr. Bates about a mile thence, near Tauton's dwelling to take the spring he makes use of and crossing the spring branch, the White Oak Branch below the Valley Road, and along the mountain to join Heldreth and to include the parcel Tauton bought, formerly John Campbell's survey.

p. 41, Aug. 23, 1791, HENRY STIFFY [STEFFY], 100 acres on South Fork of Reed Creek, beginning on Michael Nave's [Neff's] and to join Robert Buchannan.

SAMUEL FULLIN [FULLEN], assignee of William Bouren [Bourne], on treasury warrant, 4,000 acres, 1783, 80 acres on Reed Creek adjoining Michael Vanerick [Venerick], Michael Creegor, Senr., Chas. [Charles] Fullin [Fullen], to include improvements whereon Peter Creeger now lives.

pp. 41-42, MICHAEL WALTERS, assignee, 100 acres, part thereof to wit: 30 acres adjoining former entry of 30 acres which joins Michael Creegor, Nicholas Cloyn [Cline], and Henry Grub; also 70 acres adjoining the other entry of 20 acres which entry lies on the south side of Henry Grub's patent land and joining the lands of Nicholas Cloyn [Cline], and Michael Ketring, the stocking weaver's old survey on the waters of Reed Creek. The old entry was made with the surveyor of Montgomery May 18, 1782. also assignee as above, 100 acres, part thereof, beginning on Charles Fullen's deceased line and joining John Etter and Henry Humbarger [Umbarger] and Godfrey Young and along Pine Ridge to include improvements where Stroup formerly lived.

p.42, CHARLES FULLIN [FULLEN], assignee, 100 acres, joining George Houk, Duncan Gullion, William Wyrick, and Jacob Prooner (withdrawn).

August 24, 1791, PETER HEDRICK, assignee as above, 200 acres on Reed Creek beginning at the foot of Pine Ridge on the north side between his own and Moses Gordon, and to George Kinder's and to the creek and to join Joseph Ervin's patent and to the foot of Pine Ridge to include the spring.

August 25, 1791, GODFREY YOUNG, assignee as above, 100 acres on Reed Creek on southeast side of Pine Ridge, adjoining Philip Knipp and Michael Walters' new entry and Peter Stroup, to include improvements (withdrawn).

p. 43, August 27, 1791, NICHOLAS SNIDER, assignee of Arthur Campbell, assignee of Robert Rutherford, treasury warrant, 500 acres, 1780, enters 300 acres adjoining Martin Stealy (formerly James Culton) and Patterson's patent land, Birkheart Seeple [compare Cebil, Cevil], and John Ligget's entry, and Copebariger [Copybarger]. (270 acres withdrawn and all re-entered).

August 29, 1791, JAMES CULTON, assignee of William Bourn [Bourne], treasury warrant for 4,000 acres, 1783, enters 200 acres on Middle Fork of Holston adjoining his patent on south.

WILLIAM DAVIS, assignee of Robert Davis, treasury warrant, 1,200 acres, 1781, 400 acres on Nicks Creek to run agreeable to courses run by William Preston for sd. Davis, Shannon and Thos. Madison & Co.

HENRY CLEMENTS, assignee of Adam Weatherholt, assignee of James Newell, treasury warrant, 68 acres on Reed Creek adjoining John Montgomery, Senr., and to run near Simpson's Lick and Newberries "Knobb" to include spring and part of the branch.

p. 44, August 30, 1791, ADAM WEATHERHOLT, assignee of James Newell, assignee, etc., treasury warrant, 50 acres on Lick Run, branch of Coave [Cove] Creek to include Mud Lick.

JACOB BAUGH, assignee of William Bouren [Bourne], treasury warrant, 4,000 acres, 1783, enters 112 acres on Reed Creek adjoining Colo. Ward to include his improvements.

MASON COMBS enters 150 acres on Little Reed Island of New River adjoining his own and to extend up the creek on south side.

p. 45, August 31, 1791, PAUL COPENBARIGER, assignee of Wm. Bouren [Bourne], treasury warrant, 4,000 acres, 1783, 200 acres on Holston adjoining James Culton, Nicholas Snider, and James Wilson.

September 1, 1791, WILLIAM WARD, assignee as above, 100 acres on Ebbets Run, branch of Reed Creek, joining Henry Hoppes, David Vaught, Frederick Castle, Jacob Baugh and Wm. Thompson, and to run with lines of James Newell (withdrawn 40 acres and re-enters in 1793, balance withdrawn).

September 6, 1791, WILLIAM LONG, assignee, 150 acres on Peach Bottom Creek, beginning on a ridge between Peach Bottom and Elk Creek, nearly the same courses run by Captain Newell for Wm. Holland.

p. 46, ROBERT SAYERS, assignee of Wm. Bouren [Bourne], 100 acres on New River, on southwest side, adjoining Sam'l Ewing, deceased, and his own and the river (withdrawn).

September 7, 1791, WILLIAM FARMER, assignee as above, 100 acres on Peech [Peach] Bottom Creek, branch of New River, agreeable to courses run by McDonnald for sd. Farmer.

JOSEPH DAVIDSON, treasury warrant, 1782, assignee of Jas. Murphy, 50 acres on north side of Wolf Creek to include the Red Oak Bottom; transferred to Phillip Lambert.

September 8, 1791, WILLIAM KIDD, treasury warrant, assigned by Shered Adkinson, assignee of Jos. Davison, 100 acres beginning on Alexander Stewart's line below Paddy McKelyeat's Spring on the north side of the Clear Fork of Wolf Creek.

p. 47, September 12, 1791, NATHANIEL BRITTON, assignee of Robert Adams, treasury warrant, 100 acres on Walkers Creek, branch of New River, to include the improvements known by the name of Watkin's "cabbin."

September 13, 1791, JABES PERKINS, assignee of James Anderson, assignee of Stephen Creech, assignee of Joseph Maxwell, assignee of John Burton, assignee of Moses Greer, treasury warrant for 3,654 1/2 acres, 1782, enters 100 acres part thereof, and 100 acres part of a treasury warrant for 1500 acres, 1790, assigned by James Anderson, assignee of Robt. Adams, assignee of Sam'l McCraw, beginning on Couches line and down Wilson Creek on both sides for quantity.

JEREMIAH BELL withdraws 50 acres entered 13 Oct. 1790 and enters same for HENRY STOBOUGH, beginning corner to survey of Thos. Smyth on Clear Fork of Wolf Creek by John Smyth, containing 27 1/2 acres, to include Lyndsey's improvements.

p. 48, JAMES ARMSTRONG, WILLIAM ARMSTRONG, and DAVID REACE, assignees of James Hines, assignee of James Neely, assignee of John Neely, treasury warrant, 1782, 400 acres on the dividing ridge, between Snake Creek and Little Reed Island; also 341 acres on Little Reed Island Creek beginning at Suggs Spring; also 200 acres on Big Snake Creek about a mile above where Wards Gap Road crosses the creek; also 300 acres on top of the mountain, beginning near old good spur path at the head of Stotts Creek; also 400 acres beginning at the double spring; also 150 acres on West Fork of Grassy Creek near the mouth of a branch.

p. 49, DAVID REACE, assignee of James and William Armstrong, on last mentioned warrant, 200 acres on Pine Creek, beginning at Bobbetts, corner of lower survey; also 200 acres on dividing ridge between Pine Creek and Snake Creek beginning at Yeats' corner, on south near the branch.

JOHN SPINES, assignee as above, 50 acres on Big Reed Island Creek at the Narrows, beginning about the mouth of Laurel Fork.

ISAAC JONES, assignee as above, 200 acres beginning below the fork of Grassy Creek.

FRANCIS STURGION, assignee of William Bouren [Bourne], treasury warrant, 1783, 50 acres on Main Glade Branch, Potato Creek on both sides and running up to Stony Knob (withdrawn).

p. 50, ROBERT CALHOUN, assignee as above, 100 acres joining Thomas Crow and William Calhoun, deceased.

JOHN SNIEVELY [SNAVELEY], assignee of Arthur Campbell, assignee of Robt. Rutherford, treasury warrant, 500 acres, 1781, enters 100 acres joining his own patent on south side, and Thomas Crow and Henry Pickle.

HENRY PICKLE, assignee as above, 100 acres joining his own on the south and foot of Lick Mountain (?) and Wm. Davis.

JOHN LIGGET, assignee of Wm. Bourn, 50 acres on Middle Fork Holston, adjoining Jos. Patterson, his own and Abraham Goodpasture, beginning at Patterson's line.

p. 51, September 14, 1791, WILLIAM McGUIRE, assignee of Wm. Bouren [Bourne], treasury warrant for 4,000 acres, 1783, enters 100 acres part thereof, on Clear Fork of Woolf Creek, beginning at a large spring near the wagon road and up the creek above Wm. [William] Kiold's (?) line and up the creek on both sides to include Samuel Cellerd's improvement.

WILLIAM McGUIRE, assignee of James Murphy, assignee of Charles Copeland, 50 acres joining on north side of William Brown's line next to Stony Ridge and up "Writes" Creek on both sides of the waters of Bluestone.

JOHN COMPTON, assignee of Wm. McGuire, assignee of James Murphy, assignee of Chas. Copland [Copeland], treasury warrant, 500 acres, 1782, enters part thereof, 50 acres beginning at Howard Haven's line and up the north side of his own line on Bluestone Creek.

FLOWER SWIFT, assignee of David Reece, assignee of James Hines, assignee of James Neely, assignee of John Neely, treasury warrant, 524 1/2 acres, 1782, 100 acres part thereof, with William Jones' line till it joins Chas. Knuckles [Nuckolls].

p. 52, September 14, 1791, CHARLES LYNCH, assignee of James Newell, assignee of David Reece, on last mentioned warrant, 300 acres on west side of New River to begin about 1/2 mile above the mouth of Cripple Creek on the river, in a line of James Newell's and with his to Wm. Rutherford and Robt. Porter to include Thomas Muse's improvement; also 1,000 acres adjoining his own known by the name of the mines, on the west side of the New and up the river and up Cripple Creek, to join James Newell, John Brawley, Absalom Rutherford, George Keesler, and Robert Sanders.

September 15, 1791, NATHANIEL FRISBIE, assignee of James Newell on above warrant, 400 acres on Daniels Branch, a fork of Crooked Creek, branch of New River, beginning corner of Jacob Colston's and with former lines made by Newell for Thomas Herbert to include sd. survey.

p. 53, September 16, 1791, JEREMIAH PIERCEFIELD, assignee of William Neel, treasury warrant, 1,498 acres, 1782, enters part thereof, 100 acres in Rich Valley adjoining John Wilson, Peter Piercefield, and Bryant's old place.

WILLIAM THOMPSON, assignee of William Bouren [Bourne], treasury warrant, 4,000 acres, 1783, 150 acres on South Fork of Clynch [Clinch] adjoining his own and along the foot on the south side of Rich Mountain to include the place known as McAdams Run.

p. 54, JOSEPH ERVIN, assignee of Robert B. Chew, treasury warrant, 1783, 150 acres on Reed Creek on south side, beginning on Geo. Davis line and to Joseph Crockett's and John Shaver's to include improvements where Arehart Symerman [Simmerman] now lives (above entry to be surveyed in the name of Areheart Symerman [Simmerman]).

September 16, 1791, WILLIAM THOMPSON, assignee of William Bouren [Bourne], treasury warrant for 4,000 acres, 1783, 150 acres entered on north side of the plantation he now lives on, to include his mill; also 200 acres on the south side of King's plantation and both sides of Maiden Spring Fork.

p. 55, September 17, 1791, MICHAEL WALTERS, assignee of William Bourn, assignee, treasury warrant for 4,000 acres, 1783, 100 acres, to include the Snaples land contained in a survey on which Martin Wyrick lives.

September 21, 1791, DANIEL JONSTON, assignee of John Preston, 100 acres part of treasury warrant for 2000 acres, 1783, on Clynch [Clinch] River, north fork of same, agreeable to a line run by Jerh. Bell to include his mill and other improvements.

September 23, 1791, MICHAEL BROWN, assignee of William Neel, 150 acres part of treasury warrant, 1782, adjoining his old patent on west side and joining Henry Humbariger [Umbarger], Jacob Repass, Senr., Jacob Rabass [Repass],

Junr., and Wm. Finley, to include lands run for John Heldrith.

p. 56, September 24, 1791, MICHAEL FARMER, assignee of William Bell, assignee etc., of James Newell and Robert Sanders, assignee David Reece & Co., assignee of Josha. Heins (?), assignee of James Neely, assignee of John Neely, 89 acres on east side of Chestnut Creek.

September 26, 1791, JOHN BEARD, assignee of Robert Adams, 10 acres, part of treasury warrant of 4,000 acres, 1783, on Reed Creek, joining Peter Hedrick, Verner Nip [Knipp] and Joseph Erwin, to include vacant land (withdrawn and assigned to Joseph Irwin, 1794).

THOMAS WITTEN, JUNR., assignee of Robert B. Chew, 100 acres, part of treasury warrant of 2,000 acres, 1783, on Maiden Spring Fork of Clynch [Clinch], beginning near Wyns Peek on south side and to run agreeable to courses run by Capt. John Preston and to include Peerie's [Peery's] improvements.

p. 57, JOHN EVANS, on above warrant, 100 acres adjoining Archibald Thompson's Puncheon Camp survey on Maiden Spring Fork of Clynch [Clinch]; also 50 acres on North Fork of Clynch [Clinch] above Walkers Survey extending up the creek and the Hurrican Ridge.

September 27, 1791, JAMES MAXWELL, assignee of James Newell, assignee of David Reece and Co., 100 acres, part of treasury warrant, 1782, beginning on William Brooks line on Rich Mountain, and up the mountain on both sides.

p. 58, September 27, 1791, AIRHEART SYMMERMAN [SIMMERMAN], treasury warrant, assigned by William Engledove [Ingledove], assignee of Robert Sayers, 100 acres, and 73 acres on treasury warrant in his own name, 1783, enters 173 acres joining the land for Martain Nowland, Crocket, Philipp, Sayers, and Shaver lines; also for SIMMERMAN, assignee of Wm. Neel, assignee of Thos. Rutledge, treasury warrant, 1782, 150 acres on Reed Creek joining David Ross, Joseph Crockett, his own and land of James Phillips where George Davis lives (above entry was made in Montgomery County in 1780 and 1782).

p. 59, September 27, 1791, SAMUEL SHIELDS, 90 acres, part of treasury warrant, 1783, assigned by John Smyth, assignee of John Black, devisor of Sam'l Black deceased, on Clear Fork of Wolf Creek, beginning on north side of Rich Mountain to side of Buckhorn Ridge.

September 29, 1791, WILLIAM DAVIS withdraws 5 acres of May 25 entry and enters same on Walkers Creek joining his own patent on the creek to include a "situation proposed for a mill dam."

September 29, 1791, WILLIAM INGLEDOVE, 10 acres on Reed Creek, joining corner to his own line below the meeting house and along the same to the meeting house or Henry Lambert's and to Abraham Stealy [Staley], to include all the vacant land.

p. 60, October 2, 1791, EDWARD MURPHY, 50 acres on treasury warrant, undated, joining Nicholas Loser, James Finley, and Murphy to include whereon John Corvin now lives [Reed Creek?].

October 7, 1791, JOSEPH IRVEN, assignee of Robert Adams, 40 acres on treasury warrant for 1,000 acres, not dated, on Reed Creek adjoining William Ingledove, Frederick More, Henry Lambert and land Andrew Hounshell now lives on, to be laid off to include vacant land (10 acres withdrawn).

October 7, 1791, ADAM WEATHERHOLT, assignee of James Newell, 50 acres on treasury warrant for 1,000 acres, 1782, on Cove Creek beginning by John

Brackinridge's line, formerly John Wallraven.

p. 61, October 7, 1791, JOSEPH YOUNG, assignee of James Newell, treasury warrant, not dated, 100 acres beginning about 1/4 mile from father's new upland field on Canoe Ridge to include "Bens Holes."

October 10, 1791, ELISHA BLEVINS, 50 acres on treasury warrant, undated, on south side of Fox Creek, opposite Middle Fork.

DANIEL BLEVENCE [BLEVINS], 50 acres to begin at Zekiel Young's Woolf Pen and running down the creek to Jas. Cadale line.

October 11, 1791, JOSEPH PERKINS, assignee of James Newell, 50 acres of warrant for 1,000 acres, not dated, on Wilson Creek, beginning at the lower end of the improvements made by Stephen Creech.

p. 62, October 11, 1791, JABAS PERKINS, assignee of Robert Adams, 100 acres part of treasury warrant for 1,000 acres, 1782, on Wilson Creek, beginning at the mouth of Laurel Branch and down both sides for quantity.

Oct. 13, 1791, JAMES NEWELL, assignee of John Preston, on preemption warrant, 1,000 acres, 1782, enters 100 acres on Reed Creek joining Evan Williams, John Baker, Andw. Stots; also 100 acres as above on Meadow Creek, including Lunday's improvements.

JOHN BECK, on above warrant, 150 acres on Chestnut Ridge, joining William Rankin's and Joseph Middthon.

PETER KETTERING, assignee of Barnabey Hauck [Houk], 87 1/2 acres, part of treasury warrant, 187 1/2 acres, 1782, on Elk Creek adjoining his own land.

p. 63, JOHN DAVIDSON, assignee of John Smyth, devisee of Samuel Black dec'd, 400 acres on treasury warrant, 1782, on Blue Stone to begin above the mouth of App's [Abb's] Valley and to lines run by Smythe, 1785, for James Bregham and Louisa Bregham which are in Montgomery County.

JOHN COMPTON, on above warrant, 400 acres on Clear Fork of Woolf Creek, to include whereon he now lives, corner to land surveyed for Jacob Dooly on north side of Creek.

p. 64, October 19, 1791, JAMES ARMSTRONG, assignee of David Reece, 500 acres part of treasury warrant, 1782, on both sides of the West Fork of Chestnut Creek, including a cabin and other small improvements made by Armstrong, and to extend along the North Carolina line for quantity.

October 24, 1791, JOHN PEERY (blacksmith), assignee of Jas. Peery, assignee of George Peery, assignee of Zachariah Stanly, assignee of Richard Shelton, 200 acres, part of treasury warrant, 1783, on head of Clinch to include the place known as the three walnuts; 570 acres of John Peere's [Peery's] entry surveyed Nov. 26, 1792, and 100 acres of John Peery's (blacksmith's) entry withdrawn.

JAMES PERY [PERRY], on last mentioned warrant, 60 acres on west side of the Clinch River, joining Vaut's (Vaul's?), line and John Peery's new entry, beginning on the bald hill (withdrawn and assigns warrant to John Evans, March 18, 1793).

p. 65, November 9, 1791, JOHN MICHAELSON, assignee of James Newell, 100 acres, part of treasury warrant, 1782, on Brush Creek to include Porter's camp.

WILLIAM BELL, on above warrant, 100 acres joining Joseph Maxwell and Woods on Crooked Creek.

JAMES NEWELL, assignee of Robert B. Chew, 400 acres, part of treasury

82

warrant, 2,000 acres, 1783, on Glady Fork of Chestnut Creek, joining Garnet Pryant (Bryant?), John Davis, Thomas Patton, and the old survey of Walkers.

SHEDERICK GREER, assignee of James Newell, 30 acres, part of treasury warrant, 1,000 acres, 1783, on Lorrel Fork of Fox Creek, joining Abraham Jones at the lower end.

AKLES FANING, assignee of James Devour, assignee of William Hall, 60 acres, part of treasury warrant, 1782, beginning at line of Beachers (?) survey, and down the creek to include a large spring and hatter's shop.

p. 66, November 9, 1791, JAMES DEVOUR, 40 acres on creek below the place where the Widow Dunn lives and down the fork to include a small [salt] petre cave on the south side.

November 13, 1791, WILLIAM NEEL, assignee of treasury warrant for 1,498 acres, 1782, enters 350 acres on the North Fork of Holston, joining James Wilson and to run with lines surveyed by Jeremiah Bell, including the improvements of John Messersmith (withdrawn); also 100 acres on Lick Creek, on North Fork of Holston in Poor Valley between the Garden and Brushy Mountain to include the Elk Lick.

November 19, 1791, GEORGE HOWELL, 30 acres, part of treasury warrant, 1782, joining his own survey in southeast, beginning at the corner of said Howell.

p. 67, GARNER BRYANTS, 50 acres joining Thomas Lundy, Joseph Middleton, and John Davis.

November 22, 1791, ROBERT STEEL, assignee of James Doake, 50 acres, part of treasury warrant, 1,000 acres, 1781, on Walkers Creek adjoining his own land and to extend down his own spring branch and up Lindseys spring branch for quantity.

November 23, 1791, for same, as assignee of John Preston, assignee of James Hines, assignee of Sam'l Lewis, 50 acres, part of treasury warrant, 13,750 acres, 1782, 50 acres on Coolys Branch and between Coolys and Mouries (?) land, joining Edward Murphy on south and Phillip Reeder on north to include the vacant land.

p. 68, N.B. last entry was made in surveyor's office of Montgomery County, April 27, 1790.

January 3, 1792, WILLIAM THOMPSON, assignee of William Bourn [Bourne], 200 acres, part of treasury warrant, 4,000 acres, 1783, on Clinch adjoining his patent land on the south side.

JOHN THOMPSON, assignee of Wm. Thompson, assignees as above, 100 acres on Maiden Spring Fork of Clinch adjoining his own and to include the vacant land.

January 3, 1791, HENRY WILLIAMS, assignee as above, 100 acres on Maiden Spring Fork of Clinch, adjoining Wm. Thompson, Isaac More, William Hiton, and James Clansey, to include the mouth of Crab Orchard Branch and the vacant land.

p. 69, January 9, 1792, MARTIN MILLER, assignee of Robt. Adams, 60 acres, part of treasury warrant, 4,000 acres, 1783, on South Fork of Reed Creek, adjoining Adam Ketring, John Phillippy and Robert Cowden.

January 10, 1792, PETER MOIRS [MOYERS], assignee of William Bouren [Bourne], 50 acres, part of treasury warrant, 4,000 acres, 1783, joining Godfert Young to extend along the top of Pine Ridge and to cross a path called Irvin's Path, and to join Leonard Straw's line on the ridge.

THOMAS CROW, 100 acres, treasury warrant, on Middle Fork of Holston, adjoining his land (formerly Jos. [possibly Jas.] Davis) and lands of Henry Pickle, David Jonson, and Wm. Davis (92 acres surveyed).

p. 70, January 20, 1792, JAMES DUGLESS [DOUGLAS], assignee of James Newell, assignee of David Pearce, 100 acres, part of treasury warrant for 6,241 acres, 1782, adjoining his own land and the lands of Phillip Dutting on Reed Creek; also 100 acres on Chestnut Ridge, joining John Newland's new house.

February 2, 1792, JACOB KINDER, 70 acres, part of warrant for 400 acres, 1783, assigned by Jacob Baugh, assignee of Wm. Bourn [Bourne], adjoining another entry of 50 acres on south side of Reed Creek and the land of Adam Walker, Peter Hedrick, and George Kinder.

pp. 70-71, February 2, 1792 HENRY HARMON, 50 acres on treasury warrant, 1783, assigned by Richard Whiteman, assignee of John Taylor, assignee of John Mason (?), assignee of Stephen May, assignee of James Tranor (?), assignee of John Ewing, on both sides of Kimberlin's Fork joining his own land on the lower end and upper end of a survey of Robert Evans.

p. 71, February 14, 1792, JAMES PATRICK, assignee of Stophel Symerman [Christopher Simmerman], assignee of Wm. Bouren [Bourne], 25 acres part of treasury warrant of 4,000 acres, 1783, on Macks Creek, south side of New River, to begin about 150 yards up the creek from the mouth to include both sides to join Wm. Scrugs on south side of creek and to include the salt petre cave near the top of the ridge.

February 15, 1792, JAMES HAVENS, assignee of Holston Muncy, assignee of Robert Adams, assignee of Sam'l McCraw, 50 acres, part of a treasury warrant of 1,000 acres, 1790, on Walkers Creek joining the lands of John Heron and to include Heron's Sugar Camp.

p. 72, AQUILLA GREER and SHADERICK GREER, assignees of Abram Jones, assignee of Peter Saunders, 100 acres, part of a treasury warrant of 1,000 acres, 1782, on the dividing ridge between Wilson and Hilton creeks, to include the water on both sides of the ridge and also to include a grove of fir trees and to join Griffith's entry.

March 3, 1792, DANIEL HERMAN, SENR., on treasury warrant, 1783, as assignee of William Adams, assignee of Richard Whitman, assignee of James Taylor, assignee of Jos. Mason, assignee of Stephen May, assignee of James Trenor, assignee of John Ewing, 50 acres on north side of the head of Clynch [Clinch], between said Harman and along Jno. Peerie [Peery], Robert Moffet and Robert Whitley's lines.

EDWARD MURPHEY, assignee of Robert Adams, on treasury warrant, 100 acres joining Martain Wyrick, Stephen Chaplain, Alexander Stewart, John Blessly [Blessing], and his own entry of 50 acres to include the vacant land.

p. 73, March 13, 1792, CHRISTOPHER ELMS, assignee of Robert Adams, assignee of Sam'l McCraw, treasury warrant, not dated, 50 acres on Holstein [Holston], adjoining his own patent and beginning on the east to Burkhart Cebil's [Cevils?] line.

DANIEL KEISSLER, assignee of John Sneeveley [Snavely], assignee of Arthur Campbell, assignee of Robert Rutherford, 100 acres, part of treasury warrant, 500 acres, 1780, on Holstien [Holston], joining his own, Akers, and John Snider.

March 22, 1792, CHARLES BARRETT, treasury warrant, 1,012 1/2 acres, 1783, enters the same where Absalom Burton's line crosses the road near the head of Crooked Creek at or near Flower Gap and down both sides of the creek as far as Jesse Nighton's and east along Patrick County line to Armstrong's and direct course to Nighton's.

pp. 73-73, March 22, 1792, ZACHARIAH STANLEY, treasury warrant, 1010 1/2 acres, 1783, assigned by Richard Anderson, enters the same, beginning on John Ward's lower crossing on Big Reed Island Creek and down both sides to Isaac Jones and then to the lands where John Yeats now lives, and to Armstrong's entry opposite Good Spur and then with the Patrick County line.

p. 74, DAVID PATTERSON, state warrant, no date, 7,046 acres to begin at his survey and Huff's between the two Reed Island Creeks on the south side of Chiswell's Road, and up and down both sides of Big Reed Island Creek, and some waters of Greasy Creek (transferred to Zachariah Stanley).

JOHN WHITSELL, assignee of James Finley, assignee of Walter Crockett, on state warrant, no date, 250 acres on North Fork of Reed Creek joining and between the lands of three of the Zimmermans and Wileys, including an improvement the part of which was formerly surveyed for one Simmerman or Coudrey.

April 9, 1792, ERAD PURKINS and JABES PURKINS, assignee of Joseph Perkins, assignee of James Anderson, treasury warrant, 3,000 acres, 1783, enters 60 acres part of it, adjoining Aquilla Grier's entry to extend to "Cabbin" Ridge, to include some fir trees on said ridge; also as assignees of Abram Jones, assignee of Thomas Jones, assignee of Peter Saunders, treasury warrant, 1,000 acres, 1781, 50 acres part thereof, on opposite side of the above Grier's entry on Willson Creek, to include the fir trees.

April 18, 1792, PHILIP DUTTON, assignee of John Preston, assignee of John Davidson, assignee of John Smith, devisee of Samuel Black deceased, treasury warrant, 1782, 200 acres adjoining the land he lives on, on south side, and to include vacant land thrown out of a former survey and some vacant land between his line and Chestnut Ridge.

p. 75, April 19, 1792, ROBERT GRAHAM, assignee of James Newell on above warrant, 30 acres on south side of patent land and adjoining same; also 70 acres to join the patent on the north and east sides to include the vacant land.

April 18, 1792, JOHN PAXSON (?), assignee of James Newell on above warrant, 100 acres on Reed Island Creek joining the place he lives on and survey of Ben Hollins on east and south.

WILLIAM STEWART, assignee of James Newell on above warrant, 100 acres at the mouth of Poor's Branch to run up and down the river on the east side.

April 18, 1792, MARTIN MILLAR, assignee of Paul Copenbarger, assignee of William Bourne, assignee of Alexander Taite, treasury warrant, 4,000 acres, 1783, 500 acres part thereof, to include the vacant land around and adjoining his other entry of 60 acres.

RICHARD (?) HALL, assignee of James Newell, assignee of John Preston, assignee of John Davidson, assignee of John Smythe, devisee of Samuel Black deceased, treasury warrant, 2,020 acres, 1782, enters 50 acres on branch of New River known by the name of Gun Shoal Branch, to include his improvements.

April 23, 1792, ALEXANDER ORE [ORR], assignee of John Preston, assignee of John Compton, assignee of John Smythe, devisee of Samuel Black deceased, treasury warrant, 2,020 acres, 1782, 100 acres, part thereof, on Kimberland's Fork a branch of Walkers Creek, beginning corner to his inclusive survey near

William Lockhart's line, and towards Robert Evans' line and with it to Dismal Creek, including both sides.

p. 76, April 28, 1792, ROBERT STEEL, assignee of Moses Lindsey, assignee of James Murphy, assignee of Charles Copeland, treasury warrant 500 acres, 1782, 50 acres part thereof, on Walkers Creek beginning on the line of the land Moses Lindsey sold to James Waddle on both sides and towards Walkers Mountain.

May 8, 1792, MAGNUS McDONALD, assignee of William King, assignee, etc., treasury warrant, 1,000 acres, 1781, 100 acres, part thereof, beginning on Peter Bishop's line and to John Montgomery's, John Bishop's and Colonel Hancock's lines, also joining his own whereon he now lives, to include the vacant land [Reed Creek].

May 21, 1792, WILLIAM LOCKHART, assignee of Alexr. Orr, assignee of John Preston, assignee of John Compton, assignee of John Smythe, devisee of Samuel Black, deceased, treasury warrant, 2,020 acres, 1782, 200 acres part thereof, 100 acres beginning on the county line and extending up the valley between Paint Lick Mountain and Diskinses Mountain on branch of the Clinch; also 100 acres on north side of Morrisses Knob, joining William Owens' open line on Maiden Spring Fork.

June 12, 1792, PETER POWERS, assignee of James Newell, assignee of John Preston, assignee of John Smyth, devisee of Sam'l Black, deceased, treasury warrant, 2,020 acres, 1782, 100 acres part thereof, on Elk Creek adjoining Henry Kirk and Thomas Comer on head of Terky [Turkey] Fork near Dry Branch Gap in Iron Mountain.

p. 77, June 12, 1792, DAVID CAYPOLE [CLAYPOOL?], assignee of William Kidd, assignee of Sherod Adkinson, assignee of Joseph Davidson, assignee of James Murphy, assignee of Charles Copeland, treasury warrant, 500 acres, 1782, 50 acres part thereof, on upper corner of the north line of his own land.

p. 77, June 12, 1792, MICHAEL KELLEY, assignee of David Reace and Co., treasury warrant, 6,241 1/2 acres, 1782, 200 acres part thereof, beginning near the dry pons [ponds] on Salt Peter Ridge.

June 14, 1792, WILLIAM WITTEN, assignee of John Preston, assignee of John Smythe, devisee of Sam'l Black deceased, treasury warrant, 2,020 acres, 1782, 75 acres part thereof, on west side of the tract William Seissel [Cecil] now lives on, and adjoining the tract of land surveyed for Abram Lock, heir-at-law of Samuel Lock, and also adjoining the land James Witten now lives on.

p. 77, June 30, 1792, LAWRENCE MURRY, assignee of William Lockhart, assignee of Alexr. Orr, on above warrant, 100 acres beginning at William Owens' shut line, and above the Hopwood place and running towards Paint Lick Mountain; also 50 acres beginning at his open line and towards Paint Lick Mountain (withdrawn and assigned to Jeremiah Whitten).

July 9, 1792, JOHN CRAIG, JR., assignee, etc., 250 acres between and adjoining Andrew Stotts' south line and William Thomas's north line and the [New] river south and along the ridge, corner to John Craig, Sr., above his old still house and up that branch to include the head.

p. 78, July 12, 1792, WILLIAM OWENS, assignee of Laurence Murry, assignee of William Lockhart, assignee of Alexander Orr, assignee of John Preston, treasury warrant, 2,020 acres, 1782, 50 acres part thereof, adjoining Lockhart's line on the big branch (waters of Clinch).

July 12, 1792, WILLIAM LOCKHART, assignee of Alexr. Orr, on above warrant, 100 acres adjoining Andrew Lockert's line on north side of the high end of the Knob.

July 12, 1792, CONRAD RADER, assignee of Jacob Rabass [Repass], assignee of William Bouren [Bourne], treasury warrant, 4,000 acres, 1783, 100 acres part thereof, joining the land whereon he now lives and extending towards Brushy Mountain and towards Stephen Reeder's to include part of the big ridge.

July 24, 1792, JESSE EVANS, assignee of Robert Adams, treasury warrant, 1,200 acres, 1781, 100 acres part thereof, beginning corner to Valentine Mowers and with his line crossing Tates Run towards John Hutsell's and towards Peter Binkley's and his own patent and with that line towards Cove Creek and up the creek.

July 28, 1792, HENRY BEESON, assignee of Nath'l Frisbie, assignee of David Reece, treasury warrant, 6,241 1/2 acres, 1782, 100 acres part thereof, joining James Wilson on the north and Joshua Entrim on the east and to include the vacant land.

p. 79, July 31, 1792, JAMES ARMSTRONG, assignee of David Reece and Co., treasury warrant, 6,241 acres, 1782, 100 acres, part thereof, between the lands of Mathias Dickey and New River; also on same warrant, 300 acres near the Big Glade survey beginning at the Fishers Gap Road and to include part of Muddy Branch of Chestnut Creek.

August 6, 1792, AMOS JOHNSTON and JEREMIAH BARNETT, 150 acres, part of two treasury warrants, 50 acres of one which warrant is assigned by David Claypole, assignee of William Kidd, assignee of Jos. Davison, assignee of James Murphy, assignee of Chas. Copeland, warrant for 500 acres, 1782, and 100 acres assigned by [blank] out of a treasury warrant, not dated, on Walkers Creek adjoining the northern boundaries of lands on which James Rice now lives and sold to above named Amos Johnston.

August 1, 1792, EBENEZER BRUSTER, assignee of James Peerie, assignee of George Peerie, assignee of Zachariah Stanley, assignee of Richard Shelton, treasury warrant for 17,854 acres, 1783, 160 acres part thereof, on Muddy Branch of Maiden Spring Fork of Clinch beginning on the east side near Walkers line.

p. 80, WILLIAM PEERIE [PEERY], assignee of Robert B. Chew, on a treasury warrant, 2,000 acres, 1783, 50 acres part thereof, beginning at his own corner and Sam'l Ferguson (12 acres withdrawn and assigned to John Ferguson, 1794).

August 14, 1792, THOS. WITTEN, JR., assignee of Robert B. Chew, treasury warrant, 2020 acres, 1783, 100 acres part thereof, beginning near two springs and crossing a ridge with George Peerie's [Peery's] line on the east side and joining William Thompson's new survey and crossing Brier Ridge.

JAMES WITTEN, assignee of John Evans, part of the above warrant, 50 acres on east side of the tract he lives on, on Plumb Creek, branch of Clinch and with Capt. Jos. (or Jas.) Maxwell and Samuel Marrs, including the hill called the Pinnacle.

RICHARD WRIGHT, assignee of Robt. Adams, treasury warrant, 3 acres on Terky [Turkey] Fork of Elk Creek, beginning at sd. fork and to extend on both sides to include his mill.

p. 81, WILLIAM NEAL, treasury warrant, 1,492 acres (corrected to 1,498 acres), 1782, 78 acres part thereof, on South Fork of Reed Creek joining Samuel Thompson deceased, Peter Miars [Moyers, Myers], and John Houndshal

[Hounshell], to include the vacant land.

JOHN PEIRCEFIELD, on above warrant, assigned by William Neal, 100 acres on North Fork of Holston, adjoining John Bryan's and Peter Groseclose on south side, to include the vacant land.

ESAU BRADLEY, assignee of Michael Brown, 100 acres on North Fork of Holston, adjoining John Wilson, _____[blank] Custard, Peter Spangler, James Camron and his own (80 acres assigned to John Alder.)

JEFFERY HELDREATH, on above warrant, 50 acres, no location [possibly Reed Creek].

August 22, 1792, JOHN MILLER, SR., treasury warrant, 465 acres, 1782, beginning on his own patent line near Beaver Dam Creek and along the patent line to Macks Little Run, and thence towards Brushy Mountain, to include the millstone quarry.

pp. 81-82, August 31, 1792, WILLIAM NEAL, treasury warrant, 1,936 acres, 1782, enters 400 acres on North Fork of Holston, adjoining James Cameron, John Wilson, Esau Bradly, Henry Lambert, Peter Spangler, Sr., Peter Spangler, Jr., entry of Robert Davis' for 400 acres and Jacob Spangler, to include the vacant lands (50 acres surveyed for F. Sluss, 1799, and 222 acres surveyed for Wm. Neal, 1799); also on the same warrant, 300 acres on the North Fork of Holston, about two miles west of Elk Licks, on east side of Burks Garden, to include the Chestnut Ridge.

p. 82, August 31, 1792, FREDERICK SLUSS, assignee of William Neal, by last mentioned warrant, 50 acres, on North fork of Holston River, joining Esau Bradley's lands on the north side of Walkers Mountain and running towards Custars Gap, including Bradly's Sugar Camp.

August 31, 1792, JOHN PEIRCEFIELD, assignee of William Neal, by same warrant, 50 acres on the North Fork of Holston River, on Lick Branch joining Peter Groseclose, Junr. and Peter Groseclose, Senr., to include all vacant land joining said lands.

August 31, 1792, HENRY UMBARGER, assignee of William Neal, by same warrant, 100 acres on Stony Fork of Reed Creek on the south side about a mile from the head, adjoining Duncan Gullion's and to include a spur of Brushy Mountain.

August 31, 1792, WILLIAM NEAL, assignee of Thomas Rutledge, treasury warrant, 1782, 3888 1/4 acres, 500 acres entered on Reed Creek joining Christopher Brown on the west side and to extend different courses towards Brushy Mountain, and to include John Leedy's ''cabbin.'' N.B. 200 acres of above entry William Neal assigns to Henry Umbarger.

p. 83, August 31, 1792, WILLIAM NEEL, on last mentioned warrant, 100 acres joining an entry of 100 acres of Duncan Gullion's, on lower end of Stoney Fork of Reed Creek. N.B. The above entry of 100 acres assigned to Stephen Reeder.

p. 83, August 31, 1792, WILLIAM NEAL, treasury warrant, 1,875 acres, 1781, enters 400 acres on Lick Creek, North Fork of Holstein [Holston] River beginning at Burks Road and joining entry of his 100 acres on the Salt Lick so as to include all the bottom land.

September 12, 1792, JOHN KIMBERLAND, assignee of William Neal, on last mentioned warrant, 100 aces in Rich Valley, joining Benjamin Watson deceased, John Wilson, and Peter Groseclose and to extend along Walkers Mountain for quantity.

September 12, 1792, ABSALOM COX, assignee of Jenkins Williams, assignee of William Neal, by above warrant, 100 acres on Wilson Creek, beginning on the south side.

September 12, 1792, SAM'L COX, assignee as on the last, treasury warrant, 1,935 acres, 1782, enters 50 acres on Pinie (?) Mountain between Wilson and Fox Creek joining Griffiths open line to include fir trees.

September 12, 1792, JOSEPH DAVISON, assignee of Robt. Adams, assignee of Sam'l McCraw, treasury warrant, 100 acres, 1790, enters 50 acres on "Writes" Creek, waters of Bluestone, beginning on east corner of William Brown's open line.

JOHN BUCHANAN, assignee of Robert Adams, state warrant, 1790, enters 150 acres in Cove on waters of the North Fork of Holstein [Holston] River, adjoining Andrew Lammie and his own.

p. 84, September, 12, 1792, ALEXANDER ORR, assignee of John Preston, assignee of John Smythe, devisee of Sam'l Black deceased, part of treasury warrant, 2,020 acres, 1782, 45 acres part thereof, beginning in his own line and joining William Pauley on south side of Kimberlands Fork of Walkers Creek, to include the field that is cleared.

September 12, 1792, WILLIAM LONG, assignee of William Bowen, part of treasury warrant, 1783, 4,000 acres, 150 acres on head of Rock Creek, to include part of top of Point Lookout and small chopping made by Philip Dickert.

JAMES CAMRON, assignee of Robert Adams, treasury warrant, no acres, not dated, on North Fork of Holston adjoining Peter Spangler, Peter Groseclose, Sr. and Benjamin McCord.

pp. 84, September 18, 1792, ESAU BRADLEY, assignee of John Alder, assignee of William Neel, treasury warrant, 1,498 acres, 1782, 70 acres part thereof, on North Fork of Holston, adjoining Thomas Mead, John Wilson, Peter Spangler, Sr., George Baugh, and James Cameron.

pp. 84-85, September 18, 1792, HENRY HARMAN, assignee of John Preston, assignee of John Smythe, devisee of Sam'l Black deceased, treasury warrant, 2,020 acres, 1782, 100 acres part thereof, on Clinch River on southeast side of the land he lives on, and adjoining Jacob Waggoner.

p. 85, September 18, 17982, ROBERT ADAMS and ANDREW THOMPSON, assignee of Robert Davis, treasury warrant, 500 acres on Maiden Spring Fork of Clinch near the head to include a small improvement made by Thompson (100 acres withdrawn and warrant assigned to R. Davis).

September 23, 1792, NATHANIEL FRISBIE, assignee of David Reace & Co., assignee of James Hines, assignee of James Neely, assignee of John Neely, treasury warrant, 6,241 1/2 acres, 1782, 500 acres part thereof, on head of Poors Branch, Strantons Branch and Ross's Mill Creek; also 300 acres on east fork of Ross's Mill Creek at head and down the branch to join the main wagon road leading through the Flower Gap.

pp. 85-86, CHARLES HANNAGEN, assignee of James Armstrong, assignee of David Reace & Company, part of treasury warrant, 6,245 1/2 acres, 1782, 100 acres entered on southeast end of Buck Mountain, to include Kennedays Knob; also 100 acres on Crooked Creek beginning corner to Joseph Bryant's to extend to a branch that comes from Gillis' "cabbin" and down the branch; also 100 acres on Brush Creek, beginning at the old path from the River to Ozborne's settlement.

p. 86, GEORGE GIBSON, assignee of Charles Hannigan, on above warrant, enters

100 acres on Rockhouse Branch, to include the place he now lives on.

October ___, 1792, PHILIP REEDER, assignee of Robert Adams, treasury warrant, 100 acres beginning corner to his patent line and towards Mouries (Morris?) line.

October 9, 1792, JOSHUA RICHARDSON, assignee of Zach'h Stanly, assignee, etc., treasury warrant for 1,010 1/2 acres, 1783, enters 100 acres part thereof, on both sides of Little Reed Island Creek joining Isaac Green's lower line.

October 10, 1792, JOSEPH DOUGHERTY, assignee of George Oury, treasury warrant, 1781, 100 acres on Kimberlins Fork, joining Robert Garret's east line and down the creek on both sides (assigned to Nicholas Dougherty, who assigned it to George Herman).

October 16, 1792, JAMES ANDERSON, assignee of George Livse [Livesay?] on treasury warrant, 1781, enters 100 acres on branch of Wilsons Creek, to include James Wallan's improvements.

p. 87, October 16, 1792, JAMES ANDERSON, enters for GEORGE LIVSE [LIVESAY?], 200 acres on above warrant on Fox Creek, beginning at an old hunting camp; also 200 acres on a ridge between Wilson and Bear Branch, including an ore bank and joining Jebas Perkins and Bear Branch.

JOHN SMITH, assignee of George Oury, treasury warrant, 1781, 70 acres joining John Draper's patent land and John Louder's entry.

p. 87, October 21, 1792, CHARLES BARRETT, treasury warrant, 1783, no acres stated, beginning at the head of White Pine Creek to extend to Nighton's land, Absalom Burton and to the head of Little Reed Island Creek and Wards Gap.

October 21, 1792, THOMAS JACOP [JASOP?], assignee of Zachariah Stanley, assignee of John Preston, treasury warrant, 14,005 acres, enters 70 acres part thereof, joining his own on south side and to join Thomas Dillard on the north side of Reed Island.

p. 87, October 21, 1792, ZACHARIAH STANLEY, on above warrant, 50 acres beginning at Thomas Jasop's corner and to extend to Joshua Edwards' line and towards the survey made for Moses Mott.

p. 88, October 21, 1792, ZACHARIAH STANLEY and AARON COLYER, on above warrant, 200 acres beginning on a path leading from Aaron Colyer's to George Crusenberry's on the north side of Chiswell's Road on a branch of Panther Creek; also 200 acres beginning where Peck's Camp Branch and Muster Ground Branch forks on Greasy Creek.

AARON COLYER, on above warrant, 300 acres to begin on his south corner and joining Thomas Jasop and David Edwards

ZACHARIAH STANLEY, 100 acres to begin on the end of Grape Hill adjoining Moore Bell's survey on Dollons [Daltons] Creek (assigned to Isham Goard [Goad]); also 200 acres at the fork of Chiswell's Road with Jinnens [Jennings] near Elrod's cabin on Road Creek branch of Big Reed Island; also 880 acres beginning at the head of White Pine Creek adjoining Charles Barret's entry to extend north and west between Evards [should this be Edwards?] Gap Road and Flower Gap Road.

October 29, 1792, GEORGE YERYAN [YERION], assignee of Robert Adams, on treasury warrant, not dated, 100 acres joining Peter Bishop, John Montgomery, James McGavock, and to include the spring [Reed Creek].

October 29, 1792, JACOB RAPASS [REPASS], treasury warrant, 100 acres, assigned by William King, assignee of William Pendleton, 1791, and the other assignee of William Bouren [Bourne], assignee of Alexander Taite, 1790, 200 acres on

Reed Creek where Spangler's waggon road crosses Walkers Mountain on the south side and on west side of said road, adjoining the entry of William Neel's and Yost's.

p. 89, October 23, 1792, YOST SMITH, assignee of John Harkerader, assignee of William Bouren [Bourne], 1783, 100 acres on Reed Creek beginning in falls of a branch where the waggon road crosses Walkers Mountain into Rich Valley and with the road on the spur of the mountain a northeast course to joining the entry of William Neel.

October 29, 1792, JOHN HARKERADER, treasury warrant, 2,000 acres, 1783, 83 acres part thereof, assigned by William Bouren [Bourne], beginning where the road takes Walkers Mountain on the left hand of same and with Yost Smith's entry.

November 6, 1792, GEORGE DAVIS, assignee of Jacob Davis, assignee of John Whitsell, assignee of Walter Crockett attorney, on state warrant, 100 acres on Reed Creek, south side of his own, adjoining John Shaver's and Rosses, formerly Farmer's, and to extend towards Lick Mountain.

JAMES FINLEY, assignee of Robert Adams, treasury warrant, 25 acres on west side of Reed Creek between the old patent line and the land Jehue Stephens sold to Nicholas Looser and Michael Creagar.

JOHN HERKERADER, part of two treasury warrants, 150 acres to include both sides of Brushy Mountain.

p. 90, November 8, 1792, ANTHONY TONKERY [TONCRAY], assignee of William King, treasury warrant, 50 acres on Reed Creek between Ross's formerly Mc[blank] upper and lower tracts and to join Joseph White's and Maddison & Co. Gold Mine entry and another of Ross's tracts formerly Farmer's, and Airhart Zimmerman's [Simmerman's].

November 14, 1792, SAMUEL FERGUSON, assignee of John Preston, treasury warrant, 2020 acres, 1782, 50 acres part thereof, between Stanley's entry and his own, bounded on the west by William Peerie's [Peery's] entry and beginning at Peerie's [Peery's] corner and his own (assigned to John Farguson).

November 14, 1792, JOHN JENKINS, assignee of Nathaniel Frisbie, assignee of David Reace and Co., treasury warrant, 6241 1/2 acres, 1782, 100 acres part thereof, on the Fork of Pores [Poor] Branch, on the south side of Poplar Camp Mountain.

November 14, 1792, DANIEL ROBINETT, assignee of James Devor, assignee of William Hall, assignee of Adam Dean, treasury warrant, 1782, 40 acres joining a survey of Hugh Fulton that joins Robinett on the south side, to include the timber ridge.

November 14, 1792, AKELIS FANNING, assignee of William Hall on above warrant, 100 acres in Burks Garden, beginning at the head of Medleys Creek and down the creek with James Thompson's line towards Grills' old cabin.

p. 91, November 14, 1792, WILLIAM HALL, assignee of Adam Dean on above warrant, 50 acres Burks Garden, beginning in the main gap and up the creek as far as James Thompson's line, to include both sides.

November 15, 1792, ZACHARIAH STANLEY, assignee of David Petterson, assignee of Thomas Miller, treasury warrant, 1,540 1/2 acres, 1782, 640 1/2 acres part thereof, on Roaring [now Foster] Falls Mountain beginning in Thomas Foster's line on the east side and to join John Walter's and Stewart's to extend towards Conaways Mountain; also 200 acres on Little Reed Island Creek on both sides, between Ignatius Turman's two surveys; also 200 acres between Robert Commons and Robert Hicys path and to extend towards Wards Gap Road; also part of treasury warrant, 14,005 acres, 150 acres part thereof, on east side of Thomas Jessop's on Burks Fork

November 16, 1792, JOHN ROUS [ROUSE, ROUSH], assignee of Jacob Rebas [Repass], 100 acres and assignee of Robert Adams for 50 acres, enters same on branch of Reed Creek known by the name of Sugar Run, and bounded by John Ward's patent line on east side and on the north side by a survey made for Jacob Doblar, and on the west side by Michael Castle.

p. 92, December 3, 1792, ZACHARIAH STANLEY, 200 acres on treasury warrant on Beaver Dam Creek adjoining his own, John Reece's and John Green's.

THOMAS RICHISON, assignee of Zachariah Stanley, state warrant, 100 acres on Bobbit's Creek, branch of Little Reed Island Creek, adjoining an entry of John Richison for 250 acres, also a survey of John Richison's.

JONATHAN RICHESON, assignee as above, 125 acres adjoining John Richison's on Bobbet's Creek, branch of Little Reed Island of 250 acres to extend towards the land of John Walters.

JAMES WORRELL, assignees as above, 200 aces, part on Island Creek and part on Beaver Dam Creek, part on Little Snake Creek, beginning near a branch corner to Esau Worrell's survey and Zachariah Stanley's survey for John Reace, to include Meredith Shockley's improvement, and part of Red Knob for quantity.

December 3, 1792, ZACHARIAH STANLEY, state warrant, 50 acres, between his own and Francis Hamilton on the north side of Bobbit Creek and extending towards William Dalton's land; also 300 acres beginning at Thomas Jessop's corner on west side of his land on the south side of Bobbits Creek and on both sides of Dalton's Mill Road from Jessop's; also 200 acres on Cherry Creek, branch of Big Reed Island Creek, beginning on creek where path crosses from Robert Goard's [Goad's] to Spence's.

p. 93, December 3, 1792, ESAU WORRELL, assignee of Robert Adams, state warrant, 100 acres adjoining James Worrell on Island Creek, branch of Big Reed Island.

ZACHARIAH STANLEY, state warrant, 100 acres adjoining Esau Worrell, to include John Reace's improvements.

JOSHUA RICHESON, JONATHAN RICHESON and CHRISTOPHER RICHESON, assignees of Zachariah Stanley, state warrant, 250 acres on Bobbit Creek to include Jonathan Richeson's improvements and to cross Little Reed Island Creek to include the bottom and other improvements of Jonathan Richeson (225 acres surveyed and balance assigned to John Richison).

WILLIAM BOBBIT, assignee of Robert Adams, state warrant, 200 acres on branch of Big Snake Creek near Wallice's cabin to extend towards Little Snake Creek, to include Wallice's and Bowman's improvements.

PHILIP GAINES, assignee of George Ewing, treasury warrant, 956 acres, 1782, enters same adjoining Flower Swift, Charles Nicholas, Jonathan Collins, and Thomas Kinworthy.

pp. 93-94, December 1792, JOSEPH ERVINE, treasury warrant, 100 acres, 1783, assigned by William Ingledove, and 40 acres part of a treasury warrant, assignee of William Bouren [Bourne], total 140 acres on north side of Little Fork of Potatoe Creek joining William Wyatt's west line and to extend whereon Robert Osborne formerly lived; also 42 acres to include improvements whereon Moses Wells, Junr., now lives, on the north side of New River

(Ervine withdraws 40 acres of first entry June 12, 1794, and withdraws entry of 42 acres, November 1794).

p. 94, December 12, 1792, ROBERT WARRICK, assignee of Robert Davis, 100 acres on waters of Bulls Run, and Stephens Creek adjoining his own, David Farmer's and Moses Dumrett's

December 12, 1792, PHILIP GAINES, assignee of George Ewing, treasury warrant, 965 acres, 1782, 500 acres part thereof, adjoining Abner Jones, Mary Powers, Peter Kettering, Joseph Porter and George Keith.

December 12, 1790, DANIEL JUSTICE, assignee of William Hall, treasury warrant, 50 acres on Walkers Creek beginning the north corner of his patent land and extending towards Dean's line.

December 21, 1792, JOHN HURST, treasury warrant, 400 1/4 acres, 1782, 60 acres part thereof, on Macks Run on north side of New River adjoining his own. JAMES AXLEY, on above warrant, 100 acres on south side of New River, adjoining his own, Moss's and Fugat's [Fugate's].

p. 95, December 21, 1792, CHARLES DYER, on above warrant, 50 acres on south side of New River adjoining his own, on both sides of Dry Branch.

December 24, 1792, HENRY UMBARGER, assignee of William Neal, state warrant, 100 acres, beginning corner to John Etter and towards Philip Knipp's and Henry Umbarger's patent land [Reed Creek].

December 26, 1792, MICHAEL WALTERS, assignee of Robert Adams, assignee of Samuel McCraw, treasury warrant, 1,000 acres, 1790, 100 acres part thereof, beginning corner to his other survey and John Etter's and towards Charles Fullen's, Jacob Plesley's [Blessing's] and towards Pine Ridge, to include Stroup's improvements.

December 26, 1792, GEORGE LIVSY [LIVESAY], treasury warrant, 1,000 acres, 1780, 300 acres joining his other entry of 200 acres on ridge between Wilson and Bear Branch to be included in the same survey.

December 26, 1792, GEORGE WEAVER, assignee of William H. Boyer, assignee of Barnet Foly, assignee of Thomas Jones, treasury warrant, 1,000 acres, 1781, on Jumping Camp Creek of New River, beginning corner of Hamilton's survey.

p. 96, January 1, 1793, WILLIAM HALL, assignee of George Ewing, state warrant, 956 acres, 1782, 150 acres part thereof in Burkes Garden, beginning at Byrd Smith's corner at the head of his spring and with his line and to James Thompson's line and with the same towards Blue Spring to include the head of Medleys Creek; also 200 acres beginning in Thompson's line where it crosses Percifield's Camp Branch and with the line and towards Beartown and to include Percifield's Camp; also 200 acres beginning at the beach corner on the side of Haw Ridge and with James Thompson's open line, and down the creek to the other entry of 50 acres; also 200 acres beginning at James Thompson's corner where it crosses a branch near Pauley Camp and with the line towards the gap; also 100 acres beginning where James Thompson's line crosses Meadleys Creek, above where Workman lives, and to extend up the creek.

January 7, 1793, ANDREW DANNER, assignee of Nathaniel Frisbie, assignee of James Newell, 300 acres on Cripple Creek, adjoining James Campbell, his own, and George Buckleloo [Buckalew], John Hanley [Henley] and along the south side of Lick Mountain.

p. 97, January 8, 1793, JOHN BENNER, assignee of William Long, assignee of

93

Thomas Jones, treasury warrant, 50 acres part of same, on Elk Creek of New River, adjoining and beginning on his own line to the "order line" and towards Jeremiah Stone's.

January 9, 1793, HEZEKIAH BOON, assignee of Henry Banks, assignee of Jarvis Smith, treasury warrant, 50 acres, 1783, 7 acres part thereof, on the headwaters of South Fork of Holston on the north side adjoining John Vaught, David Vaught, and Zachariah Blankinspigler [Blankenbecker?].

January 9, 1793, WILLIAM ROSS, treasury warrant, 500 acres assigned by Walter Crockett, attorney in fact for James Clerk, 1782, 100 acres adjoining Thomas Whilock [Whitlock], Jos. Fugate, and James Breeden, on Little Reed Island Creek (William Ross assigned to Thos. Feeling?)

January 9, 1793, PETER RAZOR and JOSHUA JONES, assignee of John Philippee, 100 acres on the north side of Frederick Slimp's plantation joining _____[blank] and up mill creek, including the ore bank.

January 9, 1793, NATHANIEL FRISBIE and PHILIP GAINS, assignees of James Newell, 200 acres adjoining Flower Swift, Charles Knuckles [Nuckolls], Jonathan Collins and Thomas Kinworthy.

p. 97, January 17, 1793, JOHN HAYS, assignee of William Neel, 200 acres on Spruce Creek, branch of Middle Fork of Holston, beginning at the Big Lick and down the creek to include the land on both sides.

p. 98, January 17, 1793, JAMES CROCKETT, assignee of Andrew Crockett, 150 acres, state warrant, 1782, adjoining John Creager and David Sloan, and to cross Reed Creek, including the falls and to include the vacant land and part of the waters of Purgatory [Creek].

January 17, 1793, JEHU STEPHENS, treasury warrant, assigned by James Finley, assignee of Robert Adams, 5 acres beginning corner to his own land near the land of William Love, on the north side of Cripple Creek; also 20 acres beginning lower corner of Henry Cook's survey and to include the vacant land between William Love's land known by the name of the Kerr's place and said Stephens.

Feb. 1, 1793, JOHN CREAGER, assignee of James Newell, state warrant, 90 acres adjoining his own patent, Robert Graham's and another survey of his own beginning corner to patent in Hemp Field Hollow.

February 1, 1793, DAVID SLOAN, assignee of John Creager, assignee, etc., treasury warrant, 1783, 100 acres part thereof, on Reed Creek adjoining his own patent, beginning where said line crosses the creek at the Grassy Ford and up the Grassy Ford Hollow to include the spring known by the name of the Tar Kiln Spring and towards Beeson's.

February 5, 1793, JEFFERY HELDRETH, assignee of William Neel, 100 acres in Rich Valley, adjoining John Totton on the north side to include a spring that empties into the river above Mr. Bates and towards White Oak Branch to Totton's line; also 70 acres part of treasury warrant, 1,498 acres, 1783, assigned by Esau Bradley, assignee of William Neel, adjoining Philip Umbarger and with John Totten's line to his old survey, to include the spring between Umbarger and Walkers Mountain.

p. 99, February 5, 1793, WILLIAM RICHISON, assignee of William Neel, treasury warrant, 200 acres Rich Valley adjoining his own and John Totten's old line, and to include the head of White Oak Branch near the foot of Walkers Mountain.

February 12, 1793, MICHAEL BRANSTRATER [BRANSTETTER], assignee of

Jenkin Williams, assignee of William Neel, treasury warrant, 50 acres on Cripple Creek, adjoining Andrew Branstrater and to extend towards Iron Mountain.

February 12, 1793, WILLIAM TAYLOR, assignee of William Bouren [Bourne], assignee of George Underwood, treasury warrant, 2,000 acres, 1792, 100 acres part thereof, between his own survey and Thomas Pinson, to include a small improvement.

February 12, 1793, JOHN LIGGETT, assignee of William Bouren [Bourne], 50 acres and assignee of James Culton for two warrants, 50 acres, 1783, land on Middle Fork of Holston adjoining Joseph Patterson, Edward Crow, Robert Crow, Patrick Campbell, and to extend towards the Washington County line.

p. 100, February 12, 1793, NICHOLAS SNIDO, treasury warrant, 70 acres on Ancors Branch between Ancors patent line and entry and his own line.

February 12, 1793, JESSE HUBBARD, assignee of Charles Lynch, treasury warrant, 50 acres, Knob Fork of Elk Creek to include the Sang Patch.

EVAN DAVIS, assignee of William Neal, treasury warrant, 100 acres in Rich Valley on North Fork of Holston, adjoining his own on the north side; also 25 acres adjoining his own land on the south side (withdraws 44 acres and assigns to Henry Beeson).

February 18, 1793, JOHN EWING, assignee of Joshua Ewing, certificate of warrant from the principal surveyor of Greenbrier County, 1783, 200 acres on Little River, branch of New River, adjoining Joseph Robison.

p. 101, WILLIAM RIGHT, assignee of John Ewing on certificate of warrant from the principal surveyor of Bath County, 100 acres adjoining Joseph Robison and Sam'l Spelman, to include his mill.

February 18, 1793, JOHN EWING on above certificate, 100 aces adjoining William Wright's entry of 100 acres and Jacob Hays (Hecy's?) and Joseph Robinson's.

February 19, 1793, HENRY and WILLIAM MARRS, assignee of Robert Adams, treasury warrant, 40 acres on Clinch adjoining an open line of a survey made for Henry Foley, beginning corner to Foley and running toward Rich Mountain.

p. 101, February 23, 1793, PETER MIARS [MYERS, MOYERS], assignee of Henry Buck (?), assignee of Charles Fullen, 50 acres adjoining John Etter and Charles Fullen's patent land [Reed Creek].

March 4, 1793, STEPHEN REEDER, assignee of Robert Adams, assignee of William Bouren [Bourne], treasury warrant, 4,000 acres, 1783, 182 acres in Cove on Reed Creek, branch of New River to adjoin his own land on east end and southeast side, also joining Henry Reader, and down both sides of the branch that runs through the big ridge.

March 5, 1793, THOMAS PATTERSON, state warrant, 17,000 acres in Montgomery County, in Laurel Fork, Reed Island Creek to join Henry and Botetourt County lines and bounded by lines of Major Ward, in Order of Council. (copy from Montgomery County.)

p. 102, March 5, 1793, ZACHARIAH STANLEY, assignee of David Patterson, treasury warrant, 18,985 acres, 1781, 5,000 acres part thereof, on Big Reed Island on the north side of Chiswell's old mine road, a little below the mouth of Little Pine Creek which empties into Big Reed Island Creek on the north side and up both sides of the river, including the different branches as far as Montgomery and Patrick County lines, unappropriated lands and different surveys; also 3,000 acres corner to his survey of 3,700 acres near a small field cleared by Nicholas Stillwell not far from Little Reed Island Creek on both sides up to the Patrick County line; also 2,000 acres beginning near Doctor Woods upper line on Crooked Creek and up both sides towards the Patrick County line.

March 7, 1793, GEORGE YERYON [YERION], assignee of Robert Adams, assignee of Zachariah Stanley, state warrant, 100 acres adjoining his other entry of 100 acres [Reed Creek].

p. 103, March 7, 1793, NICHOLAS SNIDER, assignee of Arthur Campbell, treasury warrant, 150 acres adjoining John Snider, John McMullin, David Kirkwood, John Liggett, Joseph Patterson's patent and Patterson's hill field place, to include the vacant land.

March 18, 1793, JOHN EVANS, assignee of James Peery, treasury warrant, 1783, 60 acres beginning the east corner Walkers open line west to Henry's road, and towards Rich Mountain (withdrawn and assigned to James Peerie [Peery], 1794).

JEREMIAH WHITTEN, 20 acres between his new survey and land whereon he now lives.

HARMAN WYNE, assignee of Robert Adams, assignee of Zachariah Stanley, 125 acres between Aleanah [Alkenah?] Wynne's and Jacob Waggoner, on head of Clinch on the north side of the creek.

March 21, 1793, HUGH McGAVOCK, assignee of David McGavock, assignee of William Bourne, assignee of Alexander Taite, withdraws 100 acres part of an entry of 1791, and reassigns to David McGavock, who enters the same adjoining the lands belonging to George Hutsell, Chr. [Christopher] Symmerman [Simmerman] and Edward Murphy's old place [Reed Creek].

March 21, 1793, ANDREW LAMIE, assignee of Robert Adams, treasury warrant, 50 acres in Cove Creek, North Fork of Holston, beginning at the east corner of his old survey and across the branch towards the mountain.

p. 104, March 21, 1793, JOHN LAMIE, part of the above warrant, 70 acres in Poor Valley beginning corner to James Lamie's patent and NW course extending towards Clinch Mountain.

ROBERT EWING, treasury warrant, 703 acres, 1782, and assigned by Alexr. Wyley, 100 acres part thereof, on North Fork of Holston, to begin on the river at the north side of the river on Entrum's line and up the river 10 poles above a blind path that crosses the river; also 100 acres on North Fork of Holston to begin on a path that runs from James Gillespie's towards John Buchanan's about 10 poles from the top of the dividing ridge between said Gillaspie's and Buchanan's north side of a ridge, and northeast with the ridge; also 300 acres to begin at the top of the main dividing ridge on a path that runs from Godfrey Entrum's towards John Buchanan's and southwest course along the top of the ridge towards the entry of said Ewing and towards Thomas Gillaspie's open line. N.B. the last three entries were made in Montgomery County Surveyor's Office, March 1785.

March 21, 1793, NICHOLAS TALBOT, treasury warrant, 703 acres, 1782, 110 acres part thereof, on North Fork of Holston beginning at John Sprout's line and joining James Bates' line.

p. 105, April 1, 1793, WILLIAM NEEL, treasury warrant, 150 acres, on Stophel's Branch of Reed Creek adjoining Hezekiah China [Chaney], James Campbell, and Stophel [Christopher] Kettering, beginning on Kettering's line.

April 9, 1793, JOSEPH FANNING, assignee of Robert Adams, treasury warrant, 100 acres on Chestnut Creek, to include the surplus land in survey made for Jacob Fanning (assigned to Jacob Fanning).

MARTIN KIMBERLAND, assignee of Robert Adams, treasury warrant, 200 acres head of North Fork of Reed Creek between the mountains beginning at Rapas's [Repass's] line and along the foot of each mountain and up the creek for quantity.

April 9, 1793, PETER DELP, assignee of William Long, treasury warrant, 30 acres on south side of Iron Mountain on Dry Run Road.

April 9, 1793, ALEXANDER STEWARD, assignee of Robert Adams, treasury warrant, 150 acres on Brushy Fork of Bluestone above survey of George Perie's [Peery's] known by the name of Ingles' improvements, beginning about 40 poles from said survey.

p. 106, April 9, 1793, WILLIAM CARTER, assignee of Charles Dyer, treasury warrant, 400 1/4 acres, 1782, 90 1/2 acres part thereof, adjoining the land purchased from William Herbert, and beginning on the [New] River and with the lines of the river extending towards William Thomas's.

JACOB BEESON, assignee of Nathaniel Frisbie, treasury warrant, 100 acres in Rich Valley, adjoining James Wilson on the north side of the survey for Henry Beeson and down the river for quantity.

April 9, 1793, PATRICK ROSS, assignee of William Ross, 80 acres adjoining Laurence Stephens, Thomas Whitlock and Randal Fugate.

April 9, 1793, GEO. POWERS, assignee of Jeffery Heldrith, assignee of William Neel, 30 acres adjoining his own, William Love's and Peter Collop.

April 9, 1793, HALBERT ALISON [ALLISON], assignee of Charles Dyer, treasury warrant 400 1/4 acres, 1782, 100 acres part thereof, on Big Reed Island Creek at Probut's Foard [Ford], commonly called the big crossing, beginning below the foard [ford].

pp. 106-107, April 9, 1793, TIMOTHY ROARK, assignee of James Newell, state warrant, 100 acres joining his own on the east side and Richard Wright's; also 100 acres joining his own, Michael Thomas, Stophel [Christopher] Gose, on waters of Elk Creek.

p. 107, April 9, 1793, SHADERICK GREER, assignee of James Newell, state warrant, 100 acres beginning adjoining Abram Jones on Big Fox Creek on east side of the land, and with Jones' land.

April 10, 1793, JOHN McCOY, assignee of William Bell, assignee of James Newell, 100 acres on Crooked Creek adjoining Joseph Meas and Woods' line.

April 11, 1793, SUSANNA HELVEY, assignee of Robert Adams, treasury warrant, 400 acres beginning corner to John Davis land and to adjoin John Hutsell, John Davis, Senr., and John McNutt, to include the place where she now lives.

April 11, 1793, GEORGE REAVES, assignee of Robert Adams, treasury warrant, 50 acres on Peach Bottom Creek beginning at the lower end of Julias Bottom and up the creek to include the bottom.

April 11, 1793, ENOCH OSBORNE, assignee of James Clerk, treasury warrant, 1782, 100 acres on New River beginning on the river bank and to include the place where he now lives.

April 19, 1793, JESSE EVANS, assignee of Robert Adams, treasury warrant, 50 acres between the lands of George Kegley, Senr., Daniel Etter, Stophel [Christopher] Simmerman and Alexander Steward [Reed Creek].

p. 108, April 19, 1793, DANIEL HERMAN, treasury warrant, 1,500 acres, 1790, 30 aces part thereof, adjoining his other entry on head of the Clinch.

97

April 19, 1793, JEFFERY HEDLRITH, assignee of William Neel, treasury warrant, 50 acres in Rich Valley, adjoining Thomas Gillaspie on south, to include the spring near the path leading from Gillespie's to John Totten's and a chestnut ridge.

April 19, 1793, JOHN HERKERADER, two treasury warrants, 150 acres, on south side of Walkers Mountain to include Rocky Ridge.

JOHN TOTTON, assignee of William Bouren, treasury warrant, 100 acres, Rich Valley adjoining [Bourne], his own on south and lands of William Richardson and Philip Umbarger, and extending towards Walkers Mountain.

JOHN McNITT [McNUTT], assignee of Robert Adams, treasury warrant, 70 acres adjoining the patent land and conditional line between McNitt and James Wyley.

April 19, 1793, ALKENAH WYNNE, treasury warrant, assigned by John Preston assignee of John Smith, devisee of Sam'l Black deceased, 100 acres on head of Clynch [Clinch], adjoining his own.

p. 109, April 19, 1793, JOHN KEYS and GERRET Y. CONN, treasury warrant, 900 acres, 1783, 700 acres part thereof, in Rich Valley on Holstein [Holston], adjoining the survey made by Robert Bates on the river (withdrawn Nov. 2, 1798 and re-entered); also warrant for 200 acres in Rich Valley to include Elk Licks on the waters of Lick Creek (withdrawn).

April 19, 1793, JAMES BREEDEN, treasury warrant, assigned by Robert Adams, 100 acres between James Caffee's [Calfee's] and the river and joining Henry Davis and James Breeden and Little Reed Island Creek.

April 19, 1793, NATHANIEL POPE, treasury warrant, 1780, assigned by James Newell, 400 acres on Reed Island Creek joining John Richardson; also 20 acres joining his own and Balwins.

p. 110, April 19, 1793, JOHN PAXSON, warrant assigned by James Newell, 215 acres joining John Richardson and his own on Reed Island Creek.

JOHN POOL, assignee as above, 100 acres on Elk Creek.

RICHARD COLE, assignee as above, 100 acres on Elk Creek.

JOHN RICHARDSON, assignee as above, 60 acres on Reed Island Creek.

HERCULES OGLE, assignee as above, 60 acres on Reed Island Creek.

May 1, 1793, JOSEPH EVANS, assignee of Robert Adams, treasury warrant, 100 acres on Peek [Peak] Creek, beginning at the ford where Pepper's Ferry Road crosses said creek, near Laurel Bank.

p. 110, May 3, 1793, MICHAEL DECKERT, assignee as above, 100 acres on Peek [Peak] Creek beginning at the mouth of Mud Lick Fork and up the fork and the creek.

JOHN ADAMS, assignee, 300 acres on headwaters of Lick Run, Millers Creek and Peek [Peak] Creek to begin 50-60 poles south of a lick known by the name of White Oak Lick.

p. 111, WILLIAM ADAMS, assignee as above, 50 acres on Cove Creek beginning at the mouth of Lick Run and with the open line of the survey of Adam Weatherholt towards his own line.

June 3, 1793, PHILIP UMBARGER, assignee as above, 11 acres in Rich Valley, adjoining an entry purchased of Jeffery Heldreth.

June 6, 1793, WILLIAM NEELY, assignee as above, enters 300 [should be 500] acres on Cripple Creek, to wit: 200 acres beginning at Stephen Sanders South corner that joins with the said Neely's land and up Neely's line towards Peter Spangler's; also 300 acres on the north side of Neely's, beginning on his line and extending towards John Kerr's (?), Henley's, Campbell's and Chenies [Chaney's] at McKenlie's Run.

June 8, 1793, DAVID KIRKWOOD, assignee of Robert Adams, treasury warrant, 20 acres on Middle Fork of Holston, adjoining his own, Edward Crow and Joseph Paterson [Patterson], beginning corner to Crow's land.

p. 112, June 11, 1793, DAVID TAYLOR, assignee of Frederick Edwards, assignee of James Newell, treasury warrant, 3,062 acres, 1780, 42 acres on head of South Fork of Holston on top of Iron Mountain joining Grayson County line, to include "Goodens lick blacks."

p. 112, June 11, 1793, ADAM DUTTON, assignee of William Neel, 20 acres adjoining Gasper Vaught and extending towards Brushy Mountain.

WILLIAM CAFFEE [CALFEE], assignee of Jeffery Heldreth, assignee of William Neel, treasury warrant, 100 acres on Reed Island Creek adjoining Henry Davis, beginning at the "digging" and up the creek towards the Great Falls.

June 11, 1793, JOHN SHEAVER [SHAVER, SHAFFER], assignee of William Neel, treasury warrant, 100 acres Reed Creek adjoining Airhart Zimmerman [Simmerman] and Anthony Tonkery's [Toncray's] new survey.

p. 113, June 11, 1793, WILLIAM WARD, assignee of William Bouren [Bourne], treasury warrant, 1783, 40 acres adjoining Andrew Swallow, Lewis Able, and Ward [Reed Creek].

p. 113, June 17, 1793, JACOB COPEBARGER, assignee of Paul Copebarger, treasury warrant, 50 acres Poor Valley, adjoining lands of Burket Seaple [may be same as Civil, Cevil?] and his own entry bought of Nicholas Snider.

June 19, 1793, THOMAS WHITLOCK, assignee of Robert Adams, treasury warrant, 200 acres on Little Reed Island Creek, a branch of New River, beginning on patent line on the west side of the creek towards Laurance Stephens and with his lines crossing the creek.

June 19, 1793, JAMES BREEDEN, assignee of Robert Adams, treasury warrant, 100 acres under Roaring [now Foster] Falls Mountain, adjoining Randal Fugate and William Hurst.

June 19, 1793, JOHN BELSHEY, assignee of William Neel, treasury warrant, 100 acres adjoining Henry Umbarger, Michael Brown, Thadeus Cooly and Michael Walters [Reed Creek].

p. 114, June 19, 1793, DAVID DOAK, assignee of John King, treasury warrant, 500 acres, 1782, 49 acres adjoining his patent on south, and land of Adam Walker, on Reed Creek.

July 11, 1793, HUGH MONTGOMERY, assignee of Robert Adams, treasury warrant, 30 acres adjoining his patent line to include the improvement where Mathias Letner now lives.

July 11, 1793, WALTER CROCKETT, assignee as above, 50 acres on Cove Creek adjoining his patent.

July 11, 1793, WILLIAM WARD, assignee of Adam Dutton, assignee of William Neel, treasury warrant, 50 acres adjoining Lewis Able, Peter Kinder, Laurence Kettering, and entry of his own made in Montgomery County [Reed Creek].

July 20, 1793, JAMES FORTNEY, assignee of Robert Adams, assignee of Zacheriah Stanley, treasury warrant, 100 acres on Middle Fork of Holston, adjoining Joseph Adkins, John Snabley [Snaveley] "to sun set" [west] and Thomas Crow to "sun rise" [east].

p. 115, JOHN ADAMS, assignee of John Montgomery, treasury warrant, 1782, 50 acres adjoining Hugh Montgomery, Robert Adams, and his own, to begin at Montgomery's corner and nearly a south course with said line crossing a branch to the beginning.

August 10, 1793, JAMES BRUSTER, assignee of Robert Adams, assignee of Zacheriah Stanley, treasury warrant, 100 acres on Maiden Spring Fork of Clynch [Clinch] River, corner to Isaac Moore's survey and along the foot of the Knob Mountain to include spring and improvements bought of James Jones.

MICHAEL JOHNSON, assignee of Robert Adams, assignee of Zachariah Stanley, treasury warrant, 50 acres on Middle Fork of Holston, adjoining David Johnson, William Davis, and Henry Pickle.

p. 116, August 13, 1793, GEO. POWERS, assignee of Peter Powers, assignee of Jas. Newell, treasury warrant, 100 acres on Cripple Creek adjoining Major Love, beginning at the north corner of said land and down to William Ewings and with John Whissols [Wetzel's?] and Collops.

ANDREW THOMPSON, treasury warrant, assigned by Akelis Fannen, 1782, 50 acres beginning at his patent line and towards Sam'l Muncey's line.

NICHOLAS SNIDER, 50 acres on Middle Fork of Holston adjoining Philip Akers and Jas. Adkins on both sides of the river (withdrawn).

JOHN THOMPSON, certificate from the surveyor's office of Montgomery, 1783, assignee of Geo. Peerie [Peery], assignee of Zachariah Stanley, assignee of Richard Shelton, 45 acres part thereof, and 100 acres on treasury warrant assigned by Jeffery Heldreth, assignee of William Neel, on Maiden Spring Fork of Clynch [Clinch], adjoining the opening line of his Crab Orchard survey and with George Peerie [Peery] and Isaac Moor [Moore].

p. 117, August 13, 1793, ANTHONY TONKERY [TONCRAY], part of two warrants, 200 acres, 50 of which part of a warrant assigned by William King, 1781, 150 acres assigned by Robert Adams, assignee of Zacheriah Stanley, part of 18,985 acre, 1781, on Reed Creek adjoining his entry of 100 acres on the south and west, and the lands of David Ross.

August 28, 1793, JAMES GILLASPIE, assignee of Robert Adams, assignee of Zacheriah Stanley, assignee of David Patterson, treasury warrant, 1781, 100 acres in Rich Valley adjoining Thomas Gillaspie and his own.

pp. 117-118, September 2, 1793, JOHN REPASS, part of three treasury warrants, 300 acres, 200 acres of which was assigned by Jacob Rapass [Repass] and 100 acres assigned by Robert Adams, on Middle Fork of Holston, beginning at the head of Hayle Hollow near Henry Picle's [Pickle's] line.

p. 118, September 2, 1793, MICHAEL CASTLE [CASSELL], assignee of Jeffery Heldreth, assignee of William Neel, treasury warrant, 1,498 acres, 1782, 60 acres in Rich Valley round and adjoining two entries of Heldreth in the Valley, which is also adjoining each other.

September 9, 1793, SAMUEL SHANNAN, assignee of William Neel, treasury warrant, 1498 acres, 1782, 100 acres to join the entry made by John Shannon on Big Spring, branch of Holston River.

September 10, 1793, JOHN RADER, assignee of Robert Adams, treasury warrant, 50 acres on Middle Fork of Holston, adjoining Stophel [Christopher] Phillippee, John Ligget, and his own purchased of Sam'l Shannan.

pp. 118-119, MICHAEL BAUGH, assignee of William Neel, treasury warrant, 200 acres, headwaters of Reed Creek adjoining Jacob Dobler, Peter Snevely and Martin Staley, with his improvements and the land whereon he now lives.

p. 119, September 11, 1793, THOMAS FULLING, assignee of William Ross, 22 acres on Little Reed Island Creek adjoining James Breeden, and Henry Davis.

September 16, 1793, JOSEPH MEAIRS, assignee of Robert Adams, assignee of Zacheriah Stanley, treasury warrant, 18,985 acres, 1781, 50 acres part thereof on Peek [Peak] Creek, branch of New river, adjoining his own patent on north and Col. Pattyents [Patton's], beginning in Meaires line on ridge between two branches and with Patton's line (25 acres withdrawn).

September 19, 1793, JESSE EVANS, treasury warrants, 1781 and 1784, 176 acres on Cove Creek, beginning at the mouth of a valley and corner to survey formerly made for John McFarland near the mouth of Cove, and with Phillip Reeder's line and to his corner towards Calhoon's line, beginning corner to said line and extending towards Edward Murphey's and along the ridge, with a conditional line marked between Evans and Michael Dickert, and with Evans own line to Cove Creek and up the same.

p. 120, September 20, 1793, MICHAEL DICKERT [DECKARD], assignee of Robert Adams, treasury warrant, 50 acres on Cove Creek beginning corner to division line between Dicert [Dickert, Deckard], and Jesse Evans' patent line and with it crossing branch towards John Hutsell's entry which he sold to Jesse Evans to include the house and improvements.

JOHN LOUTHEN, assignee of Robert Adams, assignee Zacheriah Stanley, treasury warrant, 200 acres on Peek [Peak] Creek adjoining Michel [Michael] Dickert's [Deckard's] 100 acres, and up creek to survey of Henry Honaker's.

pp. 120-121, September 23, 1793, HUGH PATRICK, assignee of Frederick Edwards, assignee of James Newell, warrant not dated, 200 acres on north side of the land he lives on, including the improvements by Loveday, on Peek [Peak] Creek (withdrawn 52 acres and assigned to Isaac Grose). N.B. the above entry was made in Montgomery Surveyor's office, 1782, and 148 acres appeared to be assigned by Patrick to William Mullin and Meredith Ranes.

p. 121, October 3, 1793, PHILIP LAMBERT, assignee of Robert Adams, treasury warrant, 100 acres on Wolf Creek, adjoining and beginning at Steward's survey below Round Bottom, to include Smith's Camp.

JAS. GILBERT, assignee as above, 50 acres on Walkers Creek adjoining the land of Richard Whitman and down the north side of the creek.

October 9, 1793, JACOB WASHAM, assignee of Robert Adams, treasury warrant, 100 acres on head of Mingles Branch, Reed Creek, adjoining Frederick Castle, Adam Cook and John Rouse.

October 9, 1793, WILLIAM SMITH, assignee of Adam Dutton, assignee of William Neel, 50 acres on Middle Fork of Holston, adjoining Robert Buchanan's new survey and William Davis and David Johnson.

p. 122, October 11, 1793, JESSE EVANS, assignee of Robert Adams, assignee of Zachariah Stanley, treasury warrant, 50 acres on Cove Creek, beginning on the north side of the creek, corner to the survey of John McFarland and adjoining Phillip Reeder.

October 18, 1793, NEHEMIAH BONHAM, assignee of William Neel, treasury warrant, 100 acres on Thorn Branch of Cripple Creek adjoining John Karr, Andrew Porter, and lands he purchased of Stephen Sanders.

October 19, 1793, GEO. CREAGER, assignee of John Colvin, assignee of Susanna Helvey, assignee of Robert Adams, assignee of Zachariah Stanley, treasury warrant, 200 acres on north side of Pine Ridge to include the land on which William Crawford now lives.

p. 123, October 23, 1793, JACOB HECK and JOHN RAZOR, assignee of Peter Razor and Joshua Jones, assignee of John Phillipee, assignee of William Bouren [Bourne], treasury warrant, 4,000 acres, 1783, 50 acres on South Fork of Holston, adjoining Nath'l Morgan, Jarvis Smith, William Nelson and their own.

October 23, 1793, JAMES CAMPBILL [CAMPBELL], treasury warrant, 1782, assignee of Hezekiah Chiney [Chaney], 150 acres adjoining another entry of his on south side of Lick Mountain.

November 11, 1793, JOHN MESSERSMITH, assignee of William Neel, treasury warrant, 100 acres in Rich Valley on North Fork of Holston adjoining his open line to include the north side of a ridge on the east end of his plantation.

November 16, 1793, WILLIAM KING, assignee of William Pendleton, treasury warrant, 1000 acres, 1781, 40 acres part thereof, in Rich Valley adjoining James Camron, Adam Geerhart, Nicholas Darter, Jacob Spangler, and George Kinder.

p. 124, November 19, 1793, PETER KINDER, treasury warrant in the name of Charles Conner, 500 acres, 1780, 200 acres part thereof, on Reed Creek adjoining the land of Adam Baugh, his own, Peter Etter, the Marsh line and the Meeting-house land, to include the old survey made for Godfret [Comfir (?)]

November 25, 1793, GEORGE CREAGER, assignee of Michel Walters, assignee of Wm. Bouren [Bourne], treasury warrant, 1783, 1,771 acres on Reed Creek to include the house where Crafford [Crawford] lives and the spring and part of the improved land.

November 25, 1793, JEREMIAH BARNETT, assignee of Chrisian [Christian] Snido, assignee of John Alsup, assignee of Peter Sanders, treasury warrant, 500 acres, 1782, no acres stated, on Walkers Creek, adjoining Amos Johnson and Sam'l Dunbar, and extending down the road over the glade.

November 29, 1793, ALEXANDER BAIN, assignee of Leonard Fleming, assignee of Joseph Robertson, treasury warrant, 453 acres, 1782, 100 acres beginning on top of Garden Mountain at the end of Burks Ridge.

p. 125, November 29, 1793, WILLIAM DAY, assignee of Alexander Bain, on the above warrant, 100 acres in Burks Garden where James Thompson's line crosses the Blue Spring path, and extending towards Haw Ridge including a hollow; also on the same warrant, 100 acres in Burks Garden beginning corner of James Thompson's above Grills' place and up the mountain.

ALEXANDER BAIN, on the above warrant, 100 acres on Hunting Camp Creek, a branch of Wolf Creek, beginning at Andrew Thompson's Camp and down the creek to Smyth's line and to include both sides of the creek.

AARON INGRAM, assignee of Robert Pollard, treasury warrant, 400 acres, 1793, 200 acres part thereof, on the south side of Round Mountain, beginning at a spring by the side of the Garden Road and up the side of the mountain to include Drury Elkins' improvement.

p. 126, JOHN STOBAUGH, assignee of Aron Ingram, assignee of Robert Polard [Pollard], on above warrant, 200 acres on Little Creek beginning at William Muncy's horse pen and down the creek to Wolf Creek and including both sides of Wolf Creek (100 acres withdrawn).

p. 126, December 11, 1793, WILLIAM HAYS, assignee of Robert Adams, treasury warrant, 50 acres on North Fork of Holston, adjoining open line of the Buffalo Cow Bottom survey and east end of said survey and lands of William Orr.

December 11, 1793, JACOB DOBLAR, assignee of Robert Adams, treasury warrant,

20 acres on Reed Creek adjoining own patent land, William Johnson, and Michael Castle.

December 26, 1793, JAMES CROW, assignee of Robert Adams, state warrant, 100 acres on Middle Fork of Holston, adjoining Robert Crow, Edward Crow, John McMullen, and Washington County line.

CHAPTER III
Survey Book 1, Wythe County 1791-1800

Wythe County has preserved four early books where records of surveys and plats are recorded. They were usually signed by the court-appointed and approved county surveyors. The first book is abstracted here, detailing acreage, location, basis for the survey, with dates, and the names of adjoining owners where noted. Page numbers where the records can be found are included in the abstract. It should be noted that, for some unknown reason, the records were not entered in the survey book in chronological order.

Most of these surveys were based on treasury warrants issued by the Virginia government. These warrants were frequently assigned by one early settler to another. Many, but not all, surveys and plats were sent to Richmond to the Land Office and used as a basis for a land grant from the state. Sometimes the person who had the survey obtained the grant, and sometimes it was the person to whom the right was assigned or transferred.

The records in the first survey book probably began in 1790, but because the first four pages are missing these abstracts begin in 1791, and end in 1800. On page 5, the names are missing from the surveys. The land mentioned in the records is located in Wythe, in what is now Grayson, Carroll, Bland, part of Pulaski, Smyth, Tazewell and Russell counties. The only way to identify the general location is by determining the location of the creeks. For example, Reed Creek is in Wythe County, Fox, Wilson and Potato creeks are in what is now Grayson, Kimberling Fork is in what is now Bland, head of the Holston is in Smyth County, and Peak Creek is in Pulaski County. The Clinch River flows through parts of Tazewell and Russell, and the Tug Fork and Big Sandy are in counties further west.

The dates included may need some explanation. The first date is the date of the survey was made or completed. Following the number of acres, the date refers to the date the entry was made, although it was not always stated in the original record. The date following the specific kind of warrant is the date the warrant was issued, which is sometimes omitted in the original record. Some of the early entries were originally filed in Montgomery County before Wythe County was organized. Occasionally, the date the warrant was assigned is given in the original record.

p. 6

August 20, 1791, GEORGE KEGLEY, 40 acres, 1786 in Montgomery County and re-entered in Wythe County on a treasury warrant, 1782 (?), on Reed Creek, adjoining his old and new surveys and Daniel Etter.

Not dated, THOMAS PAULEY, 16 acres, 1790, treasury warrant, 1790, for 1,000 acres, 50 acres of which was assigned by Robert Adams, assignee of Saml. McCraw, assignee of John Netherland, assignee of Edmund Vaughn, assignee of Charles Woodson, on _____ [Walkers?] Creek.

p. 7

April 12, 1791, LEONARD STRAW, 100 acres, entered in 1786 in Montgomery County and re-entered in Wythe County, on treasury warrant, 1782, on Stony Fork of Reed Creek.

March 16, 1791, SHERROD ADKINSON, 87 acres, 1791, on treasury warrant, date missing [torn], assigned to him by Robert Adams, assignee of Saml. McCraw, assignee of John Netherland, assignee of Edmund Vaughn, assignee of Charles Woodson, on Wolf Creek.

p. 8

August 4, 1791, HENRY VICE, 279 acres, 1791, on treasury warrant, 1782, assigned by William Neel, on head of South Fork of Holston, joining John Vaught and Jarvis (Jervis) Smith.

p. 9

November 20, 1790, JAMES McGAVOCK, 2,292 acres, 1790, on part of a military warrant [date missing, torn] for 3,000 acres, and 200 acres on a treasury warrant, 1788, on south side of Lick Mountain.

p.10

March 20, 1791, JOHN CRAIG, 600 acres on 2 entries: (1) 200 acres, and (2) 400 acres, both on certificates from the Commissioners of Washington and Montgomery counties, 1782, on New River.

p. 11

November 2, 1790, LAWRENCE KETTERING, 198 acres, 1790, on Commissioner's certificate for 400 acres, 1782, adjoining Quirk, being on the north and south side of the wagon road.

p. 12

February 15, 1791, PHILIP YAUGER (YANGER?), 28 acres, 1790, on treasury warrant, 1790, assigned to him by Thomas Pauley, assignee of Robert Adams, assignee of Samuel McCraw, assignee of John Netherland, assignee of Edmund Vaughn, assignee of Charles Woodson, on Walkers Creek.

p. 13

November 17, 1791 (?), PETER HEDRICK, 200 acres, 1791, on treasury warrant, 1783, part assigned by William Bouren (?), assignee of Alexander Taite, on Reed Creek, at the foot of Pine Ridge.

Date missing, CHRISTOPHER GOSE, 250 acres, 1791, on treasury warrant, 1782, on Turkey Fork of Elk Creek.

p. 14

March 15, 1791, JOHN COMPTON, 500 acres, on an entry in Montgomery County, 1782, and re-entered in Wythe County, treasury warrant, 1781, entry assigned by David (?) Douglas, land on Clear Fork of Wolf Creek.

October 20, 1791 (?), FRANCIS STURGEON, torn, [but name provided from Montgomery County Entry Book C, p. 116], 500 acres based on an entry 1788 in Montgomery County, on a treasury warrant, 1780, assigned to him by James Lynch, assignee of William Anderson, assignee of Richard Eggleston, Junr., and re-entered in Wythe County; also entry for 100 acres in Wythe County, 1791, part of a treasury warrant for 500 acres which was assigned to him by Enoch Osborne, assignee of Walter Crockett, attorney for James Clerk, 1782; also 100 acres on entry 1791 on treasury warrant, 1783, which was assigned to him by William Bouren, assignee of Alexander Tayte, on Potatoe Creek, branch of New River, adjoining the North Carolina line.

p. 16

November 18, 1791, JACOB KINDER, 120 acres on two entries: (1) 50 acres, 1790,

104

treasury warrant, 1790, and assigned by Joseph Irwin, assignee of Robert Adams, assignee of Saml. McCraw; and (2) 70 acres, 1792, treasury warrant, 1783, assigned by Jacob Baugh, assignee of William Bouren, assignee of Alexander Taite, on Reed Creek corner to George Kinder and Henry Newman, and Peter Hedrick's line.

February 16, 1792, JACOB KINDER, 50 acres, 1790, treasury warrant, 1790, assigned by Joseph Irwin, assignee of Robert Adams, assignee of Saml. McCraw, on the north side of Reed Creek, adjoining George Kinder.

p. 17

March 12, 1792, MICHAEL WALTERS, 100 acres, 1791, on treasury warrant, 1783, assigned by William Bouren, assignee of Alexander Taite, on Reed Creek, corner to John Etter, _____ Nipp, and Henry Umberger.

p. 18

April 2, 1792, AERHEART ZIMMERMAN, 310 acres, 263 acres of which was an entry in Montgomery County and re-entered in Wythe County for 313 acres, 50 acres of the entry previously made use of, on part of a state warrant, 1782; also 47 acres part of an entry made in Montgomery County on a state warrant, 1782, assigned by Jacob Davies, assignee of John Whitsell, assignee of James Finley, assignee of Walter Crockett, on Reed Creek corner to Charles Zimmerman and Stophle Zimmerman.

p. 19

April 25, 1791, GEORGE REEVES, 400 acres, on an entry made in Montgomery County, 1784, and re-entered in Wythe County, on treasury warrant, 1782, assigned by John Cox, assignee of James Clerk's attorney, on Peach Bottom Creek.

April 26, 1791, WILLIAM BOUREN, 260 acres, 1790, on two treasury warrants, 1790, assigned by Robert Adams, assignee of Samuel McCraw, on Peach Bottom Creek, beginning in William Saxton's line.

p. 20

April 23, 1792, CHARLES LYNCH, 260 acres, 1791, treasury warrant, 1782, which was assigned by James Newell, assignee of David Reece, assignee of James Hines, assignee of James Neely, assignee of John Neely, on west side of the New River, joining Robert Porter.

p. 21

April 23, 1792, CHARLES LYNCH, 872 acres, 1791, on treasury warrant, 1782, assigned by James Newell, assignee of David Reace, assignee of James Hines, assignee of James Neely, assignee of John Neely, on west side of the New River, joining Brawley's and crossing Mine Mill Creek.

p. 22

February 9, 1792, THOMAS CROW, 92 acres, 1792, on treasury warrant, 1783, 100 acres of which was assigned by William Bouren, assignee of Alexander Taite, on Middle Fork of Holston, adjoining his own lands, Joseph Davis and near William Davises line.

January 13, 1791, BURKETT SEIBEL, 50 acres, 1790, on treasury warrant, 1790, assigned by Robert Adams, assignee of Samuel McCraw, on Middle Fork of Holston.

p. 23

December 28, 1791, JOHN LAMBERT, 100 acres, 1790, on treasury warrant, 1790, assigned by Robert Adams, assignee of Samuel McCraw, on Walkers Creek, adjoining William Davis.

July 27, 1792, ALEXANDER ORR, 50 acres, 1792, on treasury warrant, 1782, assignee of John Preston, assignee of John Smith, devisee of Saml. Black deceased, on Kimberlands Fork, branch of Walkers Creek, corner to his patent land and Robert Evans.

p. 24

July 28, 1792, JOHN HERRIN, 50 acres, 1792, on treasury warrant, 1790, assigned to him by James Havens, assignee of Holton Muncy, assignee of Robert Adams, assignee of Saml. McCraw, on Walkers Creek corner to his patent land.

p. 25

October 13, 1791, WILLIAM NEEL, 333 acres, 1791 on treasury warrant, 1782, on Stony Fork of Reed Creek, including Downing's improvement.

p. 26

October 20, 1792, WILLIAM ORR, 130 acres, 1791, on treasury warrant, 1783, 100 acres of which was assigned to him by William Bouren, the other, 1782, 30 acres of which was assigned him by Zachariah Stanley, on North Fork of Holstein in Rich Valley, beginning on a spur of Walkers Mountain and joining John Garwood.

pp. 27-29

November 23, 1792, ZACHARIAH STANLEY, 3,700 acres, on an entry made in the name of David Patterson in Montgomery County, 1782, on treasury warrant, 1782, which was assigned by Patterson to Stanley, between Big and Little Reed Island Creeks, corner to Patterson and Huff's survey, Nathaniel Pope's Island Creek survey, James Worrell's line, and John Green's line.

p. 29

November 28, 1792, ZACHARIAH STANLEY, 2,900 acres based on an entry in the name of David Patterson in Montgomery County, 1782, on treasury warrant, 1782, assigned by David Patterson to Stanley, on Big Reed Island Road Creek and Little Pine Creek, corner to Richard Bennett's land.

p. 30

December 10, 1792, ZACHARIAH STANLEY, 150 acres, 1792, on treasury warrant, assigned by John Preston, on Burks Fork, a branch of Big Reed Island Creek, corner Aaron Colyer, Thomas Jasop, and Jarret Branson's land.

p. 31

December 11, 1792, ZACHARIAH STANLEY, 230 acres, 1792, on treasury warrant, assigned him by David Patterson, assignee of Thomas Miller (?), 1782, on Beaver Dam and Island Creeks, including John Rees's improvement, corner to Esau Worrell.

p. 32

November 12, 1792, WILLIAM WHITTON, 75 acres, 1792, on treasury warrant, 1782, assigned by John Preston, assignee of John Smith, devisee of Samuel Black, deceased, on headwaters of the Clynch [Clinch] River in a line of Colo. Wm. Ingles, deceased, land.

p. 33

April 25, 1791, WILLIAM THOMPSON, 50 acres on an entry in the name of Jos. Erwin and assigned to Thompson, on treasury warrant, 1790, assigned by Robert Adams, assignee of Samuel McCraw, on Reed Creek, corner to William Ward's survey.
WILLIAM THOMPSON, 200 acres, 1792, on treasury warrant, 1783, on waters of Clynch [Clinch] River, adjoining his patent land.

p. 34

November 23, 1792, JOHN THOMPSON, 100 acres, 1792, on a treasury warrant, 1783, assigned to him by William Thompson, assignee of William Bouren, on Maiden Spring Fork of Clynch [Clinch], beginning on a spur of Morris's Knob and near a line of James Sloan's land.

p. 35

February 18, 1792, GASPER READER, 100 acres, 1791, on treasury warrant, 1790, in the Cove on the waters of Reed Creek, adjoining Walter Crockett's line.

p. 36

November 23, 1792, HENRY WILLIAMS, 76 acres, 1792 on treasury warrant, 1782, assignee of John Thompson, assignee of William Thompson, assignee of William Bouren, on Maiden Spring Fork of Clynch [Clinch] River.

November 14, 1792, ANDREW THOMPSON, 98 acres, 1792, on treasury warrant, 1790, assigned by Robert Adams, assignee of Saml. McCraw, on waters of the Clynch [Clinch], corner to Ebenezer Brewster's land.

p. 37

May 30, 1793, JOHN McNUTT, 88 acres, 1790, on a treasury warrant, 1790, on Reed Creek.

p. 38

November 17, 1792, HENRY HARMAN, JUNR., 94 acres, 1792, on treasury warrant, 1782, assigned to him by John Preston, assignee of John Smith, devisee of John Black, deceased, on headwaters of the Clynch [Clinch] River on the southeast side of his own patent land.

p. 39

January 11, 1793, JOHN SHANNON, 100 acres, 1791, on a treasury warrant, 1782, assigned to him by William Neel, on North Fork of Holstein [Holston] River.

p. 40

May 30, 1793, SUSANNA HELVEY, HENRY HELVEY and JACOB HELVEY, 265 acres, 1790, on a treasury warrant, 1790, which was assigned them by Jesse Evans, assignee of Robert Adams, assignee of Saml. McCraw, on Reed Creek, corner to John Davis and John McNitt [McNutt].

p. 41

August 24, 179_, ANTHONY TONKERY, 300 acres based on two entries (1) on treasury warrant, 1790, assigned by Robert Adams, assignee of Saml. McCraw (2) 200 acres on two treasury warrants, 1781, on Reed Creek, corner to George Davis.

p. 42

No date, JAMES GILLASPIE, 110 acres, on treasury warrant, 1781, assigned by Robert Adams, assignee of Zacheriah Stanley, on the North Fork of Holston in Rich Valley.

p.43

September 6, 1793, MICHAEL CASTLE [CASSELL], 180 acres on three entries for Jeffery Heldreth and assigned to Michael Castle, one for 70 acres, on state warrant, assigned to Heldreth by Robert Adams, assignee of Saml. McCraw, part of a treasury warrant, dated 1790, second entry for 50 acres on treasury warrant dated 1782, third entry in Castle's own name for 60 acres on the same treasury warrant, land in Rich Valley on the North Fork of Holston, adjoining Philip Umbarger's.

September 2, 1793, PHILIP UMBARGER, 61 acres based on two entries, the first 50 acres in the name of Jeffrey Heldreth and assigned to Umbarger on treasury warrant of 1783, and second 11 acres in Umbarger's own name on treasury warrant of 1781, located on the North Fork of Holston River in Rich Valley adjoining his patent land at the foot of Walkers Mountain.

p. 44

March 17, 1793, NICHOLAS TALBOT, 57 acres, based on an entry of 300 acres in Montgomery County in the name of Robert Ewing and re-entered in Wythe County and assigned to Talbot, on a treasury warrant, 1782, located in Rich Valley on the North Fork of Holston, near an old path that leads from John Buchanan's to William Beates [Bates?].

p. 45

January 28, 1793, SAMUEL SHANNON, 300 acres based on two entries: (1) 200 acres, assigned by John Shannon, who was assignee of William Neel, treasury warrant, 1782; (2) 100 acres entered in his own name on the same treasury warrant, located on Middle Fork of Holston.

p. 46

February 7, 1793, DAVID DOAK, 49 acres, treasury warrant, 1782, and assigned by John King, on Reed Creek adjoining Doak's old patent line.

January 28, 1793, ANDW. [ANDREW] DANNER, 300 acres on treasury warrant, 1782, assigned by Nathaniel Frisby [Frisbie], assignee of James Newell, on Cripple Creek, branch of New River, corner to James Campbell and going to the top of Lick Mountain.

p. 47

March 16, 1793, ROBERT BATES, 100 acres, on a treasury warrant, 1782, in the name of Robert Ewing in the surveyor's office in Montgomery and re-entered in Wythe County and assigned to Bates, in Rich Valley on the North Fork of Holston, adjoining William Bates and the river.

p.48

September 6, 1793, SIMON FOGLESONG, 1,000 acres, on entries made in 1789 and 1791 on treasury warrants, 1782, assigned by William Neel, assignee of Geo. Moore, on the main fork of Reed Creek.

p. 49

April 1, 1793, JACOB FANNING, 200 acres, on entries made 1791 and 1793, on treasury warrant, 1782, assigned by James Murphey assignee of Charles Copeland on a treasury warrant, 1781, assigned by Joseph ___, assignee of Robert Adams, assignee of Zachariah Stanley, on Long Branch of Chestnut Creek, branch of New River.

October 19, 1792, JOSEPH YOUNG, 100 acres, 1791, on a treasury warrant, 1782, assigned to him by James Newell, on Canoe Ridge, waters of Fox Creek, branch of New River.

p. 50

October 1, 1793, DAVID ROSS, agent for Ross and Trigg, assignee of Stephen Trigg, assignee of Richard Chapman and Francis Farmer, assignee of William Probat, assignee of James Sprowl, 400 acres on Commissioner's certificate, on Reed Creek.

p. 51

March 18, 1793, JOHN BUCHANAN, 550 acres, based on an entry of 400 acres on Commissioner's certificate granted Archibald Buchanan, 1781, and assigned to John Buchanan, and 150 acres in John Buchanan's name on treasury warrant, 1790, assigned by Robert Adams, assignee of Samuel McCraw, principally in Wythe County in the Cove on North Fork of Holston adjoining Andrew Lammie.

September 9, 1790, DUNCAN GULLIAN [GULLION], 100 acres based on an entry in Montgomery County and re-entered in Wythe County, treasury warrant, 1782, assigned to him by William Neel, assignee of Thomas Rutledge, on Reed Creek, branch of New River, adjoining Jacob Prooner and Martin Wyrick.

October 13, 1792, JAMES CAMRON [CAMERON], 500 acres based on entries in 1786, 1792, and 1791, on treasury warrants, 1782, 1781, and 1782, the first assigned to him by George Kincer, assignee of Michael Venerick, assignee of Michael Walters; the second assigned by Robert Adams, assignee of Zachariah Stanley, assignee of David Patterson; the third assigned by James Murphy, assignee of Charles Copeland, in Rich Valley on North Fork of Holston on side of Walkers Mountain, and corner to Thomas Mead.

February 7, 1792, JOHN MUSSER, 100 acres, 1791, on treasury warrant assigned to him by Robert Adams, assignee of Samuel McCraw, on Middle Fork of Holston adjoining his own land and Robert Davis.

March 17, 1793, EVAN DAVIS, 56 acres based on an entry in 1793 on a treasury warrant, 1781, and assigned by Jeffrey Heldreth, assignee of William Neel, in Rich Valley on North Fork of Holston, adjoining his own and Henry Beeson's.

November 1, 1793, JAMES CAMPBELL, 400 acres, entries in 1789 and 1793 part of treasury warrant, 1782, assigned to him by Adam Dean, on Cripple Creek branch of New River, corner to Campbell's patent land and Hezekiah China [Chaney].

August 17, 1793, ALKENAH WYNNE, 100 acres, 1793, on treasury warrant, 1782, assigned by John Preston, assignee of John Smith, devisee of Saml. Black, deceased, on head of Clynch [Clinch].

April 27, 1791, NATHANIEL LANDERS, 90 acres, 1790, on treasury warrant, 1782, assigned by Enoch Ozborne, assignee of James Clerk's attorney, on Saddle Creek, branch of New River, by the wagon road.

April 27, 1791, NATHAN WARD, 100 acres, 1790, on treasury warrant, 1782, assigned to him by Enoch Ozborne, assignee of James Clerk's attorney, on Saddle Creek.

May 2, 1791, GEORGE HOWELL, 100 acres, 1791, on treasury warrant, 1782, assigned by Enoch Ozborne, assignee of James Clerk's attorney, south side of New River near Andy's Branch.

December 19, 1792, WILLIAM HENRY BOYER, 33 acres, based on entry made 1782 in Montgomery County and re-entered in Wythe County in the name of Thomas Jones, assignee of Peter Saunders, on a treasury warrant, 1781, assigned to Barnet Foley, and he to Boyer, on Elk Creek branch of New River.

December 19, 1792, WILLIAM LONG, 124 acres based on an entry made 1782 in Montgomery County and re-entered in Wythe county in the name of Thomas Jones, assignee of Peter Saunders, on treasury warrant, 1781, and assigned to Barnet Foley and he to Long, on Peach Bottom Creek branch of Elk Creek, branch of New River.

December 16, 1793, GEORGE CRAGER [CRIGGER], 377 acres based on entries in 1793 on treasury warrants, 1780, 1781, the first assigned by John Corven, assignee of Susanna Helvey, assignee of Robert Adams, assignee of Zachariah Stanley, assignee of David Patterson, and second assigned by Michael Walters, assignee of William Bouren, assignee of Alexander Taite, Reed Creek on the north side of Pine Ridge.

February 6, 1794, ROBERT GRAHAM, 46 acres, 1792 and 1794, on treasury warrants, 1781 and 1782, on Reed Creek, branch of New River, adjoining his patent land on the south side.

January 19, 1793, ROBERT GRAHAM, 75 acres, 1792, on treasury warrant, 1782, on Reed Creek, adjoining his patent land on the north and east near the foot of Brushy Mountain and the wagon road.

February 10, 1794, JOSHUA JONES, PETER RAZOR, and BENJAMIN _____ (blank), 14 acres, entered on a treasury warrant, 1782, assigned by Robert Adams, assignee of Zachariah Stanley, on South Fork of Holston adjoining Joshua Jones.

March 15, 1793, WILLIAM SMITH, 200 acres based on an entry in the name of Robert Ewing on treasury warrant, 1782, in Rich Valley on North Fork of Holston adjoining Thomas Gillaspie.

September 24, 1793, MICHAEL DECKERT, 108 acres based on an entry made in Montgomery County in 1784 and re-entered in Wythe County on treasury warrant, 1782, on Cove Creek, branch of Reed Creek, corner to Jesse Evans and Peter Binkley.

January 31, 1794, JACOB DOBLER, 175 acres, based on an entry on a treasury warrant, 1781, assigned by Robert Adams, assignee of Zachariah Stanley, on Reed Creek, corner to Jacob Washam, Adam Cook, John Rouse, and Wm. Johnson.

January 31, 1794, JACOB DOBLER, 25 acres, treasury warrant, 1781, part of which was assigned by Robert Adams, assignee of Zachariah Stanley, on Reed Creek corner to William Johnson, Michael Castle, and his own land.

October 4, 1793, JOHN RABBASS [REPASS], 186 acres on an entry 1793 on two treasury warrants, 1791 and 1790, on Middle Fork of Holston adjoining Henry Pickle.

March 1, 1794, MARTIN KIMBERLAND, 190 acres, on a treasury warrant, 1782, assigned by Robert Adams, assignee of Zachariah Stanley, on Reed Creek adjoining Martin Stealy [Staley] and Michael Baugh.

October 15, 1792, DUNCAN GULLION, 100 acres on an entry in Montgomery County in 1783, and re-entered in Wythe County, on treasury warrant assigned by Walter Crockett, attorney for James Clerk, on Walkers Creek on a branch that "runeth in at the Beaver dams" corner to John Henderson, deceased.

pp. 66-67

January 23, 1793, ACQUILA GREER, 78 acres, on treasury warrants, 1781 and 1782, on Wilson Creek adjoining Solomon Cox.

pp. 68-70

March 28, 1794, WILSON CARY NICHOLAS, 300,000 acres, 1794, on 10 treasury warrants, 9 in 1794 and 1 in 1783, assigned to him, land located in Wythe and Russell, mostly in Wythe, on both sides of Sandy Creek, a branch of the Ohio, near the head of Sandy Creek in the gap of Stony Ridge called Roark's Gap about two miles from Johnson's mill on the Clinch River.

p. 71

May 1, 1794, WILSON CARY NICHOLAS and JACOB KENNEY, 320,000 acres based on two entries in 1794 on a treasury warrant in 1794 for Nicholas and one-half assigned to Kenny, located in Wythe and Russell counties, mostly in Wythe, on both sides of Sandy Creek, a branch of the Ohio River.

p. 73

February 25, 1793, GEORGE HARMAN, assignee of Nicholas Daugherty, 80 acres, 1792 on treasury warrant, 1781, on Kimberlin Fork, a branch of Walkers Creek.

p. 74

November 26, 1792, JOHN PEERY, 170 acres, 1791, on treasury warrant, 1783, assigned by James Peery, assignee of George Peery, assignee of Zachariah Stanley, assignee of Richard Shelton, land on the head of the Clinch River including a place known by the name of the three walnuts.

October 17, 1792, JOHN PERCIFIELD, 50 acres, 1792, on a treasury warrant, 1782, assigned by William Neel, located in Rich Valley, corner to Peter Groseclose, on the headwaters of the North Fork of Holston River.

p. 75

November 15, 1792, DANIEL JOHNSON, 100 acres, 1791, on treasury warrant assigned by John Preston, on North Fork of the Clynch [Clinch] River.

p. 76

November 17, 1792, DANIEL HARMAN, 80 acres based on two entries 1792 on treasury warrants issued in 1783 and 1790, located on the head of Clynch [Clinch] River.

April 8, 1794, JOHN FARGUSON, 62 acres based on entries made in 1792 and 1794 on treasury warrants, 1782 and 1783, on head of Clynch [Clinch] River.

p. 77

August 31, 1793, WILLIAM MARRS and HENRY MARRS, 40 acres, 1793, on treasury warrant, 1781, on headwaters of the Clynch [Clinch] River, corner to John Evans and James Maxwell.

p. 78

November 12, 1792, JAMES WHITTON, 50 acres, 1792, on treasury warrant, 1783, assigned by John Evans, assignee of Robert B. Chew, on Plum Creek, branch of Clynch [Clinch] River, corner to James Maxwell.

April 9, 1794, JOHN TOTTEN, 283 acres based on two treasury warrants, 1782, 1783, land located on North Fork of Holston River adjoining Philip Umbarger.

p. 79

April 10, 1794, HENRY BEESON, 90 acres based on entries made 1784 and 1793, on treasury warrant, 1781, located in Rich Valley on North Fork of Holston River, adjoining Evan Davis and his own land on the south side.

p. 80

April 16, 1794, JOHN HOGE, 187 acres, based on an entry on a treasury warrant, 1782, and a preemption warrant 1780, on Reed Creek, adjoining John Baker and Andrew Stotts, Junr.

April 28, 1791, JONATHAN OSBORN, 150 acres added on an entry made in 1782 in Montgomery County and re-entered in Wythe County on treasury warrant, 1782, assigned by James Ward and Joseph Maxwell, assignee of John Burton, assignee of Moses Greer, on New River adjoining Jesse Robinett and corner to Wells Ward.

p. 81

April 25, 1791, WILLIAM WARD, 40 acres based on an entry in Montgomery County in 1790 and re-entered in Wythe County on treasury warrant assigned by David Doak, assignee of James Doak, on Reed Creek, branch of New River, corner to Jacob Baugh.

p. 82

November 11, 1793, GEORGE ASBERRY, 1,000 acres, 1782, in Montgomery County and re-entered in Wythe County, on treasury warrant, 1781, on headwaters of East River including the Roating (Toating?) Camp Spring.

September 20, 1792, WILLIAM NEEL, 100 acres based on entry made in 1789 in Montgomery County and re-entered in Wythe County, on treasury warrant, 1781, on Reed Creek, corner to Henry Hoppess.

p. 83

April 1, 1793, DAVID McGAVOCK, 100 acres, 1793, on treasury warrant 1783, assigned to him by Hugh McGavock, corner to Charles and Stophel Simmerman, Peter Binkley, and Lewis Hutsell [on waters of Reed Creek].

p. 84

April 16, 1794, WILLIAM BROWN, 300 acres, on an entry made on Commissioner's certificate, 1782, in Write's [Wright's] Valley on Bluestone River, corner David Wallis and Henry Harman.

p. 85

August 29, 1793, HARMAN WYNNE, 125 acres, 1793, on a treasury warrant, 1791, as assignee of Robert Adams, on head of Clynch [Clinch] River.

pp. 86-87, survey and plat voided

p. 88

June 23, 1792, WILLIAM INGLEDOVE, 100 acres, 1791, on treasury warrant, 1780, on north side of Reed Creek corner to David Ross and George Armbrister.

p. 89 left blank.

pp. 90-91

September 8, 1794, DAVID PATTISON, 150,000 acres, 1794, on a treasury warrant, 1782, on waters of Tug River, fork of the Sandy River and on the Bluestone.

p. 93, left blank

pp. 94-96

September 9, 1794, WILSON CARY NICHOLAS, 480,000 acres, 1794, on 26 treasury warrants which were assigned to him, on the north side and main fork of Tug River, branch of Sandy River.

p. 97, left blank

pp. 98-100, WILSON CARY NICHOLAS, 480,000 acres, 1794, on 26 treasury warrants which were assigned to him on the north side and main fork of Tug River, branch of Sandy River.

p. 101, left blank

pp. 102-105

August 1, 1794, ROBERT POLLARD, 75,000 acres, 1794, on treasury warrant, 1794, on Reed Creek, Peek [Peak] Creek, and Walkers Creek; Peter Kitts and Jacob Tartar, chainmen and Jacob Wolf, marker. Beginning on the east side of a ridge about 1/4 mile from the road leading from John Miller's to William Patterson's in the Cove and about one mile from the wagon road leading from Wythe Court House to Peppers Ferry on the New River...crossing some branches to Robinson Tract Fork...crossing Little and Big Walker creeks....to Skidmore Muncy's...and near Philip Lambert's...by a road leading from John Heron's to Akerleaus Fanning...crossing the Stony Fork of Reed Creek... near the fields of John Leedy...crossing the head branches of Little Sally Run to near the land of John Herkerader...near William Patterson's crossing the head branches of Peack (Peak) Creek...near the land of Robert Adams...crossing the heads of Macks Run...near the land of Hugh McGavock to the beginning and boundaries including prior claims.

p. 106

September 25, 1793, MEREDITH RAINES and WILLIAM MILLER, 148 acres, based on an entry made in Montgomery County in 1782 and re-entered in Wythe County, on state warrant, 1782, assigned by Hugh Patrick, assignee of James Newell, assignee of Frederick Edwards, on Peack [Peak] Creek, branch of New river, corner to land Rains [Raines] lives on.

p. 107

November 12, 1793, ALEXANDER STUART, 192 acres, 1793, on a treasury warrant, 1781, assigned by Robert Adams, assignee of Zacheriah Stanly, on Bluestone River, branch of New River.

November 21, 1793, JOSEPH DAVIDSON, 90 acres, entered on two treasury warrants, 1782, 1790, on Right Creek, branch of Bluestone, corner to William Brown and David Wallace.

p. 108

April 12, 1793, WILLIAM ROSS, 317 acres based on an entry made in Montgomery County on treasury warrant, 1782, assigned to him by John Preston, on the New River, beginning near a branch known as Cowpen Branch.

September 15, 1794, WILLIAM ROSS, 100 acres, based on an entry on treasury warrant, assigned by Walter Crockett, attorney for James Clerk, on New River, corner to Carter.

p. 109

November 29, 1792, AARON COLYER, 300 acres, 1792, on a treasury warrant, on Big Reed Island Creek.

p. 110

November 29, 1792, ISAM GOARD [GOAD?], 100 acres, 1792, on Big Reed Island Creek in the line of Bell's survey.

November 29, 1792, THOMAS RICHISON, 100 acres, 1792, on treasury warrant, assigned by Zacheriah Stanley, assignee of John Preston, located on Bobbett's Creek, branch of Little Reed Island Creek.

p. 111

April 20, 1792, JOSHUA RICHISON, JONATHAN RICHISON, and CHRISTO-PHER RICHISON, 225 acres, 1792, on treasury warrant assigned by Zacheriah Stanley, on Bobbetts Creek and Little Reed Island Creek.

April 20, 1793, JONATHAN RICHESON, 125 acres, on an entry made on a treasury warrant assigned by Zacheriah Stanley, on Reed Island Creek.

p. 112

April 12, 1793, JOHN PAXSON, 215 acres, based on an entry on treasury warrant, 1782, assigned by James Newell, on Reed Island Creek.

April 15, 1793, JOHN RICHESON, 60 acres, on a treasury warrant, 1782, assigned by James Newell, on Reed Island Creek.

October 29, 1791, NATHAN WARD, 217 acres, on a treasury warrant, 1783, on Cole Creek, branch of Chestnut Creek, corner Maurice Davis.

p. 113

September 20, 1794, JOHN HURST, 40 acres, on treasury warrant assigned by Saml. Meredith, on west side of New River.

p. 114

September 15, 1792, WILLIAM RANKIN, 490 acres, on treasury warrant, 1781, assigned by James Newell, on west side of Chestnut Creek and Glady Fork of Chestnut Creek adjoining Davis.

April 27, 1793, HERCULES OGLE, 60 acres, on treasury warrant assigned by James Newell, on Reed Island Creek.

p. 115

February 11, 1792, THOMAS DAVIS, 50 acres, on treasury warrant, 1782, assigned by Charles Davis, on both sides of Chestnut Creek.

February 15, 1792, WILLIAM HERBERT, legatee of William Herbert, deceased, based on Commissioner's certificate, 140 acres on Reed Island, known as Read Island Spring.

p. 116

February 10, 1792, JOHN PICKERELL, 200 acres, on treasury warrant, 1783, assigned by James Newell, on Cranberry Creek.

February 10, 1792, JOHN PICKERELL, 60 acres, on treasury warrant, 1783, assigned by James Newell, on Chestnut Creek, corner to Solomon Cox and with Pickerell's old line.

p. 117

February 20, 1792, THOMAS JOHNSON, 70 acres, on treasury warrant, 1783, assigned by James Newell, on Crooked Creek.

October 3, 1794, JAMES NEWELL, assignee of John Adams, etc., 400 acres entered in Montgomery County in 1789 and re-entered in Wythe County, on treasury warrant, 1783, located on head branch of Peak Creek.

p. 118

October 13, 1794, PETER KINDER, 270 acres, 1794, on treasury warrants, 1780 and 1781, on Reed Creek, adjoining Adam Baugh and the meeting house, corner to said Kinder and John Etter.

October 1, 1794, LEONARD STRAW, 20 acres, on treasury warrant, 1782, on South Fork of Reed Creek, corner to his patent land and Andrew Hounshell and Michal Venerick.

p. 119

February 10, 1792, JOHN DAVIS, 100 acres, on two entries each for 50 acres made in 1788 in Montgomery County on treasury warrant, 1782, on west side of Chestnut Creek and both sides of Glady Fork adjoining Thomas Davis.

p. 120

September 10, 1794, THOMAS MADISON, 1,000 acres, on an entry on a treasury warrant, 1783, assigned by Henry Banks, land on Cripple Creek (withdrawn).

July 6, 1793, DAVID LOVE, 100 acres, based on an entry in Montgomery County and re-entered in Wythe County, on treasury warrant, 1783, assigned by James Newell, on Reed Creek, corner to George Kegley and Stephen Chapple.

114

October 16, 1794, WILLIAM CALFEE, 130 acres, on an entry on two treasury warrants, 1781, 1782, on west side of New River, corner to his own land and adjoining McGlister's line.

October 15, 1794, MOSES WELLS, 170 acres, on an entry in Montgomery County in 1788 for 100 acres on a treasury warrant, 1782, and an entry in 1794 on a treasury warrant, 1781, on South Fork of Holston River including his plantation.

October 20, 1794, DAVID PATTERSON, 40,000 acres, 1794, on treasury warrant, 1794, on Bluestone and Tug rivers.

January 30, 1794, WILLIAM WARD, 100 acres, based on an entry in Montgomery County in 1790 and re-entered in Wythe County, on a treasury warrant, 1782, assigned by William King, assignee of Patrick Campbell, on Ebbetts Run, branch of Reed Creek, corner to Jacob Baugh, Henry Hoppess, and Fredrick Castle.

October 28, 1794, WILLIAM WARD, 100 acres, on an entry on a treasury warrant, 1783, assigned by William Bouren, on north side of Reed Creek, adjoining Henry Hoppess and William Thompson.

October 27, 1794, WILLIAM WARD, 194 acres, on four treasury warrants, 1780, 1781, 1782, and 1790, on Evans Creek, branch of Reed Creek adjoining Lewis Able.

October 16, 1792, ADAM GEERHART, 100 acres, 1791, in the name of George Kincer, on a treasury warrant, 1782, on the head of the North Fork of Holston River adjoining Nicholas Tarter.

January 29, 1793, JOHN ROUSE, 135 acres, 1792, on a treasury warrant, 1781, on Sugar Run, branch of Reed Creek adjoining Adam Cook.

January 31, 1794, MICHAEL BAUGH, 184 acres, 1793, on a treasury warrant assigned by William Neel, on Reed Creek adjoining Martin Kimberland and Martin Staley.

October 28, 1794, WILSON CARY NICHOLAS, 500,000 acres, 1794, on 11 treasury warrants, 1794, in Wythe and Russell counties, on the Sandy and Gyandott rivers.

October 20, 1792, FLOWER SWIFT, 40 acres, on an entry on a treasury warrant assigned to him by Andrew Kincannon, assignee of Adam Dean, on Chestnut Creek.

October 22, 1792, SOLOMON COX, 30 acres, on an entry on a treasury warrant assigned by Samuel Meredith, on Wilson Creek.

June 26, 1792, FLOWER SWIFT, 80 acres, 1791, on a treasury warrant, 1782, on New River, corner to his own land and William Jones.

February 25, 1793, DAVID CLAYPOLE, 50 acres, 1792, assigned by William Kidd, on Kimberlens Fork of Walkers Creek.

p. 133

October 18, 1794, NICHOLAS DOUGHERTY, 110 acres, on a treasury warrant, assigned by Thomas Farguson, on Clear Fork of Wolf Creek.

March 4, 1794, NICHOLAS DOUGHTERY, 236 acres, assigned by Robert Adams, based on an entry on three treasury warrants, 1782, 1783, 1790, on Clear Fork of Wolf Creek.

p. 134 (a)

June 2, 1792, JOHN BRYANT, 218 acres, 1791, in the name of James Newell on treasury warrant, 1783, assignee of Robert B. Chew, on Chestnut Creek, corner to John Davis and Mahlon Collens.

p. 134 (b)

November 20, 1794, JOHN WILLIAMSON, 3,000 acres, assignee of John Mayo on treasury warrant, on Kimberlands Fork and Walkers Creek, branch of New River.

p. 135

November 26, 1794, DANIEL HARMAN, assignee of William Neel, 467 acres, on a treasury warrant, 1782, on the head of Bluestone, branch of New River, to exclude 200 acres within the bounds for which there is an allowance made in calculation.

pp. 136-138

November 28, 1794, GEORGE PUCKETT, 75,000 acres, 1794, on treasury warrant assigned by Richard C. Pollard, 1794, on the North Fork of Holston, Clinch, Walkers Creek, and Wolf Creek.

p.138

November 16, 1794, JAMES MAXWELL, 250 acres, entries made in 1791 and 1794 on treasury warrants in 178- and 1782, on Rich Mountain adjoining William Brooks.

p. 139

November 14, 1792, WILLIAM OWENS, 45 acres, 1792, on a treasury warrant, 1792, assigned by Lawrence Murry, on the north branch of Maiden Spring Branch of the Clinch River.

May 3, 1791, BENJAMIN HOULDSON [HOLSTON], 150 acres, 1790, on a treasury warrant, 1790, assigned by Robert Adams, on Elk Creek.

p. 140

February 2, 1792, GEORGE CALDWELL, 132 acres, 1790, on a treasury warrant, 1790, assigned by Robert Adams, on Flat Mountain.

p. 141

November 19, 1792, EBENEZER BREWSTER, 104 acres, 1792, on a treasury warrant, 1783, on Muddy Branch of Maiden Spring Fork of Clynch [Clinch] River.

pp. 142-143

November 26, 1794, RICHARD C. POLLARD, 75,000 acres, 1794, on East River, Bluestone, Clinch, and Wolf Creek.

p. 144

June 22, 1792, GARNER BRYANT, 50 acres, 1791, on preemption warrant, 1782, assigned to him by James Newell, on Glady Fork of Chestnut Creek, adjoining Thomas Lundy.

June 23, 1792, JOHN BECK, 150 acres, 1791, on preemption warrant assigned by James Newell, on Chestnut Creek.

p. 145

June 25, 1792, JONATHAN COLLINS, 145 acres, 1790, for James Newell and assigned to Collins, based on a treasury warrant, 1783, on both sides of Meadow Creek, adjoining John Parker.

p. 146

September 17, 1792, JACOB RABASS [REPASS], SENR., 15 acres, on an entry made by Jeffrey Heldreth and assigned to Rabass, on a treasury warrant, 1782, on Reed Creek, corner to his patent land and William Bartlett.

October 8, 1794, MICHAEL WALTERS, 87 acres on entries made in 1782 and 1791 on treasury warrants in 1781 and 1783, on Reed Creek near Tates Run, in the line of Michael Kettern's [Catron's] land, Jacob Kettern [Catron], and Nicholas Cline.

p. 147

October 8, 1794, MICHAEL WALTERS, 56 acres, 1782 and 1791, on treasury warrants, 1781 and 1783, on South Fork of Reed Creek, adjoining Henry Grubb, Michael Walters, and Jacob Creager.

p. 148

September 24, 1793, JESSE EVANS, 176 acres, 1793, on treasury warrants in 1781 and 1784, on Cove Creek corner to a survey for John Mcfarland and also to Philip Reeder, Patrick Calhoun, and Michael Dickert's survey.

p. 149

December 6, 1794, JAMES LOCKHART, heir of William Lockhart, deceased, 314 acres on an entry on a Commissioner's certificate for 215 acres in 1781, and 99 acres on a treasury warrant assigned by Robert Adams, on Middle Fork of Holston in Wythe and Washington counties, adjoining Abram Goodpasture, Henry Slegle and John Leggett.

p.150

June 21, 1794, HENRY MARS, 200 acres, on a treasury warrant, 1784, on Crab Orchard Creek, branch of North Fork of Clinch River, adjoining his own, Christopher Mars, and James Maxwell.

September 15, 1790, JAMES FINLEY, 7 acres, 1790, on a treasury warrant, 1790, assigned by Robert Adams, assignee of Samuel McCraw.

p. 151

June 28, 1792, AMOS LUNDY, 92 acres, on an entry in the name of James Newell, 1791, on a preemption warrant for 1,000 acres in 1782, on Meadow Creek of New River near the road leading to the Iron Works, corner Amos Willet's with the line of Hugh Montgomery.

p. 152

October 25, 1791, THOMAS SUGGS, 200 acres, 1782, on a treasury warrant, assigned by James Maxwell, on Grassy Creek.

May 20, 1794, JOHN HARKERADER, assignee of Phillip Herkerader, 92 acres, 1790, on a treasury warrant, 1790, assigned by Robert Adams, assignee of Samuel McCraw, in Rich Valley, North Fork of Holston, adjoining Barney Gullion.

p. 153

October 22, 1789, JONATHAN KELLEY, 100 acres, on an entry on a treasury warrant, assigned by James Newell, on Grassy Creek.

October 22, 1792, JOHN BILY, 300 acres on an entry on a treasury warrant, 1782, on Wilson Creek.

pp. 154-155

January 20, 1795, THOMAS WILSON, 57,000 acres on entries made in 1795 on treasury warrants (1) assigned by William McElery, 1794, (2) in exchange for

117

treasury warrant, 1794, assigned by William M. Elerery, on Big Creek, Cucumber Creek, and Horsepen Creek, waters of the Great Sandy River, beginning by a branch of Tug River about 8 miles above Elkhorn.

pp. 156-158

November 26, 1794, RICHARD C. POLLARD, 75,000 acres, 1794, on a treasury warrant, 1794, on East River, Bluestone, Clinch, and Wolf Creek, beginning on a spur of East River Mountain, two miles above Big Spring, branch of East River.

p. 159, blank

pp. 160-162

January 22, 1795, WILLIAM DuVAL of Richmond, 33,000 acres, on an entry on treasury warrants, 1783 and 1795 to Alexander Dick who assigned to Isaac Barr and he to DuVal, and another issued to Thomas Lewis who assigned to DuVal, and two treasury warrants issued to Joseph Smith and he to William Thomas Taylor and he to DuVal; and a treasury warrant, 1793, issued to Abram Bird and he to DuVal; and one issued in 1781 to Smith Slaughter and he to DuVal; another 1781, issued to Joel Watkins and assigned to Culip Wallace and he to DuVal; another 1782, to Patrick McGunnel and he to DuVal; land in Wythe and Grayson counties, mostly in Wythe, on Cripple Creek and Knob Fork of Elk Creek, branches of the New River, beginning about ten miles from the lead mines, corner to Doctor Thomas Ruston, William Love, William Gannaway, Thomas Gannaway, and up Francis Mill Creek to Gleaves and Love's corner, including the following prior claims: 200 acres for Isaac Newhouse, 200 acres for ____ Stroupe on head of Cripple Creek, 250 acres for Jacob Kimberland, 1,150 acres entered for William Love on Cripple Creek; 100 acres surveyed for John Harmon, 100 acres surveyed for William Burch, 150 acres surveyed for John Fielder, 150 acres for Dennis Fielder, and 200 acres for Fouts on Elk Creek, a total of 2,500 acres.

p. 163, blank page

pp. 164-167, PHILIP RICHARD FENDAL, 63,000 acres, 1795, on two treasury warrants, 1794, for Wm. McElerry, on Walkers Creek, Reed Creek, North Fork of Holston, and Middle Fork of Holston in Washington and Wythe counties, mostly in Wythe County, beginning near John Lidie [Leedy] on Stony Fork of Reed Creek, corner to Pollard's 75,000 acres, including the following prior claims: 50 acres Walkers Creek for Henry Umberger; 40 acres on Walkers Creek for Patrick Johnson; 30 acres on North Fork of Holston for Henry Tarter; 100 acres on North Fork of Holston for William Richeson; 50 acres on North Fork of Holston for Alexander Wylie; 150 acres on North Fork of Holston for Robert Davis; 50 acres on Reed Creek for William Thompson; 500 acres on Reed Creek for Henry Hoppess; 50 acres on Reed Creek for Jacob Baugh; 2,000 acres on Reed Creek for William Neel; 200 acres on west fork of Reed Creek for William Findley; 100 acres on Reed Creek for Stephen Reeder; 200 acres on Stony Fork for Henry Umberger; 40 acres on Middle Fork of Holston for Robert Davis; 60 acres on Middle Fork of Holston for James Crow; 200 acres on Middle Fork of Holston for Arthur Campbell; 100 acres on Reed Creek, patent to James Patton's executors; 100 acres on Reed Creek for Joseph Smith; and 280 acres prior claims not particularly mentioned. Pilot was Duncan Gullion; sworn chainmen were Henry Wyrick, Jacob Cline, John Lydie [Leedy], Hugh Johnson; markers were John Etter and John Henderson.

pp. 168-170

January 24, 1795, DUNCAN McLAUGHLIN and DAVID PATTISON, 41,900 acres, 1795, on several treasury warrants, 1782, 1783, and 1794, in Wythe, Washington, and Grayson counties, greater part in Wythe County, on Cripple Creek, Fox Creek, and South Fork of Holston, beginning corner to William DuVal's 33,000 acres, on Cripple Creek about one mile north of John Griffith's land on Balsom Mountain, mentions divide between Fox Creek and South Fork of Holston, and crossing Wills Creek and the wagon road leading from Rye Valley to Fox Creek, corner to Michael Bransteter, the following prior claims on South Fork of Holston excepted: 100 acres for Philip Kenneday, 90 acres for John Winman, 50 acres for Nathaniel Morgan, 40 acres for Abram Wells, 130 acres for _____ Minx, 150 acres for David Taylor, 60 acres for Joshua Jones, and a tract of 100 acres on Cripple Creek for James Williams. Pilot was John Griffith, sworn chainmen were George Ashbrook, Gideon Huddle, and marker was George Douglas.

p. 171, blank page
pp. 172-174

February 28, 1795, JOHN BEALE, 50,000 acres, 1795, on two treasury warrants, 1795, assigned by John Leyburn, assignee of Henry Heth, on East River, Brush Creek, Bluestone, and Clinch, beginning on the dividing line between Wythe and Montgomery counties.

p. 174

April 20, 1793, TIMOTHY ROARK, 320 acres, on a treasury warrant, 1782, assignee of James Newell on Elk Creek, corner to Stophel Gosses [Christopher Gose].

pp. 175-176

March 1, 1795, JOHN W. KETTERA, 20,000 acres, 1795, on a treasury warrant, 1795, on Bluestone, Clinch, and Jacob's Fork, branch of the Sandy River, beginning on the south side of Abbs Valley, ridge near John Davidson's, deceased on Bluestone, and north of plantation in Wrights Valley, called Evans place, and north of the plantation called Stinson's old place, in Wrights Valley.

p. 177, blank
pp. 178-179

March 11, 1795, JOHN W. KETTERA, 180,000 acres, 1795, on nine treasury warrants, 1795, in Wythe and Russell counties, mostly in Wythe, on Sandy River, Twelve Pole Creek, and Guyandot River, beginning on the Sandy, corner to Nicholas 500,000 acres (*see* p. 186).

pp. 180-181

March 14, 1795, ROBERT CAMP, 50,000 acres, 1795, on a treasury warrant, 1794, on Walkers, Wolf Creek, and Clinch River, beginning on Walkers Creek near southeast corner 75,000 acres for George Pickett, excluding 9,000 acres in prior claims, not listed.

p. 182

October 10, 1793, NATHANIEL BRITTON, 255 acres, on entry on treasury warrants, 1782 and 1789 and a Commissioner's certificate, on Walkers Creek, adjoining Adam Harman, William Davis, and Jerry Lambert.

p. 183

May 16, 1795, JOHN WHITSEL, 65 acres, on a treasury warrant, 1783, assigned by James Newell, on Cripple Creek, beginning on Gannaway's line.

May 16, 1795, ISAAC NEWHOUSE, 200 acres on an entry based on a treasury warrant, 1783, assigned by James Newell, headwaters of Cripple Creek, adjoining Stroup.

p. 184

March 9, 1794, WILLIAM BELSHEA, 100 acres, based on an entry on two treasury warrants, 1782, on South Fork of Maiden Spring, branch of Clinch, adjoining John Young, James Clancy, Robert Campbell, and his own lands.

April 24, 1794, JOHN DAVIS, SENR., 165 acres, 1794, on treasury warrant, 1794, on Reed Creek adjoining his own patent land.

p. 185

April 7, 1795, JONATHAN HENDERSON, 6 acres, 1795, on a treasury warrant, 1781, on Reed Creek corner to Joseph Heldrith, deceased, and Henderson's patent land.

pp. 186-189

March 11, 1795, JOHN W. KETTERA, 180,000 acres (repeat of his survey on page 178).

pp. 190-191

August 4, 1795, RICHARD C. POLLARD, 55,000 acres, 1795, on two treasury warrants, 1795, on great Guyandott (withdrawn).

pp. 192-193

August 4, 1795, THOMAS MASON, 50,000 acres, 1795, on treasury warrant, 1795, on Greasy Guyandott and waters of Sandy adjoining Pollard's 55,000 acres and excluding 8,000 acres of prior claims.

pp. 195-196

August 12, 1795, EDW. DILLAN, 21,212 acres, 1795, on four treasury warrants, 1795, between New River and Reed Island and on or near the dividing line between Wythe and Grayson counties, excluding 5,600 acres prior claims.

pp. 197-198

August 12, 1795, SAMUEL MOORE, 40 acres, in 1795, on treasury warrant, 1795, on Sandy River and Twelve Pole Creek.

pp. 199-200

August 12, 1795, JAMES TAYLOR, 9,260 1/4 acres, 1795, on three treasury warrants, in 1781, assigned by John Allen and James Reed and Geo. Blair, excluding prior claims, corner to Kettera's 180,000 acres, and 25,000 acres of Call McCregar, and Samuel Moore's 32,955 1/2 acres on Guyandotte River.

pp. 201-202

August 11, 1795, CALL. McGREAGOR, 25,000 acres, 1795, on treasury warrant, 1795, on Guyandotte River and Twelve Pole Creek, adjoining Saml. Moore, Kettera, and James Taylor, excluding 2,000 acres of prior claims.

p. 203

No date, WM. TAYLOR, 3,500 acres, 1795, on two treasury warrants, 1794, adjoining Pollard's 75,000 acres, excluding 225 acres prior claims, on headwaters of Clinch River and headwaters of Wolf Creek,

p. 204

November 24, 1794, DAVID LUSK, 100 acres, 1794, on treasury warrant, 1794, on Clear Fork of Wolf Creek, between John Compton and Wm. Kid [Kidd] and John Taylor.

p. 205

May 10, 1795, JOSEPH BEAN, 2,100 acres, on treasury warrant, not dated, on east side of New River, corner to Thos. Fauster [Foster].

p. 206

April 10, 1795, NATHANIEL FRISBIE, 28,400 acres, on two undated treasury warrants, on Middle and South Fork of Holston, corner to Straw, Bustard, Williams, and John Johnson, excluding 3,689 acres the property of Col. Arthur Campbell, and others.

pp. 209-210

May 12, 1795, MOSES AUSTIN, 3,500 acres, on south side of Reed Creek adjoining John Baker, beginning on a line of James McGavock, also mentions Pierce, and David Sloan and opposite Crockett's Ironworks, corner to Beeson, excluding 1,500 acres the property of James Newell, Richard Beeson, John Hogg [Hoge], John Baker, and Wm. Pierce.

pp. 211-213

August 31, 1795, MOSES AUSTIN, 29,000 acres, on treasury warrant assigned by James Newell, on Reed Creek, corner to James Campbell and H. Chaney, John Davis, Peter Bishop, McGavock, Michael Lease, Joseph Fanning, George Buckalew, Andrew Danner, and excluding 7,000 acres property of Thos. Madison and Co.

pp. 214-215

September 7, 1795, HENRY BANKS, 30,000 acres, 1795, on certificate from the Surveyor of Kanhawa County, on three treasury warrants; this land adjoined Pollard's 55,000 acres, and 13,000 acres of prior claims were excluded, on Great Sandy and Guyandott,

p. 216

September 7, 1795, ANDREW STEEL, 100 acres, no date of entry, on part of a treasury warrant, 1783, on Robinsons Tract Fork of Peek [Peak] Creek, crossing Peppers Ferry Road.

p. 217

October 25, 1795, JAMES CROW, 100 acres, no date of entry, on part of a treasury warrant, 1781, on Middle Fork of Holston, adjoining Edw. Crow and Robt. Crow.

p. 218

February 3, 1794, JOHN McMULLIN, 50 acres, no date of entry, on part of a treasury warrant, 1781, on Middle Fork of Holston, adjoining James and Edward Crow.

p. 219

October 5, 1793, MICHAEL JOHNSTON, 50 acres, no date of entry, on part of a treasury warrant, 1781, on Middle Fork of Holston, adjoining David Johnston's.

p. 220

October 6, 1792, MARSHALL DUNCAN, 400 acres, no date of entry, on Commissioner's certificate, 1782, on south side of Elk Creek.

p. 221

September 5, 1794, JOHN CRAIG, JNR., 250 acres, 1792, treasury warrant, 1782, assigned by James Newell, land on New River, corner to Wm. Thomas.

p. 222

September 1, 1795, NICHOLAS SNIDER, 435 acres, no date of entry, on treasury warrants, not dated, on Middle Fork of Holston, adjoining Shelton Bottom survey, corner to Leggett's and Paul Copebarger.

p. 223

March 14, 1795, ADAM SEEK, 52 acres, no date of entry, treasury warrant, 1781, on Reed Creek joining John Sheaver [Shaver], and his old survey.

p. 224

July 18, 1795, GEORGE MAY, 157 acres, no date of entry, on two treasury warrants,

1782, on Pine Run, adjoining Randle Fugate and H. Honaker.

p. 225

July 1, 1793, JAMES BREEDEN, 78 acres entry in the Montgomery Surveyor's office, part of a treasury warrant, 1782, assignee of Thomas Feiling, assignee of William Ross, on Little Reed Island Creek, corner to Joseph Fugate, Thos. Whitlock, and his own.

September 15, 1795, PETER HELVEY, 5 acres, no date of entry, on part of a treasury warrant, not dated, assignee of Wm. Davis, on Walkers Creek, corner to Wm. Davis.

p. 226

June 24, 1794, ROBERT WHITLEY, assignee of Robert Adams, on treasury warrant, 1781, on North Fork of Clinch River adjoining his own lands.

March 14, 1794, JOSIAH WYNNE, 27 acres, entry not dated, on treasury warrant, 1781, on Clinch River, corner to Zachariah Stanly and Waggoner.

p. 227

October 6, 1795, PHILIP ARMBRISTER, 824 acres on Reed Creek based on entry, not dated, for 200 acres, on part of a treasury warrant, 1782, and an entry, not dated, 124 acres, part of a treasury warrant, 1782, and an entry, not dated, for 324 acres, being surplus of part of a tract granted to James Willey, 1753, who conveyed 500 acres to Armbrister.

p. 228

November 8, 1794, WILLIAM LASLEY, 212 acres, 1794, on treasury warrant, 1783, assigned by Robert Adams, land on Bluestone, at the head of Little Valley.

p. 228, ROBERT LASLEY, 220 acres, on treasury warrants, 1782, 1783, on Bluestone called three branches, joining Little Valley.

p. 229

Apr. 19, 1793, JOHN BENNER, 40 acres, not dated, treasury warrant, 1781, assignee of Wm. Long, land on Elk Creek.

no date, ANTHONY ROSEN [probably intended for ROSENBAUM], 456 acres not dated, on a treasury warrant, not dated south side of Cripple Creek, corner to Wm. Saunders.

p. 230

February 16, 1792, JOSHUA HANKS, 100 acres, not dated, on treasury warrant, not dated, assignee of James Newell, on Crooked Creek.

February 18, 1793, JOHN JINKINS, 100 acres, 1794, treasury warrant, not dated, on both sides of Priors Branch.

p. 231

October 20, 1795, DAVID BOOTH, 20,000 acres, 1795, treasury warrant, 1795, on Guyandott River beginning at the mouth of Gilberts Creek, corner to Nicholas' 500,000.

p. 232

October 28, 1795, DAVID BOOTH, 40,000 acres, 1795, based on treasury warrant, 1795, on Guyandott and Cole rivers, adjoining Nicholas 500,000.

p. 233

September 15, 1795, NANCY, BARBARY, POLLY, and ELIZABETH THOMPSON, heirs of SAML. THOMPSON, deceased, THOMAS MADISON, ELIZABETH MADISON, MICHAEL WALTERS, and WM. BARTLETT, 2,900 acres, on treasury warrant, 1783, assigned by John Hawkins, on south side of Reed Creek, corner to David Ross, Toncray's survey, including 720 acres the property of Wm. Ingledove, Helvey's, and Jno. McNutt.

p. 234

September 18, 1795, THOMAS MADISON and COMPANY, 586 acres, on treasury warrant, 1781, assigned by John Preston, on Cripple Creek, beginning on Davis Branch.

July 30, 1795, THOMAS MADISON and COMPANY, 750 acres, entry on treasury warrant assigned by James Hawkins and others, on New River, corner to Geo. Ewing and Phil Gains.

p. 235

October 28, 1795, THOS. MADISON and COMPANY, 164 acres, based on an entry on treasury warrant, assigned by James Hawkins, on Reed Creek, corner to Grub.

October 28, 1795, WM. DAVIS, 100 acres, entry 1786 in the name of Henry Clements, assigned to Henry Pickle, who assigned to Davis, on Middle Fork of Holston, corner Henry Pickle, formerly Joseph Davis.

p. 236

October 28, 1795, HENRY PICKLE, 250 acres, on entry on three treasury warrants, 1780, 1781, 1782, on Middle Fork of Holston, adjoining Wm. Davis and line of Thomas Crow, 84 acres of prior claims excluded, leaving 250 acres.

p. 237

October 9, 1795, HENRY DAVIS, 200 acres, 1794, on treasury warrant, 1782, no location given.

February 6, 1795, PETER SPANGLER, 150 acres, 1794, on treasury warrant, 1780, as assignee of Christley Kettering on Cripple Creek, corner to Cook.

p. 238

September 14, 1795, THOS. MADISON & CO., 1,100 acres, entry 1786, on treasury warrant, 1781, and four treasury warrants assigned by Jno. and Francis Preston, on Reed Creek, corner to Grubb and including 220 acres, the property of Henry Newman.

October 15, 1795, THOS. MADISON & CO., 150 acres, 1786, on treasury warrant, assignee of John Preston, on New River adjoining Evan Williams.

p. 239

October 27, 1795, THOS. MADISON & CO., 2,000 acres, 1786, in Montgomery County, on treasury warrant, 1783, assignee of Henry Banks, on Cripple Creek, adjoining William Rogers' survey, corner to Dean's and Thos. Majors, including 500 acres the property of James McGavock.

May 15, 1795, THOS. MADISON & CO., 600 acres entry in Montgomery County as assignee of James Newell, treasury warrant, 1783, as assignee of Robt. Love, on Reed Creek, corner to Joseph Eaton and McGavock.

p. 240

October 15, 1795, THOS. MADISON & CO., 980 acres, 1786, on treasury warrant, as assignee of James Hawkins, on west side of New River, adjoining William Herbert's survey, Carter, Baker, Stotts, and Evan Williams, including 380 acres, the property of Thomas [Madison].

p. 241

September 15, 1795, THOS. MADISON & CO., 2,750 acres, 1786, on treasury warrant, 1783, on south side of Reed Creek, adjoining Colo. Stephens, including 250 acres of James Finley's and others.

February 16, 1793, SAML. HOWELL, 112 acres, entry on treasury warrant, 1783, assignee of Thos. Muse, on Chestnut and Crooked Creek.

February 16, 1793, SAML. HOWELL, 175 acres, entry on treasury warrant, 1783, assignee of Thos. Muse, on Chestnut and Crooked Creek.

February 10, 1793, WM. SEXTON, 130 acres, 1783, Montgomery County, on treasury warrant, 1782, on Rock Creek, adjoining Edward Williams.

October 20, 1795, GEO. WAMPLER, 100 acres, 1783, Montgomery County, on treasury warrant, 1782, on South Fork of Reed Creek adjoining Ratcliffs Marsh, Baugh's, Knave's [Neff's], and Peter Etter.

May 17, 1794, ADAM WEATHERHOLT, 50 acres, 1791, on preemption warrant, 1782, assigned by James Newell, assignee of Wm. Herbert, on Cove Creek, a branch of Reed Creek, adjoining Robert Breckenridge.

March 14, 1795, JOHN SHEAVER [SHAFFER], 309 acres, entry on treasury warrant, not dated, on Reed Creek, adjoining Daniel Sponsler, Joseph Kent, Airhart Simmerman, Anthony Toncrey, Adam Seek, and his own land.

October 31, 1795, JOHN DAVIS, 24 1/2 acres, entry in Montgomery County, 1783, on treasury warrant, 1782, on Reed Creek adjoining Armbrister (formerly Wyley) and Simmerman.

November 2, 1795, JOSEPH BAKER, 80 acres, entry on treasury warrant, 1782, in Cove on Reed Creek, corner to his patent land.

May 19, 1795, WM. PATTERSON, 50 acres, entry on treasury warrant, 1782, in Cove on Peek [Peak] Creek.

September 15, 1795, ADAM WEATHERHOLT, 100 acres, entry on preemption warrant, 1782, on Lick Run, a branch of Cove Creek at the foot of Lick Mountain.

July 16, 1795, LEONARD STRAW, 1,688 acres, entry on four treasury warrants, 1782, corner John Phillippe, Michael Wampler, and Buchanan.

June 7, 1795, JAMES BROOKES, 45 acres, on treasury warrant, not dated, in Rich Valley on North Fork of Holston, adjoining Thos. Dunn.

November 17, 1795, NICH. CLINE, 100 acres, entry made on treasury warrant, 1782, in the name of Henry Umbarger, 1792, assigned to Cline, adjoining Philip Nipp [Knipp] and Etter.

November 12, 1795, JOSEPH BURR, 2,500 acres, entry on treasury warrant, 1782, assignee of James Newell, on both sides of Cripple Creek, corner to George Ewing, and Gleaves, including 300 acres of William Gleaves.

November 13, 1795, THOS. MADISON & CO., 814 acres, entry 1786, in Montgomery County, assignee of Francis Preston, assignee of John Preston, on treasury warrant, not dated, on Tates Run, corner to Kincer.

November 12, 1795, THOS. MADISON & CO., 400 acres, entry on treasury warrant, 1783, assignee of Henry Banks, Cripple Creek, corner to Fanning.

November 12, 1795, THOS. MADISON & CO., 2,000 acres, 1786, in Montgomery County, assignee of John Preston, on Reed Creek.

November 14, 1795, THOS. MADISON & CO., 230 acres, entry in Montgomery County, on treasury warrant, assignee of Jno. and Francis Preston, assignee of James Newell, assignee of James McCorkle, on Lead Mine Mill Creek, corner to Richard Muse, Thomas Madison, and McGavock.

February 18, 1793, WM. STEWART, 45 acres on treasury warrant, 1782, assigned by James Newell, on east side of New River and both sides of Poors Branch.

October 1, 1793, WILLIAM HERBERT, legatee of William Herbert, deceased, 1,000 acres, entry on preemption warrant, 1782, east side of New River, corner to Foster and Ross.

November 4, 1795, JAMES NEWELL, 1,000 acres, entry in Montgomery County on treasury warrant, 1782, assignee of George Thompson, on Mine Mill Creek, corner to Jas. McGavock, and Wm. Rogers.

March 27, 1794, ABSALOM STAFFORD, assignee of John Smith, 300 acres entry in Montgomery County, 1784, on treasury warrant, 1783, on the dividing waters between the Clinch and Wolf Creek.

November 28, 1795, JOHN THOMPSON SAYERS, 465 acres, entries made 1781, 1782, on Pine Run, corner to his patent land.

February 18, 1793, HUGH MONTGOMERY, 200 acres, entry on treasury warrant, assigned by Saml. Meredith, on Crooked Creek, branch of New River.

February 17, 1793, WILLIAM HERBERT, legatee of William Herbert, deceased, 400 acres, entry in Montgomery County on Commissioner's certificate, 1782, on Reed Island Creek, known as "Rays Cabbin."

September 3, 1795, WILLIAM GLAVES [GLEAVES], 150 acres, entry on treasury warrant, 1782, assignee of James Newell, on Cripple Creek, joining Randolph Rutherford and M. Worly.

June 7, 1795, JACOB BEESON, 100 acres, entry on treasury warrant, 1782, Rich Valley, North Fork of Holston.

June 8, 1795, JOHN COX, 146 acres, entry on treasury warrant, 1784, in Rich Valley on North Fork of Holston, adjoining Henry Beeson, William Cox, and James Wilson.

November 21, 1795, WILLIAM DAVIS, 119 1/2 acres, 1795, on treasury warrant, 1795, on Mud Fork of Bluestone.

December 23, 1795, GORDON CLOYD, 7,800 acres, 1795, on treasury warrant, 1795, issued to Austin Nicholas and he to Cloyd, on east side of Gyandott, branch of the Ohio, beginning at Peter Huff's Creek.

October 8, 1795, CHARLES CALFEE, 360 acres, entry on treasury warrant, 1782, on New River, adjoining Wm. Hurst's patent land.

October 8, 1795, HENRY DAVIS, SER. [SR.], 160 acres, entry on treasury warrant, not dated, on New River, corner to 248 acres surveyed for Joseph Gray.

October 8, 1795, THOS. WHITLOCK, 140 acres, 1793, on treasury warrant, not dated, on both sides of Little Reed Island Creek, adjoining Larrance Stephens' corner and corner to patent land of Whitlock.

p. 263

October 7, 1795, HALBERT ALISON (ALLISON), 100 acres, on treasury warrant, 1782, on Pine Run, branch of New River.

January 15, 1795, JACOB WASSHAM, 100 acres, on treasury warrant, 1790, on Reed Creek, Brushy Mountain, corner to Jacob Toblas [Tobler's] patent land.

p. 264

February 28, 1795, JAMES REED, 2,000 acres, 1782, on four treasury warrants on south side of New River, corner to John Plunk and Gedian [Gideon] Moss (annulled and recorded again elsewhere due to error).

pp. 265-266

February 7, 1795, JESSE EVANS, 1,000 acres, 1796, on treasury warrant, assigned by Alexander Smyth, on Cove Creek, corner to Walter Crockett and Jesse Evans; it is understood that the plat for which above is certificate contains 1,300 acres, 300 acres of which is excluded prior claims: 200 acres for Walter Beaty adjoining Jesse Evans at the north side; 40 acres for Phillip Reeder; 10 acres for Stephen Reeder; 50 acres of other prior claims.

pp. 267-268

November 6, 1795, DAVID PATTERSON and DUNCAN McLAUGLAN, 12,000 acres, on Clinch, Sandy, and Bluestone rivers, adjoining John W. Kettera, north of the path that leads from Thomas Pickens to John Tollett's plantation and near the road that leads to Comfort Bruster's, thence to James Cecil's, to near the line dividing Wythe and Russell counties, and adjoining a survey of 150,000 acres made for David Patterson, to exclude 2,750 acres for prior claims.

pp. 269-270

February 6, 1796, DOCTOR THOMAS RUSTIN, 31,000 acres, on Holston River, based on an entry on treasury warrant, 1795, assigned by Richard C. Pollard, and an entry on treasury warrant, 1795, and treasury warrant, 1783, assigned to McLaughlan by John Powell and another entry 1782, assigned by Thomas Naper; this survey includes 11,000 acres prior claims for John Griffith, Jas. Williams, Peter Razor, James Scott, Henry Vice, David and Charles Buster, George Christly, Henry Vaught, John Newland, and others (withdrawn, error; *see* page 275). .

p. 270

February 15, 1796, JOHN TOLLET, 200 acres, 1794, treasury warrant, 1784, on Clynch [Clinch] River, corner to his patent land.

p. 271

March 7, 1796, JOHN TOLLET, 85 acres, entry on treasury warrants, 1781, 1784, on Clynch [Clinch] River, adjoining his patent land.

November 25, 1795, WILLIAM GEORGE, 100 acres, on an entry 1795 on treasury warrant, 1780, on Clynch [Clinch] River, corner 40 acres his patent land.

p. 272

October 22, 1795, STOPHLE [CHRISTOPHER] ZIMMERMAN [SIMMERMAN], 1 acre, 6 poles, 1790, made in the name of Jesse Evans on treasury warrant, 1790, on Cedar Run, branch of Reed Creek, adjoining his own and Town of Evansham; also 3/4 acres 15 poles on entry 1790 in name of Jesse Evans on treasury warrant on Cedar Run, adjoining the town.

p. 273

October 16, 1792, JOHN ALDER, 50 acres, 1792, on treasury warrant, assigned by Esau Bradley, on North Fork of Holston.

p. 274 is blank

p. 275 (a)

February 6, 1796, DOCTOR THOMAS RUSTIN, 20,000 acres, on entry on treasury warrant, 1795, assigned by Richard C. Pollard, on Holston River and Cripple Creek, with 11,000 acres of prior claims excluded: Jinkin Williams, John Griffeth, Joseph Williams, Peter Razor, James Scott, Henry Vice, Charles and David Bustard, George Christley, Henry Vaught, John Newland, and John Lastly.

p. 275 (b)

October 16, 1796, WM. McGUIRE, 92 acres, 1794, on treasury warrant, 1782, on Bluestone River, land known as Big Bottom.

p. 276

December 11, 1792, ESAU WORRELL, 100 acres, not dated, on part of a treasury warrant, 1781, on Island Creek, branch of Big Reed Island.

October 11, 1795, HENRY KIMLER, 100 acres, 1794, on treasury warrant, assigned by James McDowell, 1783, on Millers Creek corner Christly Cyphers and Long, on south side of Peppers Ferry Road.

p. 277

May 19, 1796, ADAM WALKER, 10 acres, not dated, on part of a treasury warrant, assigned by Robert Adams, 1782, on Reed Creek adjoining his patent land.

p. 278

November 19, 1795, LOE [LOW] BROWN, 388 acres, 1794, on part of a treasury warrant, 1783, on Bluestone River, corner to John Davidson.

p. 279

June 21, 1796, JOHN GREENUP, 79 acres, 1796, on part of a treasury warrant, 1783 on Clinch River, corner to his patent land.

p. 280

November 7, 1795, NATHANIEL FRISBIE, 100 acres, not dated, on part of a treasury warrant, 1782, assigned by David Pearce, on New River, corner to William Bell.

June 30, 1796, DOCTOR THOMAS RUSTIN, 20,000 acres not dated, on part of a treasury warrant, 1795, assigned by Richard C. Pollard, on Dry Fork, waters of New River.

p. 281

May 20, 1796, JACOB DOBLER, 125 acres, 1795, treasury warrant, 1782, on Reed Creek, adjoining Martin Kimberlin's, corner to his own, corner to Baugh and Sneabley [Snaveley].

p. 282

March 10, 1796, DANIEL ETTER, 250 acres, on two entries: (1) 50 acres in name of Jesse Evans, on treasury warrant, 1790; (2) 200 acres granted 1785, on Reed Creek, corner George Hutsell and George Kegley,

No date, EZEKIEL MORGAN, 128 acres, on entry on treasury warrant, 1781, on New River, corner to Richd. Ellis.

p. 283

February 13, 1796, ANDREW BOYD, 50 acres, 1794, on treasury warrant, 1788, on headwaters of Pine Run, branch of New River, adjoining Henry Honaker and crossing several spurs of Drapers Mountain.

August 26, 1796, ANDREW BOYD, 40 acres, 1794, on treasury warrant, 1788, on Pine Run, corner to Isaac Brown.

p. 284

February 6, 1796, ADOLPH FLORA, 88 acres, on entry on treasury warrant, 1794, on headwaters of Macks Run, branch of New River, adjoining William Foster, Flora, and Adam Runner.

p. 285

March 30, 1796, ISAAC DAYLEY, 50 acres, 1796, on treasury warrant, 1794, assigned by Hiram Craig, on Clinch River in Baptist Valley, corner Dayley's and to top of the divide between Clinch River and Sandy Creek; also 65 acres on entry 1796, on treasury warrant, 1794, on Clinch in Baptist Valley, corner to land he now lives on.

p. 286

April 6, 1796, ALEXR. SAYERS, 40 acres, on entry on treasury warrant, 1794, on Clinch River, corner to patent land of William Cecil and John Greenup, near the "Sault petre cave."

pp. 286-287

JAMES and ANDREW CROCKETT as tenants in common, 350 acres, 1796, on treasury warrant 1794, on Reed Creek, corner to Andrew Crockett, John Creager, and William Rogers.

p. 288

August 24, 1796, THOMAS CARTER, 100 acres, not dated, on part of a treasury warrant, 1783, on headwaters of Pine Run on south side of Drapers Mountain.

February 5, 1796, NICHOLAS HONAKER, 100 acres, not dated, on part of treasury warrants, 1783, 1794, on headwaters of Pine Run, on south side of Drapers Mountain.

p. 289

September 12, 1796, JOHN JENKINS, 75 acres, not dated, on part of a land office warrant, 1782, assigned by Nathaniel Frisbie, assignee of David Reese, on New River, adjoining his own land.

October 30, 1791, THOS. NASH, 83 acres, 1791, on part of a treasury warrant, 1783, assignee of William Bouren, in forks of Fox Creek.

pp. 290

February 28, 1795, JAMES REED, 2,000 acres, not dated, on four treasury warrants, 1782, on south side of New River, adjoining John Plink and Gedion [Gideon] Moss.

pp. 290-291

August 30, 1796, JOHN T. SAYERS, 64 acres, not dated, on part of a treasury warrant, 1783, on Pine Run adjoining Sayers, James Simpson, and Henry Honaker.

p. 291

February 16, 1796, HENRY HONAKER, 75 acres, not dated, on part of a treasury warrant, 1783, on south side of New River adjoining John Fugate, Ezekiel Morgan, and Richard Ellis.

p. 292

October 11, 1796, RICHARD ELLIS, 160 acres, not dated, on part of a treasury warrant, 1782, assigned by David Harrell, heir to John Harrell, on east side of New River.

April 22, 1796, JOHN POOL, 100 acres, not dated, on part of a treasury warrant, 1782, assigned by James Newell, on Elk Creek adjoining Richard Coles.

p. 293

November 7, 1795, JOSEPH CROCKETT, 26 acres, not dated, on part of a treasury warrant, 1790, assigned by Robert Adams, assignee of Samuel McCraw, on

Reed Creek, branch of New River, corner to Robert Crockett, Zimmerman, David Ross, and by the wagon road on Bell's Hill corner to Ross.

February 16, 1792, ANTHONY HOGGETT, 50 acres entered in Montgomery County 1788, on treasury warrant, 1783, assigned by James Newell, on Chestnut Creek adjoining Amos Williams and Johnson.

p. 294

October 10, 1792, JOHN DODSON, 68 acres, not dated, on part of a treasury warrant, 1783, assignee of James Newell, on Reed Island Creek.

October 20, 1795, JOSEPH FANNIN, 100 acres, not dated, on part of a treasury warrant 1782, assigned by James Newell, on Cripple Creek.

p. 295

October 15, 1795, SHERROD JAMES, not dated, 50 acres, on part of a treasury warrant 1782, assigned by James Newell, headwaters of South Fork of Holston, corner to Wisman.

October 25, 1793, MICHAEL BRANSTRATER [BRANDSTETTER], 50 acres, not dated, on part of a treasury warrant 1782, assignee of William Neel, Cripple Creek, corner to his own and Peter Creager.

p. 296

February 16, 1796, JOHN BAKER, legatee of Joseph Baker, deceased, 176 acres, entered on treasury warrant, 1782, on head of Little Pine Run, on south side of Drapers Mountain, adjoining Andrew Boyd, Henry Honaker, and George Draper.

October 29, 1796, ABRAHAM TRIGG, 400 acres, 1783, on Commissioner's certificate, on Hunting Camp Creek, waters of Wolf Creek, branch of New River.

p. 297

April 20, 1800, DANIEL HELT, 100 acres, 1796, on treasury warrant, 1782, on Reed Creek, corner to Michael Nave [Neff], Wampler, Cowden, and Cormany.

p. 298

No date, JOHN PEERY, 51 1/2 acres, 1795, on treasury warrant, on Clynch [Clinch] River.

December 4, 1795, WILLIAM HAYS, 164 acres, on two entries, 1793, no location given.

p. 299

December 14, 1795, JAMES WILSON, 100 acres, 1790, on treasury warrant, 1790, on North Fork of Holston.

p. 300

December 14, 1795, THOS. WITTEN, 90 acres, treasury warrant, not dated, on Clynch [Clinch] River.

p. 301

November 5, 1796, JAMES DAVIS, 660 acres entered 1791, 1792, 1796, on two treasury warrants, 1781, on North Fork of Holston.

pp. 302-303

November 1, 1796, STOPHEL [CHRISTOPHER] PHILIPPY, 89 acres, entered: (1) 50 acres in Montgomery in the name of Joseph Patterson on treasury warrant, 1780; (2) and 39 acres entered 1796 on treasury warrant, 1783, assigned by John Phillippy, assignee of Robert Adams, on Middle Fork of Holston adjoining Patterson's patent land; and separate survey for 42 acres entered 1790 on treasury warrant, 1790, on Middle Fork of Holston.

p. 303

December 5, 1795, JOHN WALKER, 148 acres, 1782, on Commissioner's certificate,

1782, on Clynch [Clinch] River, a line crossing Plumb Creek.

p. 304

No date, WM. DAVIS, 100 acres, entered on part of a treasury warrant, 1795, on Middle Fork of Holston adjoining Fristoe and Buchanan.

No date, WM. ROSS, 200 acres, entered on treasury warrant, 1782, assigned by James Newell and another by Robt. Adams, assignee of James Newell, adjoining his own and Wm. Carter.

p. 305

No date, JAMES WILSON, 350 acres, entered on treasury warrant, 1783, on Middle Fork of Holston, adjoining Adkins.

p. 306

September 10, 1795, JOHN CRAIG, 200 acres, on Commissioner's certificate, not dated, on part of above certificate and known by the name of Peirce's Ferry, on New River adjoining his former survey corner to 600 acres.

p. 307

November 15, 1796, JOHN D. BLANCHARD, 2,930 acres, 1795, on treasury warrant, 1782, assignee of James Newell, on Reed Creek, corner to 75,000 acres surveyed for Robt. Pollard and Henry Kimler.

p. 308

November 25 (26?), 1796, JOHN D. BLANCHARD, 10,000 acres entered on part of a treasury warrant, 1795, on Reed and Peak creeks, adjoining Andrew Boyd, James Crockett, and Robt. Grymes.

p. 309

November 14, 1796, JOHN MILLER, 465 acres, on treasury warrant, 1782, on Reed Creek, corner to patent land near Cove Road.

p. 310

August 18, 1796, JAMES McGAVOCK, 1,000 acres, 1794, on certificate from surveyor of Grayson County, 1783, on Reed Creek, corner to Macks Meadows, Philip Umble's [Humble's], Ramsey, John Montgomery, and Henry Clements.

p. 311

February 28, 1794, PETER BISHOP and JOHN BISHOP, 300 acres, 1791, on treasury warrant, 1781, assigned by Wm. King, assignee of Philip Pendleton, on Reed Creek, corner to John Montgomery and Philip Fry.

p. 312

March 14, 1794, JAMES PEERY, 58 acres, on treasury warrant, 1783, assigned by John Evans, on Buffalo Lick on branch of Clynch [Clinch], corner to John Peery.

p. 313

November 24, 1796, MOSES AUSTIN, 24,099 acres, not dated, on two entries on treasury warrant, 1795, on Clinch River, corner to Robert Pollard, Russell's line and corner to survey for Peterson and McGlaughlin.

p. 314

August 15, 1794, MICHL. BROWN, 300 acres, entered in name of Williams (or William _____ ?) and assigned to Brown on treasury warrants, 1782, on Reed Creek, adjoining Leedy and Stople [Christopher] Brown.

p. 315

April 22, 1797, MOSES AUSTIN, 7,000 acres, not dated, on treasury warrants, 1783, assigned by George Pickett, on headwaters of Sandy River.

October 17, 1792, PETER PERCEFIELD, 100 acres, entered in Montgomery 1787, on treasury warrant, 1782, in name of Barney Duffey, who assigned to Jas. McConnel and Joshua Antrim, who assigned to Henry Beason, who assigned to Percefield, on headwaters of North Fork of Holston in Rich Valley.

p. 316

February 10, 1793, NATHANIEL POPE, 20 acres, not dated, on part of a treasury warrant, not dated, assignee of Mathias Harmon, on Greasy Creek, a branch of Little Reed Island, corner to his old survey.

January 29, 1796, JAMES CROCKETT, 150 acres, 1793, on treasury warrant, 1782, on both sides of Reed Creek, beginning nearly opposite Crockett's Ironworks.

June 17, 1797, ANDREW CROCKETT, 150 acres: (1) 100 acres, entered in 1786, on two treasury warrants, 1782, and assigned by Jacob Fouts, assignee of John Montgomery; (2) 50 acres, entered 1797 on treasury warrant, 1782, assigned by James Crockett, assignee of John T. Sayers, assignee of Andrew Crockett, on Reed Creek adjoining 350 acres surveyed for Andrew and James Crockett.

p. 317

February 26, 1796, JAMES CROCKETT, 150 acres, assignee of John Baker, legatee of Joseph Baker, dec'd, entered in Montgomery County on treasury warrant, 1782, on Reed Creek, corner to Chas. Baker, Joseph Stevans, Chas. Carter, and John Baker.

March 7, 1797, PATRICK JOHNSON, 100 acres, on treasury warrant, not dated, on Stoney Fork, branch of Reed Creek including the mouth of the east fork, near the foot of Walkers Mountain.

p. 318

March 14, 1797, DANIEL JUSTICE, 50 acres, 1792, on part of a treasury warrant, assignee of Wm. Hall, 1782, on Walkers Big Creek, corner to Justice.

March 30, 1797, JAMES CECILL, 24 acres, 1797, on part of a treasury warrant, 1783, on Clinch River in Baptist Valley, corner to William Cecil.

March 28, 1797, JOHN McENTOSH, 80 acres, on treasury warrant, 1783, on Clinch River.

p. 319

March 29, 1797, THOMAS GREENUP, 100 acres, not dated, treasury warrant, 1783, on Clinch River, corner to John Greenup and Wm. Cecil.

p. 320

February 8, 1796, BENJAMON THURMON, 400 acres, not dated, on Commissioner's certificate, not dated, on Sandy River.

p. 321

February 23, 1797, WILLIAM LEHEW, 15 acres, not dated, entered on treasury warrant, 1794, on both sides Reed Creek corner to Wm. Pearce, said Lehew, James Crockett, and Charles Baker.

pp. 321-322

September 12, 1797, JEREMIAH WHITTON, 138 acres, 1796, on treasury warrant, 1783, on head of Clinch on north side of Pain Lick Mountain (void, see p. 401).

p. 323

August 29, 1797, JAMES HERBISON, 175 acres, 1797, on certificate from principal Surveyor of Montgomery County 1795, assigned by Gordon Cloyd and Alexander Smyth, on Robinson Tract Fork of Peak Creek, corner to land where Harbison [Herbison] now lives, near the land of Moses Chambers and Henry Patton.

p. 324

May 16, 1794, GEORGE MARTAIN [MARTIN], 150 acres, 1787, in Montgomery

County on treasury warrant, 1782, assignee of James Newell, on South Fork of Holston.

pp. 325-326

May 29, 1797, JOHN GRAYSON, 19 acres, 1797, on treasury warrant, 1794, assigned by Robt. Adams, assignee of Mathias Harman and Lovis Harman, on Walkers Creek; also 214 acres, entered 1796 on treasury warrant, 1781, assignee of Robt. Adams, assignee of James Newell and another treasury warrant, 1795, on Walkers Creek; also 100 acres, entered 1797 on head of Walkers Creek and surveyed on June 17, 1797.

p. 326

No date, WILLIAM FINLY [FINLEY], 150 aces, 1790, on treasury warrant, 1790, assigned by Robt. Adams, assignee of Saml. McCraw, on Cove Creek, branch of Reed Creek.

p. 327

May 5 (?), 1800, DANIEL PIERCE, 279 acres, 1796, on treasury warrant, assigned by Walter Crockett, attorney for James Clerk, 1782, on Cripple Creek, corner to George Vaut [Vaught], John Newland, and Andrew Irvin.

p. 328

September 25, 1797, ROBT. LOVE, 388 acres, entered in Montgomery County, 1782, on two treasury warrants, 1782, assigned by Wm. Love and George Ewing, on north side of Reed Creek adjoining Joseph Crockett.

p. 329

September 22, 1795, JAMES NEWELL, 140 acres, not dated, on treasury warrant, not dated, assigned by Jas. Laps (?) on Cripple Creek, corner to Wiley and Gleaves (plat says 140 acres, text says 200 acres).

September 10, 1796, RICHARD WILLIAMS, 135 acres, not dated, on part of a treasury warrant, not dated, assigned by Jas. Newell, on South Fork of Holston.

September 22, 1794, GEORGE WAMPLER, 140 acres, not dated, on part of a treasury warrant, 1782, assignee of Michl. Staffey [Steffey], on Tates Run, corner to his patent land.

p. 330

September 16, 1795, RANDOLPH RUTHERFORD, 35 acres, not dated, on part of a treasury warrant, 1782, assigned by James Newell, on north side of Cripple Creek.

May 12, 1797, JOHN SMITH, 15 acres, 1796, on treasury warrant, 1783, on South Fork of Holston.

p. 331

October 28, 1798, FREDRICK SLIMP [SLEMP], 350 acres, not dated, entered in Montgomery, 1783 on Commissioner's certificate, not dated, on South Fork of Holston, corner to Peter Razer [Razor].

October 18, 1798, FRANCIS KINCANNON, 95 acres, not dated, on Commissioner's certificate, 1781, on head of South Fork of Holston.

p. 332

August 13, 1795, JOHN CRAIG, SENIOR, 500 acres, not dated, on part of a treasury warrant, 1783, assigned by John Preston, assignee of Michael Ryan, on Reed Creek, corner to Wm. Rogers.

September 19, 1797, DANIEL COLLINS, 280 acres, 1797, on treasury warrant from Montgomery certified by Gordon Cloyd and Alexander Smyth, lodged in Wythe County Surveyor's Office, 1795, on New River adjoining Jacob Miller.

p. 333

no date, ADAM HINES, 250 acres, entered on two treasury warrants 1783, assigned by Hiram Craig, assignee of John Penner, assignee of Robert Adams, assignee of John Taylor, on Little Pine Run adjoining Wm. Foster, Andrew Boyd, and Adam Runner.

September 15, 1797, HALBERT ALLISON, 21 acres, 1784, on treasury warrant, 1782, on Pine Run.

p. 334

No date, URIAH STONE, 163 acres, entered on Commissioner's certificate, not dated, in Wrights Valley on Bluestone.

p. 335

September 26, 1797, HIRAM CRAIG, 100 acres entered 1797 on treasury warrant, 1794, assigned by Andrew Crockett, assignee of John Lowther, on both sides Peak Creek.

p. 336

No date, DAVID SLOAN, 290 acres, entered on treasury warrant 1781 (no description).

p. 337

June 3, 1797, HIRAM CRAIG, 400 acres, 1795, on treasury warrant, assigned by Andrew Crockett, assignee of John Louther, 1794, on New River corner to George Carter and Meredith Raines.

p. 338

February 23, 1794, ROBT. STEEL, 45 acres, 1792, on treasury warrant, 1782, on Walkers Creek; 50 acres, entered 1791 on treasury warrant, 1781, on Walkers Creek.

p. 339

October 3, 1797, ROBT. COWDEN, 80 acres, not dated, on commissioner's certificate for 300 acres, 1782, 220 acres of which was surveyed before, on South Fork of Reed Creek, adjoining Phillippi and his former survey.

p. 340

February 24, 1795, HENRY DAVIS, 200 acres, 1794, on part of a treasury warrant, assigned by James Newell, assigned by James Lapsley, 1782, on Big Reed Island, corner to James Breeden.

p. 341

February 23, 1795, WILLIAM CALFEE, 90 acres, not dated, entered in the name of Henry Davis and assigned to Calfee, on treasury warrant, 1782, and assigned to Davis by James Newell, assignee of James Lapsley, corner to his patent line [New River].

p. 342

March 28, 1794, JOHN GRILLS, 180 acres, entered in Montgomery County, 1783, on part of a treasury warrant in the name of John Grills and Joseph Cloyd, and assigned by Cloyd to Grills, in Burks Garden on East End Branch, corner to Hall.

p. 343

February 28, 1797, JAMES CROCKETT, 300 acres, 1797, on treasury warrant, 1783, assigned by Jas. Newell, assignee of George Pruett, on Reed Creek adjoining William Pierce, John Baker, and Moses Austin.

May 20, 1795, WALTER CROCKETT, 50 acres, 1793, treasury warrant, 1781, in the Cove on Cove Creek beginning at the mouth of a branch adjoining his patent line and corner to Philip Reeder.

February 26, 1797, ELENOR THOMPSON, 50 acres, not dated, on part of a treasury warrant, 1782, on Reed Creek, adjoining Samuel Crockett and Joseph Baker.

October 4, 1793, JONAS FORTNEY, 40 acres, 1793, on part of a treasury warrant, 1781, on Middle Fork of Holston, adjoining Joseph Adkins.

June 5, 1795, JOHN BRYENS, 158 acres, not dated, treasury warrant, 1795, assigned by Wm. Neel, in Rich Valley on Holston.

June 5, 1795, NATHANIEL BRYANT, 100 acres, not dated, entered in the name of John Piercefield and transferred to Bryant on treasury warrant, 1782, in Rich Valley on North Fork of Holston.

September 16, 1797, JOHN COX, 350 acres, 1795, on treasury warrant, 1790, on Walkers Creek joining the old survey and Joseph Fletcher (void, *see* p. 399).

March 3, 1793, PHILIP HARKERADER [HARKRADER], 250 acres, 100 of which was entered in the name of George Kincer, the other in the name of Hannah Alder and assigned to Harkerader on treasury warrants, 1782, on head of Walkers Creek.

March 15, 1793, WILLIAM RICHARDSON, 200 acres, 1793, on treasury warrant, 1782, assigned by Wm. Neel, in Rich Valley on North Fork of Holston, corner to patent land.

March 23, 1797, MICHAEL KERMANY [CORMANY], 494 acres, entered in Montgmery, 1782, on treasury warrant, 1782 on Reed Creek corner of the Marsh tract, Cowden, Peter Etter, and Steffy.

December 16, 1797, MICHAEL KERMANY [CORMANY], 237 acres, on two entries, (1) 150 acres, 1793, in the name of Nicholas Snider on part of a treasury warrant, 1780, assigned to him by Nicholas Snider, and transferred to Kermany; (2) 87 acres entered in Kermany's name on part of a treasury warrant, 1782, treasury warrant, 1793, assigned to him by Arthur Campbell, on Middle Fork of Holston.

February 27, 1797, JAMES CROCKETT, 60 acres, 1782, 140 acres in the name of David Sloan, on treasury warrant, 1782, assigned by Frederick Edwards, assignee of James Newell; the 140 acres was formerly surveyed in the name of Sloan and the balance of 60 acres was transferred by Sloan to James McGavock and by him to Crockett, adjoining Michael Dougherty, dec'd, and including part of David Sloan's improvement, on Reed Creek.

February 21, 1793, WILLIAM DAVIDSON, 200 acres entered in Montgomery, 1790 on treasury warrant, 1782, assigned by John Preston, on Bluestone.

March 28, 1794, WILLIAM DAY, 100 acres, 1793, treasury warrant, 1792, assigned by Alexander Bain, assignee of Leonard Fleming, assignee of Joseph Robertson, Burks Garden.

December 30, 1797, GEORGE C. TAYLOR, 4 acres, 1795, in the name of Alex. Smyth, 1783, and transferred to Taylor, on a [treasury?] warrant 1783, from Grayson County Surveyor, 1794, on Cove Creek adjoining Peter Brinkly.

December 30, 1797, GEORGE C. TAYLOR, 12 acres, 1795, on warrant from principal surveyor of Grayson County issued 1783 in the name of Robert Breckenridge, and transferred to Alex. Smyth and he to Taylor, and lodged in this office in 1794, on Cove Creek, corner to Weatherholt.

December 20, 1797, JAMES NEWELL, 1,000 acres, 1797, treasury warrant, 1796, assigned by John P. Perkins, entered 1797, on Cripple Creek.

September 5, 1795, DUNCAN GULLION, 430 acres, 1795, on warrant from the Surveyor of Nelson County, Kentucky, and lodged in this office in 1794 for Wm. Finley and he to Gullion, on Reed Creek adjoining Lewis Able and Moses Gordon.

August 29, 1797, JAMES HARBISON, 175 acres, entered on treasury warrant with Montgomery County surveyor in Robersons [Robinson] Tract Fork of Peak Creek.

No date, GEO. C. TAYLOR, 255 acres, 1794, treasury warrant from surveyor of Grayson County, issued 1783 in the name of Alex. Smyth, on Cove Creek corner to Jesse Evans and Robert and John Brackenridge [Breckenridge].

November 6, 1797, JAMES P. PRESTON, 1,000 acres, 1797, on treasury warrant, 1781, assigned by James Newell, on Cripple Creek and South Fork of Holston, corner Wm. Moor, Buster, Copenhaver, adj. Lasley.

March 17, 1798, HENRY PURKERT [BURKHART], 188 acres, on two entries: (1) 50 acres on Cripple Creek, adjoining John Newland and Philip Dutton, entered 1796 on treasury warrant 1783, assigned by Robt. Adams, assignee of James Newell, assignee of George Pickett; (2) 138 acres, entered 1798 on treasury warrant, 1797, assigned by James Newell, assignee of James P. Preston, attorney for Wm. Hilton.

no date, DANIEL HELT, 100 acres, 1796, on treasury warrant, 1782, on Reed Creek corner to Michael Nave [Neff].

no date, HENRY STIFFEY, 58 acres, 1791, on treasury warrant, 1780, Reed Creek corner to Michael Nave [Neff].

June 25, 1797, JOHN LEBURN and GORDON CLOYD, 400 acres, 1794, on treasury warrant, 1783, assigned by Daniel Weiseger, assignee of George Rowland, on headwaters of Bluestone, on second left hand fork going up Richland Creek; also 200 acres, entered 1794 on treasury warrant, 1783, assignees as above on Delashmeat Creek, branch of Bluestone; also 200 acres surveyed June 24, 1797, entered 1797, on treasury warrant, 1783, assignees as above, on Big Bottom of Wide Mouth Creek, branch of Bluestone; also 400 acres entered 1794 on treasury warrant 1783, assignees as above, on Millertons (?) Creek, branch of Bluestone.

March 30, 1798, JOSEPH CLOYD, 499 acres, 1794, on treasury warrant, not dated, same assignees as above, on waters of Bluestone.

p. 363

February 23, 1796, ANDREW DANNER, 520 acres, 1795, on treasury warrant, 1782, assignee of James Newell, on Cripple Creek adjoining his own.

p. 364

March 12, 1798, DAVID SLOAN, 290 acres, on three entries on three treasury warrants, as follows: (1) 100 acres, entered 1793 on treasury warrant, 1783, assigned by John Crager, assignee of James Newell, assignee of Thomas Madison; (2) 150 acres entered Montgomery County, 1785, and re-entered in Wythe County, 1797, in the name of Joseph Baker, deceased, and assigned by John Baker, legatee of Joseph Baker, and he to Sloan, on treasury warrant, 1782; (3) [40] acres, entered 1798, assigned by Hiram Craig, assignee of Francis Carter, attorney in fact for Samuel Woodfin, on part of a treasury warrant, 1782, land on Reed Creek adjoining his patent lands and Richard Beeson.

p. 365

July 20, 1795, DAVID DENISTON, 170 acres, not dated, treasury warrant, 1795, on Pine Run corner to Deniston and James Simpson.

p. 366

September 12, 1797, GEORGE MAY, 43 acres on two entries, 1794 and 1795, on two treasury warrants, 1782, on Pine Run, corner to James Simpson.

July 30, 1798, WILLIAM GRAHAM, 19 acres, entered 1798 on treasury warrant, 1782, Reed Creek corner to Graham, Henry Clemons, John Gibbs, and James Crockett.

p. 367

August 1798, JAMES HERBISON, 175 acres, 1798, on treasury warrant, 1798, assigned by Joseph Cloyd, on Robinson Tract, branch of Peak Creek [same as tract on p. 353].

p. 368

October 22, 1795, ARTHUR CAMPBELL, 289 acres, two entries, 1786, adjoining and above Goodwood on treasury warrant, and assigned by James Rutherford, 1780, on west side of Mill Creek on Middle Fork of Holston.

p.369

August 25, 1798, PETER SNEABLEY [SNAVELEY], 11 acres, 1798, on treasury warrant, 1797, assigned by Robt. Adams, assignee of James P. Preston, assignee of Wm. Hylton, on Reed Creek, corner to Lawrence Kettering, Peter Kinder, and John Boyd.

June 16, 1795, PHILIP HERKRADER [HARKRADER], 85 acres, 1795, on treasury warrant, 1783, on headwaters of Walkers Creek.

p. 370

March 15, 1796, PHILIP HERKRADER, assignee of James Camron, 20 acres, 1783, on treasury warrant, 1782, on North Fork of Holston.

October 29, 1796, JAMES SIMPSON, 38 acres, 1796, on treasury warrant, 1782, on Pine Run.

p. 371

July 30, 1798, JACOB BEESON, 396 acres: (1) entry in name of Henry Beeson and assigned to Jacob on treasury warrant, 1782, assigned by Nathaniel Frisbie, assignee of David Reace; (2) entry 1793 on treasury warrant and assigned by Frisbie; (3) entry 1794 on treasury warrant and assigned by James Newell and David Reace; (4) entry 1795 on (1) above assigned by Frisbie; (5) entry 1798, on treasury warrant, 1797, assigned by James Newell, assignee of James P. Preston, attorney for Wm. Hylton; in Rich Valley on North Fork of Holston.

p. 372

January 16, 1797, JAMES SIMPSON, SENR. [SR.], 105 acres, 1796, treasury warrant, 1782, on Pine Run corner to Andrew Boyd.

pp. 373-374

April 15, 1798, JOSEPH KENT, 1,339 acres based on the following right: (1) 839 acres by deed from George and Margaret Hancock; (2) 200 acres on entry for Thomas Quirk, 1786, on treasury warrant, 1782, and Quirk to Thomas Madison and by him to Kent; and (3) 300 acres in his own name on two entries, 1794, on treasury warrant, 1794, on Reed Creek, corner to Robert Sayers and John Bishop (*see* p. 449).

p. 375

October 30, 1796, GEORGE PEERY, 60 acres, 1789, on treasury warrant, 1783, assigned by Zachariah Stanley, assignee of Richard Shelton, on Wolf Creek.

p. 376

November 9, 1798, JACOB WAGGONER, 145 acres, entered: (1) 80 acres in the name of John Stobough, 1788, on treasury warrant, assigned by Jeremiah Bell, John Smith, and Zacheriah Stanley, 1783, (2) no acres stated, in his own name, 1789, on treasury warrant, 1783, assigned by George Peery, assignee of Zacheriah Stanley, assignee of Richard Shelton; and (3) 60 acres, all on headwaters of Clear Fork of Wolf Creek adjoining his own land.

pp. 377-378

_____, 1799, WILLIAM TAYLOR, 2,569 acres, on eight entries: two entries of 150 acres each and another for 69 acres, entered 1794, on treasury warrant; 100 acres entered 1794, treasury warrant, assigned by Henry Ingle, assignee of Daniel Wessiger, assignee of Daniel Kindsey; two entries one for 500 acres, the other 300 acres, 1794, on treasury warrant, assigned by John Taylor; 300 acres entered 1794 on treasury warrant, assigned by John Taylor, in Abbs Valley, the waters of Bluestone River.

p. 379

August 28, 1798, THOMAS BELL, 4,000 acres, 1782, on state warrant, 1781, at mouth of Russell Fork on Sandy River.

p. 380

September 19, 1797, SILVESTER OTT, 60 acres, on part of an entry in the name of Danl. Collins, on treasury warrant, 1795, and assigned by Gordon Cloyd and Alex. Smyth, on New River adjoining Daniel Collins, Meredith Rains.

p. 381

June 20, 1797, JAMES SIMPSON, JUNIOR, 70 acres, 1797, assigned by Hiram Craig, assignee of Francis J. Carter, attorney in fact for Samuel Woodfin, on Pine Run.

pp. 382-383

March 10, 1797, JOHN TAYLOR, 800 acres, as assignee of Benjamin Gosling, 1783, state warrant 1782, on both sides of the Sandy River.

p. 384

March 6, 1797, JOHN TAYLOR, 400 acres, assignees as above, on both sides of Sandy River and both sides of Knox Creek.

p. 385

March 1, 1797, JOHN TAYLOR, 400 acres, assignees as above, on both sides of Blackberry Creek.

p. 386, March 12, 1797, JOHN TAYLOR, 400 acres, 1783, on state warrant, on both sides Blackberry Creek.

pp. 387-388

March 10, 1797, BENJAMIN GOOSLING, 800 acres, 1782, on state warrant, 1782, on both sides of the Sandy River adjoining and below his 400 acres survey.

p. 389

March 15, 1797, BENJAMIN GOSLING, 400 acres, 1782, on state warrant, 1782, on both Louisa Fork and both sides of Russell Fork on Sandy River.

p. 390

March 9, 1797, BENJAMIN GOSLING, 400 acres, 1782, on state warrant, 1782, on both sides of Peters Creek, branch of Sandy River.

p. 391

March 8, 1797, BENJAMIN GOSLING, 400 acres, 1782, on state warrant, 1782, on both sides of Knox Creek, adjoining and above John Taylor.

p. 392

November 6, 1796, THOS. WITTEN, 238 acres on three entries: (1) 100 acres, 1792, on part of a treasury warrant, 1783, assigned by Robert B. Chew; (2) 26 acres, 1797, on part of a treasury warrant, 1783, assigned by Daniel Wissiger, assignee of Wm. McCutsheon; (3) 112 acres, 1797, on part of a [treasury] warrant, 1796, adjoining George Peery and Wm. Thompson.

p. 393

November 28, 1796, THOS. WITTEN, 150 acres on two entries: (1) 125 acres, 1794, on part of a treasury warrant assigned by James Cecil, and issued in 1783, (2) 25 acres, 1797, on part of a treasury warrant, 1783, on Horsepen Coves waters of Sandy; also 90 acres, 1794, on part of a treasury warrant, 1783, on Clinch River beginning on Spur of Rich Mountain.

p. 394

February 10, 1796, JOHN NELSON, 45 acres, 1796, on treasury warrant, 1782, assigned by James Newell, on headwaters of South Fork of Holston.

pp. 395-396

May 22, 1797, JOHN CROCKETT, 250 acres, 1794, on two warrants: (1) military warrant for 200 acres, 1780; (2) on a treasury warrant 1782, assigned by Henry Banks, on Walkers Little Creek; also 350 acres on Walkers Creek.

p. 398

March 21, 1797, LEVY CARENS, 55 acres, part of an entry in name of Gordon Cloyd and Alex. Smyth 1795, on treasury warrant, 1795, in Montgomery County, assigned by Carens on headwaters of Walkers Creek.

p. 398

February 28, 1794, AKELES FANNEN, 60 acres, 1791, on treasury warrant, 1782, assignee of James Devor assignee of Wm. Hill, on Walkers Creek.

p. 399

September 16, 1797, JOHN COX, 350 acres, on two entries: (1) 50 acres entered 1791, part of a treasury warrant, 1790, assignee of Robt. Adams, and Saml. McCraw; (2) 300 acres part of an entry in the name of Gordon Cloyd and Alex. Smyth, 1795, on part of a treasury warrant from principal surveyor of Montgomery County, 1783; said 300 acres was assigned to Cox in 1797, on Walkers Creek.

p.400

March 31, 1797, JAMES CECIL, 76 acres in the Baptist Valley on Camp Creek, a branch of the Clinch River, on part of a treasury warrant for 3,000 acres, 1783, adjoining William Cecil and Jeremiah Bell.

p. 401

September 12, 1797, JEREMIAH WITTEN, 128 acres on three entries: (1) 50 acres 1792 on part of a treasury warrant, 1783; (2) 50 acres entered 1794, on treasury warrant, 1781, assigned by Lawrence Murry (?); and (3) 38 acres entered 1797 on treasury warrant, 1796, assigned by Thomas Witten, on north side of Paint Lick Mountain on head of the Clinch.

p. 402

May 25, 1795, JOHN BOGLE, 100 acres, 1791, on warrant of 1,000 acres assigned by Robert Adams, assignee of Samuel McCraw, 1790, on Walkers Creek joining his own land near his mill.

p. 403

September 26, 1798, ALEXANDER BOYD, 220 acres, 1795, on treasury warrant, not dated, on Maiden Spring Fork, branch of Clinch River on south side of spur of Morris Griffin's Knob and near John Thompson's line.

pp. 403-404

October 19, 1798, DANIEL HERMAN, 103 acres, 1794, on treasury warrant, 1782, assigned by William Neel, on Cavets Creek, a branch of Clynch [Clinch] River; also 97 acres entered 1794 on treasury warrant, 1782, assignee of William Neel, on Cavets Creek.

p. 405

July 31, 1798, ELIZABETH VINNATTA, 130 acres, 1794, for James Workman on treasury warrant, 1783, part assigned to her by Workman, assignee of John Preston, on Clear and Muddy Forks of Wolf Creek.

April 9, 1798, WM. NEEL, 78 acres, 1792, treasury warrant, 1782, on both sides of South Fork of Reed Creek, adjoining John Hounshell, Michael Walters, Patrick Johnson, and Peter Miars (Myers).

p. 406

October 17, 1798, MOSES JUSTICE, GEORGE JUSTICE, and DANIEL JUSTICE, JUNR.[JR.], 496 acres on two entries: (1) 50 acres entered 1791 on treasury warrant 1783, in name of John Alsup and he to Justices; (2) on treasury warrant for 2,000 acres, 1796, in name of Wm. Neel, 446 acres part of entry assigned by Neel to Justices, issued 1795, on Clear Fork of Wolf Creek.

p. 407

May 10, 1797, MATHIAS HERMAN [probably HARMAN], 182 acres, part of an entry of 12,000 acres, 1795, on a certificate from the principal surveyor of Montgomery County, in name of Gordon Cloyd and Alex. Smyth, 200 acres of which was assigned to Herman, on North Fork of Holston adjoining James Davis and Jacob Beeson.

p. 407

October 17, 1797, THOMAS PEIRCE, 204 acres, 1795, on part of a treasury warrant, 1794, assigned by Robert Adams, assignee of John Taylor, on South Fork of Holston, corner to James Dougherty.

p. 408

October 17, 1797, JOHN GRIFFITTS, 34 acres, 1796, on treasury warrant for 3,000 acres, 1783, and assigned by Robert Adams, on South Fork of Holston, adjoining James Dougherty and Griffitt's patent land.

p. 408

March 9, 1797, DANIEL ROBINETT, 80 acres, part of entry of 12,000 acres in name of Gordon Cloyd and Alex. Smyth, on treasury warrant, 1795, assigned to Robinett, on Walkers Big Creek adjoining Thomas Dunn, deceased.

p. 409

August 12, 1796, STEPHEN REEDER, 87 acres, 1782, for John Syphers and Michael Cregger, Junr. [Jr.], and assigned to Reeder, on part of a treasury warrant, 1781, on Stoney Fork of Reed Creek adjoining Jacob Plesly [Blessing], Lindamood, and Verner Knipp.

p. 410

June 22, 1797, LEONARD STRAW, 558 acres, 1795, on treasury warrant, 1782 assigned by Henry Ingle, assignee of Daniel Wessiger, on Reed Creek adjoining Fred Moor, Gordon, Hedrick, Godfrey Young, Devall [Duvall] Creager, Michael Cregar, Umbarger, and Hounshell.

p. 411

October 4, 1798, JACOB BLESSING, 200 acres, 1793, for John Hays and assigned to him, treasury warrant, 1782, assigned to him by Wm. Neel, on Spruce Creek, branch of Holston.

p. 411

March 18, 1797, JAMES DEVOR, 150 acres, 1795, part of entry of 12,000 acres for Gordon Cloyd and Alexander Smyth, on treasury warrant, 1795, from the principal surveyor of Montgomery County; 150 acres assigned by them to Devor, 1796, land adjoining legatees of Thomas Dunn, deceased, on Walkers Big Creek.

p. 412

March 17, 1797, JAMES DEVOR, 150 acres on above entry, on Walkers Creek, corner to Michael Robinett, on Walkers Creek.

p. 413

August 25, 1798, WILLIAM HAYS, 163 acres on two entries: (1) 75 acres in Montgomery County 1787, in name of John Garwood and assigned to Hays, on treasury warrant for 375 acres, 1782; (2) 78 acres in his own name, entry 1798, on treasury warrant, 1787, assigned by Robert Adams and James Newell, assignee of James P. Preston, attorney for Wm. Helton, on North Fork of Holston.

p. 414

July 15, 1798, HENRY GROSECLOSE, 133 acres on part of two entries: (1) 100 acres part of entry of 12,000 acres made for Gordon Cloyd and Alexander Smyth, 1795, on treasury warrant; (2) 33 acres, 1798, on part of a treasury warrant, 1797, assigned to him by Robert Adams and James Newell, assignees James P. Preston, attorney for William Hilton, in Rich Valley.

p. 415

March 12, 1796, DAVID SLOAN, 250 acres on two entries: (1) 300 acres, 1785, made in name of Joseph Baker, 150 acres of which was assigned to Sloan by John Baker, legatee of said Joseph Baker, part of a warrant, 1782; (2) 100 acres entered 1793 on part of a warrant, 1783, assigned by John Creager, assignee of James Newell, on both sides of Reed Creek, corner to Sloan's patent land (void).

February 28, 1794, ANDREW THOMPSON, 53 acres, 1793, on treasury warrant, 1782 on Walkers Creek, adjoining his own land.

p. 416

March 13, 1797, JOHN JUSTICE and JOHN HENDERSON, tenants in common, 230 acres part of 12,000 acres entered for Cloyd and Smyth, 1795, assigned to Justice and Henderson, 1797, on both sides of Walkers Creek, corner to Daniel Robinett and Henderson; and 60 acres on the same entry, on Walkers Creek, corner to Justice and Henderson to run to spur of Walkers Mountain.

p. 417, September 27, 1797, JOSEPH CROCKETT, 460 acres on two entries: (1) 245

140

acres entered 1795, on part of a treasury warrant, 1794 assigned by Robt. Adams assignee of John Taylor; (2) 215 acres entered 1797 on treasury warrant, 1781, assigned by John Armstrong, on north side of Reed Creek, corner to his patent land (void).

p. 418

September 20, 1798, JAMES WILSON, 166 acres on two entries: (1) 24 acres part of entry of 12,000 acres, 1795, for Gordon Cloyd and Smyth; (2) 142 acres, 1798, on part of a treasury warrant, 1798, on Rich Valley adjoining his own.

p. 419

February 16, 1798, JAMES WILSON, 276 acres entered as above on North Fork of Holston, adjoining his own, corner to the meeting house survey and Jacob Spangler.

p. 420

April 27, 1797, CALEB KIRK, assignee of William Prentis, assignee of David Anderson, 1,000 acres, 1785, on treasury warrant, 1783, joining Thomas Whitten and extending to top of Rich Mountain at Northeast end of Morris's Knob.

p. 421

April 29, 1797, ZACHERIAH STANLEY, assignee of Richard Anderson, 1,381 acres, 1785, treasury warrant, 1783, joining William Thompson and William Brooks, on top of Rich Mountain at Peery's Road, near Thompson's line, Maiden Spring, branch of Clynch [Clinch] River.

p. 422

March 14, 1797, WILLIAM READER, 40 acres part of an entry, 1796, treasury warrant, 1783, both sides of Walkers Big Creek, corner to his survey of 60 acres.

March 10, 1797, WILLIAM READER, 60 acres on part of an entry, treasury warrant, 1783, on both sides of Walkers Big Creek, corner to said Reader.

p. 423

May 12, 1796, MOSES LINSEY, 200 acres, part of treasury warrant, for 2,020 acres, 1782, entered 1784, assigned to him by John Smith, on Walkers Creek, branch of New River, corner to Michael Robinett's.

March 9, 1797, DANIEL ROBINETT, 25 acres part of treasury warrant, 1782, entered 1792 (?), assigned to him by James Devor, assignee of William Hall, assignee of Adam Dean, on Walkers Big Creek, corner to Jacob Shell.

p. 424

March 18, 1797, JAMES DEVOR, 64 acres, part of 12,000 acres, treasury warrant, 1795, entered in name of Gordon Cloyd and Alexander Smith, 1795 assigned 1796 to Devor, on Walkers Big Creek.

p. 425

May 23, 1797, FREDERICK EDWARDS, 340 acres, treasury warrant, assignee of James Newell, 1782, entered 1782 in Montgomery County, on Walkers Little Creek, beginning on north side of Walkers Mountain.

p. 426

September 29, 1797, JOSEPH CROCKETT, 304 acres on two entries: (1) 245 acres, 1795, art of treasury warrant of 1,105 acres, 1794, assigned to him by Robert Adams, assignee of John Taylor; (2) ____ acres entered 1797 on part of treasury warrant of 2,000 acres, 1781, assigned by John Armstrong, on north side of Reed Creek joining his patent land.

October 15, 1798, JAMES McGAVOCK, 200 acres, entered in Montgomery County

1782, on part of a military warrant of 3,000 acres, 1780, on Reed Creek adjoining John Montgomery, Senr. [Sr.].

p. 427

July 23, 1795, JAMES BRITT, assignee of John Smith, 200 acres, 1784, on treasury warrant for 2,020 acres, 1782, on Muddy Fork of Wolf Creek waters of the New River, beginning at the foot of the Round Mountain, and along the south side of the spurs of Wolf Creek Mountain.

June 22, 1797, GODFRET YOUNG, 63 acres, 1795, on part of treasury warrant of 4,000 acres, 1783, Reed Creek, beginning on a line of Nicholas Cline and with Philip Knipp's line on south side of Pine Ridge.

p. 428

March 17, 1797, DANIEL ROBINETT, 312 acres, part of an entry for 12,000 acres, 1795, in name of Gordon Cloyd and Alexander Smyth on treasury warrant, 1795, assigned to him by James Devor, who was assignee of Cloyd and Smyth, on Walkers Creek, beginning on a line of the land of Thomas Dunn, deceased, and corner to William Grayson, a survey of Zacheriah Stanley, and corner to Jacob Shell.

p. 429

April 3, 1798, HENRY LAMBERT, JUNR. [JR.], assignee of Henry Lambert, Senr. [Sr.], 50 acres, 1794, treasury warrant, 1783, on Walkers Creek, corner to William King's land and to lines of Andrew Messersmith and John Grayson.

March 12, 1793, CONROD RADER, 100 acres, 1792, part of treasury warrant of 4,000 acres, 1783, assigned to him by Jacob Rabass [Repass], Junr. [Jr.], assignee of William Bouren [Bourne], in the Cove, beginning on William Finley's line.

p. 430

June 23, 1797, VARNER KNIP [KNIPP], 50 acres, 1790, in name of Joseph Erwin and transferred to Henry Rader and he to Knip, part of treasury warrant assigned by John Preston, 1782, Reed Creek, near the waggon road.

May 29, 1797, JOHN GRAYSON, 214 acres entered as follows: (1) 114 acres, 1796, part of warrant of 200 acres, 1781, assigned by Robert Adams, assignee of James Maxwell; (2) 100 acres part of 12,000 acres for Gordon Cloyd and Alexander Smyth, 1795, on certificate, 1795, assigned by Cloyd and Smyth, 1797, on Walkers Creek.

p. 431

June 17, 1797, JOHN GRAYSON, 100 acres, part of an entry of 12,000 acres, 1795, in the name of Gordon Cloyd and Alexander Smyth, on certificate from Montgomery, 1795, 500 acres of said entry assigned by Cloyd and Smyth to James Davis who assigned 100 acres of the 500 acres to Grayson, 1797, on headwaters of Walkers Creek, corner to Henry Lambert and Grayson's own land.

September 21, 1797, JAMES CROCKETT, 45 acres part of an entry 1797 and assigned to him by James Stotts, assignee of Hiram Craig, part of a treasury warrant, 1794, on New River, corner to land of said Crockett, Andrew Stotts, Charles Carter, and John Craig, Senr. [Sr.].

p. 432

October 16, 1798, WILLIAM KING, 170 acres on three entries: (1) 100 acres, 80 acres of which is applied to this survey, entered 1783 in Montgomery County in the name of George Kincer and by him assigned to James Camron and he to King, on treasury warrant 1782; (2) 70 acres entered 1797 in name of James Camron and by him assigned to said King on treasury warrant, 1782, assignee of

Francis J. Carter, attorney for Saml. Woodfin; (3) 20 acres in own name, 1798, part of treasury warrant of 1,152 3/4 acres, 1782, assigned to him by Francis J. Carter, assignee of Saml. Woodfin, in Rich Valley on North Fork of Holstein [Holston], adjoining Jacob Kimberling.

p. 433

October 16, 1798, WILLIAM KING, 650 acres on two entries: (1) 400 acres, 1797, on part of treasury warrant, 1782, assigned to him by Hiram Craig, assignee of Francis J. Carter, attorney for Samuel Woodfin; (2) 250 acres, 1798, on treasury warrant of 1,152 3/4 acres assigned as above, on Walkers Creek and North Fork of Holstein [Holston], corner to Philip Herklerader [Harkrader], and Andrew Messersmith's land, and John Herkerader's [Harkrader's] corner.

p. 434

October 14, 1798, WILLIAM KING, 331 3/4 acres on three entries: (1) 40 acres entered 1793 on part of treasury warrant of 1,000 acres, 1781; (2) 116 3/4 acres, 1795, on part of treasury warrant of 376 3/4 acres, 1782; (3) 175 acres, 1797 on part of treasury warrant of 1,152 3/4 acres, 1782, assignee of Hiram Craig, assignee of Francis J. Carter attorney for Saml. Woodfin, in Rich Valley, beginning on spur of Walkers Mountain, corner to Hammer's land and to bank of North Fork of Holstien [Holston] on George Kincer's line, and corner to Jacob Spangler's land.

p. 435

October 12, 1798, WILLIAM KING, 200 acres entered in two entries: (1) 100 acres, 1797, on part of a treasury warrant of 1,152 3/4 acres, 1782 assigned by Hiram Craig, assignee of Francis J. Carter, attorney for Samuel Woodfin; (2) 100 acres, 1798 on part of treasury warrant, also of 1,152 3/4 acres, 1782, assigned by Francis J. Carter, assignee of Samuel Woodfin in Rich Valley, on North Fork of Holstien [Holston] and Walkers Creek beginning at a spur of Walkers Mountain adjoining his own patent land, with lines of Philip Herkerader's land.

October 12, 1798, WILLIAM KING, 50 acres, 1798, on part of treasury warrant of 1,152 3/4 acres, 1782, assigned as in (2) above, in Rich Valley, beginning on a spur of Walkers Mountain, corner to Jacob Kimberling's land.

p. 436

June 23, 1798, JOSEPH ERWIN, 110 acres entered in two entries (1) 100 acres, 1791 on part of treasury warrant of 4,000 acres, 1783, assigned to him by Robert Adams, assignee of William Bouren; (2) 10 acres, 1794, part of a treasury warrant of 500 acres assigned to him by James Murphey, assignee of Charles Copland, on Reed Creek, beginning corner to his patent land and another tract of Erwin's, corner to Hedrick and Kinder.

p. 437

September 6, 1795, ANDREW THOMPSON, 165 acres in two entries: (1) 100 acres, 1795, on part of a treasury warrant of 4,000 acres, 1783; (2) 65 acres, 1795, on treasury warrant from principal Surveyor of Grayson County, and issued 1783, on McAdams Creek, a branch of the Maiden Spring Fork of Clinch River, corner to Ebenezer Bruster's land.

February 22, 1785, JAMES SLOAN, 145 acres, entry 1793 in the name of John Thompson, and by him assigned to Sloan, 45 acres of which on certificate from the principal Surveyor of Montgomery County, 1783, and 100 acres on treasury warrant, 1782, on Clynch [Clinch] River near More's [Moore's] land.

October 20, 1798, DAVID WALLIS, 400 acres, 1798, on part of treasury warrant of 1,152 3/4 acres, 1782, and assigned to him by Leonard Straw and William King, assignee of Francis J. Carter, assignee of Samuel Woodfin, on the waters of the Clynch [Clinch] on the divide between the Clinch and the Dry Fork of Sandy, corner to Isaac Daylie.

October 27, 1798, ROBERT WALLIS, assignee of Leonard Straw and William King, 50 acres on entry 1798 on part of treasury warrant for 1,152 3/4 acres, 1782, on waters of Bluestone, a branch of New River.

p. 439

April 30, 1793, JOHN TOTTON, 283 acres on two entries: (1) 200 acres entered 1782, in name of Matthew Alexander and assigned to I. Crabtree and assigned to Totton on part of treasury warrant, 1782; (2) 83 acres, 1793, on part of treasury warrant of 4,000 acres, 1783, assigned to him by William Bouren on waters of North Fork of Holstien [Holston], beginning at the foot of Walkers Mountain and corner to Philip Umbarger's land.

April 5, 1797, BURREL BURCHETT, 50 acres, part of an entry of 12,000 acres in 1795 in the name of Gordon Cloyd and Alexr. Smythe [Smyth] on treasury warrant, 1795, from principal Surveyor of Montgomery County, and assigned to Burchett, on both sides of Walkers Creek.

p. 440

October 26, 1798, PETER SPANGLER, 33 acres, 1798, on part of treasury warrant of 500 acres, 1782, in Rich Valley on North Fork of Holstien [Holston], beginning on John Spangler's line, corner to James Wilson's survey and John Messersmith's line.

October 28, 1798, WILLIAM FINLEY, JUNR. [JR.], 80 acres, 1798, on part of a treasury warrant of 500 acres, 1782, on Cove Creek in the Cove, corner to Crockett's land and to the north side of Queens Knob.

p. 441

October 24, 1798, THOMAS CARTER, 100 acres, 1798, part of a treasury warrant, 1782, on headwaters of Pine Run beginning on the south side of Drapers Mountain to the patent line of Andrew Boyd's land.

October 24, 1794, WILLIAM HAWL [HALL], assignee of Adam Dean, 50 acres, 1792, on [treasury?] warrant, 1782, assigned to him by George Ewing, in Burks Garden in the gap where the water runs out, beginning on a spur of the Garden Mountain, corner to the land of James Thompson.

p. 442, April 3, 1797, WILLIAM HALL, 200 acres, 1793, part of a treasury warrant, 1782, assigned by George Ewing, in Burks Garden.

April 26, 1794, JAMES LAMMIE, 150 acres on two entries: (1) 50 acres, 1793 in the name of Andrew Lammie and assigned to James Lammie on treasury warrant, 1781; (2) 100 acres 1794 on the same warrant, in Locust Cove, waters of the North Fork of Holstien [Holston].

p. 443

October 13, 1798, HENRY DAVIS, 1,110 acres on two entries: (1) 700 acres, 610 acres of which is applied to this survey, 1794, on treasury warrant, 1782, assigned by James Newell, assignee of James Lapsley; (2) 500 acres, 1798, on treasury warrant, 1798, assigned to him by Robert Adams on Reed Island a branch of New River, beginning corner to William Caffee's [Calfee's] land.

p. 444

August 26, 1796, JACOB STEALY, 125 acres, 1795, on treasury warrant from principal Surveyor of Grayson County, 1783, on Reed Creek beginning corner to John Boyd's land and on line of Michael Stiffey's [Steffey's] land, corner to Kermony's [Cormany's].

October 10, 1798, WILLIAM HALL, 350 acres on two entries: (1) 150 acres on treasury warrant assigned by George Ewing, 1782; (2) 150 acres entered 1798 on part of treasury warrant assigned by Leonard Straw and William King, assignee of Francis J. Carter, assignee of Samuel Woodfin, 1782, in Burks Garden on the headwaters of Wolf Creek, beginning corner to Henry Banks and near William Day's corner.

p. 445

October 10, 1798, WILLIAM HALL, 220 acres on two entries: (1) 100 acres 1793 on treasury warrant assigned to him by George Ewing, 1782; (2) 120 acres 1798 on part of a treasury warrant, assigned to him by Leonard Straw and William King, assignees of Francis J. Carter, assignee of Samuel Woodfin, 1782, in Burks Garden, waters of Wolf Creek, beginning corner to Thompson's.

October 26, 1794, JOHN LAMMIE, 70 acres, 1793, on treasury warrant 1781, on waters of North Fork of Holstien [Holston] River, beginning corner to John and James Lammie's patent land on spur of Clynch [Clinch] Mountain.

p. 446

October 11, 1798, WILLIAM HALL, 500 acres on two entries: (1) 200 acres 1793 on treasury warrant assigned to him by George Ewing, 1782; (2) 300 acres entered 1798 on same warrant, in Burks Garden on waters of Wolf Creek, beginning corner to James Thompson's land.

No date, DANIEL COLLINS, 280 acres, 1798, on part of a treasury warrant, 1795, assigned to him by Gordon Cloyd assignee of David Cloyd, on Racoon [Raccoon] Spring a branch of Peek [Peak] Creek, a branch of New River, beginning corner to Jacob Miller's land.

p. 447

October 12, 1798, SILVESTER OTT, 60 acres, 1798, on part of a treasury warrant, 1795, assigned to him by Gordon Cloyd, assignee of _____ Cloyd, on waters of Peek [Peak] Creek, a branch of New River, beginning corner to Daniel Collins and Meredith Rains.

No date, MAGNESS McDONALD, 78 acres, 1794, on part of a treasury warrant of 1,000 acres, 1781, assigned to him by William King, on Reed Creek, beginning corner to Daniel Sponsler, John Shaver, and Joseph Kent.

p. 448

March 6, 1797, JOHN HAMMER, 45 acres, 1795, in the name of Gordon Cloyd and Alexander Smyth, on part of treasury warrant, 1795, in Rich Valley on North Fork of Holstein [Holston] beginning corner to Jacob Kimerland [Kimberling].

p. 449

No date, JOSEPH KENT, 1,339 acres pursuant to an order of April Court 1796, for an inclusive survey which includes 839 acres conveyed from George and Margaret Hancock 1796 which was granted as follows: 200 acres to George Hancock 1792 and 500 acres to Ezekiel Calhoun, 1752 and conveyed by Calhoun to Robert, James, and William Montgomery and by them to Hancock; also 200 acres entered for Thomas Quirk 1796 on preemption warrant, entered 1782 and transferred to Thomas Madison and by him to George Hancock and by him to Joseph Kent; also 175 acres entered 1794, and 25 acres entered 1794 for Joseph Kent on treasury warrant issued 1794, on Reed Creek, branch of New River, corner to Robert Sayers, Magnus McDonald, John

Bishop, formerly Josiah Ramsey's.

p. 450

October 10, 1795, ALEXANDER MAHOOD, 140 acres entered in Montgomery County, 1786 on treasury warrant 1782, assigned to him in part by Thomas Madison and Co., on Davis Branch, waters of Cripple Creek, corner to Chenney's [Chaney's] land.

October 3, 1797, FREDRICK COPENHEIFER [COPENHAVER], assignee of Michael Brown, 200 acres, 1794, on part of treasury warrant of 6,241 acres, 1782, on South Fork of Holston, beginning corner to Slimp's [Slemp's] land and with Buster and Thomas Copenheifer [Copenhaver] lines.

p. 451

no date, WILLIAM ROSS, 100 acres, 1795, on part of treasury warrant, 1782, on waters of New River.

March 26, 1799, WILLIAM SNIDOW, 150 acres, 1794, in the names of Henry Helvey, Joseph Erwine and John Beard and assigned by them to Snidow, part of treasury warrant, 1791, on waters of Middle Fork of Holstien [Holston], adjoining lines of Henry Pickle and Rapass [Repass].

p. 452

December 1, 1798, WILLIAM TAYLOR, 625 acres pursuant to an order of court November 1798, permitting him to make an inclusive survey which includes the following tracts: 100 acres conveyed by John Taylor 1796; 88 acres conveyed by John Taylor 1796, which was granted to John Taylor; and three entries: (1) 100 acres (2) 150 acres (3) 50 acres made 1794 on part of treasury warrant assigned to him by John Taylor; 137 acres entered 1798 on treasury warrant assigned to him by James Newell, on head of the Clynch [Clinch] River, beginning in the Hurrican.

p. 453

December 20, 1797, NICHOLAS SNIDER, 310 acres on three entries, 1782 in Montgomery County on treasury warrant, 1782, 500 acres, one entry of 166 acres in the name of Nicholas Snider, another in the name of William Snider for 166 acres, 103 acres of which issued to Nicholas Snider, another of 168 acres in the name of Peter Muser [Musser] and assigned to Snider, on Reed Creek, branch of New River, beginning corner to Bastan [Sebastian] Snider's patent land, corner to Martin Kimberlan's [Kimberling's], Baugh's, and Dobler's land.

p. 454

February 4, 1794, GEORGE KEGLEY, 52 acres, 1792, in the name of Daniel Kesler and assigned to Kegley, on part of treasury warrant of 500 acres, 1780, on Middle Fork of Holston, corner to his land, John Snider's, and McPhatridge's land.

p. 455

October 26, 1798, GEORGE PEARIS, 1,000 acres, 1782, in the name of George Ashberry and he to Henry Farley and he to Pearis, on treasury warrant of 1,000 acres, 1781, on head of East River, at a place known by the name of the Big Spring.

p. 456

March 7, 1791, DANIEL WAGGONER, 50 acres, 1790, in the name of Richard Elkins and by him assigned to Zachariah Elkins and by him assigned to Waggoner, on part of a treasury warrant, 1782, on Clear Fork of Wolf Creek, beginning on Stanley's line.

March 25, 1791, ROBERT GARRETT, 200 acres, 1787, in the name of John Taylor and he to Garrett, on part of a treasury warrant, 1783, on North Fork of Walkers Creek at a place known by the name of the Clay Banks and Clay Licks, beginning on the north side of Walkers Creek, corner to land James Day now lives on.

p.457

July 1, 1797, PHILLIP DUTTON, 172 acres, 1792, on part of a treasury warrant of 2,020 acres, 1782, on waters of Cripple Creek adjoining his patent land and with James Douglas' line.

September 23, 1795, THOMAS MADISON and COMPANY, 53 acres, entered in Montgomery County, 1786, on treasury warrant, 1782, assigned to them by John and Francis Preston, on Cripple Creek, beginning in Carr's line.

p. 458

September 23, 1795, THOMAS MADISON and COMPANY, 47 acres entered in Montgomery County, 1786, on treasury warrant, 1782, assigned to them by John and Francis Preston, on Cripple Creek, beginning corner to Bonham's land, and adjoining Carr's lines.

September 23, 1795, THOMAS MADISON and COMPANY, 400 acres entered in Montgomery County on treasury warrant, 1782, and assigned as above, on Cripple Creek, beginning by a branch in William Neely's line, and corner to Chenney's [Chaney's] land, corner to James Campbell and Carr's.

p. 459

February 5, 1796, NICHOLAS HONEAKER, 167 acres on two entries: (1) 60 acres entered 1794, on part of a treasury warrant, 1783, (2) 100 acres entered 1795, on part of treasury warrant, 1794, on headwaters of Pine Run, branch of New River, beginning on the south side of Draper's Mountain to line of Andrew Boyd's line.

May 20, 1799, FREDERICK SLUSS, 188 acres entered: (1) 50 acres, 1792, on part of treasury warrant, 1782, (2) 50 acres part of an entry of 400 acres in the name of William Neel, 1792, on above warrant which was assigned to him by Neel (3) 50 acres entered 1798, part of treasury warrant of 500 acres, 1797, (4) 38 acres entered 1799 on above warrant, on waters of North Fork of Holstein [Holston], joining the lands of James Wilson in the Rich Valley.

p. 460

June 24, 1797, JOHN LEYBURN, 300 acres, part of entry of 450 acres for Joseph Hare, 1790, and assigned to Leyburn on part of treasury warrant issued to George Slauter [Slaughter], and assigned to Joseph Hare by John Preston assignee of George Slauter [Slaughter]; also 150 acres entered 1795 adjoining the above on part of treasury warrant for 18,000 acres, 1795, and assigned to him by Gordon Cloyd who was assignee of Austin Nicholas, on head of first big branch emptying into East River on south side below the mouth of the Six Mile Fork.

May 7, 1793, JEHU STEPHENS, 5 acres, 1793, part of treasury warrant, 1781, on both sides of Cripple Creek.

p. 461

October 5, 1798, DAVID HORN, 200 acres, 100 acres of which were entered 1796, on treasury warrant, 1783, and the other 100 acres, 1792, part of a treasury warrant for 500 acres, 1798, assignee of James Newell, on waters of Cripple Creek, on line of Michael Branstatter's land and corner to Douglas' land.

May 12, 1797, JOHN SMYTH, 100 acres, 1796, on treasury warrant, 1782, assigned to him by Robert Depriest on South Fork of Holston.

May 12, 1797, JACOB HECK, 34 acres, 1793, on treasury warrant, 1783, on South Fork of Holstein [Holston], corner to Morgan's patent land.

pp. 462-463

May 16, 1799, JOHN RABASS [REPASS], 186 acres, 1799, part of a treasury warrant, 1799, assigned to him by Robert Adams on the waters of Middle Fork of Holston, on a line of Henry Pickle, and John Snabeley's [Snaveley's] land, near the head of Laurel Spring.

March 15, 1799, DAVID DENIDSON (?), 170 acres entered in two entries: (1) 70 acres 1797, on part of treasury warrant, 1782, assigned by Hiram Craig; (2) 100 acres, 1799 on part of treasury warrant, 1799, assigned by Robert Adams, on Pine Run corner to his own land and corner to land of James Simpson.

p. 463

October 14, 1798, STEPHEN SAUNDERS, 294 acres, 1798, treasury warrant, not dated, assigned by Juana [Joanna] Baber, on waters of Cripple Creek, beginning on Saunders' patent line.

October 20, 1797, JNO. [JOHN] LASTLEY, 92 acres, 1797, on treasury warrant, 1781, assignee of Jno. [John] Armstrong, on headwaters of Cripple Creek, beginning in Scot's line.

October 4, 1797, JAMES JAMES, 50 acres, 1797, treasury warrant, 1781, on the head of Cripple Creek, beginning in his old line.

p. 464

January 5, 1798, ISAAC BEESON, 150 acres, 1786, in name of Joseph Baker and assigned to Richard Beeson by John Baker, legatee of Joseph Baker, and Richard Beeson to Isaac Beeson, on part of treasury warrant, 1782, on Ephraim Ward's branch, waters of Reed Creek, beginning corner to Richard Beeson.

p. 464

September 18, 1798, THOMAS TILSON, 117 acres, 1797, on part of treasury warrant, 1781, on South Fork of Holstein [Holston].

No date, RICHD. [RICHARD] WILLIAMS, 135 acres [entry is incomplete].

October 12, 1798, JOHN LASLY (?), 187 acres, 1797, on treasury warrant, 1781, assignee of Jno. [John] Armstrong, and another entry, 1798, assignee of James Newell, 1788, on waters of Cripple Creek.

p. 465

May 12, 1797, ISAAC WILLIAMS, 60 acres, 1797, on part of treasury warrant, 1794, assigned by Robert Adams, assignee of Lovis Harman, on South Fork of Holstein [Holston], corner to Morgan's land and along Moses Wells' line.

April 5, 1798, WILLIAM KING, 175 acres, 1797, in name of James Camron, and assigned to King on part of a treasury warrant, 1782, and assigned to Camron by Hiram Craig, assignee of Francis Carter, attorney for Samuel Woodfin, on North Fork of Holstein [Holston], in the Rich Valley, beginning corner to his land and with Jacob Kimberland's line and corner to George Kinder.

p. 466

October 1, 1798, WILLIAM LOVE, 1,425 acres on two entries: (1) 425 acres, 1787, on part of treasury warrant, 1782; (2) 1,000 acres, 1794, on part of treasury warrant, on waters of Cripple Creek.

p. 467

March 29, 1797, THOMAS GREENUP, 100 acres, 1797, part of treasury warrant for

3,000 acres, 1783, on Clinch River, beginning corner to John Greenup and William Cecil (by mistake twice recorded).

May 3, 1797, WILLIAM WITTEN and BENJAMIN CHRISTIAN, as tenants in common, 100 acres, 1797, on a treasury warrant, 1794, on Clinch River, beginning corner to Witten on the bank of the river and corner to survey for John McEntosh.

p. 468

March 27, 1797, JOHN McENTOSH, 70 acres, 1797, on part of a treasury warrant for 3,000 acres, 1783, on Clinch River.

November 25, 1795, JAMES MOOR, 83 acres, 1794, on part of treasury warrant, 1783, on waters of Clynch [Clinch] River, corner to survey known by the name of Locust Bottom.

p. 469

September 22, 1794, ZACHARIAH STANLEY, JOHN SMITH, and JEREMIAH BELL, 127 acres, 1786, on part of treasury warrant, not dated, on Clear Fork of Wolf Creek.

May 24, 1797, THOMAS BEGLEY, 200 acres on two entries: (1) 50 acres, 1789, in name of Thomas Smith, and transferred to Bagley [Begley]; (2) 150 acres entered 1794 on part of a treasury warrant, 1782, on Walkers Creek, a branch of New River, joining the lands of Adam Helvy and John Begley, beginning at the foot of Brushy Mountain.

p. 470

July 5, 1799, JOSEPH GILBERT, 50 acres, 1793, on part of treasury warrant, 1790, on Walkers Creek, branch of New River, beginning near John Pacer's.

August 12, 1799, JOSEPH ATKINS, 88 acres, 1789, on a treasury warrant for 1,000 acres, 1783, part of which was issued to him by Daniel Creamer, assignee of Benjamin Turner, assignee of David Anderson, on waters of Middle Fork of Holstein [Holston] joining his own lands, Crows, and Calhouns.

p. 471

March 26, 1796, JAMES FINLEY, 15 acres, 1786, on part of treasury warrant, assigned to him by James Clerk's attorney, on Reed Creek, beginning corner of Jehu Stephens.

September 18, 1797, JAMES EVANS, 100 acres, 1795, treasury warrant, 1782, on Walkers Creek, branch of New River, joining his own land, James Devor, and heirs of Thomas Dun [Dunn], deceased.

p. 472

January 16, 1797, ANDREW BOYD, 100 acres, 1796, in name of Hiram Craig, and transferred to Boyd, on part of treasury warrant, 1782, on Little Pine Run, branch of New River, beginning in line of his own land, corner to patent land of James Simpson and in line of Henry Honaker.

September 18, 1797, JAMES EVANS, 100 acres, 1795, on treasury warrant for 1,498 acres, 1782, on Walkers Creek, branch of New River, joining his own land, James Dever, and heirs of Thomas Dunn, deceased ("by mistake [entered] twice").

p. 473

February 23, 1793, JOSEPH DOUGHERTY, 50 acres, 1789, on part of treasury warrant, assigned to him by Alexr. [Alexander] Ore [Orr], assignee of John Taylor, assignee of Jonathan Isaac, 1782, on Wolf Creek of New River, adjoining the Round Bottom and survey of Alexander Steward.

May 16, 1796, JOHN PEERY, 51 acres, 1795, on part of treasury warrant of 12,500 acres, 1783, on Clinch River.

April 6, 1795, JOHN DOAK, 50 acres, 1795, on part of a treasury warrant assigned to him by David Doak, assignee of John King, 1782, on Reed Creek, beginning corner to his and George Davis' land.

November 20, 1798, WILLIAM ROSS, 200 acres, 1798, on military warrant, 1783, on New River, beginning corner to land he now lives on, on banks of Macks Run, corner to James Jones, corner to Jacob Miller's land by road leading to Ross' Mill.

August 2, 1796, WILLIAM ADAMS, 144 acres, 1795, on part of a treasury warrant, 1782, on Dry Fork on Sandy River.

May 16, 1798, JESSE EVANS, 255 acres, 1797, on part of treasury warrant of 2,000 acres, 1781, on Reed Creek, branch of New River, beginning corner to John Davis' land, and corner to William Hay.

June 6, 1799, ANDREW THOMPSON, 169 acres on two entries: (1) 50 acres entered 1794 in name of William Highton (?) and by him assigned to Thompson on part of a treasury warrant, 1783; (2) 119 acres, 1799 on part of treasury warrant of 2,000 acres, 1781, on Maiden Spring Fork of Clinch, adjoining his own land, George Peerie [Peery], and William Hitons (?).

May 17, 1793, JEHUE STEPHENS, 20 acres, 1793, on part of treasury warrant, 1781, on Cripple Creek, beginning corner to his own patent land.

March 29, 1795, WILLIAM TIPTON, 160 acres, 1793, in the name of James Breeden and transferred to Tipton, on treasury warrant, 1781, on New River beginning on line of William Hurst's land to spur of Roaring Falls Mountain.

September 17, 1798, SAMUEL WILLIAMS, 6 acres, 1797, on treasury warrant, 1782, assigned by James Newell on South Fork of Holston.

November 1, 1798, ANDREW PORTER, 133 acres, 1798, on part of a treasury warrant, 1798, assignee of James Newell, on the waters of Cripple Creek, beginning corner to Bonham's.

October 10, 1798, GEORGE BUCKALEW, 180 acres, 1798 (?), on treasury warrant, 1798, assignee of James Newell, on waters of Cripple Creek, corner to his own land.

October 27, 1798, GEORG [GEORGE] PEARIS, 200 acres, 1782, in the name of Jacob Dooley and assigned to George Asberry, and he to Henry Farley and he to Pearis, on [treasury?] warrant 1781, on East River in the Rich Valley.

October 24, 1798, JACOB PLESSING [BLESSING], assignee of John Preston, 50 acres, 1790, on part of a treasury warrant, not dated on Reed Creek, beginning on Verner Nipp's [Knipp's] line.

October 29,1798, GEORGE PEARIS, 450 acres, 1782, in the name of Jacob Dooley, and assigned to George Asberry, who assigned to Henry Farley, who assigned to Pearis, on part of a treasury warrant 1782, in forks of Brush Creek, known by the name of Fork Lick.

October 27, 1798, GEORGE PEARIS, 225 acres, 1783, in the name of Jacob Baugher and assigned to Reuben Roberts and he to Henry Farley and he to Pearis, on treasury warrant, 1782, on East River, beginning at the mouth of the Six Mile Fork, corner to Henry Farley's survey.

p. 482

October 30, 1798, HUGH CAPERTON, 200 acres, 1782, in the name of Jacob Dooley and assigned to George Asberry and he to Henry Farley and he to George Pearis, and he to Caperton, on part of a treasury warrant, 1781, at the mouth of Sand Lick Creek, a branch of Bluestone River.

p. 483

October 29, 1798, JOSIAH PERDUE, 500 acres, 1782, in the name of James Douglass and assigned to George Asberry and by him assigned to Henry Farley and by him to Perdue, treasury warrant, 1781, on waters of Bluestone and Brush Creek.

p. 484

March 28, 1795, PATRICK ROSS, 80 acres, 1793, on part of treasury warrant, 1782, on Little Reed Island Creek, corner to Lawrence Stephens.

p. 485

August 7, 1799, JOHN NEWLAND, 210 acres entered as follows: (1) 60 acres entered in Montgomery County 1788, on a treasury warrant, 1781; (2) 140 acres entered 1794 on certificate from principal Surveyor of Montgomery County; (3) 10 acres entered 1799, on part of a treasury warrant, 1799, on waters of Cripple Creek, corner to his patent land, crossing Vaught's Mill Creek, corner to George Vaught's land, corner to Henry Purkers [Burkerts], corner to Phillip Dutton, and with John Dutton's line.

p. 486

August 4, 1799, WILLIAM SPROUL, 27 acres entered in name of Joseph Mairs and transferred to Sproul, one entered 1793, the other 1795, both on treasury warrant, 1781, on Peek [Peak] Creek beginning corner to his land as purchased of Joseph Mairs and corner to Henry Patton.

August 16, 1799, JACOB DOBLER, 75 [175] acres pursuant to order of court permitting him to resurvey his land, on Reed Creek, corner to survey made for Jacob Washam, corner to Adam Cook, John Roush, and William Johnson.

p. 487

October 23, 1799, THOMAS COPEHAVER [COPENHAVER], 130 acres, entered in Montgomery County, 1788, on part of a treasury warrant, 1782, assigned by William Neel, assignee of George Moore, on Reed Creek, beginning to his corner and Meas's patent land, along Miller's line.

May 24, 1799, ADAM HARMAN, 66 acres on two entries: (1) 50 acres part of 12,000 acres entered 1795 in the name of Gordon Cloyd and Alexander Smyth on treasury warrant, 1795; (2) 16 acres entered 1798 on part of a treasury warrant on Mill Run, branch of Walkers Creek; both entries transferred to Harman by John Bagley.

p. 488

September 10, 1799, HENRY VICE, 142 acres, 1789, in Montgomery County, on part of a treasury warrant, 1782, on waters of South Fork of Holston River, with Jenkin Williams line and corner to Jarvis Smith's land.

September 26, 1799, ANDREW BOYD, 150 acres entered in Montgomery County, 1782, part of a treasury warrant, 1782, on Big Pine Run, beginning corner to his patent land.

p. 489

September 16, 1799, JOHN CROCKETT, 300 acres on two entries: (1) 100 acres,

1791, on part of a treasury warrant, 1782; (2) 200 acres, 1798, on treasury warrant, 1797, beginning corner to his own land, and with lines of Joseph Baker.

November 2, 1799, JESSE EVANS, 20 acres, 1794, entered in the name of Stophle [Christopher] Zimmerman [Simmerman], on part of a treasury warrant, 1782, on a branch of Reed Creek beginning on Stophel Zimmerman's line, and cornering on Armbrister's line.

p. 490

November 15, 1799, WILLIAM HALL, 500 acres entered [date torn], on a treasury warrant, assigned to him by Henry Davis, assignee of Francis J. Carter, 1798, in Burkes Garden on waters of Wolf Creek, a branch of New River, beginning on south side of Garden Mountain, and corner to James Thompson's land.

October 6, 179[torn], DANIEL JOHNSON, 1798, on part of a treasury warrant, on both sides of Reed Creek, beginning corner to a survey made for Samuel Thompson.

p. 491

October 6, 1799, JOSEPH ERWIN, 40 acres, 1798, on part of a treasury warrant from principal Surveyor of Nelson County, Kentucky, 1794, on waters of Reed Creek, adjoining his own land and Stephen Reeder's.

October 22, 1799, NICHOLAS SNIDOW, 57 3/4 acres, 1793, on part of a treasury warrant for 100 acres dated 178[torn], assigned to him by Arthur Campbell, assignee of Robert Rutherford, on Middle Fork of Holston, beginning at or near Aker's patent line.

p. 492

October 23, 1799, WILLIAM DAVIS, 80 3/4 acres, 1795, on part of a treasury warrant for 600 acres, 1795, adjoining the land of Aker (?), Vaught, and Perkett [Burkhart], on Middle Fork of Holston, beginning at the foot of Brushy Mountain.

pp. 493-494

October 29, 1799, JOHN THOMPSON SAYERS, 500 acres entered in Montgomery County, 1782, on treasury warrant, 1781, assigned to him by Robert Sayers, on the north side of a tract of land on Cripple Creek, formerly belonging to James Wylie, deceased, and on which one Harris formerly lived, beginning on a spur of the mountain corner to sd. tract and opposite to where said Harris formerly lived, and to corner the land of John Kerr.

p. 494

October 5, 1798, JOHN LIGGET, 240 acres in three entries: (1) 50 acres in Montgomery County, 1785, on treasury warrant; (2) 40 acres in Montgomery County, 1789, on [treasury warrant]; (3) 150 acres entered 1793 on three [treasury?] warrants of 50 acres each, beginning corner to William Patterson's patent land, on waters of the middle Fork of Holston.

p. 495

March 28, 1800, CHARLES FULLEN, 75 acres, 1794, on part of a treasury warrant of 4,000 acres, 1783, on Reed Creek, beginning corner to his patent land, and to Varner Knipp's line crossing the wagon road.

pp. 496-497

April 28, 1800, HEZEKIAH CHINEY [CHANEY], 836 acres, 1800, on part of a treasury warrant, not dated, and assigned to him by James Newell who was assignee of Alexander Smyth and David McGavock, 1800, on the waters of Cripple Creek, adjoining Gose's land, and corner to William Pattent's [Patton's] land.

No date, JOHN PEARY, JAMES SLOAN, and JOHN EVANS, 214 acres, 1799, on part of a treasury warrant assigned to them by James McCampbell, assignee of Simon Newthous (?), [not legible], on Clinch River and a line crossing the Hurricane Hollow.

p. 498

February 14, 1791, JOSEPH FLETCHER, 79 acres, 1791, on part of a treasury warrant, 1790, 100 acres of which was assigned by Robert Adams, assignee of Samuel McCraw, assignee of John Netherland, assignee of Edmund Vaughn, assignee of Charles Woodson, on Walkers Creek branch of New River, beginning corner to Fletcher's line and to John Cox, Sr.'s line.

February 19, 1799, PHILIP LAMBERT, SENR. [SR.], 100 acres, 1793, on part of a treasury warrant, 1781, on Wolf Creek, a branch of New River.

p. 499

June 22, 1797, DUVAL CREAGER, 15 acres, 1792, in the name of Peter Miars [Myers, Meyers] and assigned to Creager, on part of treasury warrant, 1783, on Pine Ridge and waters of Reed Creek, beginning corner to Godfret Young's land and corner to Leonard Straw's land.

October 28, 1799, JACOB DARTER, 50 acres, 1795, on part of a treasury warrant, assigned by Frederick Moore, assignee of James Murphy, assignee of Charles Copeland, on Reed Creek, corner to his patent land and Henry Rader.

p. 500

October 28, 1799, HENRY RADER, 50 acres, 1798, on part of a treasury warrant, 1782, on Reed Creek beginning corner to Jacob Darter's and corner to his own land.

October 7, 1799, ROBERT STEEL, 47 acres, 1791, on part of a treasury warrant, 1782, on Reed Creek, beginning on Jesse Evans' line and by a corner of Lewis Hutsell's land, to Cooley's corner and to Reeder's corner.

p. 501

April 30, 1800, PHILIP LAMBERT, 100 acres in two entries: (1) 50 acres entered 1791 on part of a treasury warrant, 1782, in name of Joseph Davidson and by him assigned to said Lambert; (2) 50 acres entered 1800 on part of a treasury warrant, 1783, on Wolf Creek, branch of New River, joining the lands of James Rice.

p. 502

May 1, 1800, PHILLIP REEDER, 46 acres, 1800, part of a treasury warrant, 1783, assigned to him by Walter Crockett, assignee of John Smyth, on the waters of Reed Creek, at Queens Knob on Cove Creek, corner to his patent land.

May 1, 1800, PHILLIP REEDER, 6 1/2 acres, 1800, on part of a treasury warrant, 1783, on waters of Reed Creek, corner to his patent land and corner to land of Jesse Evans.

p. 503

March 28, 1800, HENRY RADER, 55 acres, 1798, on part of a treasury warrant, 1782, on Reed Creek, beginning corner to Joseph Erwin's land to corner of Duncan Gullion's by foot of Pine Ridge, and corner to land of Varner Knipp and Plessley [Blessing].

p. 504

May 1, 1800, JOSEPH ERWIN, 100 acres, 1800, on part of treasury warrant, 1783, on waters of Reed Creek, corner to Peter Heddrick [Hedrick], Leonard Straw, and his own patent land.

November 10, 1796, VINCENT GRANT, 180 acres, on two entries both made in
    Montgomery County: (1) 80 acres, 1788, in name of John Stobough and by
    him transferred to Grant, on part of treasury warrant, 1783; (2) 100 acres,
    1789, in name of George Perry and assigned to Laurance Murry and by him
    to Grant on headwaters of Clear Fork of Wolf Creek.

CHAPTER IV
Wythe County Deed Book 1, 1790-1796

The documents found in Wythe County Deed Book 1 are abstracted in the
following pages. The majority of these documents are deeds for the transfer of land,
but other legal papers are included, such as militia appointments, powers of attorney,
acknowledgments of wives who were unable to travel to court, and manumission deeds
giving freedom to certain slaves. The book begins with a deed dated May 25, 1790,
the date of the first court session of Wythe County, and extends to December 13, 1796.
In many instances names appear in two or sometimes three different spellings in the
same document. All of the spellings have been included in parentheses. On a few
occasions deeds were signed by people whose names did not appear in the text. All of
these names are included here. If a name had a different spelling than might be
expected, that spelling has been added in square brackets.

p. 1, May 25, 1790, THOMAS HUTCHERSON [HUTCHINSON] and wife SARAH
    to JOHN FOSSET [FAWCETT], 261 acres on Reed Creek, part of a survey
    of 406 acres, originally surveyed for Hutcherson.
pp. 1-2, April 6, 1790, THOMAS HUTCHERSON [HUTCHINSON] and wife
    SARAH to CHRISTIAN CYBOT [SEYBERT], ____(torn) acres, part of 406
    acres as above, at the foot of the mountain.
pp. 2-3, June 14, 1790, GEORGE HOUKE to HENRY RADER, 100 acres by survey,
    1783, at a place on Reed Creek north of Pine Ridge, between Jacob Plessley
    [Blessing], and John Mcfarland.
pp. 3-4, December 20, 1787, ROBERT FRISTOE, of Franklin County, Virginia, to
    DAVID FANNEN, on a fork of Walkers Creek, branch of New River, by
    estimation 110 acres, part of survey for Fristoe of 185 acres, adjoining
    Fanning and Samuel Muncey, at the foot of Brushy Mountain.
p. 5, August 4, 1790, ROBERT DOUGHERTY, Executor of MICHAEL
    DOUGHERTY, JUNR., deceased, to JOHN CREEGAR (CRAIGER), 53
    acres on both sides of Reed Creek, part of survey ''adjoining the Boiling
    Spring tract below,'' including James Davis's improvement.
p. 6, August 4, 1790, ROBERT DOUGHERTY, Executor of MICHAEL
    DOUGHERTY, JUNR., to RICHARD BEESON, 97 acres (one place in the
    deed says land to Craiger, but *see* above), both sides Reed Creek, adjoining
    the Boiling Spring tract below.
p. 7, January 27, 1790, JOHN WALTERS and NATHANIEL POPE to NATHANIEL
    POPE of Montgomery County, Virginia, 256 acres on Beaver Dam, branch
    of Little Reed Island, corner to John Star's land, corner to Joseph Powell's.
p. 8, September 27, 1790, JOHN WALTERS to ISAAC GREEN, 180 acres, on Little Reed
    Island Creek, corner to Thomas Morgan's...to a branch of Beaver Dam Creek.

p. 9, April 17, 1789, THOMAS QUIRK and JANE, to GEORGE DAVIDSON, 400 acres on Reed Creek, adjoining Robert Sayers and Hugh Montgomery.

p. 10, April 7, 1789, THOMAS QUIRK and JANE to HANNAH DAVIS, 400 acres on Reed Creek adjoining Anchor and Hope, corner to James Chestnut.

pp. 11-12, May 4, 1790, HENRY HARMAN and wife NANCY to WILLIAM DAVIS, 200 acres on Middle Fork of Walkers Creek, joining land where said Davis now lives on, beginning near a "cabbin" on the south side of the creek.

pp. 13-14, September 29, 1790, Contract and specifications for the erection of the first courthouse of Wythe County, signed by Abr. [Abraham] Goodpasture, Walter Crockett and Jesse Evans.

p. 15, June 30, 1790, BIRD SMITH and his wife RHODA of Montgomery County to JOHN TOLLETT of Montgomery County, 200 acres on a branch of the Clinch River.

p. 16, October 26, 1790, BOSTON WYGALL and wife ELLAND to RICHARD RANES, 184 acres on waters of Peak Creek.

p. 17, November 22, 1790, JULIOUS RUTHERFORD to ABSALOM RUTHERFORD, 200 acres on Mine Mill Creek.

p. 18, December 20, 1790, JAMES McDONALD and his wife REBECCA to MAGNESS McDONALD, 222 acres on Lick Run, branch of Reed Creek.

p. 19, February 8, 1791, JOHN JENKINS to WILLIAM CARTER, 500 acres on east side of New River joining William Herbert's tract, known by the name of Poplar Camp.

p. 20, February 8, 1791, ROBERT SAYERS to NATH'L FRISBIE, 214 acres on east side of New River.

p. 21, February 8, 1791, MANITREE JONES to JAMES NEWELL, 324 acres on both sides of Cripple Creek adjoining the tract Newell lives on.

p. 22, February 8, 1791, MANITREE JONES TO JAMES NEWELL, 485 acres on Dry Branch, joining the patent land of Sam'l Ewing on New River.

p. 23, January 5, 1791, ROBERT STEEL to MOSES LINDSEY, 123 acres on Walkers Creek, branch of New River, corner to Samuel Newberry's survey.

p. 24, March 8, 1791, DOSSEL (DOSWELL) ROGERS to JESSE ROBINETT, 70 acres on headwaters of Elk Creek, with a conditional line between Rogers and Frederick Bransteter.

p. 25, December 27, 1790, CHRISTLEY PICLE (PICKLE) sells personal property to MARTIN STALY, 2 "stears," 5 years old, one black, other white, half crop in near ear for 10 pounds to be paid on or before August next.
February 12, 1791, ROBERT BEDWELL's sworn statement in regard to what he heard ABRAM WRIGHT say about SUSANAH HOUCK, which WRIGHT denied. .

p. 26, April __, 1791, DANIEL TRIGG, surviving executor of WILLIAM INGLES, deceased, to BIRD SMITH, son-in-law and devisee of William Ingles under the will, 200 acres on head springs of Wolf Creek, branch of New River in Burks Garden, granted to William Christian and Daniel Trigg, executors of William Ingles on May 3, 1785.

p. 27, April 1791, DANIEL TRIGG, surviving executor of WILLIAM INGLES, deceased, to BIRD SMITH, son-in-law and devisee of William Ingles under the will, 200 acres on a branch of the Clynch [Clinch] River, granted November 11, 1783.

p. 28, September 27, 1790, JAMES DEAN to JAMES McGAVOCK, 290 acres on a branch of Cripple Creek.

p. 29, September 27, 1790, JAMES DEAN to JAMES McGAVOCK, 53 acres adjoining the land he is now living on, adjoining the old survey.

p. 30, September 27, 1790, JAMES DEAN to JAMES McGAVOCK, 400 acres on the waters of Cripple Creek.

p. 31, September 27, 1790, JAMES DEAN to JAMES McGAVOCK, 68 acres on branch of Cripple Creek.

p. 32, April 11, 1791, WILLIAM INGLEDOW and ELIZABETH to ALMERINE MARSHALL, lot on Reed Creek, 3 acres 48 poles, part of a tract granted to James Patton, August 22, 1753, known by the name of Long Glade, beginning on Frederick Castle's line.

p. 33, February 7, 1791, WILLIAM DAVIS to JOHN MUSSER, 44 acres, no creek given, beginning at a stump in the field of said William Davis.

p. 34, April 11, 1791, HANNAH DAVIS to ROBERT SAYERS, 400 acres on Reed Creek, adjoining Anchor and Hope, same whereon George Davis now liveth.

p. 35, June 7, 1791, WALTER CROCKETT, executor, and JOSEPH CROCKETT, heir of SAMUEL CROCKETT, deceased, to CHRISTOPHER SIMMERMAN, 85 acres on Ceder [Cedar] Run, branch of Reed Creek, granted to Joseph Crockett by patent November 7, 1752, left by Joseph Crockett to his son Samuel by will.

p. 36, April 5, 1791, GEORGE CARTER to ROBERT CARTER, son of George Carter, for love and affection, 400 acres by survey Barren Springs tract on south side of New River, mentions David Sayers Island.

p. 37, September 6, 1791, HENRY MITCHELL and JANE to HENRY HONEIKER [HONAKER], 158 acres on the west side of the New River, mentions James Ingram's line, the river bank and an island.

pp. 38-39, September 9, 1791, PATRICK CASH and SARY (signed SARRAH) to JOHN FOLKS, 310 acres where Cashes now live on branch of Poplar Camp Creek.

p. 40, May 1, 1791, COLONEL CHARLES LYNCH and ANN (ANNE) to MR. HENRY DAVIS, 150 acres on unnamed creek, mentions the [New] River.

p. 41, September 10, 1791, RANDALL FEWGATE [FUGATE] and CHARITY to CHARLES DYER, 82 acres on the south side of the New River.

p. 42, September 6, 1791, RANDALL FEWGATE [FUGATE] and CHARITY to WILLIAM CALFEE, JUNR., 70 acres on south side of New River.

p. 43, September 2, 1791, RANDALL FUGATE and CHARITY to JOHN FUGATE, 100 acres on the east side of the New River.

p. 44, September 12, 1791, JOHN LOWTHAIN and ELIZABETH to ADOLPH FLOREY, 380 acres on Macks Run, branch of New River.

p. 45, September 12, 1791, JOHN LOWTHAIN and ELIZABETH to ADOLPH FLOREY, 45 acres on Macks Run, branch of New River.

p. 46, August 20, 1791, HENRY HARMAN and NANCY to JACOB NICEWANDER, no acres stated, Walkers Creek.

p. 47, September 8, 1791, ROBERT DAVIS and MARY to JOHN MUSSER, 25 acres, no creek stated.

pp. 47-48, October 11, 1791, JOHN STEVENS of Washington County, Virginia, to FREDERICK MOOR, JUNIOR of Wythe County, 130 acres on Reed Creek, near the ''waggon'' road, mentions John Nowell's line.

p. 49, October 11, 1791, THOMAS MEED and ALSABETH to PETTER [PETER] TARTER, 130 acres on Reed Creek near mountain, corner to George Kinder and near the ''waggon'' road.

p. 50, October 10, 1791, JAMES McDONALD and REBECCA to DANIEL SPONSLER, no acres, on Lick Run of Reed Creek.

p. 51, October 11, 1791, MARY KETTERING (KATRON) appoints MICHAL NAF (NEFF) attorney to recover and receive of SAMUEL ETTER, of Lebanon Township, Pennsylvania, the sum of 12 pounds, Pennsylvania currency.

pp. 51-52, October 11, 1791, CATHARINE LEETS (LITZ) appoints WILLIAM LITZ, attorney, to recover from JOHN SNOOK of Lebanon Township, Pennsylvania, my part of remainder of Leonard Dinenger's estate as under the last will of Dinenger.

pp. 52-53, December 13, 1791, EDWARD MURPHY and BRIDGET to LEWIS HUTSELL, 205 acres on north branch of Reed Creek, branch of New River (part of survey of 400 acres, corner to Henry Bean's land).

p. 54, December 13, 1791, EDWARD MURPHY and BRIDGET to LEWIS HUTSELL, 45 acres on north branch of Reed Creek, part of 400 acres, corner to Henry Bean.

p. 55, December 13, 1791, EDWARD MURPHY and BRIDGET to HENRY BEAN, 150 acres on north branch of Reed Creek, part of 400 acres where Bean now lives.

p. 56, January 29, 1791, ROGER OATES to STEPHEN SANDERS, 500 acres on south side Cripple Creek, adjoining said Sanders.

p. 57, January 10, 1792, JOHN ADAMS and ELIZABETH to ROBERT ADAMS, 160 acres on Reed Creek, mentions Robert Love's line.

pp. 58-59, December 11, 1791, CHARLES BLACKLEY and MARGARET to THOMAS CROW, 184 acres, no location given.

pp. 59-60, September 5, 1791, THOMAS BRATTON, yeoman, appoints his "trusty friend" JEREMIAH DOWLING, attorney to recover from ROBERT SANDERS, farmer, 14 pounds 10 shillings due on a note which was forcibly and illegally endorsed to NATH'L FRISBIE and also to receive from JAMES NEWELL, ESQ., 6 pounds Virginia currency, all illegally endorsed to Frisbie.

p. 61, October 13, 1791, JESSE ROBINETT to DOSWELL ROGERS, 70 acres on the head of Elk Creek, beginning on a conditional line between Doswell Rogers and Frederick Branstater.

p. 62, February 14, 1792, SAMUEL MARS, SENR., and LETTICE (LETTIS) to HENRY MARRS, 108 acres both sides of Clinch River, part of 190 acres granted to Samuel Marrs, May 9, 1787.

pp. 63-64, February 14, 1792, SAMUEL MARS, SENR., and LETTICE (LETTIS) to CHRISTOPHER MARRS, 2 acres on both sides of the Clinch River, part of 190 acres granted to Samuel Marrs, May 9, 1787.

p. 64, February 14, 1792, SAMUEL MARS, SENR. and LETTICE (LETTIS) to WILLIAM MARRS, 123 acres on Bluestone Creek, on New River, by survey dated March 11, 1784.

pp. 65-66, January 11, 1792, DOSWELL ROGERS to WILLIAM STONE, 70 acres on head of Elk Creek, mentions conditional line between Rogers and Frederick Branstater.

p. 67, October 4, 1791, JESSE EVANS to ALEXANDER SMYTH, 75 acres granted Evans December 16, 1784, adjoining the survey belonging to the heirs of Hugh Montgomery, deceased [probably waters of Cove Creek, branch of Reed Creek].

p. 68, January 11, 1792, DOSWELL ROGERS to FREDERICK BRANSTATER, 32 acres at the head of Elk Creek, adjoining Branstater and Thomas Rogers, part of survey for Rogers, December 2, 1785.

p. 69, February 14, 1792, WILLIAM OWENS to SAMUEL MARRS, no acres stated, on the north side of Rich Mountain, waters of the Clinch, near John Bradshaw's survey.

p. 70, February ___, 1792, STOPHEL ZIMMERMAN and MARGARET to ALEXANDER SMYTH, attorney at law, 1 1/2 acres including the house now occupied by the Court as a courthouse (supposed to be near center of same), corner to lot in the intended town at Wythe C.H. [Court House], on which said Smyth now lives. Lots laid off November 11 last by Robert Adams, Gent., surveyor, appear on the plat as lots known by the letters DE and F, adjoining the Cross Street, an alley called Water Alley, Milk House Alley, and Forest Alley, also a lot containing the spring northwest of the land laid off by Adams, and all interest in alleys and the spring.

pp. 71-72, February 14, 1792, SAMUEL MARRS and LETTICE (signed LETIS) 70 acres on the Clinch River, part of 160 acres by survey January 16, 1783.

pp. 72-73, March 12, 1792, WILLIAM WARD and JEAN to HENRY HOPPESS, 140 acres on both sides of Reed Creek.

pp. 73-74, March 11, 1792, JAMES DAVIS and MARY to JOHN SNIEVILY (SNAVELEY), 52 acres corner to Joseph Atkins.

p. 75, March 11, 1792, JAMES DAVIS and MARY to JOHN SNEIVELY [SNAVELEY], corner to Robert Davis, 140 acres, no creek mentioned.

pp. 76-77, February 14, 1792, JOHN BRECKENRIDGE, devisee of father GEORGE BRECKENRIDGE, deceased, who held in joint trust with son, to ROBERT BRECKENRIDGE, 185 acres, part of 400 acres on Cove Creek purchased from the executors of James Patton, Gent., deceased, corner to Patrick Calhoun.

pp. 77-78, April 9, 1792, ANDREW BOYD and MARY of Wythe County, to JOHN SMITH of Botetourt County, 550 acres on Pine Run, part of a large grant to James Patton, patent issued 20th of June 1753, corner to the land of John Thompson Sayers and Boyd.

p. 79, April 12, 1792, CHRISTOPHER ELMS and MARGARET to STOPHEL PHILIPPIE, 140 acres on Middle Fork of Holston, part of 200 acres and the place where Elms formerly lived.

p. 80, June 18, 1792, WILLIAM DAVIS and JOSEPH PATTERSON, GENT., power to take acknowledgment of MARGARET ELMS, as she is unable to travel. Examined on June 23, 1792.

p. 81, March 30, 1792, plat of lines of division between Wythe and Montgomery County.

p. 82, January 24, 1792, JOHN FINDLEY of Augusta County appoints my ''trusty friend'' WILLIAM FINLEY of Wythe attorney to make a deed to DAVID and SAMUEL FINLEY of Mercer County, Virginia, tract on Sally Run, formerly belonging to JOHN FINLEY, now deceased.

p. 82, June 12, 1792, THOMAS OGLE to JAMES OGLE, my son, for love and affection, all estate possessed at my death; no description given.

p. 83, April 11, 1792, ROBERT BUCHANAN of Wythe County, to JAMES LAMIE of Washington County, for 50 pounds to Axston Scott, assignee of Buchanan, paid by Lamie, 94 acres in Poor Valley on the North Fork of Holston and named Richlands, on Poor Valley Creek...to the foot of the Clinch Mountain.

p. 84, June 12, 1792, JOHN FINLEY of Augusta County, by WILLIAM FINLEY, attorney in fact, to DAVID and SAMUEL FINLEY of Lincoln County, Kentucky, 320 acres on Sally Run, branch of Reed Creek, granted to John Mcfarland June 20, 1753.

p. 85, June 12, 1792, CHRISTOPHER ELMS and MARGARET to BURKETT SEIBEL, 60 acres, part of 200 acres where Elms formerly lived on Middle Fork of Holston.

p. 86, April 19, 1792, GEORGE KINSER of Reed Creek to WILLIAM EWING, one ''malatto'' man named Tom, 20 years old.

p. 87, August 20, 1791, HENRY HARMAN, SENR., and NANCY to HOLTON MUNCEY, 182 acres by survey April 1754 on Walkers Creek between two mountains, part of Loyal Company grant.

pp. 88-89, June 8, 1790, WILLIAM MUNSEY and ELISBETH to HENRY HARMAN, 330 acres patent December 9, 1782, on North Fork of Walkers Creek.

pp. 89-90, June 11, 1792, JOHN ADAMS to WILLIAM ADAMS, son of John, for love and affection, 192 acres by survey granted to John Vance by patent August 1753 and sold to John Adams by P. Vance and to Robert Alcorn and he to John Adams, on the north side of a branch.

pp. 90-91, June 17, 1790, ROBERT STEEL to DANIEL ROBINETT, 150 acres on Walkers Creek whereon Robinett now lives.

pp. 91-92, June 13, 1792, MOSES LINDSEY and LETTICE to JAMES WADDLE, 123 acres adjoining Samuel Newberry, deceased, and the Green Hill on Walkers Creek, branch of New River.

pp. 92-93, no date given, PETER STROUP to MICHAEL CRAGE (CRAGER), 300 acres within the lines of Nicholas Cline's patent whereon sd. Cline now lives, known by the name of Pine Run, on both sides, joining the widow Fullen, John Etter, Godfrey Young, and Henry Umbarger; recorded September 11, 1792.

p. 93, July 24, 1792, JOSEPH DAVIS and MARGARET to THOMAS CROW, 354 acres corner to Robert Davis and John Snevely [probably waters of the Holston River].

p. 94, August 14, 1792, GEORGE WAMPLER, SR., and ELIZABETH, to GEORGE WAMPLER, JR., 200 acres on Reed Creek, part of Ratliffs Marsh where George Wampler, Junr. now lives, corner to Thomas Copenhaver, Martin Miller and George Wampler, Senr.

pp. 95-96, August 14, 1792, DAVID and SAMUEL FINLEY of Mercer County, Kentucky to WILLIAM FINLEY, JUNR., of Wythe, 327 acres on Sally Run, branch of Reed Creek, granted to John Mcfarland June 20, 1754.

pp. 96-97, August 13, 1792, THOMAS COWPEHEFER [COPENHAVER] and EULEAND (EULEANA) [JULIA ANN] to THOMAS MEAS, 115 acres on Reed Creek, branch of New River, part of Ratcliffs Marsh whereon Meas now lives.

PP. 97-98, August 10, 1792, HUGH PATRICK and SUSANA to MARY DUNN, widow and relict of THOS. DUNN, deceased, Mary being the administrator of the estate, no acres given, on both sides of New River adjoining the upper end of Jeremiah Patrick land.

pp. 99-100, September 11, 1792, JOHN McNITT and JEAN to WILLIAM HAY, 35 acres 26 poles on Reed Creek, in McNut's patent line and corner to land surveyed for the Town at Wythe C. H. [Court House], and crossing the wagon road.

pp. 100-101, August 21, 1792, WILLIAM LOCKHART and RACHEL to ALEXANDER ORE [ORR], 270 acres, no creek given.

pp. 101-102, August 23, 1792, JOHN ALCORN and JEAN, of Madison County,

Kentucky, to JOHN MILLER of Wythe, 161 acres on Lucasses Creek branch of Reed Creek.

p. 103, May 1, 1792, SOLOMON COX to DAVID PUGH of Franklin County (no state given), 330 acres on Wilson Creek, branch of New River. Deed is also signed by NEOMI COX.

p. 104, September 11, 1792, JOHN EWING and POLLY to HENRY ELLER, 225 acres both sides of Cripple Creek.

p. 105, May 9, 1792, THOMAS QUIRK to HENRY BUFORD of Bedford County, Virginia, "one Negroe man slave named Will, same I purchased of Richard Meux of Kentucky and him hired to Hon. Andrew Moore."

pp. 105-106, September 12, 1792, JAMES McGAVOCK to JAMES BABER, release of claim following a deed of trust for 480 acres, conveyed by Baber to McGavock in trust, on February 2, 1790.

p. 106, May 8, 1792, JAMES ANDERSON to WILLIAM GREEAR, 95 acres on Wilson Creek, branch of New River, also signed by MORNING ANDERSON.

pp. 107-108, September 14, 1791, THOMAS HUTCHERSON and SARAH to HENRY CLEMENS, 59 acres on Reed Creek, part of 460 acres surveyed for Hutcherson, corner to part of survey sold to Christian Cybert [Seybert].

p. 108, October 3, 1791, HARRIS McKINLEY WYLY [WYLEY] of Washington County, Territory of United States, Power of Attorney to JAMES WYLY [WYLEY] of same place to make a deed to PHILLIP ARMBRISTER, land known as Wyley's old fields. Notarized in Green County, no state given (recorded November 13, 1792).

p. 109, September 7, 1792, MOSES GORDON and HANNAH to JOHN GORDEN, 190 acres on a small branch of South Fork of Reed Creek called Pine Run.

p. 110, February 13, 1792, HENRY CLEMENS and CATHERINE to JOHN TUTWILER, 59 acres on Reed Creek, part of Thomas Hutcherson's 460 acres adjoining Christian Cybort [Seybert], at the north side of Newberry's Knob.

p. 111, February 13, 1792, WILLIAM DAVIS and LEONARD STRAW, GENT., whereas CHARLES BLACKELY and MARGARET by sale December 11, 1791, conveyed to THOMAS CROW, 184 acres, and Margaret cannot travel, the Gentlemen are to receive her acknowledgment; done November 14, 1793.

p. 112, June 16, 1791, GEORGE KINSER, yeoman, to HENRY DARTER, yeoman, all right title and interest to tract on North Fork of Holston adjoining John Stroup and John Older place, 150 acres.

p. 113 is blank

pp. 114-115, August 3, 1792, MARTIN STALEY and MARGARETT to GEORGE WEAVER, 191 acres at the head of Reed Creek and Holston River, part of a larger tract containing 130 (mistake in the original, probably should be 230 acres), corner to Michael Steffey's.

pp. 115-116, August 9, 1792, DANIEL CREAMOR of Green County, Territory South of the Ohio (Tennessee) and SARAH to DAVID KIRKWOOD of Wythe, 130 acres on the Middle Fork of the Holston.

p. 117, September 6, 1792, JAMES NEWELL and SARAH to PHILIP GAINS (?), 498 acres by survey, April 27, 1790, on headwaters of Chestnut Creek and Meadow Creek.

pp. 118-119, December 10, 1792, ROBERT and CATY SANDERS to WILLIAM SANDERS, both sides of Cripple Creek, near Henleys Branch, corner to Lucas Hood, no acres given.

pp. 120-121, December 10, 1792, ROBERT and CATY SANDERS to RANDOLPH RUTHERFORD, 157 acres by patent November 9, 1790, branch of Cripple Creek.

pp. 121-122, February 7, 1791, JAMES, ROBERT, and HARRACE OR HORRACE [HARRIS?] WYLY [WYLEY], of Washington County, North Carolina, to PHILLIP ARMBRISTER, 500 acres [probably on waters of Reed Creek] corner to McCaul's land. Signed HARRACE McKINLEY WYLY (recorded December 11, 1792).

p. 123, August 22, 1792, DAVID VAUGHT and MARGERTT (MARGRET) to JOHN GARWOOD, 58 acres on South Fork of Holston, corner Jarvis Smith, part of tract granted Joseph Crockett.

p. 124, October 9, 1792, ROBERT SAYERS and JEAN (JANE) to RICHARD MUSE, 1/2 of two tracts on east side of New River, adjoining the lead mine tract, containing 660 acres.

p. 125, August 30, 1792, RICHARD WRIGHT and SARAH to HENRY KIRK, 25 acres both sides of Turkey Fork of Elk Creek.

p. 126, October 9, 1792, RICHARD BEESON to JAMES FLACK of Franklin County, Pennsylvania, part of the "Boylin" [Boiling] Spring tract on the east side of Reed Creek adjoining Robert Graham and John Criger, where Beeson now dwells, no acres stated.

p. 127, Acknowledgment of MARY, wife of JAMES DAVIS, for deed dated March 11, 1792, signed by Justice of the peace for Western Territory south of the Ohio (Knox County), ordered November 14, 1792, done January 21, 1793.

p. 128, January 1, 1793, WILLIAM INGLEDOVE and ELIZABETH to ALMERINE MARSHALL, 12 1/2 acres on Reed Creek, part of whereon Ingledove now liveth formerly known as Paxtons Glade.

p. 129, April 5, 1793, THOMAS GILLESPY and MARGARET to JAMES GILLESPY, part of tract whereon said Thomas now lives, by survey, 61 acres on river, not named.

pp. 130-131, October 11, 1792, JAMES McCORKLE of Montgomery County and JOSEPH WHITE of Western Territory to RICHARD HALE of Wythe County, 67 acres on Elk Creek.

pp. 131-132, June 23, 1792, DAVID TAYLOR and MARY to JAMES SIMPSON, JUNR., 108 acres surveyed November 12, 1782, on Pine Run, branch of New River, granted May 9, 1787, no acres given.

pp. 133-134, October 12, 1792, BENJAMIN SMITH and JUDAH to WILLIAM LAHUGH [LAHUE], of Frederick County, Virginia, 123 acres on both sides of Reed Creek, branch of the New River.

p. 135, October 23, 1792, WILLIAM ANDERSON of Wheenton (?) County, Territory of U. S. to WILLIAM WILLIAMS, 113 acres, bearing date March 25, 1783, on Little Fox Creek, branch of New River.

p. 136, May 31, 1790, NANCY MOORE binds her daughter ELIZABETH, age 4 years and 6 months, an indentured servant to GEORGE KEGLEY, until she is 18.

pp. 137-138, February 5, 1793, SAMUEL DOACK and ANNAS to GEORGE DAVIS, 148 acres on small branch of Reed Creek, part of a larger tract granted to David Doack, October 2, 1787, and part of another tract known as Black Lick, near Brushy Mountain.

p. 139, November 1, 1792, CHARLES LYNCH and ANN, of Campbell County to JAMES NEWELL, 180 acres on the north side of the New River, opposite the lead mines plantation and on both sides of Mill Creek, being the same purchased of William Bell, including the island and the ferry.

pp. 140-141, July 20, 1793, JAIN (JEAN) EWING, relict of WILLIAM EWING, deceased, to ALEXANDER EWING, whereas William Ewing by will devised to Alexander Ewing a tract on Cripple Creek, 346 acres granted to William Ewing by patent August 6, 1782, same whereon William resided when living, subject to the life estate for Jain his wife, now she sells her life estate to Alexander Ewing.

pp. 141-142, July 2, 1793, MICHAEL CRIGGER to MICHAEL VENRICK, 87 acres on South Fork of Reed Creek, the place known as Elk Pond, in a line of William King.

pp. 142-143, July 2, 1793, MICHAEL CREAGER to PETER CREAGER, 100 acres on South Fork of Reed Creek, Elk Pond, corner to Michael Venerick.

pp. 143-144, July 2, 1793, MICHAEL GRIGGER [CRIGGER] TO JACOB GRIGGER [CRIGGER], 100 acres on South Fork of Reed Creek, Elk Pond.

p. 145, July 9, 1793, HENRY BAGLEY, of Wythe County to JAMES PEPPER of Montgomery County, 338 acres on Middle Fork of Walkers Creek, beginning about one-half mile below his house on the north side of the creek on a hill by a meadow on Joseph Pauley's line, by a ''salt Peter cave.''

p. 146, August 12, 1793, JACOB DOBLAR and ANNE to MARTIN KEMMERLEN [KIMBERLING], about 40 acres on headwaters of Reed Creek, adjoining land whereon said Dobler now lives.

pp. 147-148, November 2, 1792, MOSES AUSTIN and MARY of Wythe County and STEPHEN AUSTIN of Philadelphia, to THOMAS RUSTON of Philadelphia, one undivided 1/8th part of the lead mines tract, 1,400 acres on Banimans [Bingamans] Branch on New River, with all houses, stores, furnaces, mills, dams, and wharves.

pp. 149-150, January 2, 1794, MARY AUSTIN is unable to travel so JAMES CAMPBELL and JAMES NEWELL to take the acknowledgment of Mary; done January 6, 1794.

pp. 150-151, August 13, 1793, WILLIAM SANDERS and POLLY to NEHEMIAH BONHAM, 105 acres on Cripple Creek, part of 750 acres surveyed for Henry Francis.

pp. 151-152, March 8, 1793, GEORGE SHILLIDEAY of Wythe County appoints ''trusty friend'' ROBERT WATSON, attorney, to convey title to land on waters of Beaverdam Creek, waters of Reed Creek, to BENJAMIN LONG and JOSEPH LONG.

pp. 152-153, August 13, 1793, SAMUEL MARRS and LETTICE to WILLIAM GEORGE, 184 acres on both sides of Whiteoak branch, on waters of Clinch River, patented 15 January 1783...on Witten's line.

p. 154, August 15, 1793, JAMES MAXWELL, GENT., to take the acknowledgment of LETTICE MARRS, who is unable to travel; done on September 2, 1793.

p. 155, August 13, 1793, GEORGE DAVIDSON and ANNE to HENRY BIRD, 400 acres on Reed Creek, adjoining Robert Sayers and Hugh Montgomery.

pp. 156-157, June 11, 1793, WILLIAM SANDERS and MARY to MICHAEL LEESE, 50 acres north side of Cripple Creek.

pp. 157-158, November 1, 1792, CHARLES LYNCH, of Campbell County to ROBERT SANDERS of Wythe County, 531 acres east side of New River on Bengamons [Bingamans] Branch adjoining Herbert's, known as Benjamons [Bingamans] Bottom tract, mentions Jenkin's line.

p. 159, May 13, 1793, GEORGE FORBUSS and MARGARET to ROBERT SAND-ERS, 130 acres west side of New River, part of 600 acres on which Forbuss now lives, beginning on the river bank between Forbuss and Sanders.

pp. 160-161, July 24, 1793, WILLIAM GLEAVES and ELIZABETH to MICHAEL WORELEY [WORLEY], 81 acres on Cripple Creek.

pp. 161-162, June 6, 1793, ROBERT WYLEY of Green County, ceded territory to WILLIAM NEELEY of Wythe County, 540 acres both sides of Cripple Creek, known by the name of Wyleys place, corner to Stephen Sanders and corner Peter Spangler's.

p. 163, September 10, 1793, WILLIAM CONEWAY and RODA (RHODA) of Washington County to ZACCHEUS ELKINS, 60 acres Middle Fork of Wolf Creek, waters of New River, granted William Coneway December 26, 1792, corner to Alexander McFarland's land.

p. 164, September 10, 1793, JOHN HURST and MARY, give power of attorney to CHARLES DYER to settle business in the State of Kentucky, but more especially to convey a tract on Salt River (being our 1/3 interest of 1,000 acres granted John Hurst, by state warrant) unto Mr. Richard Parker.

pp. 164-165, July 23, 1793, JAIN (JENE) EWING, widow of WILLIAM EWING, deceased, appoints WILLIAM DAVIS, ESQ., attorney to sell, hire, or dispose of three Negroes, Jacob, Luce (?) and Sall.

pp. 165-166, October 8, 1793, WILLIAM DAVIS and JEAN to JAMES DAVIS, 260 acres on headwaters of Holston, part of 1,300 acres, Davis Fancy, being the same that James Davis, Senr., conveyed by deed of gift to Henry Davis (recorded in Augusta County), corner to William and Robert Davis, on bank of Beaverdam Creek.

pp. 166-167, September 10, 1793, JOHN CUSTARD and ELIZABETH of Wilkes County, North Carolina, to HENRY BESTERFELT of Wythe County, 192 acres on the North Fork of the Holston River.

pp. 167-168, October 7, 1793, ROBERT DAVIS and MARY to JAMES DAVIS, 100 acres on the Middle Fork of Holston, part of 350 acres corner to Thomas Crow, Junr., and John Snievely [Snaveley].

pp. 168-169, October 7, 1793, ROBERT DAVIS and MARY to PHILIP HUMBARIGER [UMBARGER], 200 acres on the North Fork of Holston River, at the foot of Walkers Mountain.

pp. 169-170, September 20, 1793, ALEX. (ALEXR.) EWING to WILLIAM GANNAWAY of Buckingham County, Virginia, 393 acres on Cripple Creek.

pp. 170-171, September 20, 1793, ALEXANDER EWING to WILLIAM GANNAWAY of Buckingham County, 346 acres on Cripple Creek, branch of New River, corner to James Douglas land.

pp. 171-172, October 8, 1793, DAVID McGAVOCK and ELIZABETH to LEWIS ABLE, 120 acres on a small branch of Reed Creek along Pine Ridge.

pp. 172-173, May 9, 1793, WILLIAM HARBERT and POLLY to WILLIAM CARTER, 367 acres known as Harberts Ferry, corner to George Forbuss

p. 174, June 12, 1793, FRANCIS PRESTON of Washington County to WILLIAM CARTER of Wythe County, 215 acres on some branches of New River, granted to Preston August 19, 1791.

p. 175, October 8, 1793, JAMES DEAN, executor of ADAM DEAN deceased, of Davidson County, Territory South of the Ohio River to JAMES McGAVOCK, 490 acres by survey June 28, 1786, on waters of Cripple Creek granted to Adam Dean, February 4, 1793.

p. 176, June 1, 1793, RICHARD BEESON to JAMES McGAVOCK, all lands owned by him on either side of Reed Creek, part of which is known and called by the name of Boiling Spring tract, and on the other is situated grist and saw mills, now occupied by Beeson.

p. 177, November 11, 1793, GEORGE SPANGLER and KATRIN to GEORGE BAUGH, 122 acres on the North Fork of Holston in Rich Valley.

p. 178, November 11, 1793, GEORGE SPANGLER and KATRIN to PETER SPANGLER, SENR., 278 acres on the North Fork of Holston in Rich Valley.

p. 179, August 24, 1793, JAMES NEWELL sold to JOHN NEWLAND one Negro man slave named Bob for 40 pounds. If paid then obligation void [may be a mortgage].

p. 179, November 12, 1793, LAWRENCE STEPHENS, following passage of an act in May 1782 to emancipate slaves, emancipated SWAN, born 1771, TOM, born 1777, LEWIS, born 1790, Stephens acting as guardian for the two youngest until they were of age.

pp. 180-181, March 12, 1793, JOHN BAKER to ISAAC SHEPHERD, no acres, on branch of Reed Creek, part of a survey for James Tuttle December 3, 1782, mentions a branch and a mill.

p. 181, October 7, 1793, WILLIAM ENGLEDOVE and ELIZABETH to DANIEL MILLER, 1 acre and 14 poles on Reed Creek, adjoining Miller and Engledove, part of a tract whereon Engledove lives, called Paxtons Glade.

p. 182, October 14, 1793, JOHN BRECKENRIDGE and MARGARET of Wythe County appointed "trusty friend" JESSE EVANS, attorney, to make a deed to ROBERT ADAMS, title to 100 acres on Cove Creek adjoining Robert Breckenridge and to run agreeable to a division line made between Robert Breckenridge and John Breckenridge and to join John Adams and William Adams, including the place known by the name of the "Wooden Bridge."

pp. 182-183, February 10, 1794, STEPHEN SANDERS and ISBELL to JOHN CARR, 50 acres on waters of Cripple Creek, part of a tract said Sanders now lives on, beginning by the Thorn Branch.

pp. 183-184, February 11, 1794, WILLIAM BUSTARD to DAVID BUSTARD, 165 acres headwaters of Cripple Creek, part of where William Bustard now lives.

pp. 184-185, February 10, 1794, THOMAS HARBERT and SARAH to MOSES AUSTIN, 225 acres on east side of New River on Binghams [Bingamans] Bottom and New River.

pp. 185-186, February 10, 1794, WILLIAM FINLEY to COONROD RADER, 32 3/4 acres beginning on the patent line [no creek mentioned...Reed Creek?].

pp. 186-187, August 31, 1793, JAMES DOUGLAS of Wythe County, Virginia, and GEORGE DOUGLAS of Lincoln County, Kentucky, to JOHN DOUGLAS of Wythe County, 330 acres both sides of Cripple Creek, corner to Alexander Ewing.

p. 188, April 9, 1793, CHARLES NUCKOLLS and wife MARY to WILLIAM BELL and WILLIAM HARBERT, 500 acres on both sides of Cripple Creek.

p. 189, September 21, 1793, SAMUEL MARRS and LETTICE to THOMAS HARRISON, north side Rich Mountain on waters of Clinch River, no acres given.

p. 190, September 21, 1793, JOHN MARRS and MARY of Wythe to JOHN EVANS, 70 acres on Clinch River, part of 160 acres surveyed January 16, 1783.

p. 191, May 13, 1794, ISAAC NEWHOUSE and CATHERINE to MICHAEL BRANSTETER, 27 acres on a branch of South Fork of Cripple Creek, branch of New River.

p. 192, May 13, 1794, ISAAC NEWHOUSE and CATHERINE to DAVID HORN, 158 acres on a branch of South Fork of Cripple Creek.

p. 193, April 8, 1794, ALMERINE MARSHALL and RACHEL to DANIEL MILLER, 12 1/2 acres on the South Fork of Reed Creek, part of Paxtons Glade, corner to fence by side of the waggon road.

p. 194, April 5, 1794, WILLIAM HARBERT and POLLY to THOMAS HARBERT, all of Wythe County, 500 acres on east side of New River known by the name of Poplar Camp tract.

p. 195, June 10, 1794, JAMES NEWELL and SARAH to STEPHEN AUSTIN of Philadelphia, NATHANIEL FRISBIE, and MOSES AUSTIN, of Wythe County, 850 acres on New River, adjoining Robert and Samuel Porter, corner to William Bell's land, at the foot of the mountain.

p. 196, July 9, 1794, JAMES CAMPBELL and STEPHEN SANDERS, gentlemen justices, ordered to get acknowledgment of SARAH NEWELL who cannot travel; done September 26, 1794.

p. 197, March 17, 1794, JAMES NEWELL to ANDREW DONALD, two tracts on Cripple Creek, 660 acres: (1) 300 acres granted Newell as assignee of Richard Muse, patented December 2, 1785, and (2) 360 acres joining Donald on which Stephen Sanders, Jr. resides, granted Newell as assignee of R. Muse, March 10, 1794.

p. 198, March 10, 1794, ROBERT SANDERS and CATY to JAMES BARNETT, 100 acres on fork of Benjamons [Bingamans] Branch, part of 531 acres.

p. 199, August 8, 1794, MATHIAS HARMAN and LYDIA to ROBERT WHITLEY, 64 acres on both sides Clinch River, part of 200 acres granted Harman October 12, 1787.

pp. 200-201, August 11, 1794, WILLIAM ADAMS and MARGARET to ROBERT ADAMS, 192 acres on Cove Creek, adjoining John Adams and said Robert Adams, beginning on north side of a branch.

pp. 201-202, March 7, 1794, ABRAM TRIGG and SUSANNA of Montgomery County, Virginia to JOHN PEERY, assignee of Robert Moffet and William Wynne, 400 acres on both sides of Clinch River, beginning in Obed. Garwood's line.

p. 203, January 8, 1793, DANIEL SPONSLER to MICHAEL WALTERS, 226 acres formerly the property of James McDonald, tanner, late of the county. [Mortgage?].

pp. 204-205, July 1, 1794, WILLIAM BELL and SARAH and WILLIAM HARBERT and POLLY to HUGH MONTGOMERY and DANIEL CARLIN (of Patrick County, Virginia), 500 acres on both sides of Cripple Creek, including houses, forges, and dams.

pp. 206-207, August 5, 1794, ROBERT SANDERS and KATHERINE to ANDREW STEEL, 125 acres on east side of Benjamins [Bingamans] Branch on Josiah Bell's line and Jenkins' line.

pp. 207-208, December 21, 1793, JOHN BAKER and PRISCILLA to DANIEL MILLER, 187 acres on Reed Creek, part of tract said Baker now lives.

pp. 208-209, January 26, 1794, MICAEL STIFY [STEFFEY] and KATRINE to MICAEL STIFFY, JUNR., 105 acres [South Fork of Reed Creek?].

pp. 209-210, November 12, 1793, JAMES WHITE and JOSEPH GREER, gentlemen justices of Knox County, Territory South of the Ohio River, whereas SAMUEL DOAK and ANNESS [AGNES] by deed February 25, 1793, sold to George Davis, 148 acres in Wythe and Annass cannot travel, ordered to get her acknowledgment for the deed; done May 23, 1794.

p. 211, December 4, 1793, JOHN ALCORN (ALLCORN) of Madison County, Kentucky, appoints ROBERT BRECKINRIDGE of Wythe County to convey 161 acres on Lucases Creek to John Miller.

p. 211, June 9, 1794, JAMES NEWELL and SARAH to STEPHEN SANDERS, 240 acres on the west side of New River, beginning on the river and crossing a branch in the fork of Mine Mill Creek, to Keesler's line, corner to Robert Sanders.

p. 212, August 12, 1794, SAMUEL BRITTON and MARY to GEORGE KEEGLY, 90 acres on Holston by survey.

p. 213, May 10, 1794, JOHN DRAPER, SENR., and JANE to JOHN DRAPER, JUNR., 230 acres on head of Macks Run, branch of New River, part of whereon John Draper, Jr., now lives.

p. 214, May 10, 1794, JOHN DRAPER, SENR., and JANE to GEORGE DRAPER, 230 acres head of Macks run, part whereon George Draper now lives, corner to John Draper, Junr., and with Dunn's and Runner's lines.

p. 215, July 22, 1794, WILLIAM MUNCEY (signed MUNSEY) and ELISABETH to GEORGE WAGGONER, 78 acres part of grant to Muncy, March 4, 1793, North Fork of Walkers Creek, commonly called Kimberland Fork, branch of New River.

p. 216, September 4, 1794, WILLIAM MUNSEY and ELIZABETH to DANIEL WAGGONER, 200 acres part of a tract granted to Munsey March 4, 1793, on the North Fork of Walkers Creek, on Kimberland Fork, branch of New River.

p. 217, September 4, 1794, RICHARD MUSE, of Wythe County, to WILLIAM GRAYSON, of Montgomery County, Virginia, 220 acres on Walkers Creek, branch of New River.

pp. 217-218, September 1, 1794, SAMUEL MARRS and LETTICE (ELETICE) to THOMAS HARRISON, 39 acres by survey as per patent, on Clinch River, adjoining his own lines.

p. 218, March 22, 1794, CORNELIUS McGLISTER to ISAAC SIMPSON, 226 acres on Pine Run, waters of New River.

p. 219, February 10, 1794, JACOB PROONER and MARY to JOHN UMBARGER, 80 acres part of 367 acres on part of said survey where Prooner now lives, corner to part of said tract sold to Jacob Rabass [Repass], Senr.

p. 220, September 9, 1794, WILLIAM FINLEY, of Wythe County, for love and affection, gift to my daughter ELIZABETH MONTGOMERY, one Negro woman named Nan and one Negro boy named Martin.

pp. 220-221, September 10, 1794, ALEXANDER EWING to WILLIAM GANAWAY [GANNAWAY], 200 acres by survey March 3, 1775, on the south side of Cripple Creek of New River, granted to Ewing March 10, 1794.

p. 221, October 14, 1794, DAVID LOVE and MARY to PATRICK JOHNSTON, 100 (?) acres on the south side of Reed Creek.

p. 222, October 13, 1794, JONHN [JOHN] COMTON [signed JOHN CUMPTON], SENR., to JOHN CUMPTON, JR., 265 acres on "Blew stone" adjoining his old survey on the south side.

p. 223, October 13, 1794, JOHN CUMPTON, SENR. [signed COMPTON] to JOHN CUMPTON, JUNR., 400 acres on Blue Stone Creek, branch of New River.

p. 224, May 10, 1794, RICHARD ELLIS and SUSANA (signed SUSANAH) to SPENCER BREEDING, 110 acres on the north side of Little Reed Island Creek, branch of New River.

p. 225, April 20, 1794, JOHN HURST and MARY to RICHARD ELLIS, 113 acres where James Axley now lives, part of Samuel Drake's old survey on the south side of New River, opposite Persimmon Bottom.

p. 226, April 6, 1794, JAMES CULTON to PHILLIP ACRE, 200 acres, no creek given, corner to Culton's land.

p. 227, April 7, 1794, JAMES CULTON to PHILIP ACRE, 274 acres at the head of the Holston River, part of 974 acres, Skillon's [Shelton's?] Bottom, being the same Culton now lives on.

p. 228, October 14, 1794, GEORGE IRVIN of Knox County, Territory South of the Ohio, to GEORGE LITTLE of Sullivan County, Tennessee, 170 acres on headwaters on North River [Fork] of Holston River.

p. 229, September 3, 1794, FREDERICK CASTLE of Tisque (?) County, New York to JOHN HUDDLE, two tracts: (1) survey of 100 acres by Commissioner's certificate, assigned to Castle by John Ward, assignee of John Ward, Senr. (2) 106 acres surveyed April 22, 1790, on a small branch of Reed Creek.

p. 230, October 13, 1794, GEORGE IRVIN of Knox County, Territory south of the Ohio and GEORGE LITTLE of Sullivan County, Territory aforesaid to GEORGE CARTER, 170 acres by survey head branch of North Fork of Holston.

p. 231, November 7, 1794, SAMUEL DAVIS and HANNAH of Knox County, Territory South of the Ohio River to HENRY BURKHART, 140 3/4 acres on Middle Fork of Holston.

pp. 231-232, November 7, 1794, SAMUEL DAVIS and HANNAH of Knox County, Territory South of the Ohio River to JOHN MUSSER, 72 3/4 acres, part of a grant of 364 acres, on the Middle Fork of Holston, corner to Burkhard.

pp. 232-233, November 7, 1794, SAMUEL DAVIS and HANNAH as above to ROBERT DAVIS, 148 1/2 acres, part of a grant of 364 acres on Middle Fork of Holston.

pp. 233-234, December 8, 1794, RICHARD MUSE and MARGARET to DANIEL JUSTICE, 180 acres on Walkers Creek, the remainder of 400 acres, part of which was sold to Thomas Dunn.

pp. 234-235, February 10, 1795, DANIEL REPASS and BARBARA to JONATHAN HENDERSON, 100 acres by patent March 15, 1793, no location.

p. 235, January 10, 1795, GEORGE CARTER to FRANCIS JACKSON CARTER, son of George Carter, 170 acres by survey on head branches of the North Fork of Holston, mentions Hugh Fulton's line, near a road and crossing a branch.

p. 236, February 25, 1793, SAMUEL DOAK and ANNASS of Knox County, Territory South of the Ohio River, to JOHN GULLION, 128 acres on the waters of Reed Creek, adjoining George Davis, George Kinder and Peter Derter [Darter, Tarter].

p. 237, August 9, 1794, GEORGE MAY, of Russell County, Virginia, to JEREMIAH PIERCIFULL of same place, 140 acres on both sides of the North Fork of Holston River.

p. 238. May 11, 1794, TRUSTEES OF THE TOWN OF EVANSHAM (A. SMYTH, WILLIAM WARD, JESSE EVANS, JOHN MONTGOMERY, DAV'D McGAVOCK), to JOHN HAY, lot #1 on north side of Main Street in Evansham [now Wytheville], being the lot adjoining on the southwest of the Cross Street, 1/2 acre, being the same lot sold to Jacob Nicewonger, who assigned to Stophel Simmerman, who assigned to Jesse Evans, who assigned to Thomas Kirk, who assigned to John Hay.

p. 239, May 11, 1794, TRUSTEES, as above, to JOHN JOHNSTON, lot #13, in the Town of Evansham [now Wytheville], on the southeast side of Main Street, the third lot northeast from the Cross Street, 1/2 acre.

pp. 239-240, May 11, 1794, TRUSTEES, as above to WALTER CROCKETT, lot in Evansham [Wytheville], number [blank] on the southeast side of Main Street, second northeastward from the Cross Street, 1/2 acre.

p. 240-241, May 11, 1794, TRUSTEES, as above to MARTIN WOLFORD (WOOLFORD), lot #19 in Evansham [Wytheville], on the northwest side of Main Street, fourth lot northeast of the Cross Street, 1/2 acre.

pp. 241-242, May 11, 1794, TRUSTEES, as above, to JOHN MONTGOMERY, lot #17 in Evansham [Wytheville], on the southeast side of Main Street, fifth lot southwest of the Cross Street, 1/2 acre.

pp. 242-243, May 11, 1794, TRUSTEES, as above to MANASSESS [MANASSAS] FRIEL, lot #3 in Evansham [Wytheville], on the southeast side of Main Street being the first lot northeast of the Cross Street, 1/2 acre.

pp. 243-244, May 11, 1794, TRUSTEES, as above to PHILLIP REEDER, lot #20 in Evansham [Wytheville], on the southeast side of Main Street, the fourth lot northeast from the Cross Street, 80 square poles.

pp. 244-245, May 11, 1794, TRUSTEES, as above to JOHN MONTGOMERY, lot #7 in Evansham [Wytheville], on the southeast side of Main Street, the fourth lot southwest of the Cross Street, 1/2 acre.

pp. 245-246, May 11, 1794, TRUSTEES, as above, to ALMERINE MARSHALL, lot #9 in Evansham [Wytheville], on the northwest side of Main Street, being the second lot southeast of the Cross Street, 1/2 acre.

pp. 246-247, May 11, 1794, TRUSTEES as above, to WILLIAM HAY, lot #2 in Evansham [Wytheville], on the northwest side of Main Street, being the first northwest from the Cross Street, 1/2 acre.

pp. 247-248, April 8, 1794, TRUSTEES as above, to MICHAEL WALTERS, lot #4 in Evansham [Wytheville], on the southeast side of Main Street, the first lot southwest from the Cross Street, that is southeast of the lot sold by Evans to Kirk across the Main Street and Southwest of Frials [Friels] lot across the street, being the same lot sold to Gerald T. Conn, assigned to Alexander Smyth who assigned it to Walters, 80 square poles.

pp. 248-249, May 11, 1794, TRUSTEES as above to STOPHEL ZIMMERMAN, as assignee of Jesse Evans, lots 8 and 11 in Evansham [Wytheville], on northwest side of Main Street, the fourth and fifth lots southwest of the Cross Street, 1/2 acre.

pp. 249-250, September 14, 1794, JAMES NEWELL to GEORGE BRECKENRIDGE, [JR.], devisee of GEORGE BRECKENRIDGE, [SR], deceased, 100 acres by survey dated June 26, 1787, granted to Newell by patent March 21, 1793, on Cove Creek, corner to Breckenridge's patent land... at the foot of Brushy Mountain.

pp. 250-251, May 11, 1794, TRUSTEES as above, to GEORGE OURY, northwest side of Main Street, the fifth lot eastward from the Cross Street, 1/2 acre.

pp. 251-252, February 9, 1795, GEORGE CREGER and ELISABETH to WILLIAM CRAFORD [CRAWFORD], 377 acres on the north side of Pine Ridge in both sides of Sifers Gap.

pp. 252-253, March 10, 1795, PETER YOUNCE and ELIZABETH to JOHN STANGER, 130 acres on Shugar [Sugar] Run, a branch of Cripple Creek, corner to Younce (signed in German script).

pp. 253-253(a), March 10, 1795, PETER YOUNCE and ELIZABETH to JOHN

STANGER, 94 acres on Sugar Run, branch of Cripple Creek, by survey dated August 2, 1784, corner to Spreager [Spraker].

pp. 253(a)-254, December 8, 1794, GIDEON MOSS to JOHN RUTHERFORD, 350 acres on Peek [Peak] Creek and New River, surveyed February 20, 1783, beginning on line of Thorn Spring tract.

pp. 254-255, April 23, 1795, JOHN MESSERSMITH to GODFREY MESSERSMITH, PETER MESSERSMITH and ANDREW MESSERSMITH, 314 acres on the North Fork of Holston.

p. 256, March 31, 1795, JOHN ADAMS and JOHN MONTGOMERY, GENT., ordered to take acknowledgment of MARGARET ADAMS as she and her husband WILLIAM ADAMS sold land to ROBERT ADAMS, and Margaret is unable to travel; done April 1, 1795.

pp. 256-257, no day or month, 1795, FREDERICK BRANSTATER and MADELEAN [MADLEONA] to JOHN SHUPE, 125 acres, no location; recorded May 13, 1795.

pp. 257-258, May 12, 1795, JOSEPH DOUGHERTY and MARY of Lee County to ROBERT GARRETT of same place, 150 acres on Kimberlins Fork, branch of Walkers Creek, patent January 15, 1793, beginning on a branch on the north side of the creek above his house.

pp. 258-259, May 12, 1795, JOSEPH DOUGHERTY and MARY to JAMES RICE, 70 acres on Wolf Creek, branch of New River, patented May 8, 1787.

pp. 259-260, March 13, 1795, JOHN YOUNG and MARY to BENGEMIN [BEN-JAMIN] PORTER MAHORNEY (?), 180 acres on northwest side of Maiden Spring Fork of the Clinch River.

p. 260, April 21, 1795, PATRICK JOHNSTON and ESTHER to PETER MOYERS, 85 acres by survey dated April 28, 1783, on Reed Creek, a branch of New River, near corner to Philip Peck's.

p. 261, May 14, 1795, MICHAEL CREAGER, SENR., and MARY to GEORGE TAWNEY, 285 acres on South Fork of Reed Creek, known by the name Elk Pond tract, beginning the corner to Jacob Creager and Henry Grubb...to the line of John King, corner to Peter Creager... to the Elk Pond.

p. 262, June 9, 1795, WILLIAM SMITH and HANNAH to JOHN LINDAMOOD, 320 acres by patent June 13, 1790 (?), on both sides of Sally Run, a branch of Reed Creek and adjoining Stophel Brown.

p. 263, June 9, 1795, ALEXANDER EWING, one of the heirs of WILLIAM EWING, deceased, to PETER KINSER, 122 acres by survey, granted William Ewing by patent March 15, 1793, on Cripple Creek. [Text of this deed uses name Peter Kinder in error in one place.]

p. 264, September 14, 1794, WILLIAM MARRS to HENRY MARRS, 123 acres on a branch of Bluestone Creek of New River, by survey March 11, 1784.

p. 265, June 10, 1795, JEREMIAH PERCIVAL and MARY to JACOB GROSECLOSE, 105 acres on both sides of the North Folk of Holston River.

p. 266, July 13, 1795, ANDREW STEELE to ISAIAH ROBERTS, now of Montgomery County, Virginia, 125 acres on Bingamin's Branch, near Josiah Bell's, Jenkins' and Barnett's lines.

p. 267, April 8, 1795, JACOB PROONER and MARY to JACOB REPASS, 107 acres on waters of Reed Creek.

pp. 268-269, July 14, 1795, PATRICK CALHOUN, ESQR., and _____ [blank] his wife, of County of Abbeville, South Carolina to JESSE EVANS of Wythe

County, two tracts: (1) the place whereon said Evans now lives, 322 acres, (2) near above tract on branch usually known by the name of Tates Run, 159 acres by survey granted Patrick Calhoun November 7, 1752. Deed signed by John Montgomery, attorney in fact for Patrick Calhoun.

p. 269, November 22, 1794, PATRICK CALHOUN, ESQ., of Abbeville County, South Carolina, power of attorney to JOHN MONTGOMERY, JUNR., of Wythe County, to convey two tracts to Jesse Evans.

pp. 270-271, October 16, 1794. JOHN THOMPSON appoints his "trusty friend" ANDREW CROCKETT, to make a deed to JOHN CROCKETT for land on Cove Creek adjoining John Crockett, 170 acres.

pp. 271-272, June 9, 1795, NICHOLAS TARTER and FINAL [FINWELL] to JOHN LEEDY, 83 acres [probably waters of Reed Creek] the northeast corner of said Tarter's patent land.

pp. 272-273, January 21, 1795, SAMUEL COWAN and JEAN of Knoxville, Territory of United States South of the Ohio River, to HUGH MONTGOMERY of Wythe County, 106 acres, patent October 30, 1752.

pp. 273-274, March 11, 1795, HUGH MONTGOMERY and EUPHAME [EUPHEMIA] to JESSE EVANS, 106 acres on Cove Creek, branch of Reed Creek, granted October 30, 1752, to Hugh Montgomery, who devised the same to Jean his daughter, the wife of Samuel Cowan, the same who conveyed to Montgomery January 21, 1795.

pp. 274-275, March 12, 1795, ROBERT SAYERS and JOHN ADAMS, gentlemen, ordered to take acknowledgment of EUPHEMIA MONTGOMERY who cannot travel; done April 11, 1795.

p. 276, July 14, 1795, THOMAS WILEY (signed WILIE, recorded WYLIE), and JENNY of Greenbrier County, Virginia, to DANIEL WAGGONER of Wythe County, 110 acres on Clear Fork of Wolf Creek, waters of New River.

p. 277, March 24, 1795, Whereas a capias executed on me by sheriff and Samuel Lewallen being my "appearance bail" at next April Court, and for indemnification of Samuel, I give up and deliver to him my Negro woman named Moll, to remain his property unless some person enters himself my special bail, signed MICH'L DUNN.

pp. 277-278, June 16, 1795, ROBERT SIMPSON and MARY to EBENEZER LISTON, 100 acres by survey April 13, 1790, on Reed Creek, adjoining William Pearce.

pp. 278-279, May 11, 1795, FREDERICK MOORE and ELIZEBATH [ELIZABETH] to SAMUEL FULLEN, 135 acres on Reed Creek, between the tract known as Paxtons Glade and Henry Lambert's, beginning near a spring corner to Henry Lambert... corner to George Kinser's land,... to line of Glade tract... and along foot of Pine Ridge (signed in German script).

pp. 279-280, July 25, 1795, JAMES CAMPBELL and WILLIAM LOVE, ordered to take acknowledgment of ISBELL SANDERS who with husband STEPHEN SANDERS conveyed on November 10, 1794, 50 acres to JOHN CARR, and she being unable to travel, the above are to obtain her acknowledgment on the deed; done August 8, 1795.

pp. 280-281, August 2, 1795, PETER TARTER and ELIZABETH to STOPHEL BROWN, 130 acres on Reed Creek, corner to George Kinder... near the "waggon" road.

pp. 281-282, August 5, 1795, JOHN HURST and MARY to CHARLES DYER, 259 acres on the north side of New River, beginning on the river bank.

pp. 282-283, August 11, 1795, WILLIAM DAVIS, GENT., and JANE to PHILLIP AKER, 314 acres on headwaters of Holston River, being part of 573 acres.

pp. 283-284, August 10, 1795, JAMES KINNAIRD and MARY to GEORGE KINNARD, 80 acres on Peek [Peak] Creek, waters of New River, beginning on Montgomery's line.

pp. 284-285, August 11, 1795, ALEXANDER SMYTH to JESSE EVANS, 75 acres granted to Evans December 16, 1784, and by him conveyed to Smyth October 4, 1791, beginning on the upper end of the survey formerly belonging to Hugh Montgomery, deceased,...with Mr.Elroy's line.

pp. 285-286, August 11, 1795, FREDERICK MOOR (signed MORE), JUNR., and CHRISTANA [CHRISTENA], to HENRY RADER, 130 acres on Reed Creek beginning near the "waggon" road... on Joseph Ervin's line.

pp. 287-288, August 8, 1795, JEREMIAH PATRICK and SARAH to RICHARD REINS, 229 acres part of a grant to Hugh Patrick, who conveyed by deed to Jeremiah Patrick, on Bradleys branch waters of New River, beginning corner to Daniel Goodwin's, it being part of said survey.

pp. 288-289, August 11, 1795, JEREMIAH PATRICK and SARAH of Wythe County, Virginia to DANIEL GOODWIN, of Botetourt County, Virginia, 30 acres on New River, beginning on the river bank, corner to Menifee's.

pp. 289-290, August 8, 1795, JEREMIAH PATRICK and SARAH of Wythe to DANIEL GOODWIN, of Botetourt County, Virginia, 171 acres, part of a grant to Hugh Patrick, and conveyed to Jeremiah Patrick on New River, beginning corner to Richard Raines (part of said survey).

pp. 290-291, August 8, 1795, JEREMIAH PATRICK and SARAH of Wythe County, to DANIEL GOODWIN of Botetourt County, 390 acres on north side of New River, by survey, where Jeremiah and Sarah now liveth.

pp. 291-292, August 8, 1795, JEREMIAH PATRICK and SARAH of Wythe County, to DANIEL GOODWIN of Botetourt County, 59 acres by survey adjoining Patrick's old patent land [probably waters of New River].

pp. 292-293, August 11, 1795, JAMES EVANS and ELIZABETH to ALEXANDER ORR, 60 acres on Walkers Creek, part of a patent of 290 acres granted said Evans December 4, 1794,...at foot of Brushy Mountain.

pp. 293-294, March 18, 1795, JAMES EVANS and ELIZABETH to GEORGE HARMAN, 230 acres on Walkers Creek, part of patent for 290 acres granted to Evans, December 4, 1794,...at the foot of Brushy Mountain.

p. 294, August 8, 1795, ALEXANDER SMYTH and NANCY to DANIEL SHEFFEY, 1 1/2 acres including the house formerly occupied by the court of said county as a courthouse supposed to cover or stand near the center thereof, being the same conveyed to Smyth by Stophel Zimmerman in February 1792, the north corner of lot in Evansham [Wytheville] on which Sheffy now keeps a store, and corner Zimmerman's meadow fence.

pp. 295-296, August 12, 1795, JOHN ALCORN and JANE of Madison County, Kentucky to JOHN MILLER, 161 acres on Lucasses Creek, branch of Reed Creek, part of survey granted James Miller by patent on June 20, 1753, signed by Robert Breckingridg [Breckinridge], attorney for John Alcorn.

pp. 296-297, August 11, 1795, ROBERT BRACKINRIDGE [BRECKINRIDGE] and MARY to ALEXANDER SMYTH two tracts on Cove Creek, waters of Reed Creek, adjoining each other: (1) 385 acres, part of 700 acres granted James Patton August 22, 1753, 400 acres of which was conveyed 24th and 25th of June, 1774 from William Thompson and William Preston, executors to

George Brackeridge and Robert Brackenridge as co-tenants, George having departed this life and by will devised to John his moiety of 400 acres (except part estimated to be 15 acres included within the fence of Jesse Evans which said George devised to Jesse and he and John by deed conveyed his part devised to him to said Robert whereby the whole tract of 400 acres (except the 15 acres above) vested in Robert, the other part being conveyed to Patrick Calhoun and (2) 148 acres granted Robert Breckinridge October 12, 1787, corner to tract #1.

pp. 298-299, August 11, 1795, ROBERT BRACKINRIDGE and MARY to ALEXANDER SMYTH, 124 acres both sides of Cove Creek, corner to grant made to James Newell, part of 300 acres granted to Robert and John Breckenridge November 21, 1793, being a share of Robert's upon partition between them.

p. 300, June 10, 1795, THOMAS GILLESPIE and MARGARET to JEFFERY HELDRITH, 139 acres in Rich Valley, on both sides of North Fork of Holston.

p. 301, August 11, 1795, JOHN BRECKINRIDGE by JESSE EVANS his attorney in fact to ROBERT ADAMS, 76 acres on Cove Creek, part of 300 acres granted to Robert and John Breckinridge, November 21, 1793, being John's share upon partition.

p. 302, August 29, 1795, JOHN MONTGOMERY and NANCY to JAMES GRA-HAM, 110 acres on Reed Creek, part of a Loyal Company grant, beginning corner to Reins' survey.

p. 303, September 8, 1795, JOSIAH BELL and PATSY to MOSES AUSTIN, 268 acres on east side of New River adjoining Austin's land known as Bingamans Bottom.

p. 304, October 10, 1795, CHARLES DYER who is about to remove to Kentucky, appoints his well beloved friend WILLIAM CALFEE, JUNR., attorney in fact, to convey land to his brother's widow or heirs [not named].

pp. 304-305, October 10, 1795, CHARLES and MARY DYER to SAMUEL GOODWIN, clerk, 82 acres by survey on south side of New River.

pp. 305-306, April 20, 1795, JOHN GARWOOD and EASTER (ESTHER) of Culpeper County, Virginia to WILLIAM HAYS of Wythe County, two tracts adjoining: (1) 220 acres on North Fork of Holston, known as Buffaloe Cow Bottom, granted Charles Campbell, August 22, 1753, and conveyed to Garwood; (2) 44 acres adjoining on the west side, on both sides of the river, granted to him by entry on a treasury warrant.

p. 307, October 13, 1795, JOHN BROWN and CATEY (CATHEREN, CATHERINE) to HENRY CHRISTLEY, 300 acres on Pine Run, branch of New River, ... in Joseph Fewgate's [Fugate's] line.

p. 308, October 13, 1795, GIDEON HUDDLE, JOHN HUDDLE and his wife MARGARET, heirs of JOHN HUDDLE, deceased, appoint their brother HENRY HUDDLE, attorney, to convey to GEORGE CAP of Shenandoah County, Virginia, a tract of 204 acres on Shenandoah River, now in possession of Cap.

pp. 308-309, October 8, 1795, PETER HEDERICK and ANN(E) to PETER STIFFY [STEFFEY], 80 acres on Reed Creek adjoining Berner [Verner] Knipp, beginning by a path near the foot of Pine Ridge.

pp. 309-310, August 12, 1795, JACOB HONECKAR [HONAKER] and MARY to HENRY HONECKER [HONAKER], 146 acres by survey on headwaters of Little Pine Run, branch of New River.

p. 311, June 9, 1795, ISAAC SIMPSON and HANNAH to FRANKLING BRIDGMAN 226 acres on Pine Run, waters of New River, corner to the survey of John Thompson Sayers.

p. 312, October 8, 1795, PALSER TARTER and MAGDALENA to GEORGE WAMPLER, SENR., 165 acres on South Fork of Reed Creek, branch of New River, corner to Robert Cowden... and John Wilson's line.

p. 313, August 19, 1795, ESTHER SHILLIDEAY of Mercer County, Kentucky, appoints GEORGE SHILLEDEAY of same place and EDWARD SHILLIDEAY of Fayette County, Kentucky, attorneys, to sell and convey lands vested in me under the will of my deceased husband, GEORGE SHILLIDEAY [SR.].

p. 314, October 13, 1795, ESTHER SHILLADAY of Mercer County, Kentucky, by GEORGE SHILLADAY of same place to SAMUEL CROCKETT, 83 acres on Cove Creek, branch of New River.

pp. 315-316, October 13, 1795, JOHN McNUTT and JEAN to WILLIAM HAY, 433 acres on Reed Creek, branch of New River, where John McNutt now lives, corner to Hays' patent land.

pp. 316-317, August (blank), 1795, GEORGE SHILLIDAY and wife JANE, of Mercer County, Kentucky, to BENJAMIN and JOSEPH LONG, of Wythe County, 272 acres, [probably on a branch of Reed Creek] beginning on the line of John Miller's land.

p. 318, October 5, 1795, MICHAEL LEESE and NANCY to HENRY KETTNOR, 300 acres on Cripple Creek.

p. 319, October 5, 1795, MICHAEL LEESE and NANCY to HENRY KETTNOR, 163 acres granted Michael Lease assignee of Adam Dean by entry on treasury warrant and by survey, on Thorn Branch, beginning on George Ewing's patent line.

pp. 320-321, September 12, 1795, HENREY [HENRY] REDER [RADER, REEDER] and CATEY to VARNER KNIPP, 100 acres Reed Creek, branch of New River, on the north side of Pine Ridge between the land of Jacob Plessley [Blessing] and Jacob Pruner, by survey May 1, 1783, beginning at the foot of Pine Ridge. Signed by Henry Rader and wife Catey Rader.

p. 321, March 10, 1795, JOHN T. SAYERS, ROBERT SAYERS, ROBERT CROCKETT, JOSEPH CROCKETT, JOSEPH BAKER, and JOHN KERR, bond for $30,000. Sayers appointed Sheriff by commission from the governor September 10 last past.

p. 322, March 10, 1795, JOHN T. SAYERS, ROBERT SAYERS, ROBERT CROCKETT, JOSEPH CROCKETT, JOSEPH BAKER, and JOHN CARR, bond for $15,000, same as above.

p. 323, March 10, 1795, JOHN T. SAYERS, ROBERT SAYERS, ROBERT CROCKETT, JOSEPH CROCKETT, JOSEPH BAKER, and JOHN KERR, bond for $15,000, same as above.

p. 324, September 11, 1792, Order of THOMAS QUIRK, "Sir, you will please to convey the title to that tract of land you sold me" of 1,200 acres on Elk Horn in "feyatt" County [Kentucky?], to CAPTAIN ANDREW KINCANNON. Order directed to CAPTAIN ROBERT SAYERS.

pp. 324-325, October 9, 1795, DUNCAN GULLION to JOHN GORDEN, all right title and interest in an entry on the waters of Wolf Creek, containing 100 acres adjoining the lands of Michael Robenit [Robinette] known by the name of the Mossy Spring.

pp. 325-326, November 9, 1795, JOHN CROCKETT to PETER SMITH 53 acres granted April 22, 1784,... beginning near the foot of a mountain...near Joseph Baker's line [probably in the Cove].

pp. 326-327, November 10, 1795, JOHN McNITT [McNUTT?] and JEAN to JOHN DAVIS, 55 acres on Reed Creek, corner to William Hay... by an old road. Marginal comment states "delivered to J. E. Brown who now owns the land February 22, 1836."

pp. 327, October 2, 1795, ROBERT PERCIVAL appeared in Washington County before Arthur Campbell, Justice of the Peace, and took oath to support the Constitution of United States and fidelity to Commonwealth of Virginia.

pp. 327-328, January 29, 1793, Articles of agreement between WILLIAM EWING and ALEXANDER EWING, nephew of said William, of Davidson County, North Carolina, in order to procure his assistance and management of domestic and foreign business, William Ewing obligates himself to give the whole of his plantation on Cripple Creek to Alexander Ewing, the same whereon William now lives, except legal dower of wife during her lifetime, and at their death to Alexander who is to render to his uncle William Ewing every possible assistance in transaction of business for the life of William Ewing.

p. 328, September 23, 1794, STOPHEL ZIMMERMAN and MARGARETT to ALMERINE MARSHALL, 3 lots adjoining George Ouries [Oury's] lots... to a stake in the side of an old road in Evansham [now Wytheville].

pp. 329-330, November 17, 1794, STOPHEL ZIMMERMAN and MARGARETT to GEORGE OURY, 15 acres on the north side of an old road, corner to Almerine Marshall, 3 lots... with the road... and joining George Hutsell's.

p. 331, November 17, 1794, STOPHEL ZIMMERMAN and MARGARETT to GEORGE OURY, 3 lots adjoining the three of Marshall as above.

pp. 332-333, September 6, 1794, JOHN GREENUP and ELIZABETH, JOSHUA DICKERSON and SUSEANA (SUSANNA), PHILLIP WITTEN and RUTH, JOHN CECIL and KEZIAH, THOMAS WITTEN and ELENOR (ELENDER), WILLIAM CECIL and ANN, JAMES WITTEN and REBECCA, WILLIAM WITTEN and LETTEY (LETTICE), all legatees of Thomas Witten to JEREMIAH WITTEN, 300 acres on Clynch [Clinch] River, beginning on Crab Orchard survey.

pp. 334-336, September 6, 1794, JOHN GREENUP and ELIZABETH, JOSHUA DICKERSON and SUSEANA (SUSANNA), PHILLIP WITTEN and RUTH, JOHN CECIL and KEZIAH, THOMAS WITTEN and ELENOR (ELENDER), WILLIAM CECIL and ANN, JEREMIAH WITTEN and SARAH, JAMES WITTEN and REBECCA, WILLIAM WITTEN and LETTEY (LETTICE), all legatees of Thomas Witten to WILLIAM WITTEN, _____ (blank) acres on Clynch, by deed from Bird Smith to John Greenup and Thomas Witten, deceased, in 1787, on the north side of the river.

pp. 336-337, December 1, 1795, NICHOLAS SNIDER and MARY to BOSTON SNIDER, 138 acres, no creek given, beginning corner to Andrew Vaught's... and Michael Baugh.

p. 338, October 10, 1795, ROBERT CROW to JAMES CROW, no acres stated, on Hunger Mother, a branch of Middle Fork of Holston, corner to Edward Crow.

pp. 339-340, September 8, 1795, PATRICK JOHNSTON and ESTHER (EASTER) to WILLIAM KING, 160 acres on head of Walkers Creek, branch of New River.

pp. 340-341, October 17, 1795, MICHAEL CRIGGER and MARY to MICHAEL

VENRICK, all interest in a tract of 88 acres on South Fork of Reed Creek, "except so much of said 88 acres as lyes within the bounds of Peter Crigger's lines," being a tract granted to Michael Crigger, part of a preemption warrant, patented June 24, 1785, corner to Peter Crigger.

pp. 342-343, December 9, 1794, JOHN LIGGET and HANNAH to HENRY SLEAGLE, 95 acres on Middle Fork of Holston, corner to William Lockheart's land.

pp. 343-344, November 10, 1795, WILLIAM ROGERS to JOHN THOMPSON SAYERS, 100 acres on waters of Reed Creek, branch of New River.

p. 344, January 12, 1796, ANDREW BOYD and MARY of Wythe County to THOMAS BOYD of Fayette County, Kentucky, 500 acres in Fayette County, Kentucky, on branches of Elkhorn Creek, a north branch of Kentucky River, part of a military survey of 2,000 acres granted to Andrew Boyd as heir-at-law of Alexander Boyd, deceased, beginning at a corner of John Boyd's land.... in Carter's military line...crossing Strouds Road, and a branch of Elkhorn... and William Anderson's line... crossing two branches and Cleveland road.

pp. 345-346, January 12, 1796, ANDREW and MARY BOYD of Wythe County, to JOHN BOYD, 500 acres in Fayette County, Kentucky, on branches of Elkhorn Creek, north branch of Kentucky River, granted Andrew Boyd as above, beginning in William Phillipps's military line...corner to John Carter's military survey...corner Thomas Boyd...corner Thomas Barnes's military line...crossing creek and Strouds Road.

pp. 346-347, January 12, 1796, STEPHEN CHAPPEL and JULIANA to CHRISTIAN KEGLEY, 100 acres by survey August 9, 1786, on waters of Reed Creek in Martin Wyrick's line.

pp. 348-351, November 16, 1795, ROBERT MORRIS, ESQ. and MARY of Philadelphia, Pennsylvania, to JAMES SWAN of Dorchester, Norfolk County, Massachusetts; whereas Morris by deed dated July 16 last conveyed to Swan all interest and also a deed December 11 to James Brackenridge, Wilson Cary, Nicholas Joseph Higby, Charles Higby, and Morris promised further assurances when requested to do so, regarding 500,000 acres by survey October 28, 1794, located in Wythe and Russell counties, the greater part in Wythe, on Sandy, Guyandott rivers... beginning on a branch of the Guyandott about six miles from the mouth of Little War Creek, a branch of the Sandy River...corner to a survey of Nicholas's 480,000 acres, and a survey for 320,000 acres for Nicholas and Jacob Kinney... down War Creek to the mouth... crossing the Sandy River at six miles... crossing Panter Creek at nine miles... to Knox's Creek... Turkey Creek, Buffalo Creek, Pigeon Creek, Gilberts (?) Creek... reserved 4,000 acres.

p. 352, April (?) 15, 1795, ENOCH OSBORN and SHADERICK GREEAR, gentlemen justices of Grayson County, whereas SOLOMON COX and NEOMI on May 1, 1792, conveyed 330 acres in Grayson County, formerly Wythe County, to DAVID PUGH. Neomi was unable to travel, they were to get her acknowledgment to the deed. Done April 22, 1795, recorded February 9, 1796.

p. 352, January 20, 1796, ABRAHAM EADS to CHARLES EADS all right title and interest to real and personal property of WILLIAM EADS, deceased, "I being his lawful heir in Kentucky."

pp. 353-354, March 8, 1796, NICHOLAS TARTER to ADAM GEARHART, 296 acres on headwaters of North Fork of Holston River.

pp. 354-355, February 17, 1796, JOHN WM. HOWE and MARY of Wythe County to GEORGE STRAMBLER of Montgomery County, 100 acres by survey December 12, 1794, on the waters of Peek [Peak] Creek and New River... beginning at John Wm. Howe's patent line.

pp. 355-356, February 15, 1796, JOHN WM. HOWE and MARY to DAVID HARBERTSON, 250 acres by survey April 11, 1783, on Peek [Peak] Creek and New River.

p. 356, October 23, 1795, JOHN WEBBER, SENR., of Campbell County, Virginia to JOSEPH DAVIDSON, 264 acres in Wrights Valley on waters of Bluestone Creek, branch of New River.

p. 357, January 9, 1796, DAVID SAYERS of Wythe, attorney for THOMAS SPENCER of York County, South Carolina, to WILLIAM THOMAS of Wythe County, 400 acres by survey on New River, beginning corner to John Baxter's...on the river opposite the upper end of Craigs Island.

p. 358, January 28, 1796, JOHN CRAIG and MARY to JOSEPH BAKER, 135 acres, part of 600 acres patented to Craig March 24, 1791, on New River.

pp. 358-359, January 28, 1796, JOHN CRAIG and MARY to CHRISTIAN BAKER, 70 acres, part of 600 acres mentioned above, on New River.

pp. 359-360, January 28, 1796, JOHN CRAIG and MARY to ISAAC BAKER, 190 acres, part of 600 acres as above, on New River.

pp. 360-361, March 9, 1796, JAMES BARNETT and wife (name blank) to JOSEPH EVANS, 100 acres on east side of New River, being part of 531 acres on fork of Bingamans Branch.

pp. 361-362, February 19, 1796, GEORGE CARTER to FRANCIS J. CARTER, all land and possessions whereon I now live, being approximately 701 acres on head of Rackon [Raccoon] branch, waters of New River.

pp. 362-363, July 29, 1795, WILLIAM GANNAWAY and ELIZABETH to GIDEON HUDDLE, 235 acres on south side of Cripple Creek, corner to James Dougless [Douglas].

pp. 363-364, March 1, 1796, HENRY HELVEY takes as indentured servant, HENRY, son of SALLY COLE, aged four, until age 21, Helvey to teach him to read and write, furnish victuals and clothes.

pp. 364-365, April 15, 1795, PATRICK JOHNSON and EASTER [ESTHER] to JOHN GREASON [GRAYSON?], 92 acres on Walkers Creek, branch of New River.

p. 365, September 16, 1794, MICHAEL CRIGER gives JOSEPH IRVEN (IRVINE) his general power of attorney.

pp. 366-367, April 15, 1794, WILLIAM FOSTER "exhibited" to WILLIAM SAYERS, deceased, a bond dated March 20, 1780, "for 2,000 pounds paper or 51 pounds by scale of depreciation, and the bond is lost. I certify as executor I have received the full amount of the amount." Signed by JOHN T. SAYERS.

pp. 367-368, April 13, 1793, JAMES WHITE of Knox County, Territory South of the River Ohio, appoints JAMES CAMPBELL, ESQ., of Wythe County to make a deed to JEHU STEPHENS for three tracts of land [may be on Cripple Creek].

pp. 368-369, March 4, 1796, JAMES HEAVEN of Botetourt County to DAVID and JOHN WALLACE, 130 acres granted Heavens by patent July 14, 1795, on Muddy fork of Bluestone, about three miles from the mouth.

pp. 369-370, March 4, 1796, JAMES HEAVEN of Botetourt County to DAVID and JOHN WALLACE, 400 acres on Bluestone, patented July 1795.

p. 371, March 15, 1796, RICHARD MUSE and MARGARET to JAMES JONES, 80 acres on Mine Mill Creek.

pp. 372-373, April 10, 1796, RICHARD MUSE and MARGARET to KONROOD KEASLER [CONRAD KEESLING], no acres stated, on Mine Mill Creek.

pp. 373-374, May 9, 1796, GEORGE CARTER and MARY to NATHANIEL FRISBEE [FRISBIE], 250 acres in Wythe and Grayson counties, adjoining Stephen and Moses Austin and Company, the lead mines, and where Mary Ginkins now lives.

p. 374, May 9, 1796, DANIEL SHEFFY to ALEXANDER SMITH [SMYTH], 1 1/2 acres same conveyed by Stophel Zimmerman to Smith [Smyth], February 1792, and afterwards conveyed by Smith to Sheffy [lot in the town of Evansham, now Wytheville].

pp. 375-376, April 12, 1796, JACOB BRUNER [PRUNER] and MARY to GEORGE MICHAEL BRUNER [PRUNER], 125 acres on branch of Reed Creek, part of 367 acres patent to John McFarland... in line of Jacob Rabass [Repass], Senr.

pp. 376-378, May 10, 1796, RICHARD MUSE and MARGARET to DANIEL LOCKETT, 300 acres on Mine Mill Creek.

pp. 378-379, May 10, 1796, JOHN KERR to WILLIAM NEELY, 56 acres, part of where Kerr now lives.

p. 379, January 21, 1796, JARVIS SMITH of Wilkes County, North Carolina, to JOHN WHISMAN, of Wythe County, 34 acres on headwaters of South Fork of Holston River...line between John Whisman and Edward Catchim (?).

pp. 380-381, January 21, 1796, JARVIS SMITH of Wilkes County, North Carolina, to JACOB DOUGHERTY of Wythe, 100 acres on headwaters of South Fork Holston, corner to Robert Allison.

pp. 381-382, January 21, 1796, JARVIS SMITH of Wilkes County, N.C. to EDWARD CATCHIM, 90 acres on headwaters of South Fork of Holston.

pp. 383-384, April 13, 1796, JOHN KERR and MARGARET to MATHIAS WHITE, 50 acres on branch of Cripple Creek, part of the tract where Kerr now lives.

pp. 384-385, April 13, 1796, JOHN KERR and MARGARET to WILLIAM BONHAM, 150 acres on a branch of Cripple Creek, part of a tract where Kerr now lives.

pp. 385-387, June 13, 1796, JOHN and JEAN BAXTER to JOHN KEIZLING [KEESLING], 400 acres on Welshires Run.

pp. 387 and 389 (no page 388), July 13, 1796, PETER HEDRICK and ANNE to YOUST SMITH, 14 acres on Reed Creek, part of 200 acres granted Hedrick November 21, 1793.

pp. 389-390, July 12, 1796, JOHN TUTWILER and JANE (signed JENET) to JOSEPH GLASGOW, 59 acres on Reed Creek, part of a survey of 460 acres originally surveyed for Thomas Hutcherson, corner to Christian Cybert [Seybert].

p. 390, July 4, 1796, MOSES AUSTIN took the oath required by law as Captain of the Militia. Signed JAMES NEWELL.

p. 391, April 23, 1796, GASPER VAUT [VAUGHT] and ELISABETH to ADAM DUTTON, 26 acres on the head of Reed Creek, part of where Vaut now lives... corner to said Dutton's line.

pp. 392-393, August 9, 1796, WILLIAM HURST and LUCY to CHARLES CALFEE, 383 acres where Hurst now lives... on New River.

pp. 394-395, August 9, 1796, JACOB DOBLAR and ANNE to HENRY HUDDLE, 217 acres on the south branch of Reed Creek.

pp. 395-396, August 10, 1796, JACOB DOBLER and ANNE (signed ANNA) to ADAM COOK, 100 acres on the North Fork of Sugar Run, a branch of Reed

Creek, adjoining John Rush, Jacob Washum, and William Ward.

p. 397, August 9, 1796, MARY CALHOON (CALHOUN), heir of WILLIAM PATTERSON, deceased, to JOSEPH PATTERSON, all interest in an undivided parcel known as Sheltons Bottom [Holston River].

pp. 398-399, August 9, 1796, SAMUEL SHANNEN and ISBALL (signed ISABLE), one of the heirs of WILLIAM PATTERSON and THOMAS PATTERSON, deceased, to JOSEPH PATTERSON, all interest in two tracts, undivided parcels: (1) Sheltons Bottom tract (2) Mountain survey [probably on Holston River].

p. 399, August 9, 1796, WALTER CROCKETT and MARGARETT to WILLIAM DROPE, one house and lot in Evansham [now Wytheville], known as lot 10, on southeast side of Main Street, second to the northeast of the Cross Street, 1/2 acre, same conveyed to Crockett by Trustees of the Town, May 11, 1794.

pp. 400-401, March 18, 1796, GEORGE OURY and ELISABETH to ALMERINE MARSHALL, three lots, being the same purchased from Stophel Zimmerman and Margrett, adjoining the lots the property of Almerine Marshal.

pp. 401-403, August 6, 1796, GEORGE OURY and ELISABETH to ALMERINE MARSHALL, 3 acres near the Town of Evansham [now Wytheville], part of a larger tract sold to Oury by Stophel Simmerman and Margaret, part of a larger tract where Simmerman now lives [waters of Reed Creek].

pp. 403-404, September 13, 1796, JAMES DEAN of Davidson County, Tennessee to JAMES McGAVOCK, 46 acres, part of a survey of 190 acres made November 17, 1753, granted to Dean March 7, 1794, on a branch of Cripple Creek... mentions the mouth of a small branch called the Middle Branch between widow Smith's and Adam Dean's old place (deed by DAVID McGAVOCK, attorney in fact).

pp. 404-405, September 13, 1796, JAMES DEAN of Davidson County, Tennessee to ROBERT MAJORS, 144 acres, part of a survey of 190 acres made November 17, 1753, granted to Dean March 7, 1794, on a branch of Cripple Creek. (Deed by DAVID McGAVOCK, attorney in fact.)

pp. 406-407, August 12, 1796, ISAAC NEWHOUSE and CATHERINE to PETER DARTER, 195 acres on south branch of Cripple Creek, same where Newhouse now lives.

pp. 407-408, September 8, 1796, JARVIS SMITH of Wilkes County, North Carolina, to SAMUEL WILLIAMS, 136 acres on the South Fork of the Holston.

pp. 408-410, September 1, 1796, MARTIN McFERREN, attorney in fact for JAMES MONTGOMERY and WILLIAM MONTGOMERY, formerly of Montgomery County, Virginia, to GEORGE HANCOCK of Botetourt County, 500 acres where Joseph Kent now lives, adjoining Robert Sayers' Anchor and Hope tract, on Reed Creek.

pp. 410-411, July 21, 1796, RICHARD RAINS and JANE to MERIDETH RAINS, 184 acres on Peak Creek of New River.

p. 412, October 12, 1796, ROBERT BUCKANNAN to JOHN GOODMAN, 118 acres on Middle Fork of Holston.

pp. 413-414, August 5, 1796, WILLIAM GANNAWAY and ELIZABETH to MONEY GANNAWAY, 116 acres on headwaters of Cripple Creek, joining John [Douglas].

pp. 414-415, October 11, 1796, DAVID BUSTERD (also signed by FRANCES BUSTERD) to WILLIAM KING, 35 acres, part of 270 acres on headwaters of Cripple Creek.

pp. 416-417, July 21, 1796, RICHARD REINS to JOHN BLACK, 250 acres, no location, beginning on Thomas Fouly's line.

pp. 417-418, October 11, 1796, SAMUEL FERGUSON and MARY to DANIEL HARMAN, 196 acres on head of Bluestone.

pp. 418-420, July 11, 1796, DANIEL MILLER and SARAH to ALMERINE MARSHALL, 13 1/2 acres and 14 perches on South Fork of Reed Creek, part of Paxtons Glade, on the side of the "waggon road" including two separate tracts: (1) 12 1/2 acres, sold by Almarine Marshall and Rachel to Miller (2) the other from William Ingledove to Miller, adjoining where Ingledove now lives.

pp. 420-421, May 13, 1796, JAMES BOGLE (signed BOGELL) to ELIZABETH DAVIS, for love and affection, 29 acres on Middle Fork of Walkers Creek (deed of gift).

pp. 421-422, October 11, 1796, HENRY SLEAGLE and CHRISTIENER [CHRISTENA] to WILLIAM JOHNSTON, 95 acres Middle Fork of Holston, corner to William Lockheart's land, corner to Patrick Campbell.

pp. 423-424, August 11, 1796, PETER COLHEP and MARY to FREDERICK COLEHEP, 117 acres on Cripple Creek.

pp. 424-426, August 17, 1796, PETER COLHEP and MARY to ADAM COLEHEP, 117 acres on Cripple Creek, corner to Frederick Colhep's 117 acres.

pp. 426-428, October 10, 1796, GEORGE DAVIS and AGNESS (signed ANN) to JACOB DARTER, 55 acres on small branch of Reed Creek, part of larger tract where George now lives...mentions Brushy Mountain.

pp. 428-430, October 11, 1796, DANIEL HARMAN and NANCY to SAMUEL FERGUSON, 40 acres, part of 380 acres where Phoeby Harman now lives, on waters of the Clinch, including three springs, mentions cleared grounds between Mathias Harman and said Ferguson.

pp. 430-431, DANIEL HARMAN and NANCY to JOHN PEERY, blacksmith, 280 acres by two grants adjoining: (1) 200 acres granted Harman July 16, 1788, corner to Mathias Harman and crossing the river and corner to Wynne; (2) 80 acres, granted Harman May 11, 1796, in line of Robert Whitley, on both sides of the Clinch River, joining Whitley, Mathias Harman and said Peery.

pp. 432-433, October 11, 1796, WILLIAM PEERY and SARAH (SALLY) to SAMUEL DUFF of Russell County, 137 acres on waters of the Clinch River, joining John Peery, Snr.

pp. 434-435, October 11, 1796, WILLIAM PEERY and SARAH (signed SERAH) to PAUL WHITLEY, 227 acres on Brushy Run, a branch of the Clinch River joining John Taylor on the northwest side.

pp. 435-437, January 14, 1796, PHILIP UMBARGER and LEAH to JOHN TOTTEN, 19 acres in Rich Valley on the waters of the North Fork of the Holston, beginning on the patent line.

pp. 437-438, November 10, 1795, WILLIAM ROGERS and MARY to JOHN GAUGH (GUGH), 130 acres on New River, part of 230 acres granted to William Rogers by patent April 2, 1795, by survey April 15, 1796.

pp. 438-439, October 24, 1796, HENRY HARMAN, SR., and NANCY of Wythe to WILLIAM DAVIS "now being on Clinch," 72 acres on the Clinch known as the Ben place, part of a survey where Henry Harman, Jr., now lives.

pp. 440-441, March 1, 1796, HENRY HARMAN, SR., and NANCY to HOLTON MUNSEY, 86 acres on Walkers Creek adjoining the land Munsey now lives on.

pp. 441-442, October 4, 1796, WILLIAM DAVIS and PRISCILLA (PRESILLAY), to ADAM HARMAN, 80 acres on Walkers Creek.

pp. 443-444, July 26, 1796, WILLIAM OWENS and NANCY of Russell County to EDLEY (EDLY) MAXWELL of Wythe County, 44 acres by patent December 17, 1789, on the waters of Plum Creek, the south branch of the North Fork of the Clinch River. [signed Owens]

pp. 445-446, July 20, 1796, WILLIAM OWEN and NANCY of Russell County to EDLY MAXWELL, 274 acres by patent July 31, 1788,...spur of Morriss ''nobb'' corner to James Brown.

pp. 447-448, July 21, 1795, JAMES MAXWELL and WILLIAM THOMPSON, Gent. Justices, to obtain the acknowledgment of LYDIA, wife of MATHIAS HARMAN, who made a deed August 8, 1794, to ROBERT WHITLEY for 64 acres, and Lydia was unable to travel. Ordered March 15, 1795, recorded October 11, 1795.

pp. 448-450, September 22, 1795, RICHARD WHITMAN and ELISABETH to MATHIAS HARMAN, 130 acres patent February 19, 1793, on the south side of the main fork of Walkers Creek, joining or near John Herren's land on the northeast side.

pp. 450-451, November 9, 1795, THOMAS ROAN, administrator with the will annexed of GEORGE DANIEL, deceased, in consideration of 48 pounds paid for and on behalf of MALVINA SMYTH, infant of Cove Creek, sold to her one Negro girl slave about 12, named Betsy, bill of sale.

p. 451, November 9, 1795, OVERTON COSBY, executor of the estate of DR. ROBERT SPRAT, deceased, quitclaims to MALVINA SMYTH, all interest in slaves which by deed of mortgage from GEORGE DANIEL, deceased to the executors of Sprat (''in which the within slave girl is contained''), is vested in executors for value received.

pp. 451-452, November 9, 1795, THOMAS ROAN(E), administrator with the will annexed of GEORGE DANIEL, deceased, for payment of 119 pounds and 10 shillings on behalf of Harold Smyth, infant, of Cove Creek, to HAROLD SMYTH, two Negro male slaves, Meariard about 16, and Armisted age 13.

p. 452, November 9, 1795, OVERTON COSBY also releases interest in slaves sold to HAROLD SMYTH, as above.

p. 453-454, October 4, 1796, WILLIAM DAVIS and PRISCILLA (PRESILLAH) to ADAM HARMAN, 145 acres on Walkers Creek... on Peter Helvey's line.

p. 454, November 7, 1796, JOHN CROCKETT produced a commission from Governor Robert Brooke appointing him Ensign in 35th Regiment of Militia, signed JOHN MONTGOMERY.

pp. 455-456, August 17, 1796, PETER COLEHEP and MARY to HENRY COLEHEP, 80 acres on Cripple Creek.

pp. 456-457, September 20, 1796, DAVID McGAVOCK to JOHN JOHNSTON, 100 acres by survey April 1, 1793, granted to David McGavock by patent September 12, 1795, on Reed Creek, corner to Charles and Stophel Simmerman, and the heirs of George Hutsel deceased... line of Michael Dickert's land.

pp. 457-458, December 1, 1796, JOHN TAYLOR of Montgomery County, Virginia to WILLIAM TAYLOR of Wythe County, two tracts: 100 acres on Brushy Run of Clinch River, beginning on his old survey; (2) 88 acres on the head of the Clinch between John and Jesse Evans.

pp. 459-460, December 13, 1796, JAMES PATTON and FLORENCE to JACOB KEASLING, 295 acres on Pek [Peak] Creek, branch of New River... on line of William Preston.

PP. 460-461, December 13, 1796, JAMES PATTON and FLORENCE to GEORGE KEASLING, 110 acres, part of 363 acres on Peak Creek, corner to William Preston's Robinson Tract.

pp. 461-462, December 6, 1796, ABRAM TRIGG of Montgomery County under power of attorney from THOMAS INGLES, dated May 20, 1790, and recorded in Montgomery County, Virginia, to WILLIAM TAYLOR, assignee of JOHN TAYLOR, 400 acres part of 1,000 acres granted William Ingles by patent July 5, 1774, and devised to Thomas Ingles, in Abbs Valley on Blue Stone Creek, branch of New River, part that lies at the upper end above and adjoining James Moore, deceased.

p. 463, September 9, 1796, ROBERT BUMPASS of Halifax County bill of sale to JOHN HOUNDSHELL, sells one Negro man, James, age 22, for £100, and shall deliver to Hounshell a Negro boy, Ben, age 7, agreeable to instrument of writing on or before 20th day of the present month, then otherwise this bill of sale to be void.

Entry for James Finley who entered 57 acres between Jehu Stephens' land and his own patent land on Reed Creek on June 26, 1786. The original was withdrawn by his order the 26th June, 1796 and re-entered, as shown by the marginal note.

Tracing from original by Mary B. Kegley.

Entry for Stephen Reeder, assignee of Robert Adams, assignee of Saml. McCraw, based on a treasury warrant for 1,000 acres, dated 21st of January 1790, enters 40 acres adjoining Joseph Erwin's land, Nowell's and his own, on August 6, 1790.

Tracing from the original by Mary B. Kegley.

John Adams Robt Sayers David McGavock Jno. T. Sayers & James Newell Senr. are appointed Commrs who, or any three of them shall direct the Surveyor in what manner to Lay of one hundred acres of Land given the County for the purpose of situating thereoff the Court house The said Commrs shall also direct the Surveyor in what manner to Lay off a Town on said Lands the number off Lotts & and also after laying off the same they shall proceed to the sale of the Lotts giving such Credit as they shall think proper taking Bond and Sufficient Security in the name of the said Commrs

---

The Wythe County Court ordered Commrs. [Commissioners] to direct the surveyor in the way 100 acres of land was to be laid off for the town [Evansham, later Wytheville] and gave them authority to sell the "Lotts."

Tracing by Mary B. Kegley from the original in the first Wythe County Order Book, p. 12, June 22, 1790.

SECTION II
Life And Death

CHAPTER I
Daily Life As Seen Through The Wythe County Orders

Every time the justices of the court met to decide cases, to install officers of the court, to recognize members of the local militia, or to review county matters presented to them, a record was made in the Court Order Books. Only one book is missing, the volume which includes the records from part of 1791 until late in 1795. All others are available at the Clerk's Office at the courthouse. In preparing this account, records have been summarized, abstracted, edited, and arranged in narrative form, but kept together on the day each court session was held. Some of the early books have no page numbers, and the index (usually a separate book) is often missing. In many cases, the only way to retrieve the original record is by date.

Wythe County was formed in December 1789, with the Act of the General Assembly requiring that the new county organize in May 1790 and meet at James McGavock's at Fort Chiswell. The first session of the new court was held on May 25, 1790.

May 25, 1790: Walter Crockett took oath as justice of the peace in the county court and chancery. James McGavock and Andrew Boyd administered the oaths. Walter Crockett then administered the oaths to the new members of the court: James McGavock, Andrew Boyd, William Davis, James Newell, R. Sayers, William Ward, William Love, John Adams, J.T. Sayers, David McGavock, Flower Swift, Jehu Stephens, and William Thompson. The commission was dated February 12, 1790. William Love, who had received his commission April 20, 1790, took oath as sheriff with Walter Crockett, Hugh Montgomery, and James Newell as securities. Robert Adams was installed as surveyor and was to be certified to the College of William and Mary.

James Maxwell, Thomas Whitten, Jr., William Peery, and John Thompson were ordered to view the best way for a wagon road from the line of Russell County near James Brown's to the road already open near Daniel Harmon's, and to make a report.

May 26, 1790: Recommendations for the local militia officers were made. Walter Crockett was recommended as a lieutenant, Jehu Stephens as colonel, William Ward as lieutenant colonel, William Love as major, James Newell, captain, William Gleaves, lieutenant, John Ewing, ensign, James Maxwell, captain, Thomas Peery, lieutenant, John Thompson, ensign, James Findley [Finley], captain, J. William Phipps, lieutenant, John Houndshell [Hounshell], ensign, Flower Swift, captain, William Bell, lieutenant, John Pikrill, ensign, Stephen Saunders, captain, Charles Bustard, lieutenant, Evan Toddhunter, ensign, Andrew Crockett, captain, John Thompson Sayers, lieutenant, William Calfee, ensign, David Doak, captain, George Kinser, lieutenant, Leonard Straw, ensign, Robert Davis, captain, James Davis, Sr., lieutenant, Joseph Patterson, ensign, Manitree Jones, captain, Lazarus Denny, lieutenant, William Ward, ensign, William Davis, captain, Daniel Robinit [Robinette], lieutenant, Thomas Polley [Pauley], ensign, John Stone, captain, Johnathan Thomas, lieutenant, Abner Jones, ensign, William Hayes, captain, Alexander Buchanan, lieutenant, Thomas Gillespie, ensign, James Anderson, captain, George Howell, lieutenant, Shederick Greer, ensign, Jesse Evans, captain, John Montgomery, lieutenant, James

McGavock, Jr., ensign, William Herbert, captain, Stephen Sanders, lieutenant, Thomas Herbert, ensign, Nathaniel Pope, captain, Lewis Harlin, lieutenant, Joseph Powell, ensign, Joseph Davidson, captain, John Listley, ensign. [The fifteen captains and their subordinates came from all parts of Wythe County and parts of what are now Smyth, Tazewell, Bland, Grayson, and Carroll counties.]

Additional justices of the peace were recommended as follows: Enoch Osburn, Manitree Jones, Alexander Buchanan, James Maxwell, Nathaniel Frisbie, William Calfee, James Campbell, Joseph Patterson, Jesse Evans, Robert Adams, James Findley [Finley], and Andrew Steele. In addition the constables for the various companies were appointed. These included James Murphy, David Miles, George Houck, Adam Aerhart, Robert Calhoun, Henry Baugh, Peter Kinser, Robert Inglish, Barnet Folie [Foley], Jesse Lynch, Archibald Buchanan, William Mairs, William Allen, Isaac Mendinall, Holton Muncey, Reubin Herrell, and John Compton, Jr.

The next order of business was the appointment of road overseers. Each of the men appointed resided within the precinct where he was ordered to work. The names of the overseers were William Ross, from Herbert's [now Jackson's] Ferry to Wolf Glade Creek [now Galax area]. John Fields to act from Wolf Glade Creek to Flower Gap. John Legget was appointed to serve from the line of Washington County to the ford of the river at Joseph Atkins [present Smyth County]. Martin Stailey's precinct was from Atkins' to the Mile Tree by the Crab Orchard. Proceeding farther to the east, George Boyd was to serve from the Crab Orchard to his own house [present Staley's Crossroads], and William Ingledove was to oversee the road from that point to the ford in the South Fork of Reed Creek. Michael Cregar was to serve from the ford of Reed Creek to the ford at the mouth of the fork. Henry Helvy was to serve from that point to the ford of the creek at Ross' which was east of present Wytheville.

East of Wytheville, overseers included Jacob Shaver, who lived near Lick Mountain and served from Ross' to Bishop's and Hugh McGavock from there to the ford of Reed Creek below Fort Chiswell. Richard Beeson served from Fort Chiswell to Mr. Boyd's [Andrew Boyd] at the intersection of present Route 100 and the old road to the Town of Draper. John Lowthain's precinct was from Boyd's to the Montgomery County line, through what is now Pulaski County.

Captain Peery was to give notice to the residents of the Blue Stone [Bluestone River] that they should send a person to show cause why they shouldn't work on the road between Rocky Gap and the head of the Clinch River. Captain Henry Harmon was appointed overseer of the road from his house to the marked tree in the Rocky Gap. John Compton was to serve from the Rocky Gap up the Clear Fork to the place where Peery's part formerly terminated. From that point Samuel Mairs was to be overseer and his precinct extended to Jacob Wagoner's on the Clinch River. Daniel Johnston served from Wagoner's to the Russell County line. Robert Evans served from Captain Harman's down to Kimberlain Fork. These roads were located in present Bland and Tazewell counties.

On the present Peppers Ferry Road, Peter Binkley [sometimes Pinkley] was appointed to serve as road overseer from the forks of the road to Captain [John] Adams who resided about two miles east of Wytheville. John Breckenridge's precinct was from that point to John Miller's. John Miller was to serve to the Draper's Road; and Joseph Mairs from that point to the Montgomery County line.

June 22, 1790: Francis Preston, George Hancock, James Blair, and Alexander Smyth were admitted to the practice of law, and James Craig was appointed deputy sheriff. The justices present for the court session included James McGavock, Andrew Boyd, William Davis, James Newell, Robert Sayers, John Adams, William Ward, Jehu

Stephens, William Thompson, and John T. Sayers.

The tithables on the "Blue Stone" [River] were exempted from working on the road leading from Captain Harman's to the head of the Clinch [River]. A report was given on the proposed road from Russell County line to Daniel Harman's and Samuel Ferguson was appointed overseer of the road from near Harmon's to the first crossing of Plumb Creek [on the Clinch River] and from that point to the line of Russell County. James Maxwell and William Thompson were to divide "the hands" [the workers].

John Adams, Robert Sayers, David McGavock, John T. Sayers, and James Newell, or any three were to direct the survey in laying off the 100 acres given to the county. This was the beginning of the county seat. John Davis gave ten acres [which included a big spring which is now located under the Wytheville Baptist Church], and Stophel [Christopher] Zymmerman [Simmerman] gave 90 acres, reserving the kitchen and barn for himself.

John Stanger was given a license to perform marriages and John Harkerader was his security. Leonard Straw was granted permission to build a mill, and Jacob Raypass [Repass] was licensed to marry people according to the ceremonies of the Presbyterian Church.

John Crockett, George Davis, W. Rogers, and James McDonald, or any three of them were ordered to view the best way from the road that was opened near Hugh Montgomery's by way of William Rogers' to the county road near David Ross' place on Reed Creek, and file a report. Phillip Reeder, Casper Rader, William Finley, and Robert Breckenridge, or any three were to view the best way from Phillip Reeder's at the Gap of the Cove [Crocketts Cove] to the Wythe Court House.

William Nelson was granted the administration of the estate of John Nelson, deceased. John Vaught, John Griffits, and Jenkin Williams were to appraise the value of the slaves and the remainder of the estate. Mary Dunn was administratrix of the estate of Thomas Dunn, deceased, and Walter Crockett, Robert Adams, and John Breckenridge were to appraise the value of the slaves and the balance of the estate.

Jeremiah Stone, William Gleaves, Stephen Sanders, and James Findley, or any three were to view the best way for a wagon road from the branch below Jeremiah Stone's to the fork of the road above Captain Findley.

The commissioners were appointed to lay off the town and prepare a plan for the Court House and prison, and also for ten acres to be used for the prison bounds contiguous to the prison building lot.

Peter Kinser took his oath as constable, George Hancock was appointed as deputy state attorney for the county, and William Davis was recommended to serve as coroner for the county. The following men were appointed to serve as appraisers on property taken under execution: Nathaniel Pope, Mathew Dickey, Lewis Hale, James Findley, James Crockett, Joseph Kent, James Devour, Joseph Davison, and James Maxwell.

July 27, 1790: The justices present included William Davis, Robert Sayers, John Adams, and John T. Sayers. At that time Charles Carter was appointed overseer of the road from the Great Road above the Big Lick to John Craig, and he was to keep the same in repair. William Foster, James Crockett, David Sayers, and Richard Beeson, or any three were to view the best way for a wagon road from Fort Chiswell to the Court House and file their report. Robert Adams produced his commission as surveyor and took the oath of office with securities John Adams and Jesse Evans.

George Davis was paid for one old wolf, and John Houndshell was appointed constable in Captain Findley's Company replacing George Houck. Phillip Gains and George Oury were sworn in as deputy sheriffs. John Houndshell, Sr., was exempt from levies.

August 24, 1790: Justices present were James McGavock, William Davis, Andrew Boyd, James Newell, Robert Sawers [Sayers], John Adams, John T. Sayers, Jehu Stephens, and William Thompson. The road from Phillip Reeder's at the Gap of the Cove to Wythe Court House was also established by Hugh Montgomery's place by where Adam Miller then lived, by Moyers to Murphy's to the Widow Hutsell's cornfield and from that point to the Court House. Phillip Reeder was to be overseer of the road, and Colonel [Walter] Crockett and Captain [John] Adams were to allot the hands.

The persons appointed to view the proposed road from Fort Chiswell to the Court House reported that in their opinion that less work will make the old way from Fort Chiswell to the intersection of Joseph Crockett's road much the best and that it is as ''nigh'' as the new way and from that point by a direction of marked trees to the Court House. Joseph Crockett was appointed overseer from Bell's Ford of Reed Creek [Kent's Mill] to the Court House.

David Love and Joseph Love had a fulling mill on Peak Creek on the land of David Love . Stephen Cole was exempted from the payment of poll tax and county levies. The inventory and appraisal of the estate of Thomas Dunn was returned to the Court. Charles Nuckels [Nuckolls] was appointed an appraiser under the execution law in the place of Mathew Dickey. John Hounshell took the oath as constable, and John Breckenridge was admitted by oath as deputy sheriff. The commissioners to lay off the town also were to let out the building of the Court House and jail to the lowest bidder.

Stophel [Christopher] Goss [Gose] and Chrisley Kettering were fined for breach of the peace. David Davies and Daniel Miller were also fined and posted their security with Joseph Kent and William Love.

September 28, 1790: Justices present were William Davis, James Newell, John Adams, and John T. Sayers. John Loathin [Lowthain] was appointed overseer of the road from the ford of Peak Creek to Andrew Boyd's. Stephen Gose was appointed overseer of the road from Elk Creek in present Grayson County, to where Sage's ''wagon oversett'' on the Dry Branch [near Speedwell], and James Campbell to be overseer from that point to the top of the ridge between Cripple Creek and Reed Creek. William Phipps was to serve from that point to the wagon road and Colonel [Jehu] Stephens, Captain Sanders, Captain Findley, and William Gleaves were to lay off the hands and clear out the road.

The following gentlemen took the oath as justices: Manitree Jones, Nathaniel Frisbie, James Findley, James Campbell, Joseph Patterson, and Robert Adams. William Davis took oath as coroner and Joseph Stephens, Robert Davis, Steven [Stephen] Sanders, Manitree Jones, John Thompson Sayers, William Davis, William Phipps, Joseph Patterson, and James McGavock, Jr., were sworn in as officers of the militia. William Adams took his oath as deputy surveyor. Jacob Cregger was exempt from county levies.

September 29, 1790: Steven [Stephen] Sanders, Jesse Evans, and Andrew Crockett took their oaths as officers of the militia, and John Baxter was appointed overseer of the road from the lead mines to the ford of Reed Creek. George Oury was paid for one young wolf.

James Findley [Finley], Jesse Evans, William Adams, Peter Binkley, and Joseph Crockett were to view the grounds proposed for a wagon road from Fort Chiswell to the Court House as reported by the former viewers to the last Court, and also to view another way which was to be shown to them by George Armbrister.

The Clerk was to hire someone to make ''a press for the papers of the County'' and the costs were to be paid out of the first county money the sheriff would collect.

The will of George Breckenridge was proven and Jesse Evans and John

Breckenridge were named executors. James McGavock, Jno. Adams, Walter Crockett, Robert Adams, and William Adams, or any three were to appraise the estate and the slaves.

The articles of agreement and the bond from the ''undertakers'' to build the Court House was returned by the commission to the court and ordered to be recorded.

November 10, 1790: A called court examined Jeremiah Breedin (?) who was charged with stealing three head of ''neat'' cattle, the property of John Combs which was valued at six pounds. After questioning by John Adams, John T. Sayers, James Campbell, and James Findley, he was acquitted. Elijah Hurst, Aaron Perry, and Byran [Byram?] Breedin were also charged with the same offense, and were also acquitted.

November 23, 1790: Present: William Davis, Jehu Stephens, Robt. Adams, James Finley, Nath'l Frisbie, and Jno. Adams.

Bounties were paid for wolf heads to Abraham Workman, John McCaslin, John Liggett, James Shannan, and Joseph Montgomery. William Calfee qualified as a magistrate and took the oath. James Newell, James Davis, and William Gleaves took their oaths as officers of the militia.

Thomas Gillespie, John S. Pratt, Samuel Davis, Robert Sayers, James Scott, and George Ewing were to appear and to show cause why they failed to appear as grand jurors.

Joseph Atkins made oath that he was not the same man that Samuel Culland obtained a judgment against in Pittsylvania Court, and the sheriff was to make a return on the execution that he was ''no inhabitant'' of the county.

William Love was brought before the court for ''swearing profanely'' and George May and Martin Miller were before the court for retailing whiskey without a license.

Samuel Ingram was brought before the court for ''profane swearing'' and Manassas Friel, Nathaniel Frisbie, William Hay, and David McGavock were brought to court for retailing goods without a license.

George Oury was charged for not keeping the road in repair, and Rebeka Oury was charged with having a bastard child. James Wilkar (?) was charged with keeping a woman contrary to law.

The jury was to assess the value of one-half acre of land of G. [probably Gideon] Moss, adjacent to D. Love's, intended as a mill seat.

Nathaniel Nuckols [Nuckolls] was appointed as overseer of the road from James Newell's to the ford of Brush Creek. William Ross was to serve from his house to Wolf Glade Creek, and William Carter from Ross' to the lead mines. Robert Sanders was overseer from the lead mines to the Boiling Springs. William Ward took oath as lieutenant colonel of the militia.

November 24, 1790: Present: William Davis, Jno. Adams, Jno. T. Sayers, Jehu Stephens, James Finley, and Robt. Adams.

Stophel [Christopher] Simmerman received a license for an ordinary and was to charge the rates that ordinary keepers could charge. The rates were established for rum, peach brandy, whiskey, a warm dinner, breakfast, supper, lodging, wine, beer, and cider.

Robert Adams was allowed six pounds for furnishing books of record in his office. John Alford was appointed constable in Captain Crockett's company replacing Reubin Harrell. Thomas Pauley took oath as an ensign of the militia, and Robert Adams, surveyor, was allowed pay for laying off the town land and lots.

The sheriff was allowed certain sums for a called court for the examination of Thomas Keys, James Breeden, Aaron Perry, Elijah Hurst, Byran [Byram?]Breedin, and for ''dieting the prisoners and guards.'' The Clerk was allowed 200 pounds of tobacco for attending the special court to examine the same men, and the sheriff was allowed 1,200 pounds of tobacco for extra services in the same connection.

Henry Umberger, Sr., was appointed overseer of the road to replace Michael Cregger, to serve from the ford of Reed Creek to the ford of said fork near Venerick's. The persons who were appointed to view the road from Fort Chiswell to the Court House reported that the way pointed out by George Armbrister was "the nighest and best" and that this road was ordered to be opened.

The sheriff was ordered to collect three shillings from each tithable. The lists of tithables were to be taken by William Davis in Captain Davis' Company; William Ward in Captain Doak's Company; John Adams in Evans' Company; John T. Sayers in Crockett's Company; Jehu Stephens in Sanders' Company; James Newell in his own company; Nathaniel Frisbie in Herbert's Company; James Findley, Manitree Jones, James Maxwell, and William Davis in their own companies; William Thompson in Davidson's Company; Enoch Osbourn in Anderson's Company; Flower Swift and William Hays in their own companies; William Calfee in Pope's Company; and James Campbell in Stone's Company.

The Clerk was allowed ten pounds for furnishing books of record for his office, and the sheriff was to pay him from the present levies.

James Findley took oath as captain of the militia and John Hounshell was recommended as lieutenant to replace William Phipps. Reubin Colley was recommended as ensign to replace John Hounshell.

November 30, 1790: Andrew Boyd, William Davis, John Adams, Robert Adams, and James Finley were members of the called court who examined John Stroupe who was charged with killing Paul Pessinger. They decided that the killing took place in self-defense.

December 28, 1790: Present: John Adams, James Newell, Robt. Adams, and James Finley.

Hugh Montgomery was appointed administrator of the estate of Mary Ewing, deceased. James McGavock, Robert Sanders, James Campbell, and N. Frisbie, or any three, were to appraise her estate.

The non-cupative will of Morris Sullivan, deceased, was proved by the oaths of Charles Blackly and William Calhoun, Jr., and ordered to be recorded.

Michael Gibb was appointed overseer of the road from Bishop's to Colonel Crockett's. D. [Duncan] Gullion was charged with stealing a hog. Almarine Marshall was sworn in as deputy sheriff. Jesse Evans, John Breckenridge, and George Oury, deputy sheriffs, were discontinued.

January 25, 1791: Present: William Davis, James Newell, Robt. Adams, James Finley, Manitree Jones, Andrew Steel, Enoch Osburn, and William Ward. William Love took the oath as major in the local militia, and Andrew Steel and Enoch Osburn the same as justices.

William Davis entered into bond for the faithful execution of the office of coroner with William Ingledow [Ingledove] as security

David Doak took oath as captain, George Kinser and George Howell as lieutenants, and Leonard Straw as ensign, in the militia. William Ingledow to be allowed for what he was overcharged in revenue tax for 1787 and 1788. Ingledove was also granted a license to keep an ordinary at his house for one year.

Jacob Colson was appointed overseer of the road from David Short's precinct to Wolf Glade Creek, replacing William Ross.

Charles Copeland and John Baldwin were appointed constables in Captain Osburn's Company, and Daniel Keeth the same in Captain Stone's Company; George

Holland the same replacing Barnet Folie; Hezekiah China [Chaney] the same in Captain Newell's Company; Sam'l Mairs the same in Captain Mairs' Company; William Allun [Allen], the same in Captain Swift's Company.

Abner Jones was recommended as lieutenant replacing Jonathan Thomas who refuses to serve. Richard Hale was recommended as ensign.

On January 15, Catherine (Catrina) Baugh, Jr., was tried for "the suspected murthering [murdering] her base born child" and was found not guilty. Catherine Baugh, Senr., and Michael Baugh were also tried for the same offense and found not guilty.

Hezekiah China [Chaney] was appointed overseer of the road replacing Stophel [Christopher] Gose.

February 8, 1791: Present: James McGavock, John Adams, Flower Swift, James Campbell, Wm. Davis, Wm. Ward, and Mani [Manitree] Jones.

John Crockett was paid for one old wolf. William Sanders was recommended as ensign, replacing Thomas Herbert who refused to serve. William Hays took oath as captain, William Herbert and Flower Swift, the same. Alexander Buchanan, the same as lieutenant. Buchanan also took oath as commissioner of the peace. Robert Warrick was appointed as constable in Captain Stone's Company replacing Daniel Keeth [Keith]; Jacob Denner, the same "in room of" Hezekiah China [Chaney] in Captain Newell's Company.

John Adams was authorized to hire someone to put a door on the courthouse, and the clerk was to give the sheriff a list of the tithables.

On the motion of James Ewing, a survey was ordered on a tract of 80 acres of land which was in dispute between Ewing, Hugh Montgomery, James Newell, and Robert Sayers.

Hezekiah China was bonded for good behavior for one year, particularly toward Mary Morgan. The bond was in the sum of £100.

Michael Walters recorded his stock mark, that is a crop in the right ear and a half crop in the left ear.

George Wampler received a license for his ordinary [it was located between present Crockett and Rural Retreat]. Peter Anderson was allowed for two old wolves.

March 1, 1791: Thomas Bratton was examined by the court and was charged with breaking open the storehouse of Frisbie and Austin, and taking goods valued at £150 [this store was in or near the present Town of Austinville]. The prisoner was questioned by the justices, denied the charge, but was found guilty after hearing the witnesses. Bratton then "begged corporal punishment." It was granted and the sheriff was ordered to give twenty-five lashes "well laid on" on his bare back. Leonard Bellur (?) was also tried on the same offense and found not guilty.

March 8, 1791: Present: William Davis, Wm. Thompson, Manitree Jones, James Campbell, James Newell, and James Finley

Persons appointed to view the grounds for a road from Richard Bailey's on "Blue Stone" [River] to Wm. Wyne's on the head of the Clinch [River], report that a passable way may be had from sd. Bailey's to Wm. Lasley's mill and by James Shannon's. Ordered that David McComas be appointed overseer of the same from Bailey's to the mill, and John Lasley from thence to the head of the Blue Stone, to a certain oak tree where the path from Samuel Ferguson's old plantation intersects the mountain fork path, and Samuel Ferguson from thence to Wynne's and that they clear out and keep the same in repair.

James Maxwell took oath as captain, Joseph Davidson, the same. John Thompson, the same as ensign. Will, a Negro man slave belonging to James Campbell, was exempted from working on the roads, and James Campbell was exempt from paying county levy and poll tax for his Negro woman slave Philes.

William Adams, Jo. Kent, Jas. Finley, Robert Sayers, and Robert Breckenridge are to view the nearest and best way for a wagon road from Fort Chiswell to the Court House.

Jeremiah Lambert was ordered to keep the peace for one year and one day, particularly toward John Hambleton, and to have two securities of 50 pounds each. Michael Dunn was fined 20 cents for contempt of court, the sum later remitted.

Joseph Atkins was granted the right to operate an ordinary at his house, security with Wm. Davis. Administration of the estate of Wm. McFarland, deceased, was granted to James McFarland. Wm. Cecil, John Greenup and Sam'l Ferguson to appraise the estate and slaves of Wm. McFarland.

Daniel Jones was appointed overseer of the road from the Gap of the Mountain between Anderson's settlement and Osburn's to the top of Iron Mountain. Benjamin Phipps, the same from Anderson's Gap to the top of the Big Ridge near Brush Creek; and George Reeves the same from thence to the ford of the New River. Jonathan Ward was appointed the same from Cox's Ford of New River to the top of the dividing ridge between Meadow Creek and Chestnut Creek. John Cox, the same from the top of the dividing ridge between Meadow Creek and the waters of Chestnut Creek to where the road goes into the Flower Gap road. Jos. Perkins, Shed. [Shadrick] Greer and Christopher Huzzy were to view the nearest and best way for a road from Samuel Cox's to the North Carolina line near Pennington's Mill. [These orders pertain to roads in Carroll and Grayson counties.]

Joseph Fields, Patrick McBridge, Wm. Muncey, and Robert Adams were paid for old wolves.

William Austin, Pet. [Peter] Whittiker, E. Osburn, Jno. Isom were appointed to view the road from the mouth of Elk Creek [present Grayson County] by way of the furnace to Whittiker's Ford on New River, and report. Lewis Hale, Jer. [Jeremiah] Stone, Jacob Kettering, and Jno. Stone, or any three were to view the nearest and best way from the mouth of Elk Creek to the top of Iron Mountain at the Blue Spring Gap.

April 13, 1791: The account of the sales of Samuel Thompson's estate was returned and David McGavock was named guardian for the children, Barbara, Polly, and Betsy Thompson because of a suit with James McCorkle.

Charles Hardy was granted a license for him to perform marriages according to the ceremonies of the Methodist Episcopal Church. Thad. Cooley and Henry Honacre [Honaker] were securities in the sum of £500.

April 14, 1791: Thomas Whitten was appointed overseer of the road from Russell County line to Plumb Creek, replacing James Brown.

Abram Gooden was recommended as ensign in Captain Sanders' Company replacing E. Todhunter.

The remainder of the court orders for 1791 are missing, all of 1792, 1793, and 1794 are also missing, as are the records for 1795 prior to September 8.

September 8, 1795: Robert Sayers, Andrew Steele, James Finley, Moses Austin, William Davis, William Love, and James Newell, justices, were present.

The Grand Jury presented John Davis for forgery and Jeremiah Percival and Nathaniel Landcraft for unlawful gaming within the past two months.

The clerk was ordered to certify to the executive that David Buster is recommended as a proper person to be added to the Commission of the Peace, and not John Buster, who was commissioned.

James Newell and James Davis ordered to examine William Taylor, touching his fitness and ability as deputy surveyor. They reported that he was qualified, and he was admitted deputy surveyor of the county. Thomas Boyd, licensed to practice law in Virginia, was admitted to practice in Wythe County.

September 9, 1795: The Court ordered that William Ramsey, Michael Brown, Andrew Thomson, Peter Binkley, David Davis, and William Henley be summoned to appear and show cause why they should not be fined for refusing to attend as jurymen. Charles Stewart and John Fannen, the same.

Stephen Saunders showed his commission as major of the 1st Battalion of the 100th Regiment, and took the oath of office.

John Ligate [Liggatt, Leggett, etc.] was permitted to keep a tavern in his house. Bond with Abram Goodpasture as security [Ligate lived in present Smyth County where he developed the Town of Leggattsville].

David Vaughn returned the list of delinquents for the revenue tax and county levy of Grayson County for 1793, and it was transmitted to the commissioner of revenue for this county. Francis J. Carter returned the list of delinquents for the year 1793 and it was also transmitted to the commissioner of revenue. Also returned were the lists of insolvents in the county levy for 1793 and the poor rates for 1792 within his district, and also the list of supernumeraries, collected by him.

October 13, 1795: On this day John Miller, overseer of the poor was to "bind out" Ann Laraman, daughter and orphan of Esther Larraman, deceased, to Caty Montgomery.

Peter Groseclose was appointed overseer of the road in Rich Valley, in place of Peter Groseclose, Senr., Robert Lastley the same, in place of John Lastley, from John Compton's to the dividing ridge between the Clinch and the Blue Stone.

Robert Sayers, Moses Austin, and Alexander Smyth were appointed commissioners to receive subscriptions towards defraying the expense of building a bridge across Reed Creek at the main ford near Joseph Crockett's [east of present Wytheville]. It was further ordered that the commissioners let out the building of the bridge on such a plan as they shall prepare to the lowest bidder and the court engage to pay the balance of the charge over and above the amount subscribed.

John Stinson was appointed constable in Captain Davidson's Company in place of John Cartmill. Richard Bailey and John Bailey were paid for wolf heads. Stephen Sanders, Junr., was appointed overseer of the road in place of John Lease, and Andrew Danner was appointed overseer of the road from Michael Lease's old place to James Campbell's, and Stephen Sanders was to allot the tithables to work on it.

Robert Sanders was appointed overseer of the road from Newell's Ferry at present Austinville to Jacob Keesler's. Thomas Foster and Richard Muse to allot the hands between Moses Austin and William Ross to work on the road from said Ross's to Evans' Ferry and from there to Newell's. William Carter was appointed overseer of the road from Evans' [now Jackson's] Ferry to the road leading from Isaac Shepperd's to John Montgomery's and keep the same in repair [this last section of the road was basically Route 52 from the ferry to Fort Chiswell].

Joseph Kent was appointed overseer of the road replacing Joseph Montgomery from John Bishop's to the ford of Reed Creek below Fort Chiswell, and that with the usual hands and the hands of his own family work on the same, and be exempted from working on any other part of the road.

November 10, 1795: The Grand Jury found against Henry Angle for selling

191

spiritous liquors without a license by the information of Nancy Moore, spinster, of Wythe County. They also found against Jacob Keasling for not having an index placed in the fork of the roads, leading from Fort Chizwell [Chiswell] to the lead mines and Herbert's Ferry; also found against the overseer of the road from Daniel Wiseley's to the ford of Reed Creek at Walters' Stone Mill, it not being made according to law.

George Armbrister, Jr., was appointed overseer of the road from the ford of Reed Creek at Bell's Hill to the Stone Mill, and Earhart Simmerman was appointed overseer of the road from the ford on Reed Creek at Joseph Crockett's [near the bridge over Reed Creek east of Wytheville] to Simmerman's.

The court ordered John Miller and Robt. Grayham [Graham] "bind Wm. McKinsey, son of Jno. McKinsey to Robertson Burg."

Robert Percival showed a certificate of having taken the oath of allegiance to the Constitution of the United States and fidelity to the Commonwealth.

On the motion of William Rogers and for reasons appearing to the court, it was ordered that the fine inflicted on him and Mary Burk, for unlawfully cohabiting together, be remitted.

Joseph Montgomery and William Steele were paid for wolf heads. Jesse Evans acknowledged his bond with security as the law directs that he will keep a ferry on New River at his plantation [this is now Jackson's Ferry site].

November 11, 1795: William Davis, Robert Adams, Jesse Evans, Leonard Straw, and Stephen Sanders justices were present and conducted the court's business.

On the motion of Robert Crockett, William Drope was discontinued from acting as deputy clerk. John T. Sayers' commission as sheriff had to be sent back to the executive because the date was missing.

Robert Crockett was allowed $27 for examining and comparing and correcting the books of the commissioners of revenue for the year 1795, for two books for the office, and one lock for the courthouse to be allowed out of the present levy.

Benjamin Holston was allowed $20.61 in the hands of Alexander Smyth for making a table for the clerk and for repairs done to the courthouse.

On the complaint of Peter Binkley, it was ordered that Isaac Alderson, his apprentice, be summoned at the next court to answer his complaint and in the meantime continue with said Binkley and "behave himself as the law directs."

Anthony Toncray was licensed to keep an ordinary at his house [it was located east of Wytheville, near the bridge over Reed Creek].

John Cypher was fined $5 and costs for contempt and refusing to serve as a juryman. Moses Wells was paid for one old wolf head.

The following rates for ordinaries were established: breakfast warm, 12 1/2 cents; cold 8 cents; dinner warm, 17 cents and cold 12 1/2 cents; supper warm 11 1/2 cents and cold 8 cents; lodging and a good bed and clean sheets 8 cents; corn per gallon 8 cents, oats per gallon 8 cents; hay or fodder and stable per night for a horse 12 1/2 cents; good pasturage for 24 hours 8 cents; whiskey per half pint 6 1/4 cents; good cyder per quart 6 1/4 cents; West India Rum per 1/2 pint, 12 1/2 cents; continent Rum 6 1/2 cents; good wine per 1/2 pint, 12 1/2 cents; peach brandy 8 cents, good French Brandy 8 cents; good Holland Gin 12 1/2 cents, good beer per quart 6 1/2 cents; methlaglin per quart, 12 1/2 cents; Cyder Royal per quart 12 1/2 cents, and boiled cyder per quart 6 1/2 cents.

Thomas Foster and William Ross were to allot the hands under Robert Sanders and William Carter, overseers of the road in different districts.

Robert Adams, John Montgomery, and Robert Crockett were ordered to settle with Jehu Stephens, late sheriff of the county, respecting the claims payable by him as sheriff and return same to the next court and that he be notified to attend Saturday the 5th of next month for this purpose.

William Hay, James Finley, and Robert Crockett were ordered to settle with the Trustees of the Town of Evansham and the trustees be notified to attend Wednesday December 9, next.

Jn.[John] Pruner in a suit against William Preston's executors was to receive a conveyance for 210 acres in fee simple.

Daniel Johnston was permitted to keep an ordinary at his house. His bond was with Robert Crockett. Andrew Thompson was admitted as deputy clerk and took oath of office.

December 5, 1795: A special court session was called for the examination of George Wyrick who was charged with stealing and carrying away one and one-half sides of leather, the property of John George Kegley, valued at $3. The justices who heard the case were John Adams, James Finley, Jesse Evans, Robert Adams, and Leonard Straw. After hearing witnesses, the criminal was allowed to choose his punishment, having been found guilty. He chose 25 lashes, and it was ordered.

December 8, 1795: The fine imposed on Wm. Love previously was set aside for illegality and he was ordered to appear and answer a new summons and indictment of the Grand Jury.

James McCampbell was appointed prosecutor of the Commonwealth in the absence of George C. Taylor. John Brawley was paid for two young wolf heads. John Leftwich was deputy under the late sheriff Jehu Stephens.

George Weaver was appointed overseer of the road in place of Martin Stealy [Staley]. Robert Adams was allowed for laying off the prison bounds, according to law out of the next levy.

George Kegley was allowed $2 out of the next levy for one day's waggoning in repairing the bridge at the Town of Evansham [Wytheville].

David Doak was ordered to open the road from Straw's Mill to the road leading up the valley on the north side of Pine Ridge and to make alterations as he thinks proper. William Ward and said Doak were to allot the hands to work on the different roads leading through Pine Ridge. Samuel Fullen, William Ward, and Andrew Swallow were to view the nearest and best way from Straw's Mill to the road leading through Hedrick's Gap to the Main Road on the north side of Pine Ridge and Jacob Kinder to be overseer. The tithables living on the north side of Pine Ridge from the Stoney Fork to Daniel Pirkey's thence by a line to Jno. Hutsell are to be exempted from further service on the main road.

John Montgomery, Robert Adams, and Robert Crockett or any two were to settle with Jehu Stephens, late sheriff of the county, respecting his collection of county and parish levies and fines for 1792 and 1793 on Saturday preceding next January Court and he is to be notified.

William Hay, James Finley, and Robert Crockett, are to settle with the Town Trustees for selling lots.

The rates for ordinaries were modified so that a warm breakfast and a warm supper were 28 cents each, and a warm dinner 25 cents.

January 12, 1796: Present: William Davis, James Newell, Jesse Evans, and James Finley.

Captain James Finley, Daniel Wiseley, and William Phipps, or any two, were to view the way proposed for an alteration of the road from Reed Creek as far as the lands of Valentine Catrine [Catron] extend and report. John Montgomery, Almerine Marshall and John Davis, or any two, were to view the way petitioned for by William

Hay through his lands, and make their report.

Hugh Montgomery, Robert Adams, Walter Crockett, John Crockett, Sener, John Adams, Joseph Kent, and Hugh McGavock, or any five, were to view the two roads leading from the Stone Mill to Fort Chizwell [Chiswell], namely, the way passing through the Town of Evansham, and the old road, sundry petitioners alleging that the new road leading through the town is sufficient and in conformity thereto, to report the conveniences and inconveniences that will result from closing the old road to individuals as well as the general public.

Jehu Stephens, late sheriff, is to attend on Monday before the February Court, to settle the business of his office, and Robert Crockett, William Hay, and Wm. Drope shall attend for that purpose.

The rates for the ordinary keepers at the November Term of 1795 were altered as follows: breakfast, dinner, and supper, warm were to be 25 cents.

February 9, 1796: Jenkin Whiteside, Nathaniel H. Claybourne, and Henry Dixon took oath and admitted to practice as attorneys in this court.

John Montgomery and Almarine Marshall reported that they had viewed and marked a way for a road through William Hay's land leaving the old road near Helvy's line nearly a direct course into the old road near Criger's line which is not inconvenient.

James Finley and William Phipps viewed the way proposed for an alternate road from Reed Creek as far as the land of Valentine Catron and it was ordered that the same be established.

Henry Davies had leave to raise and set up two gates across the road leading from Henry Honaker's to the Flower Gap.

William Neele [Neely] returned the list of delinquents and insolvents within his district as deputy sheriff for 1793.

February 10, 1796: Godfrey M. Smith [Messersmith] was appointed overseer of one-half of the road allotted to Peter Groseclose, and Alexander Buchanan and William Hays are to divide the road and the hands between the overseers.

Samuel Crockett (John's son) and Hezekiah Harman were appointed commissioners of revenue for the present year.

Andrew Thompson was discontinued as deputy clerk of this court and by motion of Robert Crockett, John Evans was admitted as deputy clerk.

March 8, 1796: Present: Wm. Davies, John Adams, Robert Adams, and Wm. Calfee.

Leonard Straw, Wm. King, George Kinser, or two of them, were to view the way from the mouth of Tawney's lane to where it intersects the main road again, and report.

Isaac Taylor was exempted from paying levys due to age and infirmity. James Patrick allowed for 45 miles coming and same returning from court, and two ferriages.

Will of Peter Spangler, deceased, partly proven by the oath of Wm. Smith, one of the witnesses, continued for further proof.

Mathias Rosenbum [Rosenbaum] was appointed overseer of the road from Kettner's to Rosenbum's Mill [on Cripple Creek] and to keep the same in repair.

John Allison showed a certificate to the court signed by Arthur Campbell showing he had taken the oath of citizen of this Commonwealth.

William Rogers, James Brawley, and William Rutherford, Junr., or any two of them, were to view the way proposed by James Newell from Rutherford's road to the lead mines and report.

George Kegley was given permission to give up and be acquitted of Elizabeth Moore, who was a servant bound to him by her mother Nancy Moore.

The following persons were recommended to act as militia officers of the county:

John Montgomery, Junr., captain in 1st Battalion, 35th Regiment, replacing Jesse Evans, promoted; Joseph Kent, same of an additional company; Stephen Montgomery, captain, replacing David McGavock, removed; John Evans, captain, replacing Wm. Adams, removed; Moses Austin, captain, in 2nd Battalion of the same regiment, an additional company; Stephen Sanders, Junr., captain, same; Francis J. Carter, captain of a company of riflemen; Joseph Evans, lieutenant in 1st Battalion, same regiment; Robert Crockett, the same; William Foster lieutenant replacing Andrew Steele, removed; Wm. Finley, Junr., same replacing Leonard Straw, promoted; and Jas. McCampbell, same, replacing John Evans, promoted.

The lieutenants in the 2nd Battalion of the 35th Regiment were to be William Ross, Samuel Grayham replacing Stephen Sanders promoted, John Crockett (son of Jas.), William Calfee, Junr., and William Sanders, the same of a Rifle Company.

The ensigns in the 1st Battalion of the 35th Regiment were Samuel Crockett (John's son), Robert Montgomery, John Crockett (son of Andrew), Jacob Ketron, replacing William Finley, promoted, John Gruget replacing Jas. Breckinridge removed.

In the 2nd Battalion of the same regiment, the ensigns were George Ewing (son of George) replacing John Lease removed, Joel Pierce, Samuel Crockett (James' son), and Samuel Crockett (Andrew's son).

Leonard Straw was recommended as captain in the 100th Regiment, replacing David Doak, resigned. It was recommended that James Neely be transferred from the 35th Regiment to the 100th Regiment.

Robert Adams was recommended as captain of a company of artillery, and John Crockett first, and James McGavock, Junr. 2nd lieutenants of the same.

Josiah Ramsey, Junr., was paid for three wolf heads. Samuel Ewing, Wm. Gleaves, James Campbell, and Wm. Ross, or any three, were to view the road from Andrew Danner's to his mill, thence by George Ewing's and thence by Samuel Ewing's and thence to the ford of New River at Samuel Porter's, thence into the mine road towards William Ross', and make their report.

Charles Fullen was entitled to £1 2/6 for apprehending John and Elizabeth Corvin charged with felonies, and for summoning twelve witnesses.

March 9, 1796: Present: Wm. Davies, Wm. Ward, Robt. Sayers, John Adams, and James Finley.

The court ordered that Robert Adams and Robert Crockett let out the building of stocks for the use of the county under such conditions "they may conceive most beneficial for the county."

Robert Adams and Hugh Montgomery were ordered to allot the hands to work on the Peppers Ferry Road from Peter Binkley's to John Miller's, and make a report.

Leonard Straw, Jas. Finley, John Hounshell, and David Doak, or any three of them to view an alteration of the road leading from George Tawney's to George Wampler's as proved by John King.

William Carter and Thomas Brooks were to allot the hands to work under Moses Austin and Wm. Ross, allowing Ross one-third of the hands to be allotted.

Samuel and Robert Crockett were to employ some person to fix and set up the stove in the courthouse. Samuel Crockett took his oath as a commissioner of revenue.

Almarine Marshall was appointed overseer of the road from Evansham [Wytheville] to the ford of Reed Creek at Jos. Crockett's, replacing Lewis Woolford; Philip Reader, same of the Cove Road, replacing Joseph Baker.

John Crockett, deputy sheriff for John T. Sayers, returned a list of delinquents in revenue tax for 1794 within his district, also a list of the same in county and parish levy.

Robert Crockett returned the same.

April 12, 1796: Alexander Smyth appeared and stated he did not accept the office of escheator of the county.

April 14, 1796: The Grand Jury held an inquest in regard to the following: William Finley and William Phipps for gaming in the house of John Johnston at cards for money by the knowledge of Wm. Henley and Wm. Gleaves, within the past two weeks; the surveyor of the Cove Road for not keeping the same in repair within six months, by the knowledge of George Owry [Oury] and Peter Binkley; George Copenbarger for offering to vote at the election a second time yesterday, contrary to law, by the information of John Thompson Sayers; the surveyors of the streets of Evansham for not keeping the same in repair; Alexander Mahood and Tabithia Cordell for fornicating and cohabiting together within the last three months by the knowledge of John Hounshell and Daniel Wiseley.

Joseph Sams (?) was appointed constable in place of John Fisher, resigned. Jacob Colson was paid for one old wolf head. Jehu Stephens took oath as justice of the County Court in Chancery. Jacob Ketrene [Catron] granted leave to keep a tavern at his house [on Old Stage Road].

John Stanger, an immigrant into this Commonwealth, appeared in court and gave satisfactory proof by oath that he intends to reside therein, whereupon by order of the court he took the oath of allegiance and fidelity to the Commonwealth, and oath to support the Constitution of the United States and become a citizen.

Isaac Shepperd was appointed overseer of the road from Jos. Montgomery's to the forks of the Great Road leading from the lead mines to Richard Beason's and William Carter, the same from thence to Evan's Ferry and that Jesse Evans and Manassas Friel divide the hands between the overseers.

The sum of 12 1/2 cents was ordered to be collected by the sheriff from each tithable in the county for discharging the claims against the same for the present year.

Joseph Crockett, Robert Adams, and Manassas Friel, or any two of them, were to view the alteration of the road lately made by George Armbrister's and make a report.

John Evans produced a commission appointing him as captain of a company of riflemen to the 1st Battalion of the 35th Regiment of the Virginia Militia; James McCampbell the same as lieutenant, and John Gruget the same as ensign.

May 10, 1796: James Newell, John Adams, James Campbell, Leonard Straw, Stephen Sanders, Moses Austin, and Jehu Stephens were present as justices of the court.

Joseph Crockett, Robert Adams, and Manassas Friel reported on the alteration of the road lately made by George Armbrister and it was in their opinion equal to the old road with a small amendment ordered to be done. Coonrod Keasler was appointed overseer of the road from Newell's Ferry [at Austinville] to the top of Lick Mountain, in the place of Moses Austin, and to clear out and keep the same in repair.

Joseph Kent was given leave to make an inclusive survey of all of his lands on Reed Creek. The clerk was ordered to insert the name of Alexander McKinsey in place of Jno. Kinsey, that being the name of the father of Wm. Kinsey whom John Miller and Robert Grayham [Graham] were directed to bind to Robertson Burgh.

John Montgomery was ordered to contract with someone to make steps to the courthouse doors and to be paid for out of the present levy. Christian Ketron [Catron], Leonard Litz, Charles and David Bustard, or any three, were ordered to view the way for a proposed road from the northwest corner of Hezekiah Chaney's field towards Spraker, and to George Wampler's, thence by Miller's, Henry Steffey's, Robert Buckhannon's or Martin Staley's to the main county road.

George Weaver was appointed overseer of the road in place of Martin Stealey [Staley].

Leonard Straw, James Finley, John Hounshell, and David Doak were to view the road from Tawney's lane to George Wampler's through John King's land and reported that the road leads through a valuable piece of ground that is cleared and under good fence, and that the way for an alternate is about 20 poles [one pole=16.5 feet] around the hill between, being very little worse than the way it now goes. Therefore the alteration proposed by King is disallowed, and the former way established. Jno. [John] Holder was allowed for one old wolf head.

A writ of *ad quod damnum* was to be issued to ascertain if any damages would be caused by erecting a mill on the lands of Thos. Crow, Junr., and to lay off one acre of land for the abutment of the said dam, and the sheriff was ordered to impanel a jury. The same for Moses Austin.

Alexr. Smith [Smyth], Joseph Kent, Francis Jackson Carter, Jos. Crockett, and Joshua Jones were recommended to serve as justices of the peace.

Stephen Montgomery was appointed overseer of the road from Draper's Road to the county line in place of Benjamin Thomas, removed, and to keep the same in repair.

James Murphy was fined $2 and costs and George Tawney $3 and costs for contempt of court.

June 2, 1796: On this date the court examined James Thompson, accused of stealing a bay horse belonging to Michael Stiffey [Steffey] worth $80, and was remanded to jail after questioning and hearing witnesses, to await trial.

June 14, 1796: The Grand Jury, composed of William Gleaves (foreman), Frederick Leonard, George Kegley, John Greenup, Robert Buchanan, Jinkin Williams, Joshua Jones, John Hounshell, Joseph Irvine, Thomas Gannaway, Francis J. Carter, Jno. Grayson, William Bonham, Nicholas Snider, John Lastley, Nathaniel Frisbie, and Alexander Smyth, heard that the highway in the precinct of Martin Stealy, surveyor, was out of repair, and that Almarine Marshall (by the hands of his wife Rachel) was selling liquor (1/2 pint brandy to John Grayson, and 1/2 pint brandy to Francis J. Carter at Evansham) without a license.

John Bishop was before the court for adultery with a "woman commonly called Mary Bishop within the last twelve months, and the said Mary, alias Mary Couder, the same for adultery with John Bishop." The Rev. Jacob Repass, preacher of the Gospel in the county, gave the information.

The court neglected to procure standard of weights and measures.

The Grand Jury recommended that a surveyor of the road be appointed from Daniel Repass' to Peter Yonce's, and that the highway in Peter Kinder's precinct was out of repair.

Robert Grayam [Graham] and Richard Muse were to bind out John Pierce, infant of _____ Pierce, deceased, to John Hurst.

An attachment was issued in the case of *Simmerman vs. Harman* against items of personal property: one pair of shoe boots, one pair of black breeches, one "weast" coat, one gray great coat, one pair of "ribed" stockings, one pair of "Jean Breaches," one pair of shoe buckles, one wallet, and one toothbrush.

Two other roads were reported out of repair: the highway between Peak Creek at McCoy's and Andrew Boyd's and the road from Wiseley's shop to the top of Lick Mountain, due to the neglect of the court to appoint an overseer.

Christian Kettering [Catron] showed his commission as captain of a company of the 1st Battalion of the 100th Regiment, and qualified.

June 15, 1796: Michael Venrick was granted a license for an ordinary at his house.

Alexander Smyth, Joseph Kent, Francis J. Carter, Joseph Crockett, Joshua Jones, James Crockett, David Busterd and William Neele were added to the commission of the peace.

Joseph Patterson declined serving as a justice of the peace and hasn't served as such, and Andrew Steele has moved outside the state. Moses Bates was granted permission to keep an ordinary at Austinville, and Moses Austin was security; same is granted Stophel [Christopher] Simmerman in Evansham [Wytheville].

June 16, 1796: Joseph Kent showed his commission as captain in the 1st Battalion of the 35th Regiment of Militia and qualified. John Fisher was reappointed constable in place of Joseph Lamins (?) removed; Julius Rutherford the same in the bounds of Captain Newell's Company; Leonard Straw qualified as captain of the ____ Battalion of 100th Regiment of Militia; Jacob Ketrene [Catron] the same as ensign in the 1st Battalion of the 35th Regiment.

John Wampler was appointed to be overseer of the road from the ford of Reed Creek to James Campbell's and with the usual hands to keep the same in repair.

June 17, 1796: Jno. [John] Miller and David Doak were ordered to bind out Jno. Grills, bastard child of Nancy Moore, to Henry Rife. Jehu Stephens refused to accept an appointment of lieutenant Colonel Commandant of the 100th Regiment of Virginia Militia.

John Phipps was examined by the court for biting off the lip of David Short, but was discharged.

July 12, 1796: James Newell returned the certificate showing Moses Austin taking the oath as captain of the militia; Francis Jackson Carter qualified as captain of the company of Riflemen in ____ Battalion of the 35th Regiment of Militia. James Davies, Junr., same as captain of a company of 1st Battalion of the 100th Regiment; Henry Stephens, the same as ensign in the same Battalion and Regiment.

William Neely, Jacob Tobler, Peter Kinder, and Robert Davis, or any three, were to view the different ways proposed for a "waggon road" from the northwest corner of Hezekiah Chaney's field into the main road leading from Evansham to the head of the Holston.

On the motion of Moses Austin, by his attorney Jinken Whiteside, John Allison is summoned to appear the second Tuesday in September to show cause if any, why an information should not be filed against him for a misdemeanor in purchasing or receiving lead from said Austin's Negro man slave, James, and encouraging and persuading him to steal lead from said Austin, his master, and sell the same clandestinely to said Allison.

James Newell was recommended as lieutenant colonel in the 100th Regiment of Militia, and William Gleaves was recommended as captain replacing James Newell, promoted. Jno. Montgomery qualified as captain of a company of the 1st Battalion of the 35th Regiment.

Stephen Sanders, William Love, Peter Spangler, and Stophel [Christopher] Ketrine [Catron], or any three, were ordered to view the way proposed for a "waggon" road from the "iron works of Stephens et als." into the road below Jno. Wampler's which leads from Cripple Creek to Evansham [Wytheville].

Andrew Porter was recommended as lieutenant of the 35th Regiment and George Ewing (son of George) the same in place of John Lease, removed.

John Cypher was appointed overseer of the road in place of George Armbrister.

August 4, 1796: An examination was held by the court for Adam Milam who was charged with stealing one sorrel horse belonging to James Patton, worth $100. The prisoner was set free.

An examination of John Williamson charged with raping Susanna Rudder; the prisoner was set free.

August 9, 1796: Henry Honaker was appointed overseer of the road from Andrew Boyd's to Jas. Crockett's. William Gleaves, William Ross, and Samuel Ewing reported on the road they viewed from A. Danner's to his mill, thence by George Ewing's and Samuel Ewing's thence to the ford of the New River at Samuel Porter's and then to the mine road and to William Ross' and concluded that "it will make a very good road with moderate labour."

Andrew Danner was to be continued as overseer from his mill to the Big Branch below Samuel Ewing's and Samuel Porter the same from Big Branch to the ford of the river at his house. Samuel Crockett was allowed for services as a commissioner of revenue.

George Weaver was appointed overseer of the road replacing Martin Staley; Peter Yantz [Yonce] was overseer of the road "in room of" Jeffrey Heldreth; Jacob Katron [Catron], blacksmith, was appointed surveyor of the road in room of John King.

William Foster showed his commission as a lieutenant of the 1st Battalion of the 35th Regiment; William Ross, the same as lieutenant in the 2nd Battalion of the 35th Regiment.

Duncan Reel (?) was appointed surveyor of the road replacing Wm. Kid [Kidd]; James Cahoun was appointed surveyor of the road replacing Joseph Patterson.

Alex. Smyth, Jos. Kent, Francis J. Carter, Joseph Crockett, and James Crockett showed commissions as justice of the peace.

Ruben Herald was appointed constable in Captain Austen's Company. The court certified that Daniel Sheffy, Gent., who wishes to obtain a license to practice law is a person of honest demeanor and is above the age of 21 years. Sam'l Newberry was allowed for one young wolf head.

Jos. Crockett, Isaac Shepperd, Ehart Zimmerman, and Manases Friel, or any three, were to view the most direct and best way for a road from Joseph Montgomery's by Peter Bishop's into the main road at or near Earheart Simmerman's, and report.

Robt. Sayers, Moses Austin, F. J. Carter, and Alex. Smyth or any three, are to draft a memorial to the Executive on the subject of the refusal of that body to commission officers in pursuance of recommendations of this court. When it was drafted it was to be "laid before the court for approbation."

Alex. Smyth was recommended as major, replacing Stephen Sanders, promoted, in the 1st Battalion of the 100th Regiment.

John Wampler was appointed overseer of the road from the ford of Reed Creek to the top of the dividing ridge between the Cripple Creek Road and Reed Creek; Jno. Stots the same from Newell's Ferry to Dick's. Thomas Crow has leave to build a mill.

August 20, 1796: The court was called for the examination of Robert Hadley who stands charged with having married Elizabeth Bishop while "he hath a former wife who is still living." The prisoner was remanded to gaol [jail] and was ordered to be taken to the circuit court for trial in Washington Court House October 7. Jacob Repass, Peter Bishop, Phillip Phry, and Valentine Keagley were witnesses bound over for their appearance in this case of bigamy.

September 14, 1796: Samuel Crockett showed his accounts for services as Commissioner of Revenue (65 days were requisite to perform the duties according to the court).

Peter Binkley was allowed eight shillings for making irons to confine McKee, a criminal. Stephen Sanders took the oath as lieutenant colonel of the 100th Regiment of Militia.

September 15, 1796: William Thompson, Alexander Buchanan, and James Maxwell were recommended as sheriffs.

September 13, 1796: (out of sequence in the order book) William Hays resigned his commission as captain in the 2nd Battalion of the 100th Regiment; Jeffrey Heldrith qualified as lieutenant in the same battalion; Evan Davies qualified as ensign in the same battalion; John Richardson, same as ensign in a company of Riflemen in the same regiment.

The Grand Jury considered the following charges: against the overseer of the road from Michael Walters to James Finley's by the knowledge of John King and Jacob Tobeas(?), yeoman; against Stephen Reader for obstructing the road from his house to George Kinder's by knowledge of Martin Woolford and Nicholas Tarter; against Mathias Rosenbaum for obstructing the road from his house to Blue Spring by the knowledge of William Gleaves and Ran. Rutherford; against John Johnston [innkeeper] for selling rum above the tavern rates, by the knowledge of John Carr and Rand. Rutherford.

William Gleaves was given permission to have an inclusive survey made of all lands on Cripple Creek, "having advertised his intent by law."

George Peary was recommended as major in the 2nd Battalion of the 100th Regiment, replacing Wm. Neelly, removed; Henry Stephens as captain in the same replacing Jas. Neely, removed; Jas. Jones, lieutenant replacing Charles Busterd, who refused to act; Samuel Williams, ensign in the same, replacing Henry Stephens, promoted; William Richardson, En. as captain replacing Wm. Hays, resigned. James Campbell enters his dissent to these recommendations because "the majority of the justices of this county were not present."

John Evans was discontinued as deputy clerk of this Court and Samuel Crockett was admitted in his place. Hezekiah Harman, one of the Commissioners of the Revenue presented his account and was allowed $65. David Busterd and Joshua Jones took oath as justices.

Barnabus Messersmith vs. William King, a suit in Chancery: the arbitrators ordered William King to convey the land, the same conveyed to King by Jacob Kinser, and his wife to join in the deed, releasing her dower.

William Adkins was recommended as lieutenant in the 1st Battalion of the 100th Regiment replacing Isaac Leftwich, who refuses to serve; Jacob Stealey [Staley] the same as ensign, replacing John Shannon who refused to serve.

Major William Neelly has not moved from the county yet, and may not soon do so, so the recommendation of George Peary to replace him is rescinded.

Edward Catcham was appointed a constable in the same bounds of Captain Neelly's Company. On September 16, 1796, Stephen Sanders showed his certificate showing he had taken the oath as captain of the militia.

"It is the opinion of the court that William Love, Esq., by coming to the bench intoxicated acts derogatory to character of a justice of the peace, and is incapable, and should be considered absent." William Love was fined 83 cents.

Captain Jas. Neelly, not having moved from the county, the recommendations of Henry Stephens as captain and Samuel Williams as ensign are rescinded. Colonel Robert Sayers was appointed overseer of the road from the house of Jno. Adams [on Peppers Ferry Road] to Millers Creek [near Max Meadows], and that with his own hands those between said road and Reed Creek, Joseph Crockett's and above Miller's Creek, those inhabiting the Cove and those north of Cove Creek and said road, but south of the Cove do keep the same in repair.

Jno. Crockett, deputy sheriff for John Thompson Sayers, returned the list of delinquents and insolvents within his district amounting to $79.94, which is allowed; Robert Crockett returned his list and was allowed 7 pounds 13 shillings, 4 1/4 pence.

Jno. Crockett also returned his account of serves in removing criminals in the amount of $34.64; also an account of Jno. Craig's for serving as guard in the amount of $11.44; also an account of Samuel Crockett for the same in the amount of $11.44.

October 11, 1796: Jesse McCollister was held and questioned on murder charges. A man was found dead near Austinville lead mines and the man's name was said to be Peter Brigs. The accused denied the charge and after examining the witnesses, the prisoner was released.

Daniel Sheffey was licensed to practice law, and took oath as an attorney, oath of fidelity to the Commonwealth and the oath to support the Constitution.

William Neele took oath as justice. William Davies qualified as captain in the 2nd Battalion of the 100th Regiment; Alex Buchanan in the 1st Battalion; Charles Busterd the same as lieutenant, and Henry Wampler the same as ensign.

In the suit *Commonwealth vs. Hadley*, Valentine Kegley (Cagley) proved one day's attendance as a witness, traveling 150 miles in coming and the same in returning and two ferriages. [This Kegley and his location have not been identified.]

John Johnston exhibited his account as jaylor [jailer] of the county for $45.99 which is allowed. Robert Crockett was allowed $45 out of the fines and present levy for his ex officio services from May 1795 to May 1796 for comparing and examining the commissioner's books of the Revenue for 1796. He also produced an account for $0.68 for criminal charges which is allowed.

Wm. Hays recommended as major of the 2nd Battalion, 100th Regiment, replacing Wm. Neely, removed; Charles Busterd recommended as captain in the 1st Regiment, replacing James Neelly removed; Henry Stephens, the same as lieutenant, replacing Charles Busterd, promoted; Samuel Williams, ensign in place of Henry Stephens promoted in the 1st Battalion.

Moses Evans was allowed for two old wolf heads and Joseph Fletcher for one.

Samuel Crockett and Jno. [John] Davies were appointed commissioners of revenue for 1797; Samuel Crockett was to act on the south side of the main road and John Davies to act on the north side of same.

Alexander Smyth qualified as major in the _____ Battalion of the 100th Regiment. William Davies, coroner of the county, returned an inquest taken on the body of a man said to be Peter Briggs.

October 12, 1796: On the motion of Henry Rife who was about to leave the state, it was ordered that he be given permission to be released of John Franklin who is bound to him as an apprentice, they both agreeing that Franklin is to be bound to Jas. Ellis.

Robert Adams was allowed nine shillings out of the next levy for the price of one book for the use of his office [he was surveyor].

Joseph Crockett, Isaac Sheperd, and Erheart Simmerman, who were appointed to view the most direct and best way for a road from Jos. Montgomery's by Peter Bishop's into the main road at or near Erheart Simmerman's report that a good road may be had without any inconvenience and residents of that area if they feel otherwise must appear at the December Court.

John Lambert, John Pacer, Adam Harman, and Thomas Pauley were to view the way for a bridle way from James Fisher's across Walker Mountain to Evansham [Wytheville]

David Doak, Frederick Whitman, Mathias Harman, Henry Beason, and William Ward are to view the way for a bridle way from Mathias Harman's to Watson's Gap by Mrs. Doak's.

November 8, 1796: It was ordered that John Wampler be appointed overseer of the road that leads to Cripple Creek from the place where the same leaves the main county road to the top of the dividing ridge.

The surveyors of the Fort Chiswell road from the ford of Reed Creek to Andrew Boyd's were reported for not keeping the same in repair based on the knowledge of Andrew Crockett and James Simpson.

Christley Stealey [Staley], Peter Kinser, Jacob Helvey, and Christley Ketren [Catron] were brought before the court for an "affray in the house of Almarine Marshall on November 7, 1796."

November 9, 1796: Leonard Straw and William King were appointed to appraise the estate of Michael Wampler deceased and applied to George Davis the administrator of the estate who informed them that there was nothing of the estate to be found.

November 10, 1796: John Montgomery had a certificate proving John Crockett qualified as ensign in the 35th Regiment. Appraisement of the estate of Charles Whitelock, deceased, recorded.

Robert Adams and Joseph Crockett ordered to settle the accounts of administration of George Lowman's estate, Earhart Simmerman, administrator.

December 13, 1796: Present: William Davis, John Adams, James Newell, William Neel, and Stephen Sanders.

Ordered that Jinken Williams be appointed overseer of the road from the top of Iron Mountain to the Cripple Creek road at Shaley (Shared?) James and that he with the hands on the South Fork of Holston keep the same in repair.

Mathias Harman, Jacob Beeson, Peter Percifield, and William Bose (Bruce?) are to view the way proposed for alteration of the road from the land of James Davis to Mathias Harman's.

James Rice appointed surveyor of the road in place of John Compton. Godfry M. Smith [Messersmith], Jacob Spangler, Peter M. Smith [Messersmith], and David Doak or any three of them to view the grounds proposed for the wagon road from Mary Doak's to Elk Licks and that James Maxwell, John Thompson, Archy Thompson, and William Scissle [Cecil] or any three of them to view the grounds proposed for continuance of said road from the Elk Licks to the foot of Rich Mountain, the other side of Wm. Thompson's.

Ordered that Henry Harman, Sr., Jacob Nisewander, and Hezekiah Harman divide the road and hands between Andrew Thompson and Robert Garrett, surveyors of the road from Henry Harmon. Sr., to the Rockey Gap.

John Montgomery hired John Gruget to make steps to the courthouse doors for 7 pounds 1 shilling 8 pence, which the court now allows to be paid.

Hiram Craig to be recommended to the executive as 2nd lieutenant in 3rd Regiment of Artillery, in place of James McGavock, who refuses to serve.

December 14, 1796: Erhart Simmerman is appointed to survey the road from the top of Lick Mountain at McDonald's Gap to the main road at Simmerman's.

Robert Adams, surveyor of the county, is appointed to run the line between Wythe and Grayson counties as the law directs. He is to employ the chain carriers and find provisions and other materials necessary for conducting business and Jehu Stephens and Stephen Sanders were to be appointed as commissioners, and ordered to attend and assist the surveyor. They were to meet February 20 at the Washington County line on the top of Iron Mountain to run said lines.

CHAPTER II
Wills And Inventories Of Wythe County

1790-1809; miscellaneous dates 1814-1845

The first will book contains 443 pages, with 171 family names mentioned as primary entries. Deed Book 1 A has only 7 items, with 4 before 1820, 2 in the 1820s, and 1 in 1845. A few of the original wills are located in the basement of the Wythe County Circuit Court Clerk's Office, at Wytheville. Occasionally, other documents such as deeds and appointments for offices of the county, are found in the will book. Spelling and handwriting are inconsistent, and alternate spellings are given here in parentheses. The wills have been abstracted, and page numbers where wills, inventories, appraisals, and sales can be found are given in parentheses. The date the will was "written" means the day it was executed or signed. Probably most were prepared by attorneys in advance for the signature of the testator. The various records for each individual have been combined even though found on separate pages of the book. For example, the will listing the heirs is mentioned first if available, and if an inventory or appraisal or settlement is recorded it is combined here with the will information. If there is no will, only an inventory or appraisal or other record is shown for that person. It should also be understood that some of the later estates may have further information in subsequent will books. The names in square brackets [ ] were supplied by the author from other sources. Abstracts of wills of Wythe County have been published before, but numerous mistakes were found, and as a result it was decided to include here the correct information from Book 1. When Will Book 1 was repaired loose pages from Will Book 2 were inserted in the front of the book. These pertain to the will and estate of William Bates, and even though these records are out of order, they are included here.

The wills in Book 1 are for residents of what are now Smyth, Grayson, Carroll, Bland, Tazewell, and Pulaski counties, as well as present Wythe county, as these counties were formed partly from Wythe County.

Wythe County Will Book I

BATES (BATS), William, will written January 11, 1811, probated March 12, 1811, wife Anable, "ears" [heirs] James, Robert, Joseph, and probably Elegah (may be Elezabeth or Elijah), Henderson, Molly, Jane, and Charles. Executors are sons Joseph and John Bats (at front of book, no page); sale recorded June 11, 1811 (front of the book, no page)[probably belongs in Book 2, p. 9].

BRACKENRIDGE [BRECKENRIDGE], George, will written May 3, 1790, probated September 29, 1790 (p. 1), names wife Agness, children Alexander, Jane Alcain [Alcorn], Elisebeath Evans, Sary Findly, John Brackenridge, Lettis Linsy; grandchild George, son of John; Robert Brackenridge (no relationship given); executors Jesse Evans and John Brackenridge; inventory, appraisal, sale, recorded October 26, 1790 (pp. 2-4).

SULLIVAN, Morris, noncupative [oral] will dated July 4, 1789, "a few hours before his death," in the presence of Charles Blakly and William Calhoun, Jr., Sullivan gave his personal property to William Calhoun, Sr., and his son James, as William, Sr., had taken care of Sullivan. Will presented in Montgomery Court on September 3, 1789, proved Wythe County, December 28, 1790 (p. 5).

THOMPSON, Samuel, appraisal and inventory recorded January 25, 1791 (pp. 5-8); sale, April 13, 1791 (pp. 8-9).

NELSON, John, inventory taken March 4, 1791, recorded March 8, 1791 (pp. 9, 10).

CALHOUN, William, will written March 6, 1791, probated June 15, 1791 (pp. 10-12) names wife Elisabeth, and children William, Andrew, Elisabeth, and Mark, Isbell [Isabell], and Elisabeth, Anne, and James are under age; executors Elisabeth and Andriew [Andrew] Calhoun; appraisal October 22, 1791 (pp. 13-15).

EWING, James, will written March 3, 1783, probated November 8, 1791 (pp. 15-16) names brother Samuel Ewing, and others no relationship given: Euphame Purnel, Robert Porter's children, and Andrew Porter's children; executors Samuel Ewing, brother, and Mineter [Minitree] Jones; inventory and appraisal recorded January 10, 1791 [should be 1792, error in original] (pp. 17-19).

JAYNE, Zophe, blacksmith, will written December 10, 1790, probated January 10, 1791 (pp. 16-17) names wife Elizabeth, children not named; wife and Moses Foley, executors.

HELVEY, Henry, millwright, will written February 23, 1790, probated May 8, 1790 (p.19) names wife Susannah (Suanah), children, Henry, Jacob, and daughters not named; executors wife, Colonel Walter Crockett, and Nicholas Tarter; inventory, September 17, 1792, recorded September 1800; settlement recorded September 11, 1800 (pp. 155-159).

HELDRETH, Joseph, will written January 24, 1792, probated August 14, 1792 (pp. 20-21) names children, Jeffery, Abigail, John, Anna, Sarah, Polly, Phebey, Ruth, and Ketturah; also Janey Cole, no relationship given; executors, Jeffery Heldreth and Robert Adams; settlement February 21, 1800, recorded March 11, 1800 (p. 151).

WIRICK [WYRICK], Nicolas [Nicholas], original dated February 28, 1791, recorded September 13, 1792. Original will is in German script; translation in the will book (p. 21) names wife Barbara, son William, and "all my children," not named. No executors were named.

EWING, William, will written July 26, 1791, probated July 9, 1793 (p. 22) names wife Jane, sister Margaret Porter's sons Sam and Robert Porter, and daughter Rebecckah Porter; sister Elanor Porter's grandson Andrew Porter; brother John Ewing's sons Alexander and William Ewing; executors Jehu Stephens, Robert Buckhannan, Robert and Samuel Porter; inventory recorded September 1808 (pp. 405-407); sale August 15, 1793, recorded September 1808 (pp. 408-409).

GOODING (GOODDING), Abraham (Abram), will written June 4, 1792, probated January 14, 1794 (p. 23) mentions "widow" not named [no executor named], eldest son Cornelius of "Caintuckee," and youngest child Samuel under age; appraisal January 23, 1794, recorded February 11, 1794 (p. 57).

CRAIG, Robert, of Washington County, Virginia, will written September 30, 1792, probated September 9, 1794 (p. 24) mentions brother James Craig land in Russell County, brother David Craig land in Washington County, brother John Craig land near Abingdon, Washington County, brother Hiram, land in Powell's Valley, four sisters not named land in Powell's Valley; executors James Craig and Robert Adams.

CALHOUN, Andrew, will written March 23, 1792, probated August 14, 1792 (p. 26) mentions wife Mary, son William, mother Elizabeth Calhoun. Guardianship of Mark has been given up; executor Joseph Patterson; appraisal February 12, 1796 (p. 52).

DOAK, Nathaniel, appraisal dated November 11, 1794, recorded January 13, 1795 (p. 27).

CRANEY [CRANY], John, inventory recorded January 28, 1794, recorded Jan. 13, 1795 (p. 28).

WITTEN, Thomas, appraisal of estate recorded February 10, 1795 (pp. 29-31); administrator's account August 5, 1797, recorded September 12, 1797 (p. 89).

BUSTERD (BUSTER), William, will written March 12, 1792, probated May 13, 1795 (p. 32) mentions wife Jane (Jean), sons Charles, David, Michael, William, and Claudious and daughters Elizabeth Byrd, Jane, and Sarah; executors are wife and son Michael.

DAVIDSON, John, will written July 22, 1791, probated June 3, 1795 (p. 33) mentions wife Marthew [Martha?], sons Andrew, John, George, William, and Joseph; land on Brushey Fork known as "Quekers Cabans" to John Burk. Mentions George Peery, Lo [Low] Brown, and John Bell (Belle), but no relationship given; land to daughter "Betse."

LOMAN, George, will written June 28, 1795, probated August 11, 1795 (p. 34) mentions wife Elisabeth, her son Erhard Simmerman, son Jacob Loman, daughters Mary, Hannagh [Hannah] and Thorotery; appraisal recorded October 13, 1795 (p. 36); John Bishop, debtor of Erhrart Simmerman, administrator of estate, October 14, 1795, recorded November 10, 1796 (p. 79).

HINES, William, appraisal ordered January Court 1796, recorded February 10, 1796 (p. 37).

HONEEKAR [HONAKER], Jacob, will written August 12, 1795, probated May 10, 1796 (p. 39) mentions wife Mary, sons Henry, Jacob, Nicholas, Joseph, Martin, Frederick, Peter, Benjamin, Isaac, Abraham; daughters Elisabeth, Mary, Christiana, and Anna; executors David Sayer and Francis J. Carter; inventory May 21, 23, 1796 recorded June Court 1796 (pp. 42-45); settlement December 12, 1807 by Andrew Boyd, Jno. T. Sayers, and William Foster, recorded January 1808 (p. 398).

SPANGLER (SPANGLAR), Peter, Sr., will written June 15, 1794, probated March 8, 1796 (p. 41) mentions wife Margrat [Margaret], sons John, and Gorge [George] Spanglar, son Jacob Spangler, and Gorge [George] Bush, no relationship given; also James Camron; Charity Camron, alias Spangler, "her children gets their part, when of age;" executors, Jacob and Peter Spangler; inventory recorded February 14, 1797 (pp. 79-81); inventory and appraisal recorded December 8, 1801 (pp. 198-200).

DUN [DUNN], Thomas, appraisal and inventory recorded August 24, 1790 (pp. 45-49).

SHILLIDEAY, George, will written September 15, 1791, probated April 14, 1792 (p. 50) mentions wife Esther (Ester), who with three sons George, Edward, and Andrew B. were to be executors; some children, not named, have their part.

DOUGHERTY, Anthony ("head of South Fork of Holstain"), inventory taken January 10, 1793, recorded February 12, 1793 (p. 51).

KATREN (CATRON, CATREN, CATTERING), Stophel [Christopher], inventory July 4, 1795, recorded July 14, 1795 (p.54); settlement May 9, 1797 (p. 82);

appraisal November 9, 1804, recorded November Court 1804 (p.301).

RORACK (ROARK, ROARKS), James, appraisal taken July 21, 1792, recorded July 8, 1794 (pp. 59,76); settlement recorded September 8, 1801 (p. 189).

CHANDLER, David, inventory, February 12, 1794, recorded February 11, 1794 (error in date in original) (p. 60).

WARNER, Jacob, appraisal not dated, recorded February 11, 1794 (p. 61).

REPASS, Jacob, inventory and appraisal, recorded November 11, 1794 (p. 62).

COLE, Jean, appraisal July 26, 1794, recorded August 12, 1794 (p. 65).

NOWELS, Edward, inventory February 8, 1794, recorded June 10, 1794 (pp. 65-66).

RUNNER, Adam, inventory, February 15, 1796, recorded May 10, 1796 (p. 67).

McGLISTER, Cornelius, appraisal July 18, 1795, recorded October Court, 1795 (p. 68).

DAVIS, Abram, inventory recorded May 13, 1794 (p. 69).

HUTSEL, George, will written March 18, 1789, probated August 13, 1793 (p. 71) mentions wife Marget, sons George, John, other boys not named; daughters mentioned but not named.

HELVEY, Susanna, will written January 27, 1794, probated March 11, 1794 (p. 72) mentions sons Henry and Jacob Helvey, and John Corven (?); daughters Peggy Bragginich, and Molly Davis; Elizabeth Davis, Susanna Hops, Christiana Helvey and are to have an equal "shear of my movables," Christiana, Catharina (not of age), and Susanna Hops are identified as daughters.

WHITLOCK, Charles, inventory September 10, 1796, recorded November 10, 1796 (p. 77).

LONG, Benjamin, will written March 7, 1797, probated May 9, 1797 (p. 82) mentions wife Agness, daughters Mary and Rachel; executors Robert Watson and Robert Miller, Sr.; inventory and appraisal October 6, 1797 (pp. 86,87); settlement October 9, 1804, recorded March 1805 (p. 316).

LEEDY, Abram (Abraham), appraisal recorded May 9, 1797 (pp. 83-86); inventory and settlement recorded April 11, 1798 (pp. 99-104).

MUNSEY, Skidmore, appraisal July 1, 1797, recorded October 10, 1797 (pp. 87,88).

DAVIS, John, Sr., will written May 18, 1796, probated September 14, 1797 (p. 90) mentions wife Mary, sons Joseph, John George [may be two sons John and George], and Jacob; three grandchildren Betsy, Polly and Susy (daughters of Abram Davis, a deceased son); daughters Betsy, Eve, Elisabeth, Barbary and Polly who have intermarried with John Hutsell, Daniel Wisely, Lewis Hutsell, Joseph and John Fannen.

CALHOUN, Elisabeth, appraisal September 29, 1797, recorded December 12, 1797 (p.91).

CROCKETT, John, will written January 25, 1798, probated February 14, 1798 (pp. 93-96) mentions wife Elizabeth, all sons under 21, Samuel, John, Joseph; daughters Esther, Racel [Rachel?], Jean, Nancy, Polly, Caty, Betsy, and Sally, some daughters under age; also mentioned Ester Ellis, late Esther Thompson; executors brother Andrew Crockett, John Montgomery, Jr., and sons Samuel and John Crockett, and wife Elizabeth executrix; appraisal recorded May 8, 1798 (pp. 106-110).

BRALLY (BRAWLEY), John, will written September 25, 1795, probated March 13, 1798 (p. 97) mentions wife, not named, sons James and John, and daughters Martha, Barbara, and Polly; executors Richard Muse and Daniel Lockett; appraisal recorded May 8, 1798 (p. 105).

REASOR (RAZOR), Peter, appraisal May 6, 1797, recorded March 13, 1798 (p. 98).

BABER (BEBBER), James, will written June 4, 1798, probated July 10, 1798 (p. 110) mentions sons James, Joel and Daniel Bebber; daughters Johannah Bebber and Nancy Hobbs; Nancy Hobbs' son Richard Hobbs; also mentions Mary Underwood, Elisabeth Draper, Fanny Holley, and Margray Henly, no relationship given, but probably daughters; executors George Ewing and William Gleaves.

THOMPSON, William, will written February 10, 1797, probated December 11, 1798 (pp. 112-114) mentions wife Lidia, sons John, Archabal, Andrew, James, Alexander, and William; daughters Jean Sloan, Nancy Ward, Rachel Thompson, Annis, Mary, and Lydia Thompson; executors son-in-law James Sloan, and sons John, Archabald, and Andrew Thompson.

BUCHANAN, Alexander, will written November 6, 1798, probated December 11, 1798 (p. 115) mentions brother Robert and his children: Alexander, John, William, and Polley Buchanan; mentions Robert McAfee and John Goodman; executors Robert Buchanan and William Hay; appraisal January 5, 1799, recorded January 8, 1799 (p. 118).

PENNER, Peter, appraisal taken and recorded December 11, 1798 (pp. 116-117).

GOOSE [GOSE], Stephen, appraisal recorded August 13, 1799 (pp. 119-121).

CARR, John, appraisal recorded September 10, 1799 (pp. 122,123).

SPROWL (SPROULL), William, will written September 4, 1799, probated October 8, 1799 (p. 124) mentions wife Elizabeth, sons Robert and Hazlet; other children not named; executors wife and son Robert; inventory December 14, 1799, recorded January 15, 1800 (pp. 128-131); appraisal of real estate, October 19, 1789, recorded October 1807 (p, 398).

CAMPBELL, James, will written March 30, 1799, probated October 9, 1799 (pp. 125-127) mentions wife Mary, children not named, called "infant family"; wife and friends Francis Preston, Arthur Campbell, and Stephen Sanders, Gentlemen, executors; inventory November 27, 1799, recorded February 11, 1800 (pp. 140-144); sale December 2, 1799, recorded February 11, 1800 (pp. 144-147).

BESINGER (BASINGER), Paul, appraisal October 19, 1799, bill of sale October 19, 1799, recorded December 10, 1799 (pp. 127,128); appraisal October 19, 1799, recorded June 10, 1800 (p. 154).

CRESS (GRESS), Nicholas, inventory, January 11, 1800, recorded January 15, 1800 (p. 131); dower in lands of Nicholas Gress deceased, April Court, 1809; commissioners to lay off land to Elizabeth Taylor, late Elizabeth Gress, May 10, 1809, recorded June 14, 1809 (pp. 438-439).

DAUGHERTY, James, appraisal May 1799, recorded January 15, 1800 (pp. 132-137).

TAWNY [TAWNEY], George, appraisal recorded January 15, 1800 (pp. 137-139); inventory February 9, 1802, recorded April 13, 1802 (p. 206).

BRUSTER, Comfort, inventory recorded March 11, 1800 (pp. 147-148).

DARTER (TARTER), Balzer, will written February 17, 1800, probated March 11, 1800 (pp. 149-150) mentions wife Magdalene (Magdalena), three youngest sons Frederick, Christian and Daniel the youngest, other sons not mentioned by name; daughters Margaret, Catharine; brother Nannikel (or Hannikel); [some have interpreted this name as Nicholas]; executors, wife and John Stanger.

GANNAWAY, William, will written November 11, 1799, probated June 14, 1800 (pp. 152-153) mentions wife Elizabeth, four sons, John, William, Thomas, and Symore; daughters Mary Williams, Betty Love, Nancy Hambleton (Hamilton),

Sally, and four youngest daughters, Caty, Susannah, Patty and Frances Gannaway; executors John Newlin [Newland] and Henry Hambleton [Hamilton]; appraisal recorded July 1804 (pp. 292, 294-295); settlement with Elizabeth Newland, late Elizabeth Gannaway widow. February 1808, recorded March 8, 1808 (p. 402); Elizabeth Newland, late Gannaway, dower laid off, 150 acres of lands of William Gannaway, February 1808, recorded March 8, 1808 (p. 402).

WALTERS, Michael, inventory recorded May 14, 1800 (pp. 160-163); sale October 25, 1798, recorded November 14, 1800 (pp. 165-172).

PHILLIPPY (PHILLIPPEY), John, will written June 23, 1798, probated November 11, 1800 (p. 163) mentions wife Barbara, sons John and Christian; daughter Barbara, "my several daughters" not named; executor Leonard Straw; appraisal November 17, 1800, recorded December 9, 1800 (p. 172).

PIERCE, Thomas, appraisal, September 12, 1800, recorded February 10, 1801 (pp. 173-175).

ADAMS, John, will written December 4, 1800, probated March 10, 1801 (p. 175) mentions wife Elizabeth, and no others.

FINLY [FINLEY], Captain James, will written October 15, 1800, probated April 15, 1801 (p. 176) mentions son William, land on Green River, Kentucky, nephew Jonathan Henderson, wife and other children not named, and some not of age; no executors named; appraisal May 8 and July 28, 1801, recorded May 12 and August 12, 1801 (pp. 179-181, 187).

KEMMERLEN [KIMBERLING], Martain [Martin], appraisal March 24, 1801, recorded May 12, 1801 (pp. 176-179); settlement December 28, 1805, recorded January 1806 (p. 340); recorded January 1806 (p. 340).

FOGLESONG, Siman [Simon], appraisal, June 2, 1801, recorded June 9, 1801 (pp. 181-183).

CARTER, Robert, appraisal ordered April 1801, recorded June 11, 1800 (pp. 183-185).

CALFEE, William, will written August 10, 1796, probated July 14, 1801 (pp. 185-187) mentioned wife Mary, nephews William and James, son of brother John Calfee and Sarah his wife; executors wife, and William and James Calfee.

CREGER, Peter, will written March 28, 1801, probated September 8, 1801 (p. 188) mentions wife Elizabeth, sons Petter [Peter], Jacob and Mickel [Michael], and daughter Margret Cridor.

FICKLE, Mathias, will written August 4, 1801, probated October 13, 1801 (p. 189) mentions wife Mary, sons Absalom, Daniel, and Mathias, and daughter Polly Crabs; executors wife, and sons Mathias and Absalom; inventory and appraisal recorded September 14, 1802 (p. 224);

CALFEE, William, will written September 16, 1801 probated October 13, 1801 (p. 190) mentions wife Mary, sons William and James, Uncle William Calfee, a John and Samuel Calfee no relationship stated, and daughters Nancy and Elizabeth Calfee; executors brother James Calfee and son William; appraisal recorded October 13, 1801 (p. 193)

GOODE, Richard, will written April 23, 1801, probated June 9, 1801 (p. 192) mentions wife Rebecca, sons Charles, Joel, Samuel, and Richard Young Good, and daughters Anne, Betty Jean, Dice, and Margaret Good; executors wife, and Peter Forde and John Zean (?).

CROW, John, appraisal June 23, 1801, recorded November 10, 1801 (p. 195); sale probably July 21, 1802, recorded June 1808 (pp. 403-404).

REEDER. Phillip, will written October 15, 1801, probated November 10, 1801 (p. 197) mentions wife Mary, sons Jacob and Josiah, and daughters Dianna, Ivana, Pamela and Mandana; executor, wife; inventory and appraisal January 8, 1802, recorded January 12, 1802 (p. 201).

FINLEY, William, will written December 15, 1801, probated February 9, 1802 (p. 202) mentions wife Judith, sons Esau, William, Jr., John Pettes, and an unborn child, and daughters Mary Aminy Finley who was under 18, Rhoda and Margaret Finley; executors wife, Judith, and friends, William Finley, Samuel Crockett, and Robert Adams; inventory March 9, 1802 (p. 204); settlement recorded March 1805 shows plat and division of land to Esau Finley by John and Samuel Crockett (p. 314).

ABEL, Lewis, appraisal September 24, 1801, recorded April 14, 1802 (p. 209); settlement recorded March 1, 1805 (p. 315); settlement recorded May Court 1805 (p. 317).

MURPHY, Edward, inventory June 2, 1800, recorded April 14, 1802 (p. 212).

CALFEE, William, Junr., inventory March 20, 1802; recorded May 11, 1802 (p. 213).

HAY, John, appraisal April 23, 1802, recorded June 8, 1802; inventory and sale, April 23, 1802, recorded June 17, 1803 (pp. 241-242); inventory May 29, 1802, recorded July 13, 1802 (p. 217); sale recorded June 1803 (p. 243).

SWAN (a Negro man), deceased June 4, 1802; non-cupative will, recorded June 10, 1802 (p. 215); Swan died 4th day of this instant; left property to Johannah Stephens, and Jane Caffey [Calfee], daughter of James Caffey [Calfee], and to his father Tommey, Sr., and mother, Jenny, slaves of Captain William Herbert [compare Swan Garner, below, p. 226].

RADER, William, inventory February 1, 1801, recorded July 13, 1802 (p. 216); settlement September 21, 1805, recorded October 1805 (p. 331).

GULLAN (GULLION), John, appraisal recorded July 13, 1802 (p. 218); inventory recorded August 10, 1802 (p. 221).

MUSE, Thomas, will written July 19, 1802, probated August 10, 1802 (p. 219) mentions wife Susanna, wife's sister Catharine Pinkley, wife's niece Malvina Smyth; executors, wife and Alexander Smyth.

FINLEY, James, Sr., will written July 23, 1799, probated August 10, 1802 (p. 220) mentions only son James Finley, and grandson William Finley.

LONG, William, appraisal June 12, 1802, recorded August 10, 1802 (p. 223).

GARNER, Swan, inventory October 6, 1802, recorded October 12, 1802 (p. 226).

WARD, William, appointed sheriff, September 4, 1802, bonds recorded November 9, 1802 (pp. 227, 228, 229).

MORGAN, Nathaniel, will written October 10, 1802, probated November 9, 1802 (p. 230) mentions wife Margaret, sons Willis, Morgan, Jonathan, Samuel, William, and Nathaniel, and daughters Margaret, Sarah, Guyney, Elizabeth and Anna.; appraisal February 15, 1802, recorded July 12, 1803 (p. 252).

BUSTER, Charles, bill of sale November 9, 1802, recorded November 10, 1802 (p. 232); appraisal not dated, recorded July Court, 1804 (p. 297).

ARMBRISTER, George, will written October 30, 1802, probated November 10, 1802 (p. 234) mentions wife Barbara, sons John, George, Henry, and Michael, and daughters Sarah (under 21), Catharine Schroeder, Barbara Rader, Betsy Armbrister, Polly, and Rebecca Armbrister; executors, Joseph Crockett, John Johnston, and John Montgomery; appraisal recorded November 1805 (p. 333); settlement November 1805 (p. 334).

HOLLEY [HAWLEY], Jonathan, bill of sale for slave girl, etc., dated June 13, 1802, recorded November 11, 1802 (p. 235).

RANKIN, David, inventory, February 16, 1802, recorded December 15, 1802 (p. 236).

SMITH, Sarah, inventory March 4, 1803, recorded March 8, 1803 (p. 238).

YOUNG, John Godfret [Godfrey], appraisal recorded March 8, 1803 (p. 239); inventory April 13, 1803, recorded April Court 1803 (p. 239).

HONAKER (HANICAR), Joseph, inventory January 14, 1803, recorded April Court 1803 (p. 240); sale January 25, 1803, recorded April 1803 (p. 243); Widow Hanicar [Honaker] sale of August 1, 1806, "widow's effects that was prais'd at her husband's death and left for her lifetime," recorded October 1806 (pp. 366-367); settlement of accounts between administrators of Joseph Honaker, deceased, to wit, Henry Honaker, and Benjamin W. Jones who intermarried with Lovice Honaker, widow of Joseph Honaker, deceased, recorded October 1807 (p. 399).

HARMAN, Mathias, appraisal recorded June 14, 1803 (p. 245); sale February 11, 1803 and July 30, 1803 recorded November 1803 (pp. 264-267).

Bonds for Joseph BARRY (BERREY), And'w [Andrew] THOMPSON, James ELLIS, Peter KITTS, Joseph RAMSEY, James WILSON, Arhart SIMMERMAN, who were appointed as constables, recorded in July Court 1803 (pp. 247-251).

CROCKETT, John, oath as commissioner of tax, March 11, 1803 (p. 253).

Bonds for John BOGLE, John JINKINS, John LOVE, William HENLEY (HANLY), Abraham (Abram) RYNO, who were appointed constables, recorded in August Court 1803 (pp. 253-256).

Power of attorney, Mathias and Mary GREENFIELD to Richard Hobbs for making title to Ably WALKER, made September 8, 1795, recorded August 1803 (p. 256).

FOSTER, William, Sr., will written May 20, 1803, probated August Court 1803 (pp. 258-261) mentions sons Thomas, deceased, James, William, and Robert, and daughters Mary, Margaret, Martha, Katharine and Isabell, grandson William (4 years old), son of Thomas and Mary Foster, granddaughter Jean (under 21), daughter of Thomas Foster; executors, sons James and William Foster; inventory December 10, 1803 recorded December Court 1803 (pp. 267, 268, 269).

BONHAM, William, bond for constable in Captain Williams Company, recorded September 1803 (p. 261).

INGLE, Henry, appraisal not dated, recorded August 1803 (pp. 262-263).

HELVEY, Henry, power of attorney to Fleming Trigg, November 25, 1803, recorded December 1803 (p. 270).

GROSECLOSE, Peter, will written November, 26, 1802, probated December Court 1803 (pp. 270-272) mentions wife Mary, sons Jacob, Henry, Peter and Adam; two daughters of Barbara Bryrant, deceased (Mary and Barbara); and daughters Elisabeth Perciful and Margaret Spangler; inventory taken December 23, 1803, recorded February Court 1804 (pp. 277-279). For another Peter Groseclose, *see* p. 212.

BISHOP, John, will written January 18, 1804, probated February 1804 (pp. 272-274) mentions wife Mary, son John (under 21), Abram Cooter, Philip Cooter, and Lawrence Cooter mentioned, but no relationship given; executors, Joseph Crockett and Robert Crockett, Clerk.

BONHAM, Joseph, will written June 22, 1803, probated February 1804 (p. 275) mentions wife Naomy, William Bonham (no relationship given), two grand-daughters, Nancy and Sarah Bell (if they stay till of age); William, Hezekiah, William, and Ephraim Bonham, and Caty Howell, Zilphy Davis, Rachel White (Whise?), and Betsy Woods who are probably his children, but not so designated; two single daughters not named; executor, wife.

GROSECLOSE, Adam, will written April 2, 1804, probated May 1804 (pp. 280-281) mentions wife Elisabeth, children, Barbara, John, Martin, Mary, Jacob, Elisabeth, Peter and Absalom Groseclose; executors Jacob Groseclose and Henry Huddle; inventory May 25, 1804, recorded June Court 1804 (p. 282); sale May 26, 1804, recorded June Court, 1804 (p. 283); inventory and appraisal "it being balance of estate which was devised to Elisabeth his wife, to be sold at decease of said Elizabeth and divided among the said Adam's children," taken January 16 and recorded February 1806 (pp. 351-353).

EWING, George [Sr.], will written March 11, 1803, probated June Court 1804 (pp. 284-289) mentions wife Elenor, sons James, Samuel, John, and George, Jr., and daughters Elenor, Mary, Margaret Purdom; executors, his four sons; inventory recorded September 1804 and September 1805 (pp. 300, 326).

ETTER, Daniel, appraisal recorded June Court 1804 (pp. 287-292); settlement September 1805 (p.329) mentions widow Mary.

DOUGLASS, James, will written April 23, 1804, probated July Court 1804 (pp. 295-296) mentions wife Jane, son John, and Jane Davenport, Molly Halfaker, Becky King, no relationship given; executors, wife, son John, and William Love.

DAVIS, Henry, will written August 10, 1804, codicil August 13, 1804, probated September Court 1804 (pp. 297-299) mentioned wife Jean, daughters Jean, Mary, Nancy, Caty, Rodah, Martha, and sons James, Wilson, and Henry, and Jameses' son Wilson; executors James Calfee and John T. Sayers; appraisal September 27, 1804, recorded November Court 1804 (pp. 300-301).

BAUGH (BOUGH), Adam, will written June 9, 1792, probated December 11, 1804 (p. 304) mentions sons, George, Henry, Leonard, Michael and Jacob, and George, oldest son of Adam Baugh, deceased, and daughters Elizabeth, and Mary; sons George and Henry Baugh served as executors.

BROOKS, Thomas, will written November 4, 1804, probated February 1805 (p. 308) mentions wife Margaret, son John John (sic) Brooks, daughter Rebeccah; others James, Robert, Jesse Brooks, and Sally Lahue, Thomas Brooks, Margaret Day, Susanna Harland (Harbard?), Ruthy Granwood and Rachel Brooks, no relationship given, but probably his children; executors, wife, Jesse and Robert Brooks; appraisal recorded March 1805, (p. 312); inventory October 6, 1805 recorded October 1805 (p. 330).

PIERCE, William, appraisal October 17, 1804, recorded February 1805 (p. 309); settlement October 17, 1804, recorded February 1805 (p. 311).

BURK, Michel, inventory not dated, recorded March Court 1805 (p. 315); settlement recorded March 1805 (p. 316).

SMITH, Samuel, settlement of real property, October 3, 1804, recorded March 1805 (p. 316).

BLOSS, Brooks, inventory recorded May 1805 (p. 318).

NICEWANDER, Jacob, Sr., will written (no date); probated June 11, 1805 (p. 319) mentions wife Mary, daughters Esther, Lydia Niswander of Frederick County, Virginia, Nancy Muncy, Christeena and Rhoda, and sons Abraham, Jacob and David, and Christiana Moore of Tazewell, no relationship given; executors

Jacob Nicewander, Jr., and William Neel, of Tazewell; inventory July 10, 1805 recorded February Court 1806 (p. 355).

GROSECLOSE, Peter, inventory recorded June 1805 (p. 321); sale July 1805 (pp. 322, 323). Henry Groseclose and Elizabeth Groseclose are administrators of the estate, and appears to be different than the Peter Groseclose mentioned above (pp. 270-272).

MONTGOMERY, John, Sr., will written July 4, 1798, recorded August 14, 1805 (p. 324) mentions wife Agness, sons Samuel, William, James, Joseph, John, and Robert, and daughters Esther Montgomery, Elisabeth Friel, Anne Craig, Catherine, Rachel, and Nancy Montgomery; executors Robert Crockett and John Crockett (sons of Samuel Crockett).

JOHNSTON, Patrick, will written May 24, 1805, probated September 1805 (p. 326) mentions wife Esther, sons John, three not named, daughter Mary.

SAUL, John, appraisal recorded November 1805 (p. 332).

ALFORD, Thomas, written, November 14, 1805, recorded December 1805 (p. 338) mentions son Moses who is to maintain his mother Elizabeth; others not named; executors Moses and Elizabeth Alford.

HENDERSON, John, settlement December 17, 1805, recorded January 1806 (p. 339) between the heirs of John Henderson: Anne, Elizabeth, Polly, Samuel, Jeane and Delilah Henderson.

COPPEHAFER [COPENHAVER], Thomas, sale January 28, 29, and March 4, 1803, signed January 13, 1806, recorded January 1806 (pp. 340-349); dower laid off for Juliana, widow of Thomas Coppehafer, October 1805, recorded February 1806,(p. 351)

SCOTT, Thomas, inventory April 1, 1806, recorded April 1806 (p. 350); will written October 14, 1805, probated February 11, 1806 (pp. 356-357) mentions wife Caty, sons John and Adam, and daughters Emulan (?) Adams, Joanah, Betsey and Fania [Fanny?].

LIGGET, John, will written September 10, 1805, probated June 1806 (p. 357) mentions wife Hanah, sons James, William, Thomas, Joseph, Alexander, and Jonathan; some of the children are under age; daughters, Mary, Hanah, Alce [Alice?] Ann, Margrit [Margaret]; executors William Ligget and wife Hanah; appraisal recorded June 1807 (pp. 376-378). Hannah Ligget, widow of John deceased dower laid off June 5, 1807 (pp. 378-379).

HANSHUE [HENSHUE], Conrod, will written February 24, 1803, probated September 1806 (pp. 359-361) mentions wife Catherine, daughter Barbara Rhinehart and her son George; all others unnamed, some under age; executor Reuben Cox; inventory not dated, recorded October 1806 (p. 361).

BLACK, James, will written February 25, 1805, probated September 1806 (pp. 364-366) mentions daughters Mary, Nelly, Jane wife of James Rodgers, Martha wife of James Louther, Jr., Ann wife of Robert Porter, and Betsy; son John, Samuel Siblott, son of daughter Jane, now the wife of James Rodgers; executors, daughters Mary and Nelly.

WISSMAN, John, inventory and sale, December 19, 1806, recorded February 1807 (pp. 368-369).

MINICK, Jacob, will written August 27, 1805, probated January 10, 1807 (pp. 370-371) mentions wife Mary and son Alleson; executors, wife, John Montgomery and John Johnston.

MILLER, John, will written January 28, 1806, probated December 1806 (pp. 371-372) mentions daughter Caty, sons Peter and Jacob, wife and other children not named; executor, wife.

GRUBB, Henry, will written June 24, 1804, probated April 1807 (pp. 372-375) mentions wife Dorothy, sons John, Lewis, Isaac, Jacob, and Francis; executors John Leftwich, John Grubb, and William Ward; appraisal, August 8, 1807, recorded August 11, 1807 (pp. 382-384).

SLIMP [SLEMP], Frederick, will written February 12, 1807, probated June Court 1807 (pp. 380-381) mentions wife Mary, sons Frederick and John, two youngest Michael, and Jacob; daughters Caty, Elisabeth, Mary, Barbrah and Ury; executors, wife Mary and son Frederick.

MILLER, Christian, appraisal ordered December 1807, recorded September Court 1807 (pp. 382-386).

JOHNSTON, Daniel, appraisal March 20 and 21, 1807, recorded December 1807 (pp. 387-388); sale March 21, 1807, recorded December 1807 (pp. 388-390).

CAFFEE [CALFEE], Charles, inventory November 19, 1807, recorded January 1808 (pp. 391-393); list of estate dated November 1807, settlement January 1808, recorded January 1808 (pp. 391-393).

SMITH, Peter, will written September 20, 1807, probated December 1807 (pp. 393-394) mentions wife Mary, sons Henry and Jacob; sole executor, son Jacob.

WHITLOCK, Mary, inventory and appraisal October 24, 1807, recorded December 1807 (p. 395); settlement October 26, 1807, recorded December 1807 (pp. 396-397).

CRAIG, John, will written May 3, 1805, probated March 8, 1808 (pp. 399-402) mentions land at Hance's Meadows, wife Molly, sons John, Jr., Hiram, James, and David; daughters Jane Allison, Sinthea Stotts, Nancy, and Idress who gets the Pearce's Ferry place; granddaughter Indiana; executors sons John, Jr., and Hiram Craig.

SIMPSON, James, will written May 6, 1804, probated April 13, 1808 (pp. 404-405) mentions sons William, James, Robert, Hugh, Isaac, and Alexander, and daughters Jean Baxter, Ellinor Mears, Mary Foster, and Margaret Smith, wife Mary; executors, wife Mary and sons James and Alexander.

RUSSELL, Joseph, will written July 24, 1808, probated October 11, 1808 (pp. 410-412) mentions brothers Albert, James, John, and Alexander, and sister Elanor Feely; nephew and nieces James Russell Feely, Margaretta Feely, Eleanor Russell, and Thomas Hewy [Hughey]; brother-in-law John Feely; inventory October 31, 1808, November 1, 1808, recorded May 9, 1809 (pp. 424, 426, 429, 430-432).

MURRAY, William, inventory November 5, 1808, recorded November 1808 (pp. 412-413).

RANKINS, David, sale September 4, 1802, by J. Carter and Milly Rankins, administrators, recorded November 1808 (pp. 413-414).

CROCKETT, Samuel, will written September 4, 1808, probated March 14, 1809 (pp. 414-416) mentions wife Elizabeth, daughters Malvina, Elizabeth, and Margaret, sons Allen Taylor Crockett and John, both under 21; executors Charles Taylor, John McC. Taylor of Montgomery County, and Joseph Crockett.

BUCKHANNAN, Robert, will written January 1, 1809, probated March 14, 1809 (pp. 416-418) mentions daughters Martha Hay, Grissal Walker, and Polly, and sons Alexander who gets land in Franklin County, Kentucky, formerly property of Alexander Buckhanan, Sr., willed to John Buckhanan (my son dec'd) and William; executors William and Alexander.

BELSHEE [BELSHA], John, inventory September 13, 1808, recorded April 12, 1809 (pp. 418-421); settlement recorded April 12, 1809 (pp. 421-424).

UMBARGER, Elizabeth, inventory April 27, 1809, recorded May 9, 1809 (pp. 432-434); sale March 11, 1809, recorded May 9, 1809 (pp. 434-436).

FOSTER, Thomas, Sr., will written May 3, 1808, probated May 9, 1809 (pp. 436-437), mentions wife Elizabeth, daughter Sarah, and sons Thomas, John, James, Samuel, and William; executors, sons Thomas and John Foster.

SIMPSON, Mary, will written August 6, 1808, recorded March 12, 1809 (pp. 437-438) mentions sons William, James, Robert, Hugh, Isaac, John, deceased, Alexander and Agness, his wife, and "thir" daughter Elizabeth; daughters Jean Backster [Baxter], Elenor Mears, Polly Foster, and Margaret Smyth; executor Alex. Simpson.

BARBSTON (BRABSTON), John, appraisal September 13, 1808, recorded June 15, 1809 (p. 439).

JANSOHN (JONSON), David, will written May 12, 1809, probated June 14, 1809 (p. 440) mentions sons William, Balsor, George, Michael, and David; wife Catharina, and daughters Catharina Clemons, Elizabeth Wampler, and Maria Zimmerman; executor John Stanger.

SPEAR (SPIAR), Robert, will written March 23, 1806, probated October 10, 1809 (pp. 441-442) mentions sons Samuel, James, John, Robert, Andrew, Amos, and Joseph, and wife not named; sole executor Joseph Spear.

MONTGOMERY, James, will written December 12, 1808, probated October 18, 1809 (pp. 442-443) mentions wife Cynthia, brothers, Joseph and John; daughters Mary W. Montgomery, Elizabeth C. Montgomery; nephew James Montgomery, son of Joseph; nephew Samuel, son of brother John, deceased; executors, Gordon Cloyd, and Robert Sproul.

COLVIN, John, will written October 18, 1809, probated November 14, 1809 (p. 443) mentions son James; brothers Isaac, Thomas, Joseph, and Samuel; Jacob Gose executor.

There are a few wills in the back of **Deed** Book 1A as follows:

WAMPLER, George, will written May 31, 1814, probated May 10, 1815 (pp. 10-11) mentions sons George, Joseph, Henry and Jacob; daughters Mary Killinger and Magdalena Stanger; son-in-law George Kinzer; sons George and Jacob to be executors; appraisal, May 19, 1815, recorded September 9, 1815 (pp. 13-20).

SAYERS, John T., will written February 28, 1816, probated May 10, 1816 (pp. 11-12) mentions sons Robert, Samuel, John T. [Jr.], wife Susanna; daughters Peggy Ingles Sayers, Lucy Sayers, Jane Crockett Sayers, and Esther Armstrong; executor wife, John Draper, Jr., Elijah Sayers, Joseph Draper, and son Robert; appraisal May 10, 1816, recorded August 8, 1816 (pp. 20-22).

WASHINGTON, John S., assignment to Dennis Kennidy of Baltimore, all debts due for merchandize at my store in Evansham for the benefit of creditors, merchants of Baltimore, October 7, 1817 (pp. 22-23).

CROCKETT, Robert, will written March 3, 1819, codicil March 12, 1819; probated May 10, 1819 (pp. 23-27), mentions daughter Maria Brown wife of James E. Brown, son Charles L. (not of age), sons Francis A., John S., Robert A., Samuel J. and Gustavus A.; daughters Agnes L., and Jane C. Crockett; wife Jane L.; wife, son Charles L. and James E. Brown, executors; inventory September 14, 1819 (pp. 27-29).

KETRING, George, appraisal May 27, 1825, recorded October 1826 (pp. 29-30).

BROWN, Margaretta, appraisal January 12, 1828, mentions Helvey place and her interest in estate of Robert Crockett dec'd at death of her mother Jane L. Crockett, recorded May 12, 1828 (p. 30).

GOSE, Ann, appraisal April 8, 1845, recorded September 8, 1845 (pp. 30-32); sale April 19, 1845, recorded September 8, 1845 (pp. 32-33).

9 Hogs	$10.00
1 Horse	40.00
1 Mare	2.00
1 Milk Cow Spotted	12.00
1 Ditto red	9.00
1 Ditto white face	9.00
1 Ditto	7.00
3 yearling heiffers red	4.50
1 yew and Lamb	1.00
Horse gears	4.67
Cutting nife and Steel	1.17
17 Geese	5.34

Partial list of personal property belonging to the estate of William Rader, deceased, February 1, 1802. The items included hogs, a horse, a mare, several cows, yearling heiffers, a "yew" and lamb, horse gears, a cutting nife [knife] and steel, and 17 geese.

Tracing by Mary B. Kegley from Will Book 1, p. 216.

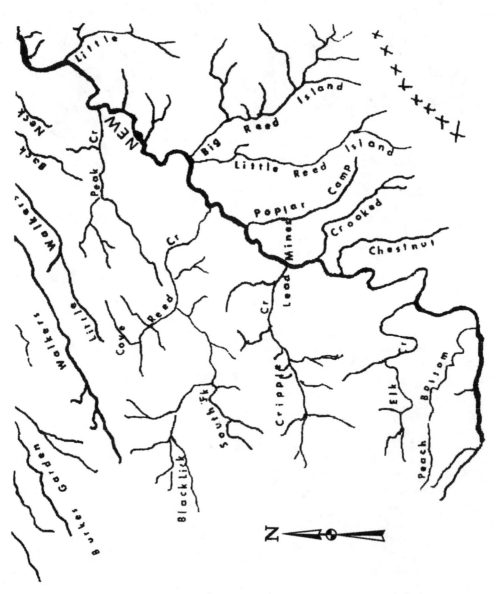

The Western Waters of the New River showing primarily the locations of creeks in what is now Wythe County. To the north are portions of Tazewell and Bland counties, and to the south portions of Grayson and Carroll counties. To the east are small areas of Pulaski and Montgomery counties.

Map by Mary B. Kegley

SECTION III
Poplar Camp, Lead Mines, Austinville, Foster Falls, And Mine Mill Creek

CHAPTER I
Creeks, Roads, And Settlements

Poplar Camp Creek runs north along present State Route 52 and empties into the New River east of the old bridge at Jacksons Ferry, draining the foothills of Poplar Camp Mountain in the southeast part of present Wythe County.

Poplar Camp itself was in existence as early as 1751, when James Patton had two tracts surveyed, designating one ''below Poplar Camp'' and the other ''above Poplar Camp.'' Edmund Pendleton made a selection of 460 acres on Poplar Camp Creek in 1748, but the creek at that time was not named.

The other choice made by Pendleton in 1748 was a 225-acre tract on the south side of the New River near the present town of Austinville. Both of Pendleton's tracts went to John Bingaman, Sr., who obtained the grants in the early 1750s. The river tract became known as Bingaman's Bottom, and the creek nearby was known as Bingaman's Branch.

Some time in the 1750s (exact date unknown), John Chiswell discovered lead on the banks of the New River and selected 1,000 acres which he located on both sides of the river. The tract was surveyed in 1760, which is the first time the mines are mentioned in any official record. The tract was later expanded to include 1,400 acres. Chiswell also anticipated an additional 1,000 acres, but no surveys were made before he died a few years later.

In 1746, Jacob Castle had lands surveyed on the south side of the river, and at his death, the improvements came into the hands of Robert Sayers, son of Alexander Sayers. As it turned out, this early selection by Castle was on the lead mines property and was included in Chiswell's survey. Many years later Sayers released his claim in return for other land.

Others in the same neighborhood were Humberston and Stephen Lyons. who settled there prior to 1746. Stephen moved on to the Holston, where he was killed by Indians. Humberston Lyons remained long enough to obtain a grant for 650 acres, but sold it in 1755, and appears to have moved to the Holston River settlement. His New River land came to Alexander Sayers, and later, the Ewings and Porters.

On the north side of the river, there was little early activity in this community. In 1748, Patton selected a tract of 650 acres, which later became Nathaniel Welshire's place. Welshire became the first settler in that area, leaving his name on the branch that flows south and empties into the New River not far from the Jacksons Ferry Bridge. More recent maps refer to this branch as Galena Creek, probably from the fact that galena was a type of lead mined nearby and that Galena Presbyterian Church is located close to the creek. The creek rises north of Laswell, approximately two miles from the Fort Chiswell High School, and parallels State Route 52 in many places, before it empties into the New River west of State Route 52. In 1857, Robert Raper had an inclusive survey made, which included much of the land south of Laswell and Raper Ridge, on both sides of the road to Jacksons Ferry, and the road known as Kincannon's Turnpike (now Route 619). Much of his land came from the Sanders, and others of the name were adjoining owners of his large holdings of 1789 acres. He later purchased Kincannon's land at the ferry and Guy Trigg's land to the north.

North of Laswell, Richard Walton and later his son George became the major developers. Richard had purchased various tracts, including over 1,000 acres, from Richard Muse, whose holdings included Evan Williams' and Joseph Eaton's land. At his death, most of his holdings went to his son George, who in 1850 at the time of his death owned 1,850 acres. His widow was to enjoy 575 acres as her dower. The land later came into the hands of his nephew Richard Walton Sanders and other Sanders relatives.

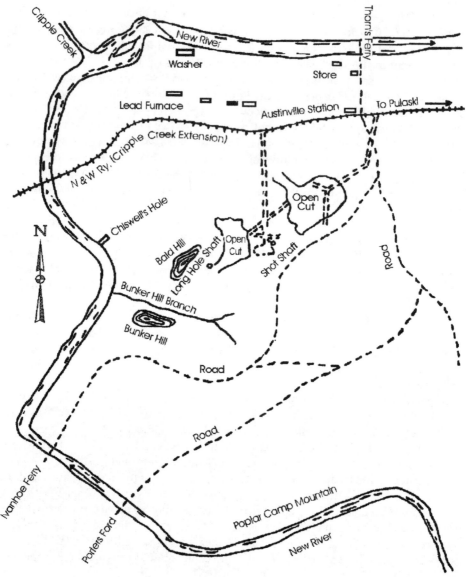

Lead and zinc mines area on the south side of the New River, about 1900. Sketch adapted by Mary B. Kegley from a drawing in Watson's *Mineral Resources of Virginia*.

With the exception of Chiswell, none of those very early settlers was known to be associated with the mining interests, but in the 1760s experienced workmen appeared in the community. William Bell and his sons, and William Herbert and his family connection were among them. Herbert developed the Edmund Pendleton land on Poplar Camp Creek, where he established a mill and a ferry before 1770, and an ordinary a few years later. Herbert's sons, William, Jr., and Thomas, were entrepreneurs in the iron and lead business, as long as they remained in the neighborhood. In addition to William Herbert, Sr., and his wife Sarah, several others, including John Jenkins, Roger Oats, David Herbert, Sr., and his wife Martha, Charles Devereaux and his wife Nancy, Evan Williams, David Herbert, Jr., and probably others, came from Bristol, England, to work in the mines in the summer of 1763. The men were referred to as the "Welsh miners."

Following the death of John Chiswell and John Robinson, partners in the lead mines, William Byrd, III, the only other partner, and later his son John, made a claim to the mines. Because of a shortage in the treasury funds, John Robinson's estate was required to repay money loaned to Robinson's friends. The mines partnership had borrowed £8,085, an amount which had to be repaid. Consequently, the mines were operated by the State of Virginia until 1781 (Dabney, "John Robinson...", p. 23,67-76).

Following William Byrd's death, and at the beginning of the Revolutionary War, an act was passed in the General Assembly to empower "the Governour and Council to employ persons for working the lead mines to greater advantage" for the purpose of making lead for the "use of the publick." An annual rent was to be paid to the estates of the former owners, unless the proprietors were going to work the mines themselves, in which case, they were to provide one hundred tons of lead annually, at the price of thirty-three pounds six shillings and eight pence per ton (Hening, *Statutes*, Vol. 9, p. 237).

Colonel Charles Lynch, Colonel James Callaway, and Henry Innes were associated with the mines in the 1770s and 1780s. In 1776, Callaway, the County Lieutenant of Bedford County, was the manager at the mines, and was ordered to send lead to North Carolina. Negroes held in jail were to be sent to the mines to work in July 1776. There was also a request for lead from Philadelphia, about the same time, and an express ordering "a large number of hands to be immediately hired, to assist those

Austinville at the zinc mines, 1930.
Photo courtesy of Graham Hankely, Dr. W.R. Chitwood Collection.

View of Austinville from the north side of the New River looking south. The Raper (Galena) Mill is in the lower foreground at the mouth of Mine Mill Creek.
Courtesy of the Norfolk and Western Railway Archival Collection,
Polytechnic Institute and State Library University Libraries.

already hired." The demand for lead at this time was very great, not only from North Carolina and Philadelphia, but on the frontiers, as the Cherokees and the settlers were involved in an Indian War. In the fall of 1776, Calloway had ten tons of lead available for the use of the Continental Army. Mr. John Talbot volunteered to provide wagons and waggoners to transport the available lead to Edmund Winston's on the James River. Calloway was directed to send 15,000 pounds of lead to Winston's. In 1777, the manager of the mines was directed "either to exchange the two thousand seven hundred and sixty-five pounds of Lead which they had on Hand for good Powder & salt petre or sell it out in small quantities to the Inhabitants at seven pence half penny per pound." (McIlwaine, ed., *Official Letters...of Patrick Henry,* Vol. 1, pp. 6, 8, 18, 53, 56, 112; Kegley, *Bicentennial History,* pp. 330-336).

The Town of Austinville appears to have received its name when the post office was established sometime prior to April 1, 1798. James Austin was the first postmaster (Post Office Records).

In the 1800s, James Newell, the Sanders (John, William, and Robert), Thomas Jackson, David Peirce, and Daniel Sheffey dominated the activities at the mines. In addition, Peirce emerged as the industrial leader in the Poplar Camp community as well. He had an iron business, operated a mill, an ordinary, several tan yards, and the iron furnace. Rapers, Waltons, and other heirs of Thomas Jackson arrived in the late 1790s (Kegley, *Bicentennial History*, pp. 336-339; 354-355).

In the 1760s, there was a reference to a "block house" in the lead mines community, probably because of the French and Indian War and the newly discovered lead deposits. In the Revolutionary War days, there was a reference to a fort in the same vicinity, as the county lieutenant was ordered to "raise a stockade fort for the Defence of the said Mines." Twenty-five men, under a subaltern were to garrison the fort, in hopes that that would be sufficient protection to prevent the Cherokees from "cutting off the persons employed at the Lead Mines." On May 7, 1782, Robert Sanders was paid "£14:11 for 291 days work on the Fort at the lead mines 1780." During the Civil War, the lead mines were a prime target for the Federal troops who attacked the mines on at least three separate occasions. The exact locations of the forts have not been discovered, either from the records or on the ground (Augusta County Entry Book 1,

p. 44; *Preston Papers,* 4QQ 57; McIlwaine, ed., *Official Letters....of Patrick Henry,* Vol. 1, p. 15; Summers, *Annals,* p. 770; Kegley, *Wythe County, Virginia,* pp. 199-201; Donnelly, ''The Confederate Lead Mines...'' *Civil War,* Vol. 5 (1959), pp. 402-414).

Although there were some agricultural pursuits in connection with the lead and iron businesses, the Poplar Camp and Lead Mines communities were primarily industrial in nature.

Mine Mill Creek

Mine Mill Creek, with its several branches, drains a wide area south of Lick Mountain west of State Route 52. The waters pass through two gaps in Rapers Ridge and flow south and east to empty into the New River opposite an island and opposite the lead mines tract of 1,400 acres. Sometimes it is called Lead Mine Mill Creek.

The name Mine Mill Creek first appeared in 1774, when John Brawley, apparently among the earliest residents on the headwaters, had 379 acres surveyed. The courthouse for Fincastle County (1772-1776) was located near the mouth of Mine Mill Creek, on the north side of the river, not far from the center of mining activities. It was ordered to be built on October 17, 1772 and on land Chiswell is said to have bought from the heirs of Colonel James Patton, a location claimed by William Byrd, Esq. In January the following year, the house next door to the courthouse was to be used for a prison. Guards were ordered to be summoned to take care of the prisoners until a prison could be built. From the beginning, the site was not suitable and the court recommended that the courthouse be established ''at a piece of land commonly called McCall's place,'' which was then the property of Ross and Company and the lands of Samuel Crockett. The reasons given were that McCaul's and Crockett's were on the ''Great Road,'' and that it was well watered, timbered and level, and was much more central than the mines, a location which was near the south line of the county, with no convenient spring, was scarce of timber, and there was very little pasture in the neighborhood, and was ''entirely off the leading Road.'' The people on the Holston River petitioned for a division of the county, and when it was finally approved and Washington and Montgomery counties were formed, the courthouse for the latter was located at Fort Chiswell (Draper Mss 2 QQ 138,139; 3 QQ 25).

In 1782, James Newell, William Rodgers, William Moore, and Alexander Neely made selections along the creek, with John Rodgers and Thomas Nelson joining them in 1783. Neely appears to have settled there in 1766, and Newell had been in the neighborhood since about 1771. Benjamin Banner, Andrew Stott, Evan Williams, Robert Hueston, Andrew Thompson, and William and Adam Dean also appear to have had early interests in that community. In 1785, William Bell took up 200 acres, later designated as only 180 acres, at the mouth of the creek opposite the island. This tract included the abandoned courthouse, and other buildings associated with it. Bell was in the community in the early 1760s. The tract on the north side of the river in Austinville was later owned by Charles Lynch, who established the ferry, then transferred the land to James Newell, and he in turn to his Kincannon connections. Later, it was known as Raper's and Thorn's Ferry. Now a new bridge crosses the river near the old Thorn house.

There are frequent references to furnaces and mills pertaining to the lead mines industry, but no exact location is ever mentioned. Because of the name ''Mine Mill'' Creek, we must assume that the earliest mill owned by the mine operation was located on the north side of the New River near the mouth of this creek. The date the first grist mill was established is a matter of conjecture, but it is clearly stated in Chiswell's time that there was no mill for grinding flour, for he obtained flour from North Carolina.

Thomas Jefferson, in writing about the lead mines in the 1780s, confirms that the pounding or stamping mill for processing the lead was on the north side of the river, as the workers transported the lead across the river in canoes. Records about the mines in the Virginia State Library show that on August 28, 1778, Charles Lynch, manager of the lead mines, paid £110.2 to John Drevough (probably Devereaux) and John Cruger for "building pearhed and flood gates, troughs and stamping mill wheel." In addition, John Hall was paid £154 and 11 shillings, for his work at the mines, and for spike nails "for stamping mill troughs & pearhead, and for making nails and repairs at the mines" in 1778. These two receipts confirm the presence of a stamping mill on the premises in 1778. The mill was used to crush rock, or the lead ore, from the mines.

In 1782, when an inventory of the mines was taken, the stamping mill and a grist mill were both in repair, but when the grist mill was built is not recorded. In more recent years, the grist mill was known as Grayson's Mill, which was still standing in the late 1970s. It operated near the mouth of the creek and the log house near the mill was used as the miller's house. In the 1890s, the mill was called the Galena Mill.

Further north on the creek, south of Rapers Ridge, 200 acres were granted to Julious Rutherford. Sometime between 1803 and 1808, the site became established as the Jacob Keesling mills. In the 1880s, the Simmermans operated a mill at the same location.

The Brawley mill has not been exactly located, but was probably on the John Brawley land in the vicinity of the present Olive Branch Methodist Church.

Daniel Lockett operated a mill and a tanyard in the neighborhood of present Walton Furnace, prior to 1824. In the 1840s, Edmund Lockett operated a still house and sawmill in the same community.

In the 1840s and 1850s, Edmund Lockett was operating from Red Bluff and the Cripple Creek forge, developing iron deposits in the community. The Blairs, later owners of the land, leased about four acres "upon which to erect a blast furnace and other buildings necessary for the manufacture of pig iron." The lease was for ten years, beginning in January 1872, with R. W.. Sanders and John M. Howard as lessees. The Walton furnace still stands on the site, but has been inactive since 1888. The furnace was named for George Walton, an early resident.

Early houses in the community were traditionally made of log. However, Howe in his *History of Virginia* written in the 1840s, states that Chiswell built the first frame house in the settlements and that it was located at the mouth of Mine Mill Creek. The exact location is not known, but could have been near the mill mentioned above, or at the place later chosen for the courthouse up on the high ground above the river, near the present marker which commemorates the Fincastle County Resolutions.

Foster Falls

The falls along the New River in southeastern Wythe County were first known as the Roaring Falls, or the Great Falls. They are presently known as Foster Falls, and were apparently named for Thomas Foster and his family. In the 1880s, the falls were referred to as Peirce's Falls, because William Peirce owned the land. It was on the inclusive survey that the Foster Falls Mining Company, the town, post office, station, and hotel were established. In recent years, much of the property was owned by the Valleydale Packing Company, and the access to the falls is prohibited because of private ownership.

The records which follow are those pertaining to the Poplar Camp, Lead Mines, Foster Falls, and Mine Mill Creek communities. They come from the counties of Augusta, Botetourt, Fincastle, Montgomery, and Wythe.

CHAPTER II
The Land Records

Poplar Camp, Lead Mines, Foster Falls, And Mine Mill Creek

AUGUSTA COUNTY SURVEYS: Staunton, Virginia

1748/49, JAMES PATTON, 650 acres on the north side of Woods River; "this is the place called Wilshire's place."

1749, EDMUND PENDLETON of Caroline County, Virginia, 460 acres on a branch of Woods River; 184 acres on south side of Woods River; both granted to John Bingaman, Sr., 1753.

1751, JAMES PATTON, 86 acres below the Marsh of Poplar Camp on the northeast side of New River, granted 1755; 63 acres on a branch of Poplar Camp Creek, a branch of New River, above Poplar Camp, on the east side of the New River, granted 1755.

1753, THOMAS WALKER for the Loyal Company, 180 acres on the east side of New River; 80 acres on the west side of New River.

1760, JOHN CHISWELL, ESQ., 1,000 acres on New River, the lead mines tract.

MISCELLANEOUS PRESTON PAPERS:

1746, 180 acres surveyed, no name; written on the back was a note that stated that this tract was sold to JACOB CASTLE "where he lives." This statement is not dated, but is presumed to be between 1746 and 1749 (Preston Papers, Wytheville Community College Library). See copy of plat, and entry mentioned below.*

1746, a tract with no acres stated, on both side of Woods River on part opposite Steven Lyons, part of 100,000 acres granted Colonel Patton & Company, no name mentioned (Virginia Historical Society, Richmond, Virginia).

PATTON-PRESTON NOTEBOOK:
Wytheville Community College Library, Wytheville, Virginia.

NATHENIEL WILLTSHEIR, " to 640 acres at £5 pr. 100; to surveirs and patent fees; to 14 rights at 5/ each; interest from 1 April 1749 = Total £40.4.3"

JACOB CASTEL, "to 80 acres where he lives, surveirs and patent fees; 4 rights at 5/ each; interest on same from 1 April 1749, Total £12.6.4." Compare with above.* [probably should be 180 acres as edge of book is worn].

Nathaniel Willtsheir   Dr

to 640 acers at £5 pr 100 ——— 34 0 0
to surveirs & patent fees ——— 2 1 4
to 14 rights at 5/ for Each £ 4 7 6
intrest on do from 1 aprail 1749 £ 40 9 3

Jacob Castel   Dr

180 acres where he Lives ——— 9 0 0
surveirs & patent fees ——— 2 1 9
4 Rights At 5/ for Each ——— 1 50
intrest on do from 1 aprail 1749 12 6 9

Records from the Patton-Preston Notebook showing the entry made for Nathaniel Willtsheir (Welshire) and Jacob Castel (Castle), 1749.

Tracing from the original by Mary B. Kegley.

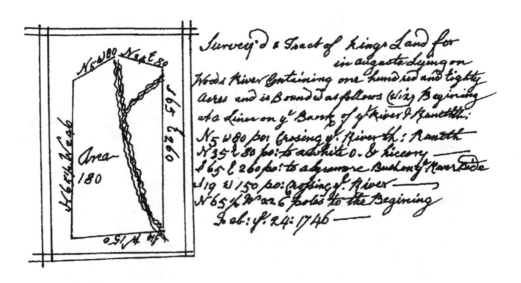

A tract of 180 acres which was sold to Jacob Castle, where he lives.

Tracing from original by Mary B. Kegley.

AUGUSTA COUNTY ENTRY BOOK 1: Staunton, Virginia.

1752, ANDREW LEWIS, four tracts on head branches of New River Creek on south side of New River on Indian Road, 100 acres on ye head branches of New River Creek, 100 acres on another branch of the same creek, 200 acres at a meadow on south side of New River on ye Indian Road, 100 acres on a branch between ye aforesaid meadow and head of said creek.

1760, JOHN CHISWELL, 400 acres at Block House on east side of New River; 400 acres east side of New River at a large spring in Reed Island Barrens running toward Short Mountain; 400 acres adjoining above; 400 acres beginning at Humberston Lyons' upper corner, west side of the river; 400 acres from Lyons' upper line on his spring branch.

1761, CHARLES LEWIS, 300 acres on both sides New River, opposite Steven Lyons.

1762, JAMES MONTGOMERY, 400 acres at a place called Poplar Camp, between New River and the mountains.

1762, JACOB CASTLE, 100 acres between Welshire and the Great Falls.

1762, JOHN BINGEMAN, 100 acres on both sides of mouth of Poplar Camp Creek; 100 acres on both sides Great Falls of New River; 150 acres south side Great Falls of New; 400 acres upper forks of Cripple Creek.

1763, CHARLES CAMPBELL, 400 acres at Great Bottom below "ye falls of New River."

AUGUSTA COUNTY: From *Executive Journals* Vol. 6

May 6, 1760, On the petition of JOHN CHISWELL, ESQR., leave is granted him to take up and survey One Thousand Acres of Land lying on both Sides of New River, beginning on the South Side, at Humberstone Lyons's lower corner, and running down the said River so as to include that Quantity (p. 157).

May 6, 1760, On the petition of JOHN ROBINSON, ESQR., leave is granted him to take up and survey One Thousand Acres of Land, on both Sides of the New River, beginning on the South Side, joining the Lines of John Chiswell's Grant, and running down the said River, so as to include that Quantity (pp. 157-158).

January 21, 1764, WILLIAM BYRD, ESQR., in consequence of his Majesty's Proclamation dated 7th of October 1763, and published in the *Virginia Gazette* in Jany. 1764, applied as Colonel of the late Virginia Regiment for Five Thousand acres lying upon the New River in Augusta on both sides thereof, including the tract known by the name of the Lead Mines (p. 700).

AUGUSTA COUNTY DEEDS: Staunton, Virginia.

1755, ALEXANDER SAYERS from Humberston Lyons, 650 acres on Woods [New] River, granted Lyons 1752.

1762, THOMAS STANTON, JR., of Broomfield, Culpeper County, Virginia., from John Bingeman and wife Elizabeth of same place, 184 acres on Woods River, patented to John Bingaman, Sr., 1753; and 460 acres on Woods River, Poplar Camp, granted John Bingaman, Sr., 1753.

1767, WILLIAM HERBERT from Richard Stanton and wife Charity, the tract Thomas

Stanton, Sr., purchased from John Bingaman, Sr., who received the patent 1753, 460 acres on Woods [New] River at a place called Poplar Camp.

BOTETOURT COUNTY DEEDS: Fincastle, Virginia.

1770, JOHN JENKINS from Thompson and Preston, executors of James Patton, 63 acres on the east side of New River above Poplar Camp.

1770, WILLIAM HERBERT from Richard Stanton, slaves and personal property.

1770, WILLIAM HERBERT from Thomas Stanton and wife Charity of Orange County, North Carolina, 184 acres on New River, granted to John Bingeman, Senr.

FINCASTLE COUNTY ENTRIES: Christiansburg, Virginia.

1774, WILLIAM BYRD, ESQ., 1,000 acres at and near the Lead Mines on both sides of the New River, joining George Forbus and William Herbert's land including the Mine Hill and buildings on the east side of the river.

FINCASTLE COUNTY DEEDS: Christiansburg, Virginia.

1774, SAMUEL EWING from ROBERT SAYERS, heir of ALEXANDER SAYERS, 650 acres [on New River] patent to Humberston Lyons 1752, and sold to Alexander Sayers in 1755.

1774, JAMES EWING from Samuel Ewing, 80 acres on the south side of New River.

1775, JAMES MONTGOMERY from Thompson and Preston, executors of James Patton, 86 acres east side New River, below the mouth of Poplar Camp Creek, granted 1755.

FINCASTLE COUNTY SURVEYS: Christiansburg, Virginia.

1774, WILLIAM BELL, 64 acres on the southeast side of New River corner to the land he lives on, and adjoining Chiswell; Montgomery County, 200 acres west side of New River some distance below the mouth of Cripple Creek, beginning opposite a point of an island.

1774, WILLIAM HERBERT, 213 acres opposite a creek known as Poplar Camp, on the north side of the New River; 1782, Montgomery County, 367 acres on the west side of New River; 1790, 425 acres on east side of New River.

1774, JOHN BRALEY [BRALLEY], 379 acres on Mine Mill Creek, branch of New River, grant 1816 to sons, James and John Bralley (otherwise called Braley).

1774, ALEXANDER THOMPSON, 190 acres on headwaters of Welcher's Run, corner Robert Huston.

1774, GEORGE FORBIS, 235 acres on Little Reed Island Creek, south branch of New River, Loyal Company, adjoining David Herbert's survey.

MONTGOMERY COUNTY ENTRIES: Christiansburg, Virginia.

1780, COLONEL CHARLES LYNCH, 500 acres adjoining the land he bought from Jennings and that formerly Ray's in the fork between Little Reed Island Creek and New River, to bind on the land he formerly bought of Abraham Price; 1781, 1,200 acres to begin on Mr. Welsher [Welshire's] lines and running west on Mines lands to Mill Creek (both withdrawn).

1781, ADAM DEAN, assignee of John Rutherford, "commonly called Black John," 400 acres on Commissioner's certificate [Mine Mill Creek of New River].

1782, WILLIAM BUTLER, assignee of William Moore, Commissioner's certificate, 200 acres on Mill Creek.

1782, ALICK NEALY, assignee of Benjamin Banner, assignee of Evan Williams, assignee of Robert Hueston, Commissioner's certificate, 400 acres on head of Mill Creek.

1782, JOHN BRAWLEY, Commissioner's certificate, 379 acres on Lead Mine Mill Creek.

1782, JAMES NEWELL, JUNR., and JAMES McCORKLE, assignees of Newell's state warrant, 1,000 acres on north side of Rodgers at or near the fork of Mine Mill Creek (*see also*, Cripple Creek section for more)

1782, WILLIAM MONTGOMERY, military warrant, 50 acres, on both sides of Wilshire's Run, branch of New River to join the land where Nathaniel Wilshire lately lived and where Jno. Baxter now lives; also 138 1/2 acres joining the entry of 50 acres.

1782, WILLIAM RODGERS, Commissioner's certificate, 400 acres on head of Lead Mine Creek.

1782, WILLIAM MOORE, assignee of Adam Dean, enters 400 acres on Mill Creek joining the land of the Mines land, also Mr. Welsers [Welshire's] and the land of Alexr. Neely on the south side.

1781, ANDREW STOTT (STOTTS), assignee of William Moore, assignee of William Dean, 190 acres on New River, adjoining his own land; 178 acres, assignee of James McGavock, 20 acres on a military warrant, so as to make 210 acres.

1782, JOHN JENKINS, JUNR., assignee of Thos. McGeorge, assignee of Caleb Hall, 500 acres between John Jenkins, Senr.'s patent land and mountain, to join Poplar Camp land.

1782, THOMAS FOSTER, military warrant, 50 acres joining and below his patent line on west side of New River at the Roaring Falls.

1782, CHARLES DEBERIX [DEVEREAUX], Commissioner's certificate, 400 (100?) acres on New River adjoining the upper part of George Forbes' line...and not to interfere with land granted Thos. Nelson, Esqr., and his successors; 1784, 400 acres on west side of New joining George Forbuss and the land sold by Forbuss [Forbes] to William Herbert, deceased, assigned after survey to James Newell.

1782, PATRICK CASH, assignee of John Long, assignee of Thomas Foster, assignee of Morgan Murrey, Commissioner's certificate, 400 acres on branch of Poplar Camp Creek.

1782, ROBERT SAYERS, heir-at-law of Alexr. Sayers, deceased, assignee of Jacob Castle, Commissioner's certificate 400 acres on the southwest side of New River to include Jacob Castle's improvements and adjoining Mine Hill; also 1,000 acres on preemption certificate from same Commissioner's on southeast side of New River adjoining his settlement; 1783, preemption warrant, 1,000 acres, enters 206 acres joining the upper end of Charles Devereaux land and to include the Ash Bottom at the end of the Little Mountain on the head of Bingeman's Branch.

1782, THOS. NELSON, ESQR., Governor of Virginia and his successors, assignee of John Jenkins, Commissioner's certificate, 400 acres on both sides of Mill Creek, joining James Thompson, Jno. Brawley, and survey made for Henry Arnold in the Loyal Company grant, lying on Cripple Creek, branch of New River.

1782, THOS. MADISON and LEAD MINES COMPANY, assignee of Alexr. Sayers, Commissioner's certificate, 400 acres on New River, above Mine Hill known by the name of Pasture.

1782, WILLIAM HERBERT, legatee of William Herbert, deceased, assignee of John Bingeman, Commissioner's preemption certificate, 1,000 acres on south side of New River adjoining above right established to said Herbert half mile below Poplar Camp and to include the mill and the ferry; also Commissioner's certificate, 400 acres on north side of New River known by the name of Herbert's Ferry; also 400 acres on south side of New River about half a mile below the mouth of Poplar Camp Creek, to include the improvements and the ferry.

1782, EVAN WILLIAMS, Commissioner's certificate, 400 acres on branch of New River adjoining his old line.

1782, RICHARD MUSE, assignee of John Hays, assignee of Wm. Sexton, Commissioner's preemption certificate, 1,000 acres on New River below a branch of Bingeman's Bottom; and as assignee of Walter Crockett, assignee of James Clerk, on state warrant enters same as follows: 350 acres lying between the lands of James Newell on Cripple Creek and Saml. Ewing on New River; 100 acres joining John Brawly and Saml. Smith on both side of the wagon road (withdrawn); 300 acres joining the settlement called Hobbs Cabin and to join east side and south side of George Ewing's patent land (withdrawn); 100 acres on east end of Charles Deavereaux land (withdrawn and entered 20 June 1786).

1782, JOHN RODGERS, assignee of James Newell, 200 acres on Mill Creek, a branch of New River.

1782, JAMES NEWELL, assignee of Richard Muse, 300 acres joining the land he lives on and the land purchased for the lead mines of Charles Devereux and the lands Samuel Smith lives on; 1790, 150 acres, on east fork of Poplar Camp Creek, to include Lee's cabin, assigned to William Ross. see also, Cripple Creek section.

1782, JOSEPH EATON, Commissioner's certificate, 400 acres on New River, adjoining Thos. Fauster's claim; also 300 acres on New River joining Thos. Fauster's claim.

1782, JAMES NEWELL, JUNR., assignee of Walter Crockett, 500 acres [Mine Mill Creek?]on state warrant, enters 100 acres between Alexr. Neelys and John Brawleys to join both their lines.

1782, PAUL RAZOR, assignee of Walter Crockett, assignee of James Clark, 500 acres on New River opposite the upper end of Saml. Ewing's to join sd. Ewing's and the place Sayers lives on called the Pasture, to include improvements said Razor lives on and those made by Wm. Burk and Saml. Byrd, and back for quantity.

1782, JAMES TUTTLE, assignee of Jeremiah Doaty, assignee of Nathaniel Banks, Commissioner's certificate, 400 acres Sinking Branch below Roaring Falls [New River]; assigned to John Johnson and Thomas Spencer.

MONTGOMERY COUNTY SURVEYS: Christiansburg, Virginia.

1782, ROBERT SAYERS, 396 acres on southeast side of New River, including Jacob Castle's improvements; 794 acres southeast side of New River adjoining settlement survey; 1783, 470 acres south side of New River, adjoining the lead mines.

1782, JOHN BAXTER, 400 acres on Welsher's Run, on certificate from Commissioners of Montgomery and Washington counties, grant 1785; 1784, 167 acres assigned by Samuel Ewing, on Welshere's Run.

1782, EVAN WILLIAMS, 337 acres on Commissioner's certificate, both sides of Welshire's Branch, corner to an old survey.

1782, ALEX NEELY, 400 acres head of Mine Mill Creek, granted to Richard Muse, 1785.

1782, JAMES NEWELL, 164 acres on Mine Mill Creek, granted to Richard Muse, 1785.

1782, WILLIAM RODGERS, 374 acres head of Mine Mill Creek, adjoining John Brawley.

1782, THOMAS SPENCER, 400 acres on New River, corner to John Baxter and opposite the upper end of Craig's Island, entry assigned by John Johnston who was assignee of James Tuttle.

1782, JOSEPH EATON, 383 acres on New River between Evan Williams and John Baxter, on certificate from the Commissioners of Washington and Montgomery counties, granted 1788; 1783, 112 acres, assignee of William Ingledove, assignee of Henry Stafford, located on Welshire's Run, granted 1800; 149 acres assigned as above, located on Welshier's Run, granted 1800.

1783, ADAM DEAN, 400 acres on the head of Mine Mill Creek, granted 1785.

1783, PAUL RAZOR, 274 acres opposite Samuel Ewing, delivered Jacob Razor, 1791; assigned to David McGavock who obtained the grant, 1792.

1783, JOHN RODGERS, 200 acres on both sides of Mine Mill Creek, grant to John Brawley, 1796.

1783, THOMAS NELSON, 722 acres on a pre-emption warrant, on both sides of Mine Mill Creek, John Brawley's line; 400 acres same location, Commissioner's certificate, both sides of Mine Mill Creek, adjoining Herbert and opposite the lower part of the island.

1783, JACOB CAIN, 413 acres on New River at the foot of Poplar Camp Mountain, grant to William Carter, 1796.

1783, PATRICK CASH, 310 acres on branch of Poplar Camp Creek, granted 1785.

1783, WILLIAM ROSS, 170 acres east side of New River.

1783, JOHN JENKINS, 500 acres at Poplar Camp, granted 1785.

1783, THOMAS MADISON and LEAD MINE COMPANY (THOMAS MADISON, JACOB RUBSEMAN, WARREN LEWIS, WILLIAM NELSON, EDMUND PENDLETON, PETER LYONS, administrators of JOHN ROBINSON, deceased), 322 acres on east side of New River, at a place called the Pastures, granted to Robert Sayers 1788; 240 acres adjoining the lead mines; 338 acres east side New River, adjoining the mine survey, granted to Robert Sayers, 1788; 214 acres adjoining the Pastures, assigned by Madison to Robert Sayers, who received the grant, 1788; 573 acres on east side New River on

Bingamans Branch, adjoining Jenkins and Jacob Cain; 1786, for THOMAS MADISON and THE GOLD MINE COMPANY, 435 acres joining Joseph Eaton, Richard Muse, and James McCorkle; 1789, 66 acres, River Hill.

1784, WILLIAM RUTHERFORD, SENR., 200 acres on Mine Mill Creek based on a commissioner's certificate.

1784, THOMAS MUSE, 531 acres east side New River, joining a place known as Bingaman's Bottom.

1786, WILLIAM LOCKETT, assignee of William Herbert, deceased, 180 acres [no location, but may be Mine Mill Creek] part of Loyal Company grant, granted to Lockett, 1800.

1787, THOS. FOSTER, 41 acres part of a military warrant of 50 acres dated May 17, 1780, on east side of New River, adjoining his patent land, granted 1793.

1789, CHARLES LYNCH in trust for LEAD MINE COMPANY, 1,400 acres to include several claims in one survey, including part of 1,000 acres surveyed for John Chiswell 1760, 240 acres surveyed in 1783 for Thomas Madison and the Lead Mines Company, and 470 acres surveyed for Robert Sayers, 1783, located on the south side of the New River and to include the lead mines, granted to Lynch, 1791.

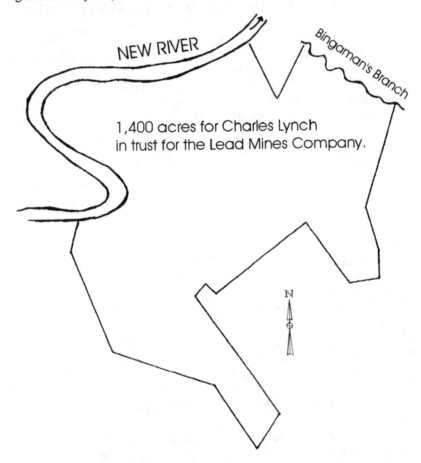

In 1789, a survey of 1,400 acres on the New River was made for Charles Lynch, in trust for the Lead Mine Company.

Tracing from the original in Survey Book D, Montgomery County, by Mary B. Kegley.

1789, JOHN ROSS, 80 acres on west side of New River.

1789, GEORGE BYRD, 100 acres New River, assigned by Charles Lynch, granted 1796.

1789, ROBERT PARSONS, 160 acres west side of New River, corner to James McDonald and Joseph Glover (Glavens?).

1789, JACOB STALLINGS, 125 acres corner to Porter, west side of New River.

1789, STEPHEN AUSTIN, 150 acres, east side of New River, beginning on River Hill.

1789, HENRY CHRISTLEY, 100 acres, on west side of New River.

MONTGOMERY COUNTY DEEDS: Christiansburg, Virginia.

1780, GEORGE FORBIS from James Patton's Executors, 680 acres on the north side of Woods River, granted to Patton's executors, December 12, 1779 [the Welshire place].

1785, ROBERT SANDERS from James Newell, 400 acres on the west side of New River, adjoining George Forbush and the land Forbush sold William Herbert deceased, grant to James Newell, 1785.

1786, WILLIAM HERBERT from David Herbert, Sr., and Marthew [Martha] his wife, of Surry County, North Carolina, all of a tract on the north side of New River, adjoining Herbert's Ferry, where David Herbert, Jr., now lives, in return for payments of £6 per year for the life of David Herbert and wife.

1787, CHARLES LYNCH of Campbell County, Virginia, from William Bell, 180 acres on west side of New River at the mouth of Mine Mill Creek, and opposite Mine Hill.

1789, WILLIAM ROSS from William Herbert, 130 acres on Poplar Camp Creek.

For the list of Commissioner's certificates issued in Montgomery and Washington counties, *see* Kegley, *Early Adventurers*, Vol. 2, pp. 102-119.

GRANTS: Virginia State Library, Archives, Richmond, Virginia.

1785, JULIUS RUTHERFORD, 200 acres on Mine Mill Creek.

1789, CHARLES LYNCH, 531 acres on east side of New River, adjoining Bingaman's Bottom.

1791, FRANCIS PRESTON, for the LOYAL COMPANY, 215 acres surveyed 1753.

1793, STEPHEN AUSTIN, NATHANIEL FRISBIE, and MOSES AUSTIN, 75 acres on the west side of the New River by James Newell's.

1793, THOMAS MUSE, 338 acres [on Mine Mill Creek?].

1796, WILLIAM ROSS, 150 acres, on east fork of Poplar Camp Creek, to include Lee's cabin; 190 acres on Poplar Camp Creek adjoining his land.

WYTHE COUNTY SURVEY BOOK 1: Wytheville, Virginia.

1792, CHARLES LYNCH, 260 acres on west side of New River, adjoining Robert Porter; 872 acres adjoining Brawley on Mine Mill Creek.

1793, WILLIAM ROSS, 317 acres on New River, beginning near a branch known as Cowpen Branch; 1794, 100 acres on New River corner to Carter; 179- (no date given), 200 acres adjoining his own land and William Carter; 100 acres on New River.

1793, WILLIAM HERBERT, legatee of William Herbert, deceased, 1,000 acres on east side of New River.

1793, JOHN JINKINS, 100 acres on both sides Prior's Branch, granted Stephen and Moses Austin, 1800; 75 acres on New River, adjoining his own land.

1794, JOHN HURST, 40 acres on west side of New River.

1795, JAMES NEWELL, 1,000 acres on Mine Mill Creek, corner James McGavock and William Rogers.

1795, THOMAS MADISON, 230 acres on Lead Mine Mill Creek, corner to Richard Muse, Thomas Madison, and McGavock.

1795, MOSES AUSTIN, 3,500 acres south side Reed Creek, adjoining John Baker, but survey includes 1,500 acres property of James Newell, Richard Beeson, John Hogg, John Baker, and William Pierce; 29,000 acres on Reed Creek, [should be Cripple Creek], corner James Campbell and H. Chaney, John Davis, including 7000 acres, property of Thomas Madison & Company.

1795, NATHANIEL FRISBIE, 100 acres on New River, corner to William Bell.

WYTHE COUNTY DEED BOOK 1: Wytheville, Virginia.

1790, JULIOUS RUTHERFORD to ABSALOM RUTHERFORD, 200 acres on Mine Mill Creek (p. 17).

1791, JOHN JENKINS to WILLIAM CARTER, 500 acres on east side of New River joining William Herbert's tract known by the name of Poplar Camp (p. 19).

1791, ROBERT SAYERS to NATH'L FRISBIE, 214 acres east side of New River (p. 20).

1791, PATRICK CASH AND SARY (signed SARRAH) his wife to JOHN FOLKS, 310 acres where Cashes now live, on a branch of Poplar Camp Creek (pp. 38-39).

1791, COL. CHARLES LYNCH and ANN (ANNE) his wife to HENRY DAVIS, 150 acres on unnamed creek and the river (p. 40).

1791, THOMAS BRATTON, yeoman, appoints "trusty friend" JEREMIAH DOWLING, attorney, to recover from ROBERT SANDERS, farmer, the sum of £14 and 10 shillings due on the note which was forcibly and illegally endorsed to Nathaniel Frisbie and also to receive £6 Virginia currency from JAMES NEWELL, ESQ., a note also illegally endorsed to Frisbie (pp. 59- 60).

1791, JESSE EVANS to ALEXANDER SMYTH, 75 acres [Cove Creek?] granted Evans on December 16, 1784, adjoining a survey belonging to the heirs of Hugh Montgomery, deceased (p. 67).

1792, ROBERT SAYERS and JEAN (JANE) to RICHARD MUSE, one-half of two tracts on east side of New River, adjoining the Lead Mines tract, containing 660 acres (p. 124).

1792, CHARLES LYNCH and ANN, of Campbell County, Virginia, to JAMES NEWELL, 180 acres on the north side of the New River opposite the Lead Mines plantation and on both sides of Mine Mill Creek, being the same purchased of William Bell, including an island and the ferry (p. 139).

1792, MOSES AUSTIN and MARY, and STEPHEN AUSTIN of Philadelphia, to THOMAS RUSTON, of Philadelphia, 1/8th undivided interest in the lead mines tract of 1,400 acres, houses, stores, furnaces, mills, and all other improvements. (pp. 147-148); January 6, 1794, separate acknowledgment of Mary Austin who was unable to travel (pp. 149-150).

1792, CHARLES LYNCH of Campbell County, Virginia, to ROBERT SANDERS, 532 acres on the east side of New River on Bingamans Branch, adjoining

Herbert's tract of Bingamans Bottom, adjoining Jenkins' line (pp. 157-158).

1793, GEORGE FORBUSS and MARGARET to ROBERT SANDERS, 131 acres on west side of New River, part of 600 acres on which sd. Forbuss now lives (pp. 159-160).

1793, WILLIAM HARBERT [HERBERT] and POLLY his wife to WILLIAM CARTER, 367 acres known as Harbert's Ferry, corner Forbuss (pp. 172-173).

1793, FRANCIS PRESTON of Washington County, Virginia, to WILLIAM CARTER, 215 acres on some branches of New River, granted to Preston, August 19, 1791 (p. 174).

1794, THOMAS HARBERT [HERBERT] and SARAH his wife to MOSES AUSTIN, 225 acres on east side of New River, Bingamans Bottom tract (pp. 184-185).

1793, CHARLES NUCKOLLS and MARY to WILLIAM BELL and WILLIAM HARBERT, 500 acres on both sides of Cripple Creek (p. 188).

1794, WILLIAM HARBERT and POLLY to THOMAS HARBERT, all of Wythe County, 500 acres on east side of New River known by the name of Poplar Camp tract (p. 194).

1794, JAMES NEWELL and SARAH to STEPHEN AUSTIN of Philadelphia, NATHANIEL FRISBIE, and MOSES AUSTIN of Wythe County, 850 acres on New River, adjoining Robert and Samuel Porter, corner to William Bell's land, at the foot of the mountain (p. 195).

1794, ROBERT SANDERS and CATY to JAMES BARNETT, 100 acres on fork of Benjamons [Bingamans] Branch, part of 531 acres (p. 198).

1794, WILLIAM BELL and SARAH and WILLIAM HARBERT and POLLY to HUGH MONTGOMERY and DANIEL CARLIN (of Patrick County, Virginia), 500 acres on both sides of Cripple Creek, including houses, forges, and dams (p. 204).

1794, ROBERT SANDERS and KATHERINE to ANDREW STEEL, 125 acres on east side of Benjamians [Bingamans] Branch on Josiah Bell's line and Jenkins' line (p. 206).

1794, JAMES NEWELL and SARAH to STEPHEN SANDERS, JR., 240 acres on the west side of New River, beginning on the river and crossing a branch in the fork of Mine Mill Creek, to Keesler's line, corner to Robert Sanders (p.211).

1795, JOSIAH BELL and PATSY to MOSES AUSTIN, 268 acres on east side of New River adjoining Austin's land known as Bingamans Bottom (p. 303).

1796, JAMES BARNETT and wife (name blank) to JOSEPH EVANS, 100 acres on east side of New River, being part of 531 acres on fork of Bingamans Branch (p. 360).

1796, RICHARD MUSE and MARGARET to JAMES JONES, 80 acres on Mine Mill Creek (p. 371).

1796, RICHARD MUSE and MARGARET to KONROOD KEASLER [CONRAD KEESLING], no acres stated, on Mine Mill Creek (p. 372).

1796, RICHARD MUSE and MARGARET to DANIEL LOCKETT, 300 acres on Mine Mill Creek (p. 376).

1796, JOHN and JEAN BAXTER to JOHN KEIZLING [KEESLING], 400 acres on Welshires Run (p. 385).

1795, WILLIAM ROGERS and MARY to JOHN GAUGH (GUGH), 130 acres on New River, part of 230 acres by patent granted to William Rogers April 2, 1795 (p. 437).

1797, JOHN and EVE KEASLING to JOHN DICK, 259 acres, part of 400 acres granted to John Baxter on Wilshers Run, a branch of New River (p. 63).

1797, JAMES and MARY MONTGOMERY to THOMAS FOSTER, 86 acres on east side of New River below the mouth of Poplar Camp Creek (p. 69).

1797, MOSES AUSTIN to JOHN MILLER, 3 acres on both sides of Welshers Branch (p. 103).

1797, JOHN and ELIZABETH MILLER to MOSES AUSTIN, all their claim to land [on New River] sold to them by Robert Buchanan which comes within lines of a survey granted to George Forbes by right of Nathaniel Welshire (p. 105).

1797, WILLIAM and RACHEL ROSS to GREENBERRY G. McKINSIE and CALEB BOBBITT of Grayson County, 130 acres on Poplar Camp Creek (p. 115); also 170 acres on east side of the New River adjacent to Cashes on Poplar Camp (p. 116); also 190 acres on Poplar Camp Creek adjacent to said Ross (p. 117).

1797, MOSES and MARY AUSTIN of Austinville, merchant, to STEPHEN AUSTIN of Philadelphia, Pennsylvania, merchant, for $3,660 milled silver dollars, two tracts on the New River, one known as Bingham's [Bingaman's] Bottom, adjoining the lead mines tract, adjacent to Charles Lynch, for 300 acres; and the second known as the "New Fields," at forks of White Oak Branch running with Bingham's [Bingaman's] Bottom to the river, down the river to Major Evan's line, to William Carter's line and to David Monroe's for 260 acres (p. 147).

1796, ROBERT and JEAN SAYERS and RICHARD and MARGARET MUSE to THOMAS JACKSON, two tracts containing 660 acres on east or south side of New River called the Pasture (p. 185).

1796, JOHN and SUSANNAH JENKINS to NATHANIEL FRISBIE of Grayson County, Virginia, 83 acres on the east side of the New River adjacent to George Carter (p. 230).

1796, JOHN and SUSANNAH JENKINS to MOSES AUSTIN, 6 3/4 acres [on New River], part of an entry made by George Carter now belonging to Jenkins, adjacent to the land whereon Jenkins formerly lived (p. 235).

1798, ELIZABETH WILLIAMS, the elder, WILLIAM WILLIAMS, JOHN STOTTS and wife POLLY, and ELIZABETH WILLIAMS, the younger, to RICHARD MUSE, 367 acres on both sides of Welshires Branch of New River (p. 245).

1798, JAMES NEWELL purchased a tract of land on New River opposite the lead mines from CHARLES LYNCH and some time later Moses Austin & Co., purchased the mines. In 1792, the Virginia Assembly passed an act to put a ferry across the river at the mines, which Newell by his purchase from Lynch was entitled to. MOSES and STEPHEN AUSTIN relinquish their claim to the said ferry (p. 254).

1798, MOSES and MARY AUSTIN to JAMES AUSTIN, 500 acres on the north side of New River adjoining Robert Sanders, being the tract from Nathaniel Forbus and Nathan Buchanan to Moses Austin (p. 264).

1798, JAMES and MARGARET AUSTIN to STEPHEN and MOSES AUSTIN, 500 acres on north side of New River, being the land sold by Nathaniel Forbus and Nathaniel Buckanen to Moses Austin, adjoining Sanders (p. 265).

1798, GREENBERRY G. McKINZIE and CALEB BOBBITT of Grayson County and THOMAS BLAIR, agreement regarding a partnership for the iron furnace at Poplar Camp that McKinzie and Bobbitt purchased of William Ross (p. 286).

1798, MOSES and MARY AUSTIN to THOMAS JACKSON, 214 acres on New River adjacent to said Jackson (p. 288).

1799, WILLIAM MOOR to ROBERT SANDERS by Thomas Fauster [Foster] his attorney, 170 acres on New River adjacent to George Keasler, John Dicks and Sanders (p. 309).

1799, THOMAS and SARAH HARBERT [HERBERT] of Grayson County, to THOMAS FAUSTER [FOSTER], 306 acres part of 1,000 acres on south side of New River, adjoining Fauster, Thomas Brooks, Jesse Evans and others (p. 339).

1795, ROBERT and JEAN SAYERS to MOSES AUSTIN, land on east side of New River adjacent to Samuel Ewing (p. 411).

1795, GEORGE FORBUSH, NATHANEL FORBUSH and NATHANIEL BUCHANAN to MOSES AUSTIN, 410 acres on west side of New River adjacent to Robert Sanders (p. 413).

1799, DANIEL GUTHRIE of Augusta County, Virginia, to CHARLES AUSTIN, 125 acres on east side of Binghamans Branch adjacent to Josiah Bell and Jenkins (p. 492).

1796 The justices of Wythe County were ordered to take the separate acknowledgment of MARGARET MUSE, wife of RICHARD MUSE, who "cannot conveniently travel" to the court for the transfer of 300 acres to DANIEL LOCKETT (p. 517), same to KOONRAD KEASLER [KEESLING], dower on Mine Mill Creek (p. 518).

The justices were ordered to obtain the acknowledgment of Margaret Muse who "cannot conveniently travel to the County Court of Wythe." The document is dated August 1st, 1796.

Tracing of part of the document from Wythe County Deed Book 2, p. 517 by Mary B. Kegley.

235

Moses Austin
(1761-1821)

Photo courtesy of the
Texas State Archives.

Stephen Fuller Austin

Son of Moses and Maria Brown
Austin was born in Austinville on
November 3, 1793. He later be-
came known as the "Father of
Texas."

Photo courtesy of the
Texas State Archives.

CHAPTER III
The Families

Moses And Stephen Austin

Moses and Stephen Austin were brothers, sons of Elias and Eunice Phelps Austin of Durham, Connecticut. Stephen, born in 1747, was the oldest and, Moses, born in 1761, was the youngest (Gracy, *Moses Austin*, hereinafter *Austin*, p.11). Both of these men had interests in the lead mines and land on the New River. Stephen, the son of Moses, and namesake of his uncle, was born on New River and later became famous as a founder of Texas.

Moses formed a partnership with Moses Bates, his brother-in-law, who also came to the New River. They were dealers of dry goods in 1782. In the following year, Austin formed a partnership with Manning Merrill. They opened a store in Philadelphia, and in 1784 one in Richmond, Virginia (Gracy, *Austin*, pp. 17, 18, 21, 22).

Moses Austin was married on September 28, 1785, to Maria (Mary, sometimes Polly) Brown, the oldest child of Abia and Margaret Sharp Brown, born January 1, 1768, at Sharpsborough Furnace, New Jersey (Gracy, *Austin*, pp. 22, 23, 24).

For the next few years, Moses lived in Richmond, and Stephen in Philadelphia. In May 1789, Moses and Stephen Austin, formed a partnership, which leased the lead mines on the New River in present Wythe County for a period of ten years. Moses may have visited the location before the lease was signed, but there is no record to confirm this. About the same time as the lease was signed, Moses Austin established a plant on Cary Street in Richmond to manufacture shot, said to be the first business of its kind in America. To protect their lead industry, the Austins were successful in persuading the Federal government to impose an import duty on lead in 1791 (Gracy, *Austin*, pp. 34, 35, 39, 51).

Stephen Austin had a survey made in 1789. The land was located on the east side of the new River, the lines to begin on River Hill (Montgomery County Plat Book D, p. 64).

Moses came to the New River in August 1789 to begin operation of the mines. He had asked for and received on loan from the state thirty tons of lead, located at the mines. This advance was to help the Austins rebuild and replace the buildings, furnaces and mills, which had deteriorated over the years. A few weeks after his arrival, Moses reported to his brother Stephen that he had put ten men to work and that they were producing 1,000 pounds of lead a day. He also reported that they had located a new rich vein. By the end of November the first shot had been produced in Richmond as promised (Gracy, *Austin*, pp. 34,35; Moses and Stephen Austin to the Governor, Executive Papers).

Stephen recruited in the Philadelphia area men who were willing to work at the mines. He is said to be responsible for the arrival of Robert Percival, Nathaniel Frisbie (who probably came from Connecticut), and probably many others. About this time, R. [Robert] Sayers, Arthur Campbell, and William Montgomery prepared a report on the mines for Governor Randolph, who passed it on to Thomas Jefferson. In 1790, there were sixty men working seven different veins to a depth of seventy feet. They obtained six to eight tons of ore each day. New crushing and washing techniques were used and the furnace was repaired. They were then recovering a ton and a half of lead per day. (*Calendar of State Papers*, Vol. 5, p. 119 names Frisbie as the manager of the mines; Gracy, *Austin*, pp. 36,37, 39, 42).

Thomas Jefferson described the lead mines in his book, *Notes on Virginia*, written and published in the 1780s. At that time, thirty to fifty men were at the mines, producing 20-60 tons of lead a year. The furnace was on the opposite side (north side) of the river from the mines. The lead was transported by wagon to canoes, taken across the river, reloaded into wagons and carried to the furnace. From there the lead was transported to Lynch's Ferry [Lynchburg on the James] and Westham [Richmond]. The pounding mills and furnace were at the mouth of Mine Mill Creek on the north side of New River (Jefferson, *Notes*, pp. 26-27).

In 1792, the mines were sold by the State at the Eagle Tavern in Richmond, and the 1,400 acres brought £6,505. The purchasers were Moses and Stephen Austin. Moses and his company owned a two-thirds interest, and Stephen and his company one-third. The Austins immediately advertised for fifty to sixty men to work the mines. At this time, they built houses, stores, mills, and furnaces, as well as shops for the blacksmith, hatter, and other craftsmen. The furnace was moved to the south side of the river, and washing and smelting techniques improved because of the importation of Englishmen, who were familiar with these processes. Thomas Jackson, later owner of a share of the mines, came from Westmoreland, England, in 1793, and was probably accompanied by others from the same area. By the end of 1794, the lead mines was a place of "great Trade & business." It is also documented that a Presbyterian congregation, part of the Abingdon Presbytery, was located in Austinville. It was said to have been organized in 1790 and had twenty-five families. The exact location is not known (Gracy, *Austin*, pp. 42,43,45,46; Hanna, *The Scotch-Irish Families in America*, p. 111).

In 1792, there was such expansion in the operation that the Austins were forced to borrow thousands of dollars. With establishments in Philadelphia and Lynchburg, and with markets in New York, Connecticut, and Kentucky, among others, it soon became apparent that they could not meet expenses. For this reason they sold a one-eighth interest in the lead mines tract of 1,400 acres with "houses, stores, furnaces, mills, and all other improvements," to Thomas Ruston, of Philadelphia, for the sum of $15,000 (Wythe County Deed Book 1, pp. 147-150; Gracy, *Austin*, pp. 46, 47).

In 1794, Moses purchased 225 acres on the east side of the river from Thomas Herbert and his wife. This was the Bingamans Bottom tract (Wythe County Deed Book 1, pp. 184-185). James Newell sold him 850 acres in 1794, and the following year Josiah Bell sold him 268 acres adjoining Bingamans Bottom land already owned by Austin. A small tract of 6 3/4 acres was added in 1796 (Deed Book 1, pp. 195, 303; Book 2, p. 235). In 1795, Moses took up by survey 3,500 acres on Reed Creek adjoining John Baker [later David Graham], and 29,000 on Reed [should be Cripple Creek] corner to James Campbell and H. [Hezekiah] Chaney and others (Wythe County Survey Book 1, pp. 209-213). In 1795 Moses purchased land on the west side of the river adjoining Robert Sanders from George Forbush and others (Wythe County Deed Book 2, p. 413).

On November 3, 1793, Stephen Fuller Austin, son of Moses and Maria Austin, was born somewhere in this revitalized community, but the exact location is unknown. None of the deeds show where Moses and his family lived. On June 22, 1795, Emily Margaret, a second child was born at Austinville. The only other child was James Elijah Brown Austin, born at Mine à Burton (Potosi), Missouri, in 1803 (Gracy, *Austin*, p. 52; Barker, *Austin Papers*, p. 37).

Meanwhile, Stephen Austin traveled to England in an attempt to sell the mines. However, when he arrived there in 1794 he was arrested and put in debtor's prison for an old debt of more than $4,000. After more than two years abroad, he finally raised the money to pay the debt and was allowed to leave. But he was unable to sell the lead mines. Ruston, who had been helpful with credit, also found himself in a poor financial situation, and about this time the State began to ask for repayment of the loan of the lead (Gracy, *Austin*, pp. 49,50).

In spite of these financial difficulties, Moses Austin, Stephen Austin, and Nathaniel Frisbie purchased additional land: 850 acres from James Newell, 225 acres on Bingaman's Branch from Thomas Herbert, 268 acres from Josiah Bell, and the land on the north side of the river from Forbush (Wythe County Deed Book 1, pp. 184, 195,303; Book 2, pp. 413, 414).

In 1796, Moses Austin was serving as a justice of the peace of the Wythe County Court and was appointed as a captain in the 2nd Battalion of the 35th Regiment of the local militia. Moses Bates, the brother-in-law of Moses Austin, received a license to operate an ordinary at Austinville in June the same year (Wythe County Order Book, 1795-1796, pp. 66, 88, 96, 101).

In the winter of 1796-1797, Moses Austin and Jos. [probably Josiah] Bell made an extraordinary journey from the lead mines to the lead-mining district west of Ste. Genevieve, Missouri. They traveled through the Cumberland Gap into Kentucky, and in Stanford saw several former residents of the New River including Nathaniel Forbus, whose land near the lead mines in Wythe County, Austin had purchased in 1795. After experiencing severe winter weather, near starvation, and miles of wilderness, they finally arrived at Whitesides Station sixty miles from Kaskaskia. After visiting the lead mines in Ste. Genevieve and making arrangements for their purchase, Austin returned by way of Nashville and Knoxville, having traveled 2,000 miles in three months and nine days (Wythe County Deed Book 2, p. 413; *see,* Forbush sketch; Garrison, ''A Memorandum...'' *The American Historical Review*, Vol. 5, pp. 518-542).

After his return to Wythe County, Moses Austin began to make arrangements for his permanent departure to Missouri. His partnership with Thomas Ruston and John D. Blanchard was terminated. James Austin, son of Jesse Austin, a cousin, became the superintendent of the mines, and sometime prior to April 1, 1798, the first postmaster of Austinville. Moses and wife Mary transferred 500 (originally 410) acres of the Forbush land on the north side of the river to James Austin in 1798, who in the same year, conveyed it back to Stephen and Moses jointly. In the same year, Moses conveyed 214 acres to Thomas Jackson. Stephen and Moses Austin dissolved their partnership and Moses transferred two tracts at the mines to pay debts owed to Stephen. About this time Congress dropped the duty on lead and lead products, which eventually caused the price of lead to drop about forty-five percent, spelling economic disaster for the Austins' lead mines in Wythe County. In the fall of 1797, in order to prepare for his arrival in Missouri, Moses Austin sent Elias Bates and Judather Kendal with a map, supplies, seven men, and tools, to build the furnace and mills and other necessary buildings (Wythe County Deed Book 2, pp. 147, 264, 265, 288, 413; Barker, *Austin,* pp. 35-37; Gracy, *Austin,* pp. 66-68; Post Office Records).

On June 8, 1798, Moses and wife and two children (including his five-year old son, Stephen F.), his brother-in-law Moses Bates and his wife and two sons, slaves, and workers for the mines-forty in all-set out with horses, nine loaded wagons, and a coach and four, for Missouri. Unexpectedly they traveled through what is now West Virginia to the ''Boat Yard'' on the Kanhawha near present Charleston, instead of going through Cumberland Gap. Austin purchased a flat boat and for three months he and his family members and associates, probably only twenty in all (others appear to have returned with wagons), floated down the Kanawha, the Ohio, and eventually to the Mississippi. Henry, son of Moses Bates, drowned near the falls of the Ohio at Louisville, and Parsons, his other son, and Martha Bates, his wife, also died on the trip. On September 7, when they arrived at Kaskaskia, only two of the remaining seventeen were able to walk ashore. After several days of recuperation, they crossed the Mississippi to begin their life at the Missouri lead mines. Stephen Austin had returned to Connecticut (Gracy, *Austin,* pp. 68-69; Barker, *Austin,* Vol. 2, pp. 36-37).

Charles Austin, first cousin of Moses Austin, wrote of the difficulties at the mines in 1798, after Moses and the others had departed. There was so much rain that the mine holes had filled up. The corn crop was almost ruined. The expenses for the trip noted as the ''Illinois Adventure'' from September 1797 through June 16, 1798 were also mentioned. Among the items included were shot, bar lead, bacon, tools, the coach, horses, the transportation, and the ''flatt'' boat. The total amount was $7,897.78 (Barker, *Austin,* pp. 39-41).

Charles Austin was a member of the Wythe County Militia, an ensign in 1798, and being recommended as a lieutenant in 1799 (Summers, *Annals,* pp. 1368,1370).

Stephen Austin later returned to Philadelphia from Connecticut, and learned that a Mr. Sanders (Robert or William?) had rebuilt the furnace at Austinville, and that salt had been ordered from Norfolk to prepare meat for the winter. He wanted to raise pigs to ''vitual'' the people at the mines. Daniel Hall, a blacksmith was to be sent to the mines, and young Ambrose, a slave, was to be apprenticed in the shop. Harry Elliot, a nephew of Austins, was to come and live with James Austin and Hall at ''the tavern'' on New River (Barker, *Austin* pp. 43-45).

In 1800, Stephen Austin and his wife Huldah, then of New Haven, transferred to Charles Austin of Austinville, two tracts of land, the Bingaman's Bottom tract and the place known as Josiah Bell's (Wythe County Deed Book 3, p. 40).

In 1801, a suit was filed against Moses, Charles, Stephen, and James Austin, by the State of Virginia, which was trying to collect debts owed by the Austins. Charles was then living in New Haven, stating that he had no property belonging to Moses and Stephen. Governor James Monroe stated that the Austins had promised to deliver twenty-two tons of lead to James McGavock, and had signed a bond to that effect on May 25, 1789. They had not delivered any of it. Moses was then living in the Spanish Territory; Stephen was insolvent in Connecticut. Samuel Paine, one of the sureties on the bond, also unable to meet his obligation, stated that James Newell, ''present possessor of the lead mines'' (in 1806) had nineteen tons of lead ready to be delivered to the agent of the state, but recognized that James McGavock was unable to serve as agent. In January 1801, the mines owned fourteen mules, ten horses, six steers, six milch cows, two yearlings, two calves, hogs, twenty-eight Negroes (including six small children), unwashed ore, shot, wagons, ox carts, tools, and ''slaggs'' at the furnace and hill equal to 12,000 pounds of lead worth about £18,000. Debts, judgments, and real estate were also included (*Monroe vs. Austins,* NS 36 OS 106, Augusta County, Circuit Court Clerk's Office; *Calendar,* Vol. 4, p. 624; Vol. 9, p. 474; Barker, *Austin,* Vol. 1, pp. 60-61).

In 1803, Charles Austin transferred the two tracts known as Bingaman's Bottom and Josiah Bell's place to James Newell. In 1806, he was ''late of Wythe County,'' and transferred 648 acres to William Sanders. James and Margaret Austin conveyed 100 acres to Isaac Green in 1802 (Wythe County Deed Book, 3, pp. 208; Book 4, pp. 99, 366).

In Missouri, Moses Austin planned for a Texas Colony with arrangements to move families there for settlement. However, he died from exposure on June 10, 1821. His wife Maria died on January 8, 1824, and they are both buried in St. Francis County, Missouri. Their son Stephen continued the work and became known as the "Father of Texas" (Gracy, *Austin*, 214, 215, 220; Barker, *Austin*, Vol 1, p. 5).

Although Moses and Stephen Austin were visionaries and developed businesses in Philadelphia, Richmond, and Wythe County, their success was limited. Although they did establish the Town of Austinville, enlarge and improve the operation at the mines, encourage and support immigration and importation of skilled workers from various places, they were not financially successful.

John Baxter

John Baxter (also spelled Backster) is mentioned on the early tithable lists of William Herbert in 1771 and 1772. He appears to have resided on Wilshire's Run, at the place where Welshire formerly lived (*see* entry of William Montgomery, 1782; Kegley, *Tithables,* pp. 12,17*)*.

In 1775, the Fincastle County Court ordered that Cornelius Deforrest with such tithables as Captain Herbert "may appoint shall open & keep the road in repair from Baxter's smith shop to the Court House." (Summers, *Annals,* p. 647). At this time the courthouse was located on the river in the west end of present Austinville. It appears that Baxter was the neighborhood blacksmith.

In 1773 and 1785, Baxter served on the jury. On June 6, 1775, Baxter sued James Newell, Jr., on a debt (Summers, *Annals,* pp. 620,782; Fincastle County Order Book 2, p. 142).

In 1783, Baxter entered two tracts, one for 400 acres and the other 200 acres, both on a Commissioner's certificate on Clover Branch, a branch not presently identifiable. In 1782, he also entered 169 acres which had been assigned to him by Samuel Ewing. This tract adjoined his settlement. An additional tract of land was entered in 1784 for 200 acres (Montgomery County Entry Book B, pp. 26, 37, 68). In 1784, Baxter had two tracts of land surveyed on Welshire's Run, one for 167 acres and the other for 400 acres. In 1796, the latter tract was granted to Baxter who with his wife Jean sold the land to John Keizling (Keesling). (Montgomery County Surveys; Summers, *Annals,* p. 879; Wythe County Deed Book 1, p.385). The other tracts were probably assigned to someone else before the grants issued. In 1790, he was appointed overseer of the road from the lead mines to the ford of Reed Creek (Wythe County Orders, September 29, 1790). About 1796, the Baxter name disappears from the Wythe County records.

Although no marriage record has been found for Baxter, the will of James Simpson mentions a daughter Jean Baxter. Also, the will of Mary Simpson mentions a daughter Jean Baxter. The Simpsons may be the parents of John's wife (Wythe County Will Book 1, pp. 404, 437).

William Bell

William Bell (ca. 1740-1801) was associated with work at the lead mines, probably beginning in the early 1760s. He testified in a lawsuit that he had worked for two years for Colonel John Chiswell in an attempt to make lead, but was unsuccessful until Chiswell went to England and brought the Welsh miners to the mines in 1763 (Deposition of William Bell, July 20, 1795, *W. Herbert vs. Joseph Farrell,* Box 32, *Chiswell Judgments,* May Term, 1827, Wythe County Circuit Court Clerk's Office, Basement).

Bell shows up in the records of Augusta County as early as 1765, when the record shows "William Bell lives at Col. Chiswell's mines" (Chalkley, *Chronicles*, Vol. 1, p. 351). He may be the same William Bell who applied for a marriage license on January 15, 1765 in Augusta County. His wife is said to be Mary Foster, daughter of Thomas Foster for whom Foster Falls is named (McConnell, *Sänders*, p. 237).

Bell lived on a tract of land south of John Chiswell's survey for 1,000 acres. In 1774, he had 64 acres surveyed on the southeast side of the New River, corner to the land he lived on and adjoining Chiswell (Montgomery County Plat Book A, p. 123). In 1785, he had a survey made for the land on the other side of the river, a tract which would include the old courthouse of Fincastle County, and the mouth of Mine Mill Creek, as well as the island in the river (Montgomery County Plat Book C, p. 561). This may have been based on the entry made by him in 1784, which was to begin on the river bank on the west side, about 200 yards above Mine Mill Creek, and to include Jinkins' improvements as well as "the mill, works, and improvements." At the time of the survey the tract was designated as 200 acres, but when William Bell sold the tract to Charles Lynch it was only 180 acres (Montgomery County Entry Book B, p. 82; Montgomery County Deed Book A, p. 429). It was on this tract that Lynch established the ferry which crossed the river to the mines. This is the site of Thorn's Ferry, which was located immediately west of the present bridge at Austinville.

In 1793, William Bell and William Herbert purchased 500 acres on Cripple Creek from Charles and Mary Nuckolls. The following year, the tract was transferred to Hugh Montgomery and Daniel Carlin, then to Robert Sanders, and in 1800 to David Peirce. This tract was probably associated with the iron industry (Wythe County Deed Book 1, pp. 188, 204; Book 2, p. 416; Book 3, p. 56).

In 1799, Bell was exempt from paying further county levies in Wythe County (Summers, *Annals*, p. 1371). There is no will recorded for him, and no settlement of the estate is mentioned. However, Jouett Boyd, a former historian of Wythe County, provided a list of Bell's children, though her source for this information is not known. They included William Bell, Jr., who moved to Kentucky, Samuel who married Margaret Edmiston and moved to Tennessee; Mary who married David Peirce of Poplar Camp, Wythe County; Mattie who married Thomas Smythe; Silas Bell and Robert Bell who moved to Kentucky; Joseph Bell who married Sally Kincannon and spent much of his life in Wythe County; and James Bell who married Mary Carter, the daughter of William and Unity Carter, who remained in Wythe County. Descendants claim that William Bell had sons Thomas and Josiah who moved to Kentucky with their brothers William, Jr., and Samuel, about 1797. Catherine McConnell in her book lists ten children: Samuel, Mary, Martha, Silas, William, Joseph, Robert, Thomas, James, and Elizabeth (who died young) (McConnell, *Sänders*, p. 237).

Marriage records in Wythe County show only two Bell marriages prior to 1810: Js. Bell married Sally Kincannon on June 13, 1805, and a Josiah Bell married Patsey Herbert in the 1790s. The Js. refers to Joseph Bell who married Sally Kincannon as mentioned below (Wythe County Marriage Book 1, pp. 4, 30).

Land records show that a Josiah Bell and his wife Patsy Bell sold 268 acres on the New River in 1795 to Moses Austin. They apparently left Wythe County at the time of Austin's removal, and in 1821 claimed land in the West through Stephen F. Austin (Wythe County Deed Book 1, p. 303, Book 3, p. 40; Barker, ed., *The Austin Papers*, Vol. 1, p. 63).

Joseph, son of William Bell, was the one who married Sallie (sometimes Sarah) Kincannon. She died on April 6, 1845, age about 67 years, and her tombstone in the Trigg Cemetery states she is "the consort of Joseph Bell." Joseph was involved with the iron industry on Cripple Creek and owned and probably operated the ironworks located at the Raven Cliff Furnace. It was located on 28 acres and was established in 1810 by Bell and Andrew Kincannon, who was probably his father-in-law. In addition, Bell owned other tracts, all of which were mortgaged at various times. Three other tracts were owned jointly with Andrew Kincannon (90 acres bought from Richard Hobbs, 310 acres from James Newell, and a survey purchased from Henry Stephens). He also owned the "black ore bank" of 50 acres, 13 acres from Martin Powell, 90 acres from Valentine Fry, and mountain land (McConnell, *Sänders*, p. 281; Wythe County Book 1A, p. 5; Book 5, p. 126; Book 6, p. 34; Deed Book 7, pp. 130, 131, 246; Book 8, pp. 240, 367; Book 9, pp. 423, 495, 558).

Joseph left Wythe County in November of 1824, intending to return. However, he died in South Carolina in August 1825. He was survived by his widow, Sarah (Sally) Kincannon, who was the daughter of Andrew and Catherine McDonald Kincannon of Surry County, North Carolina. Their surviving children were Andrew K. Bell, James N. Bell, Catherine McD. [probably McDonald] Bell, George H. Bell, Francis Bell, and Elizabeth F. Bell. Sarah Kincannon Bell died April 6, 1845, age about 67, and she is buried in the Trigg Cemetery in the west end of Austinville (*Raper, surviving partner of Raper and Jackson vs. Bell; Preston vs. Andrew K. Bell et als.*, Box 38, 1828, Wythe County Circuit Court Clerk's Office, Basement).

On December 20, 1825, a few items belonging to Joseph Bell, as shown by the sheriff James Davis, were appraised. The items included 18 hogs, pine plank, a bull, a steer, three calves, about 80 bushels of corn, a stack of oats, some rye, wheat, and hay. The total value was $93.66 1/2. Other records of inventory and appraisal taken in March and October in 1827 revealed Bell's ownership in "kittle pattrons" [kettle patterns], ladles and old irons, "pattrons and flasks including stove pattrons," (valued at $500), castings for a nail factory and rolling mill (valued at $100), stove plates, and other items of iron. The appraised value was $644.00, but the sale only brought $202.62 1/2 (Wythe County Will Book 3, pp. 184, 318).

Following her husband's death, Sarah's dower land was laid off by the Commissioners of the Court, and maps filed with the deeds (Wythe County Deed Book 10, pp. 642-644). She did not obtain dower in the forge and furnace land which were purchased by Leonard Straw at auction.

At Sarah's death, Thomas J. Boyd acted as administrator and recorded a sale of her property on July 14, 1845. Her heirs were listed in the settlement as James N. Bell, Andrew K. Bell, Francis K. Bell, Edward Walker and wife, and Alexander Peirce and wife (Wythe County Will Book 8, pp. 442, 443; McConnell, *Sänders*, p. 281).

James, son of William Bell (b. ca 1779, died ca. 1866) married Mary (Polly) Carter about 1800. She was born about 1782 and died December 12, 1831, in Wythe County. She was the daughter of William and Unity Bates Carter and is buried in the Gregory Cemetery in Wythe County. Bell was part owner of a gold mine in Rowan County, North Carolina (Wythe County Deed Book 18, p. 582) and had interests in the lead mines in Austinville, and the salt works in Saltville. James and Mary Bell had ten children: Unity Bates Bell married Daniel Walker; Malinda Bell married Robert Porter; William Thorn Bell married Sarah Ann Williams; Evalina Bell married Isaac Painter; Mary S. (Polly) Bell married David G. Shepherd; John C. Bell married Martha A. Porter; Thomas, James and Emily died young; and Jane C. Bell who married Andrew Gregory died at age 24 (McConnell, *Sänders*, pp. 237-238). James Bell left an extensive will written 15 February 1864, with a codicil added on 21 November 1865. The will was probated 12 February 1866, and sale, appraisal and settlement recorded (Wythe County Will Book 11, pp. 19, 77, 82, 285).

Bralley

John Bralley (Braly, Braley, Brawley, Brally, etc.), Sr., settled on Mine Mill Creek in 1770, where he took up 379 acres of land under the Loyal Company. He appears on William Herbert's list of tithables in 1771, and took the oath of allegiance in 1777. In 1786, he was given permission to build a mill. Some descendants believe he came from County Cork, Ireland, but this has not been proved, although the name with its various spellings are found often in Ireland (Kegley and Kegley, *Early Adventurers*, Vol. 1, pp. 32, 95, 148; Kegley, *Early Adventurers*, Vol 2, p. 105, quoting the Record of Certificates of Commissioners of Washington and Montgomery Counties, 1767-1788, p. 44; Summers, *Annals*, p. 810; for detailed family information and discussion of Irish origins, *see* Edgar M. Bralley's book, *Leabher Clainne O. Brollaigh or The Book of the Clan Bralley*, hereafter cited as Bralley, *Clan*).

In 1788, John Braley served as an appraiser of the estate of George Keesling (Keesler). (Montgomery County Will Book B, p. 130). In 1782, Brawley claimed reimbursement for a bag taken in 1780 by General William Campbell to carry powder during the Revolutionary War (Kegley and Kegley, *Early Adventurers*, Vol. 1, pp. 120, 124).

John Bralley (Brawley) Jr., married Martha Hoge, daughter of James and Elizabeth Howe Hoge, Sr., of Back Creek in present Pulaski County. The marriage took place on November 26, 1792, and was turned in by Daniel Lockett on February 8, 1793 (Montgomery County Marriage Book A, p. 349; for further information about the Hoges of Back Creek, *see* Kegley, *Early Adventurers*, Vol. 2, pp. 294-298).

John Bralley, Sr., died in 1797 (see documentation below) and his will written September 25, 1795 was recorded on March 13, 1798 (Wythe County Will Book 1, p. 97). Inventory of his estate was taken March 8, 1798, and indicated that there were sheep, hogs, a "yoak" of oxen, cows, calves, yearlings, wagons, plow irons, currying knife, carpenter's tools, iron pots a Dutch oven, and pot racks. There was also a quantity of pewter and Delph ware, with table knives and forks, a flax wheel, a check reel, and two little wheels, beds, cotton wheel, loom and slays, sleds, a chest, and four chairs (Wythe County Will Book 1, p. 105). Bralley's widow, mentioned in the will but not named, was to have all land and possessions with stock and household furniture, although the executors Richard Muse and Daniel Lockett were given the authority to rent her part of the land. At her death, the land went to two sons, James and John, equally. The stock and furniture were to be divided between the three daughters Martha, Barbara, and Polly. Martha married Benjamin Rodgers, Jr., James Bralley married Hannah Smythe (daughter of Samuel Smyth), and Barbara Bralley married Joseph Hoge and moved to Tennessee in 1793. Polly Bralley married John Rodgers, brother of Benjamin mentioned above, and John Bralley, Jr., married Martha Hoge as mentioned above (Wythe County Marriage Book 1, p. 18; *see also* Rogers sketch).

In 1816, a declaration was forwarded to the land office stating that John Brally owned 379 acres of land by survey made in 1774, and that he died in 1797 leaving James, John, Martha, Barbara, Mary, and a wife who died in 1815 (Wythe County Order Book, 1815-1820, p. 54). The land survey was recorded in Montgomery County Plat Book A, p. 13, and this tract was granted to James and John Brally, sons and devisees of John Brally (otherwise Braley) on July 3, 1816 (Copy in the hands of descendants. *See also* Kegley and Kegley, *Early Adventurers*, Vol. 1, p. 32).

The children of James Bralley included: Samuel Guy Bralley, John Smythe Bralley, Anselem Bralley, Jonathan Bralley, Louisa Bralley Sanders, Elizabeth and Julia Bralley. James Bralley was married to Rachel, the daughter of James Smyth

John S. Bralley, son of James and Hannah Smyth Bralley was born Jan. 7, 1797 died April 16, 1866 married Jane Ann Carter, daughter of Mitchell and Idress Craig Carter on October 15, 1822. She was born June 28, 1803, and died July 30, 1872. They are buried at Olive Branch Methodist Church. Photos courtesy of Helen Umberger.

Samuel Guy Bralley home near Olive Branch Methodist Church.
Photo made in 1973 by Mary B. Kegley.

(Smith), as mentioned in a power of attorney given to her brother Benjamin in 1805. The son Anselem was married to Susan Hutsel in 1831 and moved to North Carolina. John Bralley, Jr., had ten children, three sons and seven daughters: William, Almarine, James, Elizabeth (married John Catron), Lucinda (married Robert Highley), Eleanor (married James O. Burnes), Nancy (married Thomas Highley), Eliza (married William Nixon), Mary Guy (married William King), and Julia Ann (1817-1853, married James Shaffer). Wythe County Marriage records also show that Elizabeth, daughter of John Bralley, married John Kettering (also known as Catron) in 1815, and Juliana married James Sheffer (Shaffer) in 1834. Almarine moved to South Carolina, and was married to Partha (Martha?) Scruggs, and Mary Pope of S. C. He came to Carroll County, Virginia, in 1866, and married third Mrs. Jane Cash. He died in Carroll County in 1875 (Wythe County Marriage Book 1, pp. 52, 112, 117; Bralley, *Clan*, p.83; Wythe County Will Book 8, p. 278; Wythe County Deed Book 4, p. 234; Wythe County Death Record Book, p.2; information from James C. Spraker).

In 1829, John Brawley sued the widow and heirs at law and the administrator of John Catron's estate. The case grew out of the debts of John Brawley, who was in jail for the same, until his son-in-law John Catron put up bond and security on a note due under a deed of trust. The land was to be sold after Brawley's release from jail. The agreement was that Catron would settle the note and also support two of Brawleys unmarried daughters and Brawley himself in a comfortable manner during his life. In addition, he would give the two daughters a Negro girl. Catron died and Brawley received no deed for the Negro girl (*Brawley vs. Catron*, Box 58, 1835, Wythe County Circuit Court, Basement).

William Carter

William Carter (born November 20 1759) was the son of Captain George and Mary Carter, and is said to have married Unity Bates (April 8, 1754-September 4, 1824) in Wythe County about 1791 (Family Records). No marriage record has been found. Some members of the family believed that Unity was the daughter of Fleming Bates, who was a captain in the Revolutionary War, but no proof appears in the Wythe County records. This seems to be impossible, based on the birth dates, if the Captain Fleming Bates, who was born in 1747, just seven years before Unity, was the same one mentioned as a Virginia Captain in the Revolutionary War (Carter family papers in possession of the author, dated September 22, 1920; *DAR Patriot Index*, p. 43).

In 1791, William Carter purchased 500 acres of land from John Jenkins on the east side of the New River at the place known as Poplar Camp. Two years later, he purchased 215 acres surveyed in 1753, from Francis Preston, agent for the Loyal Company who obtained the grant in 1791. No exact location is given (Wythe County Deed Book 1, p. 174). He also purchased 367 acres on the west side of the New River from William Herbert, Jr. This was the western or northern terminus of the Herbert's Ferry, now known as the Jackson's Ferry (Wythe County Deed Book 1, pp. 19, 172). In 1801, Carter sold the Jenkins tract to Walter Crockett (Wythe County Deed Book 3, p. 79).

In 1808, William and Unity Carter sold 366 3/4 acres of the ferry land to Stephen Sanders, and the remaining 1/4 acre to Jesse Evans, Sr., for his ferry landing. He also helped settle overlapping claims to land on the south side of the river by joining James Newell in a deed to make the correction. They also transferred 333 acres in the same location to James Reddus (Wythe County Deed Book 5, pp. 66, 89, 104, 110).

It was probably about 1808 that William Carter settled on the Cumberland River in Kentucky. He wrote his will in 1847, and it was probated in Wayne County, Kentucky, on November 27, 1848, a short time after his death in September of that year. He mentioned his children: Braxton, Susan Shephard, Milly Dibrell, Mary Bell, deceased, and her children, John Carter, deceased, and his children, and Elizabeth Montgomery, deceased, and her children (Wayne County Will Book, p. 101). Mary or Polly mentioned in the will had been married to James Bell of New River. John Carter married his cousin, Margaret Carter, daughter of Robert and Jane Crockett Carter. A Wayne County history states that Elizabeth was married first to a Crockett, and second to R. Montgomery; Susan was married to John Moore of Monticello, Kentucky; Mildred married Anthony Dibrell of Sparta, Tennessee; Jackson married a Carter cousin (this probably should read John Carter) and his wife was Margaret Carter, daughter of Robert Carter and Jane Crockett) and moved to Tennessee, and where he died in Monroe County, on September 5, 1827. Braxton (1792-1965) married three times--Mary Ewing, Mrs. Burnetta Taylor, and Mrs. Ellen Worshan Chaplin (Johnson, *A Century of Wayne County, Kentucky*, p. 235; Bunce, *Hull-Stephenson...*, pp. 65-67, and Carter sketch).

Jacob Castle

Jacob Castle, one of the earliest adventurers to arrive on the New River in the lead mines neighborhood, is mentioned as an early road-worker in 1746 and again in 1750. He may have been the Jacob Castle who bought land on the Shenandoah from Jacob Stover in 1740 and sold it by 1742 (Chalkley, *Chronicles*, Vol. 1, pp. 23,40; Vol. 3, p. 304).

In 1746, a tract of 180 acres on both sides of the New River was surveyed and sold to Jacob Castle, probably about 1749, the year the entry appears in Patton's notebook (Patton-Preston Notebook; Virginia Historical Society document).

In May 1749, Castle was charged by Adam Harman with "threatening to aid the French." He was acquitted (Chalkley, *Chronicles*, Vol. 1, p. 38). In April 1749, Valentine and Adam Harman were committed for "violent robbery of the goods of Jacob Castlean" (Chalkley, *Chronicles*, Vol. 1, p. 433). The name Castlean is probably a misspelling of the name Castle, and this arrest of the Harmans may have led to the false accusation that Castle was threatening to aid the French.

In 1762, Castle, John Welshire, and Alexander Sayers were appointed to view and value improvements made by John Stanton on two tracts of land on the New River (Chalkley, *Chronicles*, Vol. 1, p. 102). These were the Bingaman's Bottom tract, and Poplar Camp lands later purchased by William Herbert.

Castle entered 100 acres of land between Welshire's and the Great Falls (Foster Falls), but no survey or grant has been found for him at this location (Augusta County Entry Book I).

On June 22, 1764, Jacob Cassall is one of those who withdrew from Augusta County, Virginia, as mentioned in County Court Proceedings (Kegley, *Virginia Frontier*, p. 296).

Jacob Castle is not mentioned on any of the New River tithable lists, but there is a Jacob Castle mentioned in 1782 in Washington County. Traditionally Jacob is said to have been a hunter, and is said to have moved to the frontier and settled in what is now Russell County. Castlewoods in that county is said to be named for him. Numerous undocumented statements have been made about this elusive frontiersman while he was a resident of Montgomery County, but there is no record of him living in Montgomery County. All of his early records are in Augusta County, the county which had jurisdiction over all of Southwest Virginia prior to 1769. It is clear from the land records that he claimed his bit of New River soil in what is now Wythe County and made some kind of an improvement, which was later assigned and included in a survey of 396 acres for Robert Sayers (Montgomery County Surveys)

The Russell County history claims that Jacob Castle had at least two sons, Jacob Castle, Jr., and Joseph. Consequently, other information about a Jacob Castle may pertain to the son and not the father, although that is not clear from the records *(The Heritage of Russell County, 1786-1986,* Vol. 1, p. 5).

In 1815, a tax assessment ticket for Russell County shows that a Jacob Cassle [Castle, Cassell] had a farm on Copper Creek containing 170 acres with a dwelling house of wood, one story, 20 feet by 16 feet, one barn of wood, one stable, one corn house, one loom house, all valued at $425 (Kegley, *Tax Assessments...,* p. 58).

It is also possible that Benjamin Castle, listed on the New River tithables in 1773, may have been from the same family. He died prior to August 5, 1779, when Robert Sayers was granted the administration of his estate, and James Newell, Richard Muse, and John Rutherford were appointed as appraisers. All of these men were residents in the lead mines neighborhood. The reports were returned to the court on September 8, 1779 (Summers, *Annals,* pp. 721, 724).

Bazle (Baswell) Castle

Bazle or Baswell Castle stated that he was the son of Jacob Castle. He was living in Lawrence County, Kentucky, in 1834, when he filed for and received a pension for his service in the Revolutionary War. His declaration was taken on February 2, 1834, when he was 73. He served under Colonel Preston, Captain Lewis, and Lieutenant Robinson in the State of Virginia, from Montgomery County, formerly Fincastle County. The following information is from his pension statement which is filed at the National Archives (S15369).

In April 1779, Bazle Castle began service as an Indian spy, a service for which he was drafted. He served one year in this capacity. He was in no battle during this time because as he stated, ''Indian spies was not so organized as to engage in battles.'' The country through which he marched was at the head of the Holston River and on the Bluestone River that empties into the New River. His first march was to the head of Bluestone, because the Indians had committed several murders in that neighborhood and some on Walkers Creek, and they had taken Jenney Wiley and her children down the Big Sandy River. She afterwards escaped from the Indians. (For full details of this captivity see *Bland County History,* p. 33, as condensed from ''Founding Harman Station'').

In explaining how the Indian spies operated, Castle noted that two of them worked together, taking a certain range and at night they met at an appointed place. The first four months were spent on Bluestone River. In September, the whole company had to march to Fort ''Blackamore,'' a great distance down the Clinch River. The Indians were always most troublesome in the fall of the year. Castle arrived at the fort late in September 1779, and scouted out from that fort until December. During most of December, he stayed within the fort. About the first of February, he and his company marched back to Bluestone, arriving on the head of that river in March 1780. From there he went to ''Fort Chiswel Hill'' (meaning Fort Chiswell) in Montgomery County (now Wythe) and was discharged from duty.

He also noted that in the latter part of that year, his father, Jacob Castle, was away from home under Campbell [William] at the Battle of Kings Mountain, and he, Bazle, remained at home until his father returned in the winter of 1780.

In February 1781, in Montgomery County, he entered the service as a volunteer for six months in the militia of the State Line, under Colonel Sayers, Captain Newell, and Lieutenant McGavock. He left the army in July 1781. He was in the Battle of Reedy Fork of Haw River, the Battle of Guilford in North Carolina and in the skirmish at Whitsel's Mills. He marched through Pittsylvania County and stopped at the Court House. From there he went to the Little Banister River in Halifax County, and at this place his company remained until General Greene retreated into Virginia. From this place he marched to Guilford Court House and from there returned and recrossed the Dan River and came through Pittsylvania County to Campbell County to a place called New London (Bedford County) and then returned to Campbell County Court House. From there he went to Charlottesville at the barracks where the militia was disbanded and he received his discharge.

When General Greene was retreating from Lord Cornwallis and Colonel Tarleton a great number of militia collected and marched to join him on the borders of North Carolina and about the Haw River. The Tories gathered in "great bodies" and a skirmish took place between the American troops and the Tories, and the Tories were defeated, or as Castle stated, "all cut to pieces." Castle marched to the Battle of Guilford and was wounded there, causing him great disability "under which he now labors." The wound was in his arm. Castle added that he had served the whole time in the State Troops of Virginia, and not in the Continental service.

To this pension statement, an affidavit of John Castle, son of Bazle, was added. It stated that his father had died on October 8, 1846, and that he left no widow and that he was then the only living child. At the time of the affidavit (December 29, 1851) John Castle was living in Johnston County, Kentucky (Pension S15369).

John Chiswell

Although John Chiswell was a citizen of Eastern Virginia, he had a great influence on the New River settlements in the lead mines community. His name is still prominent in the eastern end of Wythe County, where the Fort Chiswell community and various businesses carry the name.

John was the only son of Charles Chiswell of Williamsburg. When John was about ten or eleven years old he moved with his parents to Hanover County where Charles claimed land rich in iron ore and soon became an authority in that industry. His mansion house was known as "Scotch Town," later the home of Patrick Henry. Charles Chiswell was Clerk of the General Court of the Colony, and died on April 8, 1737, at Williamsburg (Shephard, "Col. John Chiswell," pp. 3, 7,8).

John Chiswell was married to Elizabeth Randolph, daughter of William Randolph of Turkey Island, in 1737, and became a merchant, planter, and land owner of importance. In addition, he became a member of the House of Burgesses, and part owner of the Raleigh Tavern in Williamsburg (Shephard, "Col. John Chiswell," pp. 12, 15, 16, 27; *Executive Journals,* Vol. 6, 391).

John Chiswell prospected for minerals in several locations in Virginia and this interest brought him to the New River area, probably in the late 1750s, although no exact date is known. According to legend, he was chased by Indians and hid in a cave along the banks of the river, where he discovered the lead deposits. The cave was later called Chiswell's Hole and the discovery was the beginning of more than two hundred years of mining activity in the area. It is a matter of record that on May 6, 1760, he obtained permission to have 1,000 acres surveyed beginning on the south side of the New River adjoining Humberstone Lyons' corner. The survey was made on both sides

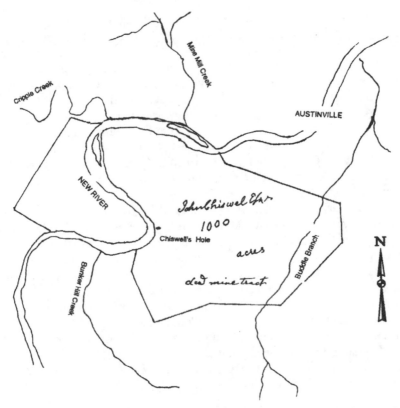

Survey made for John Chiswell, Esqr., for 1,000 acres known as the lead mines tract, completed on October 31, 1760. The land was on both sides of the New River at present Austinville.

Map by Mary B. Kegley.

Chiswell's Hole on the southeast side of the New River at the mines is believed to be the site of the discovery of lead by John Chiswell.

Photo courtesy of the Norfolk and Western Railway Archival Collection, Virginia Polytechnic Institute and State University Library.

of the river on October 31, 1760, at a time when all surveying on the New River had been halted because of the French and Indian War, and because of the claims of the Indians to that territory. The survey was "lodged" in the Land Office on March 27, 1761. In addition, Chiswell claimed through entries 400 acres at the Block House on the east side of the river in November 1760, and five other tracts of 400 acres each on both sides of the river, one in the Reed Island "barrons", and two of them joining Humberston Lyons (Augusta County Survey Book 1, p. 91; Augusta County Entry Book 1, p.44; Chalkley, *Chronicles,* Vol. 2, p. 255; *Executive Journals,* Vol. 6, p. 157).

Sometime in 1760, Chiswell sold to John Robinson (his son-in-law) an interest in numerous mining operations including the lead mines on New River. Robinson in turn sold some of his interest without making a title before his death. Just when William Byrd became a partner is not clear. Robinson died in 1766, and it was soon discovered that many of the most prominent men of Virginia owed him money. Out of £130,000 Robinson owed the Treasury of Virginia £100,000. William Byrd owed him £14,921 and the lead mines owed £8,085 (Hening, *Statutes,* Vol. 8, pp. 270, 272; Tinling, *Correspondence of William Byrd, III,* hereafter *Correspondence,* pp. 610, 611). It appears that the business activities at the mines were carried on solely by Chiswell.

Although it has been stated numerous times by a variety of writers that the work at the lead mines began in 1756 (also 1757 and 1758), the production of lead actually began in 1761, as reported by the Moravians in their diary of 1761. In July 1762, Chiswell, then referred to as "the Virginia Colonel" visited the Moravian settlements at Bethabara and Bethania. He had a small group with him, for "they get their bread or meal from here." There was also a report that silver was being mined, but this proved to be in error. In a Wythe County lawsuit, testimony was given that although work began in 1761, the production of lead was unsuccessful because there was no one in the colonies who knew exactly how to manufacture the lead (Various newspaper accounts give the erroneous dates; Fries, *Records of the Moravians,* Vol. 1, pp. 234, 249; Vol. 3, p. 1054; *see* Bell and Herbert sketches).

As a result of the unsuccessful attempt at producing lead, Colonel John Chiswell sailed to England, found in the City of Bristol men who knew the work, and who were known generally as the Welsh miners. When he returned from England in the summer of 1763, bringing them with him, work at the mines under the supervision of William Herbert, the new superintendent, began again and by mid-summer some lead had been produced *(Herbert vs. Farrell,* included in *Chiswell Judgments,* Box 32, Wythe County Circuit Court, Basement). Sometime during this early period Chiswell's frame house was constructed at or near the mouth of Mine Mill Creek. It was said to be the only frame house on the frontier at that time; others being made of logs (Howe, *Historical Collections of Virginia,* p. 515).

On June 21, 1763, John Chiswell was appointed to serve on the new commission of the peace for Augusta County. Probably he moved to the New River about this time, after his return from England (Chalkley, *Chronicles* Vol. 1, p. 107).

The Moravians at Bethabara reported on November 7, 1763, that "people from the Hollow bought 1,200 lbs. of meal at our mill and started with it to Col. Chiswell on New River." More had been ordered and was ready and waiting for him at the mill. In June 1764, George Loesch bought 300 lbs. of lead from the "Mine on New River" for the store at Bethabara (Fries, *Records of the Moravians,* Vol. 1, pp. 276, 288).

In 1766, en route to his home in Williamsburg, Chiswell stopped at Benjamin Mosby's tavern at Cumberland Court House, Cumberland County, Virginia. Here he engaged in conversation with Robert Routledge, a merchant of Prince Edward County, and others at the tavern. Chiswell called Routledge a "fugitive rebel, a villain who came to Virginia to cheat and defraud men of their property, and a Presbyterian fellow." Routledge, who was then drunk, was provoked to throw wine at Colonel Chiswell's face. In turn Chiswell attempted to throw a bowl of toddy at Routledge but was prevented from doing so by some of those present. He then attempted to throw a candlestick at him, but was prevented in that attempt also. Then he tried to strike him with a pair of tongs, but was again prevented from doing so. He then ordered his servant to bring his sword, which was reluctantly delivered to Chiswell. Several tried to prevent him from reaching Routledge, but they were threatened with the sword, if they came near. Although it was suggested that Mr. Routledge be taken to his room, he did not leave the room, and Chiswell reached across a table in the tavern and stabbed him through the heart. In the process, a Mr. Thompson Swann was so close that the sword passed through his coat before striking Routledge. During the time prior to the murder Chiswell was orally abusing Routledge, and after his death, he continued his abuse and exclaimed, "He deserves his fate, damn him; I aimed at his heart, and I have hit it." Then he called for a bowl of toddy and drank of it freely, so that when the Justice of the Peace arrived, Chiswell was somewhat intoxicated ("Historical and Genealogical Notes," *Tylers Quarterly Magazine*, X, No. 4 (April 1929), p. 289; Purdie's *Gazette*, July 18, 1766, recounts the story and has a map showing the layout of the tavern room where the murder took place).

The court papers of Cumberland County record that John Chiswell was charged with the murder of Robert Routledge on June 3, 1766. A preliminary hearing was held on June 9, 1766, when John Fleming, John Netherland, Thomas Tabb, Carter Henry Harrison, John Mayo, William Smith, and John Woodson, Gentlemen, met for "the examination of John Chiswell who stands committed on suspicion of feloniously murdering Robert Routledge." When Chiswell was charged, he stated that he "was in no wise guilty," and after several witnesses were sworn and examined and Chiswell heard in his own defense, the court decided that John Chiswell ought to be tried before the "honorable general court for the supposed fact and thereupon is remanded to gaol." Eight men, who posted bond in the amount of fifty pounds each, promised to appear at the court in Williamsburg to give evidence in the case. Their names were: Littlebury Mosby, Thompson Swann, Jacob Mosby, James McDowall, Charles Scott, Joseph Carrington, Thomas Vines, and George Fraizer (Cumberland County Order Book 6, 1764-1766, p. 253).

Chiswell was ordered to be delivered to the "keeper of the public prison," but before he reached that place, the judges of the General Court, John Blair, Presley Thornton, and William Byrd, took him from the sheriff and admitted him to bail. This created a public outcry, published in Purdie's *Gazette*. Chiswell left for the mines to tend to his business, but later returned to Williamsburg for the trial. He learned then that John Blair, Jr., an intimate friend, was to conduct the trial. Chiswell was found dead on October 14, 1766, according to the attending physician, from "fits." The conclusion was that he had killed himself at his own house on Francis Street in Williamsburg ("Old Tombs in Gloucester County," *William and Mary Quarterly*, Series 1, Vol. 2, pp. 236, 239; Purdie's *Gazette*, June 20, July 11, July 18, August 22, August 29, October 10, October 17, 1766; Griffith, *Virginia House of Burgesses*, pp. 149-150).

Chiswell had four daughters: Elizabeth who became the wife of Charles Carter; Mary who married Warner Lewis; Susanna, the wife of John Robinson, the Treasurer of Virginia, and second William Griffin; and Lucy who married Col. William Nelson. ("Lewis Family of Warner Hall," *William and Mary Quarterly*, Vol. 9 (1900-1901), n. 4, p. 265; Chalkley, *Chronicles*, Vol. 2, p. 255).

Following the death of Chiswell, some of the local citizens, "certain" that he was not dead, went to the grave and disinterred the body to be sure he was in the grave and not gone to the mines. After his death, which followed the death of John Robinson, Treasurer of Virginia, Speaker of the House, and also a partner in the lead mines, only William Byrd remained as owner of the mines. He was not an active partner and was heavily in debt himself, so could not extricate the lead mines operation from its debt. The large sums borrowed from Robinson, as mentioned above, had to be repaid to the state of Virginia, as the money belonged to the treasury. Consequently for many years the mines were in the hands of the Virginia government until all debt was paid back. Byrd died by his own hand on January 1, 1777, which further complicated the operation of the mines. As the Herberts and others related in their lawsuit, after the death of Chiswell and Robinson the mines were soon closed and Herbert ordered to turn in his tools, house, and other property belonging to the mines (*see also* Herbert sketch; Tinling, *Correspondence*, p. 613).

Walter Crockett

Walter Crockett, known as Colonel Walter Crockett, was the son of Joseph Louis Crockett, Jr., and his wife Jane de Vigné, who settled at Shawsville, Virginia. He was born in the 1730s, the date given as 1732, 1735, and 1737 in various accounts. His brothers included: Hugh, known as Colonel Hugh; Joseph, known as Colonel Joseph; Samuel, known as Major Samuel (the blacksmith); and Robert, who was killed by Indians in 1766. His sisters were: Elizabeth, the wife of William Robertson; Mary, wife of Jacob Kent; Nancy Agnes, wife of Henry Davis; and Martha, wife of Thomas Montgomery (French and Armstrong, *The Crockett Family*, pp. 5,205,256; Augusta County Will Book 3, p. 506).

Walter Crockett's name first appears in the records of Augusta County when he appeared as a witness to John Bowen's will in 1760. A list of Colonel William Christian's Company of Militia shows that Walter Crockett served 151 days and was paid a total of 13 pounds 16 shillings and 10 pence for his service in 1764 (Kegley, *Virginia Frontier,* pp. 290, 366).

Just when he moved to what is now Wythe County is not known, but when his father wrote his will in January [1767], he bequeathed to sons Joseph and Walter Crockett, the plantation where he formerly lived and the plantation adjoining it where Walter was then living. This presumably is the land in Crocketts Cove in Wythe County (Augusta County Will Book 3, p. 506 shows that the will was probated March 17, 1767; Montgomery County Will Book B, p. 116).

Joseph left other lands in the neighborhood, including the survey on Cedar Run above Willeys (now Wytheville), to son Samuel, and he left lands on the head of Peak Creek and the tract on Camp Run above Samuel Montgomery, to his son Robert. To Walter, Joseph, and Robert he devised a tract of land on the head of the Holston, but there is no evidence that the Crocketts ever lived there. In 1773, Walter Crockett released his claim to the lands on the Holston to Allisons and Campbells (Augusta County Will Book 3, p. 506; Montgomery County Deed Book A, p. 31).

In 1769, Walter Crockett was recommended to serve as a justice of the peace for Augusta County, a position he held as each new county was formed--Botetourt (1770), Fincastle (1773), and Montgomery (1777). When Wythe County was formed in 1790, Walter Crockett served as the first Clerk of the Court (Chalkley, *Chronicles,* Vol. 1, p. 158; Summers, *Annals,* pp. 66, 69, 70, 588, 680, 681,1356).

In 1770, a deed was made from William Sayers and his wife Esther Crockett

Sayers, to Walter and Joseph Crockett for 470 acres in the Cove. Joseph Crockett gave his power of attorney to Walter Crockett in 1787, and he conveyed the land to John Crockett in 1797. At that time it was designated as part of a tract where Walter Crockett "now lives. In the same year, Walter and John Crockett were to be added to the order of court, to view the way from New River by head of Peak Creek through the Cove to Kitterings (Catron's) Mill, which stood on the old Stage Road, west of present Wytheville. In 1771, Walter and his wife Margaret sold a tract of 128 acres near the Cove to James Hollis. This is the first time Margaret is mentioned in the records. She was Margaret Steel Caldwell, a widow who married Walter Crockett about 1771 (Summers, *Annals*, pp. 81, 544; Botetourt County Will Book 1, pp. 63,307, French and Armstrong, *Crockett Family*, pp. 205, 256; Montgomery County Will Book B, p. 116; Wythe County Deed Book 2, p. 122).

In 1773, Crockett was given permission to build a mill on vacant land at the Gap of the Cove, adjoining the land he lived on, which "was entered seventeen to eighteen years before with Doctor Walker." Walker was leader and agent for the Loyal Land Company (Summers, *Annals*, p. 592).

On several occasions, Walter Crockett was appointed or chosen to look after orphans in the community. In 1773, he was appointed to direct the "binding out" of Alexander, John, and Mary, orphans of Jane (Jean) Evans. Following the death of William Herbert in 1776, he acted as guardian for Thomas Herbert, releasing his control in 1787. In 1779, he acted as guardian for Robert Wylie, son of James Wylie, deceased (Summers, *Annals*, pp. 591, 726, 803).

Crockett was often appointed to take the list of tithables (taxable persons), in the neighborhood. In 1770, his district extended from Sayers to head of Reed Creek, covering the area from the present Wythe-Pulaski line to the present Wythe-Smyth County line, except the river and Cripple Creek communities, which were covered by William Herbert. In 1771, the men in his own company and Captain Doak's Company were to be listed. In that year, he and John Montgomery were to divide and allot to William and David Sayers the tithables to work on the roads on which they were overseers (Summers, *Annals*, pp. 81, 126, 134, 629, 637). The list for 1771 follows here.

James Ellison	Charles Ellison	Andrew Littel
& his son William	& one slave Judith	George Littel
William Campbell	Robert Campbell	Mathew Little
Alixander Campbell	Gasper Kinder	Adam Walker
George Kinder	& his son Jacob	Arnel Shell
William King	Josiah Ramsey	Fredrick Moore
John King	William Montgomery, Junr.	Robert Breckenridg
John Hownshell	James Davies	James McDannel
Peter Kinder	Magness McDannel	John Alcorn
Philip Kinder	William Sayers & 3 slaves,	John Montgomery
John Messersmith	Harry, Pegg & Agg	John Boyd
Edward Sharp	Walter Kinser	Jacob Kinser
James Hollis & one slave	Jacob Dobler	Nickles Wirick
named Hannah	Alixander Bohanan	John Wirick
John Gillahan	James Hamilton	Martain Stally
Edward Chapman	William Davies	Samuel Montgomery, Sen.
Robert Buchanan	Joseph Buchanan	William Bell
John Miller & son James	David Doack & 3 of his sons	Samuel Crockett

John Kitts
Joseph Crockett
Robert Davies
John Crockett &
one slave named Lew
James Montgomery
James Hays
William Montgomery, Senr.
Henry Wagener
William Phips
Stofel Ketring
Frank Kettring
Adam Kettring
John McNit
John Leaster
Walter Crockett
& one slave Pegg
Jehu Stephens
John Kelley
John Adam
James King
George Dougherty

George Cakley
James Davies
Frederick Edwards
Thomas Bell
Thomas Geather
John Willson
James Addams
Michael Weaver
Thomas Armstrong
Michael Wompler
Job Chapman
John Addams
James Finley, Senr.
James Finley, Jun.
John Diver (Diven?)
James Buchanan
Frances Farmer
Henry Long
Patrick Jonston
John Frederick, miller *
Jacob Kettring &
his servantman

Samuel Davies
Thomas Montgomery
Alexander Willy
Samuel Montgomery, Jun.
Charles Blackley
Ashel Davies
John Willey
Thomas Willson
Adam Bough
Joseph White
William Thomson
Daniel Chapman
Archable McNeel
Jacob Beam
Joseph Montgomery
George Coon
Edward Hamman
George Whillin
David Slone
Samuel Handley
George Harbison

This list contains 111 names and a total of 125 tithables. There are seven slaves, one servant and six sons included in the total. * This name may be John Fredrick Miller.

In 1772, a list of tithables in Captain Doack's and his own company has been preserved in the Botetourt County records and this list also accompanies this sketch.

Adams, John
Alison, John and
his servantman
Blacley, Charles
Buchanan, James and his
brother William and two slaves
Bough, Adam
Chapman, Daniel
Clark, John
Crockett, James
Childers, Stephen
Crow, Thomas
Carr, Walter and his
sons John and William
Doach, David and his sons
Robert, William,
Samuel, and David
Davies, James and
his servant
Davies, Robert and
his servant

Adams, James
Adams, John
Allison, William
Brackenridge, George
Boyd, John
Brackenridg, Robert
Campbell, Alixander and his
servant man James Dooson
Crockett, John
and one slave
Crockett, Samuel
and one slave
Campbell, William
Cline, Nickless
Daughterty, Michael, Sen.
Dunkin, Joseph
Davies, James
Dutinger, Phillip
Davies, William
Ewing, Alixander & his
son James

Alcorn, John
Allison, Robert
Buchanan, Alixander
Buchanan, George
Buchanan, Joseph
Buchanan, Robert
Chapman, Edward
Carr, George
Crockett, Joseph
Campbell, Robert
Crockett, Walter
and one slave
Comfer, Godfret
Davies, Ashel
Daugherty, George
Diven, John
Dobler, Jacob
Davies, Samuel
Davies, William
Eviens, John
Edwardes, Frederick

Ewing, William & his servant
Eviens, William
Fullan, Charles
Finley, James Sener.
Farmer, Frances
Finley, George
Griger, Michael
Finley, James Juner.
Gillihan, John
Haddrel, John
Glaspy, William
Hollis, James & one slave
Harbison, George
Hamelton, Isaiah
Hamelton, Thomas
Johnston, Patrick
Hownshell, John
Hartley, John
Kinder, Jacob'
Keekley, George
Kinder, Gasper
Kinser, Walter
Kinser, Jacob
Kinser, Michael
Keetering, Stophel
Kinder, Peeter, Sener.
Kinder, Peter, Junr.
Kinder, Phillip
Kettering, Jacob
Kettring, Adam
Kettring, Jacob & his servant
King, William
King, John
Littel, Mathew
Kitts, John
Littel, Andrew
McCord, David
Littel, Felty
Littel, George
McDannal, James
Litz, William
McNeal, Archibel
McDannal, Magness
McCown, George
McFarland, John
Mackfarland, Robert and his son James
Mountgomery, John, Sener.
Morison, John
Miller, John
Moore, Moses & his son James
Montgomery, Robert, Juner
Montgomery, John, Juner.
Montgomery, Thomas
Montgomery, Samuel
Moore, Frederick
Miller, James
Montgomery, James
Neely, Alixander
Montgomery, William, Sener.
McNitt, John
Phips, William
Messersmith, Barnabas
Montgomery, William, Juner.
Ramsey, Josiah
Nulan, John
Messersmith, John
Shepler, Coonrodd
Reach, Robert & his sons John and Archabel
Ogullian, Barnaba
Stefer, Michal
Smelser, Jacob
Shell, Arnold
Thomson, William
Staley, Martian
Stephens, Jehu
Wampler, Michel
Vaught, John
Sayers, William & his sons Robert and 2 servants and 2 slaves
Walker, Adam
Waggoner, Henry
Willy, Alixander
Willy, John
Wirick, John
Walraven, John
Wirick, Nicklos
Weaver, Joshua
White, Joseph
Samuel Allison
Peeter Razor
Michael Razor
Samuel Henderson
Andrew Thomson
William Thornton
James King
Frances Kettring
Moses Gordain
George Woath
John Woath

The list includes the residents of Draper's Valley (Frederick Edwards), Crocketts Cove (John Crockett), South Fork of Reed Creek (Nicholas Cline), Black Lick (the Doaks), Fort Chiswell (John Montgomery, Sr.), Pine Run (William Sayers), head of Cripple Creek (William Ewing), and head of Holston (James Davis). There were nine servants and eight slaves listed as well as sons of the head of the household. The total was 183.

The tithable list of 1773 included all men in Crockett's own company, and all on Walkers Creek as low as Rye Bottom. In 1774, the men in his own and Doak's companies were to be listed (Summers, *Annals*, pp. 606,629).

In 1770, Crockett resumed his military career in the county militia of Botetourt County (Summers, *Annals*, p. 74). He was the logical choice to serve as captain, as he had experience under Colonel William Christian. He later held the rank of captain in Fincastle County. In the summer of 1774 when the Indians were causing trouble on the frontier, he and Doak's men were to meet at the Town House (now Chilhowie) in July. On the third, while plans were underway, an order came to draft thirty men from

Crockett's and Doak's companies. On the ninth, one company under Crockett was ordered to range the head of the Clinch and Bluestone rivers. Crockett was ordered to be ready at an hour's notice and to march towards the New River or down the Clinch whichever was needed. On July 12, William Christian reported that Crockett had forty men with him. When Captain Robert Doak died, his men were ordered to go with Crockett. By September, Crockett had marched to Rich Creek (present Giles County) and his company report from Camp Union (at present Lewisburg, West Virginia) indicated that there were in addition to himself, one lieutenant, one ensign, three sergeants, and forty men fit for duty. Two men were sick, one left at Mr. Thompson's on Back Creek in present Pulaski County, and one at Stewart's Fort. There were also five P. H.. (not explained) men and one bowman, and drivers (cattle drivers) for a total of 48 men (Thwaites and Kellogg, *Dunmore's War*, pp. 44, 52, 58, 59, 73, 75, 77, 80, 84, 137, 189).

While Crockett's Company was gone, John Montgomery reported that Michael Daugherty, Ensign, had been ordered to command a party of fifteen men to the Holston. The men were ordered to be taken from Crockett's company, but only five or six could be found as "Chief of the young men are Already gon out" (Thwaites and Kellogg, *Dunmore's War*, p. 224).

The two lists for 1774 for Walter Crockett's Company which follow, were located in the Auditor's Accounts at the Virginia State Library. The lists give the number of days served and the amount of pay received. One list was designated as a company of Rangers and probably included the men who ranged on the head of the Clinch River. The other list may be the list of those who accompanied Crockett to Rich Creek and Camp Union. There is no way to be certain which men actually were at the Battle of Point Pleasant. The days served and the pay received are omitted here, but can be found in the publication, Kegley, *Soldiers of Fincastle County, 1774*, or in the original documents.

Captain Walter Crockatt's Company (Rangers)

Captain Walter Crockatt	Jeremiah Pierce, Lieut.	Andrew Thompson, Ensign
Samuel Ewing, Sergt.	Jno. Wood	Michael Dougherty
Hugh Gullion	Jno. Johnson	Richard Dodge
Jacob Huffman	James Finley	Ashel (Askel?) Davis
Charles Mcfadden	Robert Montgomery	Job Chapman
Edward Davis	Jno. Fowler	Jesse Evans
Jno. Simpson	Jno. Montgomery	James Farland
Walter Kinser	Daniel Henderson	Jacob Kinder
Samuel Handley	Michael Walter	Thomas Bell
Jacob Baugh	David Maxwell	Conrode Shapley
James Kerr	John Reaugh	Frances Kettering
Petter Kettering	Duncan Gullion	Jacob Blesley
Henry Waggoner	Chesley Weaver	Jno. Lesley
Peter Hendrick	Patrick St. Lawrence	Michael Razor
Robert Brackenridge	James Newell	George Forbes
Benja. Price	Charles Cox	Abraham Vanhouser
Joel Beaver	William Saxton	William Stuart
Michael Woods	Richard Muse	Thomas Muse
Samuel Henley	Benja. Rogers	William Rutherford
Jno. Rutherford	Ebeneazer Mead	Valentine Pupp
Joseph Abbot	Aaron Price	Samuel Irvin

Captain Walter Crockat's Company

Most of the men named in this list served 108 days, indicating that perhaps most of them were on the expedition to Pt. Pleasant. Crockett was only paid for 68 days in this list, although on the previous list he was paid for 38 days. The spelling of names in both lists are as written in the originals. Some names appear in both lists.

Capt. Walter Crockat	Jno. Draper, Lieut.	William Buchanan, Ensign
Jno. Wood, Sergt.	Magness McDonald	Jno. Raines
William Montgomery	Joseph Crockat	James Buchanan
Jno. Montgomery	Robert Montgomery	William Cole
Richard Dodge	Job Chapman	Ashel Davis
John Long	Jno. Johnson	Jacob Huffman
Robert Sayer	Charles Mcfadden	Joseph Duncan
Robert Mcfarland	Jno. Cordory	Adam Hance
William Hall	Thomas Gross	Jacob Gross
Jonathan Ingram	Walter Quarles	Frederick Oats
Andrew Stobaugh	Matthew Hayley	Peter Gwinn
Jno. Fowler	Hugh Patrick	Joseph Hughey
Jesse Evans	Joseph Evans	Robert Kerr
Low Browne	William Vardiman	James Scott
Jno. Allison	Thomas Huston	Jno. Miller
Jacob Harman	Joseph Johnson	William Strowder
Josiah Ramsey	Jno. McBridge	Samuel Walker
Edward Davis	Henry Hickey	
Jno. Duncan	James Mcfarland	

On his return from the war in 1774, Crockett was appointed to serve on the first and second Committees of Safety. He was present at several of the meetings held in 1775 and 1776, and was a member of the committee to inspect and receive the powder. He was also part of a special sub-committee for the trial of Jacob Kettering (Catron) who was a Tory. Crockett was one of the fifteen signers of the Fincastle Resolutions on January 20, 1775 (Harwell, *Committees of Safety*, pp. 17,61,78,92).

In the spring of 1776, Peter Carton in his declaration of service, stated that he served with Crockett, ranging on the head of Clinch and Bluestone rivers and on the waters of the Sandy and Gyandotte rivers against the Shawnee Indians. They were not engaged in any battles, but the men were "about naked and suffered much fatigue and hardship" while serving these three months (Pension S15363, Peter Catron, filed in Wayne County, Kentucky, 1833).

In 1776, Crockett was recommended as sheriff, but there is no mention of service. In 1780, he entered security for his position as commissioner of tax. In 1777, he took the oath of allegiance and was appointed to administer the oath in Captain Stephens' and Thompson's companies. In 1779, he was recommended to serve as Lieutenant Colonel of the militia in place of James Robertson who had resigned. The same year, the new site for the courthouse was being considered for Montgomery County. He made an offer of land for the site, but James McGavock's Fort Chiswell land was chosen (Summers, *Annals*, pp. 648, 681, 682, 690, 722, 736). In 1778, Crockett served at the Virginia Convention. He served in the House of Representatives in 1777, 1778, 1779, and 1789 (Leonard, *General Assembly*, pp. 126, 130, 134, 173, 176).

In 1779 and 1780, Crockett was known as Major Walter Crockett and was involved with the Tory activities on the New River (*see* Tories in Kegley, *Early Adventurers*, 1, pp. 137-151). In 1779, William Campbell and Walter Crockett and others involved with the Tory insurrections on the frontier, especially in Washington County, took measures not strictly warranted by law, to suppress the conspiracy. Campbell, Crockett, and all others involved were exonerated of and "from all pains, penalties, prosecutions, actions, suits, and damages on account thereof," and if sued or prosecuted could use this Act of the Assembly passed in October 1779 as evidence (Hening, *Statutes*, Vol. 10, p. 195).

After the War was over, Crockett received a land grant in 1784 for 1,000 acres of land in Jefferson County, Kentucky. The land was kept by Crockett until about 1811 when it was sold for taxes by his brother Joseph, who was then living in Jessamine County, Kentucky (French and Armstrong, *Crockett Family*, p. 584).

In 1786, Crockett was recommended to serve as county lieutenant and took the oath of office. He resigned the position in 1790, probably about the time he became Clerk of the Wythe County Court (Summers, *Annals*, pp. 813, 819, 830).

Walter Crockett was appointed Clerk of Wythe County and posted bond on May 25, 1790. It was signed by Crockett, James McGavock, Js. [James] Newell, and D. McGavock.

Tracing excerpted from Crockett's bond by Mary Kegley.

In 1788, Walter and his brother Joseph conveyed by deed 120 acres in the Crocketts Cove to William Sayers and his wife Esther. As mentioned above, his other lands in the Cove were sold jointly with his brother Joseph to John Crockett (Summers, *Annals*, p.919).

When an academy was established in 1792 in Evansham (now Wytheville), Walter Crockett was one of the trustees. He contributed £20 and Jesse Evans contributed £30 for the construction of the academy. These two gentlemen gave approximately half of all of the contributions (Kegley, *Bicentennial History*, p. 136).

It is not clear exactly when Crockett moved to the lead mines-Poplar Camp neighborhood, but it was before June 1797, when Walter Crockett, Thomas Foster, George Carter, and Thomas Brooks were ordered by the Wythe County Court to view

Home of Walter Crockett at Poplar Camp.
Photo courtesy of the F. B. Kegley Collection.

the way for altering the highway between William Carter's and John Miller's on the "high road to Evan's Ferry." This order would place him in the vicinity of the Evans' (Jackson's) Ferry. His deed to land on the New River was dated in 1801. This was the same tract formerly owned by John Jenkins which was sold to William Carter in 1791 (Wythe County Order Book 1796-1799, p. 84; Wythe County Deed Book 3, p. 79).

Colonel Walter Crockett wrote his will on January 1, 1807, and it was probated December 10, 1811. The land where he was living (at Poplar Camp) and several Negroes were to go to his son Samuel. Daughters Jane and Kitty, were to receive certain Negroes. Son Samuel Crockett, with Joseph Crockett and Joseph Kent were to act as executors. Witnesses to the will were Joseph Potts, Joseph McGavock, and James McGavock (Wythe County Will Book 2, p. 171).

Samuel Crockett, son of Walter, sold his share of the estate in 1811 to David Peirce. The land passed into the hands of Peirce's daughter Elizabeth Chaffin, and eventually to Arthur Jackson. Samuel married Elizabeth Carter of the James River Carter family. They had a large family and moved to Kentucky (Wythe County Deed Book 5, p.387; French and Armstrong, *Crockett Family*, p. 258).

Jane or Jean Crockett (b. 1772, d. 1844), daughter of Walter, married Robert Carter in 1790. Her husband Robert died about 1801 in Wythe County. Three children survived: Margaret, wife of John Carter (son of William and Unity Bates Carter); George (the ancestor of George L. Carter) who married Elizabeth Calfee; and Mary (Polly) who married William Sayers and moved to Kentucky. The children are mentioned in the division of the Negroes belonging to the estate. Kitty or Katherine Crockett married William Sayers, a grandson of Colonel John T. Sayers (Montgomery County Marriages; Kegley, *Early Adventurers,* Vol. 2, p. 148; French and Armstrong, *Crockett Family,* pp. 258,259; Wythe County Will Books 1, p. 183; Book 2, p. 120).

Charles Devereaux

Charles Devereaux (Deverex, Deverix, Deborax, Devrox, Divereux, etc.) first appears in the records of the New River in 1771, when his name is on a tithable list. However, he immigrated to Virginia with William Herbert and his family under a contract with John Chiswell in 1763. He was hired to work with Herbert at the lead mines, and no doubt was an experienced miner in or near Bristol, England, the point of emigration to Virginia (Kegley, *Tithables*, p.12; *W. Herbert vs. Joseph Farrel*, Box 32, *Chiswell, Judgments*, May Term, 1827, Wythe County Circuit Court Clerk's Office, Basement).

In 1772 and 1773, his name appears again on tithable lists, and in 1773, he was granted a license to keep an ordinary at his house in Fincastle County, apparently in the vicinity of the lead mines (Kegley, *Tithables*, pp. 17,31; Summers, *Annals*, p. 595).

In 1774, Charles Campbell suggested to William Preston that more lead would be needed and that perhaps Charles Devereaux and Evan Williams could furnish a supply. He implied that if they were to get some assistance from the country it would be cheaper than sending to Warwick (Thwaites and Kellogg, *Dunmore's War*, p. 211, quoting Draper Manuscripts, 3QQ105).

In the same year, Devereaux appeared in court twice because of debts, and in 1775 acknowledged a deed of trust to William and James Donald & Company, merchants. Some of his personal property was mortgaged in 1775. The items included Negroes: Anthony, Peter, Flora, June, and Dina, 25 head of cattle, 50 head of hogs, 18 head of sheep, one wagon and harness, all of the plantation utensils, three beds with furniture, all other household furniture, eight pewter dishes, two dozen pewter plates, copper tea kettle, copper coffee pot, two China salts, tin ware, six iron pots, and a still and all of its utensils (Summers, *Annals*, pp. 628,634,636,669; Fincastle/Montgomery County Deed Book A, p. 88).

On March 3, 1774, Devereaux was in court on a trespassing charge brought by Peter Pinkley (Fincastle County Order Book 1, pp. 29, 54, 89). On May 6, 1774, John Cockersham brought an action against Devereaux for trespassing and assault and battery and in February 1775, Alexander Baine brought two debt actions against Devereaux (Fincastle County Order Book 2, pp. 87, 114)

During the time of the Committee of Safety for Fincastle County, Devereaux was one of those who provided lead for the American cause, acting for the benefit of the local Committee. He was also employed to carry some of the lead to Manchester (Richmond), in 1776 (Harwell, *Committees of Safety*, pp. 71,77,82,93).

In 1776, Devereaux was overseer of the road from the lead mines into the "big road" below Michael Daughterty's and in 1778 was again appointed overseer from the same location to Evan Williams'. Joseph Barren was to be overseer from there to the forks of the road at Michael Daugherty's new house (Summers, *Annals*, pp. 650, 604).

In 1777, Devereaux was one of the jury members for the trial of Lawrence Buckholder, who was tried on suspicion of being an enemy of the county. In 1780, Devereaux found himself in a similar situation. He was to face trial as a Tory, and his wife Nancy, being very apprehensive that justice would not be done, "there being a misunderstanding between Colonel [Charles] Lynch and the Welsh people" requested Preston to send for Devereaux so that his trial could be held at Price's which is located in present Montgomery County, near Blacksburg. There is no record to show whether that was done (Summers, *Annals*, p. 684; Draper Manuscripts, 5QQ58).

Devereaux's name appears on John Montgomery's list of 1777 having taken the Oath of Allegiance to the State of Virginia (Kegley, *Militia*, p. 54).

In 1782, Devereaux produced proof to the court that he ought to be paid £12 for one bay horse, four years old, fourteen hands high, a bed, and pack saddle lost in the expedition against the Cherokees in 1776. He also claimed 10 shillings for one day "waggoning" (Summers, *Annals*, p. 770).

In 1784, he had 400 acres surveyed on the west side of the New River adjoining

George Forbus and the land sold by Forbus to William Herbert, deceased. This is probably where Devereaux lived. He received no grant and the survey was assigned to James Newell who sold it to Robert Sanders in 1785 (Montgomery County Plat Book C, p. 207; Summers, *Annals,* p. 917). There is no further record of Devereaux on the New River after this date.

There is no record of any Devereaux children in the New River records, with the possible exception of a John Deboreaux who was sued by James Rodgers at the same time an action on "the case" was brought against Charles Deboreaux (Fincastle County Order Book 2, p. 17, May 3, 1774).

Jesse Evans

Jesse Evans is usually associated with the Town of Evansham, the community named for him and presently known as Wytheville. However, he had large land holdings in some of the best locations in the county, and because he owned the plantation now known as the Jackson place at the shot tower in the Poplar Camp community, he is included in this section of the history.

Evans' origins have been stated in different ways. Some believe he came from South Carolina to what is now Wythe County prior to the Revolutionary War; other accounts state he was born in Maryland and came from Pennsylvania to Virginia. The WPA biographical sketch of Evans states he came from Abbeville, South Carolina, and that is why the county seat of Wythe was first known as Abbeville. However, no documentation has been found for either statement. There is however, some circumstantial evidence to support his location as Abbeville. He purchased 322 acres and 159 acres of land from John Montgomery, who acted as attorney for Patrick Calhoun, Esq., who was a resident of Abbeville. This reference, of course, could be the reason his origins were given as South Carolina (Obituary from *Western Christian Advocate,* Wisconsin Historical Society, 16E67, hereafter cited as *Advocate;* WPA Papers, Wytheville Community College).

He was born some time in the 1750s, dates given as 1755 and 1759 (*Advocate* gives the date "about the year 1755 record lost"; Pension Record from Wisconsin Historical Society, 100157-159 says 1759; *see also,* Pension) The first time the name Jesse Evans is documented in the records of Southwest Virginia, is in 1774 when the name appears on two lists of soldiers under the command of Captain Walter Crockett. Evans served 38 days and was paid £2 and 17 shillings and served 108 days and was paid £8 and 2 shillings, for his service (Kegley, *Soldiers,* pp. 28, 30). If he was born in 1755, he would have been about 19 years old at this time of service, but if in fact he was born in 1759, he would only have been a boy of 15 years.

There is some evidence that there may have been another Jesse Evans in Southwest Virginia, although this military association with Crockett and the men of his company, places him in the present Wythe County area. There is a brief undocumented record which states that a Jesse Evans settled on the North Fork of the Clinch River in 1772, but there is no known connection, if any, to Jesse of Wythe County (Summers, *Annals,* p. 1431). In 1782, a Jesse Evans made an entry of 400 acres in Wrights Valley on the head of the North Fork of the Clinch River, but three years later the records show that he had "given up" his claim to Captain Moore (Kegley, *Early Adventurers,* Vol. 2, pp. 46, 102, citing entry and Commissioner's records.)

In March 1778, Evans was appointed by the Montgomery County Court to serve as a lieutenant of the local militia. In the same year, he was commissioned a captain in the Illinois Regiment, and marched to the Boat Yard on the Holston River where he met George Rogers Clark. He proceeded to Kaskaskia with Clark and moved on to Vincennes (Summers, *Annals*, p.688; Pension).

Following this, Evans and others were sent into the recruiting service which brought him back to Virginia, North Carolina, and South Carolina. While in North Carolina, he volunteered and fought at the Race Paths on the Haw River. He was also at the Battle of Guilford Court House. Following the battle, he and his new recruits set out to join the old regiment, but they were overtaken at Wolf Hills [now Abingdon], then an uninhabited wilderness, where they were ordered to disband because the Revolutionary War had ended (Pension).

In November 1780, Evans is again mentioned in Montgomery County records, when he was ordered to purchase fifty pounds of pork and a barrel of corn from Fort Chiswell to distribute to the wives and families of two soldiers in the service of the state. These soldiers were John Beard and Richard Gullock (Summers, *Annals*, p. 746).

In 1783, Evans had a survey made for 75 acres on Cove Creek, and a year later he received the grant from the state. The entry was made in 1782. He may have lived on this tract at this time (Kegley, *Early Adventurers*, Vol. 2, p. 46; Wythe County Deed Book 1, p. 67).

In. 1787, Evans took the oath as deputy sheriff of Montgomery County and in 1790, when Wythe County was formed, he was recommended as a justice of the peace, a position he held until 1815 (Wythe County Order Book, May 26, 1790 and September 12, 1815; Summers, *Annals*, p. 1357).

No exact date for his marriage to Elizabeth Breckenridge has been found, but when her father, George Breckenridge, wrote his will on May 3, 1790, he devised a tract of land containing 15-18 acres on Cove Creek to his daughter Elizabeth Evans, and Jesse Evans was one of the executors (Wythe County Will Book 1, p. 1). Elizabeth is believed to have been born about 1751 in Albemarle County, Virginia, the daughter of George and Ann Doak Breckenridge (family records).

The county seat of Wythe County was laid off very shortly after the formation of the county, and although lots were sold and the town began to develop, there is no record to show what early name it was given, other than Wythe Court House. It was a common Virginia practice to name the town in that way. However, in October 1792, the General Assembly approved the incorporation of the town under the name Evansham, named for Jesse Evans, one of the trustees (Hening, *Statutes*, Vol. 13, p. 593).

About this time, Evans was also instrumental in the formation and construction of the academy located in Evansham. He and Walter Crockett gave more than half of the total cost of construction and served as trustees (Kegley, *Bicentennial History*, pp. 136-138; Hening, *Statutes*, Vol. 13, pp. 583, 590-591).

Alexander Smyth and Jesse Evans were appointed to contract for the construction of the Wythe County Clerk's Office in 1797, and in 1799, Evans and John Montgomery were recommended as coroners for the county (Summers, *Annals*, pp. 1362,1373). Evans was elected to the Legislature of Virginia in 1782, representing Montgomery County, and in 1793 and 1794, representing Wythe County (Leonard, *General Assembly*, pp. 146, 193, 197).

Beginning in 1793, by entry and survey, Evans claimed additional land. There was a tract of 176 acres on Cove Creek corner to John McFarland and Philip Reeder, and his own patent land; 1,000 acres on Cove Creek, corner to Walter Crockett [who had land at the Gap of the Cove], 255 acres on Reed Creek corner to John Davis, 20 acres on a branch of Reed Creek, corner to Stophel Zimmerman and Armbrister, and 150 acres, corner to the Bowling Green survey and Friel's land (Wythe County Survey Book 1, pp. 148, 265, 475, 489; Book 3, p. 47).

In 1795, when Evans received the deed to the Bowling Green lands from Patrick Calhoun, Esq., of Abbeville, S.C., Evans was living on the place. The deed transferred two tracts, one for 322 acres on Cove Creek, and the other 159 acres on Tates Run, a branch of Cove Creek. He also purchased 106 acres from Hugh and Euphemia Montgomery, which was patented to Hugh Montgomery, deceased, and was formerly the residence of John Noble, who had married Patrick Calhoun's sister. This tract was devised by Montgomery to his daughter Jean the wife of Samuel Cowan, and transferred to Hugh and Euphemia Montgomery in 1795 (Wythe County Deed Book 1, pp. 268, 272, 273, 274; Rowan County, North Carolina Will Book E, p. 41).

Evans purchased the tract of 1,000 acres on the New River from Thomas Herbert for £2,500 in 1811. Most of the land was located on the south side of the river, but he also obtained the title to the land on the north side following a lawsuit (Wythe County Deed Book 6, p. 255; Book 1A, p. 9; Washington County Deed Book 2, p. 245; Summers, *Annals*, p. 1337; Wythe County Order Book, June 11, 1811).

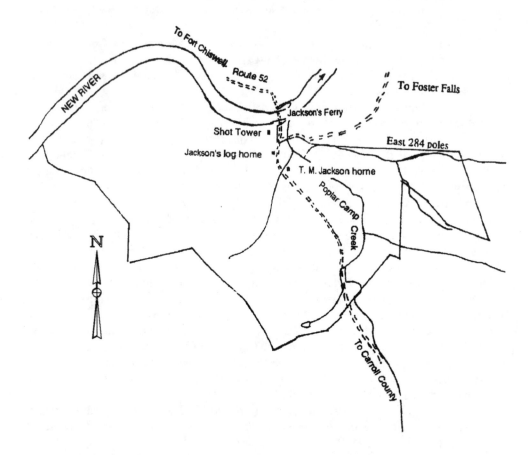

This map was prepared from Deed Book 6, pp. 255-256 showing 1,000 acres of land conveyed by Thomas and Sarah Herbert to Jesse Evans, Senr., in 1811. In 1815 the property was sold to Thomas Jackson who built the shot tower on the premises. Much of the land today is in the hands of the descendants of the brother of Thomas Jackson.

Map by Mary B. Kegley.

On June 9, 1813, Samuel Folks was appointed to be overseer of the road from Evans' Forge to Poplar Camp Furnace. The exact location and who operated the Evans' Forge has not been determined. In January 1814, Evans, owner of the public ferry, was granted a license to keep an ordinary near his house at the ferry (Wythe County Order Book, 1812-1815, pp. 54, 142).

Evans had a claim to the Helvey place located below the present Town of Wytheville. Following a lawsuit, his interests were conveyed to Robert Crockett, who also became the owner of the Bowling Green farm. This came as a result of a judgment obtained by the Treasurer of the Commonwealth of Virginia against Jesse Evans and Walter Crockett for £10,000 debt and court costs, dischargeable by paying $900.40 and costs. The sheriff levied against Evans' lands in the Cove and at the sale Jospeh Barrow bought the land and then conveyed it to Robert Crockett (Wythe County Deed Book 3, p. 16; Book 4, p. 408; Book 6, pp. 217, 219; Chalkley, *Chronicles*, Vol. 2, p. 89).

The Bowling Green land was later owned by Robert's son, Charles L. Crockett, and still later, it was owned by Lieutenant Governor R. C. Kent. The ferry farm was sold to the Jackson's in 1815, for ''$11,000 in current silver coin or $12,000 in bank notes from the Bank of Virginia or Farmers Bank or both.'' The mill seat was excluded as it had been sold to Thomas Blair, who sold it to David Peirce. The deed to the mill was made directly to Peirce (Wythe County Deed Book 6, pp. 293,313). Thomas Jackson and his brother's descendants operated a ferry there until the 1930s when it was replaced by a bridge. Much of the land in the Poplar Camp neighborhood is still owned by the Jacksons.

In 1815, when Evans was ready to leave Virginia, the Wythe County Court certified that he had represented the county ''thrice in the Legislature of Virginia, and hath filled the offices of Sheriff, Coroner, and Major in the Militia of the Commonwealth and has been a Justice of the Peace for many years'' (Wythe County Order Book, 1815-1820, p. 13).

Elizabeth Breckenridge Evans, wife of Jesse, died on June 7, 1815, in Virginia (family records). Evans and many of his family moved to Callaway County, Missouri, and in his journal he noted on September 28, 1815 ''this day, Jesse Evans moved from New River to Saint Charles on the Missouri.'' He first lived in Callaway County, but in 1828 moved to Gasconade County, about twelve miles from the city of Jefferson, and was living there when he filed his claim for a pension for service in the Revolutionary War. He was allowed $480 per annum beginning on March 4, 1831 (Pension).

In 1834, Jesse Evans, Sr., conveyed by deed for love, good will, and affection towards Joseph, James S. and Jesse R. Evans of Washington County, Missouri, his claim to bounty land and all money due in that connection. The deed was recorded in Herman, Missouri (Deed Book A, pp. 201-202).

There were several Evans marriages in Wythe County. Ann Evans and James McCampbell obtained a license signed by John Montgomery, Esq., on December 17, 1795. The McCampbells were living in Tennessee in 1812. John Evans was married on January 28, 1802 to Sally Newell. Jane Evans married Thomas Farmer sometime between 1800 and 1805 (no exact date given). Joseph Evans married Betsy Smith on March 14, 1811. Nancy Evans married George King February 4, 1813. Sarah Evans married Andrew K. Bell on January 14, 1829, and Joseph Evans's marriage bond with Scarlett Dougherty was dated May 18, 1839, for marriage with Polly Dougherty, the daughter of Scarlett. Jesse Evans, Jr., was married to Joanna, the daughter of Philip Reeder (Wythe County Marriage Book 1, 9, 26, 45, 96, 21, 44, 142; Wythe County

Deed Book 5 pp. 360, 440, 441, 442, 443).

Jesse Evans and his wife Elizabeth had ten children: John, Jesse, Jr., Ann, Joseph, Jane, Betsy or Elizabeth, Lettie, Nancy, George W., and James. Most of the children are mentioned in his will, which was recorded in O'Sage County, Missouri (Will Book, p. 34).

When Evans wrote an extensive will on November 11, 1841, he owned three slaves, Peter, Charity, and Elizabeth, who were given their freedom and received 40 acres of land jointly, as well as certain items of livestock and furniture. He also gave them the right to live out their lives in the houses where they were then living, and when the last of the three died, the land was to be sold and the money divided among his grandchildren, Jennie Farmer, Nancy King, and the children of John Evans, deceased. He provided for his children and grandchildren. He died on July 28, 1843 (Osage County Will Book, p. 43; family records).

It is not often that we have a physical description of an early pioneer gentleman, but Jesse Farmer, grandson, described his grandfather as a short thick-set man weighing 200 pounds in his old age. He recalled that his eyes were dark gray (Draper Mss 22 S229).

Joseph Evans was a lawyer, and a colonel in the War of 1812. He also served in the Virginia Legislature in 1810-1811, before moving to Missouri (Leonard, *General Assembly*, p. 263; *Goodspeeds Diary, Washington County, Missouri*, p. 985). Joseph and his son James were living at the lead mines near Cote Sans Dessein, Missouri in the 1860s. Although it is only circumstantial evidence, there may be some connection with the Wythe County lead mines by some members of this family before they moved to Missouri, and the lead mines there (family records; Draper Mss., 22S229).

Following Evans' death in 1843, the *Western Christian Advoca*te published a detailed obituary written by L. Waugh of O'Sage County, Missouri. Excerpts follow here:

> *"Major Evans was born in Maryland about the year 1755 (record lost); removed when young, with his father, to South Carolina, and again to Western Virginia, when about twenty years of age. ...He removed to Missouri and located himself at Cotesandes Seine [sic] in an early day of the settling of the state; and only removed from there to the opposite side of the Missouri River, where, in his own log cabin on the 28th of July 1843, he died in peace."*

> *"For sociality, charitableness, and genuine love of country, Major Evans was rarely, if at all surpassed. His amiableness of disposition, and firmness of principle, secured him confidence and friends wherever he was known. As a pioneer and a soldier, he endured and suffered much. ...He had a certain spot on a hill near his dwelling, to which he resorted for private prayer as long as he was able to walk. There, he told me himself, he had often sweet communion with his God.... And I always observed that when prayer was to be attended to in the family, he was particularly desirous to have all the servants come in. I have often heard him repeat two or three times, 'Tell them all to come in.' And no man ever died more lamented by his servants than he: three he left free."*

> *"Father Evans was remarkably fond of religious company; and in his house Methodist preachers always found a welcome home and a hearty friend. He was indeed liberal in the support of the Gospel. He had an abiding aversion to idleness and intemperance, and often advanced useful and impressive remarks in relation to both....He had united with the Methodist Episcopal Church."*

Evans is buried in Osage County at a location recently re-discovered by Ralph Bryant, a family researcher from Fort Collins, Colorado. The traditional site was said to be about two miles below the junction of the Missouri and Osage rivers, on the Evans farm. After considerable investigation and with the help of many local citizens, it was learned that the original junction of the river was changed in the 1930s when a levee was built as a WPA project. The property was owned by Donald Boyce in the 1990s, and there were two cemeteries located there, one of them overlooking the river. The one where Evans is said to be buried is in poor condition and no stone was found. Research continues (Ralph Bryant correspondence; Kegley, "New Evidence Uncovered on Grave of Jesse Evans," *Southwest Virginia Enterprise,* November 11, 1992).

Evans is relatively unknown in Wythe County, but his name is perpetuated in the Evansham Chapters of certain organizations and the Evansham Shopping Mall in Wytheville. He was an outstanding leader in the community and properly deserved recognition in his lifetime. Twenty-four years after he moved to Missouri, the town officials obtained a new charter and the name was changed to Wytheville. Evans' descendants have been to Wythe County to explore the town named for their ancestor.

George Forbush

George Forbus (also Forbes, Forbis, Forbess, Forbish), of New River, appears to have been the son-in-law of Nathaniel Welshire, also an early settler on the New River. He may be the same George Forbush who appears in the Augusta County records as early as September 1746. At that time it was noted that he was living in Orange County, Virginia, as of August 18, 1743 (Chalkley, *Chronicles,* Vol. 1, p. 294).

In 1747, a lawsuit was brought against a George Forbush and his wife Olive. In 1748, Forbush served as an appraiser for two estates, and in the same year he and his wife Olive sold land to John Miller on Beaver Dam Run (Chalkley, *Chronicles,* Vol. 1, pp. 33,35; Vol. 2, pp. 10, 269). About this time they disappear from the Augusta County records.

Ramsey in his book suggests that a George Forbush of Rowan County, North Carolina, spent time in Lancaster County, Pennsylvania, as early as 1735, and also in the "back parts" of Prince Georges County, Maryland, four years later. His daughter Mary married Morgan Bryan. Forbush moved to North Carolina in the fall of 1748, and settled on the west or south bank of the Yadkin two miles north of the shallow ford (Ramsey, *Carolina Cradle,* pp. 33-34). This may or may not be the same man who was on New River, although his strong connection to the Welshire, family both in Virginia and North Carolina, suggests that it is so (*see* Welshire sketch).

In 1766, a George Forbush was appointed to act as an appraiser of the estate of Robert Andrews, who was living on New River. Forbush probably moved to the New River about that time (Chalkley, *Chronicles,* Vol. 1, p. 130; Vol. 2, p. 102).

In 1771 and 1772, Forbush is listed on William Herbert's tithable list, and in 1773, on Montgomery's list. In 1773 and 1774, he served on the jury in Fincastle County. In 1774, he served with Captain Walter Crockett's Militia Company a total of 13 days and was paid 19 shillings 6 pence for his service (Kegley, *Tithables,* pp. 12,17, 31; Kegley, *Soldiers,* p. 29; Fincastle County Order Books 1, p. 101; Book 2, pp. 11, 81, 86, 88; Summers, *Annals,* pp. 610, 629).

In 1773, when William Herbert received the license for his ordinary, it was located at "the place where Forbush formerly lived" (Summers, *Annals,* p. 620; Fincastle County Order Book 1, p. 146). The following year, Forbush took up 235 acres by survey on Little Reed Island Creek (Montgomery County Plat Book A, p. 95).

When Nathaniel Welshire died, Forbush acted as one of the executors in 1777 and settled the estate in 1782 (Montgomery County Deed and Wills Book B, p. 32; Summers, *Annals,* pp. 677, 758). In 1778, Forbush received the deed for the 680 acres of the Welshire place from the executors of James Patton, being the same land noted as ''Wilshire's place'' in the original survey of 1749 (Montgomery County Deed Book A, pp. 228,229).

In 1780, during the Revolutionary War, several confessions were obtained from and about the Tories. In Peter Kinder's confession, he reported that Roger Oats told him that ''George Forbush was in the club.'' There is no record of action taken against Forbush for his Tory sentiments (Preston Papers, Virginia State Library, Archives.

In 1795, George Forbush, Nathaniel Forbush, and Nathaniel Buchanan (also heirs of Welshire) conveyed 410 acres of the Welshire land to Moses Austin. This land later came to the Sanders family, after Austin left the community. The remainder of the Welshire tract was sold by George Forbuss and his wife Margaret (notice it is not Olive as mentioned in the earlier deeds) to Robert Sanders in 1793. The entire estate remained in the hands of the Sanders for many years, and in more recent years was owned by the Cornetts and Rapers (Wythe County Deed Book 1, p. 159; Book 2, pp. 264, 265, 413).

George Forbush disappears from the New River settlements about this time, and nothing else is known of his whereabouts. An affidavit filed in 1820 states that Forbush and his wife ''reside out of the Commonwealth'' (*Herbert vs. Farrell* included in *Chiswell, Judgments,* Box 32, 1827, Wythe County Circuit Court Clerk's Office, Basement). The only others with the same surname that appear in the New River area are a John and Andrew Forbush, who are listed in the Wythe County Tax List of 1800. Both are over 16 and owned horses, John three and Andrew one (Yantis, *1800 Tax Lists,* p. 10). John Forbuss had 400 acres on the dividing ridge between Little Reed Island Creek and Crooked Creek, in present Carroll County. The land was entered in 1782, and 367 acres were surveyed in 1783. The grant was issued for 367 acres in 1785 (Alderman, *Carroll,* p. 260). Nothing else is known about John or Andrew.

In 1796, Moses Austin stopped in Stanford, Kentucky, and mentioned that there were several former residents of the New River living there, including Nathaniel Forbus (Garrison, ed., ''A Memorandum....'', *American Historical Review,* Vol. 5, pp. 518-542).

Thomas Foster

Thomas Foster, for whom Foster Falls of New River is named, was in that neighborhood as early as 1772 when he was listed among the tithables of William Herbert. He appears on Montgomery's list of tithables in 1773. In the same year, he served as overseer of the road from Herbert's Ferry to the forks of the road beyond the Boiling Spring, probably near the present Fish Hatchery (Kegley, *Tithables,* pp. 18,31; Summers, *Annals,* p. 613).

He served on the jury at least three times, 1773, 1778, and 1781. In 1777, he was a witness to the will of his neighbor, Nathaniel Welshire (Summers, *Annals,* pp. 620, 698, 752, 943).

In 1779, Foster was recommended as a first lieutenant in Captain Pearce's militia company, and in 1781 was serving in that capacity. He also appears on the list of Stephen Sanders' Company (Summers, *Annals,* p.715; Kegley, *Militia,* pp. 37, 40).

Foster served in the French and Indian War, and petitioned the Montgomery County Court in 1780 claiming that as a soldier he had never received any land for his service. Under the Proclamation of 1763, he was entitled to a military warrant, which was issued in 1780 for 50 acres. He had a survey of 41 acres made based on this warrant.

Foster Falls on the New River.   Photo by Mary B. Kegley.

The land was located on the east side of the New River (Summers, *Annals,* p. 738; Montgomery County Plat Book D, p. 521).

In 1797, he purchased 86 acres on the east side of the New River below the mouth of Poplar Camp from James Montgomery. This land was an early selection made by James Patton in 1751. In 1799, Foster added 306 acres from Thomas Herbert and his wife, Sarah. The land adjoined Brooks, Evans, his own land, and others (Wythe County Deed Book 2, pp. 269, 339).

On May 3, 1808, Thomas Foster, Senr., wrote his will, which was probated May 9, 1809 (Wythe County Will Book 1, p. 436). To his four sons, Thomas, John, James, and Samuel and to his daughter Sarah, jointly, he left his plantation where "I now live," containing 470 acres. His wife, Elizabeth, was to have a life interest, and after her death the place was to be divided so that James and Samuel would have that part adjoining the dwelling house, and Thomas was to have that part adjoining lands bought from James Newell. After the death of Elizabeth, the executors were to pay his son, William, for a horse valued at $100. James and Samuel were each to have a feather bed, and sons John and Thomas were to be executors.

There is no inventory of the estate recorded. His widow and heirs sold the plantation in 1811 to William Sanders and wife Polly, and to James Bell and his wife, who in turn sold it to David Peirce. The land then became part of a large inclusive survey of 2,100 acres made for William Peirce in 1854. It was on this land that the Foster Falls Mining and Manufacturing Company operated in the 1880s and where the furnace, depot, hotel, and other buildings were located in the village of Foster Falls (Wythe County Survey Book 4, p. 192; Wythe County Deed Book 7, pp. 133, 385; Book 30, p. 200; Book 34, p. 224).

The inclusive survey of 2,100 acres also included grants to Joseph Fulks, conveyances from Joseph Burr to David Peirce, and some of the shares of the heirs of the David Peirce estate conveyed to William Peirce. The land stretched from the mouth of Poplar Camp Creek at Jacksons Ferry to Bakers Island, and included the Foster Falls Mountain, which is sometimes referred to as the Roaring Falls Mountain (Wythe County Survey Book 4, p. 192).

Early entries for Jacob Castle in 1762, John Bingaman in 1762, and Charles Campbell in 1763, mention the "Great Falls of New River," the earliest name for Foster Falls. In the 1880s, the falls were often referred to as Pearces (Peirces) Falls, because Peirce then owned the land (Augusta County Entry Book 1; Wythe County Deed Book 30, p. 200).

269

Nathaniel Frisbie

Nathaniel Frisbie probably arrived in Wythe County about the time of its formation in 1790, as he was named a justice of the peace in that year. He is again mentioned in 1798 and as late as 1805 and possibly later (Summers, *Annals,* pp. 1357, 1367; Wythe County Order Book 1796-1799, p. 202; Order Book 1801-1805, p. 544).

Frisbie's first purchase of land was made in 1791, when he bought 214 acres of land on the east side of the New River from Robert Sayers. It was located near the "River Hill" in the lead mines community. Frisbie was associated with the Austins, and served as manager of the mines for them. He was probably the co-owner of the store with Austin: the court record shows that Thomas Bratton was charged with breaking open "the store house of Frisbie and Austin" and taking goods valued at £150 (Wythe County Deed Book 1, pp. 20, 195; *see Calendar,* February 25, 1790, Vol. 5, p. 119; Kegley, *Bicentennial History,* p. 302; Wythe County Minute or Order Book 1790 [also 1791], March 1, 1791, p. 51).

In December 1792, Frisbie was living across the county line in Grayson County, and was recommended to serve as a justice for the new county (*Calendar,* Vol. 6, *p.* 184).

In 1794, Frisbie, and the Austins (Stephen and his brother Moses) purchased 850 acres from James Newell. The land adjoined Robert and Samuel Porter, and William Bell. Two years later, Frisbie added 250 acres from George and Mary Carter. Part of this tract was located in Grayson County and part in Wythe County and adjoined the lead mines tract. It was also designated as the tract where Mary Ginkins (Jenkins) was then living (Wythe County Deed Book 1, pp. 195, 373).

In the early part of 1800, Frisbie was among the members of the Wythe Fraternal Lodge No, 55, a group organized in 1798 (Kegley, *Bicentennial History,* p. 109).

On November 10, 1813, Nathaniel Frisbie was appointed to serve as surveyor of the road from the lead mines ferry to the Poplar Camp Furnace, replacing James Reddus (Wythe County Order Book 1812-1815, p. 117).

Frisbie wrote his will on May 23, 1823, with a codicil on August 19, 1823. The will was probated in Wythe County on November 11, 1823 (Will Book 3, p. 38). To his daughter Sary (Sarah, also called Sally) Carter who married Thompson Carter in 1809, he left a Negro girl and boy for her own separate and private use, to dispose of as she wished without any control of her husband. Frisbie explained further as follows: "And whereas he has left his wife more than seven years since and hath treated her extremely ill and has done everything in his power to irque me, it is my will he shall never have any part of my estate." In addition to the Negroes, Sarah was to have one-half of the balance of his real and personal estate. Frisbie's daughter Catherine Thornbrugh (Thornborough) also received a Negro wench and her children, and the other half of the rest of the estate, both real and personal. Catherine had married William Thornbrugh in 1812 (Wythe County Marriage Book 1, p.45).

In the codicil to the will, Nathaniel mentioned his sister Thankful Frisbie, and a bequest of $100 in four yearly installments. His sister then lived in Norfolk, Litchfield County, Connecticut. To his grandson, Nathaniel Frisbie Carter, he left a silver watch.

Doubts arose regarding whether the will, as first written, could effectively prevent Thompson Carter from exercising acts of ownership over part of the estate devised to Sarah. The codicil stated that her share was to be held in trust by friends, Andrew Kincannon of Wythe County, and Eley Cook a merchant of Grayson County. Catherine died after the will was written, and in the codicil instructions were given that her share was to be divided between her children, when grandson Henry Thornbrugh became of age. Two granddaughters, Sarah and Susannah, were each to have a feather bed and bedstead, clothing and "furniture belonging to the same." Son-in-law William Thornborough was to receive the benefits from the estate until Henry was of age.

The inventory of Nathaniel Frisbie's estate was recorded and dated March 24, 1824. Among the items listed were the following: colts, mares, hogs, ox cart, still, hay stack, "gigg," harness, clock and case, looking glass, waggon, sheep, harrow, ploughs, a wheat fan, 8 still tubs, wheat, flax, oats, scythes, hoes, shovel ploughs, scythe and cradle, mattock, shovel and pick, axes, copper kettle, grindstone, bridle and saddle, two "heaps of potatoes," pots and ovens, a loom, nine Negroes, 5 more still tubs, barrels, kegs, saddle bags, two guns, a gun lock, hackle, smoothing iron, bits, pincers, plane, a silver watch, a pair of steelyards, augers, chisels, saw, candle stand, beds and bed clothes, a real [reel], table, pair of scales and weights, "frows," 50 barrels of corn, 11 "fatning hogs," 15 other hogs, two beef hides, one horse hide and five more sheep (Wythe County Will Book 3, p. 61).

Sally Frisbie Carter filed a petition with the General Assembly on November 16, 1816, requesting a divorce (Wythe County Legislative Petitions, Virginia State Library, Archives). She stated that she was married in October 1810, but the marriage records show the marriage bond was dated October 19, 1809, and that the marriage took place on October 26. She and her husband, Thompson Carter, lived together for over three years, and she had two children. Her chief complaint about her husband was that he was "very improvident, given to intoxication and idleness: and at times she was left destitute." Finally in 1813, Carter abandoned her, leaving her to live with her father, Nathaniel Frisbie.

Several prominent citizens of Wythe County gave evidence in the case, including Alexander Smyth, Thomas Smyth, Nathaniel Frisbie, Esqr., George Oury, John Evans, Esqr., Catherine Thornburg, Sally Evans, William New, and John Ginkins [Jenkins]. From their statements, it was revealed that Carter promised to join Frisbie in a store, promising to put up the sum of $1,500 when in fact he was worth nothing. Carter lived in Frisbie's house for a short time, but later moved to a rented house about a mile distant. It was during this time that he left Sally without any firewood or comfortable provisions. They returned to the Frisbie home, but Carter later left. On numerous occasions, warrants were served on Carter and all of his property was sold either by himself or the sheriff to pay his debts. Carter drank "spiritous liquors to excess and was extremely idle," and prior to his leaving "he was scarcely sober for one day." Carter had also indicated he would use every means possible to prevent Sally from obtaining a divorce, even though he never intended to live with her again. George Oury and John Evans, Esqr., both testified that Carter's general character was that of a lazy, drunken, lying man. John Jenkins stated that he had seen an advertisement on the door of Jackson and Sanders store and another at the blacksmith shop, in which Carter forewarned all persons who might trust or harbor his wife. Carter also had wanted Jenkins to set another such advertisement at the store door. In spite of all this evidence, Sally's divorce petition was rejected.

In spite of rejection in Virginia, after Sally (Sarah) Carter moved to Hawkins County, Tennessee, and established the required residency of one year, she applied for a divorce from her husband Thompson Carter in that place on November 7, 1825, and it was granted in December 1826 (copy of the case filed in *Peirce vs. Thornburg*, Box 49, 1832, packet R-Z, Wythe County Circuit Court Clerk's Office, Basement). She repeated the allegation that her husband was "addicted to intoxication" and said that she had two children after four years of marriage, and then he abandoned her and had not provided for the children, except on one occasion when "to vex the petitioner" he took away one of the children and kept the child six months. Her husband remained in Wythe County and did not appear in the court hearing. Witnesses, John A. Rogers, Jacob Miller and Joseph Wallen all testified as to Sarah's excellent character and that she had one child, a son, to whom she was "giving a good education." They confirmed Sarah's statements about her husband saying he was "a worthless dissipated man," who had spent his time "around still houses, grog shops, and houses of ill fame" in Wythe County. He had not lived with Sarah for the past ten years, and during that time one of the witnesses testified that he knew Carter had "the foul disorder" and had heard Thompson Carter say he had it many times.

In 1830, Sally (Sarah) Carter transferred all of her share of her father's estate, including all "improvements in possession of Samuel Rickey, tenant on October 31, 1827," to David Peirce. This was the same tract conveyed to Peirce by Sarah's trustees (Wythe County Deed Book 11, p. 530).

Peirce filed suit in 1831 against William Thornburg (various spellings), reciting the will of Nathaniel Frisbie, and the fact that Sarah Carter and Catherine Thornburg, daughters of Frisbie, inherited his land. Sarah's share had already been obtained by Peirce, and because Catherine died before her father, her share was left to the children with the right of enjoyment and profits to her husband. Peirce claimed Thornburg occupied the whole tract and appropriated the profits for his own use. Peirce wanted the land partitioned and compensation for profits. The case also had as defendants, the Thornburg children: Franklin B., Henry, Sarah Ann, Augustus, and Susannah (Susan), none of whom were 21 years old. Franklin, Sarah Ann, and Susannah (Susan) were not inhabitants of Virginia at the time of the suit. Thornburg denied occupying the tract belonging to Peirce, stating the land was rented and he and Sarah Carter divided the rent. When Peirce bought Sarah's part, he refused to pay the rent. Thornburg had the right to occupy the house until Henry was of "full age," and at the time of the suit, he was between 15 and 16 years of age. William grew crops, made a new fence (6,100 new rails), and put up 1,600 panels of fence to enclose the whole tract.. He made repairs to the barn in the amount of $100, and claimed that if rent were allowed to Peirce, then he should be allowed for making repairs. The tract was divided giving Peirce 206 acres and the heirs of Catherine Thornburg 197 1/2 acres.

William Thornbrough and a wife named Catherine (apparently a second wife, as the first Catherine was deceased when Frisbie wrote his will), who owned the other half of the Frisbie homeplace were living in Grundy County, Missouri, in 1845 when the deed was drawn up. In this deed, William states that he married daughter of Nathaniel Frisbie, and by her had six children, three of whom were deceased, and that the son Franklin B., sold his interest in 1834 at age 21 to James Bell, that the two other sons Henry and William had died intestate and without issue. Their interests were being conveyed to William Willis in 1845 (Wythe County Deed Book 16, p. 753; Wythe County Deed Book 13, p. 666).

Franklin was stabbed to death by Pearson Pickett on May 6, 1834. Pickett was sentenced to two years in the penitentiary on May 6, 1834 (*Commonwealth vs. Pickett*, Indictments, Box 54, 1834, Wythe County Circuit Court, Basement).

Catherine Thornbrough (apparently the widow of William) appointed Samuel Rickey her attorney to recover any and all land she was entitled to in Wythe, Carroll, or Grayson counties in Virginia. She was living in Grundy County, Missouri, in 1850, when the power of attorney was prepared. Rickey had been a tenant on the land (Wythe County Deed Book 11, p. 530; Book 18, p. 272).

Augustus Thornbrugh, as attorney for Robert J. Smith and his wife Susanna

Thornbrugh Smith, of Ray County, Missouri, sold their interest to James Bell in 1845. Augustus transferred his own share to Bell in 1842 . He states he has an interest in the land of his grandfather Nathaniel Frisbie (Wythe County Deed Book 16, pp. 80, 81, 761, 772).

Catherine Thornburgh sold her lot, assigned to her in a lawsuit (not seen) to James Bell in 1854. Four years later, Bell also received 30 acres which had been assigned to Henry Thornbrugh of Fort Lewis, Missouri (Wythe County Deed Books 18, p. 272; Book 20, p. 122; Book 21, p. 164).

The only other Frisbie mentioned in the local records is Luther, who wrote his will on January 7, 1824. It was probated on June 8, 1824 (Wythe County Will Book 3, p. 67). He left $500 to James Freeman, son of Nancy Freeman, to be left in the hands of Andrew Kincannon. Nancy was to have $12 a year until James was age fifteen. The money was to be used to give James an education. Luther mentioned his parents, David and Polly Frisbie of Norfolk, Connecticut, to whom he left $500. The balance of his estate was to be divided between Calvin Frisbey, David Frisbey, Jr., Ireney Hawley, Polly Frisby, and Miriam Homes. Nathaniel Carter was to have his silver watch. George Kincannon and Stephen Ketring were to act as executors.

On December 14, 1824, David Frisbie, Jr., of Norfolk, Connecticut, was appointed attorney for Earl T. Hawley and his wife, Irene, and for Polly Frisbie, all of Norfolk, Connecticut, and also for William Holmes and his wife Maranda of Winchester, Connecticut, who were to receive their shares in the estate of Martin Luther Frisbie. John C. Frisbie of Home, Cortland County, New York, also appointed David Frisbie, Jr., to act as his attorney in fact for the same purpose (Wythe County Deed Book 10, pp. 22, 24).

William Herbert Family

William Herbert, Sr., son of David, Sr., and Martha Herbert, was probably born in the 1730s. The date given in the family Bible is March 9, 1733, although other descendants claimed 1731 in a former DAR application. He may have been born in or near Bristol, England, but that is uncertain. However, he did marry in England on December 18, 1758, in the County of Gloucester, Diocese of Bristol. His marriage bond is dated December 13 in that year, with bondsman Phillip Tummy. His wife was Sarah Fry, and both were of the St. Philip & Jacob Parish. Witness on the marriage bond was Samuel Kindon. The bond states that Herbert was a ''smelt refiner of silver,'' and Tummy was a ''smith & farrier.'' (Bible record from typescript, original not seen; DAR application of Blanch Neal McDaniel; *DAR Patriot Index* gives March 9, 1733; Marriage Register 1755-1758, St. Philip & Jacob Parish; Bristol Marriage License Bond, copy in possession of the author, courtesy of Henrietta Herbert Cragon).

There have been numerous claims that this William Herbert first settled in Dinwiddie County, Virginia. It is likely that there is another line of Herberts in that county, as in the 1790 census of Virginia there are several Herberts mentioned as heads of families, and among them a William. It is clear, however, that the Herberts of the New River came directly from Bristol, England, as verified by documents mentioned below. There has also been a tradition that William Herbert, Sr., married Lady Humphries, nee Fry, en route to America. The Bristol marriage record refers to Sarah as a spinster and with the surname Fry, and it seems clear that this is the record for William Herbert of New River. There is some evidence that it was William Herbert, Jr., (more later) who married Polly Humphries, and perhaps that is where the confusion exists.

KNOW all Men

by these Presents, That We *William Herbert of the Parish of St. Philip & Jacob in the County of Gloucester & Diocese of Bristol* and *Philip Tumy* are held and firmly bound unto the Right Reverend Father in GOD *Philip* ————— by Divine Permission, Lord Bishop of *Bristol* ————— in the Sum of *one* Pounds of good and lawful Money of Great-Britain, to be paid to the said Reverend Father, or his certain Attorney, Executors, Administrators, Successors or Assigns: For which Payment well and truly to be made, We bind ourselves and every of us, jointly and severally, for and in the whole, our Heirs, Executors and Administrators, and every of them, firmly by these Presents. Sealed with our Seals, Dated the ——— *Thirteenth* Day of *December* in the *Thirty Second* Year of the Reign of our Sovereign *Lord George the Second* — by the Grace of GOD, King of Great-Britain, France and Ireland, Defender of the Faith, and so forth, and in the Year of our LORD, One Thousand Seven Hundred and

Fifty eight

THE CONDITION of this Obligation is such, That if hereafter there shall not appear any lawful Lett or Impediment, by Reason of any Pre-Contract, entered into before the Twenty-fifth Day of March, in the Year of our LORD One Thousand Seven Hundred and Fifty-four, Consanguinity, Affinity, or any other legal Cause whatsoever, but that the above-bounden *William Herbert & Sarah Fry of the Parish aforesaid Spinster* ——————

may lawfully solemnize Marriage together, And in the same, afterwards lawfully remain and continue for Man and Wife, according to the Laws in that Behalf provided. And moreover, if there be not at this Time any Action, Suit, Plaint, Quarrel, or Demand, moving or depending before any Judge, Ecclesiastical or Temporal, for or concerning any such Lett or Impediment between the said Parties. And if it shall not appear that either of them be of any other Parish, or of any better Estate or Degree than to the Judge at the granting of the Licence is suggested and by the said *William Herbert* ——————— sworn to

And if the said Marriage shall be openly solemnized in the *Parish Church of St. Philip & Jacob aforesaid* in the Licence specified between the Hours appointed, in the Constitutions Ecclesiastical confirmed, and according to the Form of the Book of Common-Prayer now by Law established. And lastly, if the above-bounden *William Herbert & Philip Tumy* ——————— do save harmless and keep indemnified the above-mentioned Right Reverend Father, his Vicar-General, and all other his Officers and Ministers whatsoever by Reason of the Premises, Then this Obligation shall be void, or else remain in full Force and Virtue.

William Herbert

sealed and ... in the Presence of

Marriage record of William Herbert and Sarah Fry, Bristol Diocese, England. Copy courtesy of Henrietta Herbert Cragon.

The baptismal register (1758-1774) of St. Philip & Jacob, Bristol, shows that the first child of the Herberts was born on August 19, 1759, but was born dead. The second child Joanna, was born September 16, 1762, when the family lived on Avon Street, a location in the heart of the city of Bristol, England, not far from the present shot tower. It is possible that this Joanna Herbert, born in September was the same one mentioned in the Burial Register, but this is not clear as her age is not given. The burial date was December 17, 1762. The Herbert children who lived to maturity were a Joanna, Martha, William, Jr., and Thomas.

On April 20, 1763, William Herbert made an agreement with Colonel John Chiswell, on behalf of partners John Robinson and William Byrd, to proceed to the Colony of Virginia by a vessel provided by Chiswell, from the port of Bristol with his wife and her "maid servant." Beginning on April 20, 1763, Herbert was to serve a seven year term of employment at the rate of a yearly salary of £130 sterling. In addition, Chiswell was to provide Herbert with a "good and convenient dwelling house for his station with convenient out houses for the use of his cattle and twenty acres of good pasture ground." If Herbert "should be minded to quit" and return to Bristol, England, Chiswell agreed to pay for the return of Herbert and his wife and her maid as well as any child or children they might have. This return could take place after a three year period of service and written notice (Deposition of William Herbert, *Herbert vs. Ferrell* , lawsuit included in *Chiswell, Judgments,* Box 32, May Term 1827, Wythe County Circuit Court Clerk's Office, Basement, hereinafter referred to as *Chiswell,* Judgments).

In this agreement, Herbert indicated that he was to act as ''manager or conductor'' of their ''works for smelting and refining ores and metals in the sd. colony to which art or mystery your orator [Herbert] had been regularly brought up.'' Herbert remained in the service of Chiswell at the lead mines until Chiswell's death in October 1766, and under the direction of his executors until June 21, 1767. At that time he was asked to return all tools and property of the mines and to give up his house and the land he had been using. The executors appointed one _____Gist (first name not given) to serve as manager of the mines. When Herbert applied to the executors to transport him back to Bristol, according to the terms of the agreement, they refused. The reason the suit was filed was to claim his wages then due (William Herbert Deposition, *Chiswell, Judgments).*

Charles Lynch, a later superintendent of the mines, paid the Herberts and their connection their wages, and then made a claim against Chiswell's estate and the partnership. Further evidence (uncorroborated and not accepted by the Court) in the lawsuit accused Herbert of operating a trading post when he was supposed to be tending the mines. In addition, there was an allegation that he was extracting silver from the mines for his own use *(Chiswell, Judgments).*

The lawsuit also refers to the others brought from Bristol to work for Chiswell. They were David Herbert, Sr. (William's father), David Herbert, Jr., (William's brother), and John Jenkins (William's brother-in-law who had married his sister Mary). Also included were Roger Oates (Ottes), Charles Devereaux, and Evan Williams and ''sundry others,'' not named. The men as a group were referred to as the Welsh miners, although they were hired in Bristol, England. The Mendip Hills west of Bristol, coal mines, and other mining activities in and near Bristol apparently brought the miners across the Bristol Channel from Wales (*Chiswell,* Judgments).

On March 6, 1764, Herbert wrote to William Byrd, one of the partners at the mines, and the address he used was ''The Wilsh Mines.'' Generally, the mines were, referred to as Chiswell's or Chisel's mines. The letter thanked Byrd for sending the Negroes, and was followed by Herbert's opinion of the mines, which he described as ''the aparance of the vain of the surfuis is such as I never had seen before all tho I have seen most mines of note in His Majestys Uropean dominions.'' He also expressed his concern in regard to the fact that many of the settlers were gone from their places, or were preparing to leave, and without ''any hopes of retourning any more,'' because of the Royal Proclamation of 1763 (Tinling, *Correspondence,* Vol. 1, p. 768). For further information about the Proclamation of 1763, *see* Kegley and Kegley, *Early Adventurers, Vol. 1).*

On January 10, 1765, William Herbert, designated as superintendent of the mines on New River, went to the Moravian settlement at Bethabra, North Carolina, because he had a swelling over his whole body and needed to see the doctor. There was no suitable lodging for him for so long a treatment, and he was advised to return in the spring ''when the weather was good'' (Fries, *Records of the Moravians,* Vol. 1, p. 307).

In 1766, Herbert acted as the administrator of the estate of Robert Andrew(s) (Chalkley, *Chronicles,* Vol. 1, pp. 130,465; Augusta County Will Book 1, p. 477). The next year he purchased his first land from Richard Stanton and his wife Charity. This tract was 460 acres at Poplar Camp, formerly owned by Thomas Stanton,Sr., a tract granted to John Bingaman in 1753 (Augusta County Deed Book 14, p. 424). In 1769,

Herbert was recommended as a justice of the peace for Augusta County (Chalkley, *Chronicles*, Vol. 1, p. 158). In the same year, he was listed as a representative of Boiling Springs Presbyterian Congregation, a church located in the vicinity of the boiling spring on the north side of Reed Creek near Graham's Forge (Wilson, *Tinkling Spring*, p. 171).

When the new County of Botetourt was formed, he was recommended as justice of the peace in 1770 and received the appointment (Summers, *Annals*, pp. 66, 69). The same year he purchased from Richard Stanton items of personal property (Botetourt County Deed Book 1, p. 142), including the following: a "Mallato" Negro man named Will; 12 head of cattle; 16 head of hogs, horses, mares, and colts; feather bed, "rugg" and blankets, one cattail bed; spinning wheel, large chest, table; pewter "bassons," pewter dishes, plates and spoons; brass "kittle," half dozen knives and forks, iron pots, a looking glass, a "riffle" gun, a crop of about ten "akers of Indian corn now in the ground," an ax, and pepper mill."

He presented to the Botetourt County Court, a captain's commission in the militia and took the usual oaths at the same time he took the oath as justice of the peace, and justice of the County Court in Chancery and justice of Oyer and Terminer. He was sued in Botetourt County Court by Cissilia Andrews for "Freedom Dues," and although the case was continued, a certificate of her freedom was granted to her. She was apparently an indentured servant, perhaps a relative of Robert Andrews mentioned above. From the records, it might appear that *Sissel* Andrews was the same person, and if so, she and Alexander McGee were brought to court for cohabiting and she for having a "base born" child. In 1771, William Herbert brought suit against Cisilla Andrews and he was to recover the sum of £300 besides his costs from her. No details of the suit are given (Summers, *Annals*, pp. 66, 69, 78, 79, 93, 110). Could she have been the "maid servant" of Sarah Herbert mentioned above?

On May 10, 1770, William Herbert was ordered to take the list of tithables on the New River and "waters thereof" on both sides, as high as Sayers. In June 1771, he took the list for his own company, and in 1773, John Montgomery took the list in Herbert's Company (Summers, *Annals*, pp. 82, 126, 606) The surviving lists for 1771 (which contains 123 names and a total of 156 tithables from Herbert's neighborhood) and for 1772 follow here.

List Of Tithables In My Company, William Herbert, 1771

Wells Ward	James Ward	Robert Osborn
William Hash	William Landrop	George Jones
William Jones	Moses Damron	Joseph Wallin
John Haynes ?	Moses Johnson	Neall Roberts ?
Elisah Wallin	Robert Baker	John Coxs
Francis Gilly	William Little	Jonathan Osborn
Cashin Fulsher	William Cox	John Couch
Richard Harman	Richard Wigging	Samuel Steel
Marchel Dunkam	Samuel Edmonston	Henry Gouger
William Banks	Nathaniel Banks	Jacob Atkins
William Bobbet	George Yeates (?)	John Richardson
Jonathan Jenings	Benjamin Ray	David Sayers
John Sayers	Andrew Stott	James Bell
Jeremiah Dutton	John Buchanan	Nathaniel Buchanan
Nathaniel Welsher	Alexander McKee	Benjamin Price

Abraham Price
William Perce
Evan Williams
Peter Pinkly
George Ewings
Joseph Rutherford
George Henley
William Robinson
Roger Ottes
George Forbush
James Newell, Jr.
John Retherford, Ser.
William Daniels
James Bebber, Ser.
William Sanston
Moses Clark (?Elarth?)
Joseph Hughey
William Herbert
Ezekel Yong
Moses Smith
Enoch Osborn
Vinson Jones
Charles Sanston
Jeremiah Harrison
James McDaniel
Kernelius Keith
James Watkins

William Haynes
John Jenkins
William Rogers
Samuel Ewings
William Retherford
William Henley, Sr.
Henry Francis
John Braly
Charles Devrox
Joseph Dunkin (?)
John Rogers, Ser.
John Retherford, Jr.
Michel Farmar
Thomas Hobbs
James Bebber, Jr.
Robert Elasom
Felty Pup
Barkly Green
Edward King
Beverly Watkins
Josiah Wever
John Collins
McCheger Bunch
Hugh Smith
George Keith
George Heard
John Rice

Jeremiah Perce
William Bell
James Rogers
James Ewings
Benjamin Retherford
William Henley, Jr.
Luck Woods
Thomas Fowler
Frances Copper
John Baxster
John Rogers, Jr.
Joseph Packston
William Love (?)
John Cardeman
Joseph Bebber
Henry Sordther (?)
James Thomson
James Procktor
Dutton Sweeting
George Reeves
Charles Collins
Samuel Collins
Moses Beker
Doswell Rogers
Ellott Buchanan
Joseph Massey

List Of W. Herbert, 1772

Abraham Price
Benjamin Price
Benjamin Rogers
Charles Collins
Cashen Fulsher
David Sayers
David Cocks
Enoch Osburn
Frances Hill
George Forbush
George Collins
George Jones
James Bebber, Senr.
John Braly
John Jenkins
James Ward
James Bell
Jonathan Jennings
Jonathan Richardson
John Retherford, Jun.

Andrew Stott
Barkley Green
Beverly Watkins
Charles Sanston
Charles Cocke
Dutton Sweeting
Evan Williams
Elisah Wallin
Felty Pup
George Ewings
George Keeth
George Watkins
James Bebber, Junr.
John Backster
John Husk
John Buchanan
James Cockes
Jeremiah Peirce
John Cardiman
Joseph Retherford

Alexander McKee
Benjamin Ray
Charles Devrox
Cornelius Keeth
Cornelous Deforest
Dossvill Rogers
Ezekiel Young
Efrom Osborn
Frances Gilly
George Reeves
George Heard
Hugh Smith
Joyel Benner
John Rogers
Jonas Griffith
Jeremiah Dutton
John Forbush
John Richardson
John Retherford, Ser.
James Newell

James Thomson
Isaac Wever
James McDaniel
John Rice
James Blevins
John McKee
Moses Price
Marchel Duncan
Moses Johnson
Nathiel Wilcher
Peter Binkly
Robert Steel
Stephen Osborn, Sr.
Stephen Harlin (?)
Thomas Hobbes
Thomas Davis
William Bell
William Sanston
William Henson
William Henly, Jr.
William Landrath
William Banks

James Ewings
John Collins
Joseph Massey
John Cocks
Jospeh Wallin
Joseph Houghey
Michel Farmar
McCager Bunch
Morgan Murry
Nathaniel Buchanan
Robert Elsom
Samuel Ewings
Stephen Osborn, Jr.
Thomas Ogle
Thomas Foster
Vinson Jones
Wells Ward
William Banks
William Bobbet
William Rogers
William Jones
William Roberts

James Rogers
Jeremiah Harrison
James Wallin
Jonathan Osborn
John Haynes
Luck Woods
Michel Woods
Moses Damron
Neall Roberts
Nathanel Banks
Roger Ottes
Samuel Collins
Samuel Steel
Thomas Ray
Thomas Little
Valentine Vanhouser
William Gleves
William Peirce
William Henly, Sr.
William Dencom
William Cocks
William Herbert

All had one tithable, except Beverly Watkins 2, Charles Devrox 3, Cornelous Keeth 2, Evan Williams 2, Enoch Osburn 2, George Ewing 6, George Reeves 2, Jonathan Jennings 5, John Collins 4, John Cocke, 3, Thomas Ogle 3, Val. Vanhouser 4, William Herbert 6.

In October 1770, Herbert added 184 acres (the Bingaman's Bottom Tract) on New River by purchase from Thomas Stanton and his wife Charity, of Orange County, North Carolina (Botetourt County Deed Book 1, pp. 219,220). He also made a settlement on Cubb Creek in Washington County, on waste and unappropriated land and occupied it until 1776 when his overseer, Richard Elsom, was killed by Indians. Elsom and his wife Rachel and his father-in-law, William Hays, had gone to the Clinch and settled on the land at a certain spring. In 1772, Herbert brought a stock of cattle to Hays Creek and Elsom came with them to take care of them (Chalkley, *Chronicles*, Vol. 2, pp. 74-75 quoting lawsuit, *Simon Cockrell vs. John Duncan*, O.S. 35 N.S. 12, filed May, 1796). The plantation on the Clinch was mentioned in Herbert's will and devised to his son William, Jr. The stock on the Clinch was to be divided the spring of 1777, according to articles of agreement drawn up for that purpose, "the shee kind" on shares for the benefit of the children and all the "he kind" sold for the same purpose. It is not clear how much time Herbert actually spent on the Clinch River settlement in the six years prior to his death (Fincastle-Montgomery County Will Book B, p. 31).

The exact date of the establishment of the ferry on the New River is not recorded, but the Herbert's Ferry was in operation prior to February 14, 1770. At that time, Herbert was appointed to be surveyor of the road from his ferry to the forks of the road and from his house to the Pittsylvania line. At the same time, Jeremiah Pierce was to be surveyor from Herbert's Mill to the mouth of Big Reed Island Creek (Summers, *Annals*, pp. 63, 612, 613).

When Fincastle County was formed, Herbert was again recommended to serve as a justice of the peace. A recommendation came from the Fincastle County Court to the Governor and Council, but an unnamed member of the board represented him as a "man of bad character". A recommendation was to come from Botetourt County where he served in that capacity, to the Governor of Virginia stating that he had served "with propriety and to the general satisfaction of the county." Although he served in Botetourt County, the area covered by that county at that time included the New River settlements. His recommendation was rejected (Summers, *Annals,* pp. 165, 597; *Executive Journals*, Vol. 6, p. 549).

In 1773, Herbert was appointed overseer of the road from his ferry to the head of Poplar Camp Creek, and Thomas Foster was to serve from the ferry to the forks of the road beyond the Boiling Spring. Felty Vanhouser was to be overseer of the road from the head of Poplar Camp Creek to the Pittsylvania line, and Captain Herbert was to lay off the hands between Francis (probably Henry Francis) and George Ewin (Summers, *Annals,* pp. 612,613).

With the ferry in operation and many people on the move, after the Indian problems were settled, it seemed fitting that Herbert, located at a strategic river crossing, would apply for an ordinary license. He did this on November 3, 1773, and the location was given as "where George Forbush formerly lived" (Summers, *Annals,* p. 620). In 1774, 213 acres of land opposite Poplar Camp on the north side of the river were taken up by survey (Summers, *Annals,* p. 662).

The old English derivation of the name Herbert means a soldier who was famous in battle. It seemed logical that William Herbert should also take up the sword. Already a leader of the county militia, he was well prepared to lead his men in Dunmore's War in 1774. He was among the first to be asked to draft fifty men from his company for service against the Indians. They were to join Captain Smith at his station near the head of the Clinch. Following the death of Captain Robert Doak, the men of that company were asked to go under Herbert, but none would do so, and as a result the men were assigned to Crockett and Campbell's companies. As the summer progressed, it was suggested that perhaps Herbert could stay home, but as this had apparently happened to him previously, it was decided not to ask him to drop the expedition the second time (Thwaites and Kellogg, *Dunmore's War,* pp. 59, 135, 137, 144, 145).

On August 25, there was a draft call for 30 men from Herbert's Company. On September 7, 1774, a return of his men showed that there were 1 captain, 1 lieutenant, 3 sergeants, 38 men fit for duty, 2 sick, a total of 40. The report was from Camp Union, noting that the sick had been left at Rich Creek (Thwaites and Kellogg, *Dunmore's War,* pp. 167, 189).

On October 9, there was a call for 24 men from Herbert's Company, requesting that they join Major Campbell. Herbert left Camp Union on September 12, and on October 18 at Point Pleasant he was put in charge of the men from Fincastle County. Those of Herbert's Company who crossed the Ohio River in October 1774 included 1 officer, 2 sergeants, and 26 privates, a total of 29. Their names are not known. On October 19, his return showed 1 captain, 1 ensign (James Newell), 2 sergeants, a total of 27 men for duty. Apparently after he was joined by the others from Fincastle County, his return on October 25 showed that there was 1 captain, 2 lieutenants, 2 ensigns, 6 sergeants, 110 privates, 10 sick, 20 wounded, 9 who waited on the sick, on command 6, and fit for duty a total of 65 men. Two days later a fifer had joined the group, and the total was then given as 106 men. On October 28, the same officers were noted, 63 were fit, 12 sick, 20 wounded, 9 waiting on the sick, and 5 spies and coopers, making a total of 109 men (Thwaites and Kellogg, *Dunmore's War,* pp. 241, 352, 361, 363, 366, 367, 419, 420).

Following the close of the war the auditor recorded the sum paid to each man who served in the war with the number of days he served. The accompanying list from the auditor's accounts at the Virginia State Library names 59 men of Herbert's Company. Herbert received £42 for his service of 112 days as captain. Others were paid according to rank and number of days served. (for these figures, *see*, Kegley, *Soldiers of Fincastle County, Virginia, 1774).*

Herbert's Company

Jehu Stephens	James Newell	James McDonald
William Ward	Alexander McKee	Benjamin Furman (Turman?)
Benjamin Bailey	Jno. Rogers	Benjamin Rogers
Jno. Brummet	Edmund Jennings	Joseph Abbot
Mars (Moses?) Price	Henry Louther	Isaac Lewis
Michael Woods	Francis Day	Samuel Newell
Abraham Hosier	Terrence McConnell	James Downey
Hugh Gullion	Samuel Henley	Jacob Baugh
Adam Catren	Michael Walter	Thomas Bell
Elias Bailey	Barnabus Gullion	Patrick St. Lawrence
Bazaleel Maxwell	George Carr	Conrode Shepley
William Rutherford	Richard Muse	Thomas Muse
Jno. Downing	Archibald Rutherford	Duncan Gullion
Peter Kendrick	Jno. Reah	Walter Kinsor
Charles Cox	Jno. Woods	Jno. Baxter
Aaron Price	William Barron	John Barron
James Newell	David Campbell	William Roman
Isaac Roman	James Dawson (Davison?)	Peter McLaughlin
Jno. Beck, Junr.	Jno. McFarren	James Buchanan
William Campbell		

After his return from Point Pleasant and the Ohio, Herbert was chosen to serve as a member of the Second Committee of Safety and was appointed on November 7, 1775. He attended the meetings of November 27, 1775, and January 10, 1776. He was requested to list the men of his and Captain Coxe's companies. On May 28, 1776, he wrote his will, noting that he was "sick of body." On June 11, 1776, he was unable to attend to the militia, and the Committee of Safety recommended that Jeremiah Pierce replace him as captain with Samuel Ewing, Lieutenant, and James Newell as Ensign. (Harwell, *Committees...,* pp. 17, 69, 70, 74, 89).

Sometime in the summer of 1776, Herbert died. His exact date of death and his burial place are unknown, although it is likely that he is buried somewhere on his Poplar Camp plantation. On September 3, 1776, Herbert's will was recorded in Fincastle County (Fincastle-Montgomery Will Book B, p. 31). To his wife Sarah, he left the whole of the plantation where "I now live commonly known by the name of Poplar Camp," for her lifetime. She was to have four Negro slaves.

To his eldest son, William, he left the plantation on Reed Island Creek where Joseph Barron, Jr., "is now living," and another plantation on the creek known by the name of James Bottom, and another on a branch of Reed Island Creek known as Reed Island Spring, and another on the head of the creek known by the name of Big Meadow or Tom Reah's (Ray's) Cabin, and another known as Round Meadow or Henry Goat's (Goad's?) place on a branch of Wolf Creek in the glades. William Herbert, Jr., was also to have the "Inglish Stallion known by the name of Ranter," and a mare called the Roan mare, and four Negroes. At the death of his mother, William, Jr., was to have the Poplar Camp plantation. He also was to have the plantation on the Clinch River, but the stock was to be divided as mentioned above.

To the youngest son, Thomas (born 1773), he left the plantation known as Bingaman's Bottom and the other called Forbuses and another called Paxtons and another Red Bank Meadow on Meadow Creek and the plantation where Josiah Hamilton "now lives," if it can be obtained. He was also to have a young stallion colt, a yearling filly and three Negroes. To the eldest daughter, Martha, he left a filly and horse colt and three Negroes. To the youngest daughter, Joanna, he left three Negroes, a "ball'd face" black mare and a two year old filly, and the balance of the estate.

His wife was to have her one-third (a life interest), and the remaining two-thirds was to go to the four children, but the wife was to have use of the same until the children were of age. Herbert also noted that his mother and father were living with him, and suggested that if they did not wish to live on with his wife and children, then they were to have the place over the river for their lifetime, also four cows, 2 horses, 300 pounds of pork yearly, 3 "ews," and 1 ram. At their death, the place was to go, and the stock was to be divided. The parents were also to have corn or bread for the first year, if they live by themselves.

Herbert also noted that there was money due from Mr. Ogburn, Iron monger in "West Street without lawfull gate, Bristol, in old Ingland," and it was to be obtained as soon as possible and put to use for the two daughters. John Montgomery, Senr., and Walter Crockett were executors. Witnesses were John Jenkins, John Brummet, and William Medding.

As the records show, William Herbert was a man of many talents. Trained in the mining field, recognized by Augusta, Botetourt, and Fincastle County Courts as a justice of the peace, and chosen as a member of the Committee of Safety, he showed a variety of interests and abilities. His business acumen combined ferry, ordinary and mill with stock raising and fine English horses. He owned nineteen Negroes at the time of his death, more than any of his contemporaries in the same community. He was a leader in the militia and when called to fight Indians took up the challenge. He was one of the wealthiest men of his time. His estate was appraised at more than £2,300; however there probably should be some allowance made for inflation in 1776.

The items listed in his estate (Fincastle-Montgomery County Will Book B, p. 41) show a wide variety of interesting personal property. There was a large cherry tree sea chest, iron clasps and painted; a large walnut table, a silver tankard, 9 silver teaspoons, a pair of tea tongs, a silver "salts," a large delft bowl, a stone pitcher, 7 china cups and saucers, three tea cups and one saucer; a teapot, 3 Queens china coffee cups, tea canister, delft; a sun dial; a smooth bore gun, brass mounted; a pair of copper scales, brass weights; a cherry tree tea table; a Queen's china dish, 6 plates, 1 pocket pistol, shoemaker's tools, 3 pair candle snuffers, a large coffee pot (copper); a small coffee pot (copper); a tea kettle, a still of copper with pewter worm; a smooth bore gun, and another gun; a small microscope and 12 views; a violin, a pair of velvet breeches, a cloth coat and jacket, a great coat, a feather bed, two blankets, an old coverlid, a bolster, 2 more feather beds, brass candlesticks, and several books including Bailey's Dictionary, 8 Volumes of Hume's *History* (three at James Newell's), *Acts of Virginia Assembly, Ireland Preserved, Geography Rectified, Complete English Dispensatory, Pocket Companion*, Russell's *Seven Sermons, The Christian Hero, Politicks*, Cockers *Arithmetic*, and magazines.

George Ewing, Adam Dean, Andrew Boyd, James Newell, and James Montgomery, Junr., or any three were to act as appraisers of the estate on New River, and Samuel Porter, Henry Dickerson, John Kincaid, and John Blackmore, or any three, were to appraise the estate on the Clinch River (Summers, *Annals,* p. 651).

At the time the will was presented to the court in September 1776, Sarah, the widow of William Herbert, had married Francis Day. Little is recorded about Day, but he was a private who served 104 days in Herbert's Company in 1774. When Sarah Herbert Day came to court, she objected to the will of her late husband and claimed her "thirds" in the estate. The court appointed William Preston, James McCorkle, James McGavock, Stephen Trigg, and Adam Dean, or any three to allot her dower in the estate according to law (Summers, *Annals,* p. 651; Kegley, *Soldiers,* p. 49).

On January 8, 1777, Francis Day and his wife Sarah were summoned to appear at the next Montgomery County Court to show cause why they have not allowed David Herbert, Senr., and his wife to live on the estate left them by their son William Herbert at his death. On April 2, the executors John Montgomery and Walter Crockett appeared and refused to take upon themselves the burdens of executorship. Francis Day and his wife Sarah also appeared in court and refused to represent the estate of William Herbert. The court noted that the estate "was going to waste and destruction very fast," and because the children were likely to suffer and William Herbert having no friends that would take upon themselves the administration of the estate, the court appointed Stephen Trigg and James McCorkle, Gentlemen, who lived in what is now Pulaski County. Their bond for $10,000 was acknowledged with William Preston, John Taylor, and James McGavock as securities (Summers, *Annals,* p. 676).

The disagreements continued. On September 2, 1777, Sarah was heard on her bill of complaint, and the answer of the defendant Francis Day was heard. It was ordered "that the defendant, on the 25th of December next or as soon as his dower which he claims by virtue of his marriage with the complainant, from the estate of William Herbert, deceased, be allotted to him, do give her the one-half of such dower which shall be due him from the 20th day of June next past, and in case of disagreement in such division, that Stephen Trigg and James McCorkle, Gentlemen do divide the same between them." (Summers, *Annals,* p. 682). Although there is no explanation for the day of June 20, it is my belief that was the date of the marriage of Francis Day and Sarah Herbert.

On September 2, 1777, articles of agreement were drawn up between Francis and Sarah Day, and Stephen Trigg and James McCorkle, administrators of the estate of William Herbert. The recitals give the facts of Herbert's will, and that Sarah had married again and that she was not content with the provision made for her in the will. Following her renunciation of the will, she claimed her dower in the estate, and as a result of the marriage, as was the custom of the times, Francis Day became entitled to demand and to have the dower allotted to him. It was concluded that this would result in "many inconveniences" and as a compromise, the agreement was drawn up which would bar both of them from any claims of dower. As a result of the agreement, Francis was to have Poplar Camp plantation until the 25th of December next, and to have the use of all the Negroes until that same date, for the purpose of tending and securing the crop which was to be the property of Francis, who was to have free egress and regress to move the crops off of the plantation. On December 25, he was to deliver possession of the plantation and the Negroes and to clothe the grown Negroes as follows: for each of the fellows, he was to provide a "jaiscoat," two shirts, one pair of leather breeches, shoes and stockings, and for the women, he was to provide a "jaiscoat," two shifts, petticoats, shoes, and stockings. Then the Negroes were to be divided into three equal parts, one of which Trigg and McCorkle agree to deliver up to Francis and Sarah for the lifetime of Sarah, for their use provided they enter into bond and that at the death of Sarah they were to be returned to the heirs of William Herbert. The Days were also to receive one-third of the money arising from the sale of personal property, and one-third of the money due the estate before the sale, so soon as it might be collected and also to deliver up possession of the Forbess land to Francis Day December 25 for his use during the life time of Sarah. In addition, Sarah was to make a choice of any other tract of land for her use during her lifetime, except Poplar Camp, which was left to William's father and mother. The agreement was signed by Francis Day who made his mark, Sarah Day, Stephen Trigg, and James McCorkle. It was recorded in Montgomery County on September 9, 1777 (Montgomery County Deed Book A, p. 165).

With the consent of the court, on April 6, 1779, William Herbert, orphan of William Herbert, deceased, chose Colonel Walter Crockett as his guardian. On August 6, 1784, the account of his expenses as guardian were recorded. Items included shoes, paper, blanket, suit of clothes made by George Ervin, bacon for his grandfather, leather, linen, sums paid the school master, paid Hugh Crockett boarding, and cash paid the register for two pre-emption warrants. Two Negroes were hired out for the sum of 10 pounds. The balance due the guardian was 38 pounds and 14 shillings (Summers, *Annals,* p.706; settlement from McCorkle's store book, copy in possession of the author).

On May 5, 1779, James Byrn and Joseph Cloyd were appointed guardians for Joanna and Thomas Herbert, orphans of Captain William Herbert. Joseph Cloyd's expenses for Thomas Herbert were reported to the September Court 1783, and included such items as cash paid Thomas Shannon for linen; shirts, jacket, coat, shoes, buckles, stockings, 9 months of schooling in 1782 and 8 months in 1783; and board for four years and three weeks. The total account was 26 pounds, 5 shillings and 6 pence (Summers, *Annals*, pp. 709-710; McCorkle's Account Book; Montgomery County Will Book B, p. 62).

In October 1785, Colonel Walter Crockett relinquished the guardianship of Thomas Herbert, who then chose his brother William as his guardian (Summers, *Annals,* p. 803). On October 26, 1785, William signed a bond with James Newell and Stephen Sanders binding him to the justices of Montgomery County Court in the sum of 3000 pounds on the condition that he deliver to Thomas Herbert, orphan of William Herbert, deceased, all that is due him (Montgomery County Will Book B, p. 114).

On November 19, 1788, the accounts of James McCorkle in connection with the estate of William Herbert were approved and the Court allowed McCorkle the sum of £15 and also an allowance of £60 for his trouble, ''upon which he agreed to take a bond upon Samuel Thompson of an account upon Abram Trigg, in discharge of same, which is delivered to him'' (Montgomery County Will Book B, p. 135).

Family records indicate that Sarah Herbert Day probably died in 1785-1786, but no court or other records have been found locally. A Francis Day, Jr., and Francis Day, Sr., are both mentioned in 1805 in Wythe County when Andrew Kennedy was granted an injunction to restrain the younger Day and James Newell from removing two slaves out of the jurisdiction. They were the property of Francis Day, Sr., of Kentucky (Wythe County Order Book 1801-1805, p. 528).

William, Jr., And Thomas Herbert

Thomas and William Herbert, Jr., appeared many times in the records following their father's death. The young boys were educated and trained under the supervision of their guardians, educated men of the community. As soon as legally possible, Thomas transferred his guardianship to his brother as mentioned above. William was several years his senior. Conflicting dates for the birth date of William, Jr., range from 1761 to 1765. Thomas was born in 1773.

William Herbert (sometimes Harbert), Jr.'s, first land record appears in 1782, when he had a survey made for 367 acres corner to Forbushes land (Montgomery County Plat Book B, p. 154). Other transactions followed: a survey for 129 acres on Wolf Glade Creek, a branch of Crooked Creek, on August 12, 1783; a survey of 190 acres on Poplar Camp Creek, corner to William Ross on March 1, 1787; 400 acres on Little Reed Island Creek on May 16, 1788; 116 acres surveyed on Little Reed Island Creek on April 20, 1789; and 425 acres on the east side of New River, adjoining Jenkins' line on April 29, 1790. In addition, he sold William Ross 130 acres on Poplar Camp Creek (Montgomery County Plat Book, A, pp. 96, Book C, p. 129, Book D, pp. 57, 395, 527, Book E, p. 36; Montgomery County Deed Book B, p. 17).

In the 1790s, William, as legatee of William Herbert, deceased, had several tracts surveyed in Wythe County: 140 acres on Reed Island Creek, 1,000 acres on the east side of New River, and 400 acres at Ray's cabin place on Little Reed Island (Wythe County Survey Book 1, pp. 115, 254, 257). These may have been the tracts of land mentioned in his father's will. In 1783, in Montgomery County, Thomas Herbert had 400 acres surveyed on Daniels Branch, a branch of Crooked Creek (Montgomery County Plat Book C, p. 128). In 1801, Thomas had a tract of land surveyed, being 420 acres adjoining Ross (Wythe County Survey Book 2, p.56).

In 1785, William Herbert, Jr., served as overseer of the road from Herbert's Ferry to James Coxes in ''room'' of John Jenkins. In 1786, he was an ensign in Captain Sayers' company of militia. When Wythe County was formed in 1790, he was a captain in charge of a company of local militia (Summers, *Annals*, pp. 806, 814, 1357).

William Herbert, Jr., may have married Mary or Polly Humphreys, although no marriage record has been located. Beginning in 1793, William Herbert, Jr., and his wife Polly (Mary) began to sell their land holdings in Wythe County. The ferry tract was sold to William Carter. The Poplar Camp place was transferred to his brother Thomas (Wythe County Deed Book 1, pp. 172, 194).

Thomas Herbert married Sallie or Sarah Crockett, the daughter of James and Mary Drake Crockett. Although some of the family information is incorrect in regard to the ancestry of Thomas, his wife's ancestry, their children and grandchildren are detailed in the *Crockett Family*, by French and Armstrong. Sarah Herbert (Harbert) died in Denmark, Tennessee, where she is buried. Many of her family moved to Texas and California. The children listed are James, William, John, Mary, Nancy, Aseneth, Crockett, Ephraim, Stephen, Nathaniel, Sarah, and Elizabeth *(The Crockett Family,* pp. 101-117).

In 1807, Thomas Herbert and his wife Sarah (or Sallie) and William Herbert and his wife Mary sold all of their claim to 590 acres, known as the Poplar Camp Furnace tracts, to David Peirce. This land was first owned by William Ross who had transferred it to McKensie and Bobbett of Grayson County. In 1808, William and Mary Herbert sold to brother Thomas their interest in the forge tract on Little Reed Island Creek, noting that this was where William Herbert, Jr., then lived. This is the last entry in Wythe County for William Herbert, Jr., and he probably moved about this time. He does not appear in the 1810 census of Wythe County(Wythe County Deed Book 4, p. 512; Book 5, p. 50).

The Grayson County, Virginia, records show that William Harbert (signed Herbert) and his wife Mary were living in Ashe County, North Carolina, in 1815 when they transferred a grist and saw mill on the south side of Wilson Creek in Virginia to William Thomas and Samuel Pugh (Grayson County Deed Book 3, p. 271). Also on

May 11, 1804, a conveyance in Ashe County shows that Harbert [Herbert] was of Grayson County, Virginia (Ashe County Deed Book M., p. 160). William Herbert, Jr., is said to have died in Ashe County, North Carolina, but research in the records there do not confirm this. In 1823, William Harbert conveyed his interest in 380 acres in Ashe County on the waters of Little River, and his interest in the ironworks, ore banks, and buildings belonging to the premises "with all woods, waters, mines, and minerals..." (Ashe County Deed Book E, p. 262). It is perhaps at this time he moved from the area.

Some of his children reported by family tradition are: Polly who married Col. Richard Gentry, owner of the "Old Fields," on the New River in Ashe County, North Carolina; a son David Sheffey Herbert who settled in "gold country" of California; and Elijah, born March 1800 at the lead mines in Wythe County, Virginia. From another source, the children are given as: William Herbert, III, born 1789; Katharine born May 9, 1791; Martha (Patsy) born 1792; Mary (perhaps Polly mentioned above) born 1796 or 1798; Betsy born 1799; Elijah Humphries born September 3, 1801; and David Sheffey Herbert born June 13, 1805. The dates of death of William and his wife Mary are unknown, because it is not clear where they spent their last days. One researcher claims William died in 1835 and is buried at Little River Baptist Church (Ashe County?). There is some inference that some of the family settled on the "Cherokee Purchase," in what is Clay County, South Carolina, in a location known as Herbert's Bend. (family tradition). There were Humphries (possibly William's wife's maiden name) living in Surry County, North Carolina, as indicated by the record of deeds and wills in that county. Also, a deed dated 1786 in Montgomery County, Virginia, involving the David Herberts, shows that they were living in Surry County, and three of the witnesses to the deed were David, Benjamin, and Solomon Humphreys (Montgomery County Deed Book A, p. 405).

In Cherokee County, North Carolina, in the 1850 census, there is an Elija Herbert mentioned. It states he was born in Kentucky, although his wife and all of his children were born in North Carolina. His wife was Winny, and children were: William, Nancy, Thomas, Emeline, Sheffy D., Alexander, Thompson (?), James K. P., and Frances. The reason that these records are included here is that Clay County, South Carolina, was formed from Cherokee County in 1861, and there may be a connection to the Herberts of Wythe County (1850 Census, Family 286, p. 22, courtesy of Henrietta Cragon).

In 1794, Thomas Herbert began to sell his land in Wythe County. The transfers mentioned furnaces and forges. The first transaction was the sale of Bingaman's Bottom tract on the south side of the New River, 225 acres which included houses, stores, furnaces, mill dams, wharves, etc. In 1797, a deed recorded in Washington County transferred the Poplar Camp tract of 500 acres to Jesse Evans. In 1811, Evans received the 1,000 acres at the river, and the 200 acres of the forge tract. Thomas Foster, Thomas Brooks, John Thomas, and Abner Sayers purchased other Herbert land. In 1807, when the deed was made to David Peirce, the 590 acres at the Poplar Camp furnace was transferred in four tracts, each of the Herberts conveying one-half interest in the land and improvements belonging to the furnace, and one-third interest in the Poplar Camp furnace. Excepted were the improvements of Thomas Blair as mentioned in the agreement between McKensie and Bobbett regarding the erection and operation of the furnace (Wythe County Deed Book 2, p. 339; Book 4, p. 512; Book 5, pp. 59, 60, 67, 103, 445; Book 6, pp. 156, 255, 294; Summers, *Annals*, p. 1337).

The Grayson County records show that Thomas Harbert and his wife Sarah transferred two tracts of land. The first deed was dated September 18, 1794, when 400 acres on Daniels Branch, a fork of Crooked Creek (now in Carroll County) was transferred to Nathaniel Frisbie of Grayson (*also see* Frisbie sketch). In 1808, Thomas conveyed to Greenberry G. McKenzie of Grayson County, 253 acres of land where Joseph Mee formerly lived, being the same tract he sold to Doctor Thomas Smith (deceased), and the same sold by Smith to Herbert. Caleb Bobbett and Samuel Jones were then living on the land (Grayson County Deed Book 1, p. 24; Book 2, p. 440).

Thomas Herbert disappears from the Wythe County records about 1811, probably about the time he moved to Tennessee. Records in White County, Tennessee, at Sparta, show that the inventory of the estate of Thomas Harbert was returned to the court by the administratrix, Sally Herbert, the widow, on January 21, 1817. On April 21, 1817, she was appointed guardian for children Nancy, Lucy, Crocket, Ephraim, Stephen, Nathaniel, Betsy, and Sally Herbert. William and James Herbert were bondsmen (Will Book 1, p. 65; Minute Book 1814-1817, p. 502). Deeds show that William Harbart (spelling used in Tennessee deeds), John Harbart, and James H. Jinkins and his wife Nancy, all of that county, transferred their interests in land and lots which "descended to them from their deceased father Thomas Harbart" on the 17th day of June 1822. Another deed made in 1843 mentions other Harbarts: William, John, Stephen, and Crockett Harbert as well as Sarah Ann Johnson. At that time Sarah Ann was living in Madison County, Tennessee, Stephen in Shelby County, Tennessee, and Crockett in Marshall County, Mississippi (White County Deed Books G, p. 213; Book N, p. 301). In 1841, Sarah is mentioned as being in White County, Tennessee, and at that time was claiming part of the Robert Sayers estate in Wythe County (Wythe County Survey Book 4, p. 120). Sarah died in 1854 and is buried in Denmark, Tennessee.

Mrs. Henrietta Herbert Cragon, a descendant has documented at least eleven children of Thomas Harbert (June 25, 1773-November 1816) and Sarah (Sallie) Crockett Harbert (July 16, 1773-September 15, 1854), daughter of James and Mary Drake Crockett of Wythe County. Some may have died young. These children were: James (1793), William (1794), John (1797), Mary or Polly (1799), Nancy (1800), Aseneth (1803), Crockett (1805), Ephraim (1807), Stephen (1809), Nathaniel (1811), Elizabeth (1813), and Sarah (1816). All but the last two were born in Wythe County; the others born in White County, Tennessee.

The William Herbert Daughters

The two daughters of William Herbert. Sr., and his wife Sarah Fry, married in the neighborhood. Patsey or Martha married Josiah Bell, son of William Bell, in 1793 (Wythe County Marriage Book 1, p. 4), but may have married a second time as mentioned below. No marriage record has been found for Joanna, but she married Laurence (Lawrence) Stephens, Jr., (1753-1847) probably about 1787. Joanna was said to have been born about 1761 and died on March 15, 1845, age about 84. She and her husband are buried at Barren Springs of Wythe County, in the Stephens Cemetery, off South State Route 100, near Patterson, on the homeplace. Lawrence's grave has a Revolutionary War marker, stating he was a Corporal in the 1st Virginia Regiment. An old stone on the ground gives his age as 94. The Stephens had the following children: Peter, Rhoda, James, Joseph, Elizabeth, Rebecca, Sarah (Sallie), and Martha (Patsey). Lawrence Stephens' will is recorded in Carroll County. He was the son of Lawrence Stephens, Sr., and said to be the grandson of Peter Stephens, Sr. whose wills are found in Winchester (Frederick County Will Book 2, p. 266; Holden, *The Earlys of Southwest Virginia,* pp. 192-195; family records; "Stephen's Cemetery," *Virginia Appalachian Notes,* August 1992, pp. 110-113).

On May 13, 1839, William Short of Grayson County, "a little upwards of eighty-one years," made a statement in court regarding the Herbert girls. He stated that Martha or Patsy married Joseph Dougherty and left Virginia, and that she was dead, but he did not know if she had children or not. Johanna, called Anna, married Lawrence Stephens and lived two miles from Short, who lived in that part of Grayson that became Carroll (Wythe County Order Book 1837-1840, p. 318). It should be noted that the Wythe County marriage records show that Martha or Patsy married Js. [Josiah] Bell. Perhaps she married twice, or there are two women named Patsy Herbert.

David Herbert, Sr. And David Herbert, Jr.

David Herbert and his wife Martha (sometimes Marthew) emigrated from Bristol, England, in 1763 under the agreement made with John Chiswell of the lead mines. Their known children are: William, superintendent of the mines, David, Jr., who was employed at the mines, and Mary, wife of John Jenkins, who was also employed at the mines (*see* above). There may have been others whose names are not recorded. There is an Esther Welshire Herbert, daughter of Nathaniel Welshire, who lived in the lead mines neighborhood whose relationship is not explained. Was David, Jr., married to Esther?

It appears that the elder Herberts lived with William, Sr., at Poplar Camp. Because there are two Davids, it is not always clear which one is intended in the records. For example, in 1774, David had 218 acres of land surveyed on a branch of Little Reed Island Creek (Montgomery County Plat Book A, p. 96). This is the first time the name David appears in the New River records. In 1779, the ferry was referred to as David Herbert's Ferry, when the rates were set by the county. The license as issued in the name of David Herbert, Jr. (Montgomery County Order Book 3, p. 42; Summers, *Annals*, p. 715).

In July 1786, David Herbert and his wife Marthew (Martha) were living in Surry County, North Carolina, when they joined in a lease for a tract on the north side of the New River "adjoining Herbert's Ferry, wherein David Herbert, Jr., now lives," to William Herbert, Jr. The sum of £6 was to be paid each year for the rest of the life of the elder Herberts. Witnesses to the lease were David Humphreys, Benjamin Humphreys, Soloman Humphreys, and John Jenkins, Jr., all apparently of Surry County, North Carolina, where the Humphrey names appear in numerous records (Montgomery County Deed Book A , p. 405).

On February 11, 1812, the Wythe County court noted that "for reasons appearing to the court, David Herbert is to be placed on the poor list" (Wythe County Order Book). It is not clear if David Herbert, Sr., returned from Surry County, or if this entry refers to David Herbert, Jr.

David Herbert, Jr., is mentioned in a lawsuit (*James Reddus vs. William Carter et als*, Superior Court Chancery Pleas, Vol. 6, 1812, Wythe County Circuit Court Clerk's Office). Reddus of Grayson County had purchased land in the vicinity of the lead mines, and as there were so many claims and overlapping lines, it appeared necessary to state his claim and have the lines settled. The plaintiff's bill was presented in 1812. He stated that in 177-(blank) William Herbert, deceased, held lands adjoining William Pellum (Pelham) and others, which was surveyed by the Loyal Company. William Herbert entered into a contract with his brother David and sold the land for £5 in 1774. The transfer of title was lost. David Herbert took possession of the land and sold it to John Smith, who sold it to William Rowland who sold it back to Herbert. After keeping it awhile, he sold it to Jacob Vanhoze who sold it to Jacob Cane, who sold it to William Carter, who also owned the land formerly Pellums. Carter now owning all the land, sold it to Reddus for £250. William Carter obtained the grant by settlement right on the Pellum place.

David Herbert stated in the suit that he bought the land for a black mare and a colt, and took possession in 1774. The place had a big spring and adjoined Colonel Walter Crockett, William Lockett and the Lead Mines. He sold to Rowland in 1776, and in 1777 or 1778, the property was in the hands of John Smith who sold to Jacob Hoose (Vanhoze?). William Herbert never made the title to the land, but the night before William died, David Herbert stated that he told the executors to make the title. The tract in dispute was about two or three miles from William Herbert's place, and David stated that he was living there at the time William Herbert died.

William Herbert, Jr., also entered a claim to the land and sold his claim to James Newell who sold to John Jenkins. William Carter had moved out of Virginia, and his answer in 1812 came from Wayne County, Kentucky, where he was then living and where a Roger Oats (a name that appears in connection with the Chiswell contract) was then serving as Justice of the Peace. Carter stated that he purchased 413 acres from Jacob Cane and the grant issued to Carter, who sold to Reddus. Because Newell claimed under William Herbert, Newell joined in the deed with the Carters in 1808.

James Newell's version of the ownership of the property was somewhat different. He stated that the survey made for the Loyal Company in 1753 was made in the company name for their own use and that William Pellum never resided on the land, but his name was put on the books to identify the property. Newell noted that he had lived in the neighborhood forty years and never heard anyone say that William Herbert sold the land to David Herbert, his brother. In fact, Newell doubted that David ever lived on the land in dispute, stating that he lived on a survey of 200 acres made in 1753, which covered 100 acres of William Herbert's survey of 180 acres made in 1774, but Herbert did not live within the bounds of the 180 acres.

Newell stated that he bought the claim of the 180 acres from William Herbert, Jr., in 179-(blank) and paid the Loyal Company fees and then sold it to William Lockett who actually received the grant. Then Newell bought it back. He learned that the Loyal Company grant of 180 acres was based on a survey in Herbert's name and because it contained 100 acres of the Loyal Company grant, then Newell was entitled to 100 acres of both surveys. When Cane owned the land, he had a survey made for 413 acres and this also included the Loyal Company survey of 1753. Newell and Carter realized the problem and a lawsuit was instituted to correct the lines and clear the title. They exchanged acreage between themselves, and when the land was sold to Reddus both Newell and Carter joined in the deed.

Others who testified in the case included Archibald Haslerig, surveyor, David Pierce, Jesse Evans, and William Rowland, all of Virginia; William Lockett and his wife Louisa of Wayne County, Kentucky, in 1812, and Francis J. Carter of Cocke County, Tennessee.

The court decided that the claim of Reddus be dismissed. They gave no reason, but it would appear that the fact that no title bond could be produced showing David Herbert's claim to the place in dispute, would be enough to denounce Reddus' claim.

Those familiar with the townships, sections, and quarter sections will shudder in horror at Virginia's method of obtaining boundaries for property. This particular case is cited in some detail to present the confused status of land ownership when there were overlapping lines, and when it was taken up by metes and bounds, rather than under the township system.

Repeated evidence turns up in the records to show that overlapping lines were a very common occurrence and lawsuits to settle claims to land were often filed. From this case, and others like it, certain conclusions can be drawn: titles to land were transferred many times by title bond without any evidence in the land books; lands surveyed for one person were often granted to another; lines were often overlapping, making lawsuits the only means of settlement; several surveys of different acreage could be made to include a certain spring, the same house place or disputed land; land was sometimes paid for with horses, colts, etc. in place of cash. The accompanying map shows how ridiculous the situation can become.

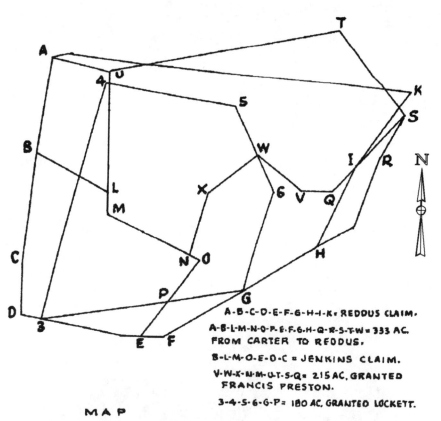

A-B-C-D-E-F-G-H-I-K= REDDUS CLAIM.

A-B-L-M-N-O-P-E-F-G-H-Q-R-S-T-W = 333 AC. FROM CARTER TO REDDUS.

B-L-M-O-E-D-C = JENKINS CLAIM.

V-W-X-N-M-U-T-S-Q= 215 AC. GRANTED FRANCIS PRESTON.

3-4-5-6-G-P= 180 AC. GRANTED LOCKETT.

MAP

REDDUS vs. WM.CARTER ET ALS.

FROM LAWSUIT SHOWING OVER-
LAPPING CLAIMS. - 1812.

Map from lawsuit *Reddus vs. Carter et als* showing overlapping claims, 1812.

Map by J. R. Hildebrand.

Shot tower on the New River built by Thomas Jackson.   Photo by F. B. Kegley

The Jackson house still stands in sight of the shot tower and is believed to be the home of Thomas Jackson. Although it has not been proved it also may have been the home of the Herberts and Evans families who lived there prior to 1815.   Photo by F. B. Kegley

Thomas Jackson

Thomas Jackson, born near Appleby, Westmoreland County, England, on November 8, 1762, came to Virginia in 1793 and settled near the lead mines. His mother, Mary Jackson, was married the second time to William Naggs (Knaggs) who operated a small grocery store in Dufton, Westmoreland County, England. Other children in the family included a sister Deborah, who remained in England with her mother, and died there about 1829 or 1830; a sister Anna, who married first William Raper and second Richard Walton and who came to Wythe County; a brother John Jackson, who married Isabelle Hastwell and also came to Wythe County. Most of this information was given by another John Jackson, son of Nathan Jackson of Westmoreland County, England, who also migrated to the lead mines community. He was not a relative of the Thomas Jackson family but knew them in England and in Virginia, and was known as "Creek" John Jackson to distinguish him from John Jackson (brother to Thomas), who was known as "River" John. Testimony in a later lawsuit given by "River" John states that Thomas had two sisters who remained in England, but he did not name them (Wythe County Order Book, 1829-1833, January 12, 1830, February 8, 1830, pp. 5, 15; *Peirce vs. Jackson,* Superior Court of Chancery Pleas, hereafter *Peirce vs. Jackson*, Vol. 9, 1830-1831, p. 86, gives the date of the arrival of Thomas in America; the date 1785 is erroneously used on the Shot Tower State Park flyer; *Sanders vs. White,* Box 87, 1840, Wythe County Circuit Court Clerk's Office, Basement).

According to information provided by Thomas M. Jackson, Thomas is believed to have spent time in New York where he had an interest in some land on Long Island. He is also believed to have spent time in Philadelphia, before coming to Wythe County (Jackson, "A sketch of the Jackson History").

Thomas Jackson never married. He died September 16, 1824, age 61 years, 10 months and 8 days, and is buried in a private cemetery located on the New Jersey Zinc property in Austinville, on the south side of the New River.

Jackson's first purchase of land was in 1796 when he bought from Muse and Sayers the 600 (660) acres known as the Pasture (*see* Sayers sketch). This is the tract where he probably lived, on the south side of the New River. In 1798, he purchased 214 acres from Moses and Mary Austin. Jackson and Robert Raper, his nephew, were partners in a store in the lead mines community, the exact location unknown, but perhaps on the road between Austinville and Poplar Camp (Wythe County Deed Book 2, pp. 85, 288; Wythe County Will Book 3, p. 140). In 1816, he purchased 1,218 acres (probably mountain land) at a tax sale which was formerly the property of Charles Austin (Wythe County Deed Book 7, p. 21; information from Thomas M. Jackson).

Thomas Jackson worked at the lead mines under the Austins, and in 1801, he and James Newell rented the mines for eighteen months (*Peirce vs. Jackson*, Vol. 9, p. 86). He learned how valuable the mines were, and agreed with David Peirce and Daniel Sheffey to form a partnership with them to purchase and operate the mines. Jackson went to Richmond and was the successful bidder on behalf of the partnership. The differences which arose over this purchase have been outlined in the David Peirce sketch. Before the lawsuit ended, Jackson had died. It was his heirs who benefited from the decision of the court that he was entitled to 11/24 of the lead mines property (*Peirce vs. Jackson*, Vol. 9, pp. 20-426; *see Peirce* sketch).

His deed for the lead mines property was not recorded until 1822 (Wythe County Deed Book 9, p. 169). The conveyance was made by John Guerrant and William Waller Hening, Commissioners appointed by Superior Court Chancery for Richmond District. The deed was made to David Peirce and Thomas Jackson. The deed followed a lawsuit in the High Court, under the style of *John Robinson, plaintiff, and widow and executors of Honbl. William Byrd and others, defendants.* According to the terms of this suit the lead mines tract of 1,400 acres was ordered to be sold on June 8 and October 7, 1802. The sale took place May 15, 1806, for the sum of £9,550. Some payments had been made by Daniel Sheffy, who had an interest with Peirce and Jackson, but in June 1821, $1,907.89 was to be paid to Sheffey, who subsequently compromised and released his interest, leaving Peirce to obtain 13/24 and Jackson 11/24 interest in the tract (Wythe County Deed Book 9, p. 169). These lawsuit papers filed in the High Court in Richmond were destroyed, so no further details could be obtained.

In 1815, Jackson purchased the old Herbert's Ferry tract from Jesse Evans. The terms of their May 19th agreement indicated that the sale also included the ferries at Poplar Camp and the land where Evans was then living. In addition, several tracts from Thomas Herbert and a tract of 150 acres by entry and grant were assigned to Jackson. Possession was to be September 1st. Jackson was to pay $11,000 ''in current silver coin or $12,000 in bank notes from the Bank of Virginia or Farmers Bank of Virginia or both.'' All dower interest was to be released. The only exception to the transfer was an 8-acre tract laid off and sold to Thomas Blair, who sold the same to David Peirce for a mill seat. The deed and the agreement were both recorded (Wythe County Deed Book 6, pp. 293, 294, 255, 230). In 1831, the heirs of Thomas Jackson in various deeds conveyed their interests in the Ferry place, the Reddish place, and the lands where he lived at the time of his death, to John, Michael, Thomas, and Robert Jackson, sons of John Jackson, the brother to Thomas (Wythe County Deed Book 12, pp. 100, 120).

On the Herbert (Evans) property, some time after his purchase, Jackson began to build the shot tower which still stands on the hill above the river (on the south side) near the old Jackson's Ferry bridge. The date of 1807 is often given as the date of construction of the tower as this was the date handed down in the Jackson family. To this author it seems very unlikely that it would have been built by Jackson on land then owned by Jesse Evans. Some family information states that the tower was incomplete at the time of Jackson's death in 1824, and others claim it was operational during Jackson's lifetime beginning in 1812. With no contemporary written record, the dates and circumstances of operation will only remain speculative. Nevertheless, Jackson is given credit for the tower's construction and design. Numerous stories persist in the community that Jackson manufactured shot for the Revolutionary War, but this cannot be true as he was not in this country at the time of the War. Also, there is no written evidence that the tower was in operation during the Civil War, although there is a tradition that Judge Fulton rented the tower and made shot there during the Civil War (family information from Mary Oewel states the tower was unfinished in 1824; family information from Thomas M. Jackson).

The tower design is unique, and the structure is one of several shot towers standing in the United States today. The purpose of the tower was to manufacture shot for shotguns, an enterprise which developed in Bristol, England, and which was still being carried on in that place in 1990 (visit to England by the author in 1990 and to two of the operating English shot towers in Bristol and Chester, uncovered information on shot towers in America and around the world).

The Wythe County shot tower was built of gray limestone, and the work was done by a good mason. In the construction, a perpendicular shaft about six feet in diameter was cut from the surface of the rock cliff to a depth of seventy-five feet, and another shaft or tunnel high enough for a man to walk through was cut from the bank of the river, at an average high-water mark, straight into the bottom of the perpendicular shaft, where a large kettle was placed to hold water carried in from the river into which the lead was to be dropped. From the surface of the cliff, the walls of the tower were erected to a height of seventy-five feet. At the base, the tower is twenty feet square, at the top fifteen feet. The walls are two feet thick. There are no windows or openings in the walls except an entrance at the bottom which gave access to the stairway winding to the furnace room at the top. There was a small balcony on the south side of the furnace room. The room is thirteen feet square and in the center there was a colander about three feet in diameter, through which the hot molten lead was poured. The lead was heated in a small furnace on the east side of the room and dropped through the colander a distance of 150 feet. Following the drop, the shot was taken from the kettle, graded, rolled and polished in a shot-house nearby. The finished product was close to the road at the ferry owned by Jackson which was convenient for loading or delivering to purchasers (Shot Tower State Park flyer; *see also* Kegley, "Shot Tower at Jackson's Ferry," *Journal of the Roanoke Historical Society*, Vol. 3, No. 1 (Summer 1966), pp. 1-7; Kegley, *Bicentennial History*, pp. 360-362).

It is not known how long the tower was in operation. It is known from the Jackson family papers that in 1835, Robert Raper had an agreement with Michael and Robert Jackson, nephews of Thomas, to operate the tower for a term of six years. The agreement is as follows:

Memorandum of an agreement made and entered into this 31st day of January 1835, between Michael Jackson and Robert Jackson of the one part and Robert Raper of the other part, witnesseth that the said Michael and Robert Jackson agrees to rent to the said Robert Raper the shot tower at their ferry for a term of six years from the date hereof for which the said Robert Raper agrees and binds himself to build a factory house of sufficient size for the manufacturing of shot and paint the tower with lime, and put the same in complete order for makeing shot. In witness whereof the parties have hereunto set their hands and affixed their seals the day and year first above written.

Michael Jackson
Robert Jackson
Robert Raper

Following the death of Thomas Jackson an appraisal of his personal estate was taken and included were the following items of interest: horses, oats, sheep hay, cows, a pony, hogs, oxen, cattle, steers, tobacco, peach brandy, apple brandy, rye, windmill, grindstone, steelyeards, beds, wool, feathers, flax wheel, cotton wheel, kettle, potatoes, cabbage, 19 Negroes, chairs, tables, a clock, cupboard, looking glass, tallow, linen, one trumpet, quilting frames, beds and bed clothes, flax wheel, hemp, castings, loom, cooper ware, wire sifter, ploughs, flax break, 8,000 shingles, beef hides, sheep skins, geese, flax, tow linen, salt, an old boat, corn, a still and 18 still tubs and 54 gallons of brandy. The appraised value of the personal property was $7,596.31. The property at the lead mines included his 11/24 share of the following items: iron, scales, smith tools, lead molds, furnace tools, bricks, rope works, mining tools, buckets, oven, wheel barrow, keg, and stacks of rye and wheat. His share amounted to $134.24 1/2 (Wythe County Will Book 3, p. 158).

The inventory at the firm of Jackson and Raper was shown by Robert Raper to the appraisers on November 2, 1824, and the store property was listed on eighteen pages (Wythe County Will Book 3, p. 140). There were 49 lots of goods mentioned with a total appraised value of $3,144.78. The first twelve categories were various kinds of materials: Bangross cord, cassinet, circassion plaid, red flannel, cassinell, cassimere, shirting, furniture check, Wilmington stripe, dark ginghams, drab cloth, red Boacking, super blue cloth, Olive cloth, white flannel, apron check, imitation circassian, gold end shirting, figured Bombazet, green flannel, Irish linen, Waterloo stripe, blue denim, cambric, bleached shirting, plaid shirting, brown shirting, N. Orleans cotton, striped "Janes," and fine white "Janes."

Among the other items listed were: suspenders, cotton balls, Dutch blankets, shawls, boys suspenders, buttons, cravats, umbrellas, edging, breast pins, silk stockings, gloves, vests, clocks, combs, hair brushes, books and stationery including readers, spelling, grammar, and arithmetic books, testaments, Bibles, playing cards, slates, paper, quills, ink and ink powder, slate pencils, dictionary, and medical companion.

Left: The brick home of Thomas Jackson (son of John and Isabella Jackson) on New River above Austinville was probably built in the mid- 1800s. Torn down in the 1990s.

Photo courtesy of Thomas M. Jackson who is in the picture with his son Delegate Tom Jackson who was then an infant.

Right: The brick home of John Jackson, Second, on the road from Poplar Camp to Austinville, later owned by Charles A. Jackson, and now owned by Mrs. Carl Shepherd. It was probably built in the mid-1800s.
Photo by Mary B. Kegley, 1994.

Home of Thomas M. Jackson near the shot tower.
Photo by Mary B. Kegley, 1994.

Stone spring house on the John Jackson (now Shepherd) property. Photo by Mary B. Kegley, 1994.

The list also included: shaving glasses, spectacles, snuff boxes, beads, coffee mills, spoons, knives, forks, scissors, gun locks, files, rasps, saws, knitting pins, thimbles, brass candlesticks, trowels, shaving boxes, curry combs, fiddle strings, bits, stirrups, fishing lines, needles, tacks, fish hooks, brass tacks, gimblets, scales, chisels, axes, frying pans, tea kettles, shovels, German and English scythes.

A list of medicines available at the store included: oil, balsom, different kinds of drops, calomel, Laudanum, camphor, cordial, Bluestone, Epsom salts, cloves, barks, aloes, and cinnamon.

There was a variety of shoes available, including prunellas, walking shoes, cordovans, boots, buckled shoes, slippers, women's and children's shoes. Also there were morocco hats, a straw Gipsy hat, and two bonnets.

The Queens Ware listed include sugar dishes, tea pots, cream ewers, tumblers, bowls, wine glasses, cups and saucers. jugs, plates and decanters. The groceries listed included indigo, rice, copperas, ginger, brimstone, allum, allspice, pepper, and lamp black.

The store also carried a supply of Whittemore's cotton cards, gallon coffee pots, bar iron, German steel, molasses, whiskey, rum, nails, powder, tobacco, chairs, crocks, feathers, wool hats, fine hats, and castings. There was also one black horse belonging to the partnership.

This excellent store inventory is interesting for several reasons. First, it gives us some idea of the wide variety of items available to the people of the lead mines area at this early date. Second, it displays such a variety that it would be difficult to find anything missing from the store. There was a great choice of material including everything from red flannel to Irish linen. Although the grocery shelf did not contain many items, this was understandable for the times. There was a selection of shoes, hats, gloves, and even silk stockings, but the only ready-made clothes mentioned were vests and cravats.

The heirs of Thomas Jackson included his brother, "River" John, who was born near Appleby, Westmoreland County, England, on August 1, 1766 and who emigrated to Wythe County in the fall of 1802. He died December 4, 1826, just two years after his brother Thomas. John's wife Isabella was born near Appleby and died March 28, 1838, age 69. His sister Ann Raper Walton and her children were also heirs of Thomas Jackson. It was agreed between John Jackson and Richard Walton in 1825, that they would divide the property as follows: John Jackson was to have the plantation where Thomas resided at his death, and the plantation known as the Reddish place. Walton was to have the Ferry place, except the shot tower, which was to be the joint property of the two. Walton was to allow Jackson and his family the privilege of crossing the ferry without paying a toll, and to have the privilege of grinding at the mill, all grain necessary for family use. In addition, Walton was to pay Jackson $5,000 within twelve months (Wythe County Deed Book 10, p. 64; tombstones of John and Isabella Jackson).

"River" John Jackson, in response to a lawsuit, stated that he was the brother of Thomas and was known as "River" John, and that his citizenship was in dispute. He explained that he was naturalized according to law as he had made his declaration and abjurance on October 12, 1812, as required by law. In May 1814, he appeared in court again and proof being made that he was under the jurisdiction of the United States between the 18th of June 1798 and the 14th of April 1802, and had continued to reside here, and was of good character, he took the oath and became a citizen. He believed that the reason his citizenship was in doubt was because of the presence of John known as "Creek" John Jackson. Richard Walton was admitted to citizenship at the same time. Also, a Joseph Jackson showed his intention to become a citizen on October 14, 1812, and Lancelot Knipe, also a native of England, appeared on May 6, 1811, to show his intent to become an American citizen (*Sanders and Walton vs. Heirs of Thomas Jackson, deceased,* Box 87, filed November 17, 1826, ended 1840, Wythe County Circuit Court Clerk's Office, Basement).

John Jackson died in 1826, leaving his widow, Isabella, and four sons, Michael, Robert, John, and Thomas. He signed his will on September 14, 1826, and it was probated on December 12 the same year (Wythe County Will Book 3, p. 251). His wife was to have $4,000 out of the personal estate and son John was to have $10,000 provided his brothers, Michael, Thomas, and Robert should not make an equal "dividend" with said John as to their uncle Thomas Jackson's estate, but if, when they are of age, they do, then John is not to receive $10,000. The land was to go to the payment of the bequests to his wife and son.

Of the four sons of John and Isabella, Robert and Michael lived in the log house, which still stands near the Shot Tower. John, known as John Second had the farm on the road from Poplar Camp to Austinville, which was later known as the Charles A. Jackson farm. He built the brick house which is now owned and occupied by Mrs. Carl Shepherd. Thomas had the farm across the river from Ivanhoe, in an area now grown up and nearly deserted. The two-story brick house on the place was built by this Thomas and in the 1960s was owned by the New Jersey Zinc Company. The house has been demolished. It was at one time known as the Simmerman place (Jackson, "A Sketch of the Jackson History").

In 1831, John Raper as attorney for William Milling of Wayne County, Indiana, released his interest in Thomas Jackson's estate (Milling being an heir-at-law) to John Jackson's four sons, Michael, Robert, John, and Thomas. They received the Reddish place, the place where Thomas lived at his death, which was purchased from Sayers and Muse, the lead mines tract of 1,400 acres excepted. The same year, George Walton and his wife Senah, and John Sanders and his wife Hannah sold their interest to the same four sons of John Jackson. This included their interest in the Ferry place, purchased from Jesse Evans, the Reddish place, purchased from James Reddish, and the two tracts where Thomas Jackson lived, purchased from Muse and Sayers. Walton and Sanders were to have the privilege of crossing the ferry, free of charge, for themselves and their families (Wythe County Deed Book 12, p. 100; Book 11, pp. 120, 467).

In 1856, Thomas Jackson (the younger) had an inclusive survey made for land formerly owned by Sayers, Muse and Austin. The land included the land known as the Pasture. The grant issued in 1860 (Wythe County Survey Book 4, pp. 264-265; Grant Book 117, p. 844).

Among the Jackson family papers is a roll of the "Company of Infantry of the line attached to the 35th Regiment of Virginia Militia on the south side of the New River" dated June 10, 1843. Michael, whose name appears first on the list, was apparently the captain. Lieutenants were Jacob Harroll and John Pearman. The list is further dated in April 1844. The time of the deletions is unknown. The names, with their original spelling, are as follows:

Michael Jackson, ferryman
Robert Hill-deleted
Wm. Bratton
Samuel Hurst
John Pierman- deleted
John Hollandsworth-deleted
Lewis Hines- deleted
Robert Calfee
Samuel Porter, Jr.
James Tolbert-deleted
Hezekiah Courtney
Levin Dickson-deleted
Wm. Bolesede-deleted
Mervin Pickett
Henry Harris
H..... Wilson-deleted
Thomas Jackson
Thomas Allford
James Pierman
Jacob Hoback
Wm. Kohler
Jacob Harrol-deleted
Alexander Chaffin
Samuel Freman?
James Tipton
Washington Taylor
Edmond Wills
Benjamin White
Wm. Beasley
Benjamin Fry

William Robertson-deleted
James Austin
Joseph Hurst
Major Hodge (?)- deleted
John King
Richard Hines
George Bicknel-deleted
Wm. Mayab
Wm. Sawyers
Martin Nelson
John Davidson
Martin Pool
Asher Pickett
Andrew Richardson
Larkin Freeman
Wm. Kzee
Patrick Inglesby
John Jackson
Jordan Welch-deleted
Andrew F. Gregory-deleted
Stephen Porter
Samuel Carrington-deleted
John Winssul [Winskell?]
John Prim
Amen ? Stoots
Henry Aker
John Graham
Wm. Fulks
Aaron Peak

Daniel Porter
Amos Private
Stephen Fry
Allen W. Hurst
Azariah Slate
Robert Wood-deleted
Joseph Alley- deleted
C. Jackson Carter
Nathan Nelson
Wm. Crawford
John Blackley-deleted
Joseph M. Baker
Anthony Wauler (?)
Henry Holt
Joseph Allen
James Lowder
John Hendrick
Elkana Green-deleted
Robert Jackson
Robt. Crawford
Wm. Pierce
Thomas Baker
James Prim-deleted
James Parkin
James Early
Coalman Warf
John Private
Doriot Victor-deleted
    corrected to Victor Doriot

Michael Jackson left a will in 1868 (Wythe County Will Book 11, p. 278), leaving all of his property to nephews Thomas and Calhoun Jackson, sons of his brother John, the place known as the Ferry place together with the ferry and all property belonging to that farm, to be equally owned by Thomas and Calhoun Jackson. It was his will that they live with his brother Robert Jackson and all of the income from the farm and ferry was to be applied to the improvement of the farm. He gave the residue of his estate and personal property to the children of his brothers John Jackson and Thomas Jackson to be equally divided between them. His brother Robert was to be executor. The will was dated August 6, 1868, and probated at the September term of court the same year. In 1876, John C. Jackson and his wife Mary G. conveyed all of his interest to Thomas M. Jackson (Wythe County Deed Book 25, p. 601). The Jackson descendants still live on the ferry farm.

John Jackson

There were two John Jacksons in Wythe County, as mentioned above, and the few paragraphs which follow pertain to John Jackson, known as ''Creek'' John, the son of Nathan Jackson of Knock, Westmoreland County, England. He was born about 1770-1772, in England (Wythe County 1850 census gives his age as 78, born England and the 1860 Census gives his age as 90, born Wales).

The family believe that ''Creek'' John married Nancy Farmer in Baltimore, following a romance on board ship coming to America. She was born between 1778-1780 according to the census, and one record states she was born in England and another states she was born in Wales. Both John and his wife Nancy lived into their nineties (Federal Census, Wythe County, 1850, 1860).

John Jackson, designated as ''Creek'' John, stated before the Superior Court of Wythe County on October 10, 1826, that he was a native of England, and that on May 6, 1811 he made a declaration of his intention to become a citizen of the United States. He having resided in the United States five years and within the State of Virginia since the date of his declaration, he then swore an oath to support the Constitution of the United States and gave up his allegiance to George the Fourth, King of Great Britain and Ireland. He was then admitted as a citizen of the United States (*Sanders and Walton vs. White*, Box 87, 1840, filed 1826, Wythe County Circuit Court Clerk's Office, Basement).

The reason John is known as ''Creek'' John is because most of his land was located on Mine Mill Creek and Cripple Creek. In 1814, James and Sally Newell conveyed 200 acres on Mine Mill Creek to John Jackson. The tract adjoined William Rodgers. In 1817, the Newells sold 273 acres on Mine Mill Creek to John. This tract adjoined Joseph Jackson, James Brawley and John Brawley. Another tract came in 1813 from Thirza Newell to a John Jackson, probably the same one, although this is not clear (Wythe County Deed Book 6, pp. 129,130; Book 7, p. 23).

According to family members, John and Nathan were the two oldest children, and they operated a tannery at the mouth of Cripple Creek before moving to Mitchell River in North Carolina, later to Illinois and Indiana. William Jackson married Charlotte Shafer in 1838; Joshua Jackson married first Sena, daughter of Nathaniel Nuckolls, the widow of Daniel Sheffey, mother of Robert S. Sheffey, and second Florence, daughter of John and Susan Pearman. James Jackson married Phebe Walridge in 1836; George Jackson married Sarah Anna Williams, daughter of Isaac and Mary Hiley Williams, in 1840. Richard Jackson married Martha Hammonds. Nancy, the oldest daughter, married Jacob Swecker in 1840. Betsy married George Aker, and Polly married William Aker. Jane married Joseph M. Baker, and Susan the youngest, married George O. Hollingsworth (Hollandsworth, Hollinsworth) in 1841 (Wythe County Marriage Book 1, pp. 150,120,75,123,87).

Beginning in 1832, conveyances were made to family members. William received 40 acres on the New River and the south side of Cripple Creek, which adjoined John Jackson, Sr., and John Jackson, Jr. In 1836, John Jackson, Senr , and his wife Nancy transferred to Joshua Jackson, 107 acres on Cripple Creek, and 95 acres to William Jackson on the south side of Cripple Creek adjoining John Jackson, Jr., Joshua Jackson, and Robert Porter (Wythe County Deed Book 12, p. 202; Book 13, pp. 362,363).

In 1850, John Jackson and his wife Nancy conveyed tracts to five of their children: Nancy Swakerd (Swecker), George Jackson, Richard Jackson, James Jackson, and Susannah (also known as Susan) Hollinsworth. Nancy received 128 acres, George 240 acres, Richard more than 300 (later resurveyed and found to be 343 1/2) acres,

Susannah 127 acres, and James 140 acres (Wythe County Deed Book 18, pp. 293, 295, 296, 298, 300; Book 19, p. 6).

Joseph Jackson who had purchased a tract of 374 acres on the head of Mine Mill Creek from William Rodgers, conveyed it to John Jackson in 1823, but it is not clear if that was John, Sr., or John, Jr. (Wythe County Deed Book 9, p. 463).

All of the children remained in Wythe County (except the two oldest, John and Nathan) and their descendants still live in the same neighborhood. William Jackson died in 1884. His estate was appraised and settled, naming Catherine A. Keister, William C. Jackson, Marion F. Jackson, Laura A. Conner, and John P. Jackson as heirs (Wythe County Will Book 14, pp. 241, 462).

George Jackson left a will written July 22, 1890, and probated in August 1890. He left the home tract to his wife (not named) for her lifetime, and at her death to his two sons John S. and James M. Jackson. He also mentioned children Joseph, George Thomas, Mary Ann wife of Thomas Pugh, Nancy wife of George Dunford, Martha wife of Frank Porter, William Burton Jackson (died about 1892), and Alfred Jackson. He also named two grandchildren, daughters of Robert Akers. They were Maggie Courtney and Sallie Akers. The executor, John S. Jackson, was to sell the land on Brushy Creek in Carroll County and the land near Ivanhoe Furnace, and all of the proceeds were to go to his wife (Wythe County Deed Book 15, pp. 299, 577). The records show that George's estate was administered over a period of years beginning in 1890 (Wythe County Will Book 15, pp. 531, 393, 459, 590; Book 16, pp. 46, 73, 245, 420 and Book 17, p. 243).

Joshua Jackson wrote his will on November 25, 1889, and it was probated September 12, 1892 (Wythe County Will Book 15, p. 536). He had already provided for his deceased son Andrew in the sum of $1,200. To his wife Florence C. Jackson, he left the farm where he resided which adjoined John P. Jackson and James T. Early, for her lifetime, and then at her death to his daughter Nancy T. Fisher wife of J. Melvin Fisher, but free from control of her husband. His wife was to have all the stock, kitchen and household furniture, wagons, plows, etc. to be hers absolutely, and all the residue of the estate was to go to his wife. His nephew John P. Jackson was to be executor. Appraisal of the estate was taken in October 1892 and recorded in November 1892 (Wythe County Will Book 16, p. 43).

Richard Jackson wrote his will on November 10, 1896, and it was probated on February 15, 1897. He devised all land he lived on, located on the south side of Lick Mountain and containing 376 acres, to his three sons, John L., Stephen, and David Jackson, the acreage to be partitioned. The same three sons were to act as executors. He mentioned the children of his deceased son Robert, daughter Jane wife of George Hudson, daughter Cynthia wife of Conly Archer, daughter Letitia Leonard, and children of his deceased daughter Anne Lavender, children of his deceased daughter Emily Ward, and children of his deceased daughter Senah Hankley. An extensive appraisal (four pages) and a sale (nine pages) and settlements were recorded between 1897 and 1901 (Wythe County Will Book 16, pp. 444, 479, 507, 565; Book 17, pp. 251, 264, 411).

John Jenkins

John Jenkins (also Jankins, Jinkins, Jenkings) first appears in the Poplar Camp neighborhood records about 1766, when he is listed in the settlement of the estate of Robert Andrews. He was paid for attending the deceased while he was sick, and for the expense of the funeral (Augusta County Will Book 4, p. 70).

In 1768, William Preston reported that he had made a survey for Jenkins on November 14, 1768. The land was located on the east side of Mine Mill Creek in the lead mines neighborhood ("Memoranda of Surveys, Item 581, Preston Family of Virginia Papers, Library of Congress). In 1770, Jenkins purchased from James Patton's executors a tract of 63 acres on a branch of the New River above Poplar Camp, on the east side of the river (Summers, *Annals*, p.539).

In 1771 and 1772, Jenkins appears on William Herbert's list of tithables. In 1776, Jenkins witnessed the will of his neighbor William Herbert, Sr., and was one of the witnesses who proved the will in court. Mary Jenkins testified that she was the sister of William Herbert, and there is a strong suspicion that she is the mother of John Jenkins, Jr., and the wife of John Jenkins, Sr. The Jenkins family were closely associated with the Herbert group who emigrated from Bristol, England and they probably came to work in the lead mines in 1763, when Herbert came. Jenkins was employed by the Fincastle Committee of Safety to provide lead for them in 1776, and he was designated as the chief smelter at the mines at this time (Kegley, *Tithables*, pp. 11, 17; Summers, *Annals*, p. 650; *Herbert vs. Ferrell*, included in *Chiswell*, Judgments, Box 32, May Term, 1827, Wythe County Circuit Court Clerk's Office, Basement; Harwell, *Committees of Safety...* p. 71; *see also* Herbert sketch*)*.

Evidence of the two Jenkins men named John appears in a land entry in 1782, when John, Jr., assignee of Thos. McGeorge, assignee of Caleb Hall, entered 500 acres between John Jenkins, Sr.'s, patent land and the mountain, to join the Poplar Camp land. In 1786, John Jenkins, Jr., was a witness to a deed for David Herbert, Senr., and his wife Marthew [Martha]. The elder Herberts were living in Surry County, North Carolina, and were renting the land where David Herbert, Jr., lived to William Herbert [Jr.]. The younger Herberts and the younger Jenkins were cousins (Montgomery County Entry Book A, p. 109; Montgomery County Deed Book A, p. 405).

In 1781, a John Jenkins appears on the list of Jeremiah Pearce's militia company, and in 1782 is designated as an ensign under Captain Saunders. In 1785, John Jenkins was replaced as overseer of the road by George Carter (Kegley, *Militia*, pp. 37,40; Summers, *Annals*, p.798).

Jenkins (which one is not clear) made a confession before Charles Lynch and Alexander Cummings on August 1, 1780, acknowledging that he had been sworn into the "secrets" by David Harbert [Herbert] last summer and before John Griffith, and was brought as a prisoner to the mines. This refers to the Tory activities in the vicinity. However, a John Jenkins took the oath of allegiance in Montgomery's Company in 1777, and it is not clear whether that is the same person who was the prisoner (Preston Papers, Draper Mss. 5 QQ 54; Kegley, *Militia*, p.54; *see also*, Kegley and Kegley, *Early Adventurers*, Vol. 1, for the chapter on Tory activities on the New River).

In 1785, John Jenkins had 500 acres surveyed for which he obtained the grant in 1785. This tract, adjoining William Herbert, was sold to William Carter and later became the property of Colonel Walter Crockett, David Peirce and his descendants (Montgomery County Plat Book C, p. 128; Wythe County Deed Book 1, p. 19).

In 1796, John Jenkins and his wife Susannah sold 83 acres of land, adjoining George Carter, to Nathaniel Frisbie. The same year, he sold a small tract of 6 3/4 acres, part of an entry of George Carter's, now Jenkin's, adjoining where Jenkins formerly lived, to Moses Austin. In 1808, Jenkins bought 110 acres on Bingaman's Branch from Newells and Carters (Wythe County Deed Book 2, pp. 230, 235; Book 5, p. 90).

In the 1800 property tax list, taken by James Newell of Wythe County, there are two Jenkins men listed: John and William. Each had one slave. The relationship is not known.

In 1810, a John Jenkins was listed on the census roll of Wythe County with one male age 10 to 16, one 16 to 26, and one over age 45 years. The only female listed was between age 26 and 45. Jenkins owned three slaves.

The only other Jenkins in the 1810 census is Mary who was over 45 years of age and who owned one slave. She is probably the same Mary, who gave a Negro girl slave to her granddaughter Susannah Jenkins, "daughter of my daughter Catherine Scott." The deed was dated March 27, 1807 (Wythe County Deed Book 4, p. 459). .

No will or settlement of the estate of either John Jenkins appears in the records of Wythe County, and no deeds show how the property was transferred.

There are two marriages for Jenkins in Wythe County: John who married Mary Jones on June 14, 1835, and Sally who married Jacob Shrader on November 11, 1824 (Wythe County Marriage Book 1, pp. 77, 115).

Minitree Jones

Minitree (Manitree, Menitree) Jones first appeared on the New River in 1780, when he selected 500 acres adjoining Samuel Ewing, being a claim purchased of James Ewing. He also entered, in the following year, 400 acres which had been approved by the Commissioners. The tract was an assignment from James Ewing, and adjoined Samuel Ewing on a branch of the New River. Some of his selections were withdrawn, and one assigned to Thomas Jones, who entered the land on both sides of Stephens Creek on the south side of Iron Mountain. In 1782, two tracts were surveyed: 90 acres, adjoining Samuel Ewing on the west side of the New River, and 395 acres on the west side of the New River, joining Samuel Ewing. In 1786, he bought 400 acres form James McDaniel on New River and Boggs Branch, and in 1787 added 140 acres from Jacob Kennaday (also Cannaday, Kennady) and his wife Jane. This tract was part of 400 acres on the west side of the New River sold to Kennady by James McDonald [probably intended for McDaniel] (Montgomery County Entry Book, Montgomery County Deed Book A, pp. 392,500; Kegley, *Early Adventurers*, Vol. 2, pp. 23, 26, 29, 44, 103; Summers, *Annals*, pp. 889, 917, 919; Montgomery County Plat Book B, p. 130).

He served on the jury in Montgomery County in 1785, and was recommended for justice of the peace in 1786. The same year he was a witness to Samuel Ewing's will and was recommended as captain in room of James McDonald. He was appointed captain the following year (Summers, *Annals*, pp. 812,814,782, 815,817, 944).

In 1787, he is mentioned in connection with a neighborhood road, "agreeable to the petition of a number of people praying a road from James Crockett's (now Grahams Forge) to Nathaniel Buchanan's on New River [Austinville area], it is ordered that Crockett and Minitree Jones, and Thompson Sayers and John Montgomery or any three of them being first sworn, do view the nearest and best way from Crockett's to Buchanan's and make their report to the next court" (Summers, *Annals*, p. 803).

In 1790, Jones took an oath to support the Constitution of the United States, and when the new county of Wythe was formed, he was a captain in the militia and recommended as a justice of the peace (Summers, *Annals*, pp. 827,1357,1356,1357).

In 1791, he sold two tracts to James Newell: (1) 324 acres adjoining Newell's residence and (2) 485 acres adjoining Samuel Ewing's patent land, on New River. Later Jones appears as a resident of Grayson County, where he was a justice of the peace at the first court, and represented the county in the Virginia Legislature, 1795-1802, and again 1814-1815 and 1817-1818 and 1820-1821 (Leonard, *General Assembly*, pp. 199, 203, 207, 212, 220, 223, 278, 290, 304; Nuckolls, *Pioneer Settlers*, pp. 2, 3; Wythe County Deed Book 1, pp. 21, 22).

According to Nuckolls, Minitree (Minitre, Manitree) Jones was the son of Churchill Jones and his wife, who was a Minitree, and a grandson of James Jones, whose wife was a Churchill. The subject of this sketch is said to have married a Miss Spotswood, and the couple had at least four children, Rosamond who married William Bourne; Minitree Jones, Jr.; Churchill; and Spotswood Jones. Some of their descendants have been traced in Grayson County (Nuckolls, *Pioneer Settlers*, pp. 153, 160).

Minitree Jones died without a will and his inventory and appraisal were made on April 5, 1821, and a sale made a few weeks later. According to Grayson County deeds, his daughters, then living were: Mary Pool, a widow; Martha Fulton, and Naomi Fulton; Euphamie Robinson, whose first husband was Christopher Catron; Julia Jones, Lucy Golden, and Nancy Swift. Minitree, Jr., is the only son mentioned in the division of the estate. Nelson P. Jones, a non-resident of Virginia, was also a son. The widow's name is mentioned as Elizabeth. The will book indicates that certain amounts of money were in the hands of the heirs. They are named as follows: Churchwell Jones, Mary Pool, William Golden, Alfred Swift, Samuel Fulton, Arther Fulton, Minitree Jones [Jr.], John Robinson, and Elizabeth Jones. Notice that here there are two men named Jones, as heirs, Churchwell [not Churchill as Nuckolls noted], and Minitree, Jr. Also there are more children than recognized by Nuckolls (Deeds of Grayson County; Grayson County Will Book 1, pp. 197,199,302).

Kincannon

Several members of the Kincannon family were associated with business ventures on the New River and intermarried with the Newell, Sanders, and Bell families of the Lead Mines community.

Francis Kincannon (1718-1795) was the ancestor of the New River Kincannons, although he settled in Washington County, Virginia, after migrating from York, Pennsylvania, at an early date. His son Andrew Kincannon, Sr., (1744-1829) and wife Catherine McDonald had nine children, and four of them were married in Wythe County: William who married Mary James in 1804; Sally or Sarah who married Joseph Bell, who is mentioned in the Bell sketch; Andrew Jr., (1780-1849) who in 1807 married Betsy (Elizabeth) Newell, daughter of Captain James Newell, Jr.; and George, who married Thirza (sometimes Thurza) Newell, sister of Betsys in 1814 (McConnell, *Sänders*, pp. 277-185; Wythe County Marriage Book 1, pp. 30, 33, 46; Wythe County Will Book 3, p. 30).

Andrew Kincannon, Sr., was a blacksmith and gunsmith and a captain in the Revolutionary War, having served at the Battle of Kings Mountain. About 1785-1786, he moved to Surry County, North Carolina, where he had an ironworks of some note. He is well documented in those records, and is found on the recently prepared historical map of Surry County settlers (McConnell, *Sanders*, p. 278; visit to the Surry County Courthouse where the map was obtained).

Andrew Kincannon, Jr., lived in the lead mines neighborhood and owned 353 3/4 acres on the north side of the New River. He died in 1849 and is buried in the Trigg Cemetery at the western end of the Town of Austinville. His death and an order for the coffin was recorded by Adams Sanders on April 20, 1849 (see illustration).

In 1837, Kincannon sold 50 acres to George Aker, adjoining Sampson Blair, and in 1849, sold 230 acres to Rosenah Bunts. This tract adjoined McGavock, Blair, and George Walton (Wythe County Deed Book, 14, p. 201; Book 18, p. 44; Book 21, p. 188). The children of Andrew, Jr., and his wife Betsy Newell Kincannon, included: Sally who married Andrew Steele Fulton; Dr. James Newell Kincannon who married

Home of Andrew S. Fulton on the south side of the New River at the lead mines.

Courtesy of Norma Greene.

List of slaves owned by Andrew Kincannon April 1, 1815.

Tracing from the original by Mary B. Kegley

Adams Sanders notified Fleming K. Rich of the death of Andrew Kincannon and ordered a coffin on April 20, 1849. Traced from the original by Mary B. Kegley.

Thorns operated the ferry at Austinville up until at least the 1930s, when this photo was taken. Ferryman was Early Green, woman is Miss Ethel Smith, a teacher, and the car is a 1929 Dodge.

Photo courtesy of Mary Grubb Henderson and Dr. W. R. Chitwood collection.

Clifton Heights, the home of William S. Thorn located at Thorn Ferry on the New River at Austinville.

Photo by Mary B. Kegley, 1985.

Mary Elizabeth Sanders, daughter of "Long Robin" and Catherine Walker Sanders; Nancy Adams Kincannon; Francis Elda Kincannon; and Rufus Drake Kincannon who married Susan Bradley Sanders, also a daughter of "Long Robin" Sanders. Rufus D. Kincannon died in 1851 (McConnell, *Sänders,* pp. 281-283; Wythe County Deed Book 21, p. 188 gives the heirs of Andrew Kincannon and a description of the land and ferry farm where he resided).

In 1815, Andrew Kincannon owned 21 slaves. After his death the inventory of Andrew Kincannon's estate showed 32 slaves, ranging in value from nothing to $800. Many of these were hired out by the administrator and were mentioned in the settlement of the estate (Wythe County Will Book 7, p. 117; Book 8, p. 14). Among the other items of interest owned by Kincannon were a dozen Windsor chairs, 1 1/2 dozen split bottom chairs, a rocker, an arm chair, beds, washstands, bowl and pitcher, curtains, dining tables, corner cupboard, candle stand, three large and 2 small wheels, 1 reel, 14 "counterpins" and quilts, a clock and case, a lounge, brass candlesticks, a "stove for stewing," andirons, tea "caddy," coffee mill, 10 extra sheets, 22 pillow cases, a press, trunks, books, a dozen extra bed blankets, and 40 pounds of feathers. Also listed in the inventory were dishes, plates, cups and saucers, knives, forks, pitchers, tumblers, bowls, waiters, a sugar dish, cream pots, 1 dozen silver spoons, soup and tea spoons, crocks, tin buckets, 18 table cloths, 10 dozen towels, carpet, dressing table. In the kitchen there were pots, ovens, lids, skillets, pothooks, about 2,500 pounds of bacon, and 1/2 bushel of salt. There were also a large kettle in the furnace, soap, lard, 40 bushels of old wheat, and 40 bushels old corn, 50 pounds of flax,

60 pounds of iron, and the "present" crops of oats and wheat. There were 8 sickles, ploughs, harrows, grindstone, blacksmith tools, hides, scythes, cradles, jugs, horses, mares, wagon, saddles, 1 yoke of oxen, 13 milch cows, 11 ten-year olds, 9 yearlings, 75 shoats and hogs, 51 sheep and 19 lambs, a bull, and old ox wagon (recorded October 8, 1849, Wythe County Will Book 7, p. 120).

In 1858, those with an interest in the land of Andrew Kincannon conveyed the 353 3/4 acres where Andrew resided, together with the ferry rights on the New River, to Robert Raper for $12,000. Those named were: Andrew S. Fulton and Sally; James N. Kincannon and Mary; Francis E. Kincannon and Sally J.; Susannah widow of Rufus Kincannon; Robert Sanders, Valerious G. Sanders; and Lockey Sanders (Wythe County Deed Book 21, p. 188). The ferry location was most recently known as the Thorn Ferry, and was located just west of the present Austinville bridge.

George Kincannon (1785-1856) and his wife Thurza (or Thirza) Newell Kincannon also owned land on the north side of the New River in the lead mines community. They were married in 1814. The following year, James Newell conveyed 400 acres to George Kincannon, the land joining John Millon, William and John Sanders and Daniel Lockett, and being an addition to the homeplace given to Thirza by her father in 1810 (Wythe County Marriage Book 1, p. 46; Wythe County Deed Book 6, pp. 224, 368). George Kincannon testified that since the year 1801 he was well acquainted with the ferry operated at first by James Newell, when he first came to the area. He stated that he moved to the county in 1816 (*Kincannon vs. White*, Box 105, 1855-1857, Wythe County Circuit Court, Basement). The Kincannons had five children: James, Mary Ann, who married Guy F. S. Trigg (for whom Trigg Cemetery is named), Andrew Newell Kincannon who died in Missouri, Sally Wood Kincannon, who married John Philpot Curran, and Catherine Josephine Kincannon, who died young (McConnell, *Sänders,* pp. 285-285).

In 1845, George and Thirza Kincannon sold the Keesling place of about 400 acres, which adjoined Andrew Kincannon and George Walton, to Guy F. S. Trigg. This was the same land conveyed to Kincannon following his marriage to Thirza. In 1870, Trigg sold 450 acres to J.P.M. Simmerman, the same tract he received from George Kincannon. The land adjoined the Rapers and Sanders. The Guy Trigg estate went through court for division, and all land which had not been sold to Simmermans was sold at auction to Robert Raper. The deed was made to his heirs, William J. and John C. Raper (Wythe County Deed Book 6, p. 368; Book 16, p. 610; Book 23, p. 616; Book 28, p. 495).

Simmerman had an inclusive survey made in 1875, for 2,490 acres in the lead mines, Mine Mill Creek vicinity. The tracts included 688 acres from Robert Sanders and others, 450 acres of the George Kincannon-Trigg land, 119 acres of the Adams Sanders land, 37 3/4 acres which was part of 113 1/4 acres of the Peirce-Kitchens land, another tract of 37 3/4 acres , also part of the same Kitchens land, 84 acres of the Burgess Wall-Flournoy land, 489 acres of the James Kincannon land, 8 acres from H. S. Bower, 380 acres which came as a result of a lawsuit in 1875, 8 1/4 acres part of 16 acres granted Samuel Rickey in 1844, two tracts of 2 2/3 acres from Dunfords (Wythe County Survey Book 4, p. 356).

Following George Kincannon's death, his wife Thirza divided her land among her three children. The part allotted to her son Andrew was sold to her son-in-law Trigg, with her consent. She left a will and mentioned three children Sally W. Currin, Mary Ann wife of Guy Trigg, and Andrew. The home place went to the Triggs. Sally's estate went to her daughter Shipton K. Sanders, and 192 1/4 acres were sold prior to her death to Robert Raper, reserving the cemetery (Wythe County Will Book 12, p. 277, Will

Guy F. S. Trigg, son of Guy Smith Trigg and his wife Frances Jackson Trigg, was born August 27, 1809 and died May 28, 1875. He was married on August 4, 1841 to Mary Ann, daughter of George and Thirza Newell Kincannon who was born December 30, 1817 and died May 10, 1895. Courtesy of Andrew Trigg Sanders, Sr.

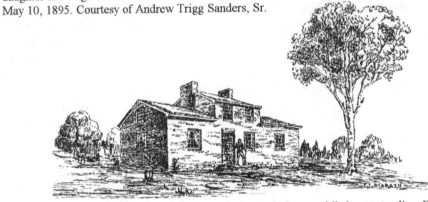

The Trigg house as remembered by persons who knew the house while it was standing. Drawing by F. C. Nisdeth about 1941. Courtesy of the F. B. Kegley Collection.

Book 15, p. 272; Wythe County Deed Book 26, p. 390; Wythe County Deed Book 20, p. 720). The cemetery was part of the S. D. Sanders farm in 1905, when Sanders made the deed to the trustees, G. B. Sanders, W. D. Sanders, C. T. Graham, and Hal C. Raper. It was on the western part of the farm of S. D. Sanders at that time, and adjoined Rapers. The cemetery probably began as a family cemetery and was in use many years before the deed of 1905 was made (Wythe County Deed Book 53, p. 583).

Lockett

Daniel Lockett probably came to Wythe County in the early 1790s. He was licensed to perform marriages and his first marriage was recorded in Wythe County on January 29, 1793. His marriage to Betsy Deforest, daughter of Cornelius Deforest, half-sister to Thomas and Richard Muse, took place on March 12, 1793 (Wythe County Marriage Book 1, p. 3).

Daniel Lockett was not too particular in recording the exact dates of the marriages he performed and on many occasions when he submitted his list to the Clerk of the Court the only date given was the date the list was submitted, and these often came long after the marriage. There has been some unnecessary confusion when researchers have cited the date of recording as the date of the marriage. For example, on February

13, 1798, he listed 15 couples he had married, and in 1805, 24 couples, and in 1816, 11 couples, with no specific dates given. The typed copy of these marriages erroneously indicate that the couples were married on the date the list was submitted.

Daniel is the son of Richard and Mary Logwood Lockett of Bedford County, Virginia. His mother came from Manchester Parish of Chesterfield County, Virginia. Daniel had siblings Mable, David, Edmund, Jeremiah, Josiah, Rodah, Jesse and Archibald Lockett. He was a descendant of Thomas Lockett I, of Bristol Parish, Henrico County, Virginia, through his son Benjamin and grandson Benjamin. Daniel and his brother William both migrated to Wythe County, and both were ministers of the gospel and both married daughters of Cornelius and Sarah Hill Deforest (Spraker, "The Lockett Family...", *Wythe County Historical Review*, No. 33 (January 1988), p. 19, hereafter Spraker, "Lockett Family"). William was married by his brother in Wythe County (Wythe County Marriage Book 1, p. 12; Scarborough, *Southern Kith and Kin, The Locketts*, Vol. 1, pp. 29,30; *see also* Muse sketch for more details about William Lockett. There are numerous references to Locketts in eastern Virginia records).

In 1796, Daniel Lockett bought 300 acres of land on Mine Mill Creek from Richard Muse, to whom his wife was connected (*see* Muse sketch). In 1803, he bought additional land in the same neighborhood from Koonrod (Conrad) Keesling and his wife Margaret, the same land that Richard Muse and his wife Margaret had sold to Keesling in 1796 (Wythe County Deed Book 1, p. 376; Book 4, p. 56).

In 1815 Daniel Lockett was assessed on his farm on Mine Mill Creek containing 469 acres with five cabbins, two barns, a stable and a corn crib. The total value was $1,500.

The assessment ticket for Daniel Lockett in 1815. He had 469 acres on Mine Mill Creek with five cabbins, two barns, a stable and a corn crib, valued at $1500.

Tracing from the original by Mary B. Kegley.

On July 24, 1824, Daniel Lockett wrote his will, and it was probated on September 13, 1825 (Wythe County Will Book 3, p.134). Out of the residue of his personal estate, if any, he left $110 to his daughter Louiza and the same to his son Edmond. His son Edmond was also entitled to six months schooling, and the expenses to be paid out of the personal estate.

To his wife Betsey E., he left the residue of his personal estate for her lifetime. In addition, she was to have all lands, tenements, and the sawmill together with the rents, profits, privileges and appurtenances for her lifetime. At her death, the estate was to be divided so that the part with the dwelling house occupied by son Richard, and the tanyard would go to his son Richard. To his son Edmond, he left the division, including Daniel's dwelling house.

To his daughter Sally Aiken, Locket left that part of the land to include the sawmill, and to his daughter Louiza, the remaining part of his land. His friends, George Kincannon and James Sanders were to act as executors.

Sally (or Sarah) Hill Lockett married Samuel Eakin in 1818 (Wythe County Marriage Book 1, p. 62). Richard Lockett married Jane Hamilton, daughter of James Hamilton, on November 26, 1818. They sold one tract of land to William Aker in 1833, and in 1834 joined with his brother Edmund W. and wife Eliza T. to sell 270 acres on Mine Mill Creek to William Blair. This included all of Richard's share and one-third of Edmund's share of their father's estate (Wythe County Marriage Book 1, p. 60; Wythe County Deed Book 12, p. 625; Book 17, p. 599).

In November 1834, Edmund and his wife Eliza were living in Chesterfield County, Virginia, and made a deed to Louisa Blair, the wife of Sampson Blair, and sister to Edmund, for 20-30 acres of land on Mine Mill Creek, part of the Daniel Lockett land on which ''a house stands in which Sampson and wife Louisa lately resided.'' Louisa Lockett and Sampson Blair were married in 1831 (Wythe County Deed Book 17, p.318; Wythe County Marriage Book 1, p. 102).

In 1846, E. W. Lockett and Eliza sold to Reuben Fisher a tract of 130 acres on Mine Mill Creek, the same they had purchased from George Walton and his wife in 1841. It was on this tract that Edmond W. Lockett had a still house and saw mill (Wythe County Deed Book 16, pp. 74, 226). This property was mortgaged twice. In addition, in 1843, certain articles of personal property were also mortgaged: one set of carding machines, 50 head of cattle, 50 head of hogs, one wagon, 11 horses, 6 sets of harness, 75 head of sheep, household and kitchen furniture, blacksmith tools and farm tools and a crop. In 1851, additional items were placed in trust as follows: 1,000 bushels of corn, 4,000 to 5,000 pounds of bacon, 400-500 cords of wood, interest in the tan yard (erected some time since by Alexander Peirce and Lockett), an interest in a brick kiln, 1,000 pounds of lard, a quantity of pig iron at Porter's Furnace, and four additional tons of iron, furniture, horses, cattle, and so forth (Wythe County Deed Book 18 pp. 546, 547).

In 1846, E. W. Lockett was selling iron from the Cripple Creek Forge, and in 1848 he sold 1,000 pounds of iron to Fleming K. Rich from Red Bluff. He was also associated with R. D. Flournoy at the Cripple Creek Forge, and in the 1840s and early 50s appears to have been in business with Robert Holliday, mentioned below (Rich Papers, various receipts).

Documents show F.K. Rich bought two lots of iron from E.W. Lockett in 1848.
Tracings from originals by Mary B. Kegley.

In the 1850 Wythe County census, Edward (Edmund) W. Lockett is listed as age 42, occupation iron master. He had a capital investment of $2,000, in an iron factory, employing twelve men, who received monthly wages of $50. His wife Eliza T. was 35 years old. Eight children were listed (Federal Census, Wythe County, family 173; Spraker, "Lockett Family," p. 20). In the same census, there were only two other iron masters, Robert Holliday and William Wilkinson, and one iron manufacturer, David Graham.

Lockett died about 1851. The appraisal of his estate was taken on August 22, 1851, and the sale was held on October 16, 1851 (Wythe County Will Book 7, pp. 484, 485). The appraisal was done by Robert Holliday, A. C. Moore, and Abner Thompson. Among the items listed were tools, scales, coal, a grindstone, old irons in the shop, an ox yoke and wagon, cast steel, balances, a coal bed, cutting boxes, gears, log chains, barrels, carpenters tools, saws, augers, iron, dye stuffs, probably items located at the forge. No household property was listed.

In the 1850s, Jerome Blair brought a suit against the heirs of Edmond W. Lockett. These included Eliza T. the widow, and children James W., Samuel D., Louisiana E., Sarah E., Hickeson H., David G., Benjamin F. and Martha P. The purpose of the suit was to obtain a deed to 250 acres on Mine Mill Creek which had been sold to him, and for which no deed had been made (*Blair vs. Lockett*, Box 102, 1853-1854, Wythe County Circuit Court Clerk's Office, Basement; for further information *see* Spraker, "Lockett Family," p. 20).

James W. Lockett, Edmund's son, was associated with Lockett's Forge on Cripple Creek, from the close of the Civil War in 1865 through March 16, 1872. The works, formerly owned by Cox, Auman, and Sexton, were destroyed by "military forces of U. S. about October 1864." After the War, Lockett made improvements and also built a house on the land and set up a blacksmith shop which he worked with a "water blast." The forge could produce 80,000 to 100,000 pounds of bar iron in twelve months. Lockett also had connections with the saltworks at Saltville, and had made an agreement with Cox, Auman, and Sexton, who were operating a furnace at Saltville, making on an average 250-300 bushels of salt a day. John G. Kegley, Sheriff of Wythe County in 1869, indicated that he had sold all of Lockett's property, and that Lockett was not solvent at that time. Lockett's interest in the forge went to David Huddle in 1871 before Lockett moved to Huntsville, Texas, where he died on July 19, 1872. A lawsuit, which provided much of this information, was continued after Lockett's death, and the widow and heirs and the administrator of the estate were made defendants. They were Sarah V., Edward, Ida W., James, and Harvey Lockett, and Peter Gallagher, the administrator (*A. G.. Cox vs. Jas. W. Lockett*, Box 143, 1884-1885, Wythe County Circuit Court Clerk's Office, Basement; Chitwood, *Deaths and Marriages*, p. 47; Whitman, *Iron Industry of Wythe County from 1792*, p. 31).

Lyons

Humberston(e) Lyon(s) and Stephen Lyon(s) were early adventurers on the New River in what is now Wythe County in the lead mines community. Humberston first appears in the Virginia records of Augusta County on March 1, 1746, when he was security for James Burk on the administration of the estate of Isaac Bean (Chalkley, *Chronicles*, Vol. 3, p. 6). In a lawsuit brought by Captain Thomas Cresap against Humberstone Lyons in 1750, it was noted that Lyons was a resident of Prince George (probably Georges) County, Maryland, in April 1743 (Chalkley, *Chronicles*, Vol. 1, p. 303). This may be the New River adventurer.

He was probably living on the New River as early as November 19, 1746, when he was ordered to serve on a road from Adam Harman's to the North Branch of Roanoke River. On November 20, the records show that he was charged with adultery with Susan, the wife of William Mires. On May 21, 1747, he was appointed Vice-Constable under James Calhoun, Constable, which would place him in present Wythe County, as that is where Calhoun lived (Chalkley, *Chronicles*, Vol. 1, pp. 23, 24, 28).

Stephen and Humberston Lyon both appear on a petition requesting road improvements, and they both were appointed to serve as road workers in 1750, from Ezekiel Calhoun's on Reed Creek to the Woods or New River (Chalkley, *Chronicles*, Vol. 1, p. 40; Vol. 2, p. 434).

In 1753, Lyons was a witness to an agreement between Benjamin Harris and Colonel James Patton for the building of two round-log houses at Springfield in present Pulaski County. At that time he signed his name Humberstone Lyon (Preston Family of Virginia Papers, Library of Congress, Folder 88).

The exact date Humberstone Lyons obtained his lands at the lead mines is not clear from the records, but he did receive a grant for 650 acres in 1752. When Alexander Sayers purchased the land in 1755, Lyons was living on it. In 1759, an agreement was recorded between Alexander Sayers and John Buchanan. These men had purchased land from Lyons jointly in 1755, Buchanan paying £38 and Sayers £12 of the purchase price. The deed was made out to Sayers alone. Sayers was to convey either in person or through his attorney in fact, Gabriel Jones, his one-half interest to Buchanan (Chalkley, *Chronicles*, Vol. 2, pp. 357, 341; Augusta County Deed Book 7, p. 294).

The agreement may not have been carried out as planned because in 1774, Samuel Ewing brought an action against Robert Sayers, the eldest son of Alexander Sayers, then deceased, and James Buchanan. John Buchanan was also deceased. Following the suit, the land was sold to Samuel Ewing, who later devised the same to his nephews Robert and Samuel Porter. James Ewing also owned a small strip of this land on the south side of the river, but devised it to Samuel Ewing at his death (Chalkley, *Chronicles*, Vol. 2, p. 370; *see also* Sayers and Ewing sketches).

It is unlikely that Lyons remained in the neighborhood after selling his land in 1755, as the settlements were abandoned during the French and Indian War. However, in 1767, Humberston Lyons is again mentioned and this time as an appraiser of the estate of Robert Andrews with George Forbush, an early resident of the lead mines community. Humberston Lyons, Jr., perhaps the same person, received a commission from the estate (Chalkley, *Chronicles*, Vol. 3, p. 102).

In May 1772, one of the men named "Humerstone" Lyons (unknown if Sr. or Jr.) was living in Pittsylvania County, when he made oath that Colonel John Chiswell agreed to give Henry Grubb £15 pounds for services "done about the lead mines" (Deposition May 26, 1772, *Herbert vs. Farrell*, in *Chiswell Judgments*, Box 32, May Term, 1827, Wythe County Circuit Court, Basement).

Following the mention of a Junior in the record, it is not clear which Humberston is in fact referred to in the following records. However, in 1773, Humberston Lyons served as a juryman for Fincastle County, and early in 1777, he appeared in the records of Washington County, Virginia, acting as security for Hannah Crabtree. He is also mentioned as a captain during the Revolutionary War period. Four tracts of land on the North Fork of Holston River were surveyed for him in 1783 (Summers, *Annals*, pp. 610, 959, 1055, 1228, 1229).

Ensign Humberson Lyon fought with General William Campbell at the Battle of Kings Mountain and was killed in action. This was probably the younger Humberson. According to White, Humberson and William Lyons were both with Campbell.

William returned and is said to have received a pension in 1833. A request for the pension record at the National Archives turned up nothing. (Draper, *Kings Mountain and its Heroes*, p. 304; White, *The King's Mountain Men*, p. 202).

Humberson Lyon (apparently the elder) died in Washington County and his will, written on October 11, 1783, was proved there on March 16, 1784 (Washington County Will Book 1, p. 71). In his will, he begins by stating, "being penitent and sorry from the bottom of my heart for my sins past, I most humbly desire forgiveness." His wife was to have one-third of the land, two Negroes, a young black mare, and one-third of the pewter, one of the pots, four sheep and one-third of the hogs. Sons mentioned were William, James, Stephen, and Jacob, who were to have the land equally. Daughter Susannah was to have £50 in gold or silver when of age. The executor, Abraham Crabtree, was to pay all of his debts.

Washington County military records show that Humberson was recommended as lieutenant in Washington County in 1780; William was recommended for ensign in the 2nd Battalion, 70th Regiment, on May 21, 1799, being replaced a few months later. He continues to be mentioned through 1807. Others in the Washington County militia included Benjamin in the 1830s, and Jacob in 1808-1810. A Humberson appears in 1831, a Jacob in 1813, and 1835, a James in 1802, 1815, and 1816, a Stephen in 1825, and William in Capt. Hayter's Company, 1803, 1815, and 1816 (Clark, *The Militia of Washington County, Virginia*, p p. 38, 118).

A Stephen Lyons, contemporary of Humberstone, had a tract of land on the New River prior to March 4, 1746, when a survey was made "opposite the lands of Stephen Lyon." The survey has no name attached to it and no acreage stated, but it was located on Woods (New) River and was part of the 100,000 acres granted to Colonel Patton. It can be seen at the Virginia Historical Society in Richmond Mss 1 P 9267). Stephen moved to the Holston River settlement and was killed by Indians there in October 1754 (Chalkley, *Chronicles*, Vol. 2, p. 510).

Muse

The Muse brothers, Thomas and Richard, first appear on the New River about 1774. In that year they both served 53 days in Captain Walter Crockett's Company, and 104 days under Captain William Herbert, and received pay for their service in the amount of £3.19.6 and £7.16.0. They may have been at the Battle of Point Pleasant (Kegley, *Soldiers,* pp. 29,49; *see* Richard's pension statement below).

In 1778, Richard was recommended as an ensign in Captain Pearce's Company of militia, and in 1779 was appointed one of the appraisers of the estate of Benjamin Castle. In 1781 and 1782, Thomas and Richard Muse appear on James Newell's list of militia. In 1782, they both appeared before the Montgomery County Court to ask for reimbursement for provisions used while on duty in North Carolina during the Revolution. Each received ten shillings. Richard Muse's name appears on Montgomery's list of those who took the Oath of Allegiance to the State of Virginia, 1777/78 (Summers, *Annals,* pp. 685, 722, 771; Kegley, *Militia,* pp. 30,31, 54).

Thomas Muse had a survey made in 1784, a tract on the east or south side of the New River, containing 531 acres. This tract was granted to Charles Lynch in 1789. Thomas had one other tract of 338 acres, for which he received the grant in 1793. This land adjoined Robert Porter and John Jackson. (Summers, *Annals,* pp. 892, 893).

Thomas Muse's will was written on July 19, 1802, and was probated August 10, 1802 (Wythe County Will Book 1, p. 219). To his faithful and affectionate wife, Susanna, he gave all his personal estate, slaves, stock, etc. and all real estate which at her death was to go to her sister Catherine Pinkley and her niece Malvina Smyth, who were to hold the property as tenants in common. His wife Susanna and Alexander Smyth were to act as executors.

The will was contested by Richard Muse when he filed suit in Staunton on August 3, 1804 (Augusta County Chancery Suit, *Richard Muse vs. Thomas Muse's executor and devisee*, OS84 NS 28; Chalkley, *Chronicles*, Vol. 2, p. 103). The Augusta County Court papers give considerable insight into community and family life. According to Richard Muse, his brother Thomas was subject to hypochondria and was under the influence of his wife and her friends. Not long before his death, Thomas wrote a will leaving everything to Richard, who claimed to be his only blood relative in the county. However, before Thomas died, he lost his eyesight, and about this time, when he was near death, he was persuaded to change his will and disinherit Richard.

The new will was drawn up by Alexander Smyth, noted lawyer of the area, who happened to be married to Nancy Pinkley, sometimes Binkley, sister of the devisee, Catherine Pinkley, and whose daughter Melvina Smyth was to inherit with her. The will was drawn up at his own house, twelve miles distant from the residence of Thomas Muse. Richard thought that Thomas would not disinherit him because he was poor and had a large family. The defendants named in the case were Susannah Muse, Alexander Smyth, and the witnesses to the will, James and Sarah Newell, Stephen and Matty Sanders.

According to Alexander Smyth's deposition, Thomas Muse was survived by, in addition to Richard Muse (his brother of the whole blood), John Chattan and Cornelius Deforest, half-brothers, and two half-sisters, Betsy Deforest wife of Daniel Lockett, and Louise Deforest the wife of William Lockett. Cornelius Deforest lived in the neighborhood for a short time.

William Lockett may have been the same one who established Lockett's Chapel in Wayne County, Kentucky, about 1800. A descendant stated that he married a DeForest, and they had come from Virginia. There was also a family story that the DeForest woman had been married before to a man (perhaps named Pepper) who made an extended trip to Europe. After more than a dozen years silence, he was presumed to be deceased. However, he did return, and made a trip from Virginia to Wayne County to see if the Locketts were happy and if they were taking care of his daughter. When he learned that they were very happy, he generously left the community without seeing his wife. Sometime later, she learned of his visit, but decided after much prayer and soul searching that her life was with Lockett, as they had children of their own (Johnson, *A Century of Wayne County*, p. 76-78). It is interesting to note that William Lockett's marriage to Louisa Butler appears in 1798 in Wythe County Marriage Book 1, p. 12. Perhaps it was Butler who made the trip to Europe. The will of Cornelius Deforest appears in York County, Virginia, in 1782 (information from James C. Spraker).

We do know that Archibald, brother of William Lockett, appointed his brother, then living in Wayne County, Kentucky, as attorney in fact to claim his part of the estate of their deceased father Richard Lockett, in Bedford County, Virginia (Power of Attorney provided by James C. Spraker; *see also* Lockett sketch for further information about the Locketts of Wythe County).

According to the Muse suit filed in Wythe County, James Newell came to Smyth's house about 1797 to write Thomas Muse's will, and gave the reasons for changing the will. He said that Richard had said Thomas was a fool for giving so much to his wife, as she would probably marry again in six months, and secondly, that Thomas had lent Richard a Negro man to go waggoning, and "for want of shoes" the Negro received frost-bite.

Smyth stated that from November 1801 until June 1802, he was confined with sciatica and had not visited the Muses during this time. In June 1802, he was again able to ride and attended court in Wythe and Washington counties. While he was in Washington County, his wife visited her sister Susannah Muse, and on her return told her husband what had happened. They asked Smyth to call on his way to Grayson Court and write a will. Thomas wanted all property to go to his wife, except the land was for her lifetime, and then to pass to Caty and Malvina.

Smyth drew up the will and visited Muse on June 25. The will was read on June 27. He heard later that Thomas was pleased with the approach of harvest at which he had "a frolic" and danced. On Sunday July 11, Thomas and Susanna planned an excursion to the mountain to gather whortleberries, but changed their minds and went to Poplar Camp Furnace, five miles away, where they dined and where Thomas purchased a sack of salt. On July 19, Thomas executed and approved the will, and on July 23 was taken with a "copious discharge from the breast," afterwards became dim sighted and lightheaded, and on the night preceding Sunday, August 1, 1802, he died.

Louisa Lockett, living in Wayne County, Kentucky in 1805, stated in her deposition that on July 20, 1802, she was informed that her brother was very sick when she went to see him. She visited again on July 24, and Thomas (whom she called Tommy) refused to see his brother Richard (whom she called Dicky). Susannah's two sisters, Mrs. Smyth (Nancy) and Mrs. Stephens (Catherine) came soon. The next day Richard and Mrs. Elisabeth Lockett (wife of Daniel) came to see him.

In her deposition in the lawsuit, Susannah Murrah (Murry) stated that she understood that Thomas and Richard Muse, John Chattan, Cornelius Deforest, Betsy Lockett, and Louisa Lockett were all children of the same mother. She also stated that Thomas and Richard lived about one mile apart. She mentioned Isaac Muse, son of Richard, who borrowed a mare belonging to her to go to North Carolina. She also referred to the Negro that drove the wagon to Pedee (South Carolina?) and froze his feet. (Lawsuit as above).

Richard Muse did not win the lawsuits, and in 1828, Malvina Smyth (Mathews) and her husband John P. Mathews sold the tract of land containing 338 acres to John, Michael, Robert, and Thomas Jackson for $2,535. The tract had been granted to Thomas Muse in 1793 (Wythe County Deed Book 11, p. 468).

On April 14, 1804, Susannah, widow of Thomas Muse, transferred the property she had inherited from her husband's estate, including real estate, four slaves, stock of horses, cattle, sheep, hogs, farm and household utensils and kitchen furniture to Stephen Sanders, Jr., in trust, because she was intending to marry William Murry and wanted the property to be free from his debts (Wythe County Deed Book 4, p. 172). Susannah Muse's marriage is recorded in Wythe County, but the groom's names is erroneously McEvoy in the typed copy. Lockett filed the marriage in April 1804, but the exact date of marriage is unknown (Wythe County Marriage Book 1, p. 23).

Susannah (sometimes Susanna) Muse Murray died sometime prior to January 18, 1828, when an account of the sales of her personal property (except Negroes) was taken. The document was recorded on December 14, 1835 (Wythe County Will Book 4, pp. 249-253). Her will was presented to the court by Robert English, but not recorded because on January 28, 1828, Alexander Smyth and others filed suit contesting the will (*Smyth and wife et als, vs. English,* Box 39, Bundle No. 1, 1830, Wythe County Circuit Court Clerk's Office, Basement). The other plaintiffs in the suit were John T. (?) Hopkins and Nancy, late Stephens, _____ and Malvina Stephens _____, his wife, Jehu Stephens, Henry Stephens, Bethia Stephens _____ and _____ her husband, heirs of Catherine Stephens, who were not inhabitants of Virginia. From the evidence presented, Dr. Jacob Haller testified that on December 27, 1827, he attended Susanna as physician, when he was called to her bedside. She asked him to write her will for her the following morning. Robert English obtained the ink, pen and paper. She stated that she did not intend to give Henry [Stephens] or any of his kin anything. When Haller mentioned that he understood the children were poor and there was one unfortunate child (a dwarf), she still did not want to give them anything. A deed in Wythe County shows that Josiah H. Hill and Nancy S. his wife (formerly Stephens), Nathaniel Watson and his wife Malvina S. Watson (formerly Stephens), were living in Monroe County, Tennessee, and were heirs of Susanna Murray. (Nancy's first husband was Hopkins as mentioned above). They appointed Col. Harold Smyth their attorney to settle with the administrators of Susanna's estate for their share of personal property and slaves (Wythe County Deed Book 12, p. 293).

By her will Susannah gave all of her slaves to Robert English: Humphreys, Tom, Charlotte and four children, Granville, Malinda, Eliza and Rufus. English was to pay $1,000 for them, certain sums to be paid to Catherine Reddish, James Madison Murray, and the children of Catherine Reddish. Nephew Harold Smyth and nieces Frances S. Piper and Nancy Smyth were to have all personal property. Frances's husband was not to have any control of the personal property, and John P. Mathews was appointed trustee for her, and he and Robert English were to be executors. The will was dated December 28, 1827.

Susanna inquired about James H. Piper, the husband of Frances, and learned that he was insolvent, requiring her to have a trustee for her property. When it came time to have the will witnessed, John Jackson the tanner who lived on Cripple Creek, was at the house, and Haller suggested that the two of them could be witnesses. She refused, saying she wanted the Messrs. Jackson over the river to be witnesses. Other visitors arrived, including Col. Harold Smyth, Mrs. English (the aunt of Susannah), Smyth and his daughter Frances Piper, and John and Michael Jackson. When asked if she wanted to sign the will Susannah refused, even though the paper was right. She was interrupted in speaking by severe sickness, but was in her right mind. This continued until Saturday night about 9 p.m. She died on Sunday. Susannah could not write.

Catherine Reddish was a sister of Robert English, and they were cousins of Mrs. Murray, who called their mother aunt. James Madison Murray was a step-son. Robert English came to live with Mrs. Murray, when he was about seventeen years old. When he grew up, he helped her attend to her business affairs, and was later in business for himself, owning a team and a Negro to drive it for him. He was hauling for the lead mines.

Mrs. Isabella Buckly testified that Susannah did not want her black people separated and wanted English to have them all. She was a sister to Robert English, and Mrs. Susannah Muse Murray was a first cousin. Catherine Stephens, deceased, was the wife of Henry, and was a sister of Mrs. Murray. Nancy Smyth, wife of Alexander, was also a sister.

"River" John Jackson stated he had often been to Mrs. Murray's home at "reapings and corn huskins" and at other times, and knew Robert English had attended to her business affairs. His mother told him that Mrs. Murray wanted him to visit, and when he did, he found her in bed at the back of the room with a curtain around the bed. He sat near the fireplace and talked to Dr. Haller. This was the only room in the house, which measured about 24 or 26 feet by 15 or 18 feet. He and his brother Michael returned on Saturday.

"Creek" John Jackson, who lived about three-fourths of a mile from Susannah, also testified, stating he had known Susannah Murray about twenty years. English had attended to Susannah's business, her "trades and dealings" as well as fixing her ploughs and farming utensils and had assisted in securing her crops of corn in harvest, often taking care of her business before his own. English lived about two miles west, and the lead mines were northeast, and there were no blood relations of Susannah living in the state, except Harold Smyth and Robert English. Smyth (son of Alexander) lived 14 or 15 miles away.

Andrew Porter, Junr., also testified. He resided within one or two miles of Mrs. Murray, and had known English for many years and knew that he took care of her business. He had seen him at log rollings, corn shuckings, and house raisings. Mrs. Murray was elderly and in poor health, and was said to be a good manager of business for a woman, and never had an overseer or any person to do business for her except English. John Foster, custodian of the estate, reported that he had on hand cash and slaves, and the appraisement was $2,896.11, although some articles had been omitted. Col. George Kincannon also testified. The will was not recorded, but the sale (except the Negroes) of Susannah's estate and the settlement can be found in Wythe County Will Book 4, pp. 249, 285. Harold Smyth received the slaves which were valued at $1,585. The "overplus" was accounted for by him to the other heirs. He acted as attorney in fact for Hall and wife and Watson and wife (no other names given) who received their share. William Stephens acted as attorney in fact for John A. Stephens, guardian for Henry H., Bethia C. and Catherine B. Stephens, the heirs of Catherine Stephens, deceased. William Stephens acquiesced in an award made between Robert English and the administrator of the estate in regard to a matter in controversy relative to a claim set up by English against the estate. The final settlement was reported on December 8, 1835, and recorded on December 14.

Richard, brother of Thomas Muse, entered several tracts in Montgomery County, and requested surveys, and several were done in Montgomery County. Among these were $1,000 acres on New River below a branch of Bingamans Bottom, 350 acres between James Newell and Samuel Ewing, 200 acres on Little Reed Island Creek joining Richard Shockley, and 150 acres, which was withdrawn, on Brush Creek which empties above Samuel Ewings', and two others which were withdrawn (Kegley, *Early Adventurers*, Vol. 2, pp. 71, 79). He also had 1,200 acres surveyed on Cripple Creek, 100 acres on Walkers Creek, and 140 acres on Little Reed Island Creek. In addition, he received a grant for 400 acres as an assignee of Alexander Neely in 1785. The Walton Furnace was built on this grant, on Mine Mill Creek. He also had 164 acres located between Brawley and Neely for which he received the grant in 1785. Other lands on Mine Mill Creek were sold to Konrood (Conrad) Keesler (Keesling) and Daniel Lockett in 1796, and James Jones in 1799. In 1805, Richard and his wife Margaret Muse sold four tracts to Richard Walton, a total of 1,000 acres on Wilshire's Run. These included the Evan Williams land, and three tracts granted to Joseph Eaton. (Wythe County Deed Book 1, pp. 371, 372, 376; Book 2, p. 245; Montgomery County Surveys; family documents).

Richard Muse and his wife Margaret had an interest in the tract known as the Pasture and joined in the deed with Sayers when it was sold to Thomas Jackson in 1796. This tract was made up of 322 acres granted to Robert Sayers in 1783, and 338 acres granted in 1788, making a total of 660 acres. Jackson later added 140 acres, part of 214 acres granted Sayers in 1788, and conveyed to Moses Austin who sold to Thomas Jackson in 1798. Jackson had an inclusive survey on the land in 1856, and it was granted to him in 1860 (Wythe County Deed Book 2, p. 185; Grant Book 117, p. 844; Wythe County Survey Book 4, pp. 264-265). In 1810, Richard Muse was living in Pulaski County, Kentucky, where he settled after leaving Wythe County (Wythe County Deed Book 5, p. 309).

In a suit regarding the land Muse sold to Walton, the evidence showed that Richard Muse, and another Thomas Muse who bought the land from the Williams heirs, were living in Pulaski County, Kentucky, in 1825. William Williams, of Tazewell County, Virginia, stated that he was one of the heirs of Evan Williams, and that he referred to Richard Muse as "uncle Muse" as he was a "connexion by marriage" but the relationship is not further explained. The others of the Williams family had moved to Kentucky, and although some of the heirs had transferred their interests in the Evan Williams land to Muse, two younger sons, Maston and Morgan Williams, had not. Although the court ordered a deed to be made, it has not been found in the deed index of Wythe County (*Richard Walton vs. Muse*, Box 35, 1827, Wythe County Circuit Court Clerk's Office, Basement; *see also* Williams sketch).

On February 18, 1839, Richard Muse, then living in Pulaski County, Kentucky, applied for a pension for Revolutionary War service (S30612, National Archives). At that time, he was "upwards of eight-six years" and stated that he was born in Lancaster County, Virginia, in 1752, but he had no record of his exact age. His service, as best he could remember, was under Captain William Harbert, with James Newell as lieutenant, and Colo. Campbell's Regiment. He marched against the Shawnee Indians, he thought in August 1775. [It was probably 1774 in the Point Pleasant expedition (*see above*)]. He also served in 1779, in the company of Captain James Newell, under the Regiment of Col. Lynch. He was stationed at the lead mines to guard and defend the mines from the British, Indians, and Tories. He offered as evidence the affidavit of Robert Sayers, of Pulaski County, Kentucky, who was unable to appear in open court because of "age and infirmity," but this document was not included in the papers sent from the National Archives. Muse lived in Wythe County until 1805, when he moved to Pulaski County, Kentucky, and where he lived most of the time in the neighborhood of his present residence. He obtained a pension in 1839, and was enrolled in Kentucky at the rate of $23.33 per year.

Newell

James Newell (1749-1823), a prominent citizen associated with the lead mines community, was the son of James Newell, Sr., and his wife Mary Drake. The Newell family migrated from Ireland about the middle of the eighteenth century and first settled in Frederick County, Maryland (McConnell, *Sänders*, p. 220). The elder Newells moved to New River in what is now Pulaski County, at a place called Persimmon (sometimes Passimon) Bottom. James Newell, Sr., or the first of the name, probably came to the New River about 1767, the date the name first appears in the Augusta County records pertaining to New River. At that time, James Newell's name was on a petition requesting a road between Ingles Ferry and Peak Creek. In 1770, his name appears on Ingles list of tithables and in 1771 on Thompson's list (Kegley and Kegley, *Early Adventurers*, Vol. 1, p. 51; Kegley, *Tithables, pp.* 3,16).

James Newell, Sr., wrote his will on December 11, 1784, and it was probated on August 22, 1786 (Montgomery County Will Book B, p. 84). His wife was to have the whole of his estate, real and personal. If the property had to be sold, the money was to be divided between two daughters, Nancy and Grizy (Grizella). The other children had received their share, but he gave sons John, James, and William, and his daughters Elizabeth and Mary, 20 shillings each. Son James, Jr., or the second, was to be executor of the will, and Nancy Newell and John Hurst, Sr., were witnesses. Other children not mentioned in the will were Samuel, Benjamin, and Drake Newell (McConnell, *Sänders*, pp. 220-222 gives some of the genealogy of this early family; see also Agnes

Graham Sanders Riley's excellent article, "James Newell, 1749-1823," *The Historical Society of Washington County, Virginia*, Series II, No. 8 (July 1970), pp. 16-34, hereafter Riley, "James Newell,").

James Newell, Sr., mortgaged 53 acres of land at "Passimon" Bottom in present Pulaski County, and several items of personal property to William Sayers in February 1774. It appears that this was because of purchases made from Donald and Company (probably for merchandise), with William Sayers as surety. Because of the war, the company left the country for Great Britain, and it was not until 1790 that Andrew Donald, Junr., came as agent to settle accounts. James Newell lived on part of the Persimmon Bottom for about twenty years prior to his death. The items of personal property included: a walnut table with hinged leaf, a large looking glass, 2 chests, a feather bed with striped tick, a green rug, 3 Dutch blankets, one one-sided rug, a coverlid, several cows and calves, sheep, and a bay mare and colt branded IM (Montgomery County Deed Book A, p. 69). This property went to James Newell, Jr., in the lawsuit filed in Staunton. The real estate was owned by James Jones at the time of the suit and his title was traced back to Thomas Walker (Chalkley, *Chronicles*, Vol. 2, p. 80, referring to *Sayers vs. Newell*, OS 227 NS 80).

James Newell, Jr., (1749-1823) was married in 1771 to Sarah Wood (1752-1831), the daughter of William and Martha Drake Wood (McConnell, *Sänders*, p. 221). It is not clear from the records where the young couple lived when they first got married, but in 1771 Newell appears on William Herbert's tithable list with other residents of the Poplar Camp-Lead Mines neighborhood. At this point, there was no evidence he had taken up any land either by survey, grant, or purchase. However, in 1819, a deed refers to 1,000 acres of the Andrew Donald land as "Newell's old place about three miles above the lead mines and below Robert Sanders ironworks, adjoining the land on which the iron works are built." It is possible this location, which later became the Christopher Catron plantation, was Newell's first place of residence (Kegley, *Tithables*, p. 12; Wythe County Deed Book 8, p. 200).

In 1772 and 1773, James Newell (probably Jr.) served on a jury. In 1773, Newell attended the wedding of Joseph Drake and Margaret Buchanan held at the Town House (now Chilhowie). In the same year he had his stock mark recorded in Fincastle County Court. The mark was to be a swallow fork on left ear and a slit in the right, and one prong cut of his brand J. N. (Chalkley, *Chronicles*, Vol. 2, p. 173; Summers, *Annals*, pp. 163, 172, 194, 609).

In 1774, Newell was involved in the Point Pleasant expedition against the Indians. He served with Captain Herbert and his company. His name appears twice on the auditor's accounts for Herbert's Company, as a private and as an officer. As a private, he served 51 days and received £3, 16 shillings and 6 pence. As an officer (ensign), he served 53 days and received £6, 12 shillings and 6 pence. Newell's name also appears on Captain Crockett's list for 1774 and in this company he served 13 days as a private and was paid 19 shillings 6 pence (Kegley, *Soldiers*, pp. 29, 49, 50). While serving on the expedition with the Fincastle Militia, Newell kept a diary of the events which took place and kept records of the number of troops on duty as well as the number of sick and wounded. Newell was wounded on or about October 23, 1774. (The diary has been published in the *Virginia Magazine of History and Biography* Vol. 11, pp. 242-253, and appears as 11 ZZ 1-12 in the Preston and Virginia Papers. *See also*, Riley, "James Newell," pp. 24-25).

In 1776, when Herbert's Company was taken over by Captain Peirce, Newell continued to serve as Ensign until 1777 when he became a Second Lieutenant. In May 1777, Newell received his pay as assistant commissary at the lead mines, the receipt being given by Thomas Madison, who was settling the accounts (Preston and Virginia Papers, 5ZZ43; Summers, *Annals,* p. 685).

At the same time, Newell was also appointed to allot the hands to work on a road from Reed Creek along by the mines and up as far as William Henley's on Cripple Creek. In 1777, he was recommended as a Justice of the Peace and in April 1778 took the oath of office of a Justice of the Peace and of Justice of the County Court in Chancery and a Justice of Oyer and Terminer, all oaths administered by William Preston, Gent. He served in this capacity many times, and when Wythe County was formed, continued to serve in that county as well (Summers, *Annals,* pp. 681,683, 688; Wythe County Order Books often mention Newell's presence at the court sessions; Riley, "James Newell," pp. 30,31).

In 1777, when his brother Samuel Newell died, James was administrator of the estate. Samuel's wife relinquished her right to undertake the administration. John and William Newell were security for James on a bond amounting to £500. In May 1778, James Newell was appointed with others to view the road requested across Poplar Camp Mountain from North Carolina to Samuel Ewing's and on to Davis' at the head of the Holston. Newell was also to allot the hands for the road from John Newland's to the lead mines, a duty assigned to him at the same court session. He was also chosen as one of the men to make the agreement regarding the construction of the Montgomery County log prison (Summers, *Annals,* pp. 678,690, 693,694).

In 1779, Newell was involved with the settlement of the estate of William Herbert, with whom he had served in the war, and was an appraiser of the estate of Benjamin Castle, a neighbor in the lead mines community (Summers, *Annals,* pp. 651, 710, 722, 729).

In 1780, Newell was recommended as a captain of the local militia in the place of Captain Henry Francis who had been killed in battle. On April 3, 1781, the Montgomery County Court appointed him captain, approving the recommendation made earlier (Summers, *Annals,* pp. 738, 751).

On April 5, 1781, Captain Newell listed the men of his company noting that several men were not fit for duty. These included Adam Dean, Saml. Smith, Richard Byrd, and James Davis. There is no way to tell which of the men, if any, actually saw service with Newell in North Carolina during 1781. Benjamin Castle describes the activity in North Carolina, and his record on previous pages may be seen for further details. It should be noted that no one by the name of Castle appears on Newell's list. The list is printed below.

Capt. James Newell's Company

James Newell, Capt.	Richard Muse, Ensign	Fran. Day
William Gleaves	Michl. Gleaves	Adam Dean
William Campbell	Isaac Campbell	James Campell
Thos. Muse	John Francis	John Doughlass
William Buster	James Rogers	George Hopkins
David Rogers	Robt. Sayers	John Rogers
Joseph Rogers	William Rogers	Reubin Rogers
John Hall	William Hall	John Ewing
Charles Rigney	William Dean.	William Henley
George Henley	John Rutherford	Julious Rutherford
Randolph Rutherford	Haza. Chinia	Joseph Love
Benjn. Rogers	Saml. Smith	William Harreldson

Richard Byrd	George Duff	James Davis
James Wylie	Henry Miller	William Jones
James Lapseley	John Carr	John Burnam
William Moor	George Culdwell	Stephen Gose
Stofle Gose	_____ Gray	_____ Gray

In 1782, another list for Newell's company was taken. It is possible that this is a tithable or tax list that he was requested to take by the court. If so, it was recorded on August 6, 1782 (Summers, *Annals*, pp. 757, 778). Newell was also to list the names of the tithables in Swift's, McDonald's [probably McDaniel's], and Ozburn's Companies. These may be the lists which appear in Kegley, *Militia...* pp. 23, 31, 32, 33, 41, 42, 43, 44. Also compare with Kegley, *Tax List...1782*). Newell's Militia list of 1782 appears here.

Newell's Militia List Of 1782

James Newell	Wm. Gleaves	William Dean
Richard Muse	Julious Rutherford	David Rogers
Isham Christian	Michl. Cortney	Rubin Rogers
James Brawley	Wm. Rogers	Joseph Rogers, Sen.
Wm. Campbell	James Dean	Adam Dean
John Rogers	John Ewing	Jas. Campbell
Geo. Ewing	Abram Razor	Saml. Byrd
Wm. Rutherford	Henry Francis	John Carr
Jas. Wylie	Robt. Wylie	David Miller
Roger Oates	Geo. Duff	Jas. Davis
Heza. Chinia	John Whealin	John Robbins
Michl. Least	Jos. Rogers	Jas. Rogers
George Henley	George Hopkins	Benj. Rogers
Geo. Culdwell	David Culdwell	Saml. Ewing, Junr.
Thos. Muse	Wm. Henley	Stofle Gose
_____ Gose	Jas. Stace? Hace?	Randolph Rutherford

In April 1782, Newell proved to the Court that he ought to be paid 41 shillings for 270 pounds of beef taken from him for the use of Captain Love's Company of Militia. On August 6, Newell and William Campbell proved that they had served 46 days each as Commissioners, and the Sheriff was ordered to pay them at the rate of 15 shillings per day (Summers, *Annals*, pp. 769, 778). Also in 1782, Newell was requested to take a list of names of all free male persons above the age of 21 years and the names of all slaves, specifying to whom they belong, and also to record the number of "nete cattle, horses, mares, colts, and mules, wheels for ridding carriadges, Billiard Tables and ordinary license and to place these articles under the names of the person to whom they belong, in Ozburn's, Swift's, Coxes and his own companies" (Summers , *Annals,* p. 757).

Beginning in 1782, James Newell took up several tracts of land on Cripple Creek, Mine Mill Creek, and along New River in the vicinity of the lead mines (*see* Montgomery County surveys and grants). There were two tracts of the Loyal Company, dated 1753, which were assigned to Newell, but no deed was made until 1799. The Newell-Loyal Company land was located between Mine Mill Creek and the mouth of Cripple Creek, along the river and extending northerly from the river towards

Mine Mill Creek and its branches (Wythe County Deed Book 2, pp. 467, 468). A clue to his first residence comes in a deed from Minitree Jones to Newell in 1791. The Jones land was located on both sides of Cripple Creek adjoining the land Newell lived on (Wythe County Deed Book 1, p. 21). The land commissioners mentioned three tracts on Cripple Creek for James Newell: 400 acres (the Robinson land), 400 acres assigned to him by Michael Woods, and 400 acres known by the name of Turkey Nobb. Entries were made for him, including a tract of 100 acres, joining his land on Cripple Creek, and 100 acres to join Samuel Ewing's land, and 300 acres (the Muse land), joining the land "he lives on" and the land purchased for the lead mines of Charles Devereux and the land "Samuel Smith lives on" (Kegley, *Early Adventurers*, Vol. 2, pp. 71, 102). Somewhere in this area was his first home. This land was included in 570, acres later given to his daughter Thurza. The later home of James Newell near the ferry was not purchased until 1792, when Lynch had left the community (Wythe County Deed Book 1, p.139; Book 6, p. 224).

In 1785, Newell sold 400 acres on the north and west side of the New River to Robert Sanders, the lands granted to Newell the same year. This was the land formerly belonging to Charles Devereaux (Montgomery County Deed Book 1, p. 418). In 1785, Newell was recommended as sheriff of Montgomery County, but did not obtain the position at that time. He was appointed to allot the tithables to work on the road from the lead mines to Fort Chiswell in June the same year. On March 28, 1786, Newell received permission to build a mill on his own lands, but the location is not given. Also, in 1786, James Newell was appointed Commissioner of Land Tax for Montgomery County (Summers, *Annals*, pp. 787, 788, 816; *see also*, Riley, "James Newell," pp. 32-33).

In April 1787, he was recommended as captain of the local militia, and took oath as captain two months later, a position he also held in Wythe County (Summers, *Annals*, pp. 818, 819,1356, 1371).

James Newell continued to buy and sell land, the many transactions recorded in Montgomery and Wythe County records (Riley, "James Newell," pp. 19-21; Wythe County Deed Book 1, pp. 117,195, 211; Book 2, p. 478; Book 4, p. 99; Book 5, pp. 74, 126, 192, 258; Book 6, p. 370; Book 7, pp. 23,261,389 among many others). Most of the land was located in and around the lead mines-Mine Mill Creek-Cripple Creek neighborhood. In 1815, the tax assessment on the James Newell property included 543 acres on the west side of New River, opposite the lead mines. There was one dwelling house of wood, two stories high, 54 feet by 28 feet, one kitchen, one barn, two stables, one corncrib, one spring house, one Negro house, one brick meat house, and another tract of 1,610 acres south of Lick Mountain with no improvements. There were also 21 slaves valued at $5,000. The total value of his property was $10,526.60 (Kegley, *Tax Assessment*, p. 139).

James Newell served as surveyor of Montgomery County as early as 1781 or 1782, and testified in various suits about his work (Riley, "James Newell," p. 21; various lawsuits, including Chaney). He was responsible for the 1790 census, reporting on Montgomery County before the formation of Wythe. At that time, there were 2,846 free white males of 16 years and upward, 3,744 white males under 16, and 5,804 white females. In addition there were 6 free persons and 828 slaves (Census of 1790, Summary of Population of Virginia by Counties in 1790, p. 9; Riley, "James Newell," p. 33; *Gose vs. Chaney*, Superior Court Chancery Book 2, Deposition of James Newell, May 19, 1820, Wythe County Circuit Court Clerk's Office).

Newell filed a lawsuit against Daniel Sheffey who had put a ferry boat on the New River at the same location claimed by Newell. Sheffey advertised at reduced rates, in the following words: "Travellers see your interest. Daniel Sheffey having built a boat

List of lands with their improvements dwelling houses and slaves owned by James Newell on the first day of April 1815 lying and being within the first district of the state of Virginia Viz in the County of Wythe —

one farm lying on the west side of new river opposite the lead mines containing five hundred and forty three acres having thereon one dwelling house of wood two stories high 54 feet by 28 one kitchen one barn — stable one corncrib one ox spinninghouse one negro house one brick meat house Valued at five thousand four hundred & thirty dollars $5430.00

one other tract of land lying south of the Lick mountain containing sixteen hundred and ten acres having no improvement — Valued at — — $96.60

Twenty one slaves of the following discription

Males 2 over 50 years
5 between 12 and 50
4 under 12
Females 2 over 50 years
6 between 12 and 50 years
2 under 12 years — Valued at — $5000.00
Total $10526.60

Jas Newell

The list of lands and slaves owned by James Newell in 1815.

Tracing from original by Mary B. Kegley.

at the Lead Mines is now ready to transport passengers across the river on the most reduced terms. Persons wishing to embrace this cheap ferriage will call for Sheffey's boat from either side, otherwise they will be compelled to pay more than double the price which Sheffey charges, viz: for a waggon and team 1/6; for cart and horse 9 and for a man and horse 4 1/2." Alexander Smyth stated there was a mistake made when the laws were revised regarding ferries. Between the time the ferry was established and the conveyance, the Austins bought the lead mines land on the south and east side of the River, but they did not buy the ferry. Smyth struck out Lynch's name and inserted Austins name by mistake. Newell bought the 180 acres from Lynch, including the ferry franchise (*Newell vs. Sheffey*, OS 218 NS77, Augusta County, filed at Staunton, Virginia).

After the Austins left the lead mines area, the mines were leased to James Newell, as mentioned elsewhere in this publication and in Riley's article, "James Newell," p. 23.

John Adams, Robert Sayers, David McGavock, John T. Sayers, and James Newell, or any three were to direct a survey in laying off the 100 acres given to the county. This was the beginning of the county seat, later named as Evansham, now Wytheville (Wythe County Orders, 1790). James Newell was recommended as lieutenant colonel in the 100th Regiment of Militia, and William Gleaves was recommended as captain replacing James Newell, promoted (Wythe County Orders July 12, 1796). Jas. Newell and Henry Stephens produced accounts of their services as Commissioners of the Revenue, and the 80 days requisite for them to perform their services. Newell was recommended as High Sheriff when the new County of Wythe was formed, and received the appointment, but could not serve because it was reported

Sarah Wood (1752-1851), wife of
Captain James Newell.
Courtesy of Andrew Trigg Sanders, Sr.

James Newell (1749-1823) from a
portrait by Fevret De Saint-Menin.
Courtesy of Mrs. Andrew Calhoun and
Mrs. Charles Motz, Sr.

that he was "about to remove from the County." He may have been involved at this time with the taking of the first Federal Census, but he never moved from the county. He eventually served as Sheriff of Wythe County, beginning on October 8, 1800 (Wythe County Orders, September 12, and November 12, 1800; Riley, "James Newell," p. 31).

James Newell (then designated as Senr. because he had a son also named James) died on March 2, 1823. His will was written on March 1, 1823, and probated April 9, 1823 (Wythe County Will Book 3, p. 30). Under the terms of the will, Sarah his wife was to have the plantation, and Andrew Kincannon was to live with her. At her death a tract of 400 acres was to pass to Andrew Kincannon for $6,000. Son-in-law Adams Sanders was to receive $300 to be paid by Andrew Kincannon, and was to receive 213 acres joining John Miller, Robert and William Sanders for $3,000. Sons-in-law, George and Andrew Kincannon, were to have 1,000 acres between the lands of Daniel Lockett and Lick Mountain adjoining John Brawley and Lockett, at a cost of $400 each. Wife Sarah was to have the slaves. Son James was to have $500; daughter Sarah (Sally) wife of John Evans was to be paid $500, but it was given to George Kincannon for her use, as her husband was to have no control over the money. Executors were George Kincannon and John P. Mathews. Sarah Newell died on April 23, 1831. Both she and her husband are buried in the Trigg Cemetery in Austinville.

The family records show that Martha (Mattie) married Stephen Sanders, son of John Sanders and Catherine Gannaway; Mary or Polly married William Sanders, son of Robert Sanders and Catherine Gannaway; a child William, died before his father; Betsy married Andrew Kincannon, II, son of Captain Andrew Kincannon and Catherine McDonald; Sarah (Sally) married John Evans and moved to Calloway County, Missouri, in 1819; James, III, married Susannah Trigg; Thirza (Thurza) married George Kincannon (brother of Andrew); and Senah married Adams Sanders, a brother of William mentioned above (Riley, "James Newell," pp. 17, 18; McConnell,

Sänders, pp. 221-222). Portraits of James and Sarah Newell were published by McConnell in *Sänders*). The Newell heirs are named in a lawsuit ended in 1833, when Leonard Straw brought suit (*Straw vs. Newell's heirs*, Box 52, 1833, Wythe County Circuit Court Clerk's Office, Basement).

James Newell, III, died April 1, 1847 at "half after seven o'clock p.m." Adams Sanders, his brother-in-law announced his death and ordered a coffin from Fleming K. Rich, a coffin-maker and a noted furniture-maker of Wytheville.

Captain James Newell was an outstanding leader in the lead mines community and provided leadership in the county for many years. His business interests included the lead mines, a mill, and the ferry. His military activities began as a young man, and he saw service in the Point Pleasant campaign and in the Revolution. His offices were among the most important in the county--justice, sheriff, surveyor, and commissioner of revenue. He was described as a "man of much good sense, sterling worth and great integrity of character" (Riley, "James Newell," p. 34), and was a notable early adventurer.

Adams Sanders announced the death of James Newell on April 1, 1847 and requested that Fleming K. Rich make a "nice coffin and case." Newell's measurements were five feet ten and twenty-two inches across the shoulder.　　　　　Tracing from the original by Mary B. Kegley.

David Peirce

David Peirce (also Pierce) was one of the outstanding business men of Wythe County and one of its most interesting adventurers. Because he was involved in so many projects, and because there is so much material available about him, the problem then becomes one of condensation without slighting the man's accomplishments.

By trade, Peirce was a gimlet maker, at least according to family tradition. A gimlet is a small tool with a screw point, a grooved shank, and a cross handle used for boring holes. He is probably better known for his leadership in the iron and lead industry with forges, furnaces, and interest in the lead mines. He also owned and operated a mill, a tavern and ordinary, and it appears from his inventory that he owned a tan yard, bark mills, and distilling equipment.

David Peirce was born in Chester County, Pennsylvania on April 8, 1756, the fifth son of George and Lydia Roberts Peirce. The exact date of his arrival in Wythe County is not known, but family records indicate that he served in the American Revolution as a private from Pennsylvania. He spent some time near Nashville, Tennessee. It was probably here that he lost all of his property by "the depradation of the savages on the Ohio." Any researcher would wonder if he lost a wife and children in that attack, especially when it is evident that he was already 42 years of age when he married in Wythe County on October 4, 1798. His wife was Mary Bell, the daughter of William Bell, who served as superintendent of the lead mines. Mary Bell was about 21 years of age at the time of the marriage. They had ten children in their thirty-five years of marriage. The marriage date appears to be the earliest record of Peirce's residence in Wythe County (Marriage Book 1, p. 17; family records; *DAR Patriot Index*, p. 534; McConnell, *Sänders*, pp. 288-289. McConnell gives the date of arrival as 1780, but the personal property tax lists for Wythe County do not show his name until 1798, the year of his marriage (*Peirce vs. Jackson*, Superior Court of Chancery Pleas, 1830-1831, Volume 9, Wythe County Circuit Court Clerk's Office).

The first land purchased by Peirce in Wythe County was 500 acres on both sides of Cripple Creek, a tract known as the Bell-Herbert forge place. It was purchased in 1800. The tract was formerly owned by William Bell and William Herbert, but was sold to Peirce by Robert Sanders and his wife Caty. The forge was operating at this site prior to July 1, 1794, as on that date the place was sold by Bell and Herbert to Hugh Montgomery and Daniel Carlin. They kept it for five years before selling to Sanders in 1799. Peirce owned and operated a mill and a forge there from the time of purchase until his death. In the partition of his estate the mill and forge passed to his son Alexander (Wythe County Deed Book 3, p. 56; Book 16, p. 54). Until recent years a large mill stood on the site with a wide sign "Peirce's Mill," painted on it.

After Peirce was situated at the ironworks, he petitioned for a road from Ahart Simmerman's to the ironworks, and on March 11, 1800, the Wythe County Court ordered that Daniel Shaver, William Rogers, John Harshbarger, John Brawley, and Robert Majors or any three, to view the nearest and best way for a road. On May 14, 1800, Shaver, Rogers, Harshbarger and Majors reported that they had viewed the road from Simmerman's to Peirce's mill works and that it "can be a convenient road" beginning at the fork of the road near Simmerman's, thence to the road near said Shaver's, thence to John Harshbarger's, thence near Julius Rutherford's, thence down the branch to the creek and up the same to the ironworks. It was ordered that the same be established, with Shaver as overseer on one side of Lick Mountain and Harshbarger on the other side. Joseph and Robert Crockett and John Shaver were to allot the hands to work on the road (Wythe County Order Book 1799-1801, pp. 147, 190).

David Peirce's three log houses at Poplar Camp, now gone. It is possible that one of the buildings was Peirce's Tavern.   Courtesy of the F. B. Kegley collection.

On July 14, 1801, Peirce and Thomas Blair asked the Wythe County Court for permission to build a grist mill on Poplar Camp Creek, and the following year on October 12, Peirce and Thomas Herbert received a license to keep an ordinary. On November 9, 1803, he received a license for a tavern at Poplar Camp (Wythe County Order Book 1801-1805, pp. 18, 134-135, 283).

The first tract of land purchased by Peirce on Poplar Camp Creek was 200 acres, from William and Rachel Ross in 1804. This is true even though he had prior permission for the mill, ordinary, and tavern (Wythe County Deed Book, p. 200).

Peirce is traditionally given credit for naming Poplar Camp Creek because he supposedly camped in a poplar tree, when he first came to the neighborhood. It is evident from the records that the name was first used by Colonel James Patton in 1751 (*see* surveys) five years before Peirce was born, and almost fifty years before he came to Wythe County. Although Peirce did not name the place, he was responsible for most of the activities that took place in that neighborhood over a period of more than thirty years. He had three log houses along the edge of the road at the intersection of present Route 52 and the road to Poplar Camp (Peirce family papers; Augusta County surveys; Kegley, *Virginia Frontier*, p. 125).

Peirce again petitioned the court for a road on May 10, 1803. He and Andrew Crockett asked that a road be opened between his Poplar Camp Furnace and James Crockett's Furnace at what was later Graham's Forge. On June 15, the Poplar Camp Furnace Road order was quashed, but the same men were to view the road to the ore bank of David Peirce, and also the road from James Crockett's Furnace to the house of James Crockett (Wythe County Order Book 1801-1805, pp. 199, 212-213).

On September 15, 1803, Robert Adams, Calvin Morgan, Daniel Lockett, and Robert Watson, four of the viewers appointed by the court to view the different grounds for that part of the roads lying between Thomas Foster's Ford and Poplar

Camp Furnace, made their report. They stated that the way proposed by Peirce measures 66 poles or thereabouts shorter than the way proposed by Major Evans. The way proposed by Peirce was not cleared and would take a great deal of labor to make it a good waggon road, but the road proposed by Evans, was with the exception of a short distance along the river, a waggon road, and could be kept in repair with very little labor. They believed that the greatest advantage would result to travellers by going by the way proposed by Evans because there were several places that they could be accommodated. The other way had no such advantages, although it would be better for Peirce in transporting his iron ore. The court decided that the Evans Road would be further considered and asked that Thomas Brooks and Thomas Foster, proprietors of the land through which the road was proposed, appear at the next court (Wythe County Order Book 1801-1805, p. 267).

In 1807, Peirce acquired the Poplar Camp Furnace from the Herberts (for further details *see* Herberts and Ross sketches). Numerous other tracts were added with locations on Cripple Creek, the Lead Mines, and Poplar Camp neighborhoods. In 1815, Peirce added the Poplar Camp Creek grist and saw mill, formerly belonging to Jesse Evans, and in 1817, he added a 200-acre "forge tract" on Little Reed Island Creek (Wythe County Deed Book 4, p. 512; Book 5, pp. 163, 278, 371, 387; Book 6, pp. 156, 220, 226, 291, 313, 319; Book 7, p. 58).

David Peirce's interest in the lead mines caused him to be involved in much litigation in the courts at Staunton and Wytheville. It is from these cases that much can be learned about the early activities of the mines. The biggest case was brought by Peirce against Thomas Jackson and can be found in Chancery Book 9. It is the lengthiest and most detailed suit ever filed in Wythe County. Needless to say, all of the story cannot be told here, but it seems to be worthwhile to condense information found in the bill presented by Peirce and the answer made by Jackson as well as from the depositions filed in the case (*Peirce vs. Jackson*, Volume 9, pp. 20-426).

In presenting the bill to the court, Peirce noted that the mines were sold by a decree of High Court chancery in Richmond to Stephen and Moses Austin, who failed to make the payments according to the terms of the sale and a new sale was ordered. He added that several years previous to the new sale that he came into the neighborhood and "by his labour and industry (after having lost all of his property by the depredation of the savages on the Ohio) acquired iron works consisting of a furnace and several forges and mills and plantations (*Peirce vs. Jackson*, p. 20).

He had heard about the new sale and mentioned it to Daniel Sheffey, a local attorney, hoping to entice him to become a partner in the purchase. Thomas Jackson, "an emigrant from England who professed superior skill in discovering, raising, washing, and smelting the lead," was living in the same neighborhood and claimed that he could carry out the operations on the "most advantageous and profitable terms." Eventually, it was agreed that Sheffey, Peirce, and Jackson would become the joint purchasers. Both Sheffey and Peirce acknowledged their ignorance of the management and superintendance of such a business, as both had other pursuits which took most of their time.

In the spring of 1806, it was agreed that each of the three would pay equal portions of the purchase price, and that Thomas Jackson would go to Richmond to make the purchase. On May 15, 1806, Jackson was the highest bidder at the sale, proposing £9,550 Virginia currency. They were to pay in annual installments, the first two being due December 1806 and the next December 1807. After bonds and securities were issued for the balance due, these three men obtained possession of the mines in January 1807. Work then began under the supervision of Jackson.

In December 1807, Sheffey and Peirce had a disagreement over the supposed failure of Peirce to pay his full portion of the first installment. Sheffey filed suit against Peirce in the court in Staunton in 1807. It lasted more than four years, causing great inconvenience for Peirce, who claimed his business at the ironworks and farms suffered because of his frequent and long absences. Peirce retained his one-third, and Sheffey was allotted 5/12 and the same was appealed. It was finally settled with a new agreement made out of court, allowing Sheffey to remain in the business until 1813. Sheffey was to convey to Jackson the Jenkins plantation and leave the slag and tools, and Jackson and Peirce agreed to make the purchase together. Other details were worked out in respect to "deferring payments, transferring smith tools, ferry boat, etc." which was supposed to compensate Peirce for his legal expenses. Even though it was all settled, Jackson changed his mind, sometimes saying one thing, sometimes another. Jackson claimed 11/24 of the mines property and according to Peirce never paid more than $30.70, even going so far as to say perhaps he was unfit to manage and carry on the business. Peirce had hoped that he and Jackson could work as a team for the common good of the business and not for individual gain.

When work began, Jackson made separate contracts with Joseph Jackson, Lancelot Knipe, and another Thomas Jackson to raise and wash ore at $40 for every ton made. Peirce, believing that the contracts were made for both of them, agreed. The men had an advantage in working the ore discovered by Sheffey, but not worked out during his time with the company.

Jackson explained in his answer (beginning on p. 29) that it was customary to let out to the miners what was called "bargains" by which the miners seek ore, raise it, sometimes wash it, and agree to their compensation by weight. Jackson did not want the mines to lie idle, so issued the contracts at $40 per ton, and also feared that because of the pending lawsuit the mines might be forfeited. He lost confidence in Peirce and resolved to trust nothing to him and to proceed on his own to make as much as he could.

They sunk six shafts, and in four they found abundant ore. During the same time period, Peirce sunk 23 shafts 40-80 feet deep and found ore in only 8 of them. Peirce claimed that each time he discovered good ore, that Jackson's men would begin shafts to intercept his, in order to exclude him, an accusation that Jackson denied. Jackson hired two "skillful able and respectable men" to work for him--William Sanders and James Bell, the latter the brother-in-law of Peirce. Jackson had several of his family connection working for him.

In January 1814, Peirce not being able to wash enough ore to keep his furnace in operation, took the ore to one of Jackson's buddles (where ore was washed), but was held off with force. Peirce then built a new buddle of his own. Jackson was also accused of cutting large quantities of wood and destroying buildings. Jackson moved from his iron furnace at Poplar Camp to the Town of Austinville, so that he could better attend to the preservation of the buildings and to the business in general. Further problems were described by Peirce. He stated that Jackson took over and rebuilt a furnace near the buddle, took possession of the location, keeping Peirce out. The Peirce waggons hauling ore to the buddles were stopped by Jackson, and the ore was thrown out of the waggons as fast "as the driver threw it in." As a result, Mr. George Spotts was brought in to superintend the whole property.

Jackson felt that the property should be divided and that only in that way could the two men carry on the business of mining lead. The final decree in the case was brought after Thomas Jackson's death, and the suit was revived in the name of his heirs. The court eventually awarded Peirce 13/24ths and Jackson's heirs 11/24ths interest in the mines, but the land was not actually divided.

In 1810, George Spotts came to live at the mines and was employed the first year keeping books. In 1811, he was employed at the buddle, overseeing the hands washing ore. The lead sold at the Wythe Court House in 1811 for £40 to £50 per ton. In 1812, Spotts was superintendent of the hands at Mine Hill. A new furnace was constructed in 1812, with brick obtained in Grayson County by John Mabe and others. The total cost was £179 and 7 shillings. Thomas Baldwin and Samuel Talbot assisted in building the furnace. William Fitzpatrick and John Mabe made bricks to build the furnace (Depositions in the case, pp. 330-426).

John Welsh, a founder for Peirce for 9-10 years, had known the ironworks for about thirty years. He was hired in 1812 to put a new hearth in Peirce's iron furnace. The snow was deep and the weather bad, and the coal was covered with snow. In the spring of 1813, the snow melted and the roads became so bad that the teams could hardly carry half a load. Ice obstructed the blast. John Mabe, John Fisher, and John Pearman were also employed by Peirce. Fisher had also worked for Major John Evans, making lead for Sheffey, and had also worked for Moses Austin. John Jackson worked for Sheffey on Mine Hill in 1812.

In September 1813, there were about 23 men employed at the mine hill, until the harvest, and then there was only 13. Of the 23, 17 were blacks. Following the harvest, 17 were employed, and 11 of them were blacks. Fifteen men were employed at the buddle, later 13, and 10 of them were black. Six hands were at the furnace, when it was in blast, and half of them were black. Charles Ballard had gone to North Carolina, where he formerly lived, to hire Negroes to work at the mines. He hired several and was well acquainted in Surry County, North Carolina. Lead sold at Wythe Court House for £56 per ton in 1813.

Michael Pearman was employed by Thomas Jackson at the mines, sometimes underground, sometimes at the windlass, and sometimes at the buddle to supervise the washing of the ore. William Sanders testified that James Bell who worked for Jackson beginning in August 1813, knew more about the lead mining business than any man in the United States, and that his salary of 750 pounds "was well laid out." Thomas Haslering (Hazelrigg, and other spellings) was clerk and manager for Jackson in 1813, weighing, selling, and keeping accounts of the lead sold. Richard Walton, George Alton, and John Millen applied to Peirce for work in 1813, and when they were refused, they went to work for Jackson. Thomas Evans moved to Wythe County in 1813, and lived at the forge where he had hands under his supervision. When all of the hands were transferred to the lead mines, Evans moved to North Carolina to live. Evans had obtained some of the hands in North Carolina. Warrick Peirce came to live with David Peirce (no relationship stated), and was superintendent of the new furnace.

William Sanders described the buildings, stating that Peirce took over in 1813, claiming the land near Jackson's plantation. All the buildings in Austinville, except the furnace house and shop, and an old shop built for pottery which Jackson had, were claimed by Peirce. This included a dwelling house, a tavern, a brick dwelling house, stone meat and spring houses, kitchen and old store house, another kitchen, stables, corn crib, and lumber house, seven cabins on Buddle Branch, a new house used as a lumber house, and a tavern with four stables. Jackson had two cabins on Buddle Branch, where he employed 28 hands at the time Peirce employed 44-50. Peirce built a three-story log house near the new furnace, with stone foundation and chimney, and two fireplaces. The 16 feet square cabin near the house was used as a kitchen. Peirce lived at the mines for two years. Sanders was manager and "labourer" for Jackson and also acted as an accountant or bookkeeper. William Sanders generally attended the buddle, James Bell attended the hands at the mine hill, and John Sanders attended to smelting ore at the furnace. Other houses on the lead mines tract not occupied were a brick house, where Mr. Jackson lived, and the house called the Austin's store house.

James Pearman, employed by Peirce as foreman, smelted the ore at the furnace. He was acquainted with the lead mines business more than twenty years, and during Austin's time, they raised blue ore. In Newell's time, they raised some blue ore, but discovered red and black ore. John Pearman, brother to James, Daniel Steel the furnace man, and three blacks were under him. In 1814, Thomas Baldwin and Thompson Carter, both stonemasons, worked at the furnace 10-20 days. Peyton Williams hauled ore, and also hauled brick from Grayson County.

James Bell stated that he began work for Jackson at the lead mines in August 1813. He worked at rebuilding a furnace, but Peirce came and told him it was his property and he wanted no assistance from Bell. Peirce ordered waggoners to unload, and Mr. Jackson drove off his horses twice or three times, and then a waggoner struck Jackson with his whip and got into a fight. Peirce told the waggoner to unload the ore. Sanders and Bell were given $500 a year by Sheffey and worked about 35 charges a month. Sheffey found them board. Jackson had no particular manager, but a bookkeeper, Archibald Hazlerigg.

John Fisher stated that in November 1813, he had sunk a shaft for Peirce and in December two more. He quit work in the shafts because of the scarcity of candles, "tallow being scarce in the neighborhood." John Sanders testified that in January 1816, he entered a partnership with Thomas Jackson for the purposes of a mercantile business at the lead mines. Jackson was to furnish the capital of $6,000 used to purchase goods from Henderson and Beaty, merchants at Abingdon. Jackson also bought goods at Baltimore.

Archibald Haslerigg was clerk and manager for Jackson and weighed the lead, sold it, and kept accounts. He lived with Peirce at the time work began on the cupulo furnace at the mines. The brick for this furnace was made in Grayson, and John Mabe and others, who were engaged in blowing rocks for the purpose of building a pot house for Peirce's iron furnace, were sent to Grayson to get the brick.

In 1814, Warrick Peirce posted the books, keeping the day book, the ledger and the time book. He came to live with Peirce April 18, 1813. He was superintendent at the new furnace smelting the slag in the cupola or slag furnace. He may have been one of the nephews referred to in an account written by a grandson of Peirce, who stated two nephews came from Pennsylvania to work for their uncle. One died shortly after arrival and the other eventually settled in Smyth County (typed manuscript, author unknown, "A Short Sketch of the Peirce Family," copy in possession of the author).

Thomas Baldwin, a stone mason, assisted in building the cupulo furnace in the winter of 1812. He estimated the total cost at $300. He also assisted Peirce in building a lead furnace in 1813, on the same ground where a furnace had stood. Part of the stone from the old one was put in the new one, and there were probably 50 waggon loads of stone used. The cost of building this furnace was estimated by Baldwin and Samuel Talbot at £179 and 7 shillings. Samuel Talbot testified about the furnaces, but added that he had piled up the logs and roof from an old mill house, on the lead mines tract, which had fallen down, and that prior to 1814 Peirce had built near the new furnace a three-story house with a dirt floor or cellar of stone, and others of logs. It measured 30 feet by 20 feet. It had two fireplaces, two floors, doors, windows, shutters and casings. The lower story had two rooms divided by a stone wall partition. The cellar had cast iron bars over the windows. There was a cabin adjoining the house, 16-18 feet square, used for a kitchen.

William Fitzpatrick was employed by Peirce in 1812 to assist John Mabe in making brick for the furnace. He helped make 21,500 brick in about 6 weeks.

Henry Sheffey was superintendent of the mines from 1808 until January 1, 1813. He noted that Major John Evans had made lead for several by contract, and that William Sanders and James Bell were fine or first rate workmen, employed at $500 a year. John Sanders was also excellent. Davy, a black, was an experienced and industrious employee in smelting. Richard Walton, as a miner, was "equal to any many affiant has ever known to take a pick in hand." John Millan was a little inferior to Walton; George Alton was industrious and apt to learn, but needed experience. Seyburn, a black, was an excellent miner. John Fisher was a man of considerable industry and judgment, perhaps a first rate miner. Joseph Jackson was slow but of good judgment. Lancelot Knipe was a good miner. James Pearman was a faithful industrious hand, and John Parker could follow a plain vein (*Peirce vs. Jackson*, Depositions).

In 1815, the tax assessor listed the lead mines land owned by Peirce and Jackson as being a tract on the east side of the New River, containing 1,400 acres, having "thereon one dwelling house of wood, two stories high with a celler under, 30 feet in length by 20 feet in width, two *kitchen* [kitchens], one office, one other dwelling house, two stories high, the length not known, one kitchen, dairy, smoke house, office, one barn, and a number of other houses say 21 for different uses, two lead furnaces and furnace houses, valued at $60,000" (Kegley, *Tax Assessments*, p. 141).

List of land and buildings at the lead mines in 1815 owned by Pierce and Jackson, valued at $60,000. Tracing from the original by Mary B. Kegley.

Photo of the portrait of Mary Bell Peirce owned by Mrs. Herbert P. Riley (Agnes Graham Sanders Riley), her great great granddaughter.
Courtesy of Mrs. Riley.

David Peirce died October 28, 1833, and is buried in a family cemetery on his land near the intersection of State Route 52 and the Poplar Camp Road Number 69. His wife Mary Bell Peirce died July 26, 1858 and is buried at the same place (tombstone inscriptions).

Following Peirce's death, there was a sale of his personal property. It was recorded in Wythe County Will Book 4, and covers 28 pages beginning on page 257. A summary of the pages follow here.

The widow purchased at the sale in November 1833 a total of more than $2,800 worth of property including the following items: part of a rye stack, a bull at the Foster place, 28 hogs, 23 cows, 36 yearlings and 2 year olds, 9 small calves, 6 stacks of hay, 53 hogs (little and big) at the Foster place, beds and furniture, 12 white counterpanes, bed clothes, table cloths, wash stand, basin and ewer, dressing glass, cloth brush, table cover, three window curtains (upstairs), 25 yards of homemade carpeting, a new carpet made up, two trunks with bed clothes and 12 pair of sheets, one set of "American State papers," one glass over the fireplace, a bureau and glass, two dressing tables and a candle stand, a large "waiter," two window curtains in the front room, a pair of brass candlesticks, snuffer tray and snuffers, clock and case, tables, dishes, cups and saucers, pitcher and bowl, chin press and contents, silverware, one bedstead furniture and curtains, beds designated as Maria's and Patsy's, three more window curtains, contents of the closet, one pair of shovel tongs, 26 chairs, two pair of andirons, kitchen furniture of every description, two old wheels, a reel (in the lower part of the office), woodwork of a wagon at the furnace, five cradles and scythes, four mowing scythes, two old oxen (blind), 100 hogs (little and big) at Poplar Camp, 36 sheep, 36 calves, one blind bay mare, 1,850 bushels of corn, 85 gallons of apple brandy, one stack of wheat.

The contents of the tavern were listed separately and sold in 1834, and included the following items: 12 beds, pillows, boulsters, sheets, counterpains, 9 wash stands, five large falling leaf tables, two dozen Windsor chairs, three small tables, two presses, a windmill, oats, fodder and rye.

At Reed Island there were yoke oxen, fur hats, tar, bar iron, pork, tobacco, deer skins, coal wagon, blacksmith tools and bellows, castings, dried fruit, and 500 pounds of salt. The sale at Bartlett's in Grayson County in 1833, listed 7 still tubs, rye, corn, buckwheat, hides and 12 1/4 gallons of brandy. At the Reed Island Forge, there was an ore pile, 1,000 cords of wood, and 2,455 bushels of "cole." At Poplar Camp there was a carding machine, flasks and patterns belonging to the furnace, a windmill, and thousands of pounds of bar iron and castings. Lead sold in Baltimore, after Peirce's death, amounted to more than $5,000. There was also a set of tanner's tools, many unfinished sole leather sides, shoemakers' casts, a bark mill, sides of upper leather, and four pounds of shoe thread.

Mrs. Peirce added to her purchases, the apple mill, three old still tubs, a still door, a "rifle gun" and shot bag, five pairs of coarse shoes, a calf skin and 18 sides of upper leather. To her privately were sold more than 100 pounds of lard, some iron and castings, beef cattle, and over 1,000 pounds of dried hides, numerous deer and sheep and calf skins.

In 1834, the property at the mines was sold and included blacksmith tools, beam scales and weights, a wheel barrow, a lot of puddle stems, and a lot of ladle "moles," and some iron. At Reed Island there were ovens and lids, steelyards, skillets and lids, pot racks, grindstone, fish pan, biscuit baker and lid, more ovens and lids, two waistcoats, one pair of socks, writing paper, a gum, an ink stand and a bottle, and a meat trough.

Other items sold included bark mills (Peirce had four in all), anvils (5 in all), kettles, ploughs, axes, a patent still and worm, three 20-gallon-kettles, grindstone, wagon wheels, more blacksmith tools, a forge hammer, a metal clock and case, eight hats, 1/2 dozen patent medicines, scales and weights, horses, bells, chisels, stoneware, a mill saw, ploughs, yoke oxen, saddles, bridles, saddle bags, carpenter's tools, tinware, blue cloth, a compass and chain, seven pairs of scissors, crocks, a shot gun, wooden clocks, eight dozen buttons, 9 whips, a cart, two rifle guns and pouch, one pair of prunella shoes, 16 pounds of powder, horseshoes, one set gun mountain, 8 ivory combs, a little wheel, sides of horse leather, upper sides of leather (more than 201), sole leather finished and unfinished, several hundred, and numerous skins in various stages of processing. There were more than 15,000 pounds of bar iron, and over 36,000 pounds of castings in the inventory.

It can be seen that Peirce had a well equipped and furnished home, including china, silver, curtains at the windows and carpets on the floors. The plantation supported every kind of farm animal, and wheat, rye, hay, and corn were mentioned. His enterprises in the iron and lead business were extensive and there were numerous references to the forge and furnace equipment and the products from them. The tavern furniture indicates that the stopping place could probably accommodate about two dozen people comfortably with 12 beds and 24 chairs mentioned.

The tanyard operation appears more extensive than expected. With tanner's tools, four bark mills and thousands of pounds of skins and leather, this operation was probably the largest of its kind in the county. Although there is only brief mention of shoes, and shoemaker's tools and thread, it appears there may have been some attempt to make shoes there too.

The distillery (or perhaps more than one) included the mention of several stills, worms, still tubs, and the finished product. Peirce seems to have limited himself to apple brandy. There were several entries for tobacco, but it may not have been grown on the plantation. The total amount of the sale was $18,243.79, a remarkable sum for the time. John Foster was the administrator of the estate.

Following Peirce's death, the land was divided by Commissioners appointed by the court. In 1838 the heirs released the lots assigned to them to each other, and their names appear in the deeds of Wythe County. The heirs were Elizabeth Chaffin, Alexander Peirce and wife Elizabeth, James R. Miller and wife Emily, David Graham and wife Martha, Alexander Mathews and wife Maria, William Peirce, James N. Peirce and wife Nancy D. (of Pulaski County), Edwin Watson and wife Malinda F.(of Pulaski County). Elizabeth Peirce married William Womack Chaffin. Two other daughters, Harriet R. and Mary S. died in infancy(Wythe County Deed Book 16, p. 54; Book 18, pp. 340, 344, 348, 352, 357, 361, 366; Kegley, "David Peirce," *Wythe County Historical Review*, No. 7, pp. 1-7 at p. 4 has further information about the children; *see also*, "Abstract of Title [Bertha Mineral Company, July 18, 1902]," *Wythe County Historical Review*, No. 15, pp. 36-41 for further information about the heirs).

Elizabeth Cloud Peirce Chaffin, daughter of David and Mary Bell Peirce was born July 22, 1799 and died July 28, 1892. She was married on September 30, 1817 to William Womack Chaffin. She is buried in a private cemetery near Poplar Camp.

Courtesy of David Davis and Rush Crockett.

The Chaffin house at Poplar Camp.   From the F. B. Kegley Collection

Brick building used as slave quarters at the Chaffin house.   From the F.B. Kegley Collection.

The land was divided as follows: to James N. Peirce, the west Crockett place 424 acres, the Anthony place in Grayson County on Little Reed Island Creek 140 acres, and the Harrel place 84 acres in Grayson on Little Reed Island Creek, and 76 acres adjoining the last mentioned place, bought from John Richardson. To Emily Miller, a house and lot in Town (Wytheville), the brick tavern, and 384 acres on Mine Mill Creek, adjoining George Walton. To Maria Mathews, in Grayson County 149 acres from Nimrod Newman and 220 acres purchased by Peirce from James Lundy, in Wythe County the Frisby place of 206 acres, and the Jenkins place of 232 acres. To Elizabeth Chaffin, the east Crockett place of 412 acres, and in Grayson the McLean place of 238 acres and the Stephen Brown place of 317 acres. To David Graham and his wife Martha, 324 acres on New River, 212 acres on Glady Fork in Grayson, 130 acres in Grayson, and in Wythe 150 acres, adjoining Robert Raper and George Walton (Wythe County Deed Book 18, pp. 340, 344, 348, 352, 357).

To William Peirce, Jerry's Hollow 500 acres in Wythe, and 145 acres on Bobbett's Creek in Grayson. To Alexander Peirce, seven tracts of land, 500 acres on both sides of Cripple Creek, 289 acres called the Sinking Spring tract on Cripple Creek, another tract of 194 acres on Cripple Creek, 158 acres on Francis Mill Creek, 88 acres on Cripple Creek, 26 acres on Cripple Creek, and 250 acres on Little Reed Island Creek in Grayson. To Malinda, wife of Dr. Edwin Watson, Lot # 7, a total of 808 acres, one tract in Wythe County and three in Grayson County (Wythe County Deed Book 18, p. 361; Book 16, p. 54).

Jeremiah Pierce

Jeremiah Pierce (Perse, Pearce, Peirce) was probably living on the New River as early as the fall of 1768. At that time, he had a tract of land surveyed on the east side of the river adjoining David Sayers. In the spring of 1769, another tract was selected and surveyed. These tracts were laid off for the Loyal Company by William Preston (Preston Family Papers, 581, Library of Congress; Kegley and Kegley, *Early Adventurers,* Vol. 1, pp. 34, 41, 42).

In 1770, he was appointed constable for the New River by the Botetourt County court. In the same year, he was appointed surveyor of the road from Herbert's Mill to the mouth of Big Reed Island Creek (Summers, *Annals,* pp. 62, 63).

He served as a lieutenant with Captain Walter Crockett for 53 days in 1774 and was paid £9.7.6 for his service. Following Captain William Herbert's death, Peirce became captain in his place in 1776 (Kegley, *Soldiers,* p. 28). He was a member of the jury for Jacob Catron's trial in 1777 (Summers, *Annals,* p. 684). Pierce appears to have served in the French and Indian War, receiving a certificate for 200 acres of land from the Montgomery County Court in 1779 (Summers, *Annals,* p. 726).

In 1781, as captain of the militia, he took the list of men which accompanies this sketch (Kegley, *Militia of Montgomery County* , pp. 1, 2, 3, 37). There is no will or settlement of an estate for Pierce in Wythe County and he probably left the New River community about 1782, when Stephen Sanders became captain of a company of militia and many of the same names appear on his list as on Pierce's. It is possible that Pierce may have moved to Kentucky as a Jeremiah Pierce is listed in 1787 tax list in Lincoln County. There is no known connection to David Peirce of Poplar Camp, or to a William Pierce, who appears in the same neighborhood.

Jeremiah Pearce's Company, April 5, 1781

Samuel Ewing
Thomas Foster, Lieut.
Alexr. Neely, Lieut.
Thos. Whitlock, Sargt.
John Hays, Sargt.
William Pierce
Benjn. Price
John Davis
Patrick Cash
Moses Waddle
Jacob Cain
John Jenkings
Saml. Price
William Stewart

Robt. Bohanon
James Craig
Robert Simpson
Anthy. Duncan
John Stephens
Sampson Steel
David Craig
Even Williams
Richd. Ellor
Roger Oats
John Forbush
Isaac (?) Shephard
------Hodge
Thos. Holland
39 for duty

Andw. Stots, Sargt.
Charles Carter
John Ross
Thomas Smith
Fredk. Davis
Wm. Lee
Geo. Forbush
Wm. Bell, Junr.
Natl. Buchanan
Jer. Harrell
Jacob Holland
Joseph Eaton
John Holland
Robt. Sayers

Captain Stephen Sanders Company

Stephen Sanders, Capt.
John Ross
John Genkins, En.
William Stuard
Jacob Holland
Thos. Holland
Francis Day
Even Williams
Charles Bright (?)
John Cain
John Whitfield (Whiserd?)
 (deleted)
Alexander Neeley
Charles Green
William Cash
Frederick Davis

Isaac Shepherd
Robert Saunders
Benjamin Bennit
William Herbert
John Abstant
John Holland
Richard Ellis
William Bell
Jacob Hufman
Andrew Stots
Thos. Foster
Bartlet Green
William Ross
Nathaniel Buchanan
Joseph Gay (Gray?)
George Gay (Gray ?)

Thomas Whitlock
Daniel Nants (?)
Wm. Hamton
Thomas Smith
James Turman
Wm. Thrift
Cornelius Linel
Howard Cash
Jacob Cain
Nath. Riever (?)
Peter Feney
Robt. Buchanan
James Craig
James Ray
Joh. Robins
Sampson Steel

John Genkins became ensign in 1782, which helps date the list.

The Raper Family

Ann Jackson, sister of Thomas and John Jackson, was born in Long Martin, Westmoreland, England. She was the daughter of _____ Jackson and his wife Mary, who later married William Naggs and operated a grocery store in Dufton, Westmoreland, England. Ann had brothers, John and Thomas, who both migrated to Wythe County, and a sister Deborah who remained in England. Ann married William Raper in England on September 14, 1764. They had five children: Mary Ann born 1787, John born 1789, William born 1792, Thomas born 1793 and Robert born 1796. All of the children were born in England, and came to Wythe County about 1801, except Thomas who only lived about a year. Ann Jackson Raper married second Richard Walton (Oewel, ''The Raper Family,'' *Wythe County Historical Review*, No. 41 (January 1992), pp. 26-27, hereinafter Oewel, ''Raper Family''; Wythe County Order Book 1829-1833, p. 5, dated Jan. 12, 1830, recites the family relationships as understood by a John Jackson, son of Nathan, of Westmoreland, England, who was not a relative of the other Jacksons, but knew them in England and in Wythe County; *see also* Walton and Jackson sketches).

Mary Ann Raper, daughter of Ann and William Raper, married twice: (1) William Millian (probably the Polly Raper who is mentioned on a typed list as marrying *John Miller* prior to February 2, 1808, in Wythe County) and (2) Joseph Parkins, and moved to Indiana. She had a son William Millian and three Parkins children: Elizabeth, John Robert, and Mary. William Millian appears to be the same person as William Milling of Wayne County, Indiana, who on June 27, 1831, appointed John Raper his attorney in fact to sell his interest in the mines and other tracts of land formerly owned by Thomas Jackson, deceased (Wythe County Deed Book 21, p.81).

John Raper, son of William and Ann Raper, married Elizabeth Keesling sometime prior to February 2, 1808 (Wythe County Marriage Book 1, p. 36). John served in the militia in the War of 1812, and received a bounty land warrant. His widow received a pension when she was living in Boston Township, Wayne County, Indiana, in 1871 (Wardell, *War of 1812: Virginia Bounty Land & Pension Applicants*, p. 265). Their seven children were heirs of Thomas Jackson and are mentioned in the Wythe County records, claiming their share of the Jackson estate. The children were: William, John, Robert, Eve, Mary, Susannah, and Ann the wife of Thomas Hasty. In 1831, at the time a suit was filed, John Raper had lately arrived in Wythe County from Indiana where he and several of his children were then living. Ann Hasty was living in Ohio. John was appointed guardian for his children, William, Robert, and John on September 8, 1831, in Wayne County, Indiana. In a letter written December 12, 1852, from Richmond, Wayne County, Indiana, to Dr. Richard Walton Sanders in Wythe County, John tells about his children who were living in various western places. His youngest daughter Susannah, wife of Abednego Hurst, was in Louisa County, Grandview Post Office, Iowa. His daughter Mary Cambel [Campbell] was living in Brown County, Mount Sterling, Illinois, and John Raper was living in Madison County, but state is not mentioned. Ann Hasty was living in Henry County, no state mentioned. His daughter Eve Fisher was living in Union County, Indiana, and son William living in Wayne County, Indiana, and John's ward, Ann Elisabeth Raper, daughter of John, was in Salt Lake City (*Sanders and Walton vs. White*, Box 88, 1840, and *John Raper and wife vs. John Raper's Children*, Chancery Box 64, 1836, 1837, Wythe County Circuit Court Clerk's Office, Basement; Wythe County Deed Book 13, p.557; copy of the letter in the author's library).

Robert Raper, son of Ann and William Raper, married Polly (Mary Craig) Crockett, the daughter of John Crockett, Jr., on December 20, 1831 (Wythe County Marriage Book 1, p.117). They had three children: William Jackson Raper born 1832, who married twice: (1) Sarah Virginia Crockett and (2) Margaret Maria Crockett, both daughters of Allen T. and Carolina Minter Crockett; John Crockett Raper born 1834, who married (Sarah) Sally daughter of J. Stuart and Margaret Taylor Crockett, and Mary Ann born 1837, who married William Samuel Thorn, son of James and Mary Ann Raper Thorn, a grandson of William Raper of Indiana (Oewel, ''Raper Family'').

On August 13, 1823, and again on September 13, 1825, Robert Raper of Liverpool, England, filed with the court his intentions of becoming an American citizen (Wythe County Order Book 1822-1826, pp. 148, 527; *see also* Kegley, *Glimpses*, Vol. 2, pp.

84, 85). The lawsuit mentioned above states that he probably never became a citizen of the United States.

Robert was closely associated with his uncle Thomas Jackson, who was part-owner of the lead mines. Raper and Jackson operated a store at the mines, which was mentioned in the estate of Thomas Jackson in 1824. When Jackson died unmarried and without a will, all of the Raper and Walton children, as well as the children of his brother John Jackson had claims to his estate (Wythe County Will Book 3, p. 140; Wythe County Deed Book 13, pp. 557,558). On June 9, 1834, Robert Raper and John Sanders applied for permission to erect a dam across "lead mine" creek to wash ore. A writ of *ad quod damnum* issued (Wythe County Order Book 1833-1837, p. 125).

William Raper, son of William and Ann Raper, married Mary McClure in Indiana, and had two daughters, Mary A. and Jane. George and Hannah Walton, children of Ann Jackson Raper and Richard Walton, also had a claim to the Jackson estate (Wythe County Deed Book 13, pp. 558, 559; Wythe County Chancery Causes, Box 88, 1840, *Sanders and Walton vs. James White's adminis. et al.; John Raper and wife vs. John Raper's Children*, Box 64 1836,1837, Wythe County Circuit Court, Basement; *see* Walton sketch).

In 1837, children of the two brothers, William and John Raper, conveyed their interest in the mines to Robert Raper by Special Commissioner, following the settlement of the lawsuit. In 1843, two of David Peirce's children, Malinda and James N. and their spouses, released their interests in the mines to Robert Raper (Wythe County Deed Book 13, pp. 557, 558; Book 16, pp. 315, 328).

Robert Raper was a large land owner, and most of his land was located on the north side of the New River. In 1857, he put several of the tracts together in an inclusive survey of 1,789 acres, which included the 300 acres, the John Millen (alias Millian) tract, 221 acres from Robert and Louisa Sanders, 339 acres and 73 poles from Robert Sanders, Jr., 6 acres and 12 poles from Robert Sanders, Sr., 525 acres from John Sanders, executor of Stephen Sanders, deceased, and 253 acres 1 rood and 22 poles, part of 384 acres granted to Henry Lee, being the land conveyed by James R. and Emily Miller, heirs of David Peirce to Raper. He continued to buy land and added to his holdings the Kincannon land and ferry, known now as Thorn's Ferry (Wythe County Deed Book, 10, pp. 415, 483, Book 15, p. 51; Book 16, pp. 315, 328, 255; Book 20, p. 638, Book 21, p. 188; Wythe County Survey Book 4, p. 278).

The John C. Raper home was sold by his widow and children to Walter M. Cornett in 1910. It stood on the south side of Route 619 east of Austinville.   Courtesy of Davy Davis.

337

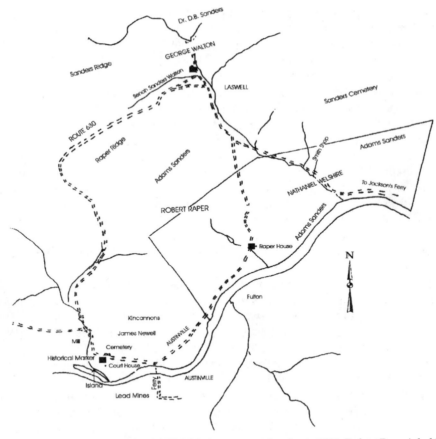

The outline represents Nathaniel Welshire's survey made prior to 1750. Robert Raper's holdings in the 1830s covered much of the same territory between Austinville and Laswell on both sides of the Jackson's Ferry Road (Route 52) and the Kincannon's Ferry Road (Route 619). Later purchases extended his acreage to the mouth of Mine Mill Creek. The 1,800 acres of the Walton land included tracts of Evan Williams and Joseph Eaton, later Richard Muse. The house of Senah Walton (widow of George) was located on an 1850s recorded plat. Locations are approximate.

Map by Mary B. Kegley from deeds and surveys.

During the Civil War, John C. Raper and W. J., Raper served in various companies at various times (*see* Kegley, *Bicentennial History,* p. 435.)

By the terms of the will of Robert J. Raper, his two sons, William, and John C. were to have the homeplace following his wife's death, and two other farms, the Stephen Sanders farm and the Trigg farm. His daughter Mary Ann Thorn was to have the Andrew Kincannon ferry place, where she was then living. His grandchildren, Mary, Annie Lee, Emma, Maggie, Lilian, Samuel Crockett Thorn, Alice Thorn, and Willie Thorn were to receive stock in the Lead Mines Company. His piano was bequeathed to his granddaughter Mary Raper Thorn. His wife was to have a life interest in the homeplace, and all other land except the interest in the Lead and Zinc Mine Company and the lands where their daughter lived. She also received all the household furnishings and the stock and tools. The sons and Mary Ann Thorn were to have shares of stock in the Wythe Lead and Zinc Co. Under his codicil, he devised the Stephen Sanders land to his sons jointly, and they were to pay the charges for the education of granddaughter Mary Raper Thorn. A new grandchild, Roberta Thorn, born since the will was written, was to have 98 shares in the mines. Raper also acquired 40 shares of stock of the Farmers

338

Bank, which was bequeathed to his wife Mary C. Raper. A second codicil noted that he had bought other lands, and he devised the farm purchased from Sallie Currin to his daughter Mary Ann Thorn. The Stephens land adjoining the ferry, being 150 acres went to his sons jointly. He also mentioned his "old servant" Sarah Hampton and daughters Eliza and Adelade, and Mary Green. Raper's will was written on December 18, 1876 with codicils added December 18, 1876 and December 20, 1877. It was probated in Wythe County in August 1878 (Wythe County Will Book 13, p. 115).

Distribution of the personal property was made by the executors and recorded in October Term 1881 (Will Book 13, p. 517). In 1879, the executors of Robert Raper conveyed the land for the Galena Presbyterian Church to the Trustees, William J. Raper, David Graham, and J.P.M. Sanders, noting that Captain Robert Raper had laid off the land, but no deed had been made in his lifetime. The church was probably organized in the 1850s and named for the type of lead mined close by (Wythe County Deed Book 31, p. 544).

Of added interest was a Legislative Petition filed with the General Assembly which mentions Captain Raper. Robert Smith, a "free man of colour," who lived in Evansham (now Wytheville) was born a slave, the property of Mann Page of Spotsylvania County, Virginia. He became the property of Doctor Coleman of Fairfax County, who sold him in 1830 to John Sanders, and he in turned sold him to Captain Robert Raper. Because of "bodily infirmities" Smith was unable to work, but "has for several years been occupied in business as a barber, hair dresser, and confectioner at Wythe Court House." He was freed by Captain Raper and wanted to remain in Virginia, even though the law stated that if freed he had to leave the state. His petition was rejected. The deed from Robert Raper was dated March 12, 1834, and mentions that Robert was generally called Robert Smith, and that he was a man of yellow complexion, about five feet five, and about 30 years old. He was lame "in the left ancle, the same having been thrown out of place." (Wythe County Legislative Petition, December 4, 1834, Virginia State Library, Archives; Wythe County Deed Book 12, p. 536).

Rogers

There are several families of Rogers (also spelled Rodgers) men mentioned in the early New River community: two Johns, two Benjamins, James, Joseph, Reuben, David, Joseph, Sr., Thomas, and Doswell (with various spellings). Of these, Benjamin, James, John, David, and Joseph were paid for Revolutionary War service in North Carolina, Doswell Rogers settled on Elk Creek, selling his land in the 1790s. James Rogers owned land at the head of Cripple Creek, but assigned it to James Scott in 1782. These men may or may not have been be related to each other (Kegley and Kegley, *Early Adventurers*, Vol. 1, p. 37; Summers, *Annals*, p. 771; Wythe County Deed Book 1, pp. 24, 65,68).

James Rogers is first mentioned as a tithable on New River in Herbert's Company of 1771. In 1774, he took up two tracts of land on Cripple Creek, and the same year he was paid by the auditors for 82 days of service with Captain Daniel Smith's Company. James is also mentioned in Doak's Company during Dunmore's War of 1774. In 1781 and 1782, his name appears on James Newell's Company roster. In 1782, he was paid for Revolutionary War service in North Carolina. A James Rogers is mentioned in several deeds describing land located not on Cripple Creek, but further east in Wythe County. The tax assessment of 1815 shows that he had one farm in Blacks Corner on the waters of New River, 50 acres having thereon one "cabben," and one stable, valued at $150. James left no will here, and deeds do not reveal the record of his family (Kegley, *Tithables*, p. 11; Kegley, *Soldiers*, pp. 21; Kegley, *Militia*, pp. 30, 31; Thwaites and Kellogg, *Dunmore's War*, p. 400; Summers, *Annals*, p. 771; Wythe County Deed Book 9, p. 117; Book 10, p. 283; Montgomery County Plat *Book A, pp. 25, 28; Kegley, Tax Assessment*, p. 143*)*.

William Rogers (Rodgers) was an early settler on Mine Mill Creek. He is mentioned in the 1771 and 1772 tithable lists and in Newell's lists of 1781 and 1782. William owned 200 acres on the head of the creek, a tract he sold in 1815 to Joseph Jackson. According to the tax assessment records, William Rodgers, Senr., owned a farm on Mine Mill Creek, on the south side of Lick Mountain, 378 acres with one dwelling house of wood, 1 1/2 stories 22 feet by 18 feet, one barn, and other ''cabbens, not worth mentioning,'' valued at $900. No wife is mentioned in local documents, and he left no will in Wythe County (Kegley, *Tithables*, pp. 11, 17; Kegley, *Militia*, pp. 30, 31; Wythe County Deed Book 6, p. 347; Kegley, *Tax Assessment*, p. 143).

John Rogers was also mentioned in the early records of Mine Mill Creek area. There was a John, Sr., and a John, Jr., mentioned in 1771 tithable list, but in 1772 and 1773, there was only one on each of these lists. In 1782, John took up 200 acres on Mine Mill Creek adjoining the upper side of James Brawley, a tract later assigned to John Brawley who received the grant in 1796 (Kegley, *Tithables*, pp. 12, 32; Grant Book 34, p. 497).

A John Rogers served 104 days with Captain William Herbert in 1774 and he was paid for his services. He is also mentioned in 1781 and 1782 on Newell's lists. He was also paid 10/ following duty in North Carolina in 1782 (Kegley, *Soldiers*, p. 49; Kegley, *Militia*, pp. 30,31; Summers, *Annals*, p. 771).

In 1778 and following, there are records of a John Rogers in Washington and Wythe counties. In Wythe County a John Rogers married Polly Brawley (Summers, *Annals*, p. 980; Wythe County Marriage Book 1, p. 18; *see* Bralley sketch. Family tradition in the Rogers family stated that Benjamin, Sr., had a son John who moved to Washington County, Tennessee, about 1791).

There were two Benjamin Rogers, one Sr., and the other Jr., and it is sometimes difficult to determine which record refers to which one. Keeping that in mind, a Benjamin Rogers appears on a tithable list for William Herbert in 1771, the first time the name appears in the New River area. The next year, John Montgomery listed Benjamin Rogers, Jr., on his tithable list (Kegley, *Tithables*, pp. 17, 32).

In 1774, a Benjamin Rogers took up a tract of 107 acres on Cripple Creek, the grant issuing to George Buckalew in 1806. In 1789, Benjamin Rogers took up 150 acres on Baber's Mill Creek, a branch of Cripple Creek. The land adjoined Benjamin Rogers, Sr. (Montgomery County Plat Book D, p. 179; Wythe County Deed Book 5, p. 366).

Benjamin Rogers served as a constable on Cripple Creek in 1774, and in 1777 Benjamin, Sr., was appointed as constable. In 1778, Benjamin is a constable in Newell's Company. In 1781 and 1782, Newell's Company included the name Benjamin Rogers. The auditor's accounts for Dunmore's War of 1774 include payments to a Benjamin Rogers for 104 days of service under Captain William Herbert and 53 days service under Captain Walter Crockett (Summers, *Annals*, pp. 602, 676, 687, 757; Kegley, *Militia*, pp. 30,31; Kegley, *Soldiers, pp. 29, 49)*.

Benjamin Rogers, Sr., moved to Washington County, Tennessee, where he is said to have died about 1802. He is probably the one mentioned in a Wythe County deed dated 1801, when he and wife Lokey sold 63 acres on Cripple Creek to Robert Majors (family information; Wythe County Deed Book 3, p. 177).

Further information was obtained about Benjamin Rogers, Jr., from his Revolutionary War service pension record (W867). On December 11, 1832, Benjamin was a resident of Campbell County, Tennessee, and was 77 years old. He stated that he was born in Culpeper County, Virginia, in 1755 although the family Bible record shows it was in January 1756. He moved from Wythe County to Blount County, Tennessee, and then to Campbell County. He was living in what is now Wythe County during the war and was called into service from there. He entered as a volunteer under Captain Harbert (Herbert) and served more than three months. In his first tour, he marched through Greenbrier and to the Kanhawa and was dismissed there [compare with the days served in Herbert's Company above].

He served a total of eight tours of duty, the last seven being service of just over three weeks each. Few of the officers were recollected, but he did mention Captain Campbell, Captain Triag (Trigg?) and Col. Prester (Preston). Sometime during these tours, he marched twice to the Moravian Towns in North Carolina and once to Bluesey Creek and once to Haw River in North Carolina He was drawn up in the line of battle at Haw River to fight the army of Lord Cornwallis, and the regulars were also at the place and were commanded by General Greene. The militia was under the command of General Preston (probably intended for Colonel Preston). Greene's aide-de-camp made an arrangement with the militia that the horses of the militia were to be given up to the care of a few men, about six horses to a man. Rogers stated that he was discharged by Preston but lost his papers.

His wife was Martha Rogers, born April 26, 1766. Her maiden name was Brawley, and they were married on March 24, 1788 (no marriage record has been found). The service was performed by a Methodist preacher named Masten, when the courts were held at Fort Chiswell. Martha lived with him for 46 years, 3 months, and 2 days, until Benjamin's death on June 27, 1834. Martha in her statement, noted that she was the widow of Benjamin Rogers of Knoxville, Tennessee, and that he had served as a private in the Virginia line and was on the roll of pensioners. He was granted $16.66 per annum.

There were no children mentioned in the service record, but William A. Wright stated that he was raised by Benjamin and his wife Martha. He too was living in Campbell County, Tennessee. Martha Brawley Rogers was probably a daughter of John Brawley, an early settler at the head of Mine Mill Creek (*see* Bralley sketch). The Bralley family history lists their children as Stephen, Sarah Coats, Polly Sherrill, and Margaret Heavley, who were mentioned in the will of Benjamin, written June 30, 1833, and probated September 20, 1834 (Family information; Bralley, *Clan*, p. 83).

By the family, I was referred to Goodspeed's *History of Tennessee,* which stated in a section about Claiborne County, that David Rogers, son of John and a grandson of Benjamin Rogers was born in 1779 in what is now Wythe County, Virginia, and came to Washington County, Tennessee, when he was twelve years of age. Other family information reveals that Benjamin and William Rogers were brothers, and that John Rogers had, in addition to David, sons William, Benjamin, John (born 1781), Jesse, and Reuben. John Rogers and his wife Polly Bralley moved from Wythe County and settled in Claibourne County, Tennessee (family information).

There are four marriages for Rogers women recorded in Wythe County. They are: Malinda who married James Magers [Majors] on January 31, 1836; Mary who married Nathaniel Knipe about November 20, 1825; Nancy who married John Kelchner December 16, 1805; and Susan who married Isaac B. Lambert on August 17, 1848. Her bond was with James Hoge, Jr., and was dated July 20, 1848. It is not known if any of these women were related to the families mentioned in this sketch (Wythe County Marriage Book 1, pp. 120, 95, 30, 170).

William Ross first appears in the records about 1782 on the militia list of Captain Stephen Sanders. He took up land in the Poplar Camp neighborhood in 1783, and in 1787 was appointed overseer of the road from Herbert's Ferry to James Cocks. In 1789, he purchased 130 acres from William Herbert (Kegley, *Militia,* p. 40; Montgomery County Plat Book C, p. 112; Summers, *Annals,* pp. 273, 920).

In writing about Poplar Camp furnace, Whitman in his book gives William Ross credit for beginning industrial activity there about 1790. He notes that Ross patented the land and erected a grist mill. However, James M. Swank in writing of the history of iron manufacturing in 1891, noted that Poplar Camp Furnace appears to have been built in 1778, as a stone bearing that date was identified with the furnace. In view of recently discovered information, the date of 1778 may be too early (Whitman, *The Iron Industry of Wythe County from 1792,* p. 12; Swank, *History...*p. 268; Legislative Petition of Owen Richardson, June 3, 1779, Virginia State Library, Archives, states that there are no iron works yet erected or begun as of this date; *see also,* Kegley, *Glimpses,* Vol. 1, pp. 134-135).

More than 600 acres were surveyed for Ross in the 1790s in the Poplar Camp neighborhood and his Macks Creek locations (Wythe County Survey Book 1, pp. 108, 304, 451, 474; Book 2, p. 1). William Ross and his wife Rachel Fugate Ross sold four tracts of land that they had acquired in 1797 for a price of $2,400. The purchasers, Greenbury G. McKenzie and Caleb Bobbett of Grayson County kept the four tracts of 590 acres for a brief period and then sold to William and Thomas Herbert, who in turn sold to David Pierce. These were the tracts connected with the Poplar Camp Furnace, which was included in the sale. In 1804, Ross also sold an additional 200 acres to Peirce. This tract, adjoining Walter Crockett, was near the lead mines (Wythe County Deed Book 2, pp. 113, 115, 116, 117; Book 4, p. 200; *Fugate vs. Fugate,* Superior Court Chancery Book 6, p. 488, discloses that Rachel, wife of William Ross, was a sister to Randolph Fugate, Sr., who died in 1814, and Randolph Fugate, Jr., married Charity Ross, daughter of William Ross. The case begins on p. 467).

William Ross appears to have moved to Persimmon Bottom on the waters of Macks Run on the New River in present Pulaski County about 1797, when he purchased from John and Mary Hurst two tracts of land containing 280 acres (Wythe County Deed Book 2, pp. 14, 165). Ross added another 200 acres by survey in 1798, designating the tract as military land office treasury warrant #528. The land cornered on the tract he was living on, also James Jones, and Jacob Miller. It was also by a road leading to Ross's Mill. The survey was repeated in 1804 (Wythe County Survey Book, 1, p. 474; Book 2, p. 1).

William Ross probably died late in 1825, as William Ross, [Jr.], was appointed administrator of the estate of William Ross, deceased, on December 13, 1825, and Rachel, the widow, was to have her dower laid off (Wythe County Order Book 1822-1826, p. 565). Rachel's dower was assigned on September 12, 1831, and transferred to Robert Sayers on September 26, 1835 (Wythe County Deed Book 12, p. 81; Book 13, p. 233). The inventory and sale of William's personal property was recorded in 1827, and at that time, he was designated as Captain William Ross, deceased. Among the items of property sold were: hammer, anvil, mattock, knives, barrels, pots, ovens, kettle, pot hooks, steelyards, cupboard and furniture, candlesticks, one gun and pouch, andirons, dining table, clock, books, decanters, two large and three small spinning wheels, sow, pigs, mares, 50 barrels of corn, oat stack, tea board, coffee mill, chest, and trunks, hay, heifers, calves, plows, pots, kettles, one man slave valued at $500; one woman slave, valued at $250, and one boy slave, valued at $200 (Wythe County Will Book 3, pp. 254, 269).

Following the death of William Ross, Catherine Ross orphan of William Ross, deceased, upwards of age 14, chose Thomas Graham her brother-in-law, as her guardian (Wythe County Order Book 1826-1829, October 12, 1829, p. 575). Several of the heirs conveyed their interests in the land to Robert Sayers, who had married Senah, daughter of William Ross, in 1824. The others mentioned included Charles Dudley who married Anne (Ann) Ross in 1827, Robert J. Yancey who married Catherine L. Ross in 1829, Samuel Slone (Sloan) who married Clarissa Ross in 1821, Thomas Graham who married Euphemia Ross in 1821, Kesiah Calfee of Monroe County, Indiana and Rachel Haines of Wythe County. Reuben and Randolph Ross (of White County, Tennessee) transferred their interest to their mother, who in turn conveyed to Sayers. (Wythe County Deed Book, 10, p. 599; Book 11, pp. 313, 496, 502; Book 12, pp. 168, 169; Book 13, pp. 230, 231, 232, 233.)

Robert Sanders

Robert Sanders, founder of the ''River'' Sanders, was one of fourteen children of Thomas and Anne Adams Sanders. He was born Jan. 22, 1749, probably in Buckingham County, Virginia, and it was from that place he came to the New River about 1780. In that year, he worked 291 days on the fort at the Lead Mines and requested in the Montgomery County Court on May 7, 1782, that he ought to be paid £14 and 11 shillings for that work. He also requested that he be paid for 15 days waggoning at 10 shillings, and £2 and 10 shillings for feeding a horse belonging to the militia of Montgomery County on their march to join General Greene in Guilford County, North Carolina, in 1781. The tax records of 1782 show that Robert was still taxed in Buckingham County. But the above records show he was at the lead mines in 1780, and apparently there permanently from at least May 1782 (McConnell, *Sänders,* p. 89; Summers, *Annals,* p. 770; Montgomery County and Buckingham County Tax Lists for 1782).

Robert's first purchase of land was 400 acres, obtained from James Newell in 1785. This tract was located on the north side of the New River, east of the present Lead Mines Bridge, and adjoined James Newell's homeplace. The deed indicates it joined George Forbush and the land Forbush sold to William Herbert, deceased (Montgomery County Deed Book A p. 418). To this tract, Sanders added 531 acres from Charles Lynch of Campbell County in 1792. In 1793, 130 acres were added from George and Margaret Forbush, being part of the 600 acres where George Forbush lived, the place originally owned by Nathaniel Welshire. In 1795, the Forbushes and other Welshire heirs sold their land to Moses Austin, 410 acres, also part of the original 600 acres. After the Austins left the community this acreage became the property of William Sanders. Robert Sanders also bought 170 acres from William Moore in 1799, adjoining George Keasler, John Dicks and his own, apparently to clear up a title, because part of this land was already included in Sanders' patent land (Summers, *Annals,* p. 917; Wythe County Deed Book 1, pp. 157, 159; Book 2, p. 309; Book 4, p. 366).

Robert sold 157 acres to Randolph Rutherford in 1792, 100 acres to James Barnett part of the 531 acres on Bingamans Branch, 268 acres to Josiah Bell on Bingamans Branch, and 125 acres to Andrew Steel on Bingamans Branch. In addition, he conveyed to his son William, 524 acres in 1810, and the Francis land mentioned below (Wythe County Deed Book 1, pp. 118, 120, 198, 205,206; Book 5, p. 274).

Robert Sanders is mentioned in connection with the establishment of roads in the lead mines neighborhood. In 1785, he and Joseph Baker were to be overseers of the road from the Lead Mines to Fort Chiswell in the ''room'' of James McCorkle, Stephen Sanders, James Newell, and Robert Sanders (also Saunders) were to lay off the tithables for the same (Summers, *Annals*, p. 788). In 1789, Robert Sanders was to serve as overseer of the road from the ferry at the lead mines to William Ross' at Poplar Camp. This road was on the south or east side of the New River, probably basically the present road between the two communities (Summers, *Annals*, p. 825). In 1790, Robert Sanders was to be overseer of the road from the lead mines to Boiling Spring. At the same time, William Carter was to take over the road from Ross' to the lead mines, and Nathaniel Nuckells was to be overseer from his own house to Wolf Glade Creek (Summers, *Annals,* p. 1359).

In October 1785, Sanders is mentioned in connection with a dispute between Joseph Eaton and Evan Williams. The dispute appears to have arisen over ''slander against hogs'' belonging to Eaton. The suit was brought by Eaton against Williams, and in order to settle the dispute several men of the neighborhood were chosen to arbitrate the suit, including Sanders. Others making the decision were John Montgomery, David Sayers, Albert (Halbert) Allison, William Foster, and George Forbush. They agreed that Evans ought to pay the cost, eighteen shillings, to Eaton. The judgment was levied accordingly (Summers, *Annals,* p. 803).

Robert Sanders obtained the grant for the Henry Francis tract of 750 acres on Cripple Creek in 1790. This land was located where the town of Cripple Creek now stands and was surveyed in 1773 for Henry Francis, who died in 1780 (Montgomery County Plat Book A, p. 35; Summers, *Annals*, p. 732). Robert Sanders also had an interest in, and was owner of the tract known as the Cripple Creek Forge. In 1799, he purchased the 500-acre tract, kept it about a year, and sold it to David Peirce. This land was known as the Bell-Herbert Forge, later Peirce's Forge. As late as 1840, it was called the Cripple Creek Forge (Wythe County Deed Book 2, p. 416; Book 3, p. 56).

List of land and slaves of Robert Sanders, Senr. The total value was $3,000.
Tracing from the original by Mary B. Kegley.

In 1815, Robert Sanders, Senr., according to the tax assessor had only one farm, and that was on the west side of the New River near Evans' Ferry, 500 acres which had one dwelling house of wood, 1 1/2 stories, 28 feet by 16 feet, one kitchen, one smoke house, one barn, one stable, one corn crib, and one spring house, and four other cabins. The value for tax assessment purposes was $1,800. At that time, he had five slaves, one male about 50 years old, one under 12, and 2 females between 12 and 50 years and one under 12 years. They were valued at $1,200 (Kegley, *Tax Assessments*, p. 144).

Robert Sanders married Catherine Gannaway born Jan. 4, 1750, and who had previously married John Sanders (brother of Robert) of Buckingham County, Virginia. No record of her marriages have been found. She had one son Stephen by the first marriage (*see* below). By her marriage to Robert Sanders she had William, John, Robert, Jr., Nancy and Adams (often erroneously Adam in the records). Catherine Sanders died about 1808, and Robert Sanders died on October 20, 1815. Both are buried in the Newell-Kincannon-Trigg Cemetery in Austinville (McConnell, *Sänders*, pp. 90-91; Wythe County Deed Book 8, p. 243).

William Sanders, son of Robert, married Polly or Mary Newell, daughter of James Newell; and Adams Sanders married her sister Senah, in 1815. John Sanders married Susan Wells Bradley; Robert, Jr., married first Martha (Patsy) Gregory and second Louisa Alexander Bralley; and Nancy married George Oury (McConnell, *Sänders*, p. 90; Wythe County Marriage Book 1, pp. 18, 22, 48).

Robert Sanders, Senr., died without a will. In 1817, in order to settle the estate, William, John, and Robert and their wives, and George Oury and his wife Nancy, conveyed the land to Adams Sanders "for love and affection and $1" because it was intended that Adams should have the homeplace. This tract contained 259 1/2 acres and was part of the Welshire-Forbush land that Robert Sanders purchased. Adams also received all interest in the personal estate of his father (Wythe County Deed Book 8, p. 243).

Adams Sanders

Adams (sometimes erroneously Adam) Sanders (1792-1860), youngest son of Robert Sanders, Sr., and his wife Catherine Gannaway Sanders, was married in 1815 to Senah Newell, the daughter of his neighbor James Newell and his wife Sally Woods (Wythe County Marriage Book 1, p.48; McConnell, *Sänders*, pp. 90, 107).

On April 13, 1813, Adams Sanders stated in the Wythe County Court that he had paid a pedlar's fee in Washington County, Virginia. On August 11, 1813, the court also noted that he had been granted a "hawker's and pedlar's license" by Franklin County, Virginia. He may have traveled to these areas as a pedlar, but how long this continued is unknown (Wythe County Order Book 1812-1815, pp. 31, 76).

In 1817, in order to settle his father's estate, he received all interest in the Robert Sanders homeplace, and here he remained throughout his life. He added to the 259 ½ acres four smaller tracts and in 1857, put them together in an inclusive survey of 384 acres, which was about 19 acres less than the deeds called for. In 1850, he had 18 slaves (Wythe County Survey Book 4, p. 281; Book 3, pp. 129, 261, 328; Wythe County Deed Book 8, p. 243; McConnell, *Sänders*, pp. 199-200).

Adams and Senah Sanders had no children, consequently their estates passed to various nieces and nephews. Under the will of Adams Sanders, written on September 10, 1859, and probated September 10, 1860, and under the will of Senah Sanders, written November 14, 1860, probated January 1861, distribution of their real and personal property was made (Wythe County Will Book 10, pp. 55, 81).

Under the terms of his will, Adams left all of his real and personal estate to his wife Senah for her lifetime, and certain slaves which she could dispose of as she wished, with several exceptions mentioned below. Adams recognized that he had three brothers and one sister, but noted that they were all dead, leaving numerous descendants. He added that to divide the estate among them all would not be of much benefit to any one of them. He therefore provided for the estate to be divided after his wife's death in four parts: one-fourth to Daniel Washington Sanders, son of nephew William Sanders, one-fourth jointly to Kitty, wife of Stephen D. Sanders, and Senah, wife of B.F. Akers, daughters of his brother John, one-fourth to Samuel G. Sanders, son of his brother Robert, and one-fourth to William B. Foster, grandson of his sister Nancy (Wythe County Will Book 10, p. 55).

At Senah's death, the slaves were to be divided, three to go to Samuel G. Sanders, but if he died then one was to go to John L. Sanders, son of his brother John; one to his brother James B. Sanders, and the other to nephew William B. Foster. Senah Aker and Kitty Sanders were also to receive certain slaves, although, if necessary to pay debts, certain slaves could be sold. The slave named Frank, who served Adams so faithfully, was to be cared for and provided for by William B. Foster.

Also mentioned in the will was nephew James B. Sanders, Edwin H. Sanders, Senah N. Walton, Thirza Trigg daughter of his wife's niece Mary Ann Trigg, Benjamin Drake Fulton, Mary E. Kincannon, nephew William Sanders son of nephew James, and his wife's nieces Mary Ann Trigg and Sally Fulton. William B. Foster served as executor of the will.

An appraisal of the estate was recorded in 1861 and included many items of interest. There were 7 mules, horses, mares, yoke oxen, many cows, 42 head of cattle, 47 sheep, 39 hogs, 18 shoats, 6 sows and 18 pigs, an ox cart, a horse cart, several wagons, carriage harness, one buggy and harness, hay rake, plows, harrows, 83 1/2 pounds of sole leather, 4 currying knives and other tools, a pair of balances, one housing mill, one iron bark mill, grain cradles, smith tools, grinding stones, wagon bed and frame, a fan mill, a jack screw, knives, augers, and forks. The total appraised value of the estate was $4,240.12. Sanders was one of the few men who had mules in Wythe County (Wythe County Will Book 10, pp. 79-81).

The Lynchburg papers carried a notice of Adams Sanders death on August 24, 1860. It reads in part: ''Mr. Adams Sanders...was suddenly summoned into eternity on Friday last. He had mounted his horse with the intention of riding over his plantation and had proceeded but a short distance when the hand of death was laid upon him. A Negro boy, who happened to be near him at the time seeing his Master was unwell, ran to the house for assistance, but ere he could return, the vital spark had fled. Mr. Sanders was a man universally respected by his acquaintances, kind, hospitable and generous, ...whose place it will be hard to fill.''

In December 1860, Senah Newell Sanders died, just a few months after her husband's death. Under the terms of her will, she disposed of Negroes and cash, and the following people were mentioned: Andrew K. Fulton; his mother, Sally M. Fulton, her niece, wife of Andrew S. Fulton; Edward William Fulton, youngest son of Judge A. S. Fulton; niece Mary Ann Trigg, wife of Guy F. S. Trigg; James Trigg, son of Guy F. S. Trigg and Mary Ann Trigg; Andrew Kincannon, son of nephew Francis E. Kincannon; nephew Daniel B. Sanders; sister Sally (Mrs. John Evans) of Missouri; niece Polly Tomlin; Sally, daughter of F. E. Kincannon; Thursy Curran, daughter of Sally Curran; Mary L. Fulton, daughter of Judge A. S. Fulton; S. G. Sanders, son of Robert Sanders; niece Mary Ann Trigg; niece Hannah Sanders, wife of John Sanders, and her brother George Walton; Nancy A. Sanders, wife of J.P.M. Sanders; Bettie N.

Green, wife of John W. Green; Polly, wife of James Sanders of Smyth County; sister Thurza Kincannon and Nancy A. Sanders (Wythe County Will Book 10, p. 81).

In the 1860s, Samuel Guy Sanders bought out the other heirs and then owned the entire interest in the homeplace, being two tracts, 384 acres, and 119 acres, adjoining John Sanders, Robert Raper, and Guy F. S. Trigg. In 1882, 384 acres were sold for $14,000 to the Lobdell Car Wheel Company of Wilmington, Delaware, by S. G. Sanders and his wife Martha A. Sanders. Also included were three horses, eight cows, 26 yearlings, 8 calves, 10 hogs, fodder and straw, two Oliver chilled plows, one harrow, three or more small plows, one horse rake, seven stacks of hay, 75 bushels of corn, 50 bushels of wheat, one yoke of oxen, and one bull (Wythe County Deed Book 23, pp. 333, 620; Book 29, pp. 360, 361). The Lobdell Company sold the 384 acres, part of the land sold to them, known as the Guy Sanders farm, to J. D. Ayres of Carroll County in 1919 (Wythe County Deed Book 66, p. 2).

The original log house was torn down in the 1930s, and a new brick house built on the site. A stone spring house nearby was built by the original owners.

Stephen Sanders

Stephen Sanders (1768-1823), son of John Sanders and Catherine Gannaway Sanders, was the only child of this marriage. His mother married second, Robert Sanders and had five children already discussed here.

Stephen Sanders (generally referred to as "the younger" or "Jr." in order to distinguish him from his uncle Colonel Stephen Sanders of Cripple Creek) married Martha (Matty) Newell, daughter of James Newell, and a sister to Polly and Senah, who married Stephen's half-brothers William and Adams Sanders. Stephen and his wife are buried in the Trigg Cemetery in Austinville (McConnell, *Sänders*, p. 5).

In 1794, James Newell sold to his son-in-law 240 acres on the west side of the New River, being part of the Newell homeplace and it was here that Stephen first lived. To this land Stephen added 263 acres in two tracts making up the Keesling farm on Mine Mill Creek, in 1807. This land joined the Jacob Keesling mills (Wythe County Deed Book 1, p. 211; Book 4, p. 457).

In 1808, Stephen Sanders purchased the river farm from William Carter and his wife Unity. This place, located on the north side of the New River contained 366 3/4 acres (Wythe County Deed Book 5, p. 66) An additional 1/4 acre had been sold as a ferry landing on the north side of the river. The ferry was operated by the Herberts, Evans, and Jacksons. In 1809, the Keesling farm was sold to James Newell, and in 1810, 240 acres of the Newell homeplace returned to Newell (Wythe County Deed Book 5, pp. 274, 317). About this time, it appears that Stephen and his wife settled permanently at the ferry farm on the river. In 1811, they added 300 acres, adjoining the ferry farm, from William and Nancy Thomas (Wythe County Deed Book 5, p. 444).

On November 14, 1810, Stephen Sanders, Jr., asked for permission to establish a ferry across the river from his own land to that of Jesse Evans on the opposite shore, but the request was continued for further study. The following day, a jury was appointed to view the proposal for the Sanders Ferry (Wythe County Order Book 1808-1812, pp. 162, 166). On June 11, 1811, the court record states that the "ferry applied for by Stephen Sanders, Jr., over the New River from his own land to the lands of Jesse Evans opposite where the road from Wythe Court House to Poplar Camp Furnace and Grayson County and North Carolina crosses, the same was ordered to be established." The rates were as follows: mare 4 cents, horse the same, for every wheel of carriage

4 cents, for each head of neat cattle 4 cents, and each hog, sheep or goat 4/5 cents. Jesse Evans appealed the establishment of the ferry. On November 14, 1811, the court ordered that one boat and two hands were to be kept by Stephen Sanders, Jr., at the ferry. (Wythe County Order Book 1808-1812, p. 204).

In 1813, an agreement was drawn up between Jesse Evans and Stephen Sanders, Jr. In this agreement, Stephen agreed to convey to Evans the ferry at Carters on New River, and Evans to pay $300 in "horses not old or broke down," one immediately worth $60 to $100, and the balance to be paid in one year. Sanders agreed not to ask for aid in establishing any other ferry across the New River at Carter's. Evans agreed to set across, at the ferry at Poplar Camp, the Stephen Sanders family, horses, carriages, etc. without charge. The Superior Court Lawsuit was to be dismissed (Wythe County Deed Book 1A, p. 9). This ferry location is now known as Jackson's Ferry.

Stephen Sanders, Jr., served as deputy sheriff of Montgomery County in 1789 and was captain of a company of Montgomery County Militia in 1790, and appointed captain in the 2nd Battalion of the 35th Regiment of Militia in Wythe County in 1796 (McConnell, *Sänders*, p. 5; Kegley and Kegley, *Early Adventurers*, Vol. 1, pp. 108, 114; Wythe County Order Book 1790-1791, p. 22; Book 1795-1796, p. 66).

On May 14, 1816, Stephen Sanders, Jr., obtained a license to keep an ordinary at his house (Wythe County Order Book 1815-1820, p. 60). How long this continued is unknown.

Stephen and his wife had ten children: James, Sally, Mary, William John, Betsy, Stephen A., William Burrows, Alexander Newell, Daniel Burton, and Martha Newell Sanders (McConnell, *Sänders*, various pages 5-48).

Stephen Sanders, Jr., died without a will on July 21, 1823. Adams and John Sanders, Jr., were administrators of the estate (Wythe County Order Book 1822-1826, p. 146). The appraisal of his estate was recorded on March 9, 1824, and included bulls, colts, calves, straw, corn (600 bushels), flax seed, hogs, waggon, wheat (about 14 bushels), plows, 19 geese, sow and pigs, 17 sheep, cattle, vegetables in the garden, crocks, pails, churn, coffee mills, stone jug, beds, saddles, bridles, kitchen furniture, glassware, plates and dishes, cups and saucers, teaspoons, sugar tongs, bottles, pitcher, coffee pot, plates, bowls, tables, candlestands, candlesticks, tea kettle, carpet, looking glass, window curtains, chest, towels, table cloths, books, 17 chairs, silver watch, carriage trunk, cupboard, shovel and tongs, hand irons, flax wheel, reels, and cards, bed clothes, three cotton wheels, loom, quill wheel, warping bar gears, 4 "Haller" chairs, 6 reap hooks, 33 gallons brandy, barrels, soap, and Negroes "rented out" including Isaac, Jim, Pompey, Jenny, Calbourn, Jane, Abby, Glosten, Allin, Evelina, and Dilsey (Wythe County Will Book 3, p. 57).

On August 13, 1823, William Burrus Sanders, orphan of Stephen, "upwards of age 14," chose John A. Sanders guardian, and he was bound out to Jacob Fisher as a house joiner and carpenter (Wythe County Order Book 1822-1826, p. 146).

On November 14, 1824, Alexander N. Sanders orphan of Stephen Sanders, Jr., upwards of 14, chose Adams Sanders as his guardian, and Fontaine Watson, a local physician, was appointed by the court to be guardian of Daniel B. Sanders, who was under age 14 (Wythe County Order Book 1822-1826, p. 379). It seems likely that Daniel B. Sanders became interested in medicine because of this association with Watson. In the 1830s, Watson and Sanders were in a partnership "in physic" and advertised in a local newspaper that they had a "handsome assortment of medicine." Dr. Watson could be found at the tavern of M. Mayse, and Sanders at the tavern of Mr.

Ingles (*Argus,* February 9, 1833). Daniel Burton Sanders was listed in the 1850 census as a 39-year old physician. He was later joined in practice by his nephew Richard Walton Sanders (McConnell, *Sänders,* p. 15; Federal Census, Wythe County 1850).

In 1815, John Sanders had a farm on the north side of the New River, near the lead mines, containing 620 acres with two old "cabbens," one gear'd grist mill and old saw mill, valued at $3,000. He also had three slaves valued at $900 (Kegley, *Tax Supplement,* p. 35).

In the division of the estate of Stephen Sanders, Jr., John was to have Carter land, and Stephen and William B., jointly, were to have the Thomas land. Their heirs sold two tracts on Mine Mill Creek to Richard Lockett in 1829 (Wythe County Deed Book 11, pp. 400, 486).

John Sanders' division of the estate included the old pioneer home, which was built very near the river. The flood of 1878 covered the lower story and washed away part of the house. At the time of the flood, John Posey Mathews (J.P.M.) Sanders, son of John and Hannah Walton Sanders, was living at the place. He built a new brick home and located it some distance from the river, so that a future flood would not damage the house. It still stands near the bridge on the north side of the river. It was known as the Edd Jennings place in the 1930s (WPA Papers).

John Sanders, mentioned above, son-in-law of Richard Walton, and Robert Raper son of Mrs. Anna Walton by her first marriage, became partners in the lead mines under the name of Raper and Sanders. From 1834 until 1838, they operated a furnace located on a branch leading from Bell's spring and their store and office near Porter's Ferry. George Walton, brother to Hannah Sanders, willed his interest in the lead mines to his nephew Stephen D. Sanders, Richard Walton Sanders, and John P.M. Sanders, but the widow retained one-third interest. About 1838, the stockholders in the lead mines consolidated their interests and operated under the name of Wythe Lead Mines Company until about 1848. John Sanders was a director and Robert Raper was Secretary for the company. In 1860, the company was chartered under the name of Wythe Union Lead Mines Company. Richard W., John, and John P.M. Sanders were still connected with the company. John was a director, and Richard was assistant to Robert Raper, the secretary. Richard and J.P.M. were part owners of the Raven Cliff Furnace and Forge tract on Cripple Creek. Richard Walton Sanders and Milton Howard built and operated the Walton Furnace in the 1880s (Kohler, "Description...of the Lead Mines," pp. 8, 14, 18,19; Wythe County Will Book 7, p. 244; Kegley, *Bicentennial History,* pp. 340,351,353).

In a deposition, Henry L. Sheffey, superintendent at the mines in 1809, described William Sanders, James Bell, and John Sanders, who were employed by Thomas Jackson, as "first rate workmen." John Sanders also had a partnership in the mercantile business at the lead mines with Thomas Jackson. Sanders was to transact and superintend the business, and Jackson provided the capital of $6,000. Jackson purchased goods from Mssrs. Henderson & Beatty of Abingdon in an exchange for a debt owed for lead. Sanders also purchased goods in Baltimore (Deposition January 1813, Henry L. Sheffey, Deposition of John Sanders, January 1816, *Peirce vs. Jackson,* Superior Court Chancery Pleas, 1830-1839, Vol. 9, pp. 349, 374).

The Thomas division of the Stephen Sanders, Jr., land went to Stephen Drake Sanders and his son S. Dixon Sanders and their heirs. Although the land boundaries in this division extend to the river, the house place is located in such a place that the river cannot be seen.

William Sanders

William Sanders (1773-1824) son of Robert and Catherine Gannaway Sanders, married Mary Newell (1774-1830) daughter of his neighbor, James Newell, in 1790 (McConnell, *Sänders,* p. 91).

Their first home was probably on the Francis land at the present town of Cripple Creek, which came into his possession in 1792 (Wythe County Deed Book 1, p. 118). The land was sold to Nehemiah Bonham, Michael Worley, and Adam Rosenbaum (Wythe County Deed Book 1, p. 150, Book 2, p. 49, Book 4, p. 332). In 1806, William Sanders probably moved to the Lead Mines on the east side of the New River when he purchased 648 acres in three tracts from Charles Austin, being the Bingamans Bottom tract and two adjoining (Wythe County Deed Book 4, p. 366). His father, Robert Sanders, transferred more than 500 acres to William on the west side of the river in 1810, part of the lands purchased from Newell and part of the Forbush land. William probably lived on this tract (Wythe County Deed Book 5, p. 274; Wythe County Deed Book 8, p. 243). In 1819, when William and his wife Polly sold 69 acres to James Newell, they designated the land as part of the tract they then lived on (Wythe County Deed Book 7, p. 389).

William was employed at the lead mines. In his own words, in October 1818, he stated that he "considers himself well acquainted with the business of making lead and he is now and has been for some years in the employment of the defendant [Thomas Jackson] making and smelting lead ore" (*Peirce vs. Jackson,* Superior Court of Chancery Pleas, 1830-1831, Vol. 9, p. 418).

In 1815, William Sanders was assessed for direct tax purposes on a farm lying on the north side of New River, one mile below the lead mines, containing 550 acres, having thereon one dwelling house of wood, two stories high, 20 feet by 18 feet, one loom house, kitchen, spinning house, one barn, one stable, one smoke house, spring house, and corn crib, valued at $3,333.34. He also owned another farm opposite the above tract known by the name of Bingaman's Bottom, containing 650 acres, having thereon one dwelling house of wood, one and half stories high 24 feet by 20 feet, one spinning house, kitchen, smoke house, barn, stable, and corn crib valued at $2,800. There was one other plantation on the south side of the river, five miles below the lead mines, containing 475 acres with one small dwelling house of wood and two other cabins, valued at $3,333.34. There were also twelve slaves: three males between 12 and 50 and 4 under 12; females, 4 between 12 and 50 and one under 12. The value of the slaves was $2,750, the total value $11,216.68 (private collection).

William Sanders moved to the Town House in what is now Smyth County about 1819, and for that reason, he is known as William of Town House. According to McConnell, he made arrangements for a five-year lease on the salt mines at Saltville. He and his brother John began work, increasing production greatly and causing James White to make an agreement with them to stop manufacturing, which they did. A deed to the Indian Fields land with 2,766 acres was promised as part of the bargain, but before the deed was written William died. The deed came to his heirs and his brother John. There is somewhat of a mystery here, as the records do not show that White ever owned the Town House land. It was Francis Smith who sold the land to the Sanders (McConnell, *Sänders*, pp. 91-93; Smyth County records).

In Wythe County, William and Polly Sanders conveyed the three tracts on the east side of the River, the Bingamans Bottom lands, to James White (Wythe County Deed Book 12, p. 70).

Robert Sanders (1792-1858), called "Long Robin" was the son of William Sanders of Town House.

William Sander's will was recorded in Washington County, Virginia on December 21, 1824 (Will Book 5, p. 193). His land on the north side of the New River, located between Andrew Kincannon and Robert Sanders, was to be sold by the executors, Polly his wife, and brother John Sanders. His wife Polly also left a will which was proved on July 20, 1830 (McConnell, *Sänders,* p. 95).

William and Mary (Polly) Sanders had fourteen children: Robert called "Long Robin" because of his height, Sallie Wood Sanders, James Newell Sanders, Catherine Sanders, Elizabeth Sanders, William Sanders known as "plain Billy," Harold, John, Valerius, Mary Alexander, Leander, Senah Newell Sanders, Andrew Kincannon Sanders, and Edwin Haller Sanders (For information on these children, *see,* McConnell, *Sänders ,* pp. 95-147).

Robert Sayers

Robert Sayers of the "Pasture" was the son of Alexander and Mary Sayers. His land was located on the east and south sides of the New River near the lead mines. When his father drowned in the New River in May 1765, Robert was a student in school in Bedford. Robert Breckinridge was chosen as his guardian in March 1767 (Chalkley, *Chronicles,* Vol. 1, p. 340; Vol. 3, p. 97).

In 1773, Robert's name appears in a deed with his mother, who had married Thomas Pritcherd (various spellings), selling lands of Alexander Sayers on Tates Run to Henry Grubb. This land was located west of present Wytheville. In the following year Robert conveyed 650 acres to Samuel Ewing, following an agreement to settle the claim of the estate of John Buchanan, deceased. Mary Ewing, wife of Samuel, received a release of interest of Robert and his mother Mary Sayers Prickett (Prichard) to any interest in the land conveyed to Samuel earlier. This land was located in the lead mines community (Summers, *Annals,* p. 668; Montgomery County Will Book B, p. 12; Montgomery County Deed Book A, pp. 34, 35, 453).

Because Robert Sayers, bachelor and colonel, son of William Sayers, was also active in the affairs of the county, it is sometimes difficult to distinguish between these two men in the records. However, Robert of the "Pasture" had a wife Jean who appears in the deeds of Wythe County. Because Colonel Robert Sayers did not live in the same community and was never married, it would appear that all land transactions or activities in the lead mines neighborhood are those of Robert of the "Pasture."

Robert Sayers appears on Pearce's Company of Militia in 1781, and Newell's Company the same year, and as Lieutenant in Captain Saunders Company in 1782 (Kegley, *Militia,* pp. 30, 37; Summers, *Annals,* pp. 754,758). He is probably the same Robert who is a lieutenant in the Wythe County militia in 1797. He may or may not have been the Robert who served on the jury several times in Montgomery County (Summers, *Annals*, pp. 723, 704, 740, 1366).

In 1782, he had a survey made, which included the improvements made by Jacob Castle. The tract contained 396 acres. The following year, he had 794 acres surveyed on the southeast side of the New River. There seems to be no record of a grant to Sayers for this tract. In 1783, 470 acres were surveyed which adjoined the lead mines, but this tract was transferred to Charles Lynch who obtained the grant as part of the inclusive survey made in 1789 (Montgomery County Plat Book B, p. 45; Montgomery County Plat Book D, p. 147).

Thomas Madison and Company also made claims for land in the same neighborhood, including 322 acres known as the "Pasture." Thomas Madison and others, acting as administrators of the John Robinson's estate, claimed 338 acres adjoining the mines, and another tract for 214 acres in the same vicinity. They were all assigned to Robert Sayers, who received the grant for all of them in 1788. The land of the "Pasture," came into the hands of Thomas Jackson, Sr., and his heirs. The younger Thomas Jackson obtained an inclusive survey for 783, acres which included the 322 acres, 338 acres, and 140 acres, part of the 214 acres. The land grant was issued to him in 1860. The land was later owned by J.P.M. Simmerman and his descendants, and was owned by the Ivanhoe Mining and Smelting Corporation in 1927 (*McGavock vs. Jackson*, Superior Court Chancery Record, Vol. 2, p. 726, and following, gives the details. Maps, records of surveys, and grants begin on p. 741, Wythe County Circuit Court Clerk's Office; *see also Virginia Reporters*, Vol. 5, *Randolph*, p. 509 for the results of an appeal to the Virginia Supreme Court in the suit involving David McGavock and Jackson; Wythe County Survey Book 4, pp. 264-265; Grant Book 117, p. 844; Wythe County Deed Book 79, p. 268; Deed Book 36, p. 339; Wythe County Will Book 45, p. 351).

Further information was obtained from the same suit, which began in 1806 and was settled in 1821. McGavock purchased 274 acres from Paul Razor by his attorney Jacob Razor. The grant was issued to McGavock. This land covered the greater part of the survey of 214 acres made for Thomas Madison and all of a survey of 66 acres surveyed for Thomas Jackson. The records indicate that sometime prior to January 1, 1778, a settlement was made on the tract near the Lead Mines called the "Pasture" and Thomas Madison and others obtained a certificate for right of settlement and a preemption warrant of 1,000 acres to adjoin the said tract. The lands were surveyed in 1783. Sayers obtained a certificate and located his preemption in 1783, and exchanged land with Madison after the surveys were made.

Razor's entry was made in November 1782, on a treasury warrant for 500 acres. McGavock believed that his claim was earlier, and also noted that the survey of 214 acres did not correspond with the location given in the warrant, as the land was to be laid off so as to adjoin the "Pasture" and Bingaman's Bottom, which is not practical (nor possible). Jackson defended his claim by a conveyance from Moses Austin, when he bought the 214 acres, which Robert Sayers sold to him and which Sayers had received as assignee of Madison. He also claimed 338 acres deeded from Sayers and Muse, as well as 66 acres as part of a preemption warrant for Richard Muse and the Lead Mines Company, but no grant was issued and a caveat was lodged by McGavock. Jackson admitted that another survey of 240 acres was made and when the four tracts surveyed were added together there was 858 acres, part of the 1,000 acres mentioned in the warrant.

In 1783, another survey was made for 573 acres for the Lead Mines Company on the same warrant, but that was in error and was corrected for another warrant. Jackson admitted that the lands had to adjoin the ''Pasture'' but to join Bingaman's Bottom was impractical. The entry, which McGavock claimed, called for joining the patent line of Samuel Ewing and the ''Pasture,'' but the survey made was one-fourth mile from the ''Pasture.''

James Newell, surveyor, stated in 1819, that certain lines were never actually run, and that Razor resided fifty miles from the surveyor's office and no interference was discovered until the patents issued.

The decree stated that McGavock had a better right to the land and Jackson was ordered to convey to him all the land included in the patent: 338 acres and 214 acres, covered by a patent for 274 acres. Jackson was also to release all claims to the 66 acres. The opinion stated that McGavock had a good right to the 274 acres and that the defendant Jackson had not shown anything to defeat it. The accompanying map shows the conflicting lines and the location of the tracts adjoining the Lead Mines and the Pasture, which were the subject of the above suit.

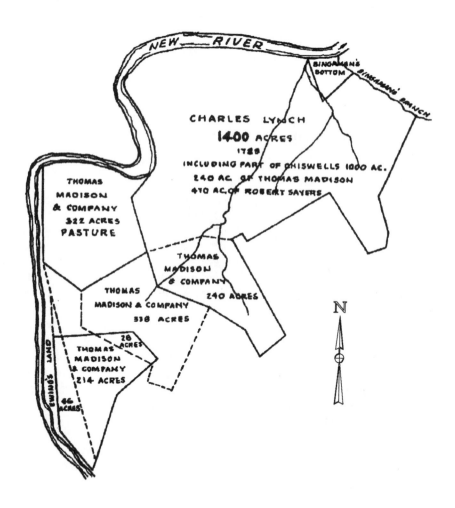

Plat from the Superior Court Chancery Record, Book 2, page 742 shows Lynch's 1,400 acres and Madison's claims at the Lead Mines. Tracing from the original by Mary B. Kegley.

The lawsuit also records the agreement between Charles Lynch and Jacob Rubsamen, on behalf of themselves and the Lead Mines Company, and Robert Sayers. It is dated August 6, 1783, and is found on page 752 of the suit. It is recorded here in its entirety as follows:

Agreement 6th June 1783, between Charles Lynch & Jacob Rubsamen in behalf of themselves and the Mine Company on one part, and Robert Sayers, heir-at-law of Alexander Sayers, deceased. It is agreed that the said Robert Sayers gives up and transfers all his right, title, and pretensions he has or may have to the Lead Mines Hills, the thousand acre survey and the bottom called Buchanan's Bottom to said Charles Lynch, Jacob Rubsamen and Lead Mines Company. For and in consideration of a certain tract of land called the "Pasture" tract which tract of land sd. Charles Lynch and Jacob Rubsamen for themselves and in behalf of the Mine Co. give in exchange and transfer to sd. Sayers according to lines now agreed upon by both parties and to be surveyed.

Witness :	*Thomas Muse*	*Signed: Chas. Lynch*
	George Duff	*Jacob Rubsamen*
	John Jenkins	*Robert Sayers.*

On July 1, 1792, Charles Lynch wrote from the Lead Mines to Thomas Madison in regard to the land, and the letter can be found on page 752 of the lawsuit. It is as follows:

Dr. Sir,
You will remember that I gave the settlement & preemption of the "Pasture" tract to Robert Sayers for his settlement & preemption of the Lands about the Lead Mines & the land or rather the warrants in your name & others, you sir assigned the warrants or surveys knowing the circumstances agreeable to my contract or Bargain with Robert Sayers & getting from under the hand of Robert Sayers administrators approving my conduct which is of record in the High Court of Chancery, it was all fixed & I obtained a pattent in my name, in trust for the company for 1400 acres, the <u>sail</u> of which is also by consent, of record in the High Court of Chancery. I see that Robert Sayers had surveyed 66 acres & sold it to Richard Muse, as he did not survey the whole at once, he surveyed that small parcel afterwards. Inclosed is Sayers order to Adams [the Wythe County surveyor], to transfer it & the certificate of survey. Now the lead Mine Co. having received all they done to have it is but right that Sayers should also receive his. You will therefore be pleased to do the need full on your part for that purpose. I am Sr. your most obedt. Huml Sert.

Chas. Lynch.

Thos. Madison Esq.

Dr. Sir, I am willing to assign for myself without recourse, but there appears a difficulty do it for the company.

Colo. Chs. Lynch   *Thos. Madison, Sept. 1795.*

In 1792, Robert and his wife Jean Sayers sold one-half interest in 660 acres, being the two tracts 322 and 338, to Richard Muse. In 1795, the 214 acres between where Sayers lived and James Ewing, were sold to Moses Austin. In 1796, Muse and Sayers joined in a deed to dispose of the ''Pasture'' tract of 660 acres to Thomas Jackson. The Sayers do not appear in the records of Wythe County after this time, and it is believed that they moved to Pulaski County, Kentucky (Wythe County Deed Book 1, p. 124; Book 2, pp. 185,411).

On September 1, 1823, based on a pension application filed in Pulaski County, Kentucky, Robert Sayers (Sayer) obtained a pension for service in the Revolutionary War. He enlisted in February 1776 in Virginia and served nine months as a private in Captain Joseph Crockett's Company, Colonel Alexander McClanachan's Virginia Regiment. He became sick and obtained a permit from General Andrew Lewis to return home. He hired a substitute as he had enlisted for two years. At the time of his application he was 71 years old and had seven children, Priscilla, age about 38, Stephen age about 36, William age about 33, Jane age about 31, Thurza age about 29, Robert age about 27, John age about 26. Priscilla and William were not married and Priscilla, Thurza, and John lived at home. Robert Sayers died on June 12, 1847. Because there is limited information in the pension application, it has not been proved that this is the same Robert as mentioned above, but it appears likely based on service with Joseph Crockett, and based on family records. A check of the deeds in Pulaski County, Kentucky, and information from the Pulaski County Historical did not provide his wife's name although he is well documented in that county (Revolutionary War Pension #S35641, National Archives; records of Janet Sayers; Irene Sayers' correspondence with clerk and Historical Society).

Walton

Richard Walton was born in Westmoreland, England, on August 4, 1778, and came to Virginia prior to June 18, 1798, settling in the lead mines area of Wythe County. He became an American citizen prior to May 5, 1811 (*Sanders v. White*, 1840, Box 87, Wythe County Circuit Court Basement; tombstone inscription; Kegley, *Glimpses*, Vol. 2, p. 83).

He purchased 1,001 acres of land on Wilshire's Run in 1805 from Richard and Margaret Muse. This estate included 357 (erroneously 367 in some records) acres deeded by Elizabeth Williams, the elder, and others to Muse, and a tract of 383 acres, adjoining it, granted Joseph Eaton in 1788, as well as two other tracts granted Eaton in 1800, one for 112 acres and the other for 149 acres (Wythe County Deed Book 6, p. 160). In 1823 Walton filed suit against Richard Muse and the Williams heirs in order to obtain a clear title to the land he purchased. Two of the sons of Evan Williams, Maston and Morgan, who were under age at the time the deed was written, did not release their interest in the land, even though they had received a share of the money. The court ordered a deed to be made, but the index does not list it (*Walton vs. Muse*, Box 35, 1827, Wythe County Circuit Court Basement; Wythe County Deed Book 2, p. 245, Book 6, p. 160; *see also* Muse, and Williams sketches).

Richard Walton married Ann Jackson Raper, sister of Thomas and John Jackson and widow of William Raper (Wythe County Order Book, January 12, 1830, p. 5; family records). William Raper died of smallpox en route to Wythe County and is buried in Richmond, Virginia. No marriage record has been located for Walton and Ann Jackson Raper in Wythe County.

Home of George Walton still stands on the western edge of State Route 52 near the intersection of Route 630.   Photo courtesy of F. B. Kegley Collection.

Richard Walton wrote his will on March 20, 1828. He died August 16, 1828, and the will was probated September 8, 1828 (Wythe County Will Book 3, p. 329). He devised to his wife Ann for her lifetime, one-third of the plantation purchased from Muse, to include the buildings occupied by John Sanders. She was also to have two feather beds and furniture, her choice of the best ''horse beast,'' and 2 cows and calves, 2 slaves, and $100 cash.

His son George Walton was to have the lands purchased of Muse and Jones, and lands bought from Robert Raper, called Millans place, subject to the dower interest. George also received the interest in the Herbert's ferry tract (Jackson's Ferry) and four slaves, but Phillis was to remain with wife Ann, until her decease.

Walton's daughter Hannah, who married John Sanders, was to have a Negro boy, a Negro woman and her three children and their increase, and another Negro woman and her five children and their increase.

Walton also noted that he had married Ann Raper and had received about £100 Virginia currency at the time. He devised the same to John, William, and Robert Raper, and Mary Parkins who were to receive $100 each, which would be the principal and interest that Walton received out of the estate. These were Ann's children by William Raper.

If Negro Lewis were purchased, he was to go to son George as he is the reputed father of Negroes Phillis and Swan ''in my possession.'' Walton added, ''I request my slaves that I have bequeathed to be treated with humanity.'' The remainder of the estate was to go to George Walton and Hannah Sanders equally.

Richard Walton is buried in the Jackson Cemetery in Austinville. His wife Ann, born September 14, 176, in Westmoreland, England, died August 12, 1844 age 73 years, 10 months and 28 days. She is buried beside her husband (tombstone inscriptions).

Ann Walton wrote her will on November 26, 1836, and it was probated on September 9, 1844. Jacob Haller was the only witness to the will. To her son Robert Raper, Ann Walton left all of her estate of every kind real and personal, subject to payment of certain legacies: to her son John Raper $500, to son William Raper $1,000, to grandchildren: Elizabeth Parkin, John Robert Parkin, and Mary Parkin, each $333.33 at the time of their marriage or when they come of age. To grandchildren: Thomas, George, and Hannah Raper, she left $160.67 each to be given to their father John Raper for their benefit until they are 21. Granddaughter Hannah Raper was to have all the silver spoons (Wythe County Will Book 6, p. 241).

All bequests were to be paid out of Ann's part of two estates, that of her late sister Debrah (Deborah) Jackson and her late brother Thomas Jackson. The estates were in the hands of her son Robert Raper. Because her other children (Waltons) inherited part of the real estate of her brother Thomas Jackson, they were not provided for by their mother.

The inventory of her estate was taken by Adams Sanders, Edmund W. Lockett, and John Allison (Wythe County Will Book 6, p. 320). The items listed included: three beds, one Jackson press, a set of silver teaspoons, a coffee pot, two candle sticks, sugar nippers and tea caddy, two tablespoons, sugar tongs, a lot of old books, a candle stand, four chairs, a table and cover, a carpet, two more chairs, a looking glass, a warming pan, shovel and tongs, a chest, a lot of curtains, bed clothes, table cloths, towels, another chest, a trunk and another press. The total appraised value of her estate was $117.00.

George Walton, born May 28, 1804, son of Richard and Ann Walton, took over at the homeplace, following his father's death in 1828. He married Senah N. Sanders, daughter of William Sanders, in 1830 (McConnell, *Sanders*, pp. 140-141 has a sketch and photos of this couple).

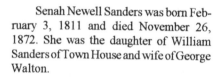

Senah Newell Sanders was born February 3, 1811 and died November 26, 1872. She was the daughter of William Sanders of Town House and wife of George Walton.

George, son of Richard Walton was born on May 28, 1804 and died in October 16, 1850. On November 4, 1830 he was married to Senah Newell Sanders.

Courtesy of David Davis and Rush Crockett.

Because George's mother was a sister to Thomas Jackson, the owner of part of the lead mines, her Walton children inherited a portion of the Jackson estate. The four Jackson nephews, sons of Thomas Jackson's brother John, and George Walton agreed on partition of the estate. By this division made in 1825, Walton was to have the Jackson Ferry farm, with the shot tower excepted. In 1831, John and Hannah Walton Sanders and George Walton and his wife Senah entered into a deed with the four Jacksons, Walton and Sanders retaining an interest in the ferry with privileges of crossing the river free of charge for their families (Wythe County Deed Book 10, p. 164; Book 12, p. 120).

In 1831, George Walton was appointed constable for the 1st District of Wythe County. The bond was dated June 4 (Wythe County Deed Book 12, p. 34). In 1834, Walton purchased 130 acres on Lead Mine Mill Creek (Mill Creek), the same tract he sold to Edmund W. Lockett in 1841 (Wythe County Deed Book 12, p. 626; Book 15, p. 373).

In 1836, Walton purchased 230 acres on Mine Mill Creek from George W. Bassett of Spotsylvania and Hanover Counties, Virginia, who also sold Walton a tract of 435 acres in the same locality in 1848 (Wythe County Deed Books 13, p. 451; Book 17, p. 538). In 1841, Walton purchased the Jenkins place from Alexander Matthews and wife, who inherited it from the estate of David Peirce. In 1856, widow Senah Walton sold it to Richard W. Sanders and his wife Elizabeth, Stephen D. Sanders and his wife Catherine, A. P. Sanders, and John P.M. Sanders, and Elizabeth Chaffin. In 1842, Walton purchased the place on the north side of the river belonging to William Sanders, with Robert and Catherine Sanders making the deed for 590 acres. In 1845, James and Louise Sanders of Smyth County released their interest in the place. The following year Walton sold the place to Stephen Sanders (Wythe County Deed Book 15, pp. 206, 413; Book 16, p. 587; Book 17, p. 259; 21, p. 200).

George Walton's will was written on July 19, 1850, with a codicil added in October of the same year. He died on October 14, 1850, and the will was presented to the court for probation in November (Wythe County Will Book 7, p. 244).

By the terms of the will, George Walton having no children left all the land he owned at the homeplace to his nephew Richard Walton Sanders. His entire interest in the lead mines on the south side of the river was devised to his three nephews, Richard Walton Sanders, Stephen Drake Sanders, and John P.M. Sanders. To his wife Senah N. Walton, he left all the family of Negroes, all the household and kitchen furniture, except the clock, and in addition his gold watch, a bay mare and colt, and a sorrel mare, and another bay mare. The clock, the farm utensils, the entire stock of horses except those devised to his wife, all cattle, sheep, hogs, and grain were left to Richard Walton Sanders. If there was not enough money to pay the debts, the executors could sell stock as they thought necessary. Nephew Richard Walton Sanders also received nine slaves, the double-barreled shot gun, and all the books. He was also to serve as executor.

The codicil noted that he had omitted one slave in the listing of the estate, and he was to go to his nephew R. W. Sanders. He also noted that Sally Adams Sanders had died and left him certain Negroes which he devised to his wife. The executor was to sell one or more of the slaves to pay the medical and funeral expenses of Sally Adams Sanders. D. B. Sanders was the physician. If Senah Walton refused these terms, then all the slaves were to go to her for her lifetime and then at her death to R. W. Sanders.

When the will was brought to the court for probation, the executor did not appear to qualify so the court appointed a curator of the estate. John Sanders with security of $20,000 was appointed curator, and assigned to collect and preserve the goods and chattels of the estate until the executor appeared. On April 14, 1851, he resigned and

Richard W. Sanders took over the management of the estate (Wythe County Will Book 7, p. 244).

On April 18, 1851, Senah Walton the widow renounced the provisions made for her in the will and following an order of May Court, 1851, her dower of 575 acres was laid off out of the estate of 1,880 acres. Her dower was to include the house. The land was located on both sides of Welshire's Run, (Galena Creek) north of the Laswell community, with the western boundary near the Walton Furnace (Wythe County Deed Book 18, pp. 601, 630; see map).

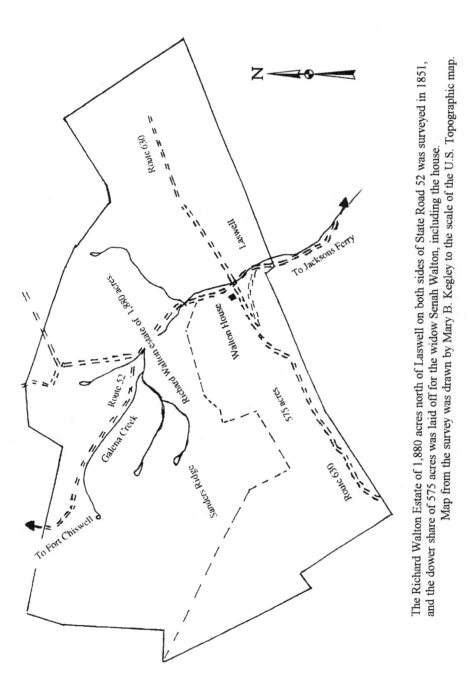

The Richard Walton Estate of 1,880 acres north of Laswell on both sides of State Road 52 was surveyed in 1851, and the dower share of 575 acres was laid off for the widow Senah Walton, including the house.
Map from the survey was drawn by Mary B. Kegley to the scale of the U.S. Topographic map.

The slaves and personal property of the estate were listed and included the following items: 21 Negroes including children ranging in price from $100 to $1,000, farm animals including mares, horses, colts, yoke oxen, cows, cattle, calves, hogs (44 fat hogs supposed to weigh 8,000 valued at $4.50 per 100), and 58 other hogs and 20 pigs, sheep and lambs. The crops included 100 bushels of wheat, 200 bushels of rye, 750 bushels of corn, 50 bushels of oats, and 7 stacks of hay, fodder and straw. There were wagons, an ox cart, a large still, a grindstone, a flax brake, a set of blacksmith tools, and a variety of other tools. There were scythes, shovels, hay forks and axes. There was an apple mill, 18 cords of wood, a salt kettle, 5 big plows, 5 shovel plows, and 5 coulter plows and an additional 4 plows. There were sheep shears, balances, steelyards, and blasting tools, a double-barrel gun, a bureau and bookcase, dining table and work tables, small and large. There was a side board, a large looking glass, a lot of bed clothes, a lounge, 2 old safes, a traveling trunk, a gold watch, 84 books valued at $60, 6 candlesticks, a dozen Windsor chairs, a dozen split bottom chairs, washstand, ewer and bason, stone jars, cotton cards, 13 1/2 pairs of sheets, 11 towels, 8 table cloths, 10 counterpanes, a Marseille counterpane, 3 quilts, 1 Calico counterpane, 5 additional table clothes and 6 bed quilts. There was also one "cumfort," an old chest, a pair of shovel and tongs, 3 smoothing irons, 3 flax wheels, a lot of kitchen furniture, 3 spinning wheels, one large copper kettle, 2 large iron kettles, 2 washing tubs, one patent churn, crocks, pails, jars, half-bushel measures. There was also one set of china tableware, a coffee mill, tumblers, 2 sets of silver teaspoons, one silver ladle, a pair of silver sugar tongs, a butter knife, and one dozen knives and forks. There was also a lot of pine plank and 12,000 shingles (Wythe County Will Book 7, p. 321).

George Walton is buried north of his residence where his grave is enclosed by a rock wall two feet thick and four feet high. His stone is the only one in the enclosure. It was erected by his nephew with the epitaph, "The noblest work of God, an honest man."

Christopher Walton, also born in Westmoreland, England, showed his intention to become an American citizen on October 10, 1826 (Wythe County Order Book 1826-1829, p. 70). Although there is probably some connection to Richard and George Walton, no record has been found locally to confirm this.

Welshire

Nathaniel Welshire (also Wilshire, Wellshire, Wiltshire, etc.) first appears on the New River in 1748/49 when he is mentioned in a survey for James Patton, which states that the 680 acres "is called Wilsher's place." The land was located on the north side of the New River between present Austinville and Jackson's Ferry Bridge (Augusta County Survey Book 1, p. 45B).

The branch on the north side of the New River, east of Austinville, was known as Wiltshire's Run, apparently named for this early settler. It drains a wide area along both sides of present Route 52, rising north of the Laswell community and emptying into the river west of Jackson's Ferry crossing. It is known today as Galena Creek (Kegley, *Early Adventurers*, Vol. 2, p.34; USGS Map, Austinville and Max Meadows Quadrangles).

The name Nathaniel Wiltshire appears in Lancaster County, Pennsylvania, in 1743, and may be the same person who migrated to the New River at an early date (Ramsey, *Carolina Cradle*, p.84, misplaces Welshire on the South Fork of the Roanoke River instead of the New River).

In 1750, Welshire appears as a tithable to work the road from Ezekiel Calhoun's eastward. He is mentioned in the papers of John Noble's estate on January 16, 1753. In 1754, he was a witness on a deed from Robert McFarland to John Downing for land on Stoney Fork of Reed Creek on the New River. On July 3, 1755, Nathaniel Welshire was wounded by Indians on the New River, and his name was recorded in William Preston's list of wounded and killed. (Chalkley, *Chronicles,* Vol. 1, p. 40; Vol. 2, p. 510; Vol. 3, p. 330; Augusta County Will Book 1, p. 480).

It appears that his removal from New River during the Indian problems, brought him to Rowan County, North Carolina. In 1756, Wiltshire bought land from John Pelham near the shallow ford of the Yadkin River, adjoining Edward Hughes, in Rowan County, North Carolina (Deed Book 3, p. 209). He kept this tract until October 1765 when the deed was recorded (Deed Book 6, p. 234).

In 1762, a John Weltshire, Jacob Castle, and Alexander Sayers were to value the improvements on John Stanton's two tracts on the New River. In 1764, a Mr. Wiltshire and others visited Bethabara, North Carolina, reporting that Little Carpenter and the Cherokees have left the New River and returned to their nation (Chalkley, *Chronicles,* Vol. 1, p. 102; Fries, *Moravian Diaries,* Vol. 1, p. 289). John and Mr. Weltshire are not further identified.

Nathaniel Welshire was a member of the Boiling Spring Presbyterian congregation and was one of their representatives in 1769 (Wilson, *Tinkling Spring,* p. 171), which would indicate that he was living on New River again, and in fact probably moved back to the place of his first settlement about 1765, when his land in North Carolina was sold. In 1771, 1772, and 1773, he appears on the New River tithable lists, and in 1773, he served on a jury in Fincastle County, Virginia (Summers, *Annals,* p. 614; Kegley, *Glimpses,* Vol. 2, pp. 149,155,170).

On November 4, 1776, Nathaniel Welshire wrote his will, and it was probated April 1, 1777 (Montgomery County Will Book B, p. 32). In his will he asked to be buried without "pomp or state" at the discretion of his dear wife and the executor. His wife (not named) was to have a Negro girl for life. The rest of the estate was divided between Nathanial Sash, son of George Sash, of North Carolina, and Nathaniel Forbis, son of George Forbis on New River. At his wife's death, the Negro was to be sold and the money divided between the two Nathaniels--Sash and Forbis. His grandson Sampson Steel was to have £25 Virginia money, and his daughter Elizabeth Buchanan was to have £15. His daughter Easter Herbert was to receive two shillings sterling. The furniture was to be divided between his grandchildren, the daughters of George Sash and George Forbis, who were not named in the will. The plantation was to go to Nathaniel Buchanan, after the death of John and Elizabeth Buchanan who lived there. The executors were James Montgomery and George Forbes.

The plantation was valued at £160 and was listed in the inventory of the estate. Other than cows, bulls, hogs, sheep and heifers, only a few items appeared on the list of personal property. There was an old cart, some old iron, knives, augers, adze, mattocks, and a wolf trap. The total value of the estate was £237 and 7 shillings (Montgomery County Will Book B, p. 47).

The clerk was paid 290 pounds of tobacco for proving the will and recording the inventory. This was an unusual kind of payment for this part of Virginia, as tobacco was not grown here. Cash was paid to Colonel Preston in the amount of £69 and 19 shillings, 1 pence. Others paid were James Tuttle, Bartlet Green, Joseph Barren, William Love, John Buchanan, and Ross and Trigg (store owners). The account was recorded on March 5, 1782 (Montgomery County Will Book B, p. 51).

The Welshire land later became the property of Robert Sanders, and in more recent years belonged to the Rapers and Cornetts (*see also,* Forbush and Sanders sketches).

Evan Williams

Evan Williams was among those "smelters and refiners of ore" who migrated to the lead mines at the time of Chiswell's ownership, arriving with William Herbert and others in the summer of 1763 (*W. Herbert vs. Joseph Farrell,* lawsuit included in *Chiswell, Judgments,* Box 32, 1827, Wythe County Circuit Court, Clerk's Office, Basement, hereafter cited as *Chiswell, Judgments).*

Williams first appears in the records of New River in 1771, when he is listed on William Herbert's tithable list. He is again mentioned in 1772 and 1773 (Kegley, *Tithables,* pp. 11, 17,32). On the Montgomery County Personal Property Tax list, he is mentioned with two tithables in 1782, 1 slave, 10 horses, and 17 cattle (Kegley, *Tax List,* 1782, p. 36). He took the oath of allegiance to the State of Virginia in 1777/78 and is listed on John Montgomery's list. He appears in the local militia companies of Jeremiah Pearce and Stephen Sanders in the 1780s (Kegley, *Militia,* pp. 37, 40, 54).

Williams was involved in several lawsuits in the early 1770s, being the defendant in a trespass suit brought by Samuel Newell, and a defendant in a suit by James Newell, Jr. He also was suited by Thomas Rodgers on a debt, and the same in a suit by James Rodgers on a replevin bond. He also was charged with slander against hogs belonging to Joseph Eaton in 1787. He brought one suit himself, against Daniel Flannery on attachment in 1775 (Cook and Cook, *Fincastle and Kentucky Counties, Virginia and Ky.,* Vol. 1, pp. 304, 318, 323, 343, 345, 356, 389, 408, 435, 451; Summers, *Annals,* p. 803).

In 1775, the Fincastle Committee of Safety authorized him to carry a ton of lead to Manchester [South Richmond] at the beginning of the Revolutionary War. He was allowed £12 for his load of salt he brought from Williamsburg, but £9 was to be deducted for 6 bushels which were lost on the road by his waggoner. The balance due him was ordered to be paid by James McGavock on June 11, 1776 (Harwell, *Fincastle Resolutions...*pp. 71,89,93).

During the time of the Tory confessions, Evan Williams, and many of the so-called Welsh miners, were named as participants of the Tory Club." However, he was also among those who took the oath of allegiance (Kegley and Kegley, *Early Adventurers,* Vol. 1, pp. 144, 148).

Although he may not have moved to Kentucky, Evan Williams' name appears on the Jefferson County, Kentucky, land entry records, having entered tracts on Beech Fork, Cane Creek, and Cedar Creek. in 1780 (Cook and Cook, *Fincastle and Kentucky Counties, Virginia, Ky,* ,Vol. 1, pp. 102,108, 111). As will be noted below, his widow and several of the family were living in Kentucky in the 1820s.

The land where Evan Williams and his family lived was a tract of 337 acres on both sides of Welshire's Run (now Galena Creek), surveyed in 1782 on a Commissioner's Certificate (Montgomery County Plat Book). He was also mentioned as assigning other tracts on Mine Mill Creek and on a branch of the New River (Kegley, *Early Adventurers,* Vol. 2, pp. 35,64, 105,107).

There is no record of the death of Evan Williams in Wythe County, and there is no recorded will or appraisal of his estate. At the time of his death, he left a widow and five children under age. In 1798, his widow Elizabeth, his daughter Elizabeth, son William (later of Tazewell County, Virginia), daughter Polly (Mary in the marriage record Wythe County Book 1, p. 12, which was turned into the court on February 13, 1798 by Daniel Lockett) and her husband John Stotts, conveyed the land of Evan Williams to Richard Muse, who in turn sold to Richard Walton. The tract was 357 acres (Wythe County Deed Book, 2, p. 245; Book 6, p. 160). In addition to the ones who signed the deed, there were two younger Williams children, Maston and Morgan, who were under age at the time. They were later ordered by the court to make a deed and convey the property to Walton, but if this was done there is no deed indexed in the Wythe County records. William Williams in his answer to the Bill of Complaint, referred to Richard Muse as ''uncle Muse'' as there was a ''connexion by marriage,'' but this is not explained (*Walton vs. Muse*, Box 35, 1827, Wythe County Circuit Court, Basement. *see also* Muse, and Walton sketches).

The Speedwell Iron Furnace is still standing on the waters of Cripple Creek. The ramp attached to the furnace, now gone, was used for loading purposes. Photo courtesy of F. B. Kegley Collection.

SECTION IV
Cripple Creek

CHAPTER 1
Creeks, Roads and Settlements

The three branches of Cripple Creek rise near the Blue Spring in the southwest part of present Smyth County, and flow eastward through the southern portion of Wythe County for approximately twenty-five miles and empty into the New River between Austinville and Ivanhoe. Numerous feeder branches enter the main stream from the north and the south. Among the major water courses are Vaught's Mill Creek, Ward Branch, Chaney (formerly McKinley's) Branch, Dry Run, Sugar Run, Thorn Branch, Fisher (now Slate Spring) Branch, Mill Branch, Henley Creek, Cook Branch, Francis Mill Creek, Dean Branch, and Rock Creek. Lesser unnamed branches and runs also appear on local maps.

The first individual tracts taken up along Cripple Creek were selected by James Patton, and James Wood before 1751. One of these tracts went to William Rutherford, and a selection made by James Rion went to William Foster in 1755. There were two early transfers by deed, the first to James Willy who obtained a 2,050-acre strip about six miles long, and the other for Alexander Noble who obtained 1132 acres from James Willy in 1755. Then the settlement appears to have been abandoned till the late 1760s and early 1770s. The Foster tract traded hands again in 1770, and John Newland became the permanent resident on the west end of Cripple Creek.

The Willys (various spellings) appear to have lived somewhere on the tract of 2,050 acres, because James Willy, the younger, stated in his Revolutionary War pension application that he moved to Montgomery County when he was young and lived about twelve miles from the lead mines on Cripple Creek. He was born in Mecklenburg County, North Carolina, on December 19, 1762. He served as a private under several local officers and was at the Battle of Shallow Ford. About seven years after the war he moved to Washington County, North Carolina, and then went to Franklin County, Georgia, and then settled in Blount County, Tennessee (Pension W26145). James Harris lived on part of the Willy land, but apparently did not own it. It was the choice land on Cripple Creek near Speedwell extending from the Stephen Sanders place to the east settled by him in the 1780s, and to William Ewing's to the west, and included a tract of Alexander Smyth he purchased from William Neely. The Willy tract also included, at various times the land of the Spanglers, Ewings, Reaghs (Rheas), Sanders, Millers, Stephens, and Loves. The furnace land west of Speedwell was part of the original grant. Those associated with the manufacture of iron at the Speedwell furnace included James White, Francis Preston, Jehu Stephens, William Love, William King, and King, Trigg and Morgan, among others. Eventually the land came into the hands of Alexander Smyth and his descendants. Adjoining the Willy tract in the eastern part and to the south was the tract of Roger Oats, later part of the Sanders and Gannaway estates. Thomas Gannaway held claim to land which covered part of the present Town of Speedwell. Peter Spangler had several tracts in and around Speedwell, and a large tract of 425 acres south of the furnace tract which eventually came to J. P. Mathews (Pension W26145).

When surveys were made in Fincastle County in 1773, only one was made on Cripple Creek and that was for Henry Francis, who had been in the neighborhood since

1768. His settlement was made in the present Town of Cripple Creek on the branch which runs south through the town and bears his name. Unfortunately, Francis was killed in battle in the Revolutionary War in 1780 and the development of the land was left to Robert Sanders, and the Rosenbaums and Jonas families.

In 1774, more than thirty additional tracts were surveyed up and down the length of Cripple Creek and its many branches. Many of these early settlers had additions or corrections to their boundaries in Montgomery County during the 1780s, with most of the grants coming after that time. Many others assigned their surveys and the grants were issued to new residents, who took over the payments and obtained the legal title to the tracts. In 1775, about a dozen surveys were made, and then all action was suspended until after the Revolutionary War.

By the 1770s, many permanent residents had settled in the community. These included Adam Dean, the Henleys, Bebbers, the Ewings, Porters, Kerrs, Gleaves, Vaughts, Reaghs (Rheas), Hobbs, and Rutherfords, among others. In the 1780s, these people added to their original selections with about two dozen deeds recorded, and about three dozen surveys obtained. This era marked the arrival of the Pattons, Spanglers, Campbells, Sprakers, Goses, and Chaneys, among others. Later arrivals included the Reverend John Stanger, the Rosenbaums, the Fishers, the Sweckers, Painters, and Peters, and others. Although Colonel Stephen Sanders was in the county, probably in the 1770s, he did not move to the upper reaches of Cripple Creek until the 1780s. General Alexander Smyth was also in the county early in the 1790s, and purchased his first land on Cripple Creek in the name of his infant son in 1796. At his death his extensive estate reached a few miles north of the present Town of Speedwell, on both sides of present State Route 21, and also included the Speedwell furnace lands to the west of the town.

Although agriculture was practiced along Cripple Creek, the farms were generally small and somewhat limited by the roughness of the terrain. Springs were numerous due to limestone formations, but it was discovered early in the development of the county that iron ore deposits were of such quantity and quality that they justified the erection of charcoal furnaces, and the instigation of mining operations soon took precedence over agriculture. With the excellent water supply, the abundance of limestone, a wealth of forest lands to provide the charcoal, and a natural deposits of iron ore, the industry was guaranteed to be a success, over a period of more than one hundred years.

Though several of the furnaces in the south and east portions of Wythe County remain standing, others have been destroyed or replaced over the years. The iron industry was known to have been operating at Speedwell as early as 1792. Several of the furnaces operated during the Civil War and provided the Confederacy with much needed iron (for further details on the furnaces and the manufacturing of iron on Cripple Creek, *see*, Kegley, *Glimpses*, Vol. 1, pp. 115-140).

The records which follow are those pertaining to the Cripple Creek region, with the emphasis on the families of Wythe County. The information comes from the counties of Augusta, Botetourt, Fincastle, Montgomery, and Wythe.

CHAPTER 2: THE LAND RECORDS

AUGUSTA COUNTY SURVEYS: Staunton, Virginia.

1746, JAMES PATTON, 428 acres on both sides of Cripple Creek.

1748, JAMES PATTON, 2,050 acres on Cripple Creek, a branch of New River (a narrow strip six miles long below the forks), granted 1753.

1749/50, JAMES WOOD, 1,200 acres on both sides of Cripple Creek above the forks, granted 1755.

1751, JAMES PATTON, 154 acres on both sides of Cripple Creek, corner to James Rion, granted 1755.

1751, JAMES RION, 87 acres on the south fork of Cripple Creek, .

1753, LOYAL COMPANY, tract 5, 75 acres on New River at the mouth of Cripple Creek, granted 1798; tract 23, 120 acres on Cripple Creek granted 1798, deed to James Newell.

AUGUSTA COUNTY GRANTS: Virginia State Library, Archives, Richmond, Virginia.

1753, WILLIAM RUTHERFORD, 428 acres on the south side of Cripple Creek.

1755, WILLIAM FOSTER, 87 acres on the south fork of Cripple Creek.

AUGUSTA COUNTY ENTRIES: Staunton, Virginia.

1761, JOHN BUCHANAN, 300 acres on a branch of the New River called Cripple Creek, at a place called Buffalo Ford, formerly surveyed.

1762, JOHN DILLARD, 400 acres on "Blew" Spring at the head of Cripple Creek.

1762, JOHN BINGAMAN, 400 acres on the upper forks of Cripple Creek.

PATTON-PRESTON NOTEBOOK: Wytheville Community College Library, Wytheville, Virginia.

JAMES HARRIS of Cripple Creek, to 2,050 acres at £4.5 total, and £87.2.6 by your bond of April 1751.

AUGUSTA COUNTY DEEDS: Staunton, Virginia.

1754, JAMES WILLY from JAMES PATTON, 2,050 acres on Cripple Creek. Witnesses were Alexander Noble and Patrick Calhoun.

1755, ALEXANDER NOBLE, GENT., from JAMES WILLY and MARTHA, 1,132 acres on Cripple Creek.

BOTETOURT COUNTY DEEDS: Fincastle, Virginia

1770, JOHN NEWLAND from WILLIAM FOSTER and MARY, 87 acres on the south fork of Cripple Creek.

FINCASTLE COUNTY SURVEYS: Christiansburg, Virginia.

1773, HENRY FRANCIS, 750 acres on both sides of Cripple Creek, granted to Robert Sanders, 1790.

1774, GEORGE BROCK, 157 acres on Cripple Creek.

1774, JAMES BEBBER, SR., 480 acres on Cripple Creek, granted 1795; 1782, Montgomery County, 85 acres on Cripple Creek.

1774, JAMES BEBBER, JR., 28 acres on Cripple Creek.

1774, ADAM DEAN, 68 acres on a branch of Cripple Creek, granted 1785; Montgomery County, 1782, 53 acres adjoining the land he lives on, granted 1785; 1783, 400 acres on the head of Mine Mill Creek, granted 1785. Additional grants: 490 acres on Cripple Creek adjoining his patent land, 1785; 290 acres on Cripple Creek, granted 1785.

1774, CHRISTOPHER ELAM, 128 acres Cripple Creek, assigned and granted to Hezekiah Chaney.

1774, SAMUEL HENDERSON, 147 acres Cripple Creek.

1774, JOHN GORDON, 270 acres on Cripple Creek.

1774, GEORGE HENLEY, 215 acres Cripple Creek assigned and granted to Hezekiah Cheney.

1774, LUCAS HOOD, 143 acres on Cripple Creek, transferred to Henry Francis.

1774, JOHN IRVINE, 196 acres on a branch of Cripple Creek.

1774, WILLIAM MEEK, 81 acres on a branch of Cripple Creek; also 395 acres on Indian Creek.

1774, JOHN LESLY (LASTLY, LASTLEY), 175 acres Blue Spring, head of Cripple Creek; Montgomery County, 1783, 250 acres at the head spring of Cripple Creek; Wythe County, 1797, 92 acres on Cripple Creek, granted 1800.

1774, THOMAS MEEK, 82 acres on Sugar Run a branch of Cripple Creek, actual settlement 1772, assigned to David Miller.

1774, THOMAS MITCHELL, 426 acres on the north fork of Cripple Creek.

1774, DAVID MILLER, 425 acres on Cripple Creek; also assignment of 82 acres on Sugar Run from Thomas Meek (*see above*).

1774, ROGER OATS, 510 acres Cripple Creek (Walker's list notes that he is co-owner with Col. Christian); grant to Oats 1783. Commissioner's certificate entitles him to 400 acres, part of 510 acres by actual settlement made in 1773.

1774, BENJAMIN RODGERS, 107 acres on Cripple Creek, granted to George Buckalew, 1806.

1774, WILLIAM ROBINSON, 254 acres at Sinking Spring on Cripple Creek.

1774, JOHN RUTHERFORD, 118 acres on Cripple Creek.

1774, JOHN VOILS, 144 acres on Cripple Creek.

1774, ANDREW VAUGHT, 364 acres on the North Fork of Cripple Creek; Montgomery County, 1782, 400 acres Cripple Creek; 1783, 172 acres on both sides of Vaught's Mill Creek, waters of Cripple Creek, grant 1785 to George and Christley Vaught.

1774, WILLIAM HENLEY, 227 acres Thorn Branch of Cripple Creek.

1774, JOHN DIVER, 120 acres on Cripple Creek.

1774, CONRAD SHEPLER (SHEPLEY?), 130 acres on Cripple Creek.

1774, JOHN HENDERSON, 195 acres on Cripple Creek.

1774, ALEXANDER COLWELL, 112 acres on branch of Cripple Creek.

1774, JOEL FIELDS, 47 acres on Cripple Creek.

1774, WILLIAM HENLEY, JR., 283 acres on Cripple Creek.

1774, THOMAS HAMILTON, 521 acres on Cripple Creek, near Lick Mountain adjoining James Rodgers, assigned to Hezekiah Chaney who received the grant.

1774, THOMAS HOBBS, 68 acres on Cripple Creek.

1774, BENJAMIN HAWKINS, 365 acres on Thorn Branch.

1774, JAMES RODGERS, 42 acres on branch of Cripple Creek; 499 acres foot of Lick Mountain, on waters of Cripple Creek.

1774, THOMAS RODGERS, 430 acres on head of Cripple Creek, corner to John Lesley, to James Scott by Commissioners, 1782.

1774, BENJAMIN RUTHERFORD, 247 acres on Cripple Creek; in 1783 "Stephen Gose owns this land."

1775, ANN EWINS, 200 acres on the south side of Cripple Creek, opposite Wm. Ewins.

1775, ALEXANDER EWING, 380 acres on Cripple Creek, south branch, to include improvements, settlement made 1770; Montgomery County, 1784, 85 acres on Cripple Creek joining the old survey; 1784, 214 acres on the north side of John Newland's, granted 1785, adjoining his settlement of 400 acres (Book O, p. 634); grant for 200 acres on the south side of Cripple Creek opposite William Ewing's, 1794.

1775, ALEXANDER EWING, JR., grants, 400 acres on Cripple Creek, 1785 adjoining James Douglas and John Newland; 1784, survey 144 acres on Cripple Creek, adjoining John Newland's patent line on the south side of the land, granted 1785; 1784, survey 156 acres with Newland's lines, granted 1785.

1775, JOHN KERR (CARR), 225 acres on the south branch of Cripple Creek corner to David Miller, granted 1795; survey 1782, 384 acres adjoining James Wylie's on Cripple Creek; grant 384 acres, adjoining the patent land of James Wyles (Wyley, Wylie).

1775, ROBERT REAGH, 150 acres on the south side of Cripple Creek.

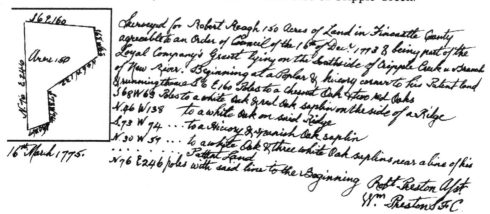

Survey for Robert Reagh containing 150 acres on the south side of Cripple Creek, was dated March 16th, 1775. The document was signed by Robert Preston, assistant to William Preston, Surveyor of Fincastle County. Tracing from the original by Mary B. Kegley.

1775, ALEXANDER HENDERSON, 182 acres on Cripple Creek headwaters.

1775, DANIEL HENDERSON, 273 acres on headwaters of the south fork of Cripple Creek.

1775, WALTER KERR, 176 acres on the north side of Cripple Creek.

1775, MICHAEL KINSER, 208 acres on both sides of Sugar Run, a branch of Cripple Creek, granted to Peter Kinser, 1802.

FINCASTLE COUNTY DEEDS: Christiansburg, Virginia

1773, JAMES and GEORGE DOUGLAS from WILLIAM EWING, 330 acres on Cripple Creek, branch of New River.

1774, PHILIP DUTTON from Thompson and Preston execs. of JAMES PATTON, late of Augusta County, 154 acres on the South Fork of Cripple Creek

MONTGOMERY COUNTY SURVEYS: Christiansburg, Virginia.

1782, HEZEKIAH CHANEY (CHINIA), 393 acres on McCendley's (McKinleys) Run, near Lick Mountain, granted 1787; 1782, 125 acres, on the north side of Lick Mountain between Stofle Kettering and James Campbell, granted 1796; 1782, 287 acres on Sugar Run, branch of Cripple Creek, granted 1787; 1782, 125 acres on the north side of Lick Mountain, survey made for George Henley and Christopher Elams, assigned to Chaney, 1799; also Thomas Hamilton survey, about the same time [*see* sketch]; and Thomas Major sold to John Sifers, two tracts of 200 acres on Cripple Creek and Sugar Run, joining William Patton on the east and James White on the south, 1784, Sifers assigned to Michael Yong (Young) who assigned it to Samuel Burks, 1787, who assigned to Chaney, 1792; 1783, 196 acres on McCendly's (McKinleys) Run, a branch of Cripple Creek, granted 1796.

1782, JAMES CAMPBELL, 400 acres on Cripple Creek, on the side of Lick Mountain, granted 1784; 145 acres on branch next to Col. Stephens, adjoining sd. Campbell where he lives, granted 1785; 55 acres on head of a branch next to Col. Stephens, Lick Mountain, granted 1785.

1782, MINITREE JONES, 90 acres adjoining Samuel Ewing on the west side of the New River, granted 1785; 1782, 395 acres on west side of New River adjoining Samuel Ewing, granted 1785; 324 acres adjoining Samuel Ewing and William Rutherford's patent land, 1785.

1782, WILLIAM HALL, 338 acres on Sugar Run, a branch of Cripple Creek, assigned to Stophell (Christopher) Spraker, granted to him 1793.

1782, WILLIAM BUSTERD, 200 acres on the head spring of Cripple Creek, granted 1785; additional grant for 426 acres on the north fork of Cripple Creek, adjoining Andrew Vaut [Vaught], 1792.

1782, FREDERICK BRANSTETER, JR., 125 acres on Cripple Creek, granted 1792.

1782, JAMES DAVIS, 357 acres on Cripple Creek, south of Lick Mountain, granted 1785.

1782, PHILIP DUTTON [DIRTING, DURTING], 328 acres on the headwaters of Cripple Creek, granted 1785; additional grants: 150 acres on head of Reed Creek, adjoining Adam Dutton, 1791; 150 acres on Cripple Creek near the head, being surplus land in old patent land, granted 1820; 172 acres on Cripple Creek, adjoining his patent land, granted 1800; 294 acres and 37 acres, adjoining Peter Deckert and Christian Vaught, granted 1810.

1782, JAMES NEWELL, 340 acres on Cripple Creek, 324 acres on Cripple Creek; 1783, 400 acres on Cripple Creek; 2,164 acres on Mine Mill Creek; 1784, 360 acres on the south side of Cripple Creek; 1783, 304 acres on Rocky Creek;

1785; 221 acres adjoining Cowden and Straw on Reed and Cripple Creeks, granted 1785; as assignee of Michael Wood, 1000 acres on Cripple Creek adjoining his settlement,1777; additional grants include 37 acres on east side of New River, 1792; 42 acres on the west side of the New River, 1792; 103 acres on west side of the New River, 1792; 872 acres on west side of New River and on Cripple Creek adjoining Brawley, 1793; 154 acres on waters of Cripple Creek adjoining William Gleaves and Hugh Montgomery, 1796; 1,000 acres on Mine Mill Creek adjoining William Rodgers, 1796; 200 acres on Cripple Creek, 1800; 460 acres on Cripple Creek, 1803; 213 acres on New River adjoining Robert Sanders and Daniel Shaver, 1812; [Newell also had grants for land on Little River, Reed Island Creek, Meadow Creek, Chestnut Creek, Crab Creek, and Elk Creek, as recorded in the grant records at the Virginia State Library, Archives]; *see also* Lead Mines section.

1782, RANDOLPH RUTHERFORD, 150 acres joining lands of Samuel Smith and Adam Dean; 1796, grant for 59 acres adjoining Lucas Hood and John Gordon; Wythe County, 1795, 35 acres on the north side of Cripple Creek, granted 1800.

1783, ANDREW BRANSTETER, 165 acres granted 1785.

1783, JAMES CRAWFORD, heir at law of JOHN CRAWFORD, deceased, 100 acres on Cripple Creek, on a Commissioner's certificate.

1783, DANIEL BABER, 99 acres on waters of Cripple Creek, on a Commissioner's certificate for 400 acres dated 1781.

1783, WILLIAM EWING, 86 acres joining his own on Cripple Creek; 193 acres on Cripple Creek; 307 acres on the south side of Cripple Creek joining his patent land, granted 1788; another tract [no acres given] on Cripple Creek, 1793.

1783, GEORGE EWING, 400 acres on Hobbs Branch of New River, granted 1785; 1783, 168 acres on a small branch running through Samuel Ewing's patent land, adjoining Manitree Jones, granted 1784.

1783, ISHAM HARRIS, 200 acres on Cripple Creek.

1783, JAMES WHITE, 11 acres on both sides of Cripple Creek.

1783, PETER COLEHEP, 80 acres on Cripple Creek, granted 1785.

1783, PETER COLEHEP and FREDRICK BRANSTETER, 235 acres on Cripple Creek, granted 1785.

1783, ROBERT WILLEY, 80 acres on Cripple Creek

1783, BENJAMIN SMITH, 350 acres on Cripple Creek

1783, THOMAS ROGERS, 430 acres on Cripple Creek

1783, NICHOLAS ANSBAUGH, 93 acres on Cripple Creek.

1783, DAVID BUSTERD, 270 acres on the head spring of Cripple Creek, on treasury warrant, assigned by John Ward, granted Creek adjoining Alex. Ewing, granted 1785.

1783, JOHN RATHBONE, 45 acres on west side of the New River.

1783, PETER CREAGER, 210 acres, assignee of John Ward, on the headwaters of Cripple Creek, granted 1788.

1783, JAMES NEWELL, JR., 300 acres on Cripple Creek; 1784, 360 acres adjoining James Newell, Sr., granted 1784; 400 acres on the west side of the New River adjoining Charles [should be George] Forbuss and land sold by Forbuss to William Herbert, deceased, granted 1785; 300 acres on the waters of Cripple Creek adjoining Adam Dean and Brawley, granted 1785; *see also* Lead Mines section.

1783, WILLIAM GLEAVES, 295 acres on Cripple Creek, Commissioner's certificate granted 1785; 1795, 150 acres on the south side of Cripple Creek; grants 1793: 90 acres on the south side of Cripple Creek adjoining the Buffalo Ford; 270 acres on Cripple Creek; grant 1796, 586 acres on Cripple Creek; grant 1798, 350 acres on Cripple Creek.

1783, ARCHIBALD REAGH, 227 acres on both sides of Cripple Creek, adjoining James White's patent land, granted 1785.

1783, WILLIAM RUTHERFORD, JR., 124 acres on Cripple Creek, adjoining James Newell, and Samuel Ewing's patent line and the Mine line, granted 1800.

1783, GEORGE POWERS, 67 acres on Cripple Creek.

1783, DANIEL PEARCE, 221 acres on Reed and Cripple creeks.

1783, RICHARD MUSE, 360 acres on Cripple Creek joining James Newell and 900 acres on both sides of Cripple Creek adjoining George Ewing; 1786, 100 acres on Walkers Creek.

1783, WILLIAM LOVE, 752 acres on Cripple Creek adjoining his patent land and James White, granted 1785; 48 acres on both sides of Cripple Creek;

1783, MICHAEL LEASE, 163 acres on Thorn Branch, assigned by Adam Dean, adjoining George Ewing's patent line, granted 1785.

1787, Executors of JOHN BUCHANAN, deceased, 150 acres on both sides of Cripple Creek, known by the name of Buffalo Ford.

1787, JOHN WITSELL (WHITSEL), 41 acres adjoining William Ewing, John Crawford and Peter Colep; 1795, grant for 65 acres on Cripple Creek; 1797, grant 150 acres on Cripple Creek adjoining Ewings.

1790, JACOB WELKER, 170 acres on the dividing ridge between Reed Creek and Cripple Creek, corner to Jacob Dicker [Deckart?].

1790, GEORGE KINSER, 142 acres on Cripple Creek.

1790, PETER YOUNCE, 130 acres on Sugar Run, Cripple Creek, corner to his own land and Spreaker; grant for 94 acres on Sugar Run, adjoining Spragers [Sprakers], 1785.

MONTGOMERY COUNTY DEEDS: Christiansburg, Virginia

1779, GEORGE EWING from William Sayers, attorney for MARY WOOD, sole executor of JAMES WOOD, and for JAMES WOOD, son of James Wood, Sr., 900 acres on Cripple Creek.

1782, WILLIAM EWING from John Montgomery attorney for ALEXANDER NOBLE of South Carolina, 556 acres on Cripple Creek.

1778, MICHAEL LEAST from William Sayers, attorney for JAMES WOOD and MARY WOOD, 300 acres on Cripple Creek.

1782, JOHN REAGH as heir of ROBERT REAGH, deceased, from John Montgomery, attorney for ALEXANDER NOBLE, 593 acres on Cripple Creek.

1782, WILLIAM LOVE, from JOHN REAGH, 149 1/2 acres on Cripple Creek.

1782, WILLIAM EWING from JOHN REAGH, 120 acres on Cripple Creek.

1783, JAMES WHITE from DAVID MILLER, 198 acres on Cripple Creek, part of a tract patented to James Patton on June 20, 1753 and by deed conveyed by John Montgomery, attorney for Alexander Noble, 1782, adjoining John Reagh and William Love.

1783, THOMAS QUIRK from JAMES WYLIE, son of James Wylie deceased, 676 acres, part of a tract known as Wylie's tract, the lower part.

1782, JAMES WHITE from JOHN REAGH, 126 acres on Cripple Creek.

1784, STEPHEN SANDERS from THOMAS QUIRK and wife JANE, 676 acres on Cripple Creek.

1784, NICHOLAS SNIDER, NICHOLAS CLINE, JACOB KETTERING from JNO. WHITSIL, the plantation he now lives on, on Cripple Creek, no acres given.

1786, JOHN EWING from GEORGE EWING, for natural love and affection, 225 acres on Cripple Creek.

1785, SAMUEL EWING from GEORGE EWING, for natural love and affection, 225 acres on Cripple Creek.

1785, JOHN NEWLAND, from ALEXANDER EWING, JR., 154 acres on Cripple Creek; also 240 acres on the north side of Jno. Newland's Paddock, and 160 acres on the north side of Newland's Paddock, on Vaught's Mill Creek; 156 acres on south side of Cripple Creek.

1785, JAMES DOUGLAS from ALEXANDER EWING, JR., 240 acres on both sides of Cripple Creek.

1786, HENRY VAUGHT from GEORGE and CHRISTLEY VAUGHT, 572 acres on the headwaters of Cripple Creek.

1786, CHRISTLEY VAUGHT from HENRY VAUGHT, 130 acres on headwaters of Cripple Creek.

1787, JACOB KIMBERLAND from ISHAM HARRIS, 200 acres on Cripple Creek.

1788, PETER SPANGLER, from ROBERT WYLEY, 15 acres on Cripple Creek.

1786, MARY EWING, from ROBERT SAYERS and MARY PRITCHARD, late wife of ALEXANDER SAYERS, 650 acres.

1787, MARGARET PORTER from STEPHEN SANDERS, 50 acres on Thorn Branch.

1786, MENITREE JONES from JAS. MCDANIEL 400 acres on New River.

ADDITIONAL GRANTS: Virginia State Library, Archives

1796, HENRY COOK, 400 acres on Cripple Creek.

1796, ANDREW DANNER, 270 acres on Cripple Creek adjoining Wm. Henley; 300 acres adjoining James Campbell granted 1796; 520 acres on Cripple Creek, adjoining Buckalew and Baber, granted 1800; 33 acres on waters of Cripple Creek adjoining Buckalew, granted 1804.

1796, THOMAS MAJORS, 195 acres adjoining George Smith and Adam Dean.

1800, DAILY WALKER, 185 acres adjoining Joseph Friend, on Cripple Creek, granted 1800.

1800, STEPHEN SANDERS, 294 acres adjoining Thomas Gannaway.

1785, CHARLES NUCKOLLS, 900 acres on both sides of Cripple Creek adjoining Jones lines; 1785, 400 acres on Cripple Creek; 1796, 300 acres adjoining Jones.

1796, GEORGE BUCKALEW (BUCKLEW), 150 acres on Babers Mill Branch, a branch of Cripple Creek adjoining Ewings.

1796, MATHIAS ROSENBAUM, 330 acres on Cripple Creek.

1792, STEPHEN GOSE, 55 acres adjoining Goose's [Gose's] old survey on Cripple Creek.

1793, JACOB NEWMAN, 142 acres adjoining where William Patton lives.

1797, NICHOLAS SNIDER, 150 acres on Blue Spring Branch, adjoining Philip Dutton, granted to Snider.

1801, ALEXANDER SMYTH, 500 acres on the north side of a tract on Cripple Creek that belonged to James Wylie deceased, and on which one Harris formerly lived.

1811, GEORGE DANNER, 1 acre 28 poles, branch of Cripple Creek, adjoining Hobbs and Gleaves.

1832, JOHN STANGER, 144 acres on branch of Cripple Creek; 110 acres on Cripple Creek corner to his patent, and also adjoining Peter Wampler, 1819.

1832, THOMAS COPENHAVER, 273 acres on the south fork of Cripple Creek.

1832, JOHN DUTTON, 187 acres on Cripple Creek.

WYTHE COUNTY SURVEYS: Wytheville, Virginia

1790, JAMES McGAVOCK, 2,292 acres, on the south side of Lick Mountain, part of military warrant # 977.

1793, JAMES CAMPBELL, 400 acres on Cripple Creek, corner to patent land and Hezekiah Chaney.

1793, MICHAEL BRANSTRATER, 50 acres on Cripple Creek, corner to his own land and Peter Creager.

1793, JEHU STEPHENS, 5 acres on Cripple Creek; 20 acres on Cripple Creek, corner to his patent land.

1795, DUNCAN MCLAUGHLIN and DAVID PATTISON, 41,900 acres in Wythe, Washington, and Grayson counties, Cripple Creek, Fox Creek and South Fork of the Holston River.

1795, ISAAC NEWHOUSE, 200 acres on the headwaters of Cripple Creek, granted 1796; also 380 acres on the south side of Cripple Creek adjoining Douglas' land, 1792.

179- [no date], ANTHONY ROSEN [BAUM], 456 acres on the south side of Cripple Creek, corner to William Saunders.

1795, THOMAS MADISON, 586 acres on Cripple Creek, Davis Branch; 750 acres on new River corner to George Ewing and Phillip Gains; 164 acres on Reed Creek; 1,100 acres on Reed Creek including 220 acres, property of Henry Newman; 150 acres on New River adjoining Evan Williams; 2,000 acres adjoining William Rogers, including 500 acres of James McGavock land; 600 acres on Reed Creek, corner to Joseph Eaton and McGavock; 980 acres on west side of New River adjoining William Herbert, Stotts, Evan Williams, including 380 acres property of [said] Thomas [Madison]; 2,750 acres on south side of Reed Creek including 250 acres of James Finley's land; 400 acres on Cripple Creek, corner to Fanning.

1795, PETER SPANGLER, 150 acres on Cripple Creek, corner to Cook.

1795, JOSEPH BURR, 2,500 acres on both sides of Cripple Creek, corner to George Ewing, Hobbs, Gleaves, and including 300 acres of William Gleaves' land.

1795, WILLIAM GLEAVES, 150 acres Cripple Creek, joining Randal Rutherford and M. Worley.

179-[no date], JOHN KERR and ANDREW PORTER, 110 acres on Cripple Creek.

1795, JOSEPH FANNIN, 100 acres on Cripple Creek.

1795, JAMES NEWELL, 140 acres corner to Gleaves; 1797, 1,000 acres on Cripple Creek.

1795, THOMAS MADISON & CO., 53 acres on Cripple Creek adjoining Carr; 47 acres on Cripple Creek, adjoining Carr; and 400 acres adjoining James Campbell.

1797, PHILIP DUTTON, 172 acres on Cripple Creek, adjoining his patent land and James Douglas.

1797, JAMES JAMES, 50 acres at the head of Cripple Creek.

1797, JAMES P. PRESTON, 1,000 acres on Cripple Creek and South Fork of Holston, corner to William Moor, Buster, Copenhafer and Lasley.

1798, HENRY PURKERT, 188 acres on Cripple Creek.

1798, DAVID HORN, 200 acres on Cripple Creek, adjoining patent land and Douglass, granted 1800; additional grants: 250 acres on headwaters of Cripple Creek, 1818; 180 acres on waters of Cripple Creek, 1825; 170 acres on Cripple Creek, 1825; 100 acres on waters of Cripple Creek, granted 1825.

1798, STEPHEN SAUNDERS, 294 acres, Cripple Creek adjoining his patent land, granted 1800.

1798, JOSEPH LASSLEY, 187 acres on Cripple Creek.

1798, WILLIAM LOVE, 1,425 acres on Cripple Creek.

1798, ANDREW PORTER, 133 acres on Cripple Creek, corner to Bonhams.

1798, GEORGE BUCKALEW, 180 acres on Cripple Creek.

1799, JOHN NEWLAND, 210 acres corner to his patent land, Daniel Peirce, George Vaught, and John Dutton, granted 1802.

1799, JOHN THOMPSON SAYERS, 500 acres, on the north side of a tract on Cripple Creek on which one Harris formerly lived, corner to John Ker [Kerr]. [This may be the tract granted to Alexander Smyth in 1801].

1800, DANIEL PIERCE, 279 acres on Cripple Creek, corner to George Vaut [Vaught], John Newland, and Andrew Irvin.

1800, HEZEKIAH CHINEY, 836 acres on Cripple Creek adjoining his own.

1800, JAMES MC CAMPBELL, 250 acres on Cripple Creek.

WYTHE COUNTY DEED BOOK 1: Wytheville, Virginia

1791, JAMES NEWELL from MANITREE JONES, 324 on both sides of Cripple Creek, adjoining the tract Newell lives on.

1791, JAMES NEWEL [NEWELL] from MANITREE JONES, 485 acres on Dry Branch, joining the patent land of Sam'l Ewing on New River.

1790, JAMES McGAVOCK from JAMES DEAN, 190 acres on a branch of Cripple Creek; also 53 acres adjoining land he is now living on, adjoining old survey; 400 acres on waters of Cripple Creek; 68 acres on Cripple Creek.

1791, STEPHEN SANDERS from ROGER OATS, 500 acres on south side of Cripple Creek, adjoining sd. Sanders.

1792, HENRY ELLER from JOHN EWING AND POLLY, 225 acres both sides of Cripple Creek.

1792, WILLIAM SANDERS from ROBERT AND CATY SANDERS, both sides of Cripple Creek, no acres given.

1792, RANDOLPH RUTHERFORD from ROBERT AND CATY SANDERS, 157 acres by patent November 9, 1790, on a branch of Cripple Creek.

1793, ALEXANDER EWING from JAIN (JEAN) EWING, relict of WILLIAM EWING, deceased, whereas William Ewing by will devised to Alexander Ewing a tract on Cripple Creek, 346 acres granted to William Ewing by patent August 6, 1782, same whereon William resided when living, subject to the life estate for Jain his wife, now she sells her life estate to Alexander Ewing.

1793, NEHEMIAH BONHAM from WILLIAM AND POLLY SANDERS, 105 acres on Cripple Creek, part of 750 acres surveyed for Henry Francis.

1793, MICHAEL LEASE from WILLIAM AND MARY SANDERS, 50 acres on the north side of Cripple Creek.

1793, MICHAEL WORELEY [WORLEY] from WILLIAM AND ELIZABETH GLEAVES, 81 acres on Cripple Creek.

1793, WILLIAM NEELEY from ROBERT WYLEY of Green County, ceded territory, 540 acres on both sides of Cripple Creek known as Wyleys place, corner to Stephen Sanders and corner to Peter Spangler.

1793, WILLIAM GANNAWAY, of Buckingham County, Virginia, from ALEX (ALEXR.) EWING, 393 acres on Cripple Creek; 346 acres Cripple Creek, corner to James Douglas.

1793, JAMES McGAVOCK from James Dean, executor of ADAM DEAN deceased, of Davidson County, Territory South of the Ohio, 490 acres by survey June 28, 1786, on waters of Cripple Creek granted Adam Dean February 4, 1793.

1794, JOHN CARR, from STEPHEN AND ISBELL SANDERS, 50 acres on Cripple Creek, part of a tract where Sanders now lives, beginning by the Thorn Branch.

1793, JOHN DOUGLAS from JAMES DOUGLAS of Wythe County, and George Douglas of Lincoln County, Kentucky, 330 acres on both sides of Cripple Creek, corner to Alex. Ewing.

1793, WILLIAM BELL and WILLIAM HARBERT, from Charles and Mary Nuckolls, 500 acres, both sides of Cripple Creek.

1794, MICHAEL BRANSTETER from ISAAC and CATHERINE NEWHOUSE, 27 acres on a branch of South Fork of Cripple Creek.

1794, DAVID HORN from Isaac and Catherine Newhouse, 158 acres on a branch of the South Fork of Cripple Creek.

1794, ANDREW DONALD from JAMES NEWELL, two tracts on Cripple Creek, 660 acres: (1) 300 acres granted Newell as assignee of Richard Muse. patented December 2, 1785 and (2) 360 acres joining Donald on which Stephen Sanders, Jr., resides, granted Newell as assignee of R. Muse, March 10, 1794.

1794, HUGH MONTGOMERY AND DANIEL CARLIN (of Patrick County) from WILLIAM and SARAH BELL, 500 acres on both sides of Cripple Creek, including houses, forges and dams.

1794, WILLIAM GANAWAY [GANNAWAY] from ALEXANDER EWING, 200 acres by survey March 3, 1775 on the south side of Cripple Creek, granted to Ewing, March 10, 1794.

1795, JOHN STANGER from PETER and ELIZABETH YOUNCE, 130 acres on Shugar [Sugar] Run, a branch of Cripple Creek, corner to Younce; 94 acres on Sugar Run, a branch of Cripple Creek by survey August 2, 1784, corner Spreager [Spraker].

1795, PETER KINSER from ALEX EWING, one of the heirs of WILLIAM EWING, deceased, 122 acres by survey on Cripple Creek, granted William Ewing, March 15, 1793.

1795, HENRY KETTNOR from MICHAEL and NANCY LEESE, 300 acres on Cripple Creek; 163 acres granted Michael Lease assignee of Adam Dean by entry on treasury warrant and by survey, on Thorn Branch, beginning on George Ewing's patent line.

1793, Articles of agreement between WILLIAM EWING and ALEXANDER EWING, nephew of said William, of Davidson County, North Carolina, in order to procure his assistance and management of domestic and foreign business, William Ewing obligates himself to give the whole of his plantation on Cripple Creek to Alexander Ewing, the same whereon William now lives, except legal dower of wife during her lifetime, and at their death to Alexander who is to render to his uncle William Ewing every possible assistance in transaction of business for the life of William Ewing.

1795, GIDEON HUDDLE from WILLIAM and ELIZABETH GANNAWAY, 235 acres on south side of Cripple Creek, corner to James Dougless[Douglas].

1796, MATHIAS WHITE from JOHN and MARGARET KERR, 50 acres on a branch of Cripple Creek, part of the tract where Kerr now lives.

1796, WILLIAM BONHAM from JOHN and MARGARET KERR, 150 acres on a branch of Cripple Creek, part of a tract where Kerr now lives.

1796, JAMES McGAVOCK from JAMES DEAN of Davidson County, Tennessee, 46 acres part of a survey of 190 acres made November 17, 1753, granted to Dean March 7, 1794 on a branch of Cripple Creek...mentions the mouth of a small branch called the Middle Branch between widow Smith's and Adam Dean's old place. Deed by David McGavock, attorney-in-fact.

1796, ROBERT MAJORS from JAMES DEAN, of Davidson County, Tennessee, 144 acres part of a survey of 190 acres made November 17, 1753, granted to Dean March 7, 1794 on a branch of Cripple Creek. Deed by David McGavock, attorney-in-fact.

1796, PETER DARTER from ISAAC and CATHERINE NEWHOUSE, 195 acres on south branch of Cripple Creek, same where Newhouse now lives.

1796, MONEY GANNAWAY from WILLIAM and ELIZABETH GANNAWAY, 116 acres on headwaters of Cripple Creek, joining John Douglas.

1796, WILLIAM KING from DAVID BUSTERD (also signed by Frances Busterd), 35 acres, part of 210 acres, at the headwaters of Cripple Creek.

1796, FREDERICK COLEHEP from PETER and MARY COLHEP, 117 acres on Cripple Creek.

1796, ADAM COLEHEP from PETER and MARY COLHEP, 117 acres on Cripple Creek, corner to Frederick Colhep's 117 acres.

1796, HENRY COLEHEP from PETER and MARY COLHEP, 80 acres on Cripple Creek.

1796, HAROLD SMYTH, infant of ALEXANDER SMYTH, 540 acres both sides of Cripple Creek from WM. and MARY NEELY of Washington County (Summers, *Annals*, p. 1327).

WYTHE COUNTY DEED BOOK 2: Wytheville, Virginia

1797, ANDREW PORTER appoints Mathias White to collect from JAMES LEPER (?) PORTER, ''legacy left me by will of Andrew Porter dec'd of Cecil County, Maryland.''

1797, MICHAEL WORLEY from WILLIAM and POLLY SANDERS, 140 acres on both sides of Cripple Creek.

1796, ANDREW BRANSTATER of Londander [Londonderry?] Twp., Dauphin County, Pennsylvania, appoints his brother-in-law Walter Kinser of Wythe County, to convey land on Cripple Creek to MICHAEL BRANSTATER of Wythe County.

1797, GEORGE DOUGLASS from JAMES DOUGLASS, 240 acres, part of 400 acres on both sides of Cripple Creek, adjacent to the patent land of James Douglas and John Newland.

1797, RANDAL RUTHERFORD from ABSALOM and MARY RUTHERFORD, 200 acres on Mine Mill Creek.

1797, ROBERT PERCIVAL from RANDOLPH and MARY RUTHERFORD, 100 acres on both sides of Cripple Creek adjoining William Gleaves.

1797, MICHAEL BRANSTATOR from WALTER KINSER, 175 acres on Cripple Creek, adjacent to Alexander Ewing.

1798, PETER TARTER from ISAAC and CATHARINE NEWHOUSE of Washington County, Virginia, 200 acres on the headwaters of Cripple Creek, adjacent to his own land.

1797, SAMUEL NUCKOLLS of Louisa County, Virginia, from GEORGE and ELEANOR EWING, two tracts on New River, adjacent to Henry Eller, Nathaniel Nuckolls, and Philip Gains, 568 acres.

1798, ROBERT PERCIVAL from MATHIAS ROSENBAUM, of Davidson County, Tennessee, 330 acres on Cripple Creek.

1798, ROBERT ELAM appointed by SUSANNAH ELAM and WALTER ELAM, to collect their legacies due them from the estate of their father, GILBERT ELAM, deceased, which is in the hands of John Godsey, Chesterfield County, Virginia, who was appointed their guardian.

1798, JOHN DUTTING [DUTTON] from PHILIP and CATHARINE DUTTING [DUTTON], 110 acres on both sides of Cripple Creek, adjoining John Newland.

1798, ADAM DUTTING [DUTTON] from PHILIP and CATHARINE DUTTING [DUTTON] 100 acres on Cripple Creek adjoining Lassleys.

1798, ROBERT PERCIVAL from MICHAEL and ANNA LEESE of Lincoln County, Kentucky, 50 acres on the north side of Cripple Creek.

1799, JOHN NEWLAND from JOHN and ELIZABETH DUTTING [DUTTON], 110 acres on both sides of Cripple Creek, adjoining Newland.

1799, JEHU STEPHENS from JACOB and MARGRET KIMMERLEN, 200 acres on Cripple Creek.

1799, THOMAS GANNAWAY from STEPHEN and ISABELLA SANDERS, 346 acres on Cripple Creek.

1793, NATHANIEL NUCKLES from CHARLES NUCKLES, 500 acres on both sides of Cripple Creek.

1799, DANIEL AND ELIZABETH CARLIN, of Patrick County, Virginia, from HUGH and EPHAMY [EUPHEMIA] MONTGOMERY of Wythe County, 500 acres on both sides of Cripple Creek adjoining Nathaniel Nuckles.

1799, JOHN KERR, JR. from heirs of JOHN KERR, THE ELDER, of Wythe County. The elder John died intestate and his estate passed to his widow, Margaret, son John, Nehemiah Bonham and wife Rachel, and Leah Kerr, daughters of John. The Bonhams and Leah conveyed the land [no acres stated, on Cripple Creek] to brother John, as their father had intended for him to have the land. John, in turn conveyed certain personal estate to the others.

1799, RANDOLPH RUTHERFORD, from JAMES and SARAH NEWELL, 35 acres adjoining Gleaves.

1799, MICHAEL WORLEY from JAMES and SARAH NEWELL, land [no acres stated]on the west side of Gleaves Branch, waters of Cripple Creek, part of 154 acres, adjacent to Randal Rutherford, William Sanders and Gleaves.

1799, SIMON FOGLESONG from JAMES and SARAH NEWELL, 110 acres on south side of Cripple Creek, adjoining Gaines.

1799, HEZEKIAH CHANEY, from JAMES CAMPBELL, 68 acres, part of a grant to Campbell 1795 [waters of Cripple Creek].

1799, GEORGE GOOSE [GOSE] from PETER and ELIZABETH DARTER, 195 acres on a south branch of Cripple Creek, the tract where Tarter now lives; also 200 acres on the headwaters of Cripple Creek, adjoining to his own land and Stroup.

1799, JAMES NEWELL from GEORGE CONWAY TAYLOR of Orange County, Virginia, 120 acres on Cripple Creek; also 75 acres on north side of New River at the mouth of Cripple Creek.

1800, FREDERICK COLLOP from ADAM COLLOP, 117 acres on Cripple Creek, adjoining the said Frederick.

1800, ALEXANDER SMYTH and JAMES NEWELL agreement. George C. Taylor sold tracts 35 and 23 to Smyth and it appears he previously had sold these tracts to Newell. Smyth quitclaims to Newell.

1799, GEORGE SPANGLER from JOHN and ELIZABETH WHITSELL, 150 acres on Cripple Creek adjoining Ewing.

1791, STEPHEN SANDERS from ROGER OATS, 510 acres on south side of Cripple Creek adjoining Sanders and Miller.

1799, ALEXANDER SMYTH from GEORGE C. TAYLOR, agent for the Loyal Company, who had grants issued for the Loyal Company, some of which may have claims to all or part, but a great length of time has passed since the surveys were done, which made it difficult to ascertain whether claims were valid, so now it seems to be expedient to sell tracts, as follows, 45 tracts containing a total of 7,345 acres, 9 tracts or 2,132 acres in Washington County, 14 tracts or 1,819 acres in Wythe County, 22 tracts or 3,394 acres in Montgomery County. Alexander is to pay $30 for each 100 acres that he can get a clear title to.

1800, ALEXANDER SMYTH from ALEXANDER WOLCOTT, of Connecticut. There were two contracts made between them and Smyth undertook to locate and have surveyed for Walcott 850,000 acres as described in the contracts [not recorded]. Following a decree from the High Court of Chancery in the Court of Appeals, the manner in the way the tracts were located and surveyed amounted to a breach of contract by Smyth. Titles may prove defective. Smyth paid considerable valuable consideration. Wolcott releases Smyth from all debts and damages by reason of the contracts of 1795, and the contracts are hereafter canceled.

The James Campbell house, drawn from an old photograph taken after the house had deteriorated. The original had a two-story log central part with one-story log wings on each end. There were two chimneys and a front porch. In later years it was covered with weather board and was known locally as the Foster, later Harris house.

By Mary B. Kegley.

CHAPTER 3: THE FAMILIES

Bebber

James Bebber, Sr., and his son, James, Jr., came to Cripple Creek about 1770, and first appear on the tithable list of Captain William Herbert in 1771. Joel (Joyel) Bebber and the others appear on the list of 1772 (Kegley, *Tithables*, pp. 12,17,31). In 1774, both James, Sr., and James, Jr., had lands surveyed on a branch of Cripple Creek, known later as Bebber's Mill Creek. The present maps identify it as Slate Spring Branch, sometimes known as Fisher Branch. The elder James selected 480 acres for which he received the grant in 1795. The Commissioners guaranteed 400 acres of the 480 acres, which was actually settled in 1770. The grant was issued on March 31, 1795. The younger James chose a small tract of 28 acres, which was settled in 1773, and which was granted to Joseph Bell and Andrew Kincannon in 1807. Daniel Baber, probably the son of the elder James as mentioned below, chose 99 acres in the same vicinity in the 1780s (Kegley and Kegley, *Early Adventurers*, Vol. 1, p. 32; Kegley, *Early Adventurers*, Vol. 2, pp. 29, 104; Montgomery County Survey (Plotts) Book A, p. 11; Plotts Book B, p. 209; Grant Book Z, p. 53).

The elder Bebber wrote his will on June 4, 1798, and it was recorded under the spelling Baber (probably identical with the English name, Beaver). The will was presented to court on July 10, 1798 (Wythe County Will Book 1, p. 110). Sons James, Joel, and Daniel, and daughters Mary Underwood, Elisabeth Draper, and Margaret Henley, were to receive one shilling sterling. The land was divided equally between two daughters, Johannah who obtained half of the plantation where James Cocks lives, and Nancy wife of Richard Hobbs, to have the other half, although Johannah was to have her preference. Executors of the will were his neighbors George Ewing and William Gleaves. Witnesses were Matthew Gleaves, James Ewing, and Absolum Gleaves.

Johannah married Martin Powell (Wythe County Marriage Book 1, p. 30), and her share of the estate was sold to Joseph Bell and Andrew Kincannon for the furnace site (Wythe County Deed Book 6, p. 34; Book 7, p. 246). Richard Hobbs and his wife Nancy sold their share of the Bebber estate (300 acres) to Leonard Straw in 1829 (Wythe County Deed Book 11, p. 19). In 1805, 93 acres was transferred to Dailey Walker (Wythe County Deed Book 4, p. 241).

Following the Bebbers, the Buckalews, Danners and Fishers took over the same location, and Hobb's division came into the hands of Elias Groseclose. The Bebber mill operated there was probably on the same site where Danner and Fishers had a mill later (Wythe County Deed Book 5, p. 109; Book 6, pp. 61, 85, 423; Book 12, pp. 607, 642; Book 17, p.60).

James Campbell

Because there are so many James Campbells in the early Southwest Virginia records, it is difficult to sort out the early ancestry of each of them. McConnell in her book elaborates on several of them, but seems to have confused the one in Wythe County with one who died in Botetourt County about 1776, and whose wife was Lettice, daughter of Isaac Taylor. James of Wythe County had a wife Mary, and appears to be the son of James and Lettice Taylor Campbell, as indicated below (McConnell, *Sänders*, pp. 258-262; Summers, *Annals*, pp. 253, 746, 943).

In the 1780s, a James, William, and Isaac Campbell appear among the Cripple

Creek settlers on James Newell's Company of Militia and may be associated with this family. William and James also appear in 1782. In 1782, William, Isaac, and James Campbell were each paid for provisions furnished when on duty in North Carolina. In 1782, the Montgomery County Tax List shows that Isaac, James, and Patrick each owned horses, cattle and land, and that James owned, in addition, seven slaves (Kegley, *Militia,* pp. 30,31; Kegley, *Tax List,* p. 5; Summers, *Annals,* p. 771).

It appears that James of Cripple Creek was recommended as a justice of the peace when Wythe County was formed in 1790 (Summers, *Annals,* p. 1357), and served in the Legislature of Virginia in 1793, representing Wythe County, and is probably the same one who served in Montgomery County with John Preston in 1783 when Montgomery County covered the part which became Wythe County (Leonard, *General Assembly,* pp. 150, 193).

In 1782, James Campbell had a preemption warrant for 1,000 acres, and selected 200 acres of the warrant to be entered on the head of a branch next to Colonel Stephens, and adjoining the land he was then living on, and joining John Francis' line and down Thorn Branch and back to Davis' to obtain the quantity. He also entered a tract of 400 acres on Cripple Creek as assignee of Isaac Campbell, assignee of David Campbell and others, based on a Commissioner's certificate. The 400 acres was approved by the Commissioners in 1782. This is probably the same tract that was surveyed in 1782 (Kegley, *Early Adventurers,* Vol. 1, pp. 40,76,113; Montgomery County Survey Book B, p. 153).

The grant books in Richmond show that James Campbell was granted 400 acres in 1784, 145 acres in 1785, and 55 acres in 1785 (Grant Book M, p. 347; Book Q, p. 481; Book R, p. 141). In Wythe County, Campbell had 400 acres surveyed, based on an entry made in 1789, and 1793, which warrant was assigned to him by Adam Dean. The land adjoined Campbell and Chaney. This tract was located on the south side of Lick Mountain and was later conveyed by the executor of Campbell's estate to Adam Rosenbaum, except 68 acres which were patented in 1795 and conveyed to Chaney by deed in 1799 (Wythe County Survey Book 1, p. 55; Wythe County Deed Book 8, p. 48).

On September 22, 1798, a slave, the property of Hezekiah Chaney, was tried for "feloniously aiding and abetting and stealing" a Negro man and two horses, the property of James Campbell, valued at $2,000. He was found not guilty (Wythe County Order Book 1796-1799, p. 244).

James Campbell lived in a two-story log house with log one-story wings. The house stood on the north side of what is now Route 651, not far from Rosenbaum Chapel. It was still standing in the 1930s but had deteriorated so badly that no one lived in it.

James Campbell wrote his will on March 30, 1799, and it was probated on October 9 the same year. He left his personal estate to his wife Mary, and his friends Francis Preston, Arthur Campbell, and Stephen Sanders, Gentlemen, were named as executors and trustees. They were to make an estimate of the estate and divide it between the children as they became of age or married. The real estate "whereon I now reside" and the land contiguous was to be sold by the executors and the proceeds to be distributed equally to the children, on the death of his wife. All other real estate was to be sold immediately. These three friends were also to be guardians of the children and Campbell appealed to them: "I most earnestly entreat my Executors that they will extend their friendship and protection to my infant family and that they will attend to the education of the sons according to their capacities and inclinations. It is to them my children must look up when I am no more, for the care and love of a father." The sons are not named. The executors were authorized at the death of his wife to emancipate his servant Caesar, ''if in their opinion he has behaved towards her dutifully and with fidelity.'' Witnesses were William Gleaves, Alexander Smyth, and Hezekiah Chaney (Wythe County Will Book 1, p. 125).

The lengthy inventory of the estate was recorded on November 27, 1799 (Wythe County Will Book 1, p. 140). There were twelve Negroes, including Caesar who was valued at £100. Others ranged in value from £15 to £75. There were 9 horses, 29 sheep, 30 hogs, 21 cows, beds and furniture and bed steads, tables, desk and bookcase, trunks, chairs, two looking glasses, a candle stand, 12 cups and saucers ''of Chaney,'' [china] 12 earthen plates, a teapot, four earthen pans, a decanter and two bottles, ''shugar'' dish, a mug, a jug, a pepper caster, a coffee pot, knives and forks, 2 sifters, a pewter dish, and two dozen spoons.

The home was well equipped for the textile industry. There was a small wheel, a large wheel, a check reel, a flax brake, swingled flax, wool and cotton. There was three pair of fire dogs [andirons], shovel and tongs, a pair of brass candlesticks, a tea board, a crib ''to sleep in,'' barrels, pots, kettle, ovens, a spider, pails, a cooler, a cheese press, a churn, two butter pots, three crocks, a barrel, wash tubs, and three sheep skins, a hog skin, three raw skins, a calf skin, a horse skin, 10 pieces of ''house paper,'' a ''spice morter,'' and a variety of tools including axes, mattocks, pitch forks, shovels, rakes, and cradles. The farm produced corn, oats, rye, and buckwheat, and had seven geese and ganders, and seven ducks and drakes, hay, a barrel of tar, and sundry books and pamphlets. The total value of the estate was £1,173.10.3. Additional inventory and the record of the sale were recorded on February 11, 1800 (Wythe County Will Book 1, pp. 142, 144, 145).

The children of James Campbell were recorded by McConnell as Elizabeth who married George Spotts; Nancy who married George Light; Polly who married William C. Morrison; James A. Campbell; John Campbell; Reuben Campbell; William S. Campbell; and Isabella who married Stephen Sanders of Cripple Creek. However, it appears from the marriage record of Isabella that she was the daughter of James and Lettice Campbell (not Mary of Cripple Creek) when she and Stephen Sanders applied for the marriage bond. They were married by the Reverend Charles Cummings on February 7, 1782. As a lawsuit filed after Mary's death shows, James was a brother-in-law of Stephen Sanders. Therefore Isabella was his sister (McConnell, *Sänders*, p. 261; Kegley, *Early Adventurers, Vol. 2*, pp. 145, 177; Summers, *Annals*, p. 758; *Caesar vs. Sanders et als, executors of James Campbell, deceased*, Box 5, 1815, Wythe County Circuit Court Clerk's Office, Basement; for details *see* below).

In 1816, a suit was brought against the executors and heirs of James Campbell by John Estill of Augusta County. Mary, Campbell's wife, was named in the suit, but was by then deceased. The heirs were named in the case as George Spotts and Elizabeth, George C. Light and Nancy, William C. Morrison and Polly, James A., John, Reuben, and William S. Campbell. Sanders and his wife Isabella were not named as heirs, but Stephen Sanders was the primary witness in the suit, and was one of Campbell's executors. The subject of the case was a debt contracted in 1781 and a judgment obtained in 1786. The court ordered that the debt should be paid, even though it was many years old, because the will revived the statute of limitations (*Estill vs. Campbell heirs*, Superior Court Chancery Book 6, p. 393).

In 1818, Stephen Sanders, executor of the will of James Campbell, deceased, conveyed to George Rosenbaum 276 acres, part of a tract divided between Rosenbaum and George Spotts. The Counselmans owned this land in 1873 and conveyed it to A. B. Harris (Wythe County Deed Book 7, p. 271; Book 25, p. 74).

In 1820, Stephen Sanders as executor for James Campbell conveyed 55 acres to George Rosenbaum. This tract was patented in 1785, and conveyed by Rosenbaum's heirs in 1854 to James Patton. In 1828, George Rosenbaum, Jr., obtained 7 acres, part of the land sold to George Spotts. Also in 1828, Stephen Sanders, the executor for Campbell, conveyed 313 acres to David Whitman. This tract was part of a larger tract divided between George Spotts and George Rosenbaum, Sr., and cornering on Adam Rosenbaum's land. Spotts gave up his claim and asked the executor to make the deed to Whitman (Wythe County Deed Book 8, p. 47; Book 10, pp. 671, 674; Book 20, p. 46).

The Whitman log house on Thorn Branch a tributary of Cripple Creek, now gone.
Courtesy of the F. B. Kegley Collection.

Caesar, the Negro mentioned in Campbell's will, did not obtain his freedom easily. He brought suit against the executors of James Campbell in 1815 in Wythe County Superior Court of Chancery, and when this failed to bring the desired results, he filed a petition in the General Assembly on December 11 the same year. Several of Campbell's neighbors testified on his behalf. Peter Spangler noted that before James Campbell went on a journey on which he died, they had spoken about the operation of his farm and Campbell was quoted as saying in regard to Caesar, "he was as good a farmer as he could get and as trusty a hand as he could get and as trusty a hand as he could put to it," and promised him his freedom. Thomas Gannaway reported that Campbell thought of Caesar as a very fine servant and promised to free him. William Henley who had lived in the neighborhood "upwards of 20 years," always heard that Caesar was a good and faithful slave. Christopher Spraker had heard similar comments. Randolph Rutherford added that Caesar had saved the life of his master, but gave no details. Jacob Gose reported that he was "one of the best and obedient slaves he ever saw." Andrew Porter made similar comments, and added that since Mr. Campbell's death the farm was not so well managed, but blamed that on the fact that they had no horses that were fit to work (Wythe County Legislative Petition, December 11, 1815, Virginia State Library, Archives).

It was revealed that Caesar had "the good fortune at the peril of his own life to save that of his said master" and that in return Campbell authorized Caesar's emancipation in his will, following Mrs. Campbell's death. However, Mrs. Campbell sold Caesar to one of the executors before she died in 1814, thus causing Caesar to file the suit in the High Court of Chancery where he obtained his freedom, but there was one hindrance to Caesar's remaining in his native Virginia. The Legislature passed a law in 1805, which provided that slaves emancipated after that time were required to leave the state. Because Caesar claimed his freedom under the 1799 will of James Campbell, he asked permission to remain near his wife and children who were slaves and the property of the children of James Campbell. He promised that he would "undertake nothing against the Republic" and his only wish was that his presence might be an example to his children proving that "duty and fidelity bring their reward even to a slave." His petition carries the names of some of the most prominent citizens of Wythe County at the time. Among them were ministers, lawyers, merchants, innkeepers, and public officials. The names were John Stanger, Alexander Smyth, George Oury, William Hay, James Calfee, John Howard, Thomas Warner, John L. Lindenberger, Adam Saftly, Taurus Marshall, Granville Henderson, Jacob T. Fishback, Abraham Ryno, Joseph Sexton, John P. Mathews, Christopher Oury, Saml. Crockett, Leonard Straw, Jr., John A. Sanders, Robert McGavock, R. Sayers, D. Sheffey. The petition was granted. As required by law Caesar, a free Negro, had to be registered. At that time he was described as 60 years of age, and 5 feet 9 1/2 inches in height, and of black complexion (Wythe County Legislative Petition, December 11, 1815, Virginia State Library, Archives; Wythe County Order Book 1815-1820, p. 22).

Much of the information filed in Richmond was also detailed in a suit decided in 1815 in Wythe County. Additional information from the suit shows that Caesar from the time he was six years of age was raised by James Campbell, deceased, and was later in possession of James Campbell, Jr., the Cripple Creek resident, who promised him his freedom for saving his life "when in the act of drowning and many other signal services." He became manager of the farm after the death of James Campbell, and became one of the best farmers in the county. However, there appeared to be friction between the widow Mary and Caesar about the operation of the farm. She knew nothing about the management but frequently would "derange the course" Caesar wished to pursue. Because of minor difficulties, and testimony that Mary was afraid of Caesar, he was sold to Stephen Sanders, one of the executors. At Mary's death, the executors refused to emancipate him. Sanders stated that because he was in the family (having married a sister to James Campbell) he purchased Caesar, and did not believe he was entitled to his freedom because he did not behave towards his mistress "dutifully and with fidelity."

Letitia Crockett (not further identified) testified she frequently heard Mary say Caesar was a "very troublesome fellow," because he would interfere with the correction of the young slaves, and then Mary would try to correct him, to which Caesar replied, "If you hit me make a sure blow." She also recalled that Mrs. Campbell sent for her father to come over and correct Caesar as she could do nothing with him. It is not clear from the statement if it was Mary's or Letitia's father who was called upon to discipline Caesar. Daughter Elizabeth Spotts often heard her mother complain, but Caesar would ask the pardon of his mistress because he gave her unbecoming language about trifles. Mrs. Campbell would then forgive him.

George Light and his wife Nancy (Campbell) had moved to Ohio and were believed to be living there in 1814. Son Reuben was only eleven years old when Caesar was sold to Sanders. John T. Campbell, another son, testified that Caesar had done the best he could about the farm. The biggest problem mentioned in numerous depositions was that too many of the farm utensils and farm animals had been sold at the sale, leaving little to work with on the farm.

William Gleaves who was acquainted with Campbell and Caesar about 30 years and lived within four or five miles of Campbell for twenty-seven years, added another reason that Campbell wanted Caesar to have his freedom. He was grateful for his conduct "with regard to a certain man by the name of Sutherlin, who had made a plot with Caesar to take him off, which plot Caesar disclosed to his master." Peter Spangler a neighbor of 28 years, William Henley and Randolph Rutherford neighbors for 20 years, and Thomas Gannaway who knew them for about 22 years, testified favorably for Caesar.

Christopher Spraker, who lived in the neighborhood thirty-three years, testified that Caesar worked for him and cleared two acres of land to discharge a debt of his mistress Mary Campbell for smith work and some calves. Caesar also worked for Jacob Gose, a neighbor of 30 years, and was highly regarded by Gose, who claimed that Caesar was one of the best and most obedient slaves. The only complaint he had heard of was that Caesar had stolen trifles and would "run after women *to* much." Because they had no horses on the Campbell farm, Caesar would borrow them from Gose (*Caesar vs. Sanders, et. als. execs. of James Campbell, deceased*, Box 5, 1815, Wythe County Circuit Court Clerk's Office, Basement).

Marriage records of Wythe County show that George Spotts and Bezy C. Campbell were married on February 1, 1804, and the bond was dated December 5, 1803, and that Polly T. Campbell married William C. Morrison sometime about 1816 (Wythe County Marriage Book 1, pp. 29,50). William S. Campbell was living in Washington County, Virginia, in 1825 when George Spotts conveyed to Campbell and Josiah N. Beatie 325 acres on Cripple Creek, known as the Thorn Spring tract (Wythe County Deed Book 10, p. 76).

In Montgomery County a William Campbell married Jini (Jene) Dean, daughter of Adam Dean, and Stephen Sanders was surety on the bond dated March 5, 1782. The connection to the family of James is unknown (Kegley, *Early Adventurers*, Vol. 2, p. 177).

Catron

Christopher (Stophel, Stuffle) Catron (also Kettering, Katron, Catren, Katren, Kettenring, etc.) who settled on Cripple Creek, was born in 1769 and was the son of Christopher, Sr., who was born in Germany and came to America on the Ship "Chance" settling first in Lancaster County, Pennsylvania. The elder Christopher and his wife Susannah Gose settled on Tates Run, in Wythe County. He died sometime prior to July 4, 1795, when his estate was appraised under the name of Stophel Katren. The accounts were presented by Adam and Christopher Catren the administrators of the estate, on May 9, 1797. The younger Christopher married Susanna Houck on August 17, 1793. His oldest brother Francis married Barbara Houck, and his brother Peter married Elizabeth Houck (1773 in North Carolina-1854) on August 17, 1793. Two others of his siblings married Goses: Barbara Catron married Stephen Gose, and Jacob Catron married Elizabeth Gose. His sister Catherine (Catharina Elizabeth) married Henry Eller (Catron, *Kettenring*, 2nd ed., pp. 251,399, 417; Catron, *Kettenring*, 1st ed. pp. 94-117 gives information on the family, *see* especially pp. 94, 97; Wythe County Marriage Book 1, p. 6 spells his name Stophield Catherien).

Christopher, Jr., and Susannah (sometimes Susan) had six children: John, Stephen, George, Felix, Elizabeth (Betsy), all mentioned below, and a son William (b. 1796), baptized at the St. Paul Lutheran Church, who died in 1802. Christopher, Jr., is said to have died on February 2, 1804, after being hit by a falling tree. However, the deed book gives his date of death as 1802. (Wythe County Deed Book 8, p. 409; Catron, *Kettenring*, 2nd ed., pp. 251, 399, 417; Kegley, *St. Paul...*, p. 17).

On September 9, 1806, Philip Gaines, was appointed guardian for George, John, Stephen, Felix and Betsy Catron, the "orphans" of Stophel Catron deceased (Wythe County Order Book, September 9, 1806, unnumbered page).

In 1815, the farm on Cripple Creek was listed by the tax assessor under the name Christopher Kattring's heirs. The tract had 1,000 acres, with one dwelling house and two out houses, valued at $1,600 (Kegley, *Tax Assessment*, pp. 131-132).

In 1815, the Christopher Kattring (Catron) place was assessed at $1,600. The farm on Cripple Creek had 1,000 acres with a dwelling house and two out houses.

Tracing from the original by Mary B. Kegley.

The Catron land on Cripple Creek was first identified as a grant to Robert Donald in 1793. Christopher had a claim to a tract of 1,100 (said to be 1,000) acres, known as the Donald tract, but also described as "Newell's old place about three miles above the lead mines and below Robert Sanders Ironworks, adding the land on which the ironworks are built." According to a lawsuit filed in 1850, Robert Crockett agent for Andrew Donald, was to make the title, but before it was done both Donald and Kettering had died. A lawsuit was brought against the heirs of Donald, and the title to the land was awarded to the widow Catron and heirs prior to 1819. The children (John, Stephen, Betsy (Elizabeth), George and Felix) were each to have one-fifth interest in the tract subject to their mother's dower. In 1820, the children of Christopher made an agreement regarding partition of the land. George conveyed his interest to Robert English, who had married Elizabeth Catron. Felix also conveyed his interest to English, who then made a contract with Henry L. Sheffey to convey land on the north side of the creek, which was in possession of Burgess Williams. English conveyed his life estate to his wife Betsy, and all interest to Thomas J. Boyd in trust for debts, and part of the original tract was sold at auction to David F. Kent. Susannah, the widow, brought suit against Kent, asking for assignment of her dower interest in the land English sold and in the share Elizabeth (called Betsy in the suit) owned. Betsy died, leaving Julia Ann English, and Darthula English, who married David William Miller and left children David K. and Elizabeth C. Miller, children of William Miller for whom William M. Chatwell was guardian. Andrew Fulton was guardian for James R., Sarah, Gordon, and David Kent, heirs of D. F. Kent. William Miller was administrator of the estate of David K. Miller, deceased, of Wise County, November 18, 1865, and William

Miller was also the administrator of the estate of Elizabeth Miller, deceased. Because his children died before he did, the court awarded William Miller their share of the property, which was 94 1/2 acres. Juliana also was assigned 94 1/2 acres. A map and description of the property can be found with the suit papers. The suit was filed before 1850, but not decided until after the Civil War (*Chatwell, guardian etc. vs. D. F. Kent heirs*, Box 111, 1861-1869, Wythe County Circuit Court Clerk's Office, Basement; Wythe County Deed Book 8, pp. 200, 249, 274, 409; Book 9, p. 178; Book 13, p. 494; Wythe County Marriage Book 1, pp. 68, 165).

Of the Catron children Stephen (1795-1835) was baptized at Zion Lutheran Church under the name Stephanus. He married Polly Porter, the daughter of Robert Porter, in 1818. They had no children. Stephen Catron wrote his will on June 14, 1835, and it was probated on November 11 the same year. (Wythe County Will Book 4, p. 237). To his wife Polly he devised all the land south of the creek, and slaves Henry, Patience, and Roof [Rufus], and one-half of the stock and farming utensils for life. At her death all was to go to the heirs (when they became of age) of brother John Catron. Negro Jeff, and the increase of Patience, were to be under the care of Elizabeth Catron [John's wife], until the children were of age. Land on the north of the creek was to go to the heirs of brother John. Negro girl Julian, daughter of Patience, was bequeathed to Malinda Porter daughter of Robert Porter. The remainder of the estate was to be sold and the money divided between wife Polly, and Susanna eldest daughter of John. Andrew Porter and Abram Painter were in charge of the estate (Catron, *Kettenring*, 2nd ed., p. 436; Kegley, *Zion*, p. 15; Wythe County Marriage Book 1, p. 58).

The appraisal of the estate of Stephen Catron was done by Lee Nuckolls, Edmund Lockett, and John Jackson, Jr., on November 20, 1835. It included 24 sheep, barrels of corn, wheat, rye, oats, cattle, a Negro boy Jeff, Negro boy Henry, Negro woman Patience, Negro boy Rufus, a wheat fan, mares, colts, hogs, a plough and gears, bureau, ten chairs, a folding leaf table, cupboard, a clock, a looking glass, candle stand and two candlesticks, three beds and furniture, small tables, two chests, four bed spreads, cupboard and furniture, a set of tablespoons, a loom, scythes, a cradle, and a wagon. The appraisal was recorded on August 8, 1836. The accounts of the estate were filed on February 8, 1847 (Wythe County Will Book 4, p. 348; Will Book 6, p. 469).

In 1820, George Catron (1798-1827) known as George H., son of Christopher, Jr., sold his interest to his brother-in-law Robert English, husband of his sister Elizabeth Kettering. The land of Christopher was described in this deed as being a total of 1,000 acres, except 75 acres claimed by David Peirce, and known as ''Newell's old place about three miles above the lead mines, and below Robert Sanders, now Peirce's Ironworks'' which adjoined where Christopher lived at the time of his death, and where the widow and children were then living. It appears from the records that the land was later conveyed to Henry L. Sheffey (Wythe County Deed Book 8, pp. 249, 409; Catron, *Kettenring*, 2nd ed., p. 422).

In 1824, John Catron and his wife Elizabeth (Bralley) Catron conveyed 233 acres of the Christopher Catron land on Cripple Creek to Burgess Williams, Guilford Wall, and Burrell Wall, equally. Part of this land was later conveyed to Robert D. Flournoy, part to Daniel Sheffey, and part to Susannah Catron (Wythe County Deed Book 12, p 238; Book 13, pp. 610, 612; Book 19, p. 133). John was born 1793, and baptized at Zion Lutheran Church. He married August 31, 1815, and died December 12, 1832. On December 28, 1832, the appraisal of his estate was taken by Adams Sanders, John Jackson, and Andrew Kincannon. Among the items listed were cows, heifers, calves, one yoke steers, cherry plank, a beef hide, plows, iron, 200 bushels of ''cole,'' a barrel,

7 still tubs, 45 hogs, 1/2 ton of plaster, wagon and gears, sheep, an apple mill and trough, 4 shovel ploughs, one bed and furniture, a clock, a candle stand and two sticks, one musical snuff box, bellows, a looking glass, fire dogs, 11 chairs, salt, a Negro girl, a "lott" of castings, tin ware, a pot and "kittel," two ovens, a stone jug, a cotton wheel, a keg of vinegar, cupboard, tables, a straw bed and furniture, a chest, bed steads, 5 dozen crocks, a walnut table, bed clothes and table cloths, a cutting box, 4 axes, a saddle, a grindstone, wash bowl, a trumpet, 12 geese, 20 [pounds?] blister steel, shot gun, hogs and pigs, a new plow, and a shelling machine (Wythe County Will Book 4, p. 98; Catron, *Kettenring*, 2nd ed., p. 426).

Major James T. Gleaves was guardian for the orphans of John Catron, named as Henry E., Catherine, Alfred, and George Catron. He obtained the rent for the land and paid Henry E., Catherine, and Alfred when they became of age. At the time of his first accounting, George was still under age and had been going to school to Miss E. Wilcox and Robert Raper. The accounts were prepared in 1850, and recorded August 12, 1850. The accounting for George A. Catron was also filed at the court by Major Gleaves, showing the balance on hand had been paid to George. This George Catron was known as George A., and he married Elizabeth Ann Rich, the daughter of Fleming Rich on November 23, 1852. George A. was an apprentice cabinetmaker and later set up his own shop in Newbern. The account was recorded on October 11, 1852. (Wythe County Will Book 7, pp. 226, 606; Rich Family papers; Wythe County Marriage Book 1, p. 202).

Catron, in his books, gives the names of the children of John Catron as Susan A. (1820), who married Robert D. Flournoy; Henry Eller (1822), who married Julia Ann English; Catherine Elizabeth (1824), who married William Miller after Darthula his first wife died; Alfred G. (1826) married Evaline P. Ewing, and George Alexander (1831) married Elizabeth Ann Rich (Catron, *Kettenring*, 1st ed., pp. 115-116; Catron, *Kettenring*, 2nd ed., p. 426).

George A. Catron conveyed all of his interest in part of the land (233 acres) and his interest in four slaves left to him by Stephen Catron, deceased, to Polly Catron in 1852. Polly sold the land within a month to James T. Early. In 1853, George A. Catron and his wife Nancy were living in Pulaski County and conveyed all their interest in certain land on Cripple Creek, adjoining James Fisher and Robert D. Flournoy to Flournoy. George moved to Tennessee and died at Chattanooga in 1882 (Wythe County Deed Book 19, pp. 291, 292; 414; Catron, *Kettenring*, 1st ed. p. 116).

Felix A. Catron (born 1801) son of Christopher, Jr., never married. On March 16, 1822, Felix Ketring conveyed 233 acres to Robert English, his brother-in-law, being his one-fifth interest in the land of his father. The title papers called for 1,000 acres, and by agreement of November 29, 1820, Felix agreed to take his one-fifth, adjoining Stephen's division and the lands of Henry L. Sheffey on the south, and was to include the dwelling, barn, and spring, and adjoined George Catron's 80 acres. This sale was to be free from any claims of his mother Susannah (Wythe County Deed Book 9, p. 178).

Felix wrote his will on September 30, 1833, when he was living in Davidson County, Tennessee. All of his property in Virginia was devised to his mother S. [Susannah, also Susan] Catron of Wythe County. He noted that he was going "to the iron works in Laurence County, Tennessee, in a few days, to live," and the will was to be deposited with Judge John Catron of Tennessee, who was to be the sole executor, and was to have his Tennessee property. Felix died December 25, 1841 in Wythe County, which was the place of his residence at the time of death. The will was probated in Davidson County in January 1843, and a copy presented to the Wythe

County Court on March 13, 1844. John Catron, executor, requested that an administrator be appointed in Virginia, and the court chose Andrew S. Fulton (Wythe County Will Book 6, p. 171).

Judge John Catron (1781-1865), was the son of Peter and Elizabeth Houck Kettenring, and was a cousin to Felix. He moved to Kentucky before settling in Tennessee. He served under Andrew Jackson in the War of 1812, and in 1815 was admitted to the Tennessee bar. He became Chief Justice of the Supreme Court of Tennessee. Peter was son of Christopher Kettenring, Sr. ,as mentioned above (Kegley, *Bicentennial History*, p. 255; *American Encyclopedia*; Catron, *Kettenring*, 2nd ed., pp. 398, 336).

Christopher's daughter Elizabeth was born in 1803. On March 14, 1820, she chose her brother John as her guardian, probably about the time she married Robert English. The exact date of the marriage is not stated in the records, but it was in 1820. It is not clear to this author if English is the same man who applied for a Revolutionary War pension on March 11, 1839. If so, he was 86 years old on March 17, 1839, and considerably older than his wife. In the pension application he stated that he was a Minute Man of a Rifle Company in Cumberland County, Pennsylvania, in 1775. He served in the neighborhood of Boston and was marching to New York acting as one of the guards of the baggage waggons. They were captured by the British and Tories and on the night following, English made his escape after serving about 17 months. After returning to his home in Pennsylvania, he moved to Frederick County, Maryland, where he enlisted in the Maryland line under Capt. Henry Harman. He served in New York State, where he was taken prisoner at the time of the surrender of Fort Washington. He escaped, after serving in the war and being a prisoner for a total of one year and eleven months. He then moved from Maryland to Botetourt County, Virginia, and in 1781 he substituted in the militia and marched to North Carolina where he was in the Battle of Guilford, and served six weeks. He again served six weeks in a company called "the flying camp," under Captain Ayre Buckner (or Buckler) of Pittsylvania. Their service involved being a guard against "the depradations of the British and Tory scouting parties." He was again in the service and was present at the surrender of Cornwallis. After the surrender, he moved to the Fort Chiswell area and settled. He also mentioned that he had volunteered to Illinois, went down the Tennessee River, burnt the towns and destroyed the property of the Chuccamugga Indians, and he then proceeded to Kaskaskia. His officers were Colonel John Montgomery and Captain Thomas Quirk. This time his service was about 8 months. His total service was claimed to be four years and four months. The land office could find no record of his service and returned his declaration (Pension R3354, National Archives; Wythe County Order Book 1815-1820, p. 429).

In 1840, English is listed in the census of Wythe County. He left no will, and no settlement of his estate was found in Wythe County. Some have suggested he moved away, but he is mentioned again in the records of 1842, when Daniel B. Sanders was ordered to pay over to William Miller, Jr., or his order, the amount of money in his hands which was levied to be applied to support Robert English, Sr., and was payable out of the levy of 1841 (Wythe County Order Book 1840-1842, August 11, 1842). He probably died without an estate sometime before 1850, as he is not mentioned in that census.

Robert English and his wife Elizabeth had two daughters: Darthula (1821-1845) and Julia Ann (born September 15, 1823-died April 4, 1906). Julia Ann married Henry Eller Catron (born March 25, 1822, died October 12, 1906) in 1847. In 1852, Henry E. Catron and his wife Julia Ann English conveyed his wife's interest in real estate, as heirs of Elizabeth English, deceased, to James N. Kincannon. No description was given, and the date of the death of Elizabeth is not recorded. Darthula daughter of Robert English married William Miller in 1840 and had two children, David Miller and Elizabeth Catron Miller (Wythe County Deed Book 19, p. 204; Catron, *Kettenring*, 2nd ed., pp. 417, 252, 253; cemetery records of Olive Branch Methodist Church Cemetery).

Susan (Susannah) Catron, widow of Christopher, Jr., filed a lawsuit in 1851 against Robert D. Flournoy. In March 1849, she made a deed to Flournoy and his wife Susan A. for land on the north side of Cripple Creek where she then resided. Also included were all the household utensils, stock, and provisions. The reason for the deed was that she was "far advanced in years, in feeble health, and living alone." Susan A. Flournoy was her granddaughter, and the elder Susan was to live with her and be cared for. After the deed was made, Susan A. and Robert broke up housekeeping and moved to Roanoke County. They agreed to re-convey the property, but they had refused to deliver the deed. The dower interest was conveyed by them to William Miller and Henry E. Catron in December 1849. Susan wanted the contract set aside or the land reconveyed to her. The case was decided in her favor in 1854. The place she claimed was the Guilford Wall place (*Susan Catron vs. Robert D. Flournoy*, Box 102, 1853-1854, Wythe County Circuit Court Clerk's Office, Basement; Wythe County Deed Book 18, p. 7).

At the time the Flournoys answered the Bill of Complaint, Robert was living in Washington County, Virginia. He at first settled in Chesterfield County, and was doing well. He thought it was impracticable to live in the same house with Susan, but the reasons are not given. Grandson, Henry Catron, also answered the Bill of Complaint. He stated that at the time of conveyance there was no objection to the 233 acres being sold. The land was sold to David F. Kent by Robert English who married Christopher's daughter. When English and his wife died, Henry Catron and William Miller claimed the title to the land.

Granddaughter Susan A. Flournoy testified that her husband was in business in Chesterfield County, and that the plantation in Wythe County was in poor condition, and that Dr. D. B. Sanders had agreed to tend to her grandmother without charge. William Miller, in his deposition, stated that Susan was about 78 years old and was sometimes confined to bed. She was living with Dr. D. B. Sanders in 1852. She had two Negro women and a Negro man hired out for her benefit.

Elizabeth Lockett, a neighbor, also testified stating that Susan was not too friendly with her other grandchildren, except Catherine Miller. She was hard to please, but always said Fluornoy was kind to her. Elizabeth lived with Susan for a week or so after the Flournoys left, but then Susan moved to Dr. Sanders.

Robert Flournoy's brother testified that he lived on Cripple Creek with his own family, on the Burwell Wall place near Susan, who was 70-80 years old. Robert was doing business for Mr. Lockett before he first went to Chesterfield, and Robert was traveling a lot in connection with his business (*Catron vs. Flournoy*).

Susan (Susannah) Kettring (Catron), widow of Christopher Catron, Jr., wrote her will on January 20, 1850, and it was probated on December 11, 1854. To her grandson George H. Ketring, she left her interest in Negro man Squire. In consideration of his many services, professional and otherwise, and agreeing to comfortably support and maintain her for the rest of her life, Susan devised to "my friend" Dr. Daniel B. Sanders, all the residue of my property, and he was to act as executor (Wythe County Will Book 8, p. 351). At the time of her death the lawsuit was still pending, and although the court ordered Flournoy to convey the property to her by a certain date, he did not do so. The court then appointed Alexander Stuart, Commissioner to make the deed. The deed was made out to Daniel B. Sanders, to whom she devised the land. It was located on the north side of Cripple Creek, and it was where Susan formerly lived (Wythe County Deed Book 20, p. 303). It was Dr. Sanders who ordered the coffin from the Fleming Rich (*see* illustration, where he states that Susan died on November 17, 1854).

Dr. D. B. Sanders ordered the coffin from Fleming Rich for Susan Catron who died on November 17, 1854. The measurements were 5 feet 8 inches long and 22 inches across the breast.

Tracing from original by Mary B. Kegley.

It appears from the records that John P.M. Simmerman obtained 500 acres known as the English place, and also purchased the Flournoy acreage (Wythe County Deed Book 21, pp. 29, 44; Book 22, pp. 305, 315).

Chatwell

The first Chatwell (also Chadwell) appears in Wythe County in the 1810 census. Isiah (Isaiah) Chatwell and his wife had five children under sixteen years at that time. His first purchase of land was in 1812, when he bought 287 acres on Sugar Run (a small branch of Cripple Creek, north of Speedwell) from Hezekiah Chaney, Jr., the same tract the elder Chaney had sold his son in 1810. In 1827, Chatwell purchased 130 acres on Sugar Run from Alexander Smyth. These were the two tracts owned at the time of his death (Wythe County Deed Book 5, pp. 289, 496; Book 10, p. 482).

Some time prior to August 1813, Isiah [Isaiah] Chatwell had established a powder mill, probably for the war effort of 1812. A special court was called on September 15, 1813, for the examination of John Deckart, who was charged with stealing five or six pounds of powder valued at 4 shillings, 6 pence per pound, on the night of August 16 from the powder mill of Isaiah Chatwell. The case was heard and the prisoner discharged (Wythe County Order Book 1812-1815, p. 77).

On December 13, 1825, Isaiah Chatwell was a witness for Robert Mills of Wythe County, who was the son of Samuel Mills of Washington County, Maryland. Chatwell stated that he knew both of them in that place. In addition, he knew that there was another son Charles Porter Mills, who had died at Seneca Creek, Maryland, leaving "neither wife nor child." There were also some other children in the same family. It is possible that Chatwell came from Maryland to Wythe County, but this has not been investigated (Wythe County Order Book 1822-1826, pp. 567-568).

In 1839, Henry and Lydia Chatwell sold 140 acres, purchased from Jacob Gose, to Isaiah Chatwell, Sr. Following his father's death, the heirs conveyed the title back to Henry Chatwell for this tract, where he was then living (Wythe County Deed Book 14, p. 176; Book 17, p. 709).

Isaiah Chatwell wrote his will May 12, 1848, and it was probated in October the same year (Wythe County Will Book 7, p. 1). To his son Isaiah, Jr., he left 100 acres on the north side of the tract "where I live," and 50 acres on the east end of the tract he bought from Alexander Smyth, and one-eighth of the residue of the estate. The other seven children were also to receive one-eighth of the residue and were named as follows: Strother, W. M., John, Henry, Eliza (Murray), Margaret (Kegley), and Sophia (Burns). If wife Margaret outlived Isaiah, the land was to be rented and the proceeds divided among the children. After her death the place was to be sold and the money divided. Sons Isaiah and W. M. Chatwell were to act as executors.

Among the items listed in the inventory of the estate were four bags of powder (supposed to be 100 pounds), one powder box and chest, one shot gun, one rifle and shot bag, 13 bee stands, a windmill, and books (Wythe County Will Book 7, p. 586).

In 1848, Strother Chatwell and his wife Catherine, William Chatwell and his wife Jane, John Murray and his wife Eliza, Daniel Kegley and his wife Margaret, Henry Chatwell and his wife Lydia, and Timothy Burns and his wife Sophia sold their shares to the estate to Isaiah Chatwell, Jr. This transaction accounted for seven-eighths of the shares of 287 acres where Isaiah lived at his death, and the 130 acres he bought of Smyth. John Chatwell, while living in Pike County, Kentucky, in 1849, owned the other one-eighth, and transferred his interest to Isaiah, Chatwell, Jr. He also deeded his interest in Henry's tract (Wythe County Deed Book 17, pp. 707, 784, 785).

The marriages of Wythe County show that Josiah (original is clearly Isaiah) Chatwell married Peggy Davis on December 22, 1822; Strother Chatwell married Katherine Gose, daughter of Jacob, on October 24, 1833; Henry Chatwell married Lydia Hines on November 5, 1833; William M. Chatwell's marriage bond with Robert Holliday was dated April 19, 1839 for the marriage with Jane, widow of Henry Eller. Daniel Kegley's bond with Isaac Chatwell, Sr., was dated May 29, 1844 for marriage with Margaret Chatwell. They were married on May 30. (Wythe County Marriage Book 1, pp. 110, 73,109, 142,155; Marriage Bond Book p. 157).

In the 1850 census William M., Strother, Isiah, and Henry are listed with their families. At this date Margaret, the widow of Isaiah, was living with her son Isiah, Jr., and was 70 years old. She is buried at Zion Lutheran Church, but there are no dates on the stone (Wythe County Federal Census; cemetery record).

In 1858, Isiah Chatwell, Jr., sold 287 acres the homeplace, to Robert W. Davidson of Tazewell County (Wythe County Deed Book 21, p. 278) This may have been about the time Margaret Chatwell died. Davidson gave part of the land in his will (written in

February 1868, probated June 15, 1868) to his son, E.G. Davidson, being on the east side of a partition line which mentions Spraker's Mill, and the road "above the old powder mill." After his wife Polly died, the remainder was to be divided between son, Samuel P. and daughter Jane wife of William Huffard (Wythe County Will Book 11, p. 258). The descendants of the Davidsons still live at the same location, south of Route 651 on the east side of Route 21 South.

William Chatwell was owner and operator of a forge on Cripple Creek. It was suggested that the forge was at first operated by Henry Eller prior to 1836 (or 1840). Eller's widow married William Chatwell. Water from Cripple Creek provided the power to operate the 800 pound hammer. There was one forge which made blister steel, a process involving placing the forged iron in a charcoal fire and allowing it to stand for several days. The iron absorbed the carbon and was converted into a mild steel. This steel was used for axes, made in a nearby blacksmith shop (Presgraves, ed., *Wythe County Chapters*, pp. 107, 108, 189).

This original document shows that Rich, a Wytheville cabinetmaker, purchased iron from Chatwell and Highley, who operated the Cripple Creek Forge. Tracing from original by Mary B. Kegley.

In the 1840s, William M. Chatwell was in partnership with Robert B. Highley in the iron manufacturing business. From a lawsuit found in the courthouse, it also appears that they purchased bar iron from Nuckolls and Jennings (*Nuckolls & Jennings vs. Chatwell & Highley*, Box 78, 1848, Wythe County Circuit Court Clerk's Office, Basement).

William owned several tracts of land in the neighborhood, and in 1855 placed a deed of trust on the property with Robert Sayers as trustee. The debts owed to Robert Gibboney and Thomas W. Carter were paid in full. The forge was a tract of 150 acres where Robert Holiday was then living. The other tract was mountain land entered by Chatwell, containing 1,100 acres. A year later Chatwell and his wife Jane conveyed the Eller land, where Chatwell was then living, the forge of 150 acres, and rights to entry and survey of 600 acres in two tracts to John P.M. Simmerman. Tracts supposed to contain 500 acres adjoining Simmerman were transferred to Isaac Painter about the same time (Wythe County Deed Book 20, pp. 294,545,774).

Carr (Kerr)

Doak's tithable list of 1772 identifies Walter Carr and his sons John and William, and a George Carr as being residents of the New River area. John took up land on Cripple Creek in 1775, being a tract of 255 acres which was patented in 1785. John's second tract was 384 acres adjoining James Wyleys [Willys] which was patented in 1795. Walter chose 176 acres on the north side of the creek, which was surveyed on March 16, 1775 under the Loyal Company (Kegley, *Tithables*, p. 14; Grant Book 0, p. 472; Grant Book 33, p. 509; Montgomery County Survey Book A, pp. 188, 192; Kegley and Kegley, *Early Adventurers*, Vol. 1, p. 36).

Walter served on a jury in several cases in May 1774, and William Henley was to pay him for appearing as a witness in the case of Alexander McGee. In 1780, a Walter Carr entered land in Lincoln County, Kentucky, in Licking Creek, but it is not known if this is the New River settler (Cook and Cook, *Fincastle and Kentucky Counties*, pp. 150,157,180, 383, 397,398,399, 417,419,420,425).

In 1796, John Kerr transferred several tracts, parts of the place where he was then living. Mathias White (Weiss) received 50 acres, William Bonham 150 acres, and William Neely 56 acres (Wythe County Deed Book 1, pp. 378,383,384).

On August 13, 1799, the Wythe County Court granted Margaret Kerr and John Kerr, Jr., the administration of the estate of John Kerr, Sr. Following the death of John Kerr, Sr., the heirs agreed that it was his intention that John Kerr, Jr., should have the land, and deeds were made to release their interest in the property. These heirs were Margaret, the widow of John Kerr, Sr., Rachel Kerr, wife of Nehemiah Bonham (married 1791), and Leah Kerr. The mother agreed to take as her dower a certain meadow and a small piece of new ground contiguous, which had been lately cleared for cordwood, being part of the home plantation, and 100 acres on the south side of Cripple Creek which had been located for Andrew Porter and John Kerr, Sr. (Wythe County Order Book 1799-1801, p. 34, August 13, 1799; Wythe County Deed Book 2, p. 433; Book 3, p. 151; Wythe County Marriage Book 1, p. 2).

Sometime prior to 1802, Walter Kerr had died and his heirs were listed as follows: George, John, James, Samuel, Walter, Jr., Jonathan, Rachel wife of Jacob Eden, Mary wife of Randal Rutherford, and Susannah wife of John Nichols (Wythe County Order Book 1801-1805, entry dated February 10, 1802, no page number).

In 1806, John Carr, Jr., and his wife Agness sold the remaining 200 acres where they were then living to Andrew Porter. In addition, Mathias Weiss (White) and his wife Rachel sold their portion of the land in 1812 to Andrew Porter. In 1803, Margaret Kerr released her interest in a 110-acre tract surveyed for her husband and Andrew Porter in 1796, and granted 1797 to Andrew Porter (Wythe County Deed Book 4, pp. 91, 397; Book 5, p. 425; Book 6, p. 225).

Nehemiah Bonham and his wife Rachel Carr were living in Tazewell County, Virginia, in 1835. Nothing else is known of the Carrs (Kerrs) and it is presumed that they left Wythe County after disposing of their land. Although there are two marriages recorded in Wythe County for John Carr, it is not clear if he is a member of this same family. One marriage was in 1822, to Esther Harbison, and the other in 1832, to Sarah Hudson (Wythe County Marriage Book 1, pp. 73,107; Wythe County Deed Book 13, p. 174).

The heirs of a Robert Karr are also mentioned in Wythe County records, although the connection to the others is not known. The widow Margaret, and heirs Henry Johnson and Mary his wife (late Karr), Willis Hicks and his wife Ellender (late Karr), William Briscoe and Sarah his wife (late Karr), and John Dunn and Margaret his wife (late Karr) of Robertson County, Tennessee, gave their power of attorney to James Karr. The land was conveyed to Joseph Russell, who was a merchant in what is now the Town of Draper, in Pulaski County (Wythe County Order Book, 1801-1805, p. 100, June 8, 1802; Wythe County Deed Book 3, p. 222; for details of Robert Karr's land *see* Kegley, *Early Adventurers*, Vol. 2, p. 397).

Chaney

Hezekiah Chaney, Sr., (also spelled China, Chinia, Cheney, Cheyne, etc.) came to the Cripple Creek community about 1775 and lived on a tract of 393 acres on McCendleys (McKinleys) Run, apparently the Chaney Branch of later maps. Chaney's name does not appear in any record of the area until 1781 and 1782, when he is listed on James Newell's Company of Militia. In 1782, he entered land on a state warrant for 200 acres, with 100 acres located on the north side of Lick Mountain "including a spring that runs by Stophel Ketterings and between Kettering's and James Campbell's," and a second tract of 100 acres on Sugar Run a branch of Cripple Creek below his plantation. He also entered a tract of 400 acres on the head of McCinney's [McKenley's] Run as assignee of George Douglas and Thomas Hamilton. This tract was near Lick Mountain. He also entered 300 acres on Sugar Run adjoining his old survey, which he later withdrew and re-entered the same on the north side of Lick Mountain, joining his last entry. In 1783, he entered 200 acres on McCenley [McKenley] Run, below and adjoining his settlement. He is mentioned in the tax lists of 1782, with two tithables, twelve horses, twenty-six cattle and land. In 1781/1782 when the land claims were settled, the commissioners confirmed to Chaney 300 acres on "Shugar" Run (settled in 1776), and 400 acres on the head of McCinneys [McKenleys] Run which included the Thomas Hamilton land (*George Gose vs. Archibald Cheyne et als*, filed October 25, 1817, Superior Court Chancery Book 2, p. 304, Wythe County Circuit Court Clerk's Office; Kegley, *Early Adventurers*, Vol. 2, pp. 113, 114; Kegley, *Militia*, pp. 30,31; Montgomery County Entry Book A, pp. 52, 72, 73; Book B, p. 8; Kegley, *Tax List*, p. 6).

On May 9, 1787, Chaney received a patent for 393 acres of land by a certificate of right of settlement given by the Commissioners for adjusted titles to unpatented lands in Washington and Montgomery counties. Sometime later, Chaney learned that James Wiley (Wyley), who had moved to South Carolina or Georgia, had 280 acres surveyed on November 16, 1753, which included part of his 393 acres. Because no fees had been paid on Wyley's tract, a grant had not been issued. Chaney paid the fees and purchased the right to the tract from Daniel Sheffey who had obtained the title from Wolcott, via Alexander Smyth and George Taylor, of the Loyal Company (*Gose vs. Cheyne*, Superior Court Chancery Book 2, pp. 304-344, gives the foregoing and the following details in regard to the dispute between George Gose and Archibald Chaney).

In 1796, Chaney obtained the grant for 196 acres, which adjoined the first tract on the east and south. On June 26, 1801, he obtained the grant for 836 acres, and he later obtained the grant for 650 acres of mountain land. These tracts had been surveyed in 1800: 650 acres and 836 acres. The 650 acres joined Kettering and Campbell, and the larger tract joined his own land, Newman, and William Patton, and was located for the most part on the east side of Sugar Run. The land between the mountain and the first mentioned tracts contained 70 acres and was "much the best" of all of his land. Chaney owned the 196 acres as early as 1783 by entry and survey. He cleared a field of 7 acres in 1797. A 20-acre field only had 12 acres cleared, and was cultivated by Chaney for nearly 40 years. In all, he had about 200 acres of cleared land. He also built a mill which was about a half mile from his house. It was located on a branch that ran at the western end of the mountain but was not connected to the plantation where he lived (*Gose vs. Cheyne;* Wythe County Survey Book 1, p. 496; Book 2, p. 40).

In 1798, Chaney owned a still with the capacity of 116 gallons, and his ownership was entered at the office of inspection. This was during the time that it was legal and when many Wythe County citizens owned and operated stills.

I Hezeciah Cheany possessor of a still marked 5 D S 6 V and numbered 33 of the capacity of 116 gallons at this time erected in the 5th division of the 6th Survey in the district of Virginia and owned by my self do hereby Enter the same at the office of Inspection No 5 for distilling by the capacity for the year To Hugh McGavock Coll of 5th division of the 6th Survey in the district of Virginia

Hezeciah X Chaney (his mark)

June 12th 1798

The record shows that Hezeciah [Hezekiah] Cheany [Chaney] had a still with the capacity of 116 gallons on June 12, 1798. Tracing from the original by Mary B. Kegley.

On March 12, 1812, Hezekiah Chaney, Sr., wrote his will and died sometime in February 1813. On April 13, 1813, the court summoned John Johnston, who had the will, to produce the same. The will was probated July 13, 1813. By the time the will was written, five of his daughters were married and had already received their shares of their father's estate, as mentioned in the will. They were: Sally Williams, Betsy Stone, Polly Stone, Jenny Cowden, and Nancy Cowden. To his daughter Caty, he left two Negro girls. To his son Abel he left land already deeded to him and 60 acres more. Hezekiah, Jr., received the land already deeded to him. To son Archibald he left the land "whereon I now live and all that tract I bought of Wiley, also 600 acres by survey joining Adam Ketterings, William Campbell and the place where Chaney lived." He was also to have a Negro boy. To his wife Jane, Chaney stated "I lend to my wife Jane, the rest of the property and she may give what she wishes to the youngest sons Hiram and Hozeah." The 300 acres between Sprakers, Stangers, and Goses were to go to Hiram and Hozeah at their mother's death or remarriage or at her discretion. A most unusual seal closed the signature of the will and is reproduced here (Wythe County Will Book 2, p. 88; Wythe County Order Book 1812-1815, April 13, 1813, p. 31).

The unusual seal used by Hezekiah Chaney on his will. Tracing from original by Mary Kegley.

By will of Hezekiah Chaney, the land in dispute passed to his son Archibald who sold it to George Gose in 1813 (deed 1821). Possession of the land was given in 1814, and a deed was to be made following a survey. It was at this time that the Chaneys discovered that the lines of the 393 acres and the 280 acres did not run along the mountain as believed. The grant for 196 acres was later discovered. Hiram Chaney conveyed this tract to Alexander Smyth in 1814. They discovered that the 70 acres was included in the grant for 196 acres instead of in the grant for 393 or the 280 acres. As Gose feared a claim from Smyth or other heirs of Chaney, he brought suit requesting the deed for the 70 acres. The suit was filed in 1817 by George Gose and revived at his death in 1819 by his wife, Anna, and his children, Stephen, George, and David Gose. It was decided on May 23, 1820, when the heirs of Gose were quieted in their possession of the land as described in the suit (*Gose vs. Cheyne*).

In 1818, Stephen Sanders, Sr., testified in the suit, stating that during the survey, he looked for marked trees and believed that chips of wood taken from the trees were made by Dr. Thomas Walker when the land was surveyed for Lewis or Hamilton. Hamilton lived there in 1776, when Sanders came to the area. He stated that Archibald Chaney was about 30 years old and Hiram was younger. James Newell, who had been a surveyor since 1781 or 1782, stated in 1820 that he had surveyed the land for Jacob Gose and by counting the rings in the trees, determined that the marks were 43 years old. He surveyed the 393 acres and the 196 acres for Chaney in November 1782. He also added that Stephen Gose, son of the plaintiff Anna, and a brother to David and George, married a daughter of Andrew Porter.

William Patton, Sr., indicated that the improvements on the land left to Hiram and Hoseah included a "cabbin" on Kirk's place. On the mill place there was a mill, but the house was built by Hiram after his father's death. There were 15-20 apple trees on Kirk's place when Chaney died. Patton also heard Hezekiah Chaney say that his son Archibald should have the old place as he had caused him to lose his eye by a "spor" [sporan] he had on. The mill plantation was chiefly cleared in Chaney's lifetime, and the timber was cut off at the time Brownlow managed Preston's Iron works and it was shortly afterwards fenced.

John A. Sanders also testified, stating he had offered to buy the part of the land Smyth later bought. The ridge between the two plantations was of considerable size through which a stream of water came from the residence of the elder Chaney to the mill, which was in the gap. The 20 acres of cleared land at the mill was on the south side of the ridge at the mill. The land sold to Gose included 200 acres of cleared land, two meadows, containing about 15 acres, and two orchards of bearing apple trees, one of them upwards of 30 years old. Gose paid $3,000 for the land. The 470 acres was conveyed by Archibald Chaney and his wife Nancy to George Gose in 1814.

Alexander Smyth filed suit against Jane Cheyne, the widow, on August 22, 1815. He stated in his Bill of Complaint that Hezekiah Chaney had received the grant for 196 acres on August 2, 1796. The land was on McKindleys Run, a branch of Cripple Creek. On June 26, 1801, Chaney received the grant for another tract of 836 acres adjoining the first. Part of this latter tract was sold to Jacob Gose. Smyth recites pertinent parts of the will of Hezekiah Chaney, and states further that Archibald leased part of the land Jane had received by the will to Kemp Thomas, who took possession of it, and that Hiram took possession of the other part, and that the residue of the land consisted of 836 acres and the 196 acres and one other tract of 125 acres (*Smyth vs. Cheyne et als*, Box 18, 1820, Wythe County Circuit Court Clerk's Office, Basement; also Superior Court Chancery Book 2, p. 435).

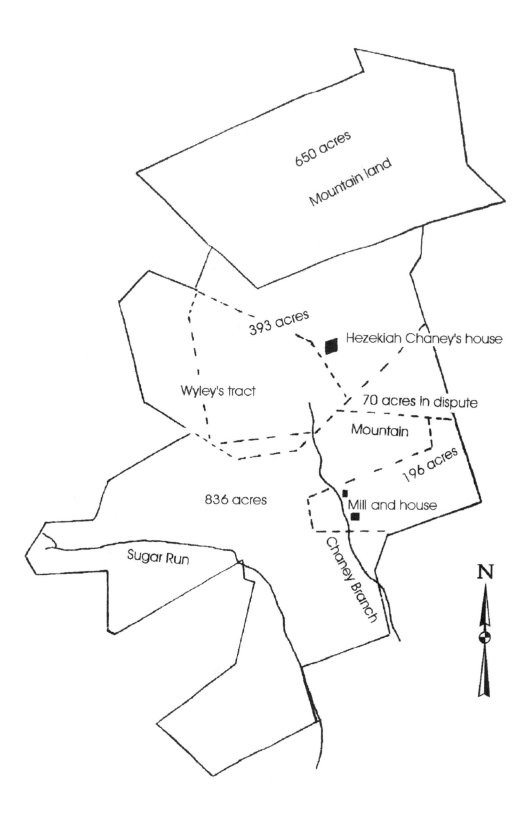

The map shows the land owned by Hezekiah Chaney on Chaney Branch and Sugar Run, with the location of his house and mill and the tracts in dispute. Tracing from the original by Mary B. Kegley.

399

The log home of the Chaneys, now gone.　　Photo courtesy of the F. B. Kegley Collection.

On February 22, 1814, Smyth purchased from Hiram Chaney with consent of his mother, one moiety of land, estimated at 840 acres and adjoining Mrs. Campbell, James Campbell's heirs, Jacob Gose, William Patton, Peter Spangler, and Harold Smyth, and including the house and mill where Hiram lived and a tract of 128 acres surveyed for Christopher Elams under the Loyal Company. The agreement with Kemp Thomas was assigned to Smyth and on March 2, 1814, Jane conveyed to Hiram one undivided moiety of the estate she had in three tracts of land under the will, one on McKinleys Run and containing 196 acres granted 1796, another on Sugar Run the residue of 836 acres granted 1801, and the third containing 125 acres on Lick Mountain, which had been conveyed by Hiram and his wife Polly Chaney on March 8, 1814, to Smyth. Jane was in possession of the house and the mill where Hiram dwelt, and the adjoining improvement was in possession of Kemp Thomas. Smyth asked for partition of the land because Hoseah Chaney was under age and had as his guardian, the Reverend John Stanger. Smyth wanted to claim the land surveyed for Christopher Elams, and so much of the land as was included in the grant "to the plaintiff [Smyth], so that he may be quieted in claim against the Loyal Company on the 128 acres."

It was also mentioned in the Smyth suit that Hezekiah Chaney had received assignment for two surveys, Elams mentioned above, and that of George Henley. Francis Smith had received payment for a survey in the name of these two and also Thomas Hamilton. Thomas Major assigned his land to John Sifers, being two tracts of land, containing 200 acres on Cripple Creek and Sugar Run, joining the William Patton land on the east and James White on the south. Sifers assigned it to Michael Yong [Young] who assigned it to Samuel Burks in 1787, who assigned it to Hezekiah Chaney in 1792. The list of the grants to Chaney were included in the suit, as well as a grant to Alexander Smyth for 500 acres as assignee of John Thompson Sayers. The land was on the north side of a tract of land on Cripple Creek formerly belonging to James Wylie, deceased, and on which "one Harris formerly resided."

Hiram Chaney testified on October 23, 1815, that he had lived on the land devised to him where his father had a mill and that he had built a new house and made other improvements, and he had sold his share to Smyth. He further stated that he had removed to Kentucky and that his mother and Hoseah had possession of the improvements made at the mill. He had no objection to the partition.

Jane, the widow, testified that Hiram lived on that part of the estate at the mill, but after a year or two his wish was to ''remove to the Western Country,'' and she agreed that the land could be rented to Kemp Thomas for three years. She claimed that Smyth knew that he would have no possession of that land until the lease expired, but she agreed to the partition.

Francis Smith, agent of the Loyal Company, reported that the so-called composition money and fees due for the Elams survey had been paid by Hezekiah Chaney. Robert Adams reported on the survey that he had divided the land with a partition line so that Smyth could claim the southern moiety joining Chatwell, Gose, Patton, and Harold Smyth, and be free from any claim for the Elams land.

Christopher Spraker, a neighbor of Chaney, brought suit in 1817 against George Gose and Archibald Chaney. Spraker noted that he had settled on the western boundary of the Wyley tract, and Chaney had settled on the eastern boundary but part was not claimed by either of them, and lay between the two settlements. As noted, Chaney's survey included part of Wyleys, and Spraker, in having his survey for 338 acres done in 1782 included a small portion of the 280 acres. Spraker's grant came in 1793 before the Wyley tract was granted, and Spraker based his claim on the older grant. The land in dispute was willed to Archibald Chaney, who sold it to George Gose in 1813, following his father's death. Chaney and Gose both refused to clear the title for Spraker, and when the case was settled in court in 1821, Spraker's claim was dismissed (*Spracher [Spraker] vs. George Gose and Archibald Cheyne*, Superior Court Chancery Book 2, pp. 767-778).

In 1802, Abel Chaney received by deed certain land on the south side of Lick Mountain from his father Hezekiah and his mother Jane Chaney. In 1810, the parents conveyed 287 acres on Sugar Run to their son Hezekiah Chaney, Jr., who sold the place two years later to Isaiah Chatwell, who lived out his days on this tract of land (Wythe County Deed Book 5, pp. 289,290; *see*, Chatwell sketch).

The Chaney marriages of Wythe County include: Jenny Chaney to Joseph Cowden in 1801; Nancy Chaney to Robert Cowden in 1807; Caty Chaney to Richard Stone, 1813; Alpha Nocles (Nuckles) to Hezekiah Chaney, Jr., in 1809; Hiram Chaney to Mary Etter in 1813; and Archibald Chaney to Nancy Ball in 1812. The Spraker lawsuit mentioned that Stephen Stone was a son-in-law but did not indicate which daughter of Chaney's he married. (Wythe County Marriage Book 1, pp. 18, 33,38, 45(2), 46; Wythe County Marriage Bond Book , p. 65; *Spracher [Spraker] vs. Gose et als*).

In 1814, Hiram Chaney sold 100 acres to Jacob Gose, and his brother Hosea sold his 465 acres, parts of 196 and 836 acres, to George Gose's heirs (Anna, Stephen, David and George Gose) in 1820. In addition, the title to the disputed 70 acres was conveyed, following the lawsuit, by Archibald Chaney who had sold his share of the land, to Alexander Smyth in 1814 (Wythe County Deed Book 6, p. 221; Book 8, p. 68; Book 9, p. 38).

Some of the Chaney family moved West, and the name disappeared from Wythe County, although Chaney Branch reminds us that the family once had large plantation holdings in that neighborhood. Descendants indicate that Abel Cheney moved to Tennessee, where he lived in Monroe County before moving to the Fort Worth, Texas, area. The records show that Abel R. Cheyne was living in Knox County, Tennessee, in 1819, and Hezekiah Chaney was living in Sevier County, Tennessee. Hiram Chaney was living in Kentucky in 1815. Hosea Chaney lived in Surry County, North Carolina, in the 1820s (*Cowden vs. Cheyne,* Box 33, 1827; *Gose vs. Cheyne,* Box 18, 1820-1821, notice to take depositions, Wythe County Circuit Court Clerk's Office, Basement; *Smyth vs. Cheyne et als,* Superior Court Chancery Book 2, p. 435).

Cook

Henry Cook was probably in Wythe County in the early 1790s as his name appears on the personal property tax list in 1793. In 1796, Cook obtained a grant for 400 acres on Cripple Creek. Although this is not certain, Cook Branch which enters Cripple Creek below the Huddle community may be named for this adventurer (Murphy and Douthat, *Tax List,* p. 12; Grant Book 37, p. 20).

.In 1815, the tax assessor indicated that Cook owned one farm on the waters of Cripple Creek on Lick Mountain containing 400 acres, with a dwelling house of wood, one and a half stories, 24 feet by 18 feet, one barn, two small stables, and one kitchen, all valued at $400 (Kegley, *Tax Assessment,* p. 117).

In 1818, Cook purchased 90 acres on Cripple Creek from Henry and Barbara Huffman (Wythe County Deed Book 7, p. 174).

In 1821, Henry Cook and his wife Caty were mentioned as heirs of Martin Kimberling who lived on Black Lick, through the latter's daughter Elizabeth who married Adam Groseclose (who died 1804). Caty appears to be a sister of Mary who married Michael Spraker, and Elizabeth, who married Peter Spraker who are mentioned below (Wythe County Deed Book 9, p.40; Gose, *Pioneers,* pp. 173-175.

On November 15, 1834 Henry Cook wrote his will, which was probated on April 13, 1835 (Wythe County Will Book 4, p. 165). All of his land and his personal estate was to be divided between Mary, wife of Michael Spraker, and Elizabeth, wife of Peter Spraker, and Catherine, wife of George Spraker. Peter Spraker was to have use of the land for one year after Cook's death. The will also indicated that Peter was to ''support me well, and keep a horse for me.'' His ''trusty friends'' Peter and George Spraker were to be executors. The witnesses were J. T. Gleaves, John Earhart, and John Ewing.

No children are mentioned in the will or any other record in Wythe County, but it appears that the Spraker men were related to his wife Caty. There may also be an earlier Spraker relationship as Eva Kook (Cook) married Jacob Spraker in 1791 (Wythe County Marriage Book 1, p. 1). In 1818, Henry Cook appears on the bond for the marriage of Eve Cook, daughter of Adam Cook, and Joseph Taid. Although there are several other Cook marriages for women of Wythe County, none seem to be directly connected to Henry Cook (Wythe County Marriage Book 1, p. 58).

The inventory of Cook's estate was taken on April 24, 1835 (Wythe County Will Book 4, p. 190). Among the items included were 6 German books, 3 small irons, shoe leather, two tables, a rifle gun, a clock, two corner cupboards and furniture; fire shovel tongs and dog irons, crockery ware, a pair of steelyards, a desk, bookcase and chest, saddlebags, a pay of powder, sugar, coffee, a Japan box, 7 chairs, beds and bedsteads, a looking glass, two baskets, harness, brass kettle, lot of leather, two hogsheads, buck wheat, shoe bench, pots, 9 bags, crout cutter and coolers, pot racks, tubs, quill wheel, plaster, 50 pounds of bacon, one fat tub, a kettle, 3 washing tubs, a ewe and a lamb, a vice, a loom, 3 axes, 3 bridles, 2 saddles, a crosscut saw, lot of iron, three whiskey barrels and measures, brandy at 50 cents a gallon ($10), stove and pipe; salt, wagon cloth, Jackscrew; tar bucket and barrels, a lot of corn, a horse, tub and flax, cows and calf, a lot of old spring house vessels, and rye. There was $525.25 1/4 in notes, and $133.18 3/4 in cash. The inventory was recorded on July 13, 1835, the same date the record of the sale was recorded (Wythe County Will Book 4, p. 192).

Danner

The Danners appear to have come to Wythe County in the early 1790s. Andrew Danner, Sr., George Danner, Hugh, Jacob, John, and Joseph are names which appear in the personal property tax lists between 1793 and 1800. The name was also spelled Dannar. By 1810, the only names listed in the census (under the spelling Dannor) were George and his wife who were 45 years and up, who had two additional males and two additional females in their household (Murphy and Douthat, *Wythe County, Virginia Tax List 1793-1800*, p. 14; Wythe County Federal Census, 1810).

Andrew Danner's name appears in the land surveys in 1793 and 1796 when he chose 300 acres on Cripple Creek, assignee of Nathaniel Frisbuy [Frisbie], a tract cornering on the land of James Campbell, which was granted in 1796. He also selected 520 acres joining his own land by his mill, and with Buckalew's line, which was granted in 1800. In 1802, he added 33 acres which again mentions the mill and Buckalew, and which was granted in 1804. He also had a grant in 1796 for a tract of 270 acres on Cripple Creek, adjoining William Henley. George Danner had a small tract surveyed in 1810, which mentions ''crossing his mill creek,'' on a branch of Cripple Creek, and which was granted in 1811. There was also a tract of 100 acres surveyed for a John Danner, and granted to him in 1833, but the land was not on Cripple Creek, and there is no known connection to the others of the name. John Danner's name appears in a deed in 1822, when he gave to his granddaughter, Polly Gill, certain items of personal property (Wythe County Survey Book 1, pp. 46, 363; Book 2, p. 113; Book 3, pp. 37, 307; Grant Book 34, p. 487; Book 35, p. 475; Book 47, p. 11; Book 52, p. 449; Book 61, p. 553; Book 82, p. 308; Wythe County Deed Book 9, p. 206).

In 1806, Andrew Danner and his wife Eve conveyed 64 acres to Jacob Fisher. In 1807, George Danner purchased 5 acres from George and Catherine Buckalew, on Bebers Mill Creek, adjoining Jeremiah Haney and Danner. The mill pond was mentioned. In 1812, Andrew Danner conveyed to George M. Danner 1,123 acres, consisting of four separate tracts (300, 520, 270, and 33 acres all of which are mentioned above). Andrew does not appear in any further records of Wythe County; it is George who remains in the community (Wythe County Deed Book 4, pp. 440, 462; Book 6, p. 423).

In 1815, George Danner's farm was described as one farm on the road ten miles above the lead mines, 700 acres, 300 acres of which is mountain land, having thereon one dwelling, two stories, one barn, one loom house, all valued at $600 (Kegley, *Tax Assessment*, p. 119).

George married Mina (also Myna, Meany, Mina, Mary, Mary Ann, Myma, etc.) Scott about 1816, but no exact date is given for the marriage. Their names appear in the deed records at various times. They sold land to Jesse Scott in 1827, and George M. Danner sold 284 acres to David Fisher in 1813 (Wythe County Marriage Book 1, p. 50 gives George's surname as Danah and her name as Meany, while other spellings appear for her in deeds, and a lawsuit; Wythe County Deed Book 6, p. 85; Book 10, p. 592).

Sometime in the fall of 1839, George M. Danner died. His wife Mima relinquished the administration of the estate to J. T. Gleaves on September 9, 1839. On the same day the appraisal was ordered to be done and his sale was held in October 1839. On November 11, 1839, an order was entered, and A. C. Moore, William M. Chatwell and William Henley were appointed as Commissioners to assign the dower of Mina Danner. It was designated as 137 acres, and was laid off on February 8, 1840. The same day Elizabeth and Julian [Julia Ann?] Danner, orphans of George M. Danner, who were above the age of 14, chose John Spraker as their guardian, and he was appointed for Malvina who was under 14 (Wythe County Will Book 5, pp. 310,312; Wythe County Deed Book 14, p. 445; Wythe County Order Book 1837-1840, pp. 395-396, 425-426).

George's appraisal revealed that he had a number of interesting items including the following: a bureau, a lot of books, a large Bible, a clock, table, cupboard and furniture, looking glass, three chairs, one pair of hand irons, a pair of candlesticks, beds and bedsteads, check reel, flax wheel, carpenter's tools, a shot gun, a wool wheel, a coffee mill, a lot of castings and harrow teeth, a cabbage knife, a loom, horse gears, shovel and barshear plows, broad axes, a wagon, a ''stake anvil and hammer,'' 18 sheep, 6 hogs, mares, cows, a beef hide, a woman's saddle, Pike's Arithmetic, and a mowing scythe. The appraisal was done by Randel Rutherford, William Henley, and Robert Henley. When the settlement was made and debts were paid, the balance remaining was only $2.16 3/4 (Wythe County Will Book 5, p. 312; Will Book 6, p. 41).

Other marriages recorded in Wythe County for Danners include Daniel who married Mary Ann Eastwood in 1842 and his mother Miney gave her consent which was filed with the marriage bond; Catharina, daughter of John Danner who married Joseph Yonce in 1844; Elisabeth who married William Miller in 1846, and who is probably the same person mentioned in the marriage bond two days earlier as Elizabeth, daughter of John, who was to marry Willouby Miller, Jr.; Malvina T. who married John Corvin in 1844; Mary A., daughter of John Danner, who married John W. Bridgeman in 1848; Dorothy who married Joseph Gill in 1821; Sarah J. A. (known as Julia Ann) who married Marshall Delp in 1845; and Joshua Danner who married Julia Ann White, 1851(Wythe County Marriage Book 1, pp. 71,151, 162, 165,195, 155, 167, 163, 190; Miscellaneous Marriages, pp. 103, 158; Wythe County Deed Book 18, p. 2).

The dower land of Mina Danner was transferred to James T. Gleaves in 1840, who the following year conveyed it back to her for her lifetime. In 1841, a lawsuit was decided in regard to the land. James Scott brought suit against Jesse G. Danner and others, who were named as Mary Ann, the widow of George Danner, and the children Jesse G., Martha, Daniel, Elizabeth, Sarah, and Malvina (the last four being under age 21 years). Scott had purchased the interests of Jesse G. Danner, who was not an inhabitant of Virginia, and wanted a deed for his part. Six divisions were made by the surveyor, but no map was found. The court ordered the parties to convey their interests to each other, and the deeds can be found in the records beginning in the 1840s. The Corvins and Elizabeth Danner were living in Russell County, Virginia, in 1850s (Wythe County Deed Book 14, pp. 491, 492; Book 15, p. 236; Book 16, p. 710; Book 20, pp. 31, 47; *Scott vs. Danner*, Box 91, 1843-1844, Wythe County Circuit Court Clerk's Office, Basement).

There was a death record for a Miss Sarah Danner who died on February 8, 1868, unmarried, at the age of 89 years 4 months and 20 days. She lived on Cripple Creek and was born in the county. She was the daughter of Andrew and Eve E. Danner. Information was given by a friend, Sarah D. Percival (Wythe County Death Register, p. 23, line 10).

James Davis of Cripple Creek is somewhat elusive. He appears on James Newell's Companies of Militia in 1781 and 1782, placing him in the community at that time. He entered 400 acres of land on Cripple Creek in 1782. He also had a claim for 200 acres on Sugar Run, which he assigned to William Hall, and received 400 acres from the Commissioners of Washington and Montgomery County, which was assigned to him by George Honley [Henley] (Montgomery County Entry Book A, pp. 107, 153; Kegley, *Early Adventurers*, Vol. 2, p. 116; Kegley, *Militia*, pp. 30,31).

In 1782, a survey was made for a James Davis on Cripple Creek. The tract of land contained 357 acres and was located on the south side of Lick Mountain, adjoining James Campbell. It was based on a 400-acre certificate from the Commissioners of Washington and Montgomery County. Davis received the grant for the tract in 1785. It appears that the 357 acres was the same tract owned by Hezekiah and Abel Chaney and later Jacob Spraker. The land was located on Mill Creek and may be part of, or adjoins, the Landreth homeplace (Montgomery County Survey Book B, p. 216; Grant Book N, p. 716; Wythe County Deed Book 5, p. 290; Book 6, p. 395). There were other men by the name of James Davis in the early records, and it is almost impossible to determine which one lived on Cripple Creek. It would appear, however, that this early James left the community after assigning his land to Chaney.

There is a group of Davises connected to Jane Davis Eller, and for information on that group *see* Eller sketch. An attempt to determine the parents of this group has been unsuccessful.

The group of Davises in the Slate Spring Branch community of Cripple Creek appears to be headed by a Jacob Davis who in 1846 purchased two tracts on Cripple Creek from James and Mary Anne Scott, the same two tracts sold to Scott in 1827 by Adam and William McKee and Shepherd Brown [merchants]. The first tract was 150 acres on Baber's Creek, corner to Benjamin Rogers, Sr., and the other was 180 acres which was the same conveyed by George Buckaloo and his wife to Joseph Bell and then to Hugh Spence and later the McKees and Brown. Davis also added 7 additional acres adjoining his own land and Elias Groseclose (Wythe County Deed Book 12, p. 597; Book 17, pp. 181, 672).

In 1867, Jacob Davis and his wife Jane conveyed land to Jezreal H. Groseclose, a son-in-law, and also transferred 50 acres to Jacob M. Davis the same year. Jacob M. is most often identified as J. M. and is the same person as Marion mentioned in the census, and family records. On April 12, 1869, Jacob gave John S. Johnson and his wife, Arminda A. Johnson, 113 acres on Cripple Creek. Arminda was Jacob's daughter, and the land was given in return for support and maintenance and payment of certain debts. There are many Johnsons still in the Slate Spring Branch community. In 1869, Jacob Davis conveyed to James W. Lockett, as trustee, one acre for a community cemetery to be known as the Davis Graveyard, or Cemetery, which is still being used as a neighborhood burial place (Wythe County Deed Book 23, pp. 209, 479, 512; Book 36, p. 556). Jacob who gave the land for the cemetery is buried there. He was born December 21, 1796, and died June 22, 1879. His wife Jane was born January 26, 1800, and died December 8, 1868. Another Jacob Davis is buried at St. John's Lutheran Church Cemetery and was born in 1790 and died August 13, 1820. A marriage record for Jacob N. (should be M.) Davis and Elisabeth K. Groseclose in 1856 indicates that the groom was born on Reed Creek, son of Jacob and Jane (no maiden name given) Davis, and was 21 years old (Wythe County Marriage Book 2A, p. 9; for a complete listing of burials in the Davis Cemetery, *see* Collins, "Davis Cemetery," *Wythe County Historical Review*, No. 41, January 1992, pp. 10-22).

The appraisal of Jacob Davis was taken on August 15, 1879 and recorded in 1880 by J. M. Davis the administrator of the estate (Wythe County Will Book 13, pp. 410,412).

Robert Eddystone Johnson, the grandson of Arminda Atkins Davis and John Shannon Johnson, was able to provide me with additional information about the family. According to his records, Jacob Davis married Mary Jane Johnston, and had the following children: Mary who married Rufus Umberger, a twin of Sarah who married Benjamin Swecker, Lucinda who married Absolem Hines, Julia who married Jesse Groseclose, Lydia who married Gordon Keister, Harriett who married Dave Hines, Martha who married Dave Grey, Marion who married Betty Groseclose, Melvin who died in Camp Chase in 1864, and is buried in Columbus, Ohio, Elic (or Alec) Davis who married Betty Walters, and Arminda Atkins Davis (1841-1915), who married John Shannon Johnson (1834-1910). John Shannon Johnson was a farmer and a carpenter, and was in charge of building the Calvary Methodist Church on Cripple Creek. He also built houses, one of which was the Simmerman home on Cripple Creek, near Speedwell, which is now gone.

Mary Jane Johnston, the wife of Jacob Davis, was the daughter of Larkin Johnston (born 1764 in North Carolina and died about 1852), and his wife Mary (Polly) Davis (born about 1772), the daughter of John Davis, II, and his wife Mary. This is confirmed by the list of ten heirs of Larkin Johnston who received their share of his estate. Jacob Davis and his wife Jane are mentioned. Jane was a granddaughter of John Davis II mentioned above. The children of John Davis, II, appear in an order book on February 14, 1816 when Jesse Evans brought suit against the heirs of John Davis named as follows: John, George, William, and Abraham Davis, Larkin Johnson [usually Johnston] and his wife Polly who was a Davis, Charles J. Woodson and his wife Caty who was a Davis, Spencer Lehue and his wife Peggy who was a Davis,

Tombstone of J. Melvin (Melville) Davis who died at Camp Chase. He is buried in the camp cemetery in Columbus, Ohio. Courtesy of Robert Eddystone Johnson.

Jacob Harrell and his wife Anne, who was a Davis, Jacob Whitmore and his wife Nancy who was a Davis, and appears to have married second Henry Hufford, William Ferguson and his wife Susanna, who was a Davis (Wythe County Will Book 9, pp. 80,81; Wythe county Order Book 1815-1820, p. 41; Order Book 1812-1815, p. 99).

Although the census records are not always accurate, Jacob and Jane and their children are listed in the 1850 census (Family 1318). Jacob was 51 and Jane 47. The children listed were Alexander age 23, Martha age 22, Julia Ann age 19, Harriett age 17, Lidy age 15, Marion (male) age 14, Arminda age 12, Melville age 8. Living with the family was Lucinda Hines, age 21, who was a daughter of Jacob. It appears that Elic (Alic) is the same as Alexander, and that Melville is the same as Melvin, a name used in the family. This is confirmed by the military record where he is named as Melville J. Davis. He was captured at Cloyd's Farm in 1864, and sent to Camp Chase, where he died from pneumonia on March 13, 1865. He is buried at Green Lawn Cemetery, grave 1638 (Scott, *45th Virginia Infantry*, p. 88).

It seems likely that Jacob Davis of Cripple Creek lived on Reed Creek near the rock quarry before moving to Cripple Creek, and that he was the one who donated the land for the Cedar Hill Methodist Church (Wythe County Deed Book 16, p. 265). It also seems likely that Jacob was the son of John Davis who left a will written in 1796 and probated in 1797 which mentioned a son Jacob as well as a wife Mary, sons Joseph, John, George, and Abram, who was deceased at the time of the will, leaving three daughters, Betsy, Polly, and Susy. John also had five daughters Betsy, Eve, Elizabeth, Barbara, and Polly who intermarried with John Hutsell, Daniel Wiseley, Lewis Hutsell, Joseph Fannon and John Fannon (Wythe County Will Book 1, p. 90).

Following the death of Jacob Davis, the administrator of the estate, his son J. M. Davis, filed suit in the court in December 1879. Jacob had 42 acres of land which had not been disposed of before his death, and as there was not enough money to pay the debts he owed, the suit requested that the land be sold, debts paid, and the remainder distributed among the heirs. From the suit papers further information was obtained about the family. The suit was brought by J. M. Davis the son, who explained that all of the family wanted the land sold, debts paid, and the balance of the money divided. He named the children of Jacob Davis as Sarah wife of Benjamin Swecker, Lucinda wife of Absolem Hines, Julia A. wife of Jezreal H. Groseclose, Arminda wife of John S. Johnson, Martha C. widow of David (published in the paper erroneously as Daniel) Gray, Alexander Davis who had been gone from Virginia and was living outside the Commonwealth for about seven years. Three of the children had died before their father and were named as Lydia E. whose husband had been Gordon Keister, Mary M. whose husband had been Rufus Umberger, and Harriett whose husband had been David Hines. Because these three girls were deceased their children inherited from the estate. The children under age were Charles and James Keister, Lydia's children, and Stephen Hines, Harriett's son, who with his father was living outside the Commonwealth of Virginia. The Rufus Umberger children were all of age and were named as Mary J. wife of J. W. Pattison [should be Patterson], Elizabeth wife of Stephen Kegley, Charles G. [Greever] Umberger, Robert T. [should be L.] Umberger, Isaack (also named as Israel which is correct) N. [Newton] Umberger, and James B. [Brown] Umberger. As a result of the suit, the deed was made to W. B. Davis and William C. Davis (*Davis vs. Swecker et als.*, Box 138, December 1883, Wythe County Circuit Court Clerk's Office, Basement; Wythe County Deed Book 37, p. 50; Notes by F. B. Kegley).

Some of the marriage records are mentioned in the Wythe County records. Rufus Umberger and Mary Malvina Davis were married on October 16, 1845, and the bond was dated three days before with Jacob Davis as surety. Benjamin Swecker married Sarah M. Davis on May 27, 1848, with Alexander W. Davis on the bond signed five days before. David Hines married Delila H. [Harriett] Davis on February 21, 1854 when she was 22 years old. Alexander W. Davis was married on August 24, 1854 at age 27 to Elizabeth, daughter of William and Molly Walters. Jacob N. (should be M.) Davis married Elisabeth K. daughter of Elias and Regina Groseclose on March 19, 1856. David Gray married Martha C. Davis on July 26, 1853, and Arminda A. Davis married John S. son of Samuel and Hester Grubb Johnson on April 8, 1869 when she was 26

(Wythe County Marriage Book 1, pp. 160; Marriage Bond Book, pp. 149, 173; Miscellaneous Marriages, p. 635, Book 2A, pp. 1 (2 on this page), 9, 47).

The main part of the Jacob Davis house on Cripple Creek was torn down, and the part that was attached and used as a kitchen and dining room was moved to another location on the farm, and was standing in 1994. John Wayne Johnson , another grandson of John S. Johnson, presently lives at the site of the Jacob Davis place.

The house of Jacob Davis house as remembered and drawn by Robert Eddystone Johnson.

Adam Dean

The name Adam Dean appears in the Augusta County records beginning about 1762. An Adam Dean is also mentioned in Albemarle County, and in 1765 an Adam Dean and his wife ''Elanor'' of Augusta sold lands to Charles Teas on the South River. Adam and ''Elinor'' Dean of Albemarle also sold their land on Stocktons Branch of Meechums River in Albemarle County on October 1, 1773. William Dean's will recorded in Augusta County in 1773, mentions a son Adam (who refused to act as executor), son John, daughters Mary and Elizabeth and a wife Sarah. It is not clear if these references relate to the Adam Dean who settled on Cripple Creek in what is now Wythe County (Chalkley, *Chronicles,* Vol. 1, pp. 149,174; Vol. 3, pp. 130, 418, 444; Augusta County Will Book 5, pp. 107,108; Albemarle County Deed Book 6, p.274).

Adam Dean of Cripple Creek appeared in the area about 1774, and had numerous tracts of land surveyed and later granted to him on a branch of Cripple Creek which was named for him. It appears on local maps as Dean's Branch. This branch runs eastward from the foot of Lick Mountain and empties into Cripple Creek some distance north of Ivanhoe. The tracts included 400 acres granted March 30, 1785, 68 acres granted September 20, 1785, 53 acres adjoining the land he lived on, September 1, 1785, and 490 acres granted February 4, 1793. He also had tracts on the Clinch River, entered for survey in Montgomery County (Kegley and Kegley, *Early Adventurers,* Vol. 1, pp. 33, 40; Kegley, *Early Adventurers*, Vol. 2, pp. 28, 75, 76, 77, 103; Grant Book R, p. 382; Book O, p. 310; Book S, p. 337; Book 27, p. 463).

Dean served as an appraiser of the estate of William Herbert in 1776/77, and was one of those asked to assign the dower of his widow, Sarah Herbert Day. He also served as a road overseer and viewer on the Cripple Creek Road. He served on the jury in 1777, and for Duncan Gullion's trial in 1779. That year, he was recommended as a fit person to be a justice of the peace and took the oath of office. He served numerous times in 1781 and 1782 (Summers, *Annals,* pp. 651, 684, 693, 694, 696, 706, 710, 717, 747, 753, 774).

Adam Dean appears on James Newell's Company of Militia in 1781, but he was not fit for service. A William Dean also appears on the list. The next year another list was recorded by Newell, and Adam, William, and a James Dean are mentioned. Adam Dean is among those who took the oath of allegiance in 1777 and appears on Montgomery's list (Kegley, *Militia...* pp. 30,31,53).

In 1785, Adam Dean was required to take the list of taxable property in Sayers' and Newell's companies and his report was returned to the court the same year. The next year his assignment was Sayers' and McKinney's old company on Elk Creek (Summers, *Annals,* pp. 784,787, 811).

Dean's will was written on June 12, 1787, and was probated September 4, 1787, when it was proved by Sarah Smith and William Love. James Dean became the executor of the estate with Stephen Sanders as surety on his bond (Montgomery County Will Book B, pp. 122, 124; Kegley and Kegley, *Early Adventurers,* Vol. 1, p. 119).

By the terms of the will, his wife Elizabeth and the family were to live on the land in Montgomery (now Wythe) County and all profits arising from it were to be used to support and educate the family. If his wife should remarry and be "inclined to remove from that way of living" then she was to take her dowry allowed by law, "after having her dowry settled in the estate of her first decist husband which is not yet done."

The work horses and farming utensils, Negro Tom and a Negro belonging to the step-children, were to labor for the support of the family until the wife had her dowry laid off in them, and from then on till the heirs were of age. Negro Tom was to go to son Robert Love Dean. Daughter Ally was to have one English mare known by the name of the "bald filley" and also a good feather bed and furniture. Daughter Elizabeth was to have one sorrel filley and a bed and furniture.

All land in Montgomery County, now Wythe County, was devised to sons James, Joseph, and Robert Love Dean. If they decided to leave, then the profits from the sale of the lands were to go to the daughters Mary, Eleanor, and Anna, each to have one-third. His step-daughter Margaret Edmiston was to have one black filley. If the land in Kentucky was obtained, it was to go to son James and son-in-law John Hustin (Hueston), provided they pay the expenses. If not, part was to go to son Robert Love Dean. All the lands that were surveyed for his wife in Kentucky, "I allow it to remain at her disposal."

He also mentioned a tract of land of about 400-500 acres, the exact quantity not known, as it was not yet patented. Adam Dean had entered the land with Thomas Madison, John Preston, and James Newell. His wife Elizabeth, and son James were to act as executors. Witnesses to the will were Samuel and Sarah Smith, and William Love.

The appraisal of Adam Dean's estate was done by Robert Saunders [Sanders], William Rogers, and Michael Lees [Lease]. Among the items listed were 14 cows, 5 steers, 7 calves, several mares and their colts, 5 horses, 8 sheep, 4 hogs, 5 feather beds, 30 pounds of feathers, a Negro man, bonds and notes, and certificates including one identified as a "militia" certificate. The appraised amount, exclusive of the certificates, was £383.0.11 (Montgomery County Will Book B, p. 136).

James Dean sold his father's land on Cripple Creek to James McGavock, who received four tracts in 1790, including 290 acres, 53 acres adjoining the land James Dean was living on, 400 acres, and 68 acres. James had a grant for 190 acres in his own name, dated March 7, 1794. Sometime between 1790 and 1796, James moved to Davidson County, Tennessee, and from there deeded his remaining holdings to James McGavock who received 46 acres, part of a survey of 190 acres made November 17, 1753, the grant issuing to James Dean in 1794, and the remainder of the 190 acres to Robert Majors, the same year (Wythe County Deed Book 1, pp. 28, 29, 30, 31, 403, 404; Grant Book 27, p. 463).

Family records show that James Dean was born on March 8, 1763, and was married in Davidson County, Tennessee, to Mary "Polly" Dickinson, and died there on September 3, 1801. He had three children: Sally who married Michael Gleaves; James who married Charlotte Horn; and Mary or "Polly" who married Thomas Gleaves and later John Fletcher (family records of Margery G. Miller).

It is clear from the will that Adam Dean's wife was married twice, but the name of her first husband is not certain. Some believe she might have been a Love, as one child had the middle name of Love, and a William Love was a witness to Dean's will. The will mentioned the step-daughter Margaret Edmiston, but this may be her married name not her maiden name. Adam's daughter Jini (Jene) is not mentioned in the will, but she married William Campbell on or about March 5, 1782, in Montgomery County. Another daughter, her first name not given in the marriage bond, but mentioned as Adam's daughter, married John Hueston on or about September 27, 1785. Some of the children may be by a second wife, but this is not mentioned in the records here. Nothing is known of the other family members who were mentioned in the will (Montgomery County Marriages as found in Kegley, *Early Adventurers*, Vol. 2, pp. 177, 178).

The James McGavock land was included in an inclusive survey made in 1821 for Joseph Kent and Gordon Cloyd (Wythe County Survey Book 3, p. 145) where the dates of the grants to Dean are recorded, and an additional 1,000 acres was included, making the new total 2,347 acres. McGavock willed this land to his daughters Peggy wife of Joseph Kent, and Betsy wife of Gordon Cloyd. All of the land became the property of the Kent family and later became the site of the Moore family homes. The brick house is now in the W. D. S. Huddle family (Wythe County Will Book 2, p. 34; Will Book 6, p. 140). Other McGavock land was sold to John Hudson in 1843 (Wythe County Deed Book 5, 345; Book 13, p. 747; Book 16, p. 534).

The Colonel A. C. Moore house, later the home of W. D. S. Huddle.

Photo by Mary B. Kegley, 1993.

Douglas

James, John, and George Douglas (also Douglass, Dugless) were early settlers on the head of Cripple Creek. James and George purchased 330 acres of land from William Ewing in 1773 (Montgomery County Deed Book A, p. 22). The same year, a John Douglas is listed in Stephen Trigg's Company, but as this company listed people in the present boundaries of Pulaski County, it may not be the same John. However, Captain Doack's (Doak's) list of 1773, mentions James and George Douglas which would place them in what is now Wythe County (Kegley, *Tithables*, pp. 25, 29).

On August 7, 1774, a John Douglas, leaving on a journey (perhaps to participate in the Point Pleasant expedition ?) devised to George Blackburn and his wife, two cows and three calves. The balance was to be divided between "my father and three brothers" who were not named. The will was recorded on March 7, 1775. James and Joseph Douglass were administrators of the estate, George Blackburn having relinquished his claim (Montgomery County Will Book B, p. 24). The inventory of his estate was taken by George Blackburn, Joseph Black, and Alexander Breckenridge and was recorded on August 1, 1775, and included an extensive selection of goods (Montgomery County Will Book B, p. 29).

In 1777, George Douglas Sr., and Jr., and James Douglass took the oath of allegiance in front of James McGavock. George Douglas is listed in Capt. William Love's Company of Militia in the 1780s. John Douglas was listed in James Newell's Company in 1781, and Thomas Douglas appears on Enoch Ozburn's militia list (Kegley, *Militia*, pp. 19, 20,30,32,52).

In the 1780s, James and John Douglas were paid 8 and 10 shillings respectively, apparently for losses during the Revolutionary War. It is interesting to note that James and Thomas Douglas were also reported as suspected Tories (Kegley and Kegley, *Early Adventurers*, Vol. 1, pp. 127, 144).

In the 1782 tax list for Montgomery County there are only two Douglas men on the list, James and Thomas. Both owned land, and James had 3 slaves, 13 horses and 28 cattle (Kegley, *Tax List,* p. 10). In 1784, in Montgomery County, there is a marriage bond for a George Douglas and Cathrine Harris, with surety by Isam (Isham) Harris. In Wythe County there is a marriage for George Douglass and Elizabeth Williams on November 14, 1795; a Jean Douglas and John Right in 1808; and Polly Douglas and Michael Huffaker in 1799 (Kegley, *Early Adventurers*, Vol. 1, p. 177; Wythe County Marriage Book 1, pp. 14,15,35).

In 1793, James Douglas of Wythe County and George Douglas of Lincoln County, Kentucky, conveyed 330 acres on both sides of Cripple Creek to John Douglas. In 1797, James Douglas conveyed to George Douglas, both of Wythe County, 240 acres part of 400 acres on both sides of Cripple Creek and Vaught's Mill Creek, corner to Newlands. This tract was sold in 1808 to James Newland (Wythe County Deed Book 1, p. 186; Book 2, p. 126; Book 5, p. 112).

James Douglas wrote his will on April 23, 1804, and it was probated in July the same year. To his wife Jane he left the whole of his estate, notes, bonds, houses, cattle, sheep, hogs, household furniture and fanning tools for her lifetime. The blacksmith tools were to go to his son John. He also mentions Jane Davenport, the heirs of Molly Halfaker (probably the same as Huffaker, mentioned above) and the heirs of Becky King. These are probably his daughters, but they are not so identified. Witnesses were his neighbors Money and John Gannaway, and Joseph Newland. Executors were wife Jane, John Douglas, and William Love (Wythe County Will Book 1, p. 195).

In 1805, John Douglas and his wife Anne conveyed 185 acres to Frederick Kinzer, corner to the Tarter land (Wythe County Deed Book 4, p. 300).

On January 28, 1826, John Douglas wrote his will which was probated on May 9 the same year. He left to his wife Ann all land, stock, and "waggon," and after her death to be divided between Logan and John, his sons. Witnesses were John Gannaway, Joshua Martin, and Patsy Martin. Executors were to be his wife Ann, Zachariah Mitchell, and Charles Vaught (Wythe County Will Book 3, p. 193). The inventory of the estate was taken on May 3, 1826, and recorded on October 10, 1826 (Wythe County Will Book 3, p. 232). Among the items listed were cattle, calves, hogs, sheep, a Negro named Jack, copper "wear," wagon and gears, castings and loom, bread tray, tin and pewter ware, saddles and saddle bags, smith tools, and other tools such as augers, saw, shovel, cradle. There were plows, mares, horses, "unbroke" flax, wheat "sives" and cutting box, and a bureau, cupboard and furniture, chests, side saddles, wheels, beds and furniture and bed coverings, several old books, 21 yards of "Genes," a pair of stillards, a grindstone, 30 pounds of wool, a pepper mill and a candle stand. The total value was $790.20.

In September 1834, the widow, Ann Douglas, and John Douglas, and his wife Ann conveyed 214 acres (being half of the plantation devised to him by his father, and being the same John now lives on) to John Gannaway, Sr., Thomas and Seymore Gannaway. Thomas L. [probably Logan] Douglas and his wife Ann, and Ann Douglas the widow of John, deceased, sold 214 acres, the other part of the old tract owned by John Douglas, to Peter Groseclose (Wythe County Deed Book 12, pp. 100, 695). This tract eventually came into the hands of John Groseclose and later David James (Wythe County Deed Book 12, p. 62; Book 29, p. 249; *see also* Gannaway sketch).

Dutton

Philip Dutton (also Dartinger, Dutinger, Darting, Dutting, Turtin, etc.) appears on the head of Cripple Creek as early as 1772, when his name appears on Doak's list of tithables. He also appears the following year. He is paid for providing two beeves and for serving in the militia eight days during 1774. In 1781, he appears on Capt. Love's Company of Militia, and in 1782 he is taxed on land, two tithables, 13 horses, and 17 cattle. Family researchers believe that he is descended from the Duttons (Dartingers) of Shenandoah County, Virginia (Kegley, *Tithables*, pp. 14, 29; Kegley, *Soldiers*, pp. 22, 59; Kegley, *Militia*, pp. 19,20; Kegley, *Tax List*, pp. 9, 11; Shenandoah County Deed Book D, pp. 252,257).

In 1774, Philip purchased a tract of 154 acres on the South Fork of Cripple Creek from James Patton's executors. His name was spelled Turtin in the deed. In 1781, he entered 400 acres on the head of Cripple Creek based on a Commissioner's certificate which was assigned to him by John Wisman, assignee of Samuel Henderson. This was to include a survey made for Henderson in 1774, and the tract was settled in 1772. In Montgomery County he had a tract of 328 acres on the headwaters of Cripple Creek surveyed and granted to him in 1785. He also had 150 acres on Reed Creek, 150 acres on Cripple Creek, 172 acres granted in 1800, and 194 and 37 acres granted in 1810. In Wythe County, he had 12 acres adjoining his patent land and James Douglas, surveyed in 1797 (Kegley, *Early Adventurers*, Vol. 2, pp. 52, 117; Montgomery County Deed Book A, p. 50; Grant Book 46, pp. 107, 116; Book 59, pp. 548, 549; Wythe County Survey Book 1, p. 457).

From various sources, it appears that Philip Dutton was involved with the Tories during the Revolutionary War. In 1779, he was tried and found not guilty, but was required to post bond for his good behavior. The following year on November 8 he surrendered himself to the court, and it was their opinion that he be dismissed and "his person and property protected whilst he behaves," otherwise he was to be tried for his past offenses as an enemy of his country (Summers, *Annals*, pp. 708, 744; Kegley and Kegley, *Early Adventurers*, Vol. 1, pp. 138,139,144, 145).

In 1798, Philip Dutting and his wife Catharine conveyed 110 acres to their son John Dutting, and on the same date conveyed to their son Adam Dutting a tract of 100 acres on Cripple Creek. The following year John sold his tract to John Newland (Wythe County Deed Book 1, pp. 291,294, 320).

Philip Dutton and his wife Catherine had six children: David, Adam, John, Catherine (wife of Christian Phillippi), Mary (wife of Henry Meas or Meese), and Elizabeth (wife of Tobias Arney). David, John, and Mary and her husband Henry were not residents of Virginia in 1824, when lawsuits were brought to settle the estate. Philip died on February 7, 1810, intestate. Tobias Arney and his wife Elizabeth purchased David Dutton's share of the estate (*Dutting vs. Arney et al*, Box 42, 1830, and *Arney vs. Phillippi*, Box 60, 1835, Wythe County Circuit Court Clerk's Office, Basement; Wythe County Will Book 3, p. 261).

In 1815, the tract of land belonging to Philip's estate at the head of Cripple Creek contained 150 acres and was valued at $400 by the tax assessors. The widow claimed one female slave under 12, valued at $300 (Kegley, *Tax Assessment*, p. 121).

Adam the son of Philip known as Adam, Jr., married Catherine Meese, daughter of Thomas, in 1795. He died in Smyth County, Virginia, in 1859. David his brother married Mary Haines, June 17, 1802, and died in Pulaski County, Kentucky, on May 21, 1869. Mary daughter of Philip was married on November 6, 1799, to Henry Meese (erroneously Muse in the marriage record, but also Mees and Meas), a son of Thomas Meese mentioned above. On April 30, 1799, Katherine (Catherine) married Christian Phillippi (Wythe County Marriage Book 1, pp. 8, 15,18,21; family records).

Catherine Dutton, widow of Philip, died March 12, 1827 (Katharine Durting in the will) names her six children in her will written on May 31, 1820, and probated on March 14, 1827. At that time the will was written, daughter Mary Meese was deceased. Catherine's Negro girl Mimy was to be sold and the money divided between the six children. All of her personal property was to be sold immediately after her death and the money divided. Because Mary was deceased, her share was to go to her children. Son-in-law Henry Meese was to have $1. Her clothing was to be divided between daughters Elizabeth and Katharine. Son-in-law *Chrisllough* (Christley or Christian) Phillippy was to be executor. However, he refused to serve and John Stanger was appointed by the court to act as administrator, with the will annexed. The court recorded her name as Catherine Dutton when the will was recorded (Wythe County Will Book 3, p. 261).

In 1826, Tobias Erney (also Arney) and his wife Elizabeth, and the widow Catherine Dutting, sold 395 acres to William W. Sanders. The tract adjoined David Horn and Adam Dutting. However, a prior claim of Nicholas Snider's representatives, by a prior right, claimed 45 acres. Also in 1816, a conveyance was made to Adam Dutting by Christian Phillippy, Peter Phillippy, Barbery [Barbara] Phillippy Copenhaver, Sally Phillippy, Mary Phillippy Steffey, John Phillippy and Catherine Phillippy Buck, the children and heirs of Catherine Phillippy, who was heir of Catherine Dutting, one of the heirs of Phillip Dutting deceased. The interest conveyed was a one-third interest in the 154 acres which was granted to James Patton and sold to Dutton in 1774, and was still owned by Philip at his death. In 1812, David Dutting, Henry Mees, and

Christian Phillippy and Tobias Erney and wife Elizabeth sold 93 acres to Peter Deckart. Although the deed was made in 1812, it was not delivered until March 17, 1828 (Wythe County Deed Book 10, pp. 461,509, 354).

In September 1824, a case was brought by Tobias Arney and his wife Elizabeth against Phillipppi and others, heirs of Philip Dutton. Arney explained that Adam and John had received their part of the land before their father's death, and agreed to make the others equal at the father's death. The Arneys were living on a small tract belonging to the estate, supposed to be about 50 acres, adjoining John Newland, Peter Decard [Deckard], and Adam Dutton. The Arneys purchased all interest of the rest of the heirs who promised title. Another tract of the estate adjoining the first contained 360 acres and Arney bought all interest of the other heirs except Christian Phillipi and his wife. Title was promised by all of the heirs but no deed was received. Arney wanted title to the land. Documents show that David Dutton (Dertinger), Christian Philippy and Henry Mees all conveyed their interest to the land, by title bond. An ad was placed in the *Wythe Gazette* in 1826 indicating that David and John Dutton, and Henry Meas and his wife Mary were not inhabitants of Virginia at the time. Adam Dutton, son of Philip, answered the suit and indicated that he had paid $130 to the others to make them equal, but no deed had been made, and he did not know that it was necessary, but he was willing to execute any deed. However, he believed that the disagreement was between the other heirs and that he was wrongfully before the Court. The case was ended in January 1835, when it was dismissed by J. Stanger, agent for the plaintiff. No deed to Tobias Arney was found in the index to deeds (*Arney vs. Phillippi*, Box 60, Wythe County Circuit Court Clerk's Office, Basement).

A second suit was filed on August 27, 1827, by Adam Dutting, Jr. [son of Philip] against Tobias Arney, Addison Davis, and William Sanders, and although some of the suit papers are missing, further information was obtained. The answer of William W. Sanders filed on May 22, 1828, explains his situation. He stated that Philip had given a 500-acre tract of land to his children David, Henry Meese and wife, and Christian Phillippe and wife. Tobias Arney bought shares of David and the Meeses, and Adam, Jr., bought the share of Phillippi and wife, but was unable to pay for it, so agreed to sell one-half to the defendant Arney. George W. Davis was called upon to do a survey and divide the same, but an error was made, and Adam, Jr., received more than expected and Arney less. Sanders bought from Arney for $2,000 and afterwards discovered that part of the land from Arney was covered by an older and better right of James and John Davis, who claimed under Nicholas Snider, believing the acreage to be about 20 acres, but in fact it was more than 40 acres. Adam, Jr., had more land due to the mistake and to the claim, and if it was corrected, it would have taken much of Adam's cleared land and would have been very injurious to him. Then an agreement was made between Arney and Sanders that Adam should execute an obligation for $66 and the line made by Davis would remain. If Davis' claim was more than 20 acres, then Adam was to bear one-sixth of the cost. Arney had moved from Virginia. Sanders understood that Adam was dissatisfied with the situation, and Sanders offered to give up the obligation and give him $10, if he would agree to set aside the latter agreement to let the parties be "remitted" to their original rights and to have the mistake in the survey corrected. Sanders also believed that although Adam made the deed, he did not have title to the land as it was in all of the heirs of Philip Dutting, deceased. Sanders denied any fraud. Depositions were taken from George W. Davis, Jacob Duttin, and Henry Crider regarding the survey and the agreement regarding the division line. The case was dismissed (*Dutting vs. Tobias Arney et als.* Box 42, 1830, Wythe County Circuit Court Clerk's Office, Basement).

It should be noted that there was another Adam Dutton. He also lived in Wythe County, but on Reed Creek in the Black Lick neighborhood.

Earhart

John Earhart, (sometimes Ahart) Sr., married Margaret Painter in Rockingham County. She was the sister of Mathias Painter who settled on Cripple Creek. The elder Earharts lived in Montgomery County, Virginia, and had six children, several of whom became residents of Wythe County. They were Margaret wife of Eli Davis of Black Lick, George Earhart, Adam Earhart, Mary (Polly) Hutsell, Henry Earhart of Black Lick, and John Earhart, Jr., who settled on Cripple Creek. The will of John Earhart, Sr., recorded in Montgomery County, and was written August 26, 1836, was probated April 5, 1841 (Montgomery County Will Book 6, p. 342). The sons John, George, and Henry were to have $50 in addition to $1,748.50 they had already received. Daughters Margaret Davis and Mary Hutsell were to have $400 in addition to $1,000 they had already received. The youngest son Adam was to have all the land, being 594 acres, and he was to pay the other legatees. Adam also was to have the personal property of the estate. Son George was to be the executor. The land in Montgomery County came from several purchases beginning in 1802 when John Earhart purchased the place on Ingles Mill Creek a branch of North Fork of Roanoke River, where Samuel and Sarah Wilson were then living (Montgomery County Deed Book C, pp. 525,538; Book D, pp. 27,128,388).

In Wythe County in 1809, Henry Keltner [also Kettner], Sr., and his wife "Barbary" conveyed to John Earhart, of Montgomery County, 444 acres, part of a survey of 1,200 acres patented to James Wood, and including the plantation where Keltner was then living. Michael Lease, the former owner, had sold two tracts of land to Keltner (also Kettner) in 1795. Nine years later, John, Sr., and Margaret Earhart, of Montgomery County conveyed to their son John, Jr., 454 acres on Cripple Creek, which was the same tract purchased from Keltner. (Wythe County Deed Book 1, pp. 318,319; Book 5, p. 213).

John Earhart, Jr., (born September 25, 1791) married Polly Stanger (born December 25, 1797, died Jan. 3, 1853) the daughter of the Reverend John Stanger in 1814 (Wythe County Marriage Book 1, p. 46). Four years later they appear to have moved to the land conveyed to them by his father, and it was there they lived out their lives. John Earhart added some of the Nathan Nuckolls' land in 1835, and it was conveyed to George Earhart in 1849. Another part of the same land was conveyed to Alexander Earhart, and a tract of 150 acres was conveyed to John S. Earhart. George Earhart and his wife Matilda conveyed their 224 acres to David Huddle (Wythe County Deed Book 13, pp. 158,159; Book 18, pp. 47,48; Book 20, p. 598).

John Earhart ordered a coffin for his wife who died January 3, 1853. Fleming K. Rich made coffins for many in Wythe County. Notice that she was five feet five inches tall.

Tracing from original by Mary B. Kegley.

In the 1830s and 1840s, there are several lawsuits involving John Earhart, Jr., and his neighbor, Alfred C. Moore. The Moore house burned on Jan. 9, 1837, and the barn and a fence were burned in February or March 1838. Moore believed that Earhart, his son-in-law Wampler, or one of his Negroes, had deliberately set the fires. Because of this belief and statements made in the neighborhood, Earhart sued Moore for slander, asking for $5,000 in damages. Moore was found not guilty, and a motion for a new trial was overruled. The case was sent to the General Court at Richmond, but no errors were found and the judgement was confirmed. Criminal charges were brought against Earhart on October 14, 1839, and continued on several days. He was to be tried before the Judge of the Circuit Superior Court of Law and Chancery, and put up bail in the amount of $1,000. John Stanger and Henry Earhart went on his bond. He was found not guilty. Some of the witnesses testified that the fire began in the garret, and that A. C. Moore was not present at the time of the burning (*Moore vs. Earhart*, Box 68, 1839, Bundle D-Z, and *Earhart vs. Moore*, Bundle 1 and 2, and *Commonwealth vs. Earhart*, Box 72, Bundle 4, Wythe County Circuit Court Clerk's Office, Basement).

John Earhart was also charged with burning the fence at the Moore place, and another suit was brought by Moore and decided in 1844. Again, Earhart was found not guilty. One of the witnesses was Thomas Rutherford, who in 1841 was living in Bloomington, Monroe County, Indiana. At the time of the fires Rutherford lived on the Earhart place, and had frequent conversations with Earhart in the summer and fall of 1837, when Earhart threatened destruction of Moore's property (*Moore vs. Earhart*, Box 75, 1844, Bundle D-Y, Wythe County Circuit Court Clerk's Office, Basement).

John Earhart, Jr., died on June 25, 1859, and is buried in a nearby Huddle Cemetery. The inventory of his estate was taken in September and a sale was held in October the same year (Wythe County Will Book 9, pp. 461,471). Following his death, a suit was brought by Rufus Wampler and wife against David Huddle and others, the heirs of John Earhart. The homeplace was sold in 1862 to the highest bidder who was Alfred C. Earhart, and contained 420 acres less 5 acres claimed by D. G. Shepherd. In 1863, Alfred (A. C. M.) Earhart was living in Monroe County, Virginia [West Virginia] and the entire homeplace of John Earhart was sold to David Huddle. John Earhart's mountain land was conveyed to Eli Earhart, also as a result of the lawsuit (Wythe County Deed Book 22, pp. 619, 620).

A family account book, which showed how much each of the children of John Earhart had received in his lifetime was filed in a lawsuit as evidence. The book began on November 5, 1837, when Earhart listed the items given to Elvira Highley (wife of Lewis). Elvira was the oldest child and was born May 22, 1816, and baptized at the Zion Lutheran Church on July 28, 1816. She married Lewis Highley on July 20, 1837. From her father, she received bed and furniture, a trunk, plates, teacups, knives and forks, a washing tub, a pail, two pots, one oven, one skillet, one smoothing iron, one looking glass, a saddle and bridle, two cows, one mare and colt, a coffee pot, spoons, and plates, and two ladles. Two years later she received a horse valued at $50. The value of the entire account was $244.50 (Wythe County Marriage Book 1, p. 123; Kegley, *Zion*, p. 75; *Earhart vs. Huddle*, Box 113, 1866-1868, Wythe County Circuit Court Clerk's Office, Basement, hereafter *Earhart vs. Huddle*).

Son, Alexander Earhart (born November 27, 1818, and also baptized at Zion Church) was given his portion on November 22, 1839. He received a horse, saddle and bridle, a colt, two cows, one "bar Shear" plow, two shovel plows, a set of harness, an axe and a mattock, one-half of a wheat fan, and one bed. Ten years later he received land valued at $1,000 for a total of $1,212. The address in the account book indicates that Alexander was living in Dayton, Cass County, Missouri, but no date is given (Kegley, *Zion*, p. 82; *Earhart vs. Huddle*).

A page from the account book of John Earhart shows that his daughter Elvira Highley received several items of personal property valued at $244.50. Tracing of original by Mary B. Kegley.

The third entry in the book was for Theresa, wife of Rufus Wampler and was dated March 10, 1841. She was born on February 3, 1821, and was baptized at Zion Lutheran Church. She married Rufus Morgan Wampler on October 26, 1840. She died on October 4, 1899, and he died on October 28, 1878, and both are buried at Kings Grove Cemetery in Wythe County. Theresa received much the same property as her sister Elvira, except she received a churn, a spinning wheel and $20 in cash. In 1853, she received three sets of dog irons [andirons] and land, and in 1858, $200 in cash for a grand total of $595 (Kegley, *Zion*, p. 83; Wythe County Marriage Book 1, p. 150; Shouse, *Wamplers*, pp. 89, 92; *Earhart vs. Huddle*).

On January 2, 1848, John S. Earhart received his share, including the usual animals, tools, a bed, some cash and land valued at $600, for a total of $1,203.16. On February 10, 1858, daughter Margaret, wife of David Huddle, received a young mare, two cows, two beds, and in 1859, six sheep, for a total of $159 (*Earhart vs. Huddle*).

David Huddle, the administrator of the Earhart estate, presented the book to the court, so that the estate could be settled and each child could be made equal. Because some of the heirs lived in Missouri, and because of war difficulties (their attorney was killed in the war), the Wamplers brought suit. In addition to the heirs mentioned in the book, there were two sons, Alfred C. M. Earhart and Eli D. Earhart. These two were in the same Confederate company during the war and served in the northwest. John S. Earhart and George Earhart, sons of John, had moved to Missouri, where Elvira and her brother Alexander were also living. Theresa, Eli D., and Margaret stayed in Wythe County, where many of their descendants remain. In a suit filed after the war, the evidence showed that George and John S. Earhart were deceased, and that Elvira Highley was a widow. Alexander, George, John S., and Elvira were ordered out of Missouri by a Federal Commander in the fall of 1862 and they went to Texas. They had gone to Missouri to "escape the Civil War" (*Earhart vs. Huddle; Earhart vs. Huddle*, 1872, Box 114, 1871-1872, Wythe County Circuit Court Clerk's Office, Basement).

David Huddle (1824-1880) and his wife Margaret P. Earhart Huddle (1831-1911) are buried in a nearby Huddle Cemetery. Following the death of David Huddle the land was partitioned by the court, and the heirs were listed as the widow, Margaret P. Huddle and children: Mary Ellen wife of M. J. Swecker; Margaret E. P. Fulton, wife of S. M. Fulton Jr., who had married since her father's death; Robert E. L. Huddle; N. E. Kyle Huddle; Garland E. Huddle; John H. Huddle; and William D. S. Huddle. All of the children were under 21 except Mary Ellen. At that time, Huddle owned several tracts totaling 1,100-1,200 acres, and a tract of mountain land 200-300 acres. A map was filed with the suit showing the division of the property. The widow received her dower, including the "mansion house" and 311 acres. Some of the land is still in possession of the Huddle family. (*Swecker vs. Huddle*, Box 136, filed February 1881, Wythe County Circuit Court Clerk's Office, Basement).

The Earhart place where the house, now owned by Huddles, is still cared for.
Photo, 1994 by Mary B. Kegley.

In 1792, Henry Eller purchased 225 acres of land on both sides of Cripple Creek from John and Polly Ewing, the same land selected by George Ewing for his son John, and part of the grant to James Woods in 1755 (Wythe County Deed Book 1, p. 104; *Eller vs. Earhart*, Box 72, 1840, Wythe County Circuit Court clerk's Office, Basement).

In 1810, Henry and his wife were both over 45 years of age and had ten slaves. No children were listed in the census (Federal Census, 1810). There is a reference that Catherine Catron was married to a Henry Eller, but which one is not clear (*see* Catron sketch). In 1831, Henry Eller married Jane Davis (Wythe County Marriage Book 1, p. 103).

Henry wrote his will on May 19, 1838, and it was probated on February 11, 1839 (Wythe County Will Book 5, p. 194). His wife Jane was to have one-half of the land and 16 Negroes, and all the bees, kitchen furniture and buildings. Brother Frederick Eller was to have $200; Henry, son of George Eller, his nephew, was to have one-half of the land. Polly Painter, the wife of Alexander Painter, was to have $100. Margaret and Rachel Eller, daughters of Frederick Eller, were to have $100 each.

On April 19, 1839, William M. Chatwell obtained a bond with Robert Holliday for his marriage to Jane, the widow of Henry Eller. George Eller, Jr. married Betsy Gleaves in 1799, and Pressley Lutteral married Elizabeth Eller in 1834 (Wythe County Marriage Book 1, pp. 15,112,142).

On April 20, 1839, Jane Eller, apparently about the time of her marriage to Chatwell, conveyed Mariah, a Negro girl about 10 years of age, to her sister Sarah Davis for love and affection. On the same day, she transferred Martha, a Negro child about 4 years of age, to her sister Elizabeth Holiday, and transferred a Negro boy named Calvin Gleaves, age about 2 years, to the children of her brother William Davis. They were Elizabeth Jane Davis, John Davis, William Davis, Jr., James Davis, Andrew J. Davis, and Henry Davis (Wythe County Deed Book 14, pp. 353,354,355).

It appears that Sarah (Sally) Davis died unmarried in 1848, and that Edmond Lockett, Abner Thompson, Isaac Painter and Alfred C. Moore, or any three, were to appraise the estate. In 1850, J.P. Mathews was ordered to settle with William Chatwell, the administer of the estate, but no record has been found in the will book. The Henry Davis mentioned above may be the same one who was deceased in 1837, and for whom James Davis was appointed administrator (Wythe County Order Book 1837-1840, October 9, 1837, p. 68; Book 1848-1852, pp. 85, 261).

In 1846, Henry Eller and his wife Sarah sold their interest in the land inherited from his uncle (except 40 acres) to William M. Chatwell, and at that time, were living in Morgan County, Indiana (Wythe County Deed Book 15, p. 30). *See also* Chatwell sketch for information about the forge.

Henry Eller filed a caveat against John Earhart, who attempted to claim 119 acres of land which was included in the James Woods' land grant. The men who served to arbitrate the case stated that the land was not vacant at the time of Earhart's entry, and that Earhart had no claim to the land. The original land grant was filed in the case along with maps of the land in question. Eller died some time after September 11, 1838, a date the court ordered the survey in the suit (*Eller vs. Earhart*, Box 72, 1840, Wythe County Circuit Court Clerk's Office).

In 1857, John P. M. Simmerman had an inclusive survey made for 1,030 acres. The tracts included were 225 acres of the John Ewing to Eller land, which Eller devised to his wife, and the same land William Chatwell obtained an interest in through his marriage to Jane Eller. The second tract was 150 acres from John Earhart to William M. Chatwell. The third tract was 10 acres part of 16 1/2, which was part of Earhart's 205 acres granted to him in 1827, which also came into the hands of Chatwell. The fourth tract was one-fourth acre of the Isaac Painter land, also sold to Chatwell. The fifth tract was 184 acres part of 506 acres granted Chatwell in 1848, and the last tract was 167 acres part of 470 acres granted to Chatwell in 1854. All of these tracts were sold to John P. M. Simmerman in 1856. Additional selections were made on treasury warrants (Wythe County Survey Book 4, p. 282).

George Eller, Sr., and George Eller, Jr., are briefly mentioned in the records of Wythe County. Both of them were on a bond the condition of which was that George Eller, Jr., was to permit Betty Brown, alias Dilly [probably a slave], to attend at the Clerk's office for a subpoena for her witness and at trial of a suit she brought against him. He was not to ill treat or misuse her, and was not to remove her out of the state. Nothing else is known of the Ellers (Wythe County Order Book 1799-1801, p. 327; Wythe County Marriage Book 1, p. 15).

George Ewing

The Ewing families of Cripple Creek are believed to be descendants of William and Eliza Ewing who migrated to Northern Ireland about the middle of the 17th Century. They had two sons, Robert (born about 1650) who settled near Londonderry, and William who settled near Coleraine. Alexander, son of Robert, came to America in 1727 and settled in Cecil County, Maryland, and it appears he may be the ancestor of at least some of those who settled on Cripple Creek. William also came to America and died in Cecil County, Maryland, in 1748. His wife was Rachel Porter, daughter of Alexander's sister Margaret and husband Robert Porter. The Porters and Ewings were intermarried many times, probably in Ireland as well as in America. Alexander's will mentions his children James, John, William, and Samuel, and two daughters who married Porters, Margaret and Elinor. These same names appear in Prince Edward County, Virginia, and also in the records pertaining to the New River and Cripple Creek Ewings. (Ewing, *From Whence We Came*, pp. 15-18; *see also* Porter sketch).

Ewings were in Amelia (later Price Edward) County, Virginia, as early as 1745, when a Samuel Ewing purchased land there. Other purchases were recorded for Alexander (1753), George, Jr., (1753), James (1757), Charles (1760), and Thomas (1755). Amelia County records also show that James Ewing appointed Joshua Ewing of Cecil County, Maryland, as his attorney to sell James' land in Maryland in 1750. The earliest Ewing will recorded in Prince Edward County was for Samuel Ewing, who wrote his will September 13, 1758. It was probated on October 10, 1758. He mentions children George, Alexander, Jane, Alener (Eleanor), Margaret and Ann. His wife was Margaret. He also mentions three grandsons, Samuel son of George Ewing, Samuel son of Alexander Ewing, and Samuel Caldwell (Amelia County Deed Book 2, p. 142; Book 3, p. 371; Book 4, p. 545; Prince Edward County Deed Book 1, pp. 27, 95, 134; Prince Edward County Will Book 1, p. 17).

In 1770, the Prince Edward County records show that George Ewing, Alexander Ewing, William Ewing, Jane Ewing, John Caldwell, Ellener Caldwell, James Ewing, Margaret Ewing, and Ann Ewing were of Prince Edward County and Botetourt County [this latter county covered what is now Wythe County in 1770], but the record does not state which ones were in which county (Prince Edward County Deed Book 3, p. 448).

The Samuel Ewing of Cecil County, Maryland, and Russell County, Virginia, has been well documented by Turnell in her article , and does not seem to be of the immediate family of Ewings of Cripple Creek. He was a descendant of William the son of Alexander, through his son Joshua. However, it should be noted that Samuel son of George was also living in Russell County, as mentioned below (*see* Turnell, "Samuel Ewing, Cecil County Md. ca. 1740-Russell County Virginia, 1817," *The Colonial Genealogist,* Vol. 6, No. 1, (Winter 1973), pp. 75-77).

Because of the intense repetition of given names in the Ewing family, it can not be determined from the court records the exact relationship of all of those who came to Cripple Creek. It is important to note, however, that a family Bible which was in existence in 1939 in Ivanhoe (Wythe County) was owned by a descendant of the Cripple Creek/New River Porters. The Bible appears to have belonged to James Ewing, who was born August 8, 1728 and entered his name in the Bible on January 21, 1746/7. Another entry shows that the Bible was bought in the year 1727 by Alexander Ewing of Ireland, who departed this life aged sixty-one, May ye 7, 1738. Another entry gives the date 1737/8. It is presumed that this is the Alexander who came to America in 1727. James appears to have had brothers, John born 1725, William, 1728/9, another child whose name is not legible born March 1729, and Samuel born March 10, 1738. There are also several entries which mentioned Porter names, including a Mary Porter who was born on November 29, 1743 (undated newspaper clipping; Bible not seen).

In 1771, the names Samuel, James, and George Ewing are mentioned in the Cripple Creek/New River records. In 1772, the names of George, Samuel, and James Ewing were mentioned on Herbert's tithable list, and in the same year, Capt. Doack's company lists William Ewing and his servant, and "Alixander" Ewing and his son James. In 1773, Alexander and his son Samuel, William Ewing, and Alexander Ewin [Ewing] appear on Doack's list of tithables (Kegley, *Tithables*, pp. 11, 14, 17,18).

In 1774, Samuel Ewing served 22 days as a sergeant in Capt. Walter Crockett's Company and was paid £2.15 for his service. A Samuel Ewing also appears in Doak's Company and was paid for four days service. In 1782, five Ewings appear on the tax rolls. They were Alexander, George (perhaps two of them), John, Samuel, and Samuel, Junr. (Kegley, *Soldiers*, pp. 28,47; Kegley, *Tax List*, p. 11). Names which appear in the local militia companies 1777 to 1790 included George, George, Jr., James, John, John, Jr., Samuel, Samuel, Jr., and William (Kegley, *Militia,* pp. 19,20,30, 31,37,51,53,54, 55). From various wills, it was determined that John, William, James, and Samuel were brothers, and had sisters Margaret and Eleanor, who both married Porters (*see below*). None of these documents mention George as their brother, and there is no mention of parents' names in the records.

It should also be noted that in 1782, George, John, Samuel and William were listed on the tax rolls of Montgomery County, Virginia, but there were also numerous Ewings in Bedford County, a few in Augusta County, and a few in Lincoln County, Kentucky, at the same time, including Samuel, John, James, and a William (Fothergill, *Virginia Tax Payers,* p. 41).

Samuel Ewing

There were at least two Samuel Ewings who appear in the early New River records. One was the brother to James, William, and John Ewing, of New River and Cripple Creek, and the other, the son of a George Ewing. Sometimes the records designate Sr., and Jr., but not in every case. It appears from the records, that Samuel,

421

the elder, was in the neighborhood as early as 1768 and probably located on 650 acres of land on the New River, which he purchased from the heirs of Alexander Sayers in 1774. This conveyance came as a result of an agreement between William Preston, who was an executor of John Buchanan, and Ewing. The claim was identified as one-half of the tract Ewing "now lives on," on New River, near the lead mines. Ewing had to pay £178 plus £6.12 for quitrents to the executors for the land. In the same year he conveyed 80 acres to James Ewing. The deeds describe the property as 650 acres which was granted to Humberston Lyon on November 7, 1752, and leased and released July 3, 1755 (Summers, *Annals*, p. 669; Montgomery County Deed Book, B, p. 12; Book A, pp. 54, 75).

In 1774, one of the Samuels served 22 days as a sergeant in Crockett's Company, and 4 days under Captain Robert Doak. In 1777, a Samuel was appointed first lieutenant in Capt. Pearce's Company and became Captain in room of Captain Pearce in 1781. In 1782, Samuel Ewing, Jr., is listed on Capt. James Newell's Company, and took the oath of allegiance to the State of Virginia. One of the Samuel Ewings took the list of tithables in 1781 in Morgan's, Newell's and Ozburn's companies (Kegley, *Soldiers*, pp. 28,47; Kegley, *Militia*, pp. 37, 31, 54; Summers, *Annals*, pp. 751,752).

In 1779, Samuel Ewing, Sr., was to serve as one of the appraisers of the estate of Benjamin Castle. The road order of 1778 refers to Samuel Ewing, Sr., as follows: "Patrick Campbell, Henry Francis, and Adam Dean are appointed to view the road from where the Carolina Road crosses Poplar Camp Mountain and thence crossing the New River at Samuel Ewings." This viewing of the road followed a petition submitted to the court by the "sundry inhabitants of the county setting forth the necessity of opening a road..." (Summers, *Annals*, pp. 693, 696, 722).

In 1779, Samuel Ewing, Jr., served on the jury and was appointed a justice of the peace and justice of the Court in Chancery and Oyer and Terminer (Summers, *Annals*, pp. 721).

The elder Samuel Ewing's will was written on June 3, 1783, and was probated in Montgomery County on May 23, 1786. His land on the Cumberland in North Carolina, containing 1,920 acres, his land in Kentucky 200 acres, and his land on the Clinch were to be sold to pay debts and funeral expenses and the balance divided. His wife Mary was to have the tract of land where he lived for life, and also certain Negroes. Two other Negroes were lent to her for a period of six years. She also had the use of the household goods and stock for life, as well as the crops in the ground. His brother James Ewing was to be maintained for life. To Robert Porter son of his sister Margaret Porter, he devised the lower end of the land in return for paying Betty Porter and Fanny Purnal £40, when of age. To his sister Margaret Porter's son Samuel Porter, he devised the other half of the land after his wife's death. He was to pay Margaret Porter and Sarah, her sister, £40 a piece when of age. His silver watch, valued at £5 sterling was to go to Alexander Ewing, Jr., son of his brother John. To his sister Margaret Porter's daughter Elender [Eleanor] Porter he bequeathed the Negro Zeb at the end of six years, and six years after his decease her daughter Rebecca Porter was to have a Negro wench named Cato. All stock and household goods to be sold and money divided equally after his wife's death. His wife Mary and James Ewing were to act as executors. Witnesses were Mainitree Jones, George Birde [Byrd], and William Birde [Byrd] (Montgomery County Will Book B, p. 81). These Porters gave the name Porter's Ford to the crossing of the New River near Ivanhoe.

The inventory of the estate of Samuel Ewing was taken by James McGavock, Samuel Smith, and Hugh McGavock, on June 14, 1786. Among the items listed were cows, heifers, calves, cows, steers, mares, colts, horses, sheep, an ox cart, two churns, pails and tub, an iron pot, a tea kettle, a copper kettle, a grid iron, pot hook, and a pair of tongs, a pair of fire dogs [andirons], a plow shear, 11 pewter plates, 4 pewter basons, 3 pewter dishes, 3 spinning wheels, a teapot, 6 cups and 5 saucers, 6 stone plates, a bowl, a pepper box, a salt "seller," a black walnut table, 6 walnut chairs, 2 looking glasses, feather beds and furniture, a plow iron, a Negro man named Zeb (valued at £70), a Negro woman Kate (valued at £60), a grind stone, a hair trunk, a tea chest, a quantity of wool, 3 axes, 20 hogs, and 16 pigs, and a quantity of feathers. The record of a sale was also recorded (Montgomery County Will Book B, pp. 98, 120).

Mary, Samuel's wife, received a release of the interest of Robert Sayers and his mother Mary Sayers Prickett (Pritchard), and in 1786 the tract was designated as where Mary Ewing now lives (Montgomery County Deed Book A, p. 453).

Mary Ewing was deceased before December 28, 1790, and Hugh Montgomery was the administrator of her estate. Appraisal of her property was ordered, but was not recorded (Wythe County Minute or Order Book 1790-1791, p. 40).

Samuel did not mention any children in his will, but was generous to his brothers and sisters and their families.

James Ewing

James Ewing appears briefly in the records, beginning about 1774, when he purchased 80 acres of land on the south side of New River from Samuel Ewing, probably his brother (Summers, *Annals*, p. 669; Montgomery County Deed Book A, p. 75; *see* map of Lead Mines tract elsewhere for location). There is no record that James was married. He wrote his will in 1783, but it was not probated until November 8, 1791 (Wythe County Will Book 1, p. 15). He devised all of his real estate to his brother Samuel [who predeceased him]. He noted that he owed Euphame (Euphamy) Purnel (Purnell) a debt and paid it by devising to her a breeding mare valued at £10. He mentions Robert Porter's children and Andrew Porter's children in his will. The Porter men had married two of his sisters, Margaret and Eleanor. James also had brothers William and John Ewing. The names of their parents are not mentioned in any local record, but this is probably the James who owned the Bible mentioned above in the George Ewing sketch, and who appears to be a son of Alexander Ewing of Ireland. Euphamy Purnell may have been the one who married Alexander Ewing, Jr., in 1786. Her mother Mary Ewing gave consent to the marriage (Montgomery County Marriages; *see also* Kegley, *Early Adventurers*, Vol. 2, p.180).

The estate of James Ewing was listed on January 10, 1792, and included horses, mare, colts, feather bed and blankets, chest, iron pot, dutch oven, pot racks, steel trap, flax hackle, a large Bible, 5 "puter" plates, a pair of spoon "moles," a prayer book, yards of "Durrant," blue broad cloth, an old saddle, a pair of leather breeches, a green jacket, a hat, a great coat, a small coat, a "callin" coat and jacket, two old shirts, a brand and iron, a pair of steelyards, a "guilt" [gilt? or quilt ?] trunk, bottle, vials, stockings, a razor strap, grindstone, bells, a candlestick, a pr. of garters, a quantity of flax, wheat and "wry," side leather, and buttons. The appraisal was done by Robert Sanders, James Newell, Robert Sayers, and Stephen Sanders (Wythe County Will Book 1, pp. 17-19).

In 1823, Samuel Porter and his wife Ursley (Usla) conveyed all interest in the land on the east side of the New River and both sides of the road that crossed the road leading to Porters Ford, being part of the land devised to Samuel Porter and others by James

Ewing's will, to Thomas Jackson (Wythe County Deed Book 9, p. 391). When Samuel Porter, Senr., died, his land at Porter's Ford was divided between Samuel E. Porter and Jordan Porter, his sons. William Porter's interest in the land at Porter's Ford actually belonged to his father, Robert Porter, Sr., but William had the tract in his possession and had cultivated it for several years. His interest passed by his will to his brother, Andrew Porter, Jr., in 1817 (Wythe County Will Book 2, p. 176; for further details about the Porter's Ferry and Ford, see Kegley, *Bicentennial History*, pp. 63, 65, 342, and a map elsewhere in this publication; for details about James, son of George Ewing, Sr., *see below.*).

John Ewing

Two John Ewings appear in the early records, one the brother to James, Samuel, and William and the other a son of George Ewing. John Ewing's will, written January 25, 1787, was recorded March 5, 1788, in Montgomery County (Will Book B, p. 128).

To his daughter Eleanor Cocke he left a brown mare with other items he had already given her. His son Alexander was to receive his desk and one young bay mare and colt. Son William was to have Negro man Zeb and a woman named Kate, and the land in Powells Valley in Russell County being 1,300 acres; also one feather bed and furniture, and one bay mare four years old.

Sons William and Charles Coake to have my whip saw and cross cut saw. Daughter Betsy was to have 300 acres of land known as Cocke's old tract, if she comes there to live, and if not to remain in the possession of son William. She was also to have one bay mare three years old next spring. Grandson John Cocke was to have 200 acres of land at the mouth of Trading Creek including both sides of the creek. The household furniture was to be divided between the two sons. William was to pay his brother Alexander £70 in horses at the valuation of two different men. Son Alexander was to have the tract on Elk Creek in Montgomery County, 1,100 acres if obtained. Sons William and Alexander were to be executors. Witnesses were five men named Montgomery: John, Senr., John, Junr., Samuel, Robert, and Joseph.

The other John Ewing appears as a soldier of the Revolutionary War, being paid 10/ for a blanket lost in the Battle in North Carolina. He also appears as an Ensign in Captain James Newell's Company in 1787 and in 1790 appears as Ensign for the Wythe County militia (Summers, *Annals,* pp. 771, 818, 1357).

This John moved to Logan County, Kentucky, where on April 3, 1833, he applied for a pension for services in the Revolution (S31015). He was then 72 years old and stated he was born in Prince Edward County, Virginia, in June 1761, and when he was about ten years old he moved with his father (not named) to Montgomery County, later Wythe County.

He entered the service in 1778, when he volunteered in the militia under Captain Henry Francis, William Gleaves as Lieutenant. He made his rendezvous at the lead mines and marched from there to the waters of the Yadkin River in North Carolina under Col. Crockett and General William Campbell. They took a captain of the Tory party and hung him. He also served thirty days at the mines, guarding the Tories who were prisoners there.

When Isaac Campbell and Robert Sawyers [Sayers] were directed to raise two companies of Light Horse or Rangers to serve for ten months and to hold themselves in readiness to march at a moments notice, Ewing again volunteered under Campbell and again rendezvoused at the lead mines. At that place, Col. Abraham Trigg took command, and they marched up the New River, crossing at Jones's Ford, proceeding across the mountain to the headwaters of the Yadkin River. Here, they met a party of Tories under the company of Captain Kyle. They killed twelve to twenty of them and dispersed the balance. It was here his former Captain, Henry Francis, was killed, being the only "Whig that was touched by the enemy." From the battle, they went to the Moravian towns where they found Col. William Campbell with about 300 men. Here, he received an account of the death of Col. Beaufort. He was then sent by General Campbell to the Waxhaw settlement not far from the Catawba River. On his return to the camp, he was informed that Sumpter had been defeated. He served six months, and never received a dollar for his services, and he furnished his own horse, equippage and arms.

In 1780, he again volunteered in a company of militia under Captain James Newell and Lieutenant William Gleaves. They met on the south side of the New River at Herbert's Ferry, at the mouth of Poplar Camp Creek. Here, he was placed under the command of Cols. Preston, Crockett, and Cloyd, and marched then across the mountains to Guilford County, North Carolina. They were joined there by General William Campbell, who had about eight men under his command. They marched to Guilford County Courthouse, but were ordered from there to General Greene's army. They contemplated capturing Col. Tarlton, but a Tory deserted from the army and gave information about the attack, and Tarlton left his camp in the night and crossed the Haw River at a place called High Rock Ford. They pursued him, until they met Col. Lee, who informed them that they must retreat for they were in the immediate neighborhood of the main British Army under Cornwallis. The morning after they reached camp, General Greene advised them to send their horses home, as they were going into battle and they might lose them. They moved out to Whitsell's Mill on Reedy Fork of Haw River and there formed the line of battle against Cornwallis. They formed their line near the old mills and fired two rounds, and then were ordered to retreat because they were almost surrounded by Cornwallis' Army. In the retreat, he recalled that an old Irish man by the name of Buckhannon took shelter in the old mill and fired upon and killed an Englishman. They were defeated and dispersed, but "rendezvoused" and were then sent home from Guilford Courthouse. The whole campaign took about thirty or forty days.

William Ewing

William Ewing, brother to John, James, and Samuel Ewing, was probably located on Cripple Creek before 1771. In that year, he appears in the records when he was taken into custody for his "contempt of laws of the County" and was to remain in custody until he proved two securities of £25 each, and until he provided a bond of £50 for himself. This bond was for "good behavior for twelve months and a day." William Herbert and Henry Francis provided the smaller bonds (Summers, *Annals*, pp. 122,123).

In 1772, Ewing is listed on Doak's tithable list with one servant. In 1773, he is listed with three tithables. In 1773 and 1779, he served on the jury. His mark was recorded in 1773, "a smooth crop of left ear, the right ear half crop and the hind part cut off." Alexander Caldwell of Fincastle County sold to William Ewing a Negro boy named Archy on March 2, 1772. In March 1775, he had 214 acres surveyed for him (Kegley, *Tithables*, pp. 14, 29,30; Summers, *Annals,* pp. 604, 617, 620,723; Montgomery County Deed Book A, p. 61; Montgomery County Survey Book A, p. 187).

In 1773, William Ewing and his wife Jane sold 330 acres to James and George Douglass, near the head of Cripple Creek and in 1782 purchased from John Montgomery, attorney for Alexander Noble of South Carolina, 556 acres "where said William Ewing now lives." This latter tract was west of the present Town of Speedwell. In 1782, he also purchased 120 acres from John Reaugh, a tract which adjoined his residence. He also had surveys made in 1783, for 307 acres and 193 acres. In 1784, he had a tract of 86 acres adjoining his own surveyed (Montgomery County Survey (Plotts) Book B, pp. 141, 142; Book C, p. 37; Summers, *Annals*, pp. 668, 913, 914; Montgomery County Deed Book A, pp. 22, 256, 259, 289).

William Ewing's will was written in 1791 and probated on July 9, 1793. He bequeathed to his wife Jane certain Negroes, Jacob, Luce and Sal, and lent her one-half of the land, including the buildings, for her lifetime. His brother John's son Alexander was to have one-half of the land, and at Jane's death to have the entire plantation. Sister Margaret Porter's son, Robert, was to receive a Negro named Jacob at Jane's death, and her daughter Rebeckah Porter was to receive a Negro woman Sal, and John's son, Alexander, was to receive a Negro boy Henry at Jane's death. Sister Elanor [Eleanor] Porter's grandson, Andrew Porter, was to have a Negro girl Peg, and brother John's son, William Ewing, was to receive the tract of land on the "Tenace" containing 640 acres, and the land on the Cumberland, if obtained. Sister Margaret Porter's son, Robert, was to have a horse. The executors were Jehu Stephens, Robert Buckhannon, Robert and Samuel Porter. Witnesses were Samuel Ewing, Marks Hart, and Peter Powers (Wythe County Will Book 1, p. 22).

The inventory of William Ewing's estate was taken and a sale held in 1793. William Neeley, John Newland and Thomas Gannaway were appraisers, and recorded the documents in September 1805. The list shows that Ewing owned Negro man Jacob, Negro boy Jacob, Negro women, Lucy, Peggy, and Sally, and a child Nancy. Also listed were horses, mares colts, waggon and gears, a cart with a yoke, steelyards, tools of many kinds (including a carpenter's hammer), a Conk Shell, a lantern and candle box, churns, pickling tubs, bee hives, ploughs, coffee mill, pot racks, spinning wheel, ovens, flax hackle, pewter of various kinds, sheep, table, copper kettle, a dozen chairs, a gun and powder horn, 18 harrow teeth, 7 geese, round table, beds, chest of drawers, looking glass, a bag of wool, two Bibles, *Confession of Faith*, a steel trap, spoon moulds, and 17 weaver spools (Wythe County Will Book 1, pp. 405, 408,409)

The William Ewing place was sold by Alexander Ewing to William Gannaway of Buckingham County, in 1793. (*see* Gannaway sketch, and also Porter sketch for lawsuit involving some of the land).

George Ewing

George Ewing, the elder, settled on part of the James Wood tract and received a deed for 900 acres in 1779 from the executors. It was probably where he lived from the time of his arrival on Cripple Creek (Montgomery County Deed Book A, p. 222). His relationship to the others mentioned above, has not been exactly determined, but he *may be* the son of the Samuel who died in Prince Edward County in 1745. However, it should be noted that there was another George who was a pensioner of the Revolutionary War, also from Prince Edward County; *see below*.

The name George Ewing appears several times in the Botetourt, Fincastle, and Montgomery County records where he served on juries in 1771, 1773, 1774, and 1779. He served as an appraiser of the estates of William Herbert (1776) and Captain Henry

426

Francis (1780). He is also mentioned in connection with roads of the Cripple Creek area. In 1773, a road was to be worked from the lead mines to John Newlands (near the head of Cripple Creek), and George Ewen [Ewing] was overseer of that part from the mines to the land of Henry Francis [now the Town of Cripple Creek], and from there Francis was in charge up to Newlands. Overseers were to take the road the nearest and best way (Summers, *Annals*, p. 608).

In 1773, William Herbert was overseer of the road from his ferry to the head of Poplar Camp Creek, and Thomas Foster from there to the forks of the road beyond the Boiling Springs, and Felty Vanhouser was to be the overseer from the head of Poplar Camp Creek to the Pittsylvania line and Herbert was to lay off the hands between Francis and George Ewen [Ewing] (Summers, *Annals,* pp. 612-613).

One of the George Ewings was recommended to the Governor as a proper person to serve as Ensign of Militia in Capt. Love's Company. This was probably the George who filed for a pension in Tennessee. Also a George (probably the same one) was paid 8 shillings for a blanket lost while on duty in North Carolina when he was in action at Reedy Fork (Summers, *Annals*, pp. 758, 771; *see below*).

In 1778, the road from the lead mines to Newlands was to be continued with Adam Dean as overseer from the mines to Thorn Branch and George Ewing from there to the land of Captain Francis, and David Miller from there to John Maxwell's, and James Douglass from there to John Newlands. James Newell and Samuel Ewing, Junr., were to allot the hands to work on the lower part of the road and William Ewing and Robert Reaugh the same on the upper part, and they were to keep the same in repair according to law (Summers, *Annals,* p. 694).

In 1777, James McCorkle, Gent., was appointed overseer of the road from the lower ford of Reed Creek to McCaul's fording in the room of James Simpson and with all the tithables on this side of Reed Creek and this side of New River along by the mines and up as far as William Henley's on Cripple Creek and across from there to the cove including all the hands below the cove from John Boyd's down to Peak Creek, and to keep the same in repair. John Crockett and James Newell were to allot the hands to work on the road including George Ewing, Samuel Ewing, Samuel Ewing, Junr., Bartlet Green, and John Rutherford on Cripple Creek (Summers, *Annals*, p. 681).

A George Ewing had two surveys made in 1783, 400 acres on Hobbs Branch, the same tract settled in 1772 and assigned by Thomas Hobbs to Ewing and certified by the Commissioners of Washington and Montgomery County, and 168 acres on a small branch running through Samuel Ewing's patent land which was granted to him (Summers, *Annals,* p. 885; Montgomery County Survey Book B, pp. 138, 140; Grant Book N, p. 365; microfilm reel, 358, p. 285, Virginia State Library, Archives).

George Ewing conveyed 225 acres, for love and affection, to his son, Samuel Ewing in 1785, and also 225 acres to his son George in 1786. These tracts were part of his "old deeded patent land" on Cripple Creek (Montgomery County Deed Book A, pp. 369,389).

George Ewing and his wife Elener conveyed 568 acres in two tracts to Samuel Nuckolls of Louisa County, Virginia, in 1797. The land adjoined Nathaniel Nuckolls, Henry Eller and Phil. Goins [Gaines] (Wythe County Deed Book 2, p. 229).

On March 11, 1803, George Ewing wrote his will, which was probated in June 1804 (Wythe County Will Book 1, p. 284). His wife Elenor was to live on part of the land "I now live on" with son James Ewing, and to use the personal property with son James. Certain Negroes were to go to son James. Other sons mentioned were Samuel, John, and George. Daughters mentioned were Anne Cozbie, Mary, Margaret Purdom, and Eleanor who was still single. Son George was to have the land on the north side of Cripple Creek where he lived with Cripple Creek as the dividing line. Son James was to have all land on the south side of Cripple Creek, where his father was living, and a meadow which "lies on mouth of a branch which runs down through George Ewing's plantation." James was to have blacksmith tools. The still was to be sold. If lands in Kentucky were obtained, they were to be sold. Some Negroes (named in the will) were to be sold. The four sons were to be executors. Witnesses were John Rogers, Richard Hobbs, and Johanner [Johanna] B. Baber. The land for George Ewing, Jr., and James Ewing included 325 acres for George, and 663 for James, and the lines were laid off according to the description in the will (Wythe County Deed Book 4, pp. 460, 461).

The appraisal and sale of George Ewing are also recorded in Wythe County Will Book 1, pp. 300, 326, 328). The goods included a wagon and gears and four horses, a Negro Bet, and a Negro boy Cuff, a still cap and worm, cows and calves, and a bull, and 7 still tubs.

James Ewing (son of George Ewing, Sr.) living in Bedford County, Tennessee, in 1822, sold 533 acres on Cripple Creek to James Bell, who conveyed the same to Isaac Painter in 1862 (Wythe County Deed Book 13, p.737; Book 22, p. 401). This was the same land laid off to James under the terms of his father's will. It was probably the same James who conveyed 130 acres to Joseph Bell in 1821 (Wythe County Deed Book 8, p. 240).

George Ewing, Jr., wrote his will on February 21, 1837, and it was probated April 9, 1838 (Wythe County Will Book 5, p. 45). His wife Margaret was to remain in the house and to be supported. Son John was to move in with her after George's death and was to attend to her comfort and to her support. Samuel, the oldest son (now in Russell County), was to have the land he resided on in that county, "the right of which now lys in my son John." The tract was purchased by George for John and Samuel. Margaret, the eldest daughter of son Samuel, and Emily, Evalina, and Polly, daughters of Samuel, were to share in the Negroes. Son John was to have the tract where George was living, and also a tract purchased of Joseph Bell, all stock, tools, blacksmith tools etc. Son Joshua was to have the land where "he now lives," to wit: purchased by me from Finney Rutherford. Other children mentioned were: George, and Sally wife of Patrick Ewing. Son John and James Gleaves were to be executors. Witnesses were Isaac Painter, James Fisher and A. C. Moore. The deed from Rutherford was dated 1833, and was a tract of 214 acres where Rutherford was living (Wythe County Deed Book 12, p. 463).

On May 14, 1838, three of the children of George Ewing, deceased, Margaret, Emily, and Evelina, "upwards of age 14," chose Andrew Porter for their guardian, and he was appointed by the court to act for Polly, who was under age 14 (Wythe County Order Book 1837-1840, p. 131).

The appraisal of the estate of George Ewing, deceased, was taken by James T. Gleaves and John Ewing, and dated May 14, 1838, and recorded on August 13 the same year (Wythe County Will Book 5, p. 90). Among the interesting items listed were 43 hogs, 800 bushels of corn, 60 sheep, a wagon and gear, harrow and plows, a wheat fan, fodder and hay, colt, mares, horses, fillys, cattle, cows, calves, a broadax and a foot ads [adz], augers, a drawing knife, some iron, a cradle, 12 bushels of salt, 50 bushels of oats, 15 bushels of buckwheat, 20 bushels of rye, and 20 bushels of wheat. There were also washing tubs, plates and crocks, 600 pounds of bacon, a loom and five wheels, castings, a bee stand, Negro boys named Stephen, Squire, Sampson, Peter, Abraham, and Charles, Negro girls named Sharlet, Charity, Mackey, Diana, and a child named Mary, a boy named Burrell, a girl Phebe, and a sick girl Frankey. There were also blacksmith tools, a pattent clock, three barrels, cupboard and furniture, tables, chests, a shot gun, rifle, a check reel, shovel tongs, a looking glass, beds and furniture, wool, chairs, flax thread, books, saddle and bridle, a coffee mill, knives and forks, tow and flannel, $105 in gold, $357.87 1/2 in silver, and $145.00 in bank notes.

On June 11, 1838, an allotment and division of slaves was done, assigning 13 slaves valued at $5,785.00 to six distributees: James Ewing, the children of Samuel Ewing, Patrick Ewing, Joshua Ewing, John Ewing, and George Ewing (Wythe County Will Book 5, p. 212). Some accounts were recorded in 1840, which mentioned legatees Joshua and Patrick Ewing, and Andrew Porter, the guardian for Margaret Highley, Emily Ewing, Evalina, and Polly Ewing (Wythe County Will Book 5, p. 335).

The John Ewing mentioned as the son of George and Margaret Ewing appears to be the one who died about 1845, when the appraisal of his estate was taken on December 19 of that year. Among the items listed in his estate were: a bureau, beds, 15 chairs, a safe, a large table, a clock, looking glass, chest, an old desk, andirons, 7 sides of underleather, a lot of tan deer skins, a piece of sole leather, a new saddle, part of a barrel of salt, old tools, 2 flax wheels, a loom, castings, 2 pot racks, a kitchen table, cupboard, 2 toe [tow] wheels, 1800 pounds of poark [pork], a barrel of salt, steelyards, a brass kettle, a grindstone, 20 bushels of wheat, 10 bushels of buckwheat and barley, hoes, sythes, cradles, 4 bushels of flaxseed, 500 bushels of corn at 40 cents each, axes, hoes, horses, colts, mares, 20 sheep, 9 cows, yearlings, steers, calves, plows, a windmill, sheaf wheat, hay, Irish potatoes, smith tools, 12 bushels of wheat, 10 tan sheep skins, 3 cow hides, 2 hog hides, currying knives, augers, chisels, iron, a Negro Phebe, a Negro Sampson, Abram, Thurza, and Elbert, a bark mill, a lot of books, and a square and a hand saw (Wythe County Will Book 6, p. 494).

In 1847, the court was ordered to assign the dower in the slaves of Mary Ewing, the widow of John Ewing, deceased. On April 12, 1847, she was assigned slaves named Sampson and Charlotte, who were among the Negroes listed above. On November 11, 1847, Mary Ewing married James B. Johnston, and on January 10, 1848 James T. Gleaves, Thomas Sanders, Alfred C. Moore, and William M. Chatwell were to assign the dower in land to Mary Johnston, late the widow of John Ewing. It was returned to court on February 14, 1848, but no record has been found in the usual books (Wythe County Marriage Book 1, p. 172; Wythe County Order Book 1842-1848, April 12, 1847, pp. 509, 597, 605; Wythe County Will Book 6, p. 480).

On March 13, 1848, James and Jane Ewing, upwards of age 14, chose Lee Nuckolls as their guardian, and the court appointed him for Elizabeth, Kent, Caroline and Amanda (Wythe County Order Book 1848-1852, p. 2).

In the 1850s, Lee Nuckolls, guardian for James, Mary Jane, Elizabeth, Kent, Caroline, and Amanda Ewing, minor children of John Ewing deceased, brought a suit in court to have the 369 acres of land owned by them sold. They also owned eleven slaves and had between $1,500 and $2,000 in money. The first three children were over fourteen and the last three under that age. Both parents were deceased. James, Jane, and Elizabeth filed an answer agreeing to the sale in 1851 (*Lee Nuckolls guardian vs. James Ewing*, Box 103, 1850-1854, Wythe County Circuit Court Clerk's Office, Basement).

In 1851, Lee Nuckolls had certain slaves belonging to the children, (Phoebe, Charlotte, Sampson, Abraham, Thirza, Elbert, Sarah and Wythe) in his possession. The accounts list them by age (Wythe County Will Book 7, p. 290). Numerous settlements were made by Nuckolls in the 1850s in which the children and their expenses are listed. In the 1857 settlement he mentions that Margaret E. married E. G.

Greggons, and later mentions that Elizabeth has married E. F. Gregory (Wythe County Will Book 7, pp. 319, 545, 554; Book 8, pp. 62, 364, 444; Book 9, pp. 95, 272, 395, 554).

On September 23, 1853, Mary Jane Ewing wrote her will and it was probated on June 12, 1854 (Wythe County Will Book 8, p. 253). She mentions money from her father's [John's] estate to go equally to her brothers and sisters, including her half sister Laura A. Johnson. Negro Thirza was to go to Lydia C. Ewing, and if she had any children Amanda C. Ewing was to have the first child and Laura A. Johnson the second. If more children, they were to be divided between her other brothers and sisters.

George Ewing

It is interesting to note that another George Ewing whose wife was also named Margaret, at one time lived on Cripple Creek. He filed his Revolutionary Service claim in Blount County, Tennessee, in 1832, when he was 72 years old (Pension W9, National Archives). He stated that he was born in Prince Edward County in 1760 and at an early age moved to Montgomery County, where he was drafted into service in 1778 for a period of eighteen months. He served under Lieut. James Crawford, and marched to guard the frontier station on the head of the Clinch River. He also marched to the lead mines under Captain Love, Col. William Campbell's Regiment. He was also under Captain Isaac Campbell, who had about 100 men under his command and marched to various places, sometimes in Virginia and sometimes in North Carolina. In the latter state, they had a skirmish with the British on Reedy Fork of Haw River, following which he was detached and sent off to the Moravian towns with the wounded. He then returned home.

In 1783, he moved to Tennessee, to a county not then formed. He resided there, in the area which became Blount County, for 48 years and was an acting justice of the peace there for 37 years. He married Margaret Caldwell on January 3, 1786, and their children were John, Rachel, Alexander, Eleanor, Margaret, and Samuel.

Additional affidavits were taken in 1844, and at that time James Ewing, age 76 of Monroe County, Tennessee, stated that he was present at the wedding of George and Margaret. Robert Rhea of Blount County, Tennessee, age 84, stated that he knew both of them, and knew George had served in the Revolutionary War because they served together under Colonel Walter Crockett and Major Joseph Cloyd. They marched from the New River to North Carolina through Burke and Rutherford counties, and hung several Tories on their route. They were in the skirmish at Shallow Ford, under Cloyd. They met a party of 400 Tories at that place, and ''put them to flight,'' James Wyly (Wyley), age 82, of Blount County, Tennessee, stated that he had served in the same company with George Ewing.

There is no relationship stated between James and George, and no mention is made of the parentage of this George Ewing. Extensive family Bible records were filed with the pension request. George was born February 3, 1760, his wife Margaret Caldwell was born February 13, 1765, and they were married Jan. 3, 1786. Their children were: John Ewing born 1787, died October 7, 1819; Rachel, born 1788, died August 20, 1820; Alexander, born 1791; Eleanor, born 1792; Margaret, born, 1795; Samuel, born 1797 died December 16, 1822. Marriages and death records were also given for George's children and some of his grandchildren. Margaret, the widow of George Ewing, filed her declaration for a pension in Blount County, Tennessee, in 1844.

Alexander Ewing

In the Cripple Creek community, there were two Alexander Ewings, Sr., and Jr. On Walter Crockett's list of tithables in 1772, there was an Alexander with a son James, and in 1773 Alexander and a son Samuel appear on Doak's list (Kegley, *Tithables*, pp. 14, 29).

Alexander Ewing had his mark recorded in 1773, a "crop and a slit on the right ear and a steeple fork on the left ear." In the same year he served on a jury. In 1774, he raised 793 pounds of "neat winter rotted hemp." An Alexander appears as an ensign of the militia from January until June 1776 (Summers, *Annals*, pp. 602, 615, 621).

Alexander's first land was taken up in 1775, when a survey of 380 acres was made, and was to include the improvements as the year of settlement was 1770. In 1784, 85 acres and 400 acres were added, and in 1785, he received a grant for 400 acres adjoining James Douglas and John Newland, and 144 acres adjoining Newland, and another tract of 156 acres adjoining Newland. An Ann Ewing also had a tract of 200 acres, opposite William Ewins [Ewings], surveyed in 1775. In 1779, Alexander and William Ewing, James Douglas, and William Love were to act as appraisers of the estate of Nathaniel Christian (Summers, *Annals*, p. 702; Montgomery County Survey Book A, pp. 37, 176, 187, 234).

Alexander Ewing, Jr., had 214 acres on Cripple Creek, adjoining his settlement of 400 acres and adjoining Newland's, surveyed in 1784, and a tract of 156 acres and another of 144 acres in the same location surveyed in the same year (Montgomery County Survey Book C, pp. 177, 178). In 1785, Alexander Ewing, one of the heirs of William Ewing, deceased, conveyed 122 acres to Peter Kinser who in turn sold it to Michael Wiseley in 1821 (Wythe County Deed Book 1, p. 263; Book 8, p. 21; Montgomery County Survey Book C, pp. 177, 178).

In 1782, an Alexander Ewing was reimbursed in the amount of 10/ following service in a battle in North Carolina. In 1785, he gave proof to the court that he was entitled to pay for the use of a mare 83 days service, at 1/6 per day, and for 100 weight of flour, this being certified to the auditor of public accounts (Summers, *Annals*, pp. 772, 788).

Alexander is mentioned in the wills of Samuel and William Ewing, who are brothers to his father, John Ewing, who bequeathed him a desk and a young bay mare and colt (Montgomery County Will Book B, p. 128). From William Ewing, Alexander received the whole of his Cripple Creek plantation containing 346 acres, subject to the dower interest of Jane Ewing. The recorded agreement states that Alexander was then living in Davidson County, North Carolina (Wythe County Deed Book 1, p. 327, 1793), and was entitled to the plantation for "every assistance in transaction of business during the life of said William Ewing." Following the death of William, Alexander received the entire estate, and in 1793, he deeded the farm to William Gannaway of Buckingham County, who also purchased 393 acres and 200 acres belonging to Alexander Ewing. Ewing's other land was sold in 1785 to John Newland and James Douglass. An additional tract was sold to Peter Kinser in 1795 (*see* William Ewing, William Gannaway, Newland, and Douglas sketches; Montgomery County Deed Book A, p. 22).

Samuel Ewing's will refers to his son, Alexander Ewing, Junr., to whom he bequeathed his silver watch (Montgomery County Will Book B, p. 81). There is a marriage record for an Alexander Ewing and Euphemy Purnell, daughter of Mary Ewing who gave consent, dated 1786 (Montgomery County Marriages; Kegley, *Early Adventurers*, Vol. 2, p. 180).

There is a Revolutionary War service record for an Alexander Ewing, whose wife was Sally (Pension W152, National Archives). He states that he was born March 10, 1752, and was commissioned September 3, 1777, Second Lieutenant of the 14th Virginia Regiment, and on February 14, 1779 Lieutenant of the 10th Virginia Regiment, and served until January 1, 1782. He was married in Davidson County, Tennessee, to Sally Smith, who was born August 12, 1761. Alexander Ewing died on April 9, 1832, and she died June 15, 1840. Their children were as follows: John Love Ewing, James Ewing, Lucinda Ewing, Louisa Ewing, William Ewing, Alexander C. Ewing, Randal McGavock Ewing, Oscar Smith Ewing, and William Black Ewing. On February 12, 1853, the son, William Black Ewing, of Davidson County, Tennessee, applied for the pension and the same was allowed on behalf of himself and the only other surviving child, James Ewing. There is no proof that this is the same Alexander Ewing who resided in Wythe County, but it does seem possible, especially since Randal McGavock was from Wythe County and was connected to the Ewings in Tennessee as well as in Wythe County.

The marriages for Ewings in Wythe County include: Andrew B. Ewing who married Eliza M. McGavock on May 1, 1821; John Ewing who married Polly Painter, December 23, 1830; Patrick Ewing who married Sally Ewing, April 17, 1834; Emily Ewing who married Abram Painter, April 22, 1841; Margaret Jane Ewing, daughter of George Ewing, who married Robert B. Highley, March 22, 1839; Goelina Ewing who married Alfred G. Catron, October 8, 1845; Mary E. Ewing who married George A. Sanders, August 14, 1845; Mary Ewing who married James B. Johnston, November 11, 1847; and William Ewing who married Margaret L. McGavock, on September 14, 1850 (Wythe County Marriage Book 1, pp. 71,100,112,146,135,163,159,172,180).

Fisher

There are numerous Fisher families mentioned in the records of Wythe County, and it is not clear just when they arrived in the county, or how they are all related, but it appears that two Jacob Fishers, a John and a David Fisher were settled here before the 1810 census. Both Jacobs were between 26 and 45 years old (Federal Census, 1810).

The records of one of the Jacob Fishers (born 1775), can be found in the family Bible, written in German script. This appears to be the one who settled on Cripple Creek and later moved to Grayson County. A descendant claimed he came from Shenandoah County to Wythe. The children mentioned in the Bible include: Rebekah, Catharine, Joshua, Joseph, Reuben, Elijah, James (1810), and Andrew, all born between 1799 and 1812. Family records add another child Hester Ann Rogers, but no date is given. Jacob's wife was said to be Susana, born 1777, probably Susanna Peters, as the marriage of their son James shows (family Bible records; Wythe County Marriage Book 2A, p. 63).

Jacob of Cripple Creek appears to have settled on what is now Slate Spring Branch of Cripple Creek about the same time as the Sweckers, Painters, and Peters, probably about 1806. He is said to be the same Jacob Fisher who was married in Rockingham County to Mary Painter on December 27, 1798, but this may be in error, in view of the marriage record of James mentioned above. (Wayland, *Virginia Valley Records*, p. 10).

Jacob's first purchase of land on Cripple Creek was 64 acres owned by Andrew Danner. The tract joined Hobbs and George Ewing, and was purchased in 1806. In 1808, he added 30 acres from Henry and Barbara Keltner, and in 1834 he added 61

1/2 acres from Leonard and Lucy Straw. The 1815 tax assessment records show that Jacob owned 104 1/2 acres on Cripple Creek, with a dwelling house of wood, one and a half stories, 20 feet by 17 feet, one kitchen, one smoke house, two stables, one corn crib, one loom house, one "double-geard" grist mill, all valued at $850. He signed his name in German script. The WPA records show that the log house was L-shaped with weather boarding, and was two stories with a large basement which was used for a kitchen and dining room. In the 1930s, the house was in poor condition and was on property owned by Bert Dunford (Wythe County Deed Book 4, pp. 435, 440; Book 5, p. 39; Book 12, p. 607; Kegley, *Tax Assessment*, p. 123; WPA collection, Virginia State Library).

In 1816, Jacob applied to the court to officially establish a water grist mill, which he had built on his own land, and a jury determined the possible damage which the dam might cause. It was decided that the land of Henry Kook (Cook) would be damaged to the extent of $3.75 (later given as $7) which amount Fisher was to pay. Although there was some concern about George Ewing's land below if the dam should break, they did not assess any damages. They agreed that the passage of fish and ordinary navigation would be completely obstructed, but it was determined that the mill would be of "more public utility" than the problems caused by the obstructions. The health of the neighborhood was also considered and it was decided that "it would not be annoyed by stagnation of the waters." Those who viewed the site were neighbors: And. Kincanon, Joseph Bell, William Gleaves, Richard Hobbs, James Ewing, Martin Powell, Henry Arnol, Henry Ellar, Joseph Jackson, John Brawley, Heinrich Hofman (?), and Thomas Jackson (Wythe County Deed Book 6, p. 516).

This Jacob Fisher moved to Grayson County, where he bought two tracts of land on Elk Creek in 1831. Sometime in 1836 he apparently married Elizabeth Robinson (no marriage record in Wythe or Grayson Counties), with whom he had a premarital agreement. His land was put in trust prior to the marriage, and at his death it was to go to his wife Elizabeth. If she died first, then the land would revert to Jacob and his heirs, unless there were issue of the marriage, in which case it would go to them (Grayson County Deed Book 6, pp. 200,205; Book 7, p. 251).

This Jacob left a will in Grayson County (Will Book 2, p. 328), written November 7, 1846, and probated at the November Term of Court 1846. His sons Andrew and Reuben were to act as executors and were to sell his land in Wythe County. Other children named were: Joshua, Joseph, Elijah, James, Rebecca, and Catharine wife of Joseph Hutzell (married August 19, 1819). The will also mentions Catherine's two daughters, Rebecca and Lucinda. Jacob's youngest daughter was named as Hester Ann R., perhaps a daughter of wife Elizabeth, and perhaps the same as the Hester Ann Rogers named above. The widow Elizabeth received certain furniture and kitchen items as well as a mare and a cow. According to an 1858 deed, Joseph lived on a one-acre tract on Meadow Creek in Grayson County. The property in Wythe County was sold in 1853 by Reuben Fisher as executor of Jacob, deceased, following a public sale and was purchased by John A. Sanders. The tract contained 204 acres and adjoined John Ewing, deceased, George Fisher, deceased, David Fisher, David Harkrader, Peter Spraker, and John Earhart (Grayson County Deed Book 11, p. 449; Wythe County Deed Book 19, p. 519; Wythe County Marriage Book 1, p. 64).

According to family notes written in 1892, Rebecca Fisher married Peter Spangler (married December 23, 1847) but raised no children. She is said to have died at an old age on Cripple Creek some time between 1880 and 1890. However, the 1850 census of Wythe County shows several Spangler children in the household. Catherine Hutzell, as mentioned in the will, died in Grayson County at an advanced age. Joshua moved to Missouri. Joseph married twice: (1) Sarah Repass (May 10, 1832) and (2) Sarah Harkrader, widow of Isaac Harkrader, and had seven children, two by the first wife, and the others by the second. Joseph died May 9, 1866 (family records; Federal Census, Wythe County, Family 625; Wythe County Marriage Book 1, pp. 106, 172).

The other Jacob Fisher appears to have lived in Evansham (now Wytheville), arriving there about 1806 when he and George Cook and Jacob Cook, Junr., purchased Lot 25 on Main Street from John P. Nye. All three were from Botetourt County. In 1809, Jacob Fisher and Rebecca his wife and the Cook men, mentioned above, sold the lot to John Haller, Jr., who was the town's first resident physician (Wythe County Deed Book 4, p. 435; Book 5, p. 175).

This Jacob Fisher was born in Pennsylvania in 1780 and died in Cleveland, Bradley County, Tennessee. His wife was Rebeckah Rader (1778-November 15, 1854, Chattanooga, Tennessee) whose marriage record in Wythe County was dated 1808. This Jacob appears to be a house carpenter, who lived on the northwest side of Main Street, on the 9th lot from the Cross Street in the Town of Evansham, now Wytheville. On this lot he built a frame house and a woodworking shop and other outbuildings. This was the lot purchased from Alexander Thompson in 1816. At the time of the sale of this lot in January 1837, Jacob and his wife Rebecca were living in Athens, McMinn County, Tennessee. Fisher also owned a lot on Monroe Street on which he had erected a house, kitchen, etc. as mentioned in a deed of 1830. Jacob and Rebecca Fisher had ten children, nine of whom were born in Evansham [now Wytheville]. They moved to Tennessee about 1835, and in Athens the Fishers opened a carpenter's shop, where they made furniture and other treasured items which are still to be found in Athens today. It should be noted that Flavius Fisher, a distinguished portrait artist, was a son of Jacob and Rebecca Fisher, and was internationally known Although Jacob Fisher is credited with work in the Haller Rock House in Wytheville, the records in Haller's accounts show that the work was done while the Hallers lived on Main Street. Jacob's son Augustus O. Fisher, and son-in-law Henry H. Rider, moved to Knoxville, Tennessee, where they are credited with building two dormitories and other buildings for the University of Tennessee (Wythe County Marriage Book 1, p. 36; Wythe County Deed Book 6, p. 460; Book 11, p. 461; Book 13, p. 547; *Jacob Fisher vs. Minerva and Stephen Thompson*, Box 38, 1822, Wythe County Circuit Court Clerk's Office, Basement; correspondence from Reba Boyer to Wythe County Historical Society, *Wythe County Review*, No. 44 (July 1993), p. 7; Kegley, *Bicentennial History*, p. 250).

David Fisher settled in Wythe County sometime prior to the fall of 1808, when his first land was purchased. He was born November 8, 1777, and died August 26, 1855. According to the marriage records of Rockingham County, David married Rachel Peters on February 26, 1798. A lawsuit in Wythe County shows that he owned land in Rockingham County. The 1850 census shows that David was living with son Absalom, and that he was born in Maryland. No wife has been named in any available Wythe County record (Federal Census, Wythe County 1850, Family 1327; family records; Wayland, *Virginia Valley Records*, p. 9; *Vance admins. vs. David Fisher et als*, Box 36, 1828, Wythe County Circuit Court Clerk's Office Basement; Wythe County Deed Book 4, p. 440).

David Fisher's first land was 106 acres in two tracts (4 acres and 102 acres) from Jean and Peggy Haney, followed by 196 acres from Daly and Joanna Walker, and 284 acres from George Danner. In 1815, David had one farm on Cripple Creek, containing 679 acres with four cabins, a barn and a saw mill. He signed his name in German script. One tract of 98 acres was conveyed to John Swecker in 1838, and in 1855 land was conveyed to Jacob Hoback (Wythe County Deed Book 5, p. 109; Book 6, pp. 61, 85; Book 14, p. 39; Book 20, pp. 239, 244; Kegley, *Tax Assessments*, p. 123).

David wrote his will on September 26, 1851, and it was probated on September 10, 1855 (Wythe County Will Book 9, p. 5). All of his land and his personal estate were to be sold at auction. His granddaughter Judith Archer, child of his daughter Sally, was to have $50 when of age. Son Absalom was to receive $200 one year after he became 21. The balance of the estate was to be divided five ways: to son John one-fifth, to son Jacob one-fifth, son-in-law John Phillipps, who married Polly, his daughter one-fifth; to his son-in-law James Adkins, who married daughter Ludy's (Lydia), the use of one-fifth interest, provided he gave security for the payment of the same in equal shares, without interest, to his five children by daughter Ludy, as they arrive at age 21 [This only accounts for 4/5ths of the estate; for resolution of this problem, see details of lawsuit which follows]. According to the will, reasons, "which seem to me entirely just and proper," David saw fit to exclude some of the children from his estate, and he left it up to the others whether they would have any part of the estate. Son Absolum and son-in-law James M. Adkins were executors.

There was a lawsuit following the death of David Fisher, and the executors brought suit against John Fisher and others and asked the court for an interpretation of the will. It appears that after the will was written and before the death of David Fisher, he sold part of his land to Jacob Hoback (about 100 acres). Also, they proposed to the court that one-fifth of the proceeds from the land was to be given to Absalom, although it was not clear in the will, and appeared to be an oversight. The court agreed. The suit brought by Absalom Fisher and James M. Atkins, executors, also names John Fisher, Jacob Fisher, John Phillips and wife Polly, Absalom Fisher, Sampson Archer and his wife Sally, granddaughter Judith Archer, and George Fisher's children and heirs: Harvey G., Minerva, Malvina, John, Thomas, and George W. Fisher, Jane Groseclose (daughter of Jane Fisher, daughter of George), and Daniel, Isaac N., Abram P., other heirs of Jacob. Of these children, John, Jacob, Daniel, Isaac N. and Abraham P. Fisher were living out of state. John Phillips lived in Grayson County, but in 1856 his wife Polly had been dead for years. The Archers were found in Mercer County, Virginia (now West Virginia) in 1856 (*Fisher's execs. vs. Fisher*, Box 106, 1857-1858, Wythe County Circuit Court Clerk's Office, Basement).

There was a George Fisher who purchased, from Leonard and Lucy Straw a tract of 134 acres of land, being the northwest part of the tract of 480 acres which was surveyed in 1774, and granted to James Bebber, Senr., in 1795. It adjoined Jacob Fisher. George Fisher married Sarah Jane Jones, daughter of Ezekiel Jones, on October 24, 1827. Following his death, his land was laid off for his widow Sarah and other heirs, who were: Wiley S. and Sarah W. Fisher, infants, Samuel B. Williams, Mary J. M. Groseclose, William S. Spraker and wife, Harvey Fisher, and Thomas J. Fisher. The deed suggested that the part of the infants be sold for their benefit, and that the part designated for Mary J. M. Groseclose be rented for her benefit, as long as she is single or until she arrives at age 21, "there being on it a comfortable house." Thomas J. Fisher died without a will and without issue, but left a widow also called Sarah. His widow Sarah M. was assigned 16 acres and the house with right to use the spring. Also mentioned were Malvina H. Groseclose wife of E. H. Groseclose, and Mary J. Johnson granddaughter of George Fisher, and wife of William F. Johnson (Wythe County Deed Book 12, p. 605; Book 40, p. 515; Book 42, p. 407; Wythe County Marriage Book 1, pp. 90, 95).

James Fisher son of Jacob, of Cripple Creek and Grayson County, was a Methodist minister, and received permission to marry citizens of Wythe County. He posted bond on December 14, 1846. Those who gave security on the bond were Joseph Fisher, Andrew Fisher, and James L. Yost (Wythe County Minister's Bond).

James purchased 209 1/2 acres from Joshua and Martha Ewing in 1841. The land adjoined Col. George Kincannon (Wythe County Deed Book 15, p. 247).

Following the death of James Fisher in 1888, his wife Nancy J. brought suit against Josiah Brown and others. James owned about 270 1/2 acres, two miles northeast of Ivanhoe, and he died intestate. He had been married three times, and had three sets of children who were his heirs-at-law. They were named as Josiah Brown and his wife Nickati Fisher Brown; Thomas Fry and his wife Fannie Fisher Fry:, Caroline M. Fisher; R. G. Epperson and Sarah J. Fisher, his wife; Guy S. Brally and Mary E. Fisher his wife; James K. Hollandsworth and Ann E. Fisher his wife; Stuart Wohlford and Catherine Fisher his wife; Jacob M. Fisher; Stephen M. Jackson and his wife Viola Fisher Jackson; Stephen F. Dean and his wife Lucy B. Fisher Dean; Samuel H. Ward and Nannie E. Fisher Ward his wife; and six infants under 21; James T. and Maud K. Fisher (both over 14), Guy M. Fisher, Pearl R. Fisher, John K. Fisher, and Charles Fisher. The widow had 60 acres of the total 270 acres laid off for her dower, which adjoined Simmerman and included the mansion house and outbuildings (*Fisher vs. Brown, et als*, Box 157, 1889, Wythe County Circuit Court Clerk's Office, Basement).

When Olive Branch Methodist Church was organized in 1833, Jacob Fisher was one of the trustees, and in the church there is a memorial to the Rev. James Fisher who served the community for many years. The inscription states:

The righteous shall be in everlasting remembrance
The Rev. James Fisher was born December 17, 1810.
Died December 27, 1888. Aged 78 years 10 days.
He was 60 years a faithful Christian, 2 years an exhorter
and 47 years a faithful preacher.
Full of faith and of the Holy Ghost, he served his gen-
eration with zeal and fidelity, and was not, for God
took him. Many were the sheaves which he gathered
for the Master.

James Fisher was also a trustee of the Bethany Methodist Church. On Slate Springs Branch, in 1855, David Fisher conveyed an acre of land to Absalom Fisher, Reuben Fisher, Jacob Davis, H. J. Fisher and George Sanders, Trustees of the Methodist Episcopal Church South, to include the Slate Spring Church. Absalom and Thomas Fisher were among the trustees of a Methodist Church which later became the Berea Christian Church. Absalom and Abraham Fisher were also ministers, who served the Methodist Church and whose bonds were posted in the Clerk's Office of the Wythe County Court. According to notes made by F. B. Kegley, noted historian of the county, Jacob Fisher's home was the first Methodist preaching place in that section of the county. It was a favorite haunt of the Reverend "Bob" Sheffey. A place had been arranged for a torch light for reading in the sitting room near the fireplace (Presgraves, ed., *Wythe County Chapters*, pp. 145,146, 156, 157, 159; F. B. Kegley notes; Wythe County Deed Book 23, p. 391).

William Fisher (born about 1796) was a soldier in the War of 1812, and it is from his pension application that much of this information was taken. At the time of his discharge in March 1815, he was 19 years old, had dark hair, brown eyes, fair complexion, and was five feet eight inches high, and was a blacksmith. He was born in Wythe County, but no parent's names are given. He married Amy Hudson (sometimes Hutson) on May 1, 1816 (1817?), and was listed in Captain Isaac T. Preston's Company, 45th Regiment of the United States Regular Soldiers, and was stationed at Norfolk during the full period of the war, and was discharged on March 18, 1815. He applied for a pension in 1871, at age 75, when a widower. William W. Phelps of Wytheville and George Hollinsworth of Cripple Creek testified to the accuracy of his statement. His pension was awarded at the rate of $8 per month, beginning February 14, 1871 (Pension, National Archives).

The marriage record appears in Wythe County, but was filed by Rev. Lockett, who did not note the exact date of marriage. He filed his report on December 25, 1817 (Wythe County Marriage Book 1, p. 57). William Fisher died on October 11, 1873, at the home of James P. Wade, Tazewell, Virginia, with whom he was living in 1860 in Wythe County, and who paid for the expenses of his last sickness and burial (Pension, National Archives; Federal Census).

The relationship of David, Jacob, George, and William Fisher is not indicated in any public records, but it seems that all of those living on Cripple Creek were probably related in some way before they came to the area.

Henry Francis

Henry Francis was one of the earliest settlers on Cripple Creek, being in the neighborhood as early as 1768 when his tract of 750 acres was settled. At this date his name is also found on a roster of purchasers at James Cartie's sale (Kegley, *Early Adventurers*, Vol. 2, p. 116; Chalkley, *Chronicles*, Vol. 3, p. 106).

In 1770, he was appointed constable for the Cripple Creek area and served on the jury several times. He served on the grand jury in 1779, and was a member of the jury for Jacob Kettering's Tory trial in 1780. He was also called upon to be overseer or viewer of the first road along Cripple Creek, which connected Newlands at the headwaters with the lead mines at the river (Summers, *Annals*, pp. 62, 122, 608, 620, 729, 740).

In January 1773, he was given "leave to build a mill on land where he now lives," hence the name Francis Mill Creek, which is still on the map of Wythe County. His selection of 750 acres included the present location of the Town of Cripple Creek. He recorded his mark in 1774, "crop and half a crop on right ear and single crop left ear." He also obtained 143 acres which had been surveyed for Lucas Hood in 1774, and which adjoined his own land (Montgomery County Survey Book A, pp. 30, 35; Summers, *Annals*, pp. 593, 602).

In 1776, he was an ensign in the militia for the Committee of Safety, and a few months later was lieutenant in the new company on Cripple Creek led by Captain Andrew Thompson. In 1778, Francis replaced Thompson as captain (Harwell, *Committee*, pp. 75, 86; Kegley, *Militia*, p. 1).

In 1779, he proved to the Montgomery County Court that he was entitled to 200 acres of land under the Proclamation of 1763 for his services in the French and Indian War (Summers, *Annals*, p. 728). The Montgomery County Minute Book (April 1779, p. 94) gives additional details as follows:

"Henry Francis served as a Sergeant in 1st Virginia Reg't under different commanders and continued in service about 6 1/2 years and was legally discharged by Col. Adam Stephens. He never received a warrant for land and is an inhabitant of this state and has been since his discharge and he is thereby entitled to 200 acres of land under the Proclamation of 1763." In the same book, Henry claimed land as heir of his two deceased brothers as follows: "Henry Francis, eldest brother and heir at law of William Francis, deceased, states that William served three years in the 1st Battalion of Royal Americans and he died and never received a certificate for land. He is thereby entitled to 50 acres." He also claimed 50 acres as brother and heir at law of John Francis, deceased, who served for three years as a soldier in the 1st Virginia Reg't commanded by Washington. John was killed by Indians.

In 1777, Henry and his sons John and Henry took the oath of allegiance to the State of Virginia. In 1778, Francis, already an experienced soldier and as captain of his local militia company, rendezvoused at the lead mines and proceeded to North Carolina. In 1779, John was appointed to serve as constable in his father's company. In 1780, on another mission to North Carolina, Henry was killed in the fight with some Tories under Captain Kyle, and James Newell was recommended to replace him (John Ewing's Revolutionary War Service Claim S31015, National Archives; Kegley, *Militia*, pp. 1, 51, 52, 56; Summers, *Annals*, p. 715).

On November 7, 1780, Leah Francis, the widow of Henry, was granted the administration of the estate and William Love, William Campbell, George Ewing, and James White, or any three were to undertake the appraisal. On May 9, 1782, on the motion of Adam Dean and James Newell, it was ordered that Leah and John Francis be asked for counter-security for the administration of the estate (Summers, *Annals*, pp. 742, 771).

The inventory of the estate was recorded on November 10, 1780. Among the items listed were: one Negro girl, a gun barrel and locks, a rifle, one pair of money scales, three beds, two chests, one trunk, five pewter teaspoons, kettles, dutch oven, fry pan, loom, shoemaker's tools, still and vessels, and many tools including saws, axes, adzes, augers, mattocks, and knives. Many animals were listed. There was also cash in paper money amounting to £750. The total value of the estate was £33,357.10, an amount which probably reflects the severe inflation of the period (Montgomery County Will Book B, p. 45).

Son John appears in Captain James Newell's Company in 1781, and as heir of his father claimed land on Cripple Creek. Son Henry appears on Newell's list of 1782, and he claimed 150 acres which had been settled by George Brock in 1771, and 143 acres surveyed for Lucas Hood which adjoined John Francis. The Hood land was surveyed in February 1774, and was assigned to Henry Francis (Kegley, *Militia*, pp. 30, 31; Kegley, *Early Adventurers*, Vol. 2, pp. 53, 69, 116, 117,118; Montgomery County Survey Book A, p. 30). Both John and Henry served in the Revolution.

From the Revolutionary War service record (R3746) for John and Nancy (sometimes Ann) Francis, it was learned that John served as a lieutenant in the Revolutionary War and was in the Battle of Shallow Ford, Yadkin River, North Carolina, and was in service most of the war. Witnesses who spoke for John stated that he had served near his father Henry, who was shot by a Tory at Shallow Ford and John in turn shot at the man who killed his father, and believed that he had killed him. John moved to Lincoln County, Kentucky, where he married Nancy Ann Mounts (born in Maryland in 1761) on May 15, 1784. He was probably born about 1760. In 1800, John Francis was in Cumberland County, Kentucky, and in 1801 was sworn in as High Sheriff of Wayne County, Kentucky, an office he held until 1813. He served as a judge of the quarterly court in Wayne County, Kentucky, and died there October 9, 1829. His widow Nancy, age 90, was living in Livingston County, Missouri, when she made a new declaration in 1852. She had moved from Kentucky in 1849 (Pension R3746, National Archives; Harris, Clawson and Harris, "Captain Henry Francis of Montgomery County, Va..., *Detroit Society for Genealogical Research*, Vol. 32, Nos. 1, 2, 3, 1968-1969, hereafter Harris, "Captain Henry Francis").

The John Francis family consisted of twelve children, all born in Kentucky: Leah, Mary ("Polly"), Henry, Tabitha, Elizabeth, Nancy, John, Elisha, Peggy, Jane ("Fanny"), George W., and Mahaley (Harris, "Captain Henry Francis").

Henry Francis, Jr., was living in Pulaski County, Kentucky, in the late 1790s, and in 1837, he applied for a pension which was denied (R3739). He stated that his father died at the Battle of Shallow Ford, and that he was also present at the same battle. He was born in Virginia but later lived in Kentucky and Missouri, and at the time of the pension application, he was living in Johnson County, Arkansas, having lived there seven years. He died there on June 28, 1840, age 83 (Harris, "Captain Henry Francis."

If Captain Henry Francis had other children their names do not appear in the local records. (For further details of sons John and Henry, see Harris, "Captain Henry Francis.").

Valentine Fry

Valentine Fry, son of Valentine Fry, Jr., (born 1749 Lancaster County, Pennsylvania) was born on August 9, 1786, and probably married in North Carolina about 1803 or 1804. His family settled there about 1759. Valentine, known as the third, first appears in Wythe County in the 1810 census record with three male children under ten years, and he and his wife both between 16 and 26 years of age. He purchased his first land in 1814, from Frederick Worley and wife Sally Fry Worley (married 1797), of Hawkins County, Tennessee, who inherited the land from his father Michael Worley. This tract of 180 acres was on Francis or Garner's Mill Creek. In the 1820s and 30s, Fry added a total of 136 1/2 acres to his estate. He sold one tract of 130 acres to Joseph Bell in 1821 (Federal Census, Wythe County 1810; Wythe County Deed Book 8, pp. 271, 367; Book 9, p. 422; Book 11, p. 26; Book 12, p. 517; Wythe County Marriage Book 1, p. 14; family Bible records and family history manuscript).

Valentine Fry died on September 3, 1833, and is buried above the house where he lived, located on route 602 about a mile south of the Town of Cripple Creek. His great-great granddaughter now owns the house. On the 14th of October, Catherine Fry, the widow of Valentine renounced the administration of the estate of her deceased husband in favor of James T. Gleaves and Joseph Sanders, who were to act as administrators. Joseph Sanders married Valentine's daughter Matilda Fry in 1831 (Wythe County Marriage Book 1, p. 102; Wythe County Order Book 1833-1837, p. 37; *Dunaway vs. McRea et als*, Box 105, 1855, Wythe County Circuit Court Clerk's Office, Basement).

On August 11, 1833, Isaac Fry (born 1814), an orphan of Valentine Frye, upwards of age 14, chose Catherine Fry (his mother) as his legal guardian. The court appointed her as guardian for Susanna (born 1822), Delila (born 1823), Abraham (born 1827), Jane (born 1829), and Margaret (born 1831) who were under age 14. Delila married Absalom Slimp (Slemp) in 1839; Susanna married Charles Dunaway in 1844. Other children were: Jacob (born 1804), Andrew (born 1808), Hiram (born 1810), Absalom (born 1811), Matilda (born 1812), Nehemiah (born 1816), Mary (born 1818), and Elizabeth (born 1820) (Bible records; Wythe County Order Book 1833-1837, pp. 158; Wythe County Marriage Book 1, pp. 143,161).

On October 28, 1833, an appraisal of the estate was done and recorded on December 14, 1835 (Wythe County Will Book 4, p. 247). There were cows, calves, 35 geese, hay, steers, heifers, 2 sows and 9 pigs, 24 hogs, 2 ploughs, waggons, harrow, mares, filleys, and colts, a wheat fan, a cutting box, pitch forks, 3 riddles, saddle, blacksmith tools, a kettle, 3 washing tubs, 3 grindstones, "sythes" and cradles, 80 sheep, a pair of "stilliards," sheep shears, 2 pair of andirons, beds and furniture.

The home was well prepared to process flax and wool. There were 5 flax wheels, 3 large reels, 2 check reels, and a loom. There were also 3 slates and books, 9 chairs, bridles and bells, axes, 11 bags, a quantity of castings, churn and pails, and a man's saddle. The items selected by the widow at the sale and some settlement information were also recorded (Wythe County Will Book 4, pp. 124, 334).

In August 1835, Catherine's dower was laid off, a tract of 75 acres which included the house of Valentine Fry. Anticipating her marriage to Daniel D. MacRae, Mary Katherine (Catherine) Fry, the widow, conveyed to John Yonce and Nehemiah Fry, acting administrators of Valentine's estate, all cattle, furniture, etc. into a trust. Witnesses were Lucinda, Mary, and Susan Fry (Wythe County Deed Book 14, p. 206). On February 5, 1839, the marriage bond was secured and the couple married. They were both living in 1850 when the census was taken. She gave her age as 64 and her birthplace as North Carolina. Her husband Daniel was 76 years old, and he was also born in North Carolina (Wythe County Deed Book 13, p. 167; Book 14, p. 206; Federal Census, Wythe County 1850; Wythe County Marriage Book 1, p. 132).

Hiram Frye (born March 8, 1810) married Polly Yonce in 1833, and Nehemiah Fry (December 7, 1816) who married Lucinda Eastwood in 1838. These are among the children of Valentine Fry who were named in the lawsuit filed by his daughter Susannah and her husband Charles Dunaway against her mother and others. The purpose of the suit was to obtain her share of the estate. She complained that her mother did not turn over her share to her when she became of age. In the suit, title bonds show that Hiram and Absalom Fry conveyed their interest in the land to their brother Isaac, who in turn conveyed his interest, with his wife Margaret (both of Giles County, Virginia), to his brother Nehemiah Fry. Absalom Slemp of Smyth County, conveyed his interest to Nehemiah Fry in 1842, and Andrew Fry of Smyth County also conveyed his interest in his father's estate to Nehemiah Fry. John Shupe conveyed his interest in his father-in-law's estate to Nehemiah Fry in 1843. Joseph Sanders conveyed his interest in his father-in-law's estate to Mary Katherin Fry, and at the time of the suit was not living in Virginia. Another child, Polly, who married William Arnold, had not responded to the suit and was probably out of state. Another child, Jane married a Porter, and was also mentioned. Margaret another child of Valentine Fry, died in the fall of 1845 at age 14. Susannah became of age (21) on February 14, 1843. Hiram is buried at Evergreen Cemetery, not far from where he lived, and Nehemiah is buried in the Frye family cemetery near Cripple Creek (Wythe County Marriage Book 1, pp. 109,127; *Dunaway vs. McRae*).

The case also reveals that Susannah had two children and that her mother assisted her during her confinement. She had also given her daughter a spinning wheel, a cow, and beds and furniture. The records show that the difference between the two accounts was $29.74, and the court ruled that Susannah and her husband were required to pay this amount to her mother. In 1849, the 206 acres of land was sold by the commissioner to Nehemiah Fry for $550 (*Dunaway vs. McRae*).

Hiram Fry settled on Venricks Run, a branch of Reed Creek, near the Evergreen Church. He bought the land from Jacob and Rosanna Gose, who had purchased it from Michael Venrick. The Fry log house still stands at the site (Wythe County Deed Book 13, p. 222, Deed Book 10, p. 559).

Nehemiah, Hiram, and Abraham Fry appear in the 1850 Wythe County Census. Following the death of Daniel McRae in 1868 or 1869 the widow moved to Tazewell County, Virginia, and died there (Federal Census, Wythe County 1850; family records).

Gannaway

The Gannaways settled in Bath, England and the first immigrant to Virginia probably was connected with these English families. John Gannaway appears as a resident of King William County by actual recorded date 1721, but he was probably in Virginia several years before this date. He is known to have had two sons, John and William (b. 1723). There were seven Gannaway families in Buckingham County in 1782. The elder John died about 1783 in Buckingham County, Virginia. His son John, Jr., died there in 1770. The younger John had married Mary Gregory and had twelve children: William, John, Catherine, Thomas, Gregory, Mary, Robert, Frances, Patty, Edmund, Betty, and Susanna. Several of these children moved to Wythe County, probably about 1793, the year their mother died and the year William Gannaway purchased his first land on Cripple Creek. These tracts came from Alexander Ewing, as heir of William Ewing, and were near the headwaters of Cripple Creek. In 1795, William Gannaway and his wife Elizabeth sold 235 acres to Gideon Huddle, and in 1796 sold 116 acres to Money (Monney) Gannaway, and in 1797 sold a tract to William Williams (family records quoting *William and Mary Quarterly*, St. Peter's Parish Records, New Kent County, and the family Bible; Buckingham County Tax List 1782; Wythe County Deed Book 1, pp. 169,170,36,413; Book 3, p. 12).

William Gannaway wrote his will on November 11, 1799, and it was probated on June 14, 1800. To his wife Elizabeth (formerly Wright, the daughter of Archibald and Elizabeth Shepherd Wright) he lent the 150 acres "where I now live, with the house and plantation." He also lent her certain Negroes. Daughter Mary Williams was to have 114 acres "where she now lives," and daughters Nancy Hambleton, Sally Gannaway, and the four youngest, Caty, Susannah, Patty, and Frances were to receive certain Negroes as well. The four sons, John, William, Thomas, and Seymore, were to have the balance of the land equally and the wife's share at her death. Executors were to be his wife Elizabeth, John Newlin (Newland) and Henry Hambleton. Witnesses were Thomas and William Gannaway, William Love, and Elisha Williams (Wythe County Will Book 1, p. 152).

Following the death of her husband, Elizabeth Wright Gannaway married her neighbor, John Newland, the marriage agreement dated August 23, 1803. Because of the marriage, differences arose in regard to the land, Negroes, and other property left to her by her husband, and in "order to restore harmony which is always desirable in families" John and Elizabeth Newland released all interest to the land, houses, plantation, etc., to John, Thomas, and Seymore Gannaway. John also obtained his brother William's share (Wythe County Deed Book 5, pp. 148,262; Book 8, p. 212).

Daughters Caty, Susanna, and Patty, who married Joseph A. Brownlow (1804), Joseph Atkins (1808) and George Winniford (1808), respectively, and Frances Gannaway by her guardian Joseph Atkins joined in the deed recorded in 1809. This release resulted from the lawsuit in which Elizabeth explains that Stephen Sanders and Henry Hamilton were to be trustees for her children at the time the marriage agreement was drawn up. By some mistake the profits all went to the daughters and this had to be corrected. The original papers are filed in the Staunton courthouse and the suit is mentioned in Chalkley (Chalkley, *Chronicles*, Vol. 2, p. 99; *Gannaway vs. Sanders, Trustee*, OS77 NS26, Augusta County; Wythe County Deed Book 5, p. 148).

In 1841, William Ward and his wife Nancy conveyed land for the Methodist Episcopal Church in Speedwell. The trustees were John Gannaway, Sr., James H. Piper, Seymore W. Gannaway, Thomas Gannaway, David Whitman, Peter Keesling, and Stephen Porter (Presgraves, ed., *Wythe County Chapters*, p. 155).

The youngest son of William and Elizabeth Gannaway was Seymore, who apparently never married. He wrote his will on April 8, 1846, and it was probated on May 11, 1846. He left the part of the old tract where he lives to his brother John and in addition 80 acres he bought from Andrew Porter, Sr. His brother Thomas was to have his part of the Douglass tract. Elizabeth R., daughter of John Gannaway, Sr., was to have a yellow horse. Each of John's other children was to get $50. The rest of the estate was to be divided between his five surviving sisters, Nancy Rogers, Sarah Gannaway, Susannah Atkins, Martha Winniford, and Frances Atkins. John T. Gannaway, son of his brother John, was to have a Negro. His brother John and Thomas Sanders were to be executors. Witnesses were William Ward, Stephen Huddle, and William Davis (Wythe County Will Book 6, p. 386).

Sally (probably the same as Sarah) Gannaway, married her cousin Robertson Gannaway (son of Gregory Gannaway), who was born in Cumberland County, Virginia, on July 7, 1770. He came to Cripple Creek the winter of 1801 and worked as a carpenter at the Speedwell Ironworks. He married Sally on December 24, 1801. He later became a minister. There is another Sally who married William Gannaway in 1804 (Presgraves, ed., *Wythe County Chapters*, p. 87; Wythe County Marriage Book 1, pp. 21, 27).

Robertson Gannaway, a resident of Smyth County on July 19, 1853, filed a declaration when he was 72 years old. He stated that his father, Gregory Gannaway, was a soldier in the Revolutionary War from the County of Buckingham. He served at the Battle of Guilford in North Carolina. Gregory married in Cumberland County in the summer or fall of 1779 and died in 1804, survived by his widow, who died in February 1852 in the State of Missouri. Gregory died before filing for a pension. His widow could have filed for a pension under the law of 1831, but apparently did not do so. The heirs were claiming the pension which accrued from March 4, 1831 to the 15th day of February 1853, a period of twenty-two years. The children of Gregory were listed as Robertson, Jeffery, Polly Harris, Catharine Oury, Sally Gannaway, John Gannaway, Norval Gannaway, William Gannaway, Pamela Rader, Thomas Gannaway, and Martha McDearman. The claim was not allowed because no proof of service was provided by the applicant. Robertson Gannaway is buried at the Sulphur Springs Cemetery, Chilhowie, where his stone says he was born July 7, 1780, and died January 12, 1859 (R3893, National Archives; also filed in Smyth County Order Book; Sturgill and Sturgill, *Smyth County, Virginia, Cemeteries*, Vol. 1, p. 178).

Other marriages recorded in Wythe County include: Norwell to Bezy Sanders (1819); Mary daughter of John to Henry Hamilton (1848); Elizabeth to William Love (1795); Mary to Robert H. Richardson (1848). Joseph A. Brownlow, son of Joseph and Caty (Catherine) Gannaway, moved to Tennessee in 1826, and became a preacher serving for ten years. He then entered politics and was elected Governor of Tennessee following the Civil War. He later served as U.S. Senator. He died in 1882 (Wythe County Marriage Book 1, pp. 9, 35, 36, 64, 15, 21,196; Kegley, *Bicentennial History*, p. 256).

On September 11, 1848, Sarah F. Gannaway, over fourteen, chose John Gannaway her guardian, and the court appointed him to act for Emiline, Martha, and John T. Gannaway who were under age fourteen. These may be children of John Gannaway, but the record does not specify the relationship (Wythe County Order Book 1848-1852, p. 66).

Thomas Gannaway (age 64 in the 1850 census) was living with brother John (age 69) and his wife Kesiah (daughter of Adam Barringer of Montgomery County, whom he married about 1819), and their children in 1850. Thomas and John Gannaway, both died in 1850, both wills being probated on December 9. Thomas wrote his will on

September 7, 1850, and left his interest in the old tract where "I now live" to his nephew John, son of brother John. To his six nieces, daughters of his brother John, he left the interest in Douglass and Phillippe tracts, and certain Negroes. These nieces were: Mary C. Richardson, and Elizabeth W., Nancy R., Sarah F., Anne E., and Martha W. Gannaway (Wythe County Will Book 7, p. 215; Kegley, *Early Adventurers,* Vol. 2, p. 204).

John Gannaway wrote his will on March 15, 1850. To his wife Kesiah, he gave his interest in the estate but the slaves were to be sold. Son John was to have interest in the old tract "where I now reside" after his wife's death. The remainder of the land was to go to daughters Elizabeth W., Nancy R., Sarah F., Ann E., Martha W. and Mary C. The executors were to be his wife Kesiah and Thomas Sanders (Wythe County Will Book 7, p. 213).

All of the land mentioned in the various wills was located between Speedwell and Cedar Springs, and formerly belonged to William and Alexander Ewing, and then William Gannaway and his sons and grandchildren. A rock house, known as the Jack Gannaway place, three miles west of Speedwell, was later known as the Gabe Davis-Calvin James house. It was weather boarded, but in later years this covering was removed as the house was to be remodeled. The house is now gone. It is not clear from the records who built it.

The Gannaway brick house at Speedwell.   Photo courtesy of F. B. Kegley Collection.

The Jack Gannaway rock house, now gone, was formerly located about three miles west of Speedwell, and was later known as the Gabe Davis-Calvin James house.

Photo courtesy of F. B. Kegley Collection.

443

Thomas Gannaway

Thomas Gannaway, Sr., born May 18, 1752, was the brother of William Gannaway, Sr., who settled on the headwaters of Cripple Creek. Thomas probably moved to Wythe County from Buckingham County about the same time as his brother. The deed to his first land was dated 1799 and came from Stephen and Isabella Sanders, who sold him 346 acres, located just east of the present town of Speedwell. In 1802, he added 90 acres, part of 294 acres granted Sanders in 1800. An additional tract of 250 acres was surveyed in 1805 and granted to Thomas Gannaway in 1807. The census of 1810 shows that Thomas had eleven slaves (Federal Census, Wythe County 1810; Wythe County Deed Book 2, p. 384; Book 3, p. 199; Wythe County Survey Book 2, p. 213).

In 1820, Thomas Gannaway and his wife Sarah made a deed to John Gannaway, Jr., (their son) for the homeplace, a tract of 361 acres part of the land where Thomas was presently living. Thomas retained a life interest in the land for himself and his wife. The spring was to be shared by Thomas and John equally (Wythe County Deed Book 8, p. 9).

On November 14, 1818, Thomas Gannaway, Sr., wrote his will which was witnessed January 7, 1819, and probated on August 8, 1820. His wife Sally and sons Martin and John were to be executors. Daughters Patsy and Betsy and son John were to get beds, furniture, etc. The balance was to be equally divided between the children, except Polly Gregory, but one-eighth part was to go to her children. It was understood that son Martin was going to Kentucky and intended to settle on his father's land there, and this was confirmed in the will. Witnesses were John, Thomas, and Seymore Gannaway (Wythe County Will Book 2, p. 313).

In 1821, William Love as attorney for William Gannaway of Breckenridge County, Kentucky, sold his interest to his brother John. The land sold was his interest in three tracts where his father Thomas formerly lived, and where "John Gannaway now lives," being 250 acres granted in 1807, and the two tracts from Sanders (Wythe County Deed Book 8, p. 212).

With the title to the land secured, John Gannaway, probably sometime in the 1830s, built a brick house which still stands in Speedwell. In the 1850 census, this John is 57 and his wife Ann (Trigg) was 53, and their four children were John, 21, Thomas, 15, Catherine 18, and James L., 15 (Federal Census, Wythe County 850).

It is not clear from the records which John Gannaway was the justice of the peace and sat on the Wythe County Court. He was commissioned June 1, 1820, and qualified July 11, 1820. Also, a John Gannaway served as sheriff of Wythe County, but the extent of his term and which John actually served has not been determined (Wythe County Order Book 1822-1826, front unnumbered pages, has a list of acting magistrates for the county; Wythe County Order Book 1848-1852, March 13, 1848, p. 3).

John Gannaway, son of Thomas, Sr., wrote his will on August 13, 1864, and it was probated in September 1865. His wife Ann was to have control of the plantation and slaves and at her death the land was to go to son Thomas. A dividing line was run through the place in 1852, and all that land lying northwest of the line, "embracing the Dry Run place on which there is a brick house," was to go to Thomas. Sons William and James and daughter Catherine and her heirs were to receive Negroes. Each of his children, William, John, Thomas, and Catherine were to receive a horse and certain furniture. Son William was to have the share of stock in the Virginia Tennessee Railroad valued at $100. Three sons were to act as executors. Witnesses were David Gose and Daniel Stoner (Wythe County Will Book 10, p.641). The brick house mentioned here is still standing, but is unoccupied.